D0205641

THE PAPERS OF
WOODROW WILSON

VOLUME 18
1908-1909

SPONSORED BY THE WOODROW WILSON
FOUNDATION
AND PRINCETON UNIVERSITY

THE PAPERS OF

WOODROW
WILSON

ARTHUR S. LINK, *EDITOR*

DAVID W. HIRST AND JOHN E. LITTLE
ASSOCIATE EDITORS

JOHN M. MULDER, *ASSISTANT EDITOR*

SYLVIA ELVIN FONTIJN, *CONTRIBUTING EDITOR*

M. HALSEY THOMAS, *CONSULTING EDITOR*

Volume 18 · 1908-1909

PRINCETON, NEW JERSEY
PRINCETON UNIVERSITY PRESS
1974

INTRODUCTION

THE documents in this volume, covering a period of less than a year—from March 2, 1908, to January 19, 1909—richly reflect Wilson's busy life as public lecturer, educator, administrator, political scientist, and prolific correspondent.

During these months, Wilson speaks to such varied groups as the Traffic Club of Pittsburgh, the American Bankers' Association, the Commercial Club of Chicago, the Chamber of Commerce of Toledo, the City History Club, the Southern Society, and the National Democratic Club, all of New York. He is no less active on the alumni circuit, addressing groups in New York, Boston, Chicago, Pittsburgh, and Baltimore. Nor does he neglect opportunities to speak before students at Yale University, the Woman's College of Baltimore, the Lawrenceville School, the Hotchkiss School, the Newark Academy, high schools in Jersey City and in New York, the Chicago Latin School, and the University School for Boys in Chicago. To all these speeches must be added his notable and much-quoted oration on Robert E. Lee at the University of North Carolina.

In his public lectures, Wilson reiterates his earlier stand against direct regulation of business by government, or what he calls government by commission. This, he claims, is the first inexorable step toward socialism. The only safe regulation, he insists, lies in "the incorruptible instrumentality of the law, not through the choice of government officials."

He continues to criticize William Jennings Bryan—once by name and frequently indirectly—for his "foolish and dangerous theories." Clearly, he is offering himself as spokesman for a new conservative Democratic coalition. How seriously he is considering such a role is revealed in his letter to Mary Allen Hulbert Peck of November 2, 1908. "Two years from now," he writes, "I can retire on a Carnegie pension of $4000. I have $2000 of my own. I shall not willingly wait more than two years for the Princeton trustees to do what it is their bounden duty to do with regard to the reform of university life. At the end of that time I would be glad to lend my pen and voice and all my thought and energy to anyone who purposed a genuine rationalization and rehabilitation of the Democratic party on lines of principle and statesmanship!"

In his addresses to Princeton alumni, Wilson makes it abundantly clear that he intends to take at face value the statement with which the trustees accompanied their withdrawal of support of his quadrangle plan—that he was free to continue advocacy of the plan within the Princeton community. Again and again, he reminds the alumni of his firm conviction that only through major social reorganization can the university concentrate on its single purpose, the training of the intellect. "If I have done nothing else," he tells the Princeton Club of Chicago, "I have started a subject which you cannot drop."

Wilson's career as a scholar comes to a climax and an end in this volume with the publication of *Constitutional Government in the United States*. In it he offered, to use his own words, a "fresh analysis" of the American system of government "with an eye to practice, not to theory." The book is significant for what it reveals about the evolution of Wilson's political thought since *Congressional Government*. In *Constitutional Government*, he abandons his earlier calls for adoption of the cabinet form of government and now recognizes the great potentialities of presidential leadership. If the President, Wilson writes, can "rightly interpret the national thought and boldly insist upon it, he is irresistible. . . . His office is anything he has the sagacity and force to make it."

In university affairs, Wilson continues to oversee meticulously the expansion of the university in the completion of Palmer Physical Laboratory and the beginning of a large new dormitory, Holder Hall. In the controversy over the location of the graduate college, Wilson seemingly wins a signal victory over the Pyne-West faction when the trustees approve a location between Prospect and Seventy-Nine Hall, in the heart of the campus.

Several poignant references to persistent "neuritis" in his right arm reveal that Wilson has by no means recovered from the small stroke he suffered in December 1907, and that he still has great difficulty in writing. This prompts his decision to spend the following summer in England in his beloved Lake District. From this journey comes the most descriptive and lyrical letters, to his wife, that Wilson ever wrote. In addition, he gives a fascinating account of a visit to Skibo, the Highland residence of Andrew Carnegie, and of the famous persons he met there.

Readers are again reminded that *The Papers of Woodrow Wilson* is a continuing series; that persons, institutions, and events that figure prominently in earlier volumes are not re-identified in subsequent ones; and that the Index to each volume gives cross references to fullest earlier identifications. We reiterate that we print texts *verbatim et literatim*, repairing words and phrases in brackets only when necessary for clarity or ease of reading; and that we make silent corrections only of obvious typographical errors in typed copies.

We are grateful to Lewis Bateman of Princeton University Press for editorial help and to Marjorie Sirlouis for deciphering Wilson's shorthand. We are additionally indebted to Mary Yates of Rydal, England, for supplying new materials and information relating to Wilson's visit to the Lake District of England in 1908, and to Dr. Charles Howard Hopkins for making available letters from the Papers of John Raleigh Mott.

THE EDITORS

Princeton, New Jersey
March 18, 1974

CONTENTS

CONTENTS

ILLUSTRATIONS

Following page 322

Drawing of Wilson in 1908, by Frederic Yates
Princeton University Library

A Newly-Discovered Collection of Wilson Family Photographs
Margaret Wilson, c. 1887
Margaret Wilson and Jessie Woodrow Wilson, c. 1891
Ellen Axson Wilson and Eleanor Randolph Wilson, c. 1890
Margaret Randolph Axson, c. 1894
Ellen Axson Wilson, c. 1890
Princeton University Library

Wilson's letter to Ellen Axson Wilson, July 23, 1908
Princeton University Library

Map of the Lake District of England
Princeton University Library

Palmer Physical Laboratory, shortly after completion, 1908
Princeton University Archives

ABBREVIATIONS

ALS	autograph letter(s) signed
CCL	carbon copy of letter
EAW	Ellen Axson Wilson
hw	handwriting, handwritten
LPC	letter press copy
T	typed
T MS	typed manuscript
TCL	typed copy of letter
TL	typed letter
TLS	typed letter signed
TRS	typed report signed
WW	Woodrow Wilson
WWhw	Woodrow Wilson handwriting, handwritten
WWhw MS	Woodrow Wilson handwritten manuscript
WWsh	Woodrow Wilson shorthand
WWsh MS	Woodrow Wilson shorthand manuscript
WWT	Woodrow Wilson typed, typewritten
WWTLS	Woodrow Wilson typed letter signed

ABBREVIATIONS FOR COLLECTIONS AND LIBRARIES

Following the National Union Catalog
of the Library of Congress

CtHC	Hartford Seminary Foundation, Hartford
CtY	Yale University, New Haven
CtY-D	Yale University, Divinity School
DLC	Library of Congress
MH-Ar	Harvard University Archives
MH-BA	Harvard University, Graduate School of Business Administration
NIC	Cornell University, Ithaca
NN	New York Public Library
NNC	Columbia University, New York
NjP	Princeton University, Princeton
RSB Coll., DLC	Ray Stannard Baker Collection of Wilsoniana, Library of Congress
TxHR	Rice University, Houston
UA, NjP	University Archives, Princeton University
WC, NjP	Woodrow Wilson Collection, Princeton, University
WHi	State Historical Society of Wisconsin, Madison
WP, DLC	Woodrow Wilson Papers, Library of Congress
WWP, UA, NjP	Woodrow Wilson Papers, University Archives, Princeton University
WyU	University of Wyoming, Laramie

[March 3, 1908]	publication date of a published writing; also date of document when date is not part of text
[[March 14, 1908]]	delivery date of a speech if publication date differs
[*March 24, 1908*]	composition date when publication date differs
⟨you⟩	matter deleted from document by Wilson and restored by editors

THE PAPERS OF

WOODROW WILSON

VOLUME 18
1908-1909

THE PAPERS OF
WOODROW WILSON

From Lewis Eugene Pierson[1]

Dear Doctor: New York Mar. 2, 1908

Referring to our talk in Bermuda regarding our desire to secure you as one of the speakers at the Annual Convention of the American Bankers' Association, the writer is very much pleased to herewith confirm his talk and also to further say first that the Convention will very likely be held in Chicago, Illinois, and second that the date is still open, but, from present indications may be set for September or October.

If you can, as far as possible, keep this matter open in your diary we shall be able to advise you of the exact date some time in May.

The writer's associates are much pleased to learn of the possibility of our having you with us and we trust that nothing will prevent your attendance when the date may finally be set.[2]

With kind personal regards,

Yours sincerely,   Lewis E Pierson

TLS (WP, DLC).

[1] President of the Irving National Exchange Bank of New York and chairman of the Executive Council of the American Bankers' Association.

[2] Further correspondence with Pierson is missing, but, as it turned out, Wilson did accept this invitation and spoke to the American Bankers' Association in Denver on September 30, 1908. The text of his address is printed at that date.

An Interview

[March 3, 1908]

DR. WOODROW WILSON.

Last week a representative of The Royal Gazette in the course of a conversation with Dr Woodrow Wilson, President of the Princeton University, collected some of his views on the question of Woman's Franchise, State Feeding of children, and other matters of much public interest at the present time. Women, says President Wilson, do not really want the Franchise and it would not be an unmixed blessing for the rest of the world if they had it.

"It may be true," he said, "that women in various parts of the world have to fight against severe odds, but in America, at least, they are almost too much protected. Not that I would have this otherwise, because I think a woman should have all the protection that is legitimately possible."

"There are many public questions which are the better for the attention of women," Dr. Wilson agreed. "In my own little town, Princeton, they are interested in everything and do a great deal of good by taking such an active part in its life. But, as a rule, women prefer goodness as a quality, to ability, and are apt to be not a little influenced by charm of manner."

"That is why," he went on thoughtfully, "I have almost wished, sometimes, that every fool could be a knave, instead of being, as they often are, very fascinating people. Take our Mr. Bryan, for example, personally, he is the most charming and lovable of men, but his theories are both foolish and dangerous."[1]

Dr. Woodrow Wilson thinks that in many of the States, the Women's Franchise soon became a dead letter after it had been granted. "They simply don't use the privilege," he said.

Asked for his opinion on the State feeding of children he said he was opposed to it on principle. "You cannot," he said, "even enforce work on the father in order that the State may feed his neglected offspring. That would throw a burden on future generations that must not be thrown. Besides, if the State accepts burdens of this kind what becomes of the individual opportunity? The solution of such problems seems to me to lie in the realization, by the individual, of his responsibility to each member of the community in which he lives, and in education."

In speaking of England Dr Wilson said he always looked on it as a delightful holiday place. He and Mrs. Wilson kept house for six months in the Lake District and made many friends amidst the family surroundings of Mrs. Humphreys [Humphry] Ward. Dr. Wilson enjoys Mrs. Ward's books and considers her the ablest writer in England today.[2]

Dr. Woodrow Wilson has enjoyed his holiday in Bermuda extremely. He came for a rest and change and now his tall active figure looks the picture of health.

The President of Princeton has great charm of manner. His words seems [seem] to be the outcome of calm consideration. His face is generally in repose but is lighted every now and then by a delightful smile.

He particularly enjoyed watching the balls at the [Hotel] Hamilton. "It is a very pretty sight and I enjoy it very much," he said, cordially, as he rose from his chair and stood as the band played "God Save the King!"

Printed in the Hamilton, Bermuda, *Royal Gazette*, March 3, 1908.
    [1] Portions of this interview to this point were quoted in an editorial in the Jersey City *Evening Journal*, March 10, 1908.
    [2] Mary Augusta Arnold (Mrs. Humphry) Ward, a granddaughter of Dr. Thomas Arnold of Rugby. Though born in Tasmania, she spent much of her childhood at the Arnold family estate, Fox How, near Ambleside.

To Frank Frost Abbott

[Princeton, N. J.]
My dear Professor Abbott: March 3rd, 1908.

I have returned once more to my duties and have learned with the utmost interest of the conversations and correspondence Dean Fine and Professor Capps have had with you.

I write now merely to give myself the pleasure of saying in person how warmly I desire your acceptance of our call.[1] It would be, in my own mind, one of the most gratifying things that has happened in my administration if we could have the pleasure of adding you to the number of men who are now devoting themselves to classical studies here in an atmosphere and with a programme which I trust will not fail to give to classical study a very great distinction and an unusual academic advantage.

With most cordial regards,
            Sincerely yours,   [Woodrow Wilson]

CCL (WWP, UA, NjP).
    [1] Abbott, at this time Professor of Latin at the University of Chicago, had in fact already accepted the call to Princeton, as the documents will soon reveal.

To Edwin Grant Conklin

Princeton, N. J.
My dear Professor Conklin: March 3rd, 1908.

Thank you for your letter of February 28th with its enclosed copies of your correspondence with Mr. Crampton.[1] I am sincerely glad that you have secured his services and am very pleased to confirm the appointment.[2]

My stay in Bermuda was of the greatest benefit to me, and I have come back feeling very fit in every respect. They have opened a new aquarium down there which is likely to be both interesting and valuable. It is arranged in the corridors of an old magazine on an island, and they hope, after the spring and winter catches, to have it stored with practically every variety of fish to be found in those parts. Their collection is already various and interesting and is attracting a good deal of attention.

Hoping that you are yourself very well,

Cordially and sincerely yours, Woodrow Wilson

TLS (E. G. Conklin Papers, NjP).
    [1] Conklin's letter and its enclosures are missing.
    [2] Guy Chester Crampton, Princeton 1904, was appointed Assistant in Biology for the coming academic year.

From James Hay Reed

My Dear Dr Wilson   Pittsburgh.   Mch 3/08

I understand you are to speak at the Traffic club dinner on April 3d[1] and Mrs Reed and I (and in fact the whole family) want you to stay with us during your stay in Pittsburgh. You can come and go with the same freedom as if at a hotel

Yours Truly   J H Reed

PS I will even agree to go to the dinner and listen to your address.

ALS (WP, DLC).
    [1] Wilson's abstract of his address to the Traffic Club of Pittsburgh on April 3, 1908, is printed at that date.

From Robert Hunter Fitzhugh

My dear Doctor: Lexington, Ky.   March 4th, 1908.

Your letter conveying your usual valued liberality to my negro work has greatly refreshed me. Because of the delay in hearing from you I had feared that my conscious unworthiness had come to be shared in also by you.

Now if I can get night riders,[1] mad dogs, and Bryan off my mind I will be a comparatively happy man.

I don't see why a surface-skimming, phrase-making talking machine should be so peculiarly fitted to represent a democracy the founder of which never made a speech in his political life.

O, for a man who is so busy thinking, and executing that he don't have time to talk—a sort of Washington or Lee, or another Virginian that I might mention.

I sincerely trust that you and your family (if you had them with you) greatly enjoyed the sea trip, and islands, and got back home refreshed in mind and body.

With very high, and warm regard,

Sincerely yours   R. H. Fitzhugh.

ALS (WP, DLC).

1 The "night riders" were members of various extralegal and paramilitary groups which were at this time terrorizing the countryside in the tobacco-growing areas of western and central Kentucky and Tennessee. They were an outgrowth of several associations of tobacco growers formed between 1904 and 1906 for the purpose of pooling their crops in an attempt to force a rise in the price of tobacco, most of which was sold to the American Tobacco Company and other components of the so-called Tobacco Trust. When peaceable methods failed to gain this end, extremist elements in the planters' associations, with the covert support of most of the other members, formed secret organizations of night riders forcibly to prevent tobacco from reaching the market and to compel all tobacco growers to support the boycott. From late 1905 onward, the night riders burned down or dynamited warehouses and other property of the Tobacco Trust; destroyed crops and barns; beat and sometimes murdered men and women; intimidated local courts and law officers; and even invaded and terrorized whole towns.

Fitzhugh's concern was well founded, for by March 1908 the activities of the night riders were reaching a peak and had spread from the areas of western Kentucky and Tennessee, where dark tobacco was grown, to the burley growing sections of central Kentucky. As it turned out, the night riders were soon to receive their first effective checks, and their violent activities then rapidly died out. The new Governor of Kentucky, Augustus E. Willson, elected in November 1907, used the state militia to subdue the riders, and Governor Malcolm R. Patterson of Tennessee soon followed suit. In May 1908, a jury in the United States Circuit Court at Paducah, Kentucky, found twenty-eight members of the night riders guilty in a civil suit brought by members of a family attacked by them, thus opening an effective avenue of legal redress for others similarly molested. Encouraged by a rise in tobacco prices, public opinion in the region also gradually turned against the night riders. By early 1909, most of the illegal activities had ended.

During their period of greatest activity in 1907-1908, the night riders were the subject of much comment and criticism in newspapers and magazines throughout the United States. For the fullest and most sympathetic scholarly study of the night riders, see James O. Nall, *The Tobacco Night Riders of Kentucky and Tennessee, 1905-1909* (Louisville, Ky., 1939). John G. Miller, *The Black Patch War* (Chapel Hill, N. C., 1936), is much more critical of the night riders.

From Henry Burchard Fine, with Enclosure

My dear Tommy,   [Princeton, N. J.]   March 4, 1908

I enclose Abbott's letter of acceptance rec'd this morning fearing that I may not see you before leaving Princeton tomorrow. I go to Atlantic City to join Mrs. Fine, thence to Phila. to attend the Alumni Banquet Friday evening, & thence to Washington, returning to Princeton Sunday evening.

                    Affectionately yours,   H. B. Fine

I leave information as to my whereabouts while away at the room.

E N C L O S U R E

Frank Frost Abbott to Henry Burchard Fine

My dear Dean Fine: Chicago, March 2, 1908

I have sent to President Judson[1] today my formal resignation, and this note may serve as an informal acceptance of the Professorship at Princeton. It has seemed to me only fair to write you at once, now that my formal decision is made known to the University authorities here, because I realize how important it is to issue the programme for next year as soon as possible.

My work here comes to an end June 12, and I am looking forward with great pleasure to the prospect of joining you in the autumn. In your letter notifying me of the appointment you were good enough to offer me the alternative of teaching the full year or a half year during 1908-9. Please count upon me for the entire year. I am eager to see our plans carried out, and to take up for good the life of which Mrs. Abbott and I had such a pleasant foretaste a fortnight ago.

Very sincerely yours   Frank Frost Abbott

ALS (WP, DLC).
    [1] Harry Pratt Judson, President of the University of Chicago.

From Melancthon Williams Jacobus

My dear Dr. Wilson: Hartford, Conn., March 5, 1908.

I thank you most heartily for your kind note of yesterday.[1] It was simply the necessity under which I was of making the train in order to reach home before midnight that compelled me to go without having a word with you.

I cannot but feel that the outcome of the afternoon's discussions[2] [was] most hopeful, and it seems to me that when the Subcommittee reports, we will be assured of the practicability of the site on which most of us seem to be agreed. I suppose, of course, that Mr. Cram should be conferred with by the Sub-committee in order to present before the entire Committee as complete an opinion regarding the proposed location as possible. Indeed, I have wondered whether more than one sanitary engineer outside of Princeton should not be consulted. But this perhaps is not necessary.

On the way out from Princeton, Mr. Cadwalader said that Mr. John S. [A.] Stewart had been urging the name of Mr. Halsey for the clerical vacancy in the Board,[3] assuring him that all the ministerial members were agreed to have him presented. I was compelled to say to Mr. Cadwalader that if his name was presented, I would not be able to support it; and I know nothing which I have ever said to Mr. Stewart that would give him to believe that Mr. Halsey would be my choice for that vacancy. I may have expressed my opinion as to his general desirable characteristics as a minister and a man and an alumnus of Princeton; but this, to my mind, is very different from saying that he would be my choice for a vacancy, in the present condition of Princeton's affairs. I am absolutely convinced that when it comes to the matter of the clerical vacancy, we must—all the more because it is a clerical vacancy—decide upon the very best man we can get, irrespective of location or institutional relationship, and I shall reserve my vote until such a man as this is proposed.[4]

Of course, further than this I dare not go without seeming to urge upon the Committee on Vacancy a reproposal of the name of Dr. Mackenzie;[5] but as I did not propose his name in the first place, and have kept as clear as possible from seeming to urge him in any way, I do not wish now to make even any suggestion regarding a possible further action in his direction. I do not wish to irritate either Dr. Stewart or Dr. DeWitt, especially at this time when the harmonious spirit of the Board is such a desideratum, and I trust you will not think that I am writing this in order to renew that discussion. I am simply anxious that my position regarding Mr. Halsey shall be clear to you, whether it is to anyone else or not.

After hearing what I had said, Mr. Cadwalader said he would certainly not vote in Mr. Halsey's favor, for he was determined to vote for no one upon whom the clerical members of the corporation could not agree.

I trust that you are going to be in good health and spirits for your Alumni Association visits, and I am perfectly sure that what we agreed upon last Saturday is going to be of first value towards conserving all future action of the Trustees in matters relating to the great interests of Princeton.[6]

With kindest regards and renewed thanks for your kind note,
Yours very sincerely,   Melancthon W Jacobus

TLS (WP, DLC).
    [1] It is missing.
    [2] That is, the meeting on March 2 of the trustees' Committee on the Graduate School, when a subcommittee consisting of Grover Cleveland, chairman, Woodrow Wilson, and Edward W. Sheldon was appointed to make an early recommendation on a site for the proposed Graduate College.
    [3] That is, the vacancy created by the death of Elijah Richardson Craven on January 5, 1908. Halsey was Abram Woodruff Halsey '79.
    [4] Craven was replaced by Thomas Davies Jones, elected on October 15, 1908.

5 William Douglas Mackenzie, President of Hartford Theological Seminary.
6 The documents give no clues as to the subject of their conversation on Saturday, February 29, 1908.

From Ambrose White Vernon[1]

My dear Mr. Wilson: New Haven, Conn., March 6, 1908

I am delighted to be sure of hearing you once more when you come to Yale.[2] I have wanted to thank you for that noble speech before the Philadelphian Society which the Alumni Weekly reported for us[3] and thereby made good much of its barrenness. It did a great deal for me, and now I am to have the treat of *hearing* you.

I am writing to know if it can in any way fall to our lot to entertain *ourselves* by having you with us for a meal or for a cup of tea or for anything while you are here. There are two or three of us Princeton fellows here and if you would like it, I could have them around to meet you. Will you be good enough, then, to designate any hour or meal that we may have you in our house? If you are already too overloaded during your visit, do not hesitate a moment to say so; but it was too rare and good a chance to allow to pass.

With warmest regards to Mrs. Wilson, believe me
Very sincerely yours   A. W. Vernon

ALS (WP, DLC).
1 Princeton 1891, at this time Professor of Practical Theology at Yale Divinity School.
2 Wilson was to deliver the address at a Phi Beta Kappa dinner on March 18, 1908. The text of his address is printed at that date.
3 See n. 1 to the news report printed at Oct. 25, 1907, Vol. 17.

A News Report of an Address in Baltimore to the Princeton Alumni Association of Maryland

[March 7, 1908]

PRINCETON MEN CHEER

Dr. Woodrow Wilson Dines With Maryland Alumni.

PLEADS FOR MEN WHO THINK

Dr. Woodrow Wilson, president of Princeton University, was the principal and most enthusiastically cheered speaker last evening at the annual banquet of the Princeton Alumni Association of Maryland, in Arundell [Arundel] Club Hall. . . .

Dr. Wilson spoke on Princeton, saying that it was the aim of that university to train men to think and reason comprehensively, and to organize their lives so that they may become of good to the country. He said that a leading class of clear-thinking, level-headed men should be formed, and that the country could not refuse the leadership of such a class.

Princeton's president was received to the tune of "Mr. Dooley"[1] and was given some cheers, several "sisses," a tiger or two and a few "ahs." His welcome was as lusty and full-voiced as the singing of "Old Nassau."

Mr. Wilson said that a university that takes a man's money and sends his son back without an education is a fraud on the public, and that an institution that does not sober a man's mind and give him a sense of the tasks he will have to undertake in the world is unfaithful to its trust. Speaking of a thorough understanding of the world, he said:

"One of the things most misleading about socialism is the simplicity of its theories. You cannot by mere criticism combat them. The point is that they will not work, and a man cannot see how they will not work unless he is in touch with the complexities of life, and an educational institution should put a man in the position to see these complexities.

"We must organize our own thinking before we try to straighten out the complications of our national affairs."

In many universities, Dr. Wilson said, the attention of undergraduates is so absorbed by the attention to the organization of the college that they have not time to organize their lives. He said that college life now was sounder, cleaner and much better than he ever knew it to be.

"The universities," he went on, "must give the country a leading class so competent that the country cannot reject that leadership. The country now says that Princeton knows what to do, and God forbid that Princeton will ever lose that leadership. We must keep ours the leading light of the country.

"We must see and solve the distemper there is in our nation; we must see the hope, for our province is not a material province, but one for salvation and not for our material success."[2]

Printed in the Baltimore *Sun*, March 7, 1908; one editorial heading omitted.
[1] See n. 1 to the news report printed at Dec. 13, 1902, Vol. 14.
[2] There is a WWhw outline of this address, dated March 6, 1908, in WP, DLC.

To John Van Antwerp MacMurray[1]

My dear Mr. MacMurray: Princeton, N. J.   March 9th, 1908.

Your very interesting letter of December 29th[2] came during my absence from home in Bermuda and was forwarded to me there. I greatly enjoyed it, and it gave me a most vivid and satisfactory picture of your new life and duties and gratified me particularly in the evidence it contained that you were not only enjoying your work but thought that it was thoroughly worth while.

It is very pleasant to think that I was in any degree of service to you,[3] and I shall look forward to the several steps of your career with the greatest interest. If I can ever be of service to you in any other way, I hope that you will not hesitate to call upon me.

Affairs go here now quietly enough. There was the deepest and most wide-spread excitement about the proposals that I made for a systematic reform of the social life of the University, but now that those proposals have, at the request of the Board, been for the time at any rate withdrawn, the excitement seems to have subsided, and those who opposed the plan seem to be slowly recognizing the fundamental difficulty of the task they have assumed of proposing something else in its stead. I cannot help thinking that it will be found necessary in the end to do substantially what I proposed. I am not at all bent upon pressing the matter too fast, because I have the firmest possible conviction that there is no other way out of our present difficulties, and it heartens me not a little to have such words of sympathy and encouragement as your letter contains.[4] I confidently hope that thoughtful men everywhere will sooner or later come to the same decision.

There is no news with us, except that Professor Westcott is to marry very soon Miss [Marian] Bate,[5] whom you may possibly remember as Professor Marquand's assistant in the Art Museum for a time, a most attractive and admirable woman, whom everybody expects to be a very delightful addition to our circles. The distinguished Latinist, Professor Abbott of the University of Chicago, has accepted a call to Princeton and we are now rejoicing in the fact that we have what must without question be accepted as the strongest Classical Department in the country. It is growth of this kind that constitutes the reward of such duties as I am seeking to carry.

Mrs. Wilson joins me in warmest regards. I am,
Always faithfully and cordially yours,
                                        Woodrow Wilson

TLS (J. V. A. MacMurray Papers, NjP).
1 Princeton 1902, Secretary of the United States Legation and Consul General in Bangkok, Siam.
2 J. V. A. MacMurray to WW, Dec. 29, 1907, ALS (WP, DLC). In this twenty-four-page letter, MacMurray tells of his experiences in the diplomatic service at Bangkok during the four months since his arrival at his post.
3 About this matter, see S. Axson to J. V. A. MacMurray, Dec. 14 and 16, 1905, and WW to J. V. A. MacMurray, Dec. 21 and 26, 1905, all in Vol. 16.
4 MacMurray had written: "Though the Quadrangle Scheme has been laid on the table, I devoutly hope that its purpose has been partially fulfilled by the mere agitation, bringing to the realization of the undergraduates the abuses that have grown up about the clubs."
5 They were married on March 25, 1908.

To James Curtis Hepburn[1]

My dear Dr. Hepburn: [Princeton, N. J., c. March 11, 1908]

I am about starting West for Chicago, but before doing so must give myself the pleasure of congratulating you on reaching your ninety-third birthday, as I understand you are to do on Friday next.[2]

I hope you realize the high honor in which you are held by all who know you and all who know of your work, and that you realize in particular the very great pride that all Princeton men have in the lifework by which you have won such honorable distinction.

It is a real pleasure to have you still with us, and I know that I am expressing the general feeling when I wish you continued good health and send you a godspeed in the name of all Princeton men.

With warmest regard,

Faithfully yours,   Woodrow Wilson.

Printed in the *Princeton Alumni Weekly*, VIII (March 18, 1908), 385-86.
1 Princeton 1832, retired medical missionary to China and Japan, at this time the oldest living graduate of Princeton University. For additional biographical information, see WW to the Board of Trustees of Princeton University, March 8, 1905, n. 2, Vol. 16.
2 March 13, 1908.

From Ralph Adams Cram

My dear Dr. Wilson: Boston, March 11, 1908.

I am just in receipt of your very kind letter of March 10, asking if I can be in Princeton for the 23rd., or the 25th of March.

As you know, I hold myself entirely at your orders in all matters connected with Princeton, and if the dates you have given are the only ones on which a conference with regard to the Graduates' College site is possible, then I shall certainly arrange to come, only it would be necessary for me to choose the 25th of March, rather than the 23rd., as I have a very important Committee meeting here in Boston on the former date. I confess, however, I shall come to Princeton on the 25th with some inconvenience, as I have just arranged with Mr. Thompson to make another visit to Princeton on the first of April, in connection with a meeting of the Grounds and Buildings Committee. Both these conferences are of extreme importance, and if it is impossible for the two to coincide, either about the 25th of March, or about the first of April, why then no course is open to me except to make the two visits.

As you know, I always welcome any excuse for coming to Princeton, but just at the present time it is a bit inconvenient, particularly as I have to leave for Cincinnati, Cleveland and Detroit next Sunday, and shall not be back in Boston until the following Saturday, so if I come to Princeton for the 25th, and again for the first, I shall be spending most of my time travelling.

I don't know whether you know that Mrs. Cram has been very terribly ill for the last two months, and only within the last week have we been able to feel that she was entirely out of danger. We have had two nurses constantly in the house for the last seven weeks, so of course I can get away whenever it is necessary, still I am not looking for chances to be absent just at this time.

I think I will write Mr. Thompson and ask if there is any possibility of his getting the meeting of the Committee on Grounds and Buildings for the 25th or 26th. If this can be done, then I could combine the two visits, which would work out most satisfactorily for myself.

I repeat, however, I shall come cheerfully, both on the 25th, and on the first, if other arrangements prove impossible.

I am particularly glad to be called into consultation at this time with regard to the Graduates' School, for it would be difficult to overstate my interest in the question of its location, which is certainly one of the most important to be considered at this time.

I am delighted to know that you are back again in Princeton, and hope that your trip South has restored you to perfect health again. Very faithfully yours, R A Cram.

Supervising Architect.

TLS (WP, DLC).

From Henry Smith Pritchett

Dear President Wilson: New York March 11, 1908.

You perhaps have had but little time since your return to run over the minutes of the last meeting of the executive committee. When you do, you will notice that I have agreed practically to a sharply limited compromise in the matter of the state universities. I have been led to this from the following considerations and I am writing to you because I have felt all along that I had your thorough support in this matter: (1) the representatives of the state universities have submitted a paper practically agreeing that it is the obligation of the state to furnish its retiring allowances, but insisting that with help from us for a limited time they can hope to establish a system successfully, but that without it they have no prospect of such success; (2) I found that their feeling in this matter was so deep that it was likely to split educational institutions into two groups—the tax-supported and the non-tax-supported—a result much to be regretted; (3) I felt that there was much in the argument that the educational influence of the Foundation might be extended if it might have a grip for a limited period of years on these institutions.

All these considerations have led Mr. [Charles William] Eliot and myself, after listening to the state university arguments, to feel that a compromise was on the whole preferable at this time. Meantime, I may say to you confidentially that Mr. Carnegie has quite changed his own attitude and desires now the admission of the state universities without any conditions whatsoever and without any limit of time, a conclusion to which, however, I have not been able to bring myself. All this information I felt I should like to have you know before the next meeting of the executive committee.

I had a note from Mr. Carnegie this morning at Dungeness, stating that he expects to reach here early next week.

Yours faithfully, Henry S. Pritchett

TLS (WP, DLC).

A News Report

[March 12, 1908]

GIVES PUPILS A TALK ON GOOD CITIZENSHIP

President Woodrow Wilson of Princeton University
Pays a Visit to Two Chicago Schools.

President Woodrow Wilson of Princeton University, on his first visit to Chicago in several years, began his day's work this morning by giving students of the Chicago Latin School and the University School for Boys advice on the subject of good citizenship, a subject it is expected he will not forget to refer to in his formal address to-night as the guest of honor at the annual dinner of the Princeton Club of Chicago.

Marry early, have ideals and cherish them, cultivate the spirit of service and remember that the citizen owes a great deal to the country and its institutions was the gist of the advice which was given the youngsters.

At each of the schools the arrival of the Princeton president was made an event to be remembered by the students. At the Latin School all of the pupils were marshaled in the large gymnasium, and at the conclusion of the address rose and gave the school cheer with the name Woodrow Wilson substituted for the usual final words.

President Wilson was accompanied on the trip to the schools by Cyrus H. McCormick, whose guest he will be while in Chicago. When he was leaving the Latin School he was asked if he would see any of the Democratic chieftains while in the city.

"No, I am afraid not," he answered, smilingly, with an honest twinkle of enjoyment in his eyes, which seemed to indicate that he was not allowing any possibilities of the Democratic presidential nomination to interfere with his chosen work.

At noon to-day he was the guest at luncheon, in the Chicago Club, of Mr. McCormick and several of the other local Princeton alumni. To-night he will make the principal address at the Princeton annual dinner to be given in the University Club, and an enthusiastic reception has been arranged for him by the sons of "Old Nassau."

The university and its affairs will be the theme of his address, and a good many of the local alumni, especially those who are members of upper-class clubs, are awaiting the talk with a great deal of interest, as the president's position is expected to determine in large part the future of these thriving organizations.

The material progress of the university will be outlined for the older graduates, and the outcome to date of some of the scholastic innovations at the school, notably the new preceptorial system, which has proved highly successful, will be described.

To-morrow President Wilson will go to Madison and the University of Wisconsin, where he will see several of the men who have been associated with him in various organizations of educators. On Saturday he will return to Chicago to address the members of the Commercial Club at its dinner in the Congress Hotel.

Personally, President Wilson strikes those who meet him as an unusual combination of the scholar and man of affairs. There is a look of seasoned scholarliness about him which accents his affability and charm. He is of medium height, inclined to be spare of frame, and shows in his long, lean face the features of his Virginia Presbyterian antecedents.

He goes to a good deal of pains to find the words which lie closest to the meaning he has in mind for expression, but a clear, unhesitating delivery deceives the hearer as to the care which has been taken.

Though he has not yet completed his tenth year as president of Princeton, he has revolutionized the institution and through new methods of collegiate instruction placed it in the eyes of the educational world.

Printed in the *Chicago Evening Post*, March 12, 1908; some editorial headings omitted.

An Address to the Princeton Club of Chicago

[March 12, 1908]

Mr. McCord[1] and gentlemen: It is with sincere pleasure I find myself in Chicago again. I remember with the greatest pleasure the cordial greetings that you have given me on former occasions, and there is always a feeling with me, whether it comes from the sounds or whatever else, of being upon a familiar scene when Princeton men are together. This is a season when Princeton men want to hear something in particular about the University; indeed, I believe that the whole country in recent years has got in the habit of hearing something in particular about Princeton. It is absolutely necessary, if a University would re-

[1] Alvin Carr McCord, Princeton 1889, President of McCord & Co. of Chicago (manufacturers of railway equipment) and of the Western Steel Car and Foundry Co.; also President of the Princeton Club of Chicago.

tain its self respect, that the country should be hearing something in particular about it all the time.

It seems a very short time, but probably it must be three years, since I stood in this place and spoke to you before,[2] and a great many things have happened in those three years at Princeton.

Looking back upon those years it seems to me a very interesting circumstance, gentlemen, that when we revolutionized the course of study at Princeton and absolutely changed the method of instruction[3] and [it] raised hardly a ripple upon the surface of the alumni.

They were interested when they heard that things had been done that were considered noteworthy; they were gratified; but in accepting what had been done evidently thought of it as a purely intellectual matter and entirely our business (Laughter). But when we came to touching the social life of the University,[4] that was another matter; not a ripple of excitement (Laughter), not a mere ripple of excitement, but a storm of excitement swept the body academic, and we knew at last that we had at last touched the vital matter.

Now, notwithstanding the fact that the revolution of the curriculum and the change in the method of instruction is not in your estimation the vital matter of university life, I have a few words to say about it. (Laughter).

We have changed the curriculum for the purpose of systematizing the instruction,—I am not going into the details of it, because I know that would be tedious to you,—and we have done so because we perceived, as all thoughtful persons did, that the courses of instruction had simply gone to pieces. There was no system, there was no pretenses [pretense] of ordered sequence, there was no intelligent guidance offered anybody. We had fallen into case so wittily described by Mr. Robert Annin,[5] who supposes the Harvard faculty to say that nobody but a freshman understands what anybody ought to take, and therefore, to relieve themselves of all responsibility in the matter by leaving it entirely to the freshmen. That had come to be considered naturally a very undesirable state of affairs; but apparently nobody had felt ready

[2] In fact, Wilson had not spoken to the Princeton Club of Chicago since November 28, 1902. A news report of his address is printed at Nov. 29, 1902, Vol. 14.

[3] Wilson referred, of course, to the new undergraduate curriculum adopted by the faculty on April 25, 1904, and to the preceptorial system established in 1905. See the Editorial Note, "The New Princeton Course of Study," Vol. 15, and the many references to the preceptorial system in Vol. 16.

[4] That is, his quadrangle plan for the social reorganization of the university.

[5] Robert Edwards Annin, Princeton 1880, of South Orange, N. J., at this time in the stock brokerage business in New York.

to tackle the very difficult enterprise of systematizing the course of study. The minute we did it at Princeton, we were congratulated on all hands for having had the courage to do so, and surprise was expressed that it had turned out to be so practicable a thing to do.

Then we found that it was all very well to have a systematic course of study, but it was in danger of not being very serviceable to those who undertook it: that, while the symmetry of the course on paper and theoretically was very gratifying to us as constructive educators, it was still going to be necessary to induce undergraduates to get interested in it. And so, by the preceptorial system, we changed the system of instruction. We brought instruction so close home to the undergraduates that it became embarrassing to them not to attend to it. I mean that literally; I mean socially embarrassing; because, as one undergraduate explained to me, "I live in the same entry with my preceptor, and I often drop in and smoke a pipe with him. I did not like to go into his conferences with only two or three other fellows and not know anything about what we were talking about. The next time I 'drop in' I am embarrassed."

Now, that is exactly the kind of embarrassment that we wish to create, the social embarrassment of associating with men who know that you do not know anything. (Applause). It puts you at a distinct disadvantage, a disadvantage which one does not like to rest under permanently.

I have seen things recently in Princeton which I never dreamed I should see. Certainly when I was an undergraduate I never dreamed of it; and when I first went back into the faculty I never would have dreamed of it. I have seen undergraduates taking walks with members of the faculty, and without any sense of strangeness or distance between them.

But, while all that is very gratifying, it necessarily leads up to something else. We cannot stop there. It is not sufficient to have given a system to study and made study necessary,—not necessary by compulsion of law, but necessary by social compulsion.

It is desirable that the boundary of knowledge should be extended. It does not satisfy any University to impart to a body of undergraduates the accepted items of knowledge. It is necessary for the welfare of a University that the process should go further: that there should be a considerable number of advanced students, and that it should be known as a place where the boundaries of knowledge are steadily pushed forward into the undiscovered territories of the mind. Therefore we have set our hearts at Princeton upon building up a strong graduate department, and we have begun at the right end; we have begun by slowly but steadily calling to Princeton's faculty men whom advanced students cannot afford not to study under, men who will themselves be the only kind of advertising that a University should condescend to. We have now a body of mathematicians and physicists whom men in these lines must study under, if they wish to get the best that there is to be had in the country. We feel certain that next year we shall have a classical department which will be without rival in respect to the most advanced studies, will be without rival in the United States. Department by department, as we have the means, we are fitting Princeton for the things which will give her intellectual distinction and intellectual primacy in this country.

For, after all, gentlemen, a University has as its only legitimate object intellectual attainment. I do not mean that there should not go along with that a great deal that is delightful in the way of comradeship; but I am sure that men never thoroughly enjoy each other if they merely touch superficially. I do not believe that men ever thoroughly know or enjoy each other until they lay their minds along side each other and make real test of their quality. You are tying in perfectly to your friend only when you have shared his thoughts, when you have discussed his ideals, when you have cried an echo to his purposes; then there begin to be wrought those links of steel which bind you to him for life. Every other kind of comradeship is superficial, can be broken; but the comradeships which are of the mind are more than comradeships, they are partnerships. Men who are united in that way are united in such a way that their strength is doubled[,] their purpose increased. When I say, therefore, that a University is a place for intellectual achievement, I also think of it as a place for the most vital social comradeship, a partnership of life. You cannot by pushing the intellectual purposes of Princeton impair the life of Princeton. No life is impaired by being lifted to a higher plane, no life is weakened by being enriched; no life is made less worth living by being beautified by the best things that can come into a human mind and into a human spirit; and if you will add these things to the splendid but superficial foundations of comradeship which already exist at Princeton, you will lift Princeton men to a power such as no University men have yet as a class exerted in this country.

It seems to me that there ought to be a very specific answer to the question which Mr. McCord just now propounded, "What use ought a University Education to be to a man?" For my part I do not believe that the use of an education, of a University training, is merely to impart bodies of information. To judge by our own imperfections, our minds are very much like a sieve. Most things that come into them pass through them, and all that remains sticks to the meshes in some purely accidental fashion. Systematic bodies of information are almost impossible to retain, but there is possible to every man an habituation to the orderly processes of correct thinking. It is possible by close association with trained minds to get the habit of using your mind like an instrument of precision, instead of using it carelessly and dispersing its powers.

There is such a thing as, after four years of discriminating attention to things worth studying, going away with a habit of giving facts and principles a discriminating attention and being able to study things in such wise as to search out their interior and essential substance. That is what a University ought to do for men, teach them the processes which are the real processes of penetrating to the heart of things. And there never was a time in this country, gentlemen, when a training in that sort was more needed, there never was in this country a period of looser, more reckless, more disconnected thinking than the present. (Applause).

The number of things that men now know that are not so is discreditably large, and the number of things that are so that they do not know is equally large. Moreover, they are thinking with their emotions and not with their minds (Applause). Now, a man ought to get out of University the habit of thinking with his mind and not with his emotions, of knowing when he hears trustworthy evidence, and when he does not hear trustworthy evidence, of knowing the kind of talker to believe and the kind of talker to discredit. We have some very attractive talkers in this country, and if one or two of them should ever happen to have a real, tested idea they would be irresistible. Never having been able to distinguish an idea from a mere notion, from an interested purpose, from a personal antipathy, they have lacked convincing power. The power to discriminate between an idea and a preference is a very important power, and that is the kind of power a University ought to give men. It ought to give them the power of clear and disinterested thinking, the power of catholic thinking, so that they will be at once careful of old ideas and hospitable to new. A University education should teach a man to expect that there are things that are true that he never heard of; to expect every now and again to have a new idea swim into his ken, and not to be taken off his feet because it is a new idea; to show a spirit of hospitality for the things he has not heard, a willingness to discuss unusual propositions and not be shy of them because they are unusual; to do clear thinking not only, but catholic thinking also, and, above all, detached and disinterested thinking. The fear I have of the kind of education which starts a man to look only for those things which are going to serve him in his profession, is that from the start to the finish he will have his thoughts so immersed in that profession that he never can think outside of it.

If we had no body of men in this country who could be counted on to think outside of their professions, we would have no trustworthy public opinion at all; because in order to form a just public opinion, you must form a disinterested, a detached opinion, an opinion which does not stick fast in your particular interests, which does not ask first of all "How will that touch me?" The particular creed, the particular rule of life which a University man should *not* have is the rule of life I once heard a cynical person profess. He did not mind, he said, what happened provided it did not happen to him. Now, University men ought to be very much interested in the things that happen that do not happen to them; they ought to have a disinterested and detached view so that they will be able to assess events and tendencies on their merits.

Not only so, gentlemen, but in a country like this it is absolutely necessary that we should do democratic thinking. The particular threat that seems to me the most alarming to our life at the present moment is that we are beginning to think in classes, that we are beginning to think in the terms of the capitalistic interest or in terms of the labor interest or in terms of some other one interest, like the mining interest or the agricultural interest; that we are not putting our minds in the true American attitude of trying to combine the interests, of trying to ignore particular interests, if it be necessary to do so in order to combine them; of putting ourselves in absolute sympathy with that order of life which has made America and which will preserve it if it is to be preserved,—that order under which every man's chance was rendered as free as every other's and under which there was no preferrment of persons or classes in the law-making of the country; the feeling that you must not discriminate against any class, and must not discriminate in favor of any class; that there must be absolutely a free field and no favor for anybody.

There are some of you to whom I have expounded the doctrine of freedom in a political sense and to whom I have used that very phrase in expressing what I understand to be political freedom, "A free field and no favor." That does not mean that every man is going to be kept back to the pace of the slowest. It does not mean on the racing track, any more than it means in the formula as I have used it, that men are to be obliged to hold back and shirk with the loafer and that nobody is going to be permitted to win the race; it means that the best man is going to be permitted to win the race and that no man less than the best is by any unfair method to be allowed to come out in front (Applause). It means exactly what it says, a free field and no *favor*, no favor to the sloth, no favor to those who can take care of themselves, but an absolute equality. Let the race go always to the swiftest and to the best. You cannot heighten enterprise, you cannot secure the best energy of nations, if you suppress the energy of the most capable; you are not going to lift the nation by keeping it on the level of those who are the least capable among those who undertake enterprise.

That is what I mean by democratic thinking, not stopping to ask a man's origin, not stopping to ask a man's influence, but regarding a man, every man, as different from his fellows only in capacity, only in trustworthiness, only in character. The world has been enriched by that idea, and by no other idea. Whenever you have shut classes up tight, nations have begun to rot, because the individual worth has been checked and individual opportunities denied.

Now, if that is the case, you must organize the life of your Universities also in that spirit.

The executive committee of this club was kind enough to ask me to come here and speak particularly on the things which have been most discussed recently with regard to the life of the University. I am going to try to lay before you as candidly as I can the conditions at Princeton as I understand them. I am not going to avail myself of the kind invitation of the committee to discuss the remedies which seem to me necessary. I have proposed a systematic change in the life of the University. I believe more and more as the months go by in the necessity of that change; moreover I am a good fighter, gentlemen,—on the whole I would rather fight than not (Applause), but I have made it a rule never to fight in my own family. (Applause). I so thoroughly believe that the Princeton feeling is a family feeling, and that the Princeton family is a candid family, that will deal frankly with itself in the long run but I am not at all in a fighting mood.

I have been invited, in the matter of remedies, to go and sit down (laughter). I have always been able to take a hint; and this has been more than a hint. I am perfectly willing to sit down for a little while; but I want you to understand what the penalty of my sitting down is,—somebody else has got to do the job; it has got to be a systematic job, and it has got to be thoroughly done. The persons who tell me to sit down are shouldering the responsibility of doing something of their own. I think it is perfectly fair, if I am told to sit down, you should say to the persons who have told me to sit down, that the job is now theirs; it cannot be let alone or ignored; and I can say to them with the utmost heartiness, I am at their service to spread any promising design they may set afoot (Applause), because we are not after bad schemes, we are after a particular result, and for my part I do not care a peppercorn how that result is achieved provided it is achieved. All that I do say is that the result must be achieved (Applause). There is no hurry; I hope there will be no excitement; it is not necessary that anybody should be excited, or suppose that somebody else is going to spring something on them over night; no such tactics are contemplated by anybody that I know of. There is plenty of time, but there is no time for anything but effective thinking. There is no time to do nothing, but there is plenty of time to do the right thing; and if the time is used in doing something intelligent, I don't care how long the time is. If we can see results coming, the speed with which they come is a matter of comparative indifference. That is my position, but I want to lay before you very candidly the things that are to be done.

In the first place, Princeton shares with the other Universities of the country a general situation which puts all the Universities at a disadvantage as teaching bodies. I am going to take the liberty of assuming that Universities are teaching bodies; and Universities everywhere in America are embarrassed as teaching bodies by the fact that the attention of the undergraduates is necessarily withdrawn to other things. The chief reason why their attention is necessarily withdrawn to other things is that nowhere in the United States does any University attempt to unite the life of its undergraduates with its own life. The organization of undergraduate life is left entirely to the undergraduates. You know we speak of residential colleges, but we really have no residential colleges in the United States. We have dormitory colleges. We have colleges which supply a certain number of rooms for men to sleep in. But men must get up in the morning, and after they are up they must go somewhere for breakfast, must find a place for lunch, somewhere to dine; and in between getting up and going to bed, the most of their life that they are interested in has to be lived and to be organized.

Now, all that, everywhere in America, is left to the undergraduates themselves. Their natural tendency is to organize this independent life of theirs in a way which will be agreeable, in a way which will afford them all the indulgences of comradeship, and comradeship with agreeable persons, which they can have; which will give them good food, which will give them pleasant and comfortable surroundings. When you think of it, this is just what absorbs the attention of the greater part of the world. Most of us are engaged all day at a business because we have to provide houses and breakfast and lunch and dinner. We are struggling day after day as business men and as professional men to increase the comfort with which we do these very things, with which we eat and take our ease, and sleep and live. Very few men engage in business for the luxury of engaging in business; if they ask themselves why they are trying to make money, they will say to themselves, not in order to spend it in business, but in order to spend it on the persons whom we love and delight in associating with and who are dependent upon us; that is the burden of life.

When the alumni show by their sudden interest, by their unusual degree of interest, that you have touched their lives when you speak of these things, though you have not touched their lives when you change the curriculum and the method of instruction, they are showing a thing natural enough and universally true. That is life, so far as the material aspects of it are concerned, and it is a very difficult thing to organize successfully. If you leave the undergraduate body to organize it, the energy and initiative of the best men among them must be absorbed in the endeavor.

We have been turning our attention in the wrong direction, when we have said that the reason men do not study is that athletics absorb their interest. Athletics do absorb interest, the interest of the teams, I dare say, during the season, particularly the foot-ball season, because foot-ball is played all night. I mean to say that a foot-ball team is not through for the day when it has had its afternoon practice; it is not through even when it has done with attempting large exercises in digestion at the training table. It sits up at night with the coaches and goes over the signals and discusses the strategy of the game, and the men go to bed jaded with the intellectual strain and absorption of foot-ball. You know this, those of you that have been on teams; you have to study the thing as you would study the diagrams in geometry, and it takes a great deal quicker brain to learn all the signals than it does to remember the demonstrations in geometry. It is an absorbing thing, and I for my part cannot imagine how members of a foot-ball team find any time to study. But most un-dergraduates, you need not be told, are not members of a foot-ball team or any team, although they go, whether they wish to or not, to the practice; because if they did not they would bring upon themselves a lecture from the *Princetonian*. No Princeton man can afford, if he would retain the respect of his fellow stu-dents, to stay away from the practice. The under-classmen, at any rate, go to the practice, whether they want to or not; the enthusiasm which they show at practice is a duty. They cheer when they are told to cheer. But, after all they do not spend the day at the practice field; and we have managed by a great endeavor to prevent their talking exclusively about athletics. I am credibly informed that subjects of study are sometimes men-tioned in conversations at Princeton, and there is a great deal of quiet seclusion in rooms because of the necessity of studying. So far as mere athletics are concerned, I would abide the intellectual rivalry of study with athletics without much misgiving.

But when it is necessary for undergraduates to be busy about a score of practical things that must be done, and which are in themselves desirable things, which can be done with a great deal of credit and result in a great deal of pleasure,—things which involve some of the most delightful and interesting sides of life, I despair of getting their attention. As a matter of fact what we call "undergraduate activities," occupy quite two-thirds of every undergraduate's time, of the conscientious man's time as well as of the loafer's time.

We are trying to part with men who will not work at all at mid-year examinations, and we are succeeding in parting with a considerable number of them, so that we can take care of the deliberately negligent; but, it is not such men who organize un-dergraduate life; it is the best men in the University that organize it, and we would very much like to have a good deal more of their attention. That is the whole truth of the matter; and Princeton is not singular in it. Other Universities cannot get the attention of their undergraduates for the same reason.

When you turn to our own particular organization of under-graduate life, some very interesting things that we all know about are easily seen to be true. It does not make any difference to us for the purposes of our present discussion how far they are true of other Universities. And we cannot, besides, be sure about the details of any other University than our own. It may be that many of the things we regard as characteristic of Princeton are to be found elsewhere also—indeed I am told as I go about the country, by Yale and Harvard men, that their problem is practically the same as ours, and it is very interesting to see how Yale and Harvard want us to make the beginning at reform; they are anxious to see the plans which I have proposed tried by us. They realize that in their case, as in ours, a certain period of excitement and trouble would have to be gone through with; and they are perfectly willing we should lead the way through that *pro bono publico,* and to save them the trouble. They seem to feel that just as certainly as we do it, they will have to do it. I suppose they would rather be obliged to do it than do it voluntarily.

The things that concern me most and illustrate what I have been talking about are the present social ambitions, struggles, and disappointments of undergraduate life. We talk a good deal of nonsense about aristocracy and aristocratic caste and all that sort of thing at college. I do not believe that "aristocracy" is the proper term or is in its real meaning possible among a lot of American youngsters. It is very difficult to find the terms in which to define existing circumstances which are not extravagant and which will not seem exaggerated. It is putting the whole question in a false light, for example, when you discuss the situation at Princeton as a question of the character of the clubs. There is no club at Princeton that I know of whose character I object to in the least. I mean that the character of any given club is clean and legitimate and excellent, as you would expect among self-respecting young men.

That is not the point. The point is, how does the club system work viewed from outside the club and looking at the general life of the men who enter the Universities?

You know what ordinarily happens. In the first place, a numerous group of men coming from some one preparatory school is very likely to contain a larger number of club men than another equally numerous group from scattered sections. That is to say, if men know how to keep together in freshman year and stay together for social purposes, they are more certain to get into an upper-class club than those who enter as individuals and are alone and who have to commend themselves to organized groups of their classmates in order to get into the running.

It is very simple if you become an athlete and so become specially distinguished, or win immediate fame in some other way individually. It will not avail you socially to become distinguished as a scholar, but you may become distinguished in some other way and attract attention enough to get into the running. But if you do not attract attention individually, you must attract it collectively, must get into some organized group.

What does that lead to? It leads in the first place, and this is merely a matter of fact, to absorbing the attention of men even before they get to Princeton with this question, first of all, whether they are going to "make" a club or not.

Observe how important that question is. It is not merely a social question, it is a question whether you are going to get digestible food or not, a question whether you are going to get comradeship, a question of the organization, decency, and pleasure of your whole life as an undergraduate. It is not merely a question of social ambition. There is no other way [to] live at Princeton so desirable as can be found by getting into a club. What is the temptation, then, that a freshman is under? In such circumstances his temptation is to do the very thing that Universities ought to discourage, namely, to *standardize* himself. Do you understand what I mean? I mean to do exactly what he sees others do,—to conform to every practice and every suggestion that is made to him when he gets there; not to be singular in any respect. Underclassmen at Princeton attempt to do what everybody else does; not to express unusual notions; not to do any unusual thing; not to get "queered" by having any individuality whatever. And yet the object of intellectual training is individuality. The object of training a man's mind is to show how one mind differs from every other mind, the thing which each mind in particular can do. The mind which standardizes subordinates and belittles itself, denies itself, sacrifices itself, submerges itself. America cannot afford to have a University which demands of every man that he conform to a type;[6] cannot afford to have Universities—you will not have a University if you oblige men to standardize themselves, it will not be a University, it will not be an intellectual process, it will be a social process, pure and simple, a social process, the penalty of which is laid upon the man who insists upon being himself. That is the serious side of it, and another serious side of it as is shown in the results of the mid-year examinations, seventy-three men were dropped the other day, and when so many men are dropped it makes

[6] At this point Wilson stopped revising this stenographic report.

a noise that the whole country hears. When I hear the figure "seventy-three" where ever I go, they are more sinister than "Twenty-three."

Now, of these, all I believe except ten were in the freshman and sophomore classes, and only one or two seniors and only six or eight juniors were dropped; they are established in life, they know what is going to happen to them; either they did or they didn't. Their minds are at any rate at ease; they are finally disappointed or finally gratified. There is really time to attend to the business of the University for them, except those of them who have to conduct these elaborate organizations and are responsible for their successes, but the under classes have not yet arrived any way, they are guessing, hoping, struggling, combining their whole attention; the whole object of the emotions is absorbed in the thing which makes it impossible for us to get their serious attention particularly at this time of the year, because the [club] elections are coming next month, and the other courses in mathematics and physics, made up of the picked scholars; at any rate at this time all the sophomore class practically does not do anything at all between the first of March and the middle of April. Men cannot think mathematics or reason out physics when their whole future happiness hangs upon something they have to be attentive to.

Now, I am very anxious indeed to get the attention of these young gentlemen. We have something interesting to tell them, and it is a great pity they should wait until the junior year to hear it.

How are you going to relieve that state of affairs? Mind you, it is a very artificial state of affairs. You know very well that when you talk about—when you say you must allow University students to draw together in congenial groups, you know you are putting up a bluff. Do you really mean to tell me that groups of men who get together and form a club, that the clubs are formed on lines of pure congeniality? They are not. Men who do not care particularly for each other, will combine in these groups to get into a particular club, and some of the dearest friends will be separated in the process. I can suggest to you some very much better way to get congenial groups of men together. In the most part, in most of the clubs, they are not chosen by the club, but by themselves, by a process, before the clubs choose them; take one, you got to take the rest; that is the general rule, they come in bodies, they come in conventions, that is the difficulty about the whole process; it becomes artificial. If it were truly natural, most of the objections, at any rate many of them, would disappear, but it is universally admitted to me by the undergraduates, they are not natural, but they are artificial, and that therefore the main thing you are after is not really in several cases, or at any rate, many cases, attained. In other words, the minute you allow a system of that kind to crystallize or grow hard, it defeats the very purposes for which it was originally created, and loses the character which it at first had. But, in one sense it is neither here [n]or there to me; as one of the teaching bodies, it is in one sense neither here [n]or there to me, whether a man finds congenial companions or not, but they should not be so absorbed in undergraduate activities that I cannot get their attention.

Now, that is what every University in this country must face; it must reorganize its life, so that the men will not have to think chiefly of how they are going to live, so that some sort of natural and agreeable life will be provided for men whether they struggle for social preferment or not.

Every where I go I find that Universities and not only Universities but secondary schools may not have their attention centered upon that point, but they are discovering that nine-tenths of what happens in Universities has nothing whatever to do with the classroom.

I hear a man say "my son got this or that out of the college, he got experience I mean, he came out of it a very mature fellow," very true, but what did he go to college for, why didn't he go into the bigger or more real and serious life as soon as he left the high school or secondary school? He could have got it there just as thoroughly and much better, but if you are going to give him that at the University, then the University is going to have a greater hold upon his time and his attention, so that if you really want him to have a University training, you must let him call for this other kind of discipline, which is the discipline of organized life. It all inevitably swings around to that kind of an organization which will make a man's life from day to day and from hour to hour conscientiously in contact with the University itself. In other words, gentlemen, the preceptorial system acquired all over this country has now come, after only three years of operation, to a dead wall; mind you, that wall stands a great distance beyond where the University stood when this system was introduced; something like a revolution has been wrought in the habits of study in Universities. Why, preceptors cannot get more than a certain amount of attention from the undergraduates,—not only that, but you cannot really get hold of a man unless you live with him, and the necessity in the re-organization of the Universities is, that the teachers should live with the pupils, live with them as members of the same organization, of the same family, so that a man outside of study hours, and the hours which he regards as hours of task should be conscious of the intellectual force which we present in this place.

Why, I remember distinctly when I left Princeton and went to the University of Virginia, I went to a place by no means organized as I thought it ought to be organized, but so geometrically constituted that we were daily in contact with some of the most celebrated men in the faculty of the University. I shall never forget the influence upon me of merely passing every day of my life one of the most distinguished scholars in America[7] and exchanging a few words with him and feeling that I was a campus comrade of his. Upon my intellectual maturity merely to know that this man who upon certain topics could hold the attention of the world was my daily comrade, gave me some conception of what a University was for, an idea I never got at Princeton. The Princeton campus, the place where all forces are centripetal, where a man coming for certain constructive purposes and then falls apart and all the pull is outward, all the pull is away off; they have exchanged the messages that they have for each other and after that they had their conference, given their lecture, they have nothing more to do with each other unless they deliberately call each other out and that is not considered an ordinary thing to do, and merely to tie,—to socially tie together the teacher and pupil part of the University is a thing that is now necessary, if the progress of the University is not to be estopped.

I believe really one of the most enlightening kind of influences that has ever happened to me, I would go off some where where I was known merely as a very instructive person, as a president of a University or professor of this, that or the other, and I would be thrown into intercourse with some person who would presently after a day or two express a surprise about things which he would put in very guarded language, but which would go to this, that he had found me to be a human being, that he had found that I was interested in a lot of things besides things that I taught. That I was a man that kept my eyes open to what was going on in the world and liked a good story as well as the next fellow and could tell some that could be repeated in polite company. And it has

[7] It is impossible to know to whom Wilson was referring. He almost certainly was not referring to John Barbee Minor, his principal law professor, for his contacts with him were far from casual.

changed,—I know that it has changed the conception of Universities for some men, merely to socially know members of the faculties and find they are made as other men and are just as intelligible, if you take them reasonably and don't expect too much of the average man.

One of the trials of my life is that wherever I go people endeavor to engage me in conversations on very serious subjects and I want to get out of the school occasionally and I remember being a guest at the hearth of a very interesting gentleman who took me very seriously at the dinner table and when I arrived he invited a company of persons to meet me, all as he supposed seriously minded. I got so tired of discussing all the high themes there are that I presently kicked over the traces and I asked him if he would like to hear my favorite lyric. He seemed surprised but he expressed himself as desirable of hearing it and I said my favorite lyric is "There was a poor Monk of Siberia, found his lot growing drearier and drearier, so he broke from his stall [cell], with a hell of a yell, and eloped with the Mother Superior" (Applause).

I found that limbered up the conversation and after that I was allowed the ordinary freedom and prerogatives of a human being. It would be for the benefit of the undergraduates to discover that we are living with human beings, and that these gentlemen, bent upon their intellectual improvement, were an excellent kind of a comrade. If you knew that gentlemen, you cannot go away from the University with your horizon limited to the undergraduate point of view.

The new undergraduate is a very interesting person with regard to the matters which he has experience about and which he understands. He is as old as anybody; I don't want any better balanced judgment than I can get from an intelligent undergraduate about undergraduate things, but with regard to things he has never had any experience in, he is a child, and sometimes a very diverting child. I think some of the editorials I have read in the Princetonian would make the fortune of any comic journal, read by some persons, when they are out of the editor's balliwick [bailiwick] probably the things he may have notions about is very large because I think you have no greater freedom than when you discuss anything you do not understand. You are not limited then by any knowledge, and it is extremely wholesome to come into contact on these matters with older minds.

Part of my discipline I think I gained from an uncle of mine[8] who had one of these painfully clear minds and to whom I used

8 Dr. James Woodrow.

to make very expansive statements. He would proceed without excitement to trim them down to their natural size and I learned a certain discretion in his presence which I otherwise would never have learned, and it occurred to me on several occasions I ought to be informed before I expressed an opinion; and the discipline did not come with any painfulness because he was an extremely affable man, kind old gentleman, very fond of me, but I got what was coming to me, and there was no abatement of the process, notwithstanding its joviality and the interesting manner in which he flayed me on occasions when he took me on excursions to see what I was really talking about, things which I thought I could penetrate at a glance and which I found contained more than I could penetrate at a glance.

Our object is to unite these. That cannot be done by the present system; if you do it with the present system you hermitically [hermetically] seal the two apartments. If you make the existing thing work perfectly then you have completed the separation and if you have completed the separation you have absolutely estopped the intellectual permeation of the undergraduate body; you cannot afford to do that and I for my part do not care how you prevent it providing you do completely prevent it.

I have a private opinion that there is a plan by which it can be done and I think that any plan by which it is to be done must more or less resemble that plan but then that is for the time being my private opinion. I may publish that opinion but for the time being it is withheld from publication, and we are eagerly awaiting for the publication of some other plan and we cannot dispense with the thing; we cannot turn our backs upon it, we cannot forget it. If I have done nothing else I have started a subject which you cannot drop (Applause), and I want to end this part of my address as I began it by expressing my greatest confidence in the candor of Princeton undergraduates, my confidence that they will not drop this subject, that they will go to the bottom of it, that they will at length come to some candid, as nearly as necessary uniform opinion. I am not afraid of anything which may befall this particular discussion. I believe with Doctor [blank] that the truth is not an invalid, you need not be afraid of treating her roughly; she will survive the process. If what I have said is not true, it is desirable of being shown to be false. If, what I have proposed is not the right remedy, there is a better remedy some where lying undiscovered. I am perfectly willing to leave it to the candor of Princeton's men and to their undoubted and earnest love for their alma maters here, which is at least fundamental, which gets to the heart of her life and to the heart of every life or the life of every University of this country, for here again gentlemen, if we find the solution, we have, as we have already attained in so many other respects, the leadership of America. (Great Applause).[9]

T MS with WWhw emendations (WP, DLC).
  [9] There is a WWsh abstract of this address, dated March 12, 1908, in WP, DLC. Wilson's transcript of this shorthand draft was printed in the *Princeton Alumni Weekly*, VIII (March 25, 1902), 402-405.

From John Lambert Cadwalader, with Enclosure

My dear Mr. President: New York.   12 March, 1908.

I have made one or two attempts to go to see Mrs. Sage,[1] but I could not quite arrange it at a time to suit her, and I finally wrote a letter (of which a copy is enclosed herewith) to Henry W. de Forest, who represents her and through whom the suggestion of what she proposed to do was communicated to me.

I told de Forest that I would go to see Mrs. Sage today, if agreeable to her and that I was going away this afternoon for ten days; but the hour which would be agreeable to her was so late that I was compelled to leave it at de Forest's suggestion until I come back. He had read to her the substance of my letter and said that it was satisfactory to her and that she would be glad to talk over the details with me; so I assume the matter is on an entirely proper basis.

I said, however, to de Forest that he, as a University man,[2] would understand that it was hardly feasible to put in a Freshman building alone, because it would lead to disorder and objectionable surroundings and would not work. He said he entirely understood it and that that would not do.

I suggested also whether he thought it would be agreeable to Mrs. Sage if we should bind ourselves, as you suggested, that there should be accommodation upon the campus for as many freshmen as the building would hold, whether they roomed in the building or not, and he said that seemed to him a reasonable proposition.

On my return in ten days I will choose an occasion to go and see Mrs. Sage and do something to clinch the business and make it possible to hereafter arrange the details.

I assume that it would be agreeable to you if I offered the hospitalities at Princeton to Mrs. Sage.

                    Yours faithfully,   John L. Cadwalader

TLS (WP, DLC).
¹ Margaret Olivia Slocum (Mrs. Russell) Sage, with whom Cadwalader had been negotiating through her adviser, Henry Wheeler de Forest, about the gift of a dormitory to the university. Discussion of this matter begins in Vol. 17.
² A.B., Yale 1876; LL.B., Columbia 1878.

E N C L O S U R E

John Lambert Cadwalader to
Henry Wheeler de Forest

My dear de Forest: [New York]   10 March, 1908

I have tried once or twice, unsuccessfully, to get you on the telephone in regard to Mrs. Sage.

I saw the President of the University and explained to him Mrs. Sage's liberal intentions in regard to Princeton, and he requested me to call on Mrs. Sage, in the way most agreeable to her, to intimate that the University was greatly delighted at the interest she took in presenting them with a dormitory, that they accepted the gift and that we would make every effort, in every respect, to most distinctly follow her inclinations and intentions in the matter. I had proposed to suggest, to show our appreciation, that I go and see Mrs. Sage and make the statements in person. On Thursday, however, I am compelled to go away to the South for ten days. I could go on Thursday morning, if you thought it wise to do so and it would be agreeable to Mrs. Sage, or I can leave it until my return.

We would like very much if she would come down to Princeton on some day a little later and look over the ground and assist the University authorities to choose a site. The President would be delighted if she would lunch with him, and see how attractive a place Princeton is.

We all quite appreciate what Mrs. Sage proposes to do, and we will faithfully carry it out. My thanks to you.

Yours faithfully,   [John L. Cadwalader]

TCL (WP, DLC).

An Address to the Commercial Club of Chicago

[[March 14, 1908]]

THE GOVERNMENT AND BUSINESS

MR. PRESIDENT AND GENTLEMEN:—I esteem it a particular compliment that you should have invited me to speak again to this club. I cannot but remember that it is now five years since I addressed the club;[1] I must suppose that most of you have forgotten my former address.

I do not feel that I come here to-night as a college president but rather as one of the citizens of the United States, interested in this question, because every man of public spirit, conscientiousness and intelligence must be interested in it. And every man must accept any opportunity that is offered to take part in the universal public counsel now going on regarding it—for certainly we stand very much in need to take counsel with each other.

We are being governed by many impulses, but we are not being governed by well thought out conclusions. It is certainly a time of excitement, of excited action which is being made more excited by excited speech; and in such a time there is special need that we should take counsel with one another as to what it is wise to do.

I feel that in attempting to discuss so great a subject as that which I have had the temerity to undertake I at least give myself the advantage of plenty of sea room. There are many phases in which one might regard the subject of "The Government and Business."

A member of your Executive Committee told me the other day when I had the good fortune to travel a little way with him on the train that one thought of your Committee had been that I should discuss the constitutional aspect of the government to business. I am afraid that the constitutional aspect of these questions are not taken very seriously now. I am afraid that constitutional discussions sound very academic. I am afraid that we have got impatient of constitutional restraint—that we regard it a little old fashioned to ask what the government of the United States for example, has the right to do, and have fallen into the fashion of asking only what we would desire it to do. Constitutional restraints we are apt to think are only for persons who are bringing themselves to political maturity. We have come to political maturity; and now, if there be no constitutional powers definitely suitable to our business needs we must find them; must make shift to find them in the doubtful phases, if there remain any doubtful phases, of the constitution itself. Undoubtedly it is one of the most interesting sides of this question—what the government of the United States can do. It is also most interesting

[1] The text of Wilson's first address to the Commercial Club of Chicago, "The Relation of University Education to Commerce," is printed at Nov. 29, 1902, Vol. 14.

to ask where the line lies between what the states can do and what the federal government can do. But, after all, can we not for the moment postpone that question so far as our evening's discussion is concerned, in order to deal with the other and larger question, What *ought* the government, whether it be government of the state or the United States, to do in respect of the regulation of business under its modern conditions.

A perfect mania for regulation has taken hold of us. We have got in a fever of activity with regard to legislation; and I suspect that after having acted we shall think; after having attempted a dozen remedies we shall then carefully set our selves down and ascertain whether any of the remedies remedy. Is it not the wiser part to ask what it is that we want to remedy and what will be likely to remedy it?

Of course it is no longer debatable that there are a great many things to remedy. It is no longer debatable that a great many practices have sprung up under the modern conditions of business which are very undesirable practices indeed, very demoralizing to the public welfare, and very demoralizing to the men who engage in them—things not founded in righteousness, not founded in fair dealing, not founded in the right interpretation of law. And these things have been done under the cover of corporate organization. They do not seem to have been done so much by individuals as by combinations of individuals, which, in the old phrase, have no bodies to be kicked or souls to be damned—intangible, invisible, multiple persons, given their existence only by the theory of law, and not susceptible to ordinary moral standards.

In fact, we feel that we have lost the wrongdoers in the complex organization of modern business, and, instead of undertaking to find them again, we are undertaking to handle the organizations and not the persons, and so are changing the whole theory and practice of our legal system. For in respect of all things hitherto punishable it has been regarded as the sound theory of the law that the persons responsible should be punished, and not the business of the country. We have been trying to regulate the business when we should have been trying to regulate transactions. We have been trying to regulate the affirmative constructive administrative conduct of business when we should have been discriminating between those transactions which are detrimental to the public welfare and those which are not, seeking to check the one and to let the other go free of restraint.

Now the pursuit of the responsible person has become necessary, because in his concealment he has brought reproach and suspicion upon all other persons similarly circumstanced with himself. We hear a great deal about dishonest transactions, but we do not hear the names of the men who have conceived the dishonesty. It will not do to cast suspicion upon hundreds of thousands of honest men because you can not find half a score of dishonest men. No man in his senses will believe that the business of this country is essentially corrupt. No man who has any experience in dealing with men of affairs in this country will suppose that the majority of them are dishonest. Everybody knows that, upon the practiced philosophy of business, business would break down if the majority of the men who conducted it were dishonest. If men could not trust each other they would not enter into transactions with each other.

I was talking to-day with a gentleman as much interested in the administration of law as I am myself, and we were commenting upon the interesting circumstance that where there are no courts, at least no courts that can be trusted, a man's word is always as good as his bond in business transaction; because that is then the only thing to rely upon. If you can not cite him before the courts and enforce his promises against him, why then you will not accept his promises unless you know that it is unnecessary to resort to courts in order to enforce them. And, inasmuch as most business everywhere rests upon foundations lying outside the courts, most business undoubtedly rests upon the trustworthiness of the individuals engaged in it. The great transactions of this country could not have been carried to the perfection to which they have been carried if the majority of men were wrong in their principles and dishonest in their methods.

There is no doubt such a thing as predatory wealth but if wealth were all of it predatory—if every man were preying on every other man, a condition of things would arise which would be a condition of warfare and not of peace, a condition not of organization but of confusion and disorganization. Such a condition has not arisen, but these [there] are undoubtedly bad practices and it is none the less necessary, if we would moralize our business, that we return to a possible basis of morality.

Now morality is never corporate. Morality is never aggregate. The only way you get honest business is from honest men. I know that there are methods by which men cover the uncomfortable emotions of their consciences. I know that men accept in business which is corporate certain compromises which they conceive to have been forced upon them by the action of those with whom they must act in corporate transactions. I know that men salve their consciences by saying it was necessary to do this, that, or the other thing because they had to do it by way of compromise and in combination with others. But in the long run a man's conscience never lies easy under that kind of salve. It it [is] necessary for every one of us, sooner or later, to go to bed. It is necessary for every one of us, sooner or later, to put out the light and lie down with our consciences. It is necessary, if men would retain the momentum of their best energy, that they should retain their respect for themselves when they are alone and closeted with their own consciences; and society itself cannot exist upon any other basis. Men know they are not going to be saved from responsibility by those who judge of the essence of the matter by any combination with others. They know they must be judged separately and individually, and there is no valid system of law which can be based upon any other feeling than that.

What I want particularly to point out this evening is this: We are making in our generation a radical choice by choosing between various sorts of practices. We are choosing between opposite sorts of principles. The principle upon which we shall choose our course of action, we of this generation, is a principle which will either retain or alter the character of our government. That is the serious aspect of the whole matter.

I have heard it said that certain kinds of governmental regulations must be adopted in order to stop the drift towards socialism in this country, and yet the very kinds of governmental regulation which are contemplated in such arguments are regulations which are themselves essentially socialistic in principle. After you start a little way on that road it is merely a question of time and choice as to how far you will go upon it. You can not, after you have got on the road, arbitrarily call a halt at any one point upon it. Let me proceed at once and tell you what I mean.

The regulation of the transactions is not socialistic in principle, no matter how far you carry it. If you say that the law shall prohibit such and such transactions, transactions of such and such kinds and classes, that is not socialistic; that has been time out of mind the process of law and is quite possible to be handled by the judicial machinery of the country. But if you propose that the government shall keep its hand on business by way of direct administrative regulation, through the instrumentality of commissions which will have it in their discretion to guide business in this direction or guide it in that, to determine which is best method and practice here, which the best there, you have adopted *in principle* the same thing as government ownership itself. You have not adopted government ownership with candid bravery; but you are on the way towards it. You are saying: Let the private individual have the burden and risk of the active administration, but let the government say what the character of the administration shall be. Let the individual take all the risks, let the individual spend all the money, but let the government say how the business shall be conducted.

Now in principle there is no difference whatever between that and government ownership, no difference whatever between the direct regulation of business and the ownership of business enterprises. For the only safe way by which the government can pick its steps is by picking them upon the basis of experience, and the only thing that experience can yield is the revelation, item by item, of the things, the particular transactions, which society wishes to control.

What is it that is wrong with the business of this country? In the first place, certain monopolies, or virtual monopolies, have been established in ways which have been unrighteous and have been maintained in ways that were unrighteous; and have been used and intended for monopolistic purposes. In the second place, the business of the country has come near to being regulated, at one crisis and another, by what is no business at all, but the mere manipulation of those securities which represent business. The chief things that have gone wrong with the business of the country have not been based upon monopolistic undertakings at all, but have been based upon such things as overcapitalization and the foisting upon the public, that does not know the process by which this thing has been done, of securities that were not worth the purchase price that was paid for them. At the same time that purchase price, a perfectly artificial thing in itself, brought millions of dollars into the pockets of men who had managed the unrighteous transaction. Now the men who did these things are not always the men who administer the actual business of the country. In most instances they are not. The other day the directors of the United Railways of New Jersey were lunching in Princeton, and the inevitable topic of discussion arose—the topic of railway regulation. President [James] McCrea of the Pennsylvania Railroad, who was the guest of the occasion, said, what I believe, that he did not know of a particular in which the Pennsylvania Railroad was being dishonestly administered.

I do not think that any man, at any rate any man who is informed upon such matters, supposes that the Pennsylvania Railroad is administered in any way but in the best business way; and the same can be said of most of the greater railway systems of the country. But the difficulty about the whole situation is that the responsible administration of the railroads is too often disconnected with the management of their finances.

The management and manipulation of securities in the market may be and often is disconnected from the actual way in which the business is being conducted. The business may be earning a great deal of money or it may be earning a very little money, but the men who manipulate the securities make certain representations and certain deals which bring about artificial changes in value in the money market. Now the minute these artificial values are discovered to be artificial the credit of a perfectly sound institution is apt to suffer and collapse as a consequence.

I believe you will all agree with me that there has been more of an exhibition of predatory wealth in that field than in any other. The men who have preyed upon us have not been the men who were manufacturing or who were actually running the railroads of this country. They have been the men who deceived us with regard to the values of securities. They have preyed upon us and they have got something for nothing. I do not object, and I do not believe that any citizen of the United States objects, to any amount of money that has been earned, but every man objects to the accumulation of vast sums of money that have not been earned except by a wrong use of the wits of the men who acquire it.

Now it is a very nice problem of law how you are going to define these offenses and how you are going to put your finger on the men who are guilty of them. I do not believe, for my part, that the government can say how great bodies of business ought to be administered. Neither do I believe that any discretionary action of the government with regard to who shall be caught and who shall not be caught at these nefarious transactions will accomplish the object that we are after.

What we need just now is a very peculiar thing, which I am afraid we are not very likely to get. We need the advice of very experienced corporation lawyers. What I mean to say is that the men who have stood inside the corporations as counsel and who have been trying to defend those corporations from the action of the law, are, as I know, some of them the chief critics of what our legislation has been. We ought not to heed their criticisms in the least unless they will come forward and say what the legislatures ought to do. They know what has gone wrong if anything has, and they know how to get at it if anybody does.

Now the situation is simply this. If these gentlemen will come forward and disclose the exact nature of such transactions and show the way in which they may be limited or prohibited, if they will assist us to distinguish between the transactions which are legitimate and the transactions which are not legitimate, and show us how to make that discrimination in the prohibitions of the law, they will save their corporations from the mob, and will have saved this country from what may be a fatal period of experimentation. Are they going to do it?

I can speak very glibly about the theory of this thing and what ought to be done. But these gentlemen know in detail what it is practicable to do and what ought to be done. If I were called upon at this moment to draw up any measure whatever, by way of suggestion, the first thing I would have to do would be to call them in to tell me what the measure ought to be. They know how to discriminate between one kind of transaction and another because they have been trying to steer their corporations on the leeward side of the law, and they know which is the leeward side and which is the windward side. Now I am a lawyer myself, and I haven't very much hope that they will do it. (Laughter). Almost all lawyers are on the defensive. Almost all lawyers think that the thing to do is to "stand pat" and defy the law, and see whether the legislator can do what he wants to do or not; and the reckoning justified by many past experiences is that he won't find a way to do it after all. But, gentlemen, there is blood in the eye of the American people now and they are not going to be stopped from wrecking something if you do not guide them into remedying something. You have the choice between wreckage and remedy.

Now I have a few ideas which are not vague on this subject. I believe that with regard to the administration of corporations it is possible to pick out the individual who is responsible. I do not know of any corporation which cannot itself pick out the person connected with its administration who is responsible when anything goes wrong. And if the corporation itself can pick out the responsible person I am sure the corporation can be induced to disclose the responsible person to the officers of the law. I am sure that if every corporation has in its own mind, in the mind of its own managers and owners, that which will enable it to put its hand on the man responsible for each transaction it can be made to disclose for the benefit of the public the requisite information, so that the officers of the law can find that man; and then you have found your man before the offense—for there is a certain play of hide and seek after the offense. After you have got your information and your fingers pointing to the man, and the transaction prohibited is engaged in, it is easy enough to get your man.

You will say that the corporation will put up a dummy; but I venture to predict that the corporation won't put up more than one dummy. You can not hire a capable man to go to the penitentiary, and you can not afford, even when the government is not looking at you, to employ an incapable person. You can not get dummies of the stuff you need for the administration of your business for a price that will induce them to run the risk of going to the penitentiary. If you will fine individuals, if you will imprison individuals, if you will bring the responsibility home to the person who did the thing, then the things that you complain of will stop. They will stop by unanimous consent. I want to use an illustration, which if it were misunderstood would be offensive. I hope it will not be misunderstood.

Let us assume that the corporation is doing something which it detrimental to the public welfare. Our present method of treating it is such that it would encourage a lot of burglars, for example, to form a burglarizing corporation, if it were possible, in the expectation that when a burglary was committed and detected, you would fine the corporation of burglars and allow it to retain the services of its most expert burglars. That is closely analogous to the operation of some of our present legal arrangements. You allow corporations, when you occasionally detect their breaches of the law, to retain the services of the men who can easily make good by their wits the fines which you impose upon the corporation, and so do not check the very thing that you are intending to check when you impose the fine.

I do not believe that we shall ever by that process check the things we are intending to check. I am not criticising the imposition of fines by the courts, because they are obliged in the performance of their duties to go in that direction at the present time. I am discussing what the law might be, not what the courts might do, because the courts must execute the law as it is. I do not believe that laws of that kind will have the effect we intend them to have.

I know that it is a very difficult matter, standing outside a corporation, to put your finger, for example, on gentlemen who are manipulating business in their own interest; because the real difficulty, as I understand it, in getting individuals convicted now is the opinion of the country and the opinion of jurors that generally the person you are trying to convict is not the real person who is responsible—that a great many of the most objectionable transactions are brought to pass by pressure from those who are the real masters, but not the acknowledged masters of the business. There is the point of most difficult distinction. Cannot the corporation lawyers enable us to detect these outside masters, as well as the inside servants who are responsible for the over-capitalization, and for the secrecy of method which makes it impossible for the investor to find out whether securities are worth the price he pays or not? These are the things which render the situation in the stock market from time to time disastrous and uncertain. If they can not, it seems to me that we have little hope of remedy. You may make business on its administrative side as clean as possible and yet leave the business of the country in a feverish condition, because you have not checked the disturbing evils.

If you undertake the old-fashioned program of finding and punishing the individual, what have you got to do? In the first place, you have got to have public officials who won't be respectors of persons. You must have public officials who will promptly, zealously, and fearlessly execute the law against anybody, no matter what the consequence is—men who will not exempt those whom they may consider serviceable to the community, but will proceed against anybody, in any circumstances, who breaks the law. I am afraid that is not the present situation. We hear of a great many discriminations as between individual and individual. There are many men in this country—I won't say many, but there are several—who are known to be responsible for certain outrageous transactions, against whom no attempt to put the law into operation has been made.

No government can regulate anything, gentlemen, unless that government is of the right sort and is thoroughly trustworthy. I remember talking with a member of a reform club not long ago, a reform club in the city of New York. He said that for twenty years he had been going to Albany to get reform measures passed and that little had been accomplished although many promising measures had been passed; and that he had the humiliating confession to make that, after all those twenty years of effort to get a good government by good legislation, he had found that the only way to get good government was to elect good men to conduct it; that the best laws did not operate successfully unless the best men were put behind them to execute them.

Not only that, but, on the other side of the law itself, you must simplify and speed the processes of the law. Our present law is intricate, and it is too expensive for the ordinary litigant. I suppose there is hardly a man of moderate means engaged in business in this country who has not allowed himself to be preyed upon in instance after instance because of the difficulty and expense of the processes of the law.

I was present at a banquet the other evening given to the retiring chancellor of the state of New Jersey, the distinguished Judge [William Jay] Magie, and of course a great deal was said about the chancery practice in that state. New Jersey is one of the few states which has retained a distinct set of chancery courts as contrasted with the courts of common law and every thoughtful student of our judicial system must be very much interested in the chancery procedure of that state. It has been not a little altered from the old chancery practice in England, except in its form of procedure, and it seems to come to this: It is the direct and informal side of the administration of the law. You can go into a chancery court in New Jersey, for example in the case of a stock company, and get the court to look into all the circumstances and make a sort of family arrangement for the benefit of the stockholders without impeding itself by any of the technicalities of suit and procedure which hamper the common law courts. It is an instrumentality for getting things informally disentangled by the simplest and most direct methods on the part of the courts themselves. Now I am not sufficiently acquainted by experience with that practice to commend it in such a connection as that of which I am now speaking. I use it merely as an illustration of what we must do in order to get at the modern complex situations in business and disentangle modern rights.

For, gentlemen, we are about, should we keep our present tendencies, to embark upon experiments which may bring us deep disappointment and confusion. We are apparently trying to establish a system by which the government will take care of us and tell us how our business is to be directed. I am referring of course to the discretionary powers of the various commissions which we have set up. I have yet to hear, for example, of a state railway commission that has had the courage to discriminate in its regulations between one line of railroad and another. I know of a particular state with whose affairs I am familiar in which one of the main lines of railway runs through a flat country where there is an abundant population, where the operating expenses of the road, because of the absence of heavy grades, etc., are comparatively light, where the rolling stock is easily kept in order; but in which another main line runs a great distance through a mountainous country, where all the operating expenses are heavy and where there are practically no earnings at all worth mentioning in the way of freight and passenger traffic. It is manifestly unfair to impose the same rates upon those two systems of railway. The one road can make profit at the rate which is imposed, and the other road cannot; and yet the railway commission of that state has not the courage, in the face of present public opinion, to discriminate between the two lines in framing its regulations. What is the consequence? You are bringing pressure to bear upon the owners of the unprofitable road to do what you profess to wish to prevent—namely to sell out and pool its profits and losses with those of some bigger system—those of rival and competing roads—the very thing you have aimed so much of your legislation against. By selling out, and only by selling out, by uniting with other interests, by combining, by lessening their administrative expenses, it will pay them to do things which they are obliged by the railway commission of the state to do.

You are merely tempting Providence by some of the experiments you are trying. While there is a responsible governor in the State of New York, I have no doubt that the public service commissions of the state and of the city of New York will be very public spirited commissions; but there is going to come a time when we will be drowsy and inattentive about these things, when we will forget to keep our eye upon them, when there will be other sorts of governors (as there have been other sorts of governors), and when the appointment to such commissionerships will furnish an opportunity for a system of graft such as we never yet dreamed of in this country. For the first time in America the business of the country will be at the discretionary disposition of the officers of the government. I do not believe that we shall ever come out upon a firm basis of law on that side.

You will see that I am simply going round and round about a single theme. I am simply going back at every turn of what I have been saying to what seems to be the crux of this whole business. We have acted without analysis. There never was a time when it was necessary that we should do franker or clearer or more comprehensive thinking about the business transactions of the country. We ought to discriminate what we really want from what we do not want.

At present we say in our law that we want every great corporation to be broken up. For more than twenty years a large number of states in the Union have been engaged in the attempt to prevent the formation of corporations which might operate their businesses as a monopoly. They have not required in those laws that they should operate them as a monopoly in order to become obnoxious to the law. It is only sufficient that they are of a kind to have power to operate as a monopoly, and if they are of that kind they are illegal.

What has been the consequence? Have those corporations been broken up? On the contrary they have multiplied. They have enormously multiplied. Have you heard any man who knew the way in which business was conducted and must be conducted in this country suggest that we should go back to the operation of business by small individual firms? Have you heard anybody suggest that we should go back from the corporate organization and attempt an entirely different one? You have heard nobody who knew anything about business suggest anything of that kind; but you continue to try to break up organizations which have the opportunity to be monopolistic without inquiring whether they have become monopolistic or not. Have you ever defined in your law what a monopoly is? Have you ever defined under the law what kind of restraint of trade you regard as undesirable? Have you ever defined under the law what constitutes over-capitalization and what kind of capitalization you regard as desirable, what process of capitalization you regard as desirable? Have you ever tried to define under the law what you mean by unfair competition? Have you ever defined under the law what you mean by the kind of business which must not be forced out of operation by competition, and the kind that ought to be forced out of operation by competition? Do you wish to save men from being forced out of business if they won't operate their business in the way that is best or most serviceable for the public? Do you wish to save the weak and check and discourage the strong? Do you mean to keep business on a level as low as that to which some trade unions try to depress their members by keeping it down to the level of that which is worst conducted? Have you ever determined any of those things? Has any legislator ever attempted to define them?

The real trouble about our present situation is that we do not know what law it is that we are required to conform to. We have not been required to conform to these destructive statutes. They have never been enforced; and the whole thing that we stand in need of is summed up in the word "definition." It is an old saying of the lawyer that certain injustice is a great deal more endurable than uncertain justice. If you know you are "Going to get it in the neck" to-morrow you can at least dodge, but if you do not know that you are "going to get it in the neck" you do not know when you are going to get hit and you can not even dodge. (Laughter). You can not accommodate your business to an uncertain to-morrow, but you can accommodate it to a certain to-morrow.

Definition is not compatible with the present system—with discretionary management. Definition is the very opposite of the kind of regulation we are now attempting. Such regulation is in its very nature insusceptible of definition. Can you find any definition from beginning to end in the Sherman Act? Hasn't the Supreme Court of the United States itself found two sets of definition of that Act hardly consistent with each other? Has anybody found out how to conform to all the decisions of the Supreme Court of the United States with regard to the Sherman Act? It is a body of regulation apparently undefined; and apparently, too, adjudged by the Supreme Court to be indefinable. That is what makes the situation so perilous and lamentable. Any business can be accommodated to a definite obligation, a definite requirement, but no business can be accommodated to an indefinite requirement.

I have been very much interested in the theory of government adduced by certain prominent persons. There is one very prominent person in the United States, for example, who won't trust corporations, but will, to any extent, trust the government of the United States. Now the government of the United States is made up of individuals just as a corporation is, and I have observed that there have been periods when corporations were made up of just as trustworthy persons as the government of the United States. Moreover the corporations have the advantage of understanding their own business. They must understand their own business or go into bankruptcy and the government of the United States has not yet produced a body of geniuses who can understand other people's businesses. (Laughter). Until the government of the United States or the government of a state can understand a complex body, not of one business, but of a number of businesses, conducted by other persons for their profit, better than the persons whose fortunes are embarked in it understand it, they cannot by any discretionary measure justly regulate that business.

I was interested to hear Mr. Farwell[2] say that some very great number of years ago—I think he said one hundred years ago—the colleges thought that the less government there was the better. I still think that the less administrative government there is the better. I still think that the governing, in respect of business and of all private transactions, ought to be done by the courts and not by the executive officers of our state and federal governments. I still think that the only safety of the individual in any government is under the safeguard of judicial process. Now, I don't care for my part, so far as I am intellectually concerned, I do not care whether you think so or not, because I have this interesting advantage, that all history is on my side—all of it.

I was saying to a body of public men the other day who were assessing each other that the interesting thing for the college man in such a company was that they might think what they pleased, and then some quiet college student would sit in a remote room and determine the whole thing: tell future generations what they were to think of them. The thoughtful writers have the last word. They sum up the evidence after the glamour and noise have passed—after the actors have gone off the stage and things have quieted down; and they who sit down and read books are the final arbiters of fate and of fame.

Now history is inexorable. History does not indulge populistic parties. History has no atom of encouragement for socialistic processes. History says power, if you accumulate it in governors, will certainly sooner or later become oppressive and impossible to be borne. The only reign under which any self-respecting men can live is the reign, not of authority, but of law—the exact definition alike of his rights and of his obligations; definitions enforced by men whose object and interest are not political but judicial, who determine without administrative bias what is the true and ancient and lasting intent of the law of the land. The twenty-ninth clause of Magna Charta is just as permanent as any law of human nature, because it is founded in human nature.

There is no liberty unless a man's privileges be determined by the judgment of his peers and the law of the land. So soon as I have to go to Washington to ask how I may conduct my business I have ceased to live under an American polity. There is then no longer any difference between the polity which we established

2 John Villiers Farwell, President of the John V. Farwell Co., dry goods, Chicago, who also spoke.

this government to escape and the polity which we ourselves, childishly, have returned to.

Government regulation? Yes, but through the ancient, the stable, the incorruptible instrumentality of law, not through the choice of executive officials. A country not to be upset by the scolding of magistrates but only to be upset by the corruption of its citizens—a country that knows its own mind, knows its own law, upholds its own magistrates is sure of the future because it is sure of its own principles.

Gentlemen, we shall not escape the necessity of making a fundamental choice. Wrong practices must be stopped, but they must be stopped in such a way that we shall not substitute the wrong of tyranny for the wrong of private oppression. I can resist my neighbor but I can not resist the government; and when the government is made strong against me and interferes in everything that I attempt to do, then my life is the life of a man enslaved and not of a man standing upon the ancient privileges of a free race. Have we not the self-possession to diagnose the case? Have we not the self-possession to determine exactly what it is that is the matter with us and that we want to correct? Have we not the intelligence and capacity to define the remedy in law? Have we not had courts which could be depended upon to enforce the law? I would despair of the intelligence of this people if I thought that there was more than one answer to that question.

The answer may not come soon. I admit to you in this presence that I am not hopeful of the immediate future; but I would be deeply hopeless of any future, immediate or remote, if we did not begin now to think straight about these things. We are going, apparently, to act first and think afterward; and God help us in the process of saving the fragments. But the sooner we begin to think the less the fragments will be scattered and the less impossible it will be to put them together again. The sooner we make up our minds that we are going to act upon tested principles and not upon doubtful experiments, the sooner we strip ourselves of individual interests and prejudices in the matter, the better.

Look what has been taking place in Washington: Conference after conference with regard to the amendment of the Sherman Act—not leading anywhere in particular, so far as I can learn, because of several sets of opposing interests; somebody afraid that somebody else is going to get the advantage of him; the manufacturer and the railway man afraid that the law will be so changed that they can not control the labor organizations;

the labor organizations afraid that the law will be so changed that the corporations will get the upper hand of them; every man standing off for fear he cannot get as much advantage out of the new law as he can get out of the present law. That temper is the certain precursor of revolution. If you want to save this country from revolution, forget your own interests and think for a little while upon the public interest. Forget your antagonisms. Forget that there is somebody that you want to get the better of —some organization that you want to keep under your hand, and ask yourself what ought to be the position of the organization that you are interested in. Think of your common partnership— that liberal principle of give and take which is the only foundation of any lively commonwealth.

The real thing which a gathering of gentlemen like this should realize is that they must, for the salvation of their country, adjourn their own individual and particular interests for a very serious effort of public counsel; for we are on the eve of a political choice in this country which may be a permanent choice. We are upon the eve of a critical choice which may turn us in this direction or in that; and God help us if we do not know which direction we have chosen. We stand in the presence of the necessity of choosing a direction. We must recover by one process or another the ancient principles of morality, the ancient principles of public spirit, the ancient principles of common purpose, and then there will be no difficulty in putting a stop to the things which are against the public welfare. (Prolonged applause).[3]

Printed in *The Government and Business: An Address before the Commercial Club of Chicago* . . . (Chicago, n. d.).

[3] There is a WWsh outline and a WWT outline, both dated March 14, 1908, and a WWsh undated draft of an abstract of this address in WP, DLC. The typed transcript of the abstract is in WC, NjP. A printed version of the abstract, *Government by Commission* (n. p., n. d.), is in WP, DLC.

From Joseph Bernard Shea

Dear Mr. President: Pittsburgh   March 14, 1908.

I should have written this letter three or four weeks ago; at least so they now tell me, but I certainly did not know that I was to have written it or it would have been written long before this.

The Executive Committee of the Princeton Club of Western Pennsylvania informed me yesterday that I was to have either seen or written you and urged upon you that you be present to represent the University at our Annual Dinner on May 2nd. You know the Western Association of Princeton Clubs meets in Pittsburg this year and we do not feel as if the meeting would be what it should be unless you respond to "Princeton."[1]

I am very much annoyed to find that by some misunderstanding I should not have written you as early as the Committee desired, and I sincerely trust that my delay will not have resulted in your having made some other engagement which will prevent you coming to us for that date.

Hoping and anticipating a favorable reply, I remain,

Most sincerely yours,   J B Shea

TLS (WP, DLC).

[1] Wilson did accept; the text of his address is printed at May 2, 1908.

From Ralph Adams Cram

Dear Dr. Wilson: Boston, March 14, 1908.

I have just heard from Mr. Thompson that it is impossible for him to change the date of the meeting of the Grounds and Buildings Committee from the first of April, and he suggests, therefore, that I give up any attempt to be present at this meeting if it is impossible for me to come to Princeton, both for the 25th, and for the first. Assuming that the 25th remains as the date fixed on for the meeting of the Sub-Committee with regard to the location of the Graduate School, you may certainly count on my being in Princeton on that day, and I shall make every effort to come again for the first, as I particularly wish to go over the general scheme for the development of the University with the Grounds and Buildings Committee.

Very sincerely yours,

R A Cram, Supervising Architect.

TLS (WP, DLC).

From Henry Smith Pritchett

Dear President Wilson: New York   March 16, 1908.

The admission of the state universities even to a limited participation in the Carnegie Foundation is going to excite a feeling which has been voiced on the part of many denominational institutions that the action of our executive committee toward these institutions is more rigid than our charter would justify. For example, institutions have applied for admission in which a small minority of trustees were elected by a denominational body, the others being self-perpetuating and under an agreement that they should be chosen without regard to denominational affiliations. Up to this time we have declined to accept such institutions, the executive committee taking the position that it had received no instructions from the trustees and that such institutions might well await a more lengthy examination of the question. I should be glad to know whether, in your judgment, it would be wise for us to assume a limit in this matter within which such institutions might be admitted, for example, to admit institutions in which not more than one fourth of the trustees are chosen from some denominational body.

Very sincerely yours, Henry S. Pritchett

TLS (WP, DLC).

An Address at a Yale Phi Beta Kappa Dinner

[[March 18, 1908]]

THE TRAINING OF INTELLECT

Mr. Toastmaster,[1] Mr. President,[2] and Gentlemen:—I certainly considered it a compliment to myself when Mr. Phelps made the comparison he made a few moments ago, but it was hardly a compliment to Princeton.

I do not feel that in coming to Yale I am coming among strangers. I believe that a man who is accustomed to living among college men finds everywhere the same spirit, the same atmosphere. I feel toward you as a friend of mine felt toward an acquaintance who slapped him on the back familiarly. He looked at the fellow coldly and said, "I do not know your name, but your manners are very familiar." And so I feel with regard to every college gathering that their manners are familiar, but I also feel that there is a quickness of mutual comprehension that is very reassuring to a speaker. And then I feel particularly at ease in appearing before a strange audience because they have not heard my stories, and, moreover, because it is not so difficult to maintain a boast of dignity where you are not known as it is where you are known. When I appear before a Princeton crowd and try to live up to an introduction, I feel like the old woman who went into the side show at the circus and saw a man reading a newspaper through a two-inch board. "Let me out of this place," she exclaimed, "this is no place for me to be with these thin things on." I have an uncomfortable feeling in such circumstances that

[1] William Lyon Phelps, Lampson Professor of English Literature at Yale.
[2] Arthur Twining Hadley, President of Yale University.

the disguise is transparent, but perhaps I can maintain a disguise for a little while among you.

I must confess to you that I came here with very serious thoughts this evening, because I have been laboring under the conviction for a long time that the object of a university is to educate, and I have not seen the universities of this country achieving any remarkable or disturbing success in that direction. I have found everywhere the note which I must say I have heard sounded once or twice to-night—that apology for the intellectual side of the university. You hear it at all universities. Learning is on the defensive, is actually on the defensive, among college men, and they are being asked by way of indulgence to bring that also into the circle of their interests. Is it not time we stopped asking indulgence for learning and proclaimed its sovereignty? Is it not time we reminded the college men of this country that they have no right to any distinctive place in any community, unless they can show it by intellectual achievement? that if a university is a place for distinction at all it must be distinguished by the conquests of the mind? I for my part tell you plainly that that is my motto, that I have entered the field to fight for that thesis, and that for that thesis only do I care to fight.

The toastmaster of the evening said, and said truly, that this is the season when, for me, it was most difficult to break away from regular engagements in which I am involved at this time of year. But when I was invited to the Phi Beta Kappa banquet it had an unusual sound, and I felt that that was the particular kind of invitation which it was my duty and privilege to accept. One of the problems of the American university now is how, among a great many other competing interests, to give places of distinction to men who want places of distinction in the classroom. Why don't we give you men the Y here and the P at Princeton, because after all you have done the particular thing which distinguishes Yale? Not that these other things are not worth doing, but they can be done anywhere. They may be done in athletic clubs where there is no study, but this thing can be done only here. This is the distinctive mark of the place.

A good many years ago, just two weeks before the mid-year examinations, the Faculty of Princeton was foolish enough to permit a very unwise evangelist to come to the place and to upset the town. And while an assisting undergraduate was going from room to room one undergraduate secured his door and put this notice out, "I am a Christian and am studying for examinations." Now I want to say that that is exactly what a Christian undergraduate would be doing at that time of the year. He would not be attending religious meetings no matter how beneficial it would be to him. He would be studying for examinations not merely for the purpose of passing them, but from his sense of duty.

We get a good many men at Princeton from certain secondary schools who say a great deal about their earnest desire to cultivate character among our students, and I hear a great deal about character being the object of education. I take leave to believe that a man who cultivates his character consciously will cultivate nothing except what will make him intolerable to his fellow men. If your object in life is to make a fine fellow of yourself, you will not succeed, and you will not be acceptable to really fine fellows. Character, gentlemen, is a by-product. It comes, whether you will or not, as a consequence of a life devoted to the nearest duty, and the place in which character would be cultivated, if it be a place of study, is a place where study is the object and character the result.

Not long ago a gentleman approached me in great excitement just after the entrance examinations. He said we had made a great mistake in not taking so and so from a certain school which he named. "But," I said, "he did not pass the entrance examinations." And he went over the boy's moral excellencies again. "Pardon me," I said, "You do not understand. He did not pass the entrance examinations. Now," I said, "I want you to understand that if the Angel Gabriel applied for admission to Princeton University and could not pass the entrance examinations, he would not be admitted. He would be wasting his time." It seemed a new idea to him. This boy had come from a school which cultivated character, and he was a nice, lovable fellow with a presentable character. Therefore, he ought to be admitted to any university. I fail to see it from this point of view, for a university is an institution of purpose. We have in some previous years had pity for young gentlemen who were not sufficiently acquainted with the elements of a preparatory course. They have been dropped at the examinations, and I have always felt that we have been guilty of an offense, and have made their parents spend money to no avail and the youngsters spend their time to no avail. And so I think that all university men ought to rouse themselves now and understand what is the object of a university. The object of a university is intellect; as a university its only object is intellect. As a body of young men there ought to be other things, there ought to be diversions to release them from the constant strain of effort, there ought to be things that gladden the heart and moments of leisure, but as a university the only object is intellect.

The reason why I chose the subject that I am permitted to speak upon tonight—the function of scholarship—was that I wanted to point out the function of scholarship not merely in the university but in the nation. In a country constituted as ours is the relation in which education stands is a very important one. Our whole theory has been based upon an enlightened citizenship and therefore the function of scholarship must be for the nation as well as for the university itself. I mean the function of such scholarship as undergraduates get. That is not a violent amount in any case. You cannot make a scholar of a man except by some largeness of Providence in his makeup, by the time he is twenty-one or twenty-two years of age. There have been gentlemen who have made a reputation by twenty-one or twenty-two, but it is generally in some little province of knowledge, so small that a small effort can conquer it. You do not make scholars by that time, you do not often make scholars by seventy that are worth boasting of. The process of scholarship, so far as the real scholar is concerned, is an unending process, and knowledge is pushed forward only a very little by his best efforts. And it is evident, of course, that the most you can contribute to a man in his undergraduate years is not equipment in the exact knowledge which is characteristic of the scholar, but an inspiration of the spirit of scholarship. The most that you can give a youngster is the spirit of the scholar.

Now the spirit of the scholar in a country like ours must be a spirit related to the national life. It cannot, therefore, be a spirit of pendantry. I suppose that this is a sufficient working conception of pedantry to say that it is knowledge divorced from life. It is knowledge so closeted, so desecrated, so stripped of the significances of life itself, that it is a thing apart and not connected with the vital processes in the world about us.

There is a great place in every nation for the spirit of scholarship, and it seems to me that there never was a time when the spirit of scholarship was more needed in affairs than it is in this country at this time.

We are thinking just now of [with] our emotions and not with our minds, we are moved by impulse and not by judgment. We are drawing away from things with blind antipathy. The spirit of knowledge is that you must base your conclusions on adequate grounds. Make sure that you are going to the real sources of knowledge, discovering what the real facts are before you move forward to the next process, which is the process of clear thinking. By clear thinking I do not mean logical thinking. I do not mean that life is based upon any logical system whatever. Life is essentially illogical. The world is governed now by a tumultuous sea of commonalities made up of passions, and we should pray God that the good passions should out-vote the bad passions. But the movement of impulse, of motive, is the stuff of passion, and therefore clear thinking about life is not logical, symmetrical thinking, but it is interpretative thinking, thinking that sees the secret motive of things, thinking that penetrates deepest places where are the pulses of life.

Now scholarship ought to lay these impulses bare just as the physician can lay bare the seat of life in our bodies. That is not scholarship which goes to work upon the mere formal pedantry of logical reasoning, but that *is* scholarship which searches for the heart of a man. The spirit of scholarship gives us catholicity of thinking, the readiness to understand that there will constantly swing into our ken new items not dreamed of in our systems of philosophy, not simply to draw our conclusions from the data that we have had, but that all this is under constant mutation, and that therefore new phases of life will come upon us and a new adjustment of our conclusions will be necessary. Our thinking must be detached and disinterested thinking.

The particular objection that I have to the undergraduate forming his course of study on his future profession is this—that from start to finish, from the time he enters the university until he finishes his career, his thought will be centered upon particular interests. He will be immersed in the things that touch his profit and loss, and a man is not free to think inside that territory. If his bread and butter is going to be affected, if he is always thinking in the terms of his own profession he is not thinking for the nation. He is thinking for himself, and whether he be conscious of it or not, he can never throw these trammels off. He will only think as a doctor, or a lawyer, or a banker. He will not be free in the world of knowledge and in the circle of interests which make up the great citizenship of the country. It is necessary that the spirit of scholarship should be a detached, disinterested spirit, not immersed in a particular interest. That is the function of scholarship in a country like ours, to supply, not heat, but light, to suffuse things with the calm radiance of reason, to see to it that men do not act hastily, but that they act considerately, that they obey the truth whether they know it or not.

The fault of our age is the fault of hasty action, of premature judgments, of a preference for ill-considered action over no action at all. Men who insist upon standing still and doing a little thinking before they do any acting are called reactionaries. They want actually to react to a state in which they can be allowed to think. They want for a little while to withdraw from the turmoil of party controversy and see where they stand before they commit themselves and their country to action from which it may not be possible to withdraw.

The whole fault of the modern age is that it applies to everything a false standard of efficiency. Efficiency with us is accomplishment, whether the accomplishment be by just and well-considered means or not; and this standard of achievement it is that is debasing the morals of our age, the intellectual morals of our age. We do not stop to do things thoroughly; we do not stop to know why we do things. We see an error and we hastily correct it by a greater error; and then go on to cry that the age is corrupt.

And so it is, gentlemen, that I try to join the function of the university with the great function of the national life. The life of this country is going to be revolutionized and purified only when the universities of this country wake up to the fact that their only reason for existing is intellect, that the objects that I have set forth, so far as undergraduate life is concerned, are the only legitimate objects. And every man should crave for his university primacy in these things, primacy in other things also if they may be brought in without enmity to it, but the sacrifice of everything that stands in the way of that.

For my part, I do not believe that it is athleticism which stands in the way. Athletics have been associated with the achievements of the mind in many a successful civilization. There is no difficulty in uniting vigor of body with achievement of mind, but there is a good deal of difficulty in uniting the achievement of the mind with a thousand distracting social influences, which take up all our ambitions, which absorb all our thoughts, which lead to all our arrangements of life, and then leave the university authorities the residuum of our attention, after we are through with the things that we are interested in. We absolutely changed the whole course of study at Princeton and revolutionized the methods of instruction without rousing a ripple on the surface of the alumni. They said those things are intellectual, they were our business. But just as soon as we thought to touch the social part of the university, there was not only a ripple, but the whole body was torn to its depths. We had touched the real things. These lay in triumphal competition with the province of the mind, and men's attention was so absolutely absorbed in these things that it was impossible for us to get their interest enlisted on the real undertakings of the university itself.

Now that is true of every university that I know anything about in this country, and if the Faculties in this country want to recapture the ground that they have lost, they must begin pretty soon, and they must go into the battle with their bridges burned behind them so that it will be of no avail to retreat. If I had a voice to which the university men of this country might listen, that is the endeavor to which my ambition would lead me to call.[3]

Printed in the *Yale Alumni Weekly*, xvii (March 25, 1908), 637-39.
[3] There is a WWhw outline of this address, dated March 18, 1908, in WP, DLC.

From John Robertson Dunlap[1]

My dear Sir: New York, March 18, 1908.

Confirming my telephone message of yesterday, I now beg to say that the following Committee from the National Democratic Club[2] will call upon you at the University Club, New York City, to-morrow (Thursday) afternoon at 3 o'clock, for the purpose of asking your cooperation in our celebration of Mr. Jefferson's birthday on the 13th proximo, namely:

Hon. John Fox, President, National Democratic Club,
Hon. C[harles]. V[incent]. Fornes, Member of Congress from New York,
Stephen Farrelly, Esq., Pres. Friendly Sons of St. Patrick,
Judge Thomas L. Fietner, ex-President, N. Y. Tax Dept.,
Mr. John R. Dunlap, Editor, The Engineering Magazine.

As I mentioned over the telephone, we were so profoundly impressed by your address at Chicago on the 14th inst., in the course of which you pointed out the fallacy underlying the current craze for "government by commissions," instead of government by law, that we are especially anxious to have you again emphasize this statesmanlike and essential point in an address at our forthcoming Jefferson Day Dinner. Of course, you understand that we do not desire to have you confine yourself to this single point; but because of the vital importance of the subject, we trust sincerely that you may be able to honor us by accepting an invitation to again emphasize it.[3]

Looking forward with pleasure to meeting you on Thursday, and with great respect, I am,

Very truly yours,   John R. Dunlap.

TLS (WP, DLC).
   [1] Founder and editor of *The Engineering Magazine*.
   [2] A New York organization with close ties to Tammany Hall.
   [3] Wilson accepted; a press release of his address is printed at April 13, 1908, a news report at April 14, 1908.

To Harriet Hammond McCormick[1]

Princeton, N. J.

My dear Mrs. McCormick: March 20th, 1908.

Neuritis has first and last made it so difficult to use my pen that I feel sure you will pardon the informality of my use of a typewriter in writing to report my safe arrival home. I had to be off again the very next day after I got home, to make a speech for the Phi Beta Kappa Society at New Haven, and am at last settled for a few days of quiet work in Princeton and can look back with the greatest satisfaction upon my delightful visit with you. You were most thoughtfully kind to me in every way and made me feel, what it is most delightful to feel, that you regarded me as a member of the family in all my privileges, and altogether made my stay very happy. I shall look forward with the greatest pleasure to seeing you again in April.[2]

Please give my love to Cyrus. Mrs. Wilson joins me in warmest regards.

Always sincerely yours,   Woodrow Wilson

TLS (WP, DLC).
   [1] Mrs. Cyrus Hall McCormick.
   [2] When he was to return to Chicago to speak at the semi-centennial of the Chicago Y.M.C.A. A news report of his address is printed at April 28, 1908.

To Cyrus Hall McCormick

My dear Cyrus: Princeton, N. J.   March 20th, 1908.

Thank you very much indeed for the clippings.[1] They are very interesting, and I appreciate your kindness in having had them collected.

I was not at all satisfied with my address before the Commercial Club, but certainly they received it with the greatest courtesy, and I look back upon my whole visit with great pleasure and satisfaction. It was altogether delightful to be with you.

Always affectionately yours,   Woodrow Wilson

TLS (WP, DLC).
¹ A group of clippings from Chicago newspapers reporting on his recent addresses there.

To Henry Smith Pritchett

[Princeton, N. J.]
My dear President Pritchett: March 20th, 1908.

. . . I am sincerely sorry that we shall have to make even a compromise with the State universities. I cannot help thinking that a compromise is or will eventually turn out to be a surrender, particularly if you think that Mr. Carnegie's feeling in the matter has changed so decidedly. But you may be sure that when it comes to the discussion of the matter in the committee I will not insist upon my objections in any way to embarrass you but will concur in any necessary conclusion.¹

As for a new basis for admission for denominational institutions, I think that if we admit State universities we shall certainly have to consider it very carefully. I have not yet been able to make up my mind just what proportion in the make-up of the Boards of Trustees we should fix upon. I have felt very uneasy, as you know, with regard to the whole matter because it has not seemed to me that we were frankly dealt with in all cases, and the mere matter of the proportion contained on the Board of Trustees of an institution does not seem to be a real index of its essential character. No doubt, however, we can fix upon some formal test of proportion in the make-up of the Boards and at the same time be very careful to investigate the real relations of the institution to the church to which it is attached.²

Thank you very much for what you tell me of Mr. Carnegie's movements. I could see him, if it suited his convenience, on the afternoon of either Friday the twenty-seventh, Saturday the twenty-eighth, Sunday the twenty-ninth, or Monday the 30th of this month.

Unhappily my calendar is so crowded with appointments that if he cannot see me on one of those dates, I shall have to ask for some date after the ninth of April, when our Board of Trustees meets. I will be in New York for a dinner on Monday, the 13th of April, and could also be free on the afternoon of Tuesday the 14th, Wednesday the 15th, or Friday or Saturday the 17th and 18th.

I would like very much to talk with you about the matter I am going to lay before him,³ if I might have an opportunity before I see him, because I feel sure that if you approve of it, it would help me in no small degree with him.

Always with warmest regard,

Cordially and sincerely yours,   [Woodrow Wilson]

CCL (WWP, UA, NjP).

[1] Carnegie soon added $5,000,000 to the endowment of the Carnegie Foundation for the Advancement of Teaching to provide pensions for faculty members in state-supported institutions.

[2] The trustees of the Carnegie Foundation continued to exclude denominational colleges from participation in the pension plan. However, they did admit Wesleyan University on May 5, 1910, on the ground that, although approximately one fourth of its trustees were chosen by various conferences of the Methodist Church, the full board of trustees was pledged by the university's charter to the maintenance of an undenominational administration. See Carnegie Foundation for the Advancement of Teaching, *Fifth Annual Report* . . . (New York, 1910), pp. 26-30.

[3] That is, the quadrangle plan, for which Wilson hoped to secure Carnegie's aid.

From Theodore Dreiser[1]

Dear Sir: New York   March 20, 1908.

The accompanying booklet we believe will interest you. It is the text of an article "What is the matter with the Public Schools?" that we are soon to publish in The Delineator.[2] We are in advance submitting it to the leading educators of the country because we want to know what you who are experts in this line of the world's work, think of it.

To our trained investigator the writer of the article, as also to President Woodrow Wilson of Princeton University, it appears that there is something radically wrong with the public school system of the United States. We have compiled and are here presenting evidence that shows this to be true. It is an ex[h]ibit worth looking at. New York, Cleveland, Kansas City, and Chicago, bear testimony to the facts. A school principal has told us, "The average grammer school graduate is the most ignorant little animal on earth." Yet as a nation we spent on our schools in 1906 the sum of $307,765,659. If they are not right it is a matter for all of us to reason together about. Won't you read about it? It is in behalf of the educational welfare of the youth of the land, that we ask you to take the time for the perusal of these few pages submitted.

Then, having read the story we have to tell you, won't you also write us just briefly—a sentence or two will do—your opinion in answer to these two questions:

What is wrong with the public school system of the United States?

What can be done to right it?

The Editor at his desk wants very much to know these things. You are one of the few who can tell him.

Won't you?

Yours Educationally,   Theodore Dreiser

TLS (WP, DLC).

1 The novelist, at this time editor of *The Delineator.*

2 Rheta Childe Dorr, "What's the Matter with the Public Schools?" *The Delineator,* LXXII (Oct. 1908), 551-53, 643.

To Melancthon Williams Jacobus

My dear Dr. Jacobus: [Princeton, N. J.]   March 21st, 1908.

I have been rushing so constantly from one alumni meeting to another and from appointment to appointment of every kind that I have not before had time to acknowledge the receipt of your kind letter of March 5th.

The sub-committee on the site of the Graduate School has made plans to secure the opinion of two sanitary engineers,[1] one of whom [Hering] has already looked over the ground and the other of whom will visit Princeton today. Mr. Cram is coming down to meet the sub-committee next week and I think that by the time appointed for the meeting of the whole committee we shall have a complete and, I hope, satisfactory report ready.

I entirely agree with you in your feeling about Halsey. I have a strong personal affection for him, but I think that it would be most unwise to add another man to the Board who would not in any way enlarge or vary our representation in the country. I also feel as strongly as I ever did that it would be most desirable to have Dr. Mackenzie in the Board. These matters have become matters of great delicacy in view of recent circumstances, but I shall certainly do my best to lead the Committee of Suggestion in another direction. Allow me to thank you for expressing your opinion in the matter so frankly and fully.

I had a very interesting and successful visit to Chicago, and on Wednesday night last was in your immediate vicinity dining with the Phi Beta Kappa Society at New Haven.

I sincerely hope that you are all now quite well.

Mrs. Wilson joins me in warmest regard,

Always faithfully yours,   [Woodrow Wilson]

CCL (RSB Coll., DLC).

[1] Rudolph Hering of Rudolph Hering & George W. Fuller, Hydraulic & Sanitary Experts of New York, and George C. Whipple, of Allen Hazen & George C. Whipple, Consulting Engineers of New York.

From Edward Wright Sheldon, with Enclosures

My dear Woodrow: [New York]   March 21, 1908.

I will hold myself in readiness to go to Princeton on Wednesday by such train as will enable to meet you and Mr. Cram. If I could take the 12.20 and thus have the morning here, it would be a convenience to me, but I will do whatever you say. Mr. Cleveland, I assume will not be with us. I enclose a copy of a letter which I received from him last Tuesday, and a copy of the opinion of Chancellor Magie. You will notice how much importance Mr. Cleveland attaches to a consultation between Prof. Brackett and the New York engineers. I have talked with Mr. Herring about this and think that it can be arranged.

The ex-chancellor's opinion is interesting. I do not see, though, how he could have come to any different conclusion. As I read the opinion, it finally excludes Merwick as a possible site, and leaves open only the question as to whether land incorporated into "the grounds" of the University after Mrs. Swann's death would be available. For myself, I have not been able to see any sufficient reason why the time of acquisition should be deemed controlling, provided the land fairly became an integral part of the territorial unit known as "the grounds" or campus. But that point is arguable, I have no doubt.

Yours most sincerely,   Edward W. Sheldon

TLS (WWP, UA, NjP).

E N C L O S U R E   I

William Jay Magie to Grover Cleveland

March 13, 1908.

My opinion is asked in respect to the land upon which the Trustees of Princeton University may properly apply the proceeds of the residue and remainder of the estate of Mrs. Swan, given to said Trustees by the 13th paragraph of her will, in the erection of the building provided for by that paragraph.

Testatrix's direction is that it shall be erected "upon the grounds of the said University." The Trustees, in performing their trust, must obey that direction.

Grounds (in the plural) has a meaning distinct from the meaning of land or lands. According to the lexicographers and in common usage, *grounds* means lands connected with, contiguous to and used with a dwelling or homestead, such as gardens, lawns, etc. Such is the meaning in which Mrs. Swan used the word many times in the 12th paragraph of her will by which she left trustees her "house and grounds" and provided for the care of the buildings and "said grounds."

A University literally speaking has no homestead or dwelling but it has buildings in some of which students and others live and in others of which its functions are carried on. When the word "grounds" is applied to a University it is in a figurative sense, but we are not justified, in my judgment, in considering it to have lost its restricted sense and to cover all lands owned by the University. The *grounds* of a University consist of the land surrounding the Buildings in which its work is done or contiguous thereto and used therewith. The building must be erected on land answering that description.

In considering this will, the circumstances surrounding the testatrix may be considered. She had been a resident of Princeton for many years and was thoroughly familiar with the location of the Buildings of the University and the lands around the same. This, in my judgment adds force to the construction of the word grounds which I have given.

I am further asked whether upon this construction, the building may properly be erected (1) on land which was within the grounds when Mrs. Swan made her will or (2) on land which was within the grounds when the will took effect on her death or (3) on land acquired by the University after her death and in contemplation of the erection of the Building.

The building may no doubt properly be erected on any part of what were *grounds* in the meaning given, at the date of her will.

In my judgment, it may properly be erected on any land which between the date of her will and her death had been acquired by the University and become part of its grounds. Although we resort to the circumstances surrounding testatrix to discover in what sense she used a word in her will yet her will speaks from her death and the meaning we have found is then applicable.

The third question is more difficult of solution. The view above expressed leads to the result that the building could not properly be erected on lands which are not part of the University grounds although acquired for the purpose of the erection. Whether it could properly be erected on lands, which since Mrs. Swan's death, have been acquired, or which may be acquired and have become or may become "grounds" of the University, I have doubt about. If that concrete question is presented I will consider it.

ENCLOSURE II

Grover Cleveland to Edward Wright Sheldon

My dear Mr. Sheldon: Princeton, N. J., 14 March, 1908.

I have received your letter of the 12th instant.

Yesterday Chancellor Magie's opinion reached me on the legal question involved in the will which has been the matter of some conversation and discussion between us. I gather from it that the location which you know I have favored[1] would probably in his judgment not meet the provisions of the will. I will have a copy of this opinion made and sent to you.

I have at last felt obliged to give way to the doctors who have me in charge, deeming it no longer wise to fight against their opinion (and my own too for that matter) that I should have a change of scene. I expect, therefore, to start for Lakewood on Monday, where I hope to soon discover whether or no the climate and surroundings there can be expected to benefit me. I shall not be able, it seems to me, to take any part for the present in the things which are necessary to be done in order to arrive at some conclusion on this question of locality. Of one thing I am absolutely convinced, and that is that in every view of the case Dr. Brackett should be consulted on the question as to the desirability in regard to healthfulness of the location last proposed.[2] Within the last two or three days I have, for the very best of reasons, also become thoroughly convinced that it will not do to neglect the executors in determining this matter. I do not think it should be made a merely perfunctory, formal affair, resorted to only after our conclusion has been definitely reached. I say these things because I am as sure as I can be that they enter largely into the disposition with which the final determination reached will be received and considered by the Board.

In submitting the legal proposition to Chancellor Magie, I was very careful to do it in such a manner as to avoid the least hint of the preferences I had expressed, or the opinion of any others. I barely stated to him the legal proposition as plainly as I could, without mentioning the locations which these involved. I confess that I expected he would arrive at a different conclusion than that expressed in his opinion. Although one question which I intended to submit plainly to him, is left in abeyance, I shall not be surprised if the availability of the location which I have favored is disposed of in the early part of his opinion.

My understanding of the order of procedure has been as you intimate, that the New York engineers are to be here next week and the architect, Mr. Cram, the week after. I do hope that there will be no mistake made in failing to associate Dr. Brackett with the New York engineers in their examination. Of course I am anxious to make a definite recommendation to the Board at its next meeting, but I would rather face another delay than to leave undone anything that may aid the committee and the Board to arrive at the wisest conclusions in the premises.

Yours very sincerely,   Grover Cleveland

TCL (WWP, UA, NjP).

[1] That is, the grounds of Merwick on Bayard Lane.

[2] A wooded knoll on the eastern side of Washington Road, which Wilson had suggested at the meeting of the trustees' Committee on the Graduate School on March 2, 1908. See Andrew F. West, "A Narrative of the Graduate College of Princeton University . . . " (mimeographed MS in UA, NjP), pp. 35-36.

From Isaac Sharpless[1]

Dear President Wilson: Haverford, Pa. 3/21/1908.

I wrote you some weeks ago asking if we could have the pleasure of an address from you on the occasion of the 75th. anniversary of the founding of Haverford on October 16th. next.

You were absent at that time in Bermuda, as your secretary informed me, and I fear that in the confusion of business which followed your return my letter has been mislaid.

We should be very glad if you could speak from thirty to forty minutes on the occasion. Harvard and Pennsylvania will be represented and we should be glad to have Princeton on the list in the person of its President.[2]

You know so well what Haverford is that I feel that I need not go any further into detail.

Yours truly,   Isaac Sharpless

TLS (WP, DLC).

[1] President of Haverford College.

[2] Wilson did accept; the text of his address is printed at Oct. 16, 1908.

From Lewis Charles Everard[1]

My dear Mr. Wilson: New Haven, Conn.   March 21, 1908.

The Yale Chapter wish me to express their hearty appreciation of your visit and especially of your scholarly and effective talk at the dinner. It was certainly a most impressive and fitting climax to the evening and contained a great many things that needed to be expressed not only for the good of Phi Beta Kappa and Yale but of the cause of learning in America. It will always be to me a memory full of both pleasure and inspiration.

Hoping that this may be only the beginning of closer relations along the fundamental lines of University life between Yale and Princeton, I remain,

Fraternally yours,   Lewis C. Everard

TLS (WP, DLC).
[1] Yale 1908, undergraduate president of the Phi Beta Kappa chapter of Yale University.

To Theodore Dreiser

Editor The Delineator   Princeton, N. J.   [c. March 23, 1908]

I have been very much impressed by the article you sent me, entitled "What is the Matter with the Public Schools?" The address which I delivered before the Association of Colleges and Preparatory Schools of the Middle West [Middle States and Maryland], and from which Mrs. Dorr quotes the sentence which she puts at the head of her paper, contains in part, at any rate, an answer to the question.[1]

With much appreciation,

Sincerely yours,   Woodrow Wilson

Printed in *The Delineator*, LXXII (Dec. 1908), 1024.
[1] The quotation, which appeared under a photograph of Wilson in Rheta Childe Dorr, "What's the Matter with the Public Schools?" *The Delineator*, LXXII (Oct. 1908), 551, was: "We all know that the children of the last two decades in our schools have not been educated. With all our training we have trained nobody. With all our instructing we have instructed nobody." The text of the address from which the quotation is taken is printed at Nov. 29, 1907, Vol. 17.

A Treatise

[*March 24, 1908*]

CONSTITUTIONAL GOVERNMENT IN THE UNITED STATES[1]

PREFATORY NOTE

These lectures are not intended as a systematic discussion of the character and operation of the government of the United States. They are intended merely to present it in some of its more salient features from a fresh point of view and in the light of a fresh analysis of the character and operation of constitutional government. It is hoped that they will be thought, for this reason, to be serviceable in the clarification of our views as to policy and practice.

WOODROW WILSON.

Princeton, New Jersey,
March 24, 1908.

I

WHAT IS CONSTITUTIONAL GOVERNMENT?

My object in the following lectures is to examine the government of the United States as a constitutional system as simply and directly as possible, with an eye to practice, not to theory.

And yet at the very outset it is necessary to pause upon a theory. The government of the United States cannot be intelligently discussed as a constitutional system until we clearly determine what we mean by a "constitutional" government; and the answer to that question is in effect a theory of politics.

By a constitutional government we, of course, do not mean merely a government conducted according to the provisions of a definite constitution; for every modern government with which our thoughts deal at all has a definite constitution, written or unwritten, and we should not dream of speaking of all modern governments as "constitutional." Not even when their constitutions are written with the utmost definiteness of formulation. The constitution of England, the most famous of constitutional governments and in a sense the mother of them all, is not written, and the constitution of Russia might be without changing the essential character of the Czar's power. A constitutional government is one whose powers have been adapted to the interests of

---

[1] About the provenance of this book, see WW to EAW, Jan. 14, 1907, ns. 2 and 12, Vol. 17; the news item printed at Feb. 19, 1907, *ibid.*; and WW to W. H. Carpenter, Oct. 9, 1907, and Feb. 17, 1908, *ibid.* All notes Editors'.

its people and to the maintenance of individual liberty. That, in brief, is the conception we constantly make use of, but seldom analyze, when we speak of constitutional governments.

Roughly speaking, constitutional government may be said to have had its rise at Runnymede, when the barons of England exacted Magna Carta of John; and that famous transaction we may take as the dramatic embodiment alike of the theory and of the practice we seek. The barons met John at Runnymede, a body of armed men in counsel, for a parley which, should it not end as they wished it to end, was to be but a prelude to rebellion. They were not demanding new laws or better, but a righteous and consistent administration of laws they regarded as already established, their immemorial birthright as Englishmen. They had found John whimsical, arbitrary, untrustworthy, never to be counted on to follow any fixed precedent or limit himself by any common understanding, a lying master who respected no man's rights and thought only of having his own will; and they came to have a final reckoning with him. And so they thrust Magna Carta under his hand to be signed,—a document of definition, which spoke of rights which had been disregarded and which must henceforth be respected, of practices until now indulged in which must be given over and remedied altogether, of ancient methods too long abandoned to which the king must return; and their proposal was this: 'Give us your solemn promise as monarch that this document shall be your guide and rule in all your dealings with us, attest that promise by your sign manual attached in solemn form, admit certain of our number a committee to observe the keeping of the covenant, and we are your subjects in all peaceful form and obedience;—refuse, and we are your enemies, absolved of our allegiance and free to choose a king who will rule us as he should.' Swords made uneasy stir in their scabbards, and John had no choice but to sign. These were the only terms upon which government could be conducted among Englishmen.

That was the beginning of constitutional government, and shows the nature of that government in its simplest form. There at Runnymede a people came to an understanding with its governors, and established once for all that ideal of government which we now call "constitutional,"—the ideal of a government conducted upon the basis of a definite understanding, if need be of a formal pact, between those who are to submit to it and those who are to conduct it, with a view to making government an instrument of the general welfare rather than an arbitrary, self-willed master, doing what it pleases,—and particularly for the purpose of safeguarding individual liberty.

The immortal service of Magna Carta was its formulation of the liberties of the individual in their adjustment to the law. The day of Magna Carta was not a day in which men spoke of political liberty or acted upon set programs of political reform; but the history of constitutional government in the modern world is the history of political liberty, the history of all that men have striven for in the reform of government, and one has the right to expect to get out of it at least a workable conception of what liberty is. Certainly the documents of English history and the utterances of the greater public men on both sides of the water supply abundant material for the definition. "If any one ask me what a free government is, I reply, it is what the people think so," said Burke, going to the heart of the matter. The Declaration of Independence speaks to the same effect. We think of it as a highly theoretical document, but except for its assertion that all men are equal it is not. It is intensely practical, even upon the question of liberty. It names as among the "inalienable rights" of man the right to life, liberty, and the pursuit of happiness, as does the Virginia constitution and many another document of the time; but it expressly leaves to each generation of men the determination of what they will do with their lives, what they will prefer as the form and object of their liberty, in what they will seek their happiness. Its chief justification of the right of the colonists to break with the mother country is the assertion that men have always the right to determine for themselves by their own preferences and their own circumstances whether the government they live under is based upon such principles or administered acording to such forms as are likely to effect their safety and happiness. In brief, political liberty is the right of those who are governed to adjust government to their own needs and interests.

That is the philosophy of constitutional government. Every generation, as Burke said, sets before itself some favorite object which it pursues as the very substance of its liberty and happiness. The ideals of liberty cannot be fixed from generation to generation; only its conception can be, the large image of what it is. Liberty fixed in unalterable law would be no liberty at all. Government is a part of life, and, with life, it must change, alike in its objects and in its practices; only this principle must remain unaltered,—this principle of liberty, that there must be the freest right and opportunity of adjustment. Political liberty consists in the best practicable adjustment between the power of the government and the privilege of the individual; and the freedom to alter the adjustment is as important as the adjustment itself for the ease and progress of affairs and the contentment of the citizen.

There are many analogies by which it is possible to illustrate the idea, if it needs illustration. We say of a boat skimming the water with light foot, 'How free she runs,' when we mean, how perfectly she is adjusted to the force of the wind, how perfectly she obeys the great breath out of the heavens that fills her sails. Throw her head up into the wind and see how she will halt and stagger, how every sheet will shiver and her whole frame be shaken, how instantly she is "in irons," in the expressive phrase of the sea. She is free only when you have let her fall off again and get once more her nice adjustment to the forces she must obey and cannot defy. We speak of the 'free' movement of the piston-rod in the perfectly made engine, and know of course that its freedom is proportioned to its perfect adjustment. The least lack of adjustment will heat it with friction and hold it stiff and unmanageable. There is nothing free in the sense of being unrestrained in a world of innumerable forces, and each force moves at its best when best adjusted to the forces about it. Spiritual things are not wholly comparable with materal things, and political liberty is a thing of the spirits of men; but we speak of friction in things that affect our spirits, and do not feel that it is altogether a figure of speech. It is not forcing analogies, therefore, to say that that is the freest government in which there is the least friction,—the least friction between the power of the government and the privilege of the individual. The adjustment may vary from generation to generation, but the principle never can. A constitutional government, being an instrumentality for the maintenance of liberty, is an instrumentality for the maintenance of a right adjustment, and must have a machinery of constant adaptation.

English writers have not often enough noticed that in the very generation which saw Magna Carta formulated and signed in England, a similar transaction was witnessed in Hungary. Magna Carta was signed in 1215; seven years later, in 1222, the Magyar nobles of Hungary exacted of their king a document which ran upon singularly similar lines, a "Golden Bull," to which those who struggled for privilege in Hungary always looked back as Englishmen looked back to Magna Carta. But two remarkable differences existed between Magna Carta and the Golden Bull which it is worth while to dwell upon for a moment, because of their significance with regard to the question we are discussing,—the nature of constitutional government. For all she made a similar beginning, Hungary did not obtain constitutional government, and England did. Undoubtedly the chief reason was that the nobles of Hungary contended for the privileges of a class, while the barons of England contended for the privileges of a nation, and that the Englishmen were not seeking to set up any new law or privilege, but to recover and reëstablish what they already had and feared they should lose. Another and hardly less significant reason was that the Englishmen provided machinery for the maintenance of the agreement, and the Magyars did not.

Of course the parliament of England runs back in its origins beyond 1215; but the parliament which Simon of Montfort set up in 1265 and Edward confirmed in 1295 was the first that definitely received and accepted the trust of preserving the liberties, the free choices, of England against the wilful preferences of her kings, upon the basis laid in Magna Carta; and until that parliament was set up, with its burgesses and knights of the shire, the barons had attempted, as again and again they forced upon their kings a renewal of the great charter, to provide against its infringement by the watchfulness of representatives delegated from their own ranks to see that faith was kept. They had the practical instinct to see that promises upon paper are only promises upon paper, unless the party that demands privilege is as alert and as ready for action as the party that exercises power. The Magyar nobles provided no such machinery of maintenance and adjustment, and lost what they had gained. No doubt free parliaments are as important as definite charters.

And yet the other difference is the deeper and, in a sense, the more essential. The barons at Runnymede were not speaking for themselves as a class, but for Englishmen of every rank and privilege, and they were claiming nothing novel or of their own peculiar preference and invention, but rights which they conceived to be as old as Edward the Confessor. They were speaking, not out of theory, but out of practice and experience, for the maintenance of privileges which they conceived themselves time out of mind to have possessed. They were insisting that government should be adjusted to their actual lives, accommodated to their actual experience. And so Magna Carta speaks of no new rights. It grants nothing. It merely safeguards. It provides methods and reforms abuses. It does not say what men shall have by way of freedom and privilege; it speaks only of what restraints the king's government shall observe in seeking to abridge such freedom and privilege as Englishmen already of right enjoy. Let the famous 29th clause serve as an example. It says nothing of the grant to any man of life, liberty, or property: it takes it for granted that every man has the right to these, as our own Declaration of Independence does, and enacts simply that "no man shall be deprived of life, liberty, or property, save by the judgment of his peers and the law of the land." It is seeking to regulate the exercise of power, to adjust its operation, as safely and conveniently as may be, to that general interest which is the sum of the interest of every man; that he may be dealt with, not as the king arbitrarily pleases, but as his own peers, men of his own kind and interest, deem just, and as laws which deal equally with all men impartially direct.

Look into any constitutional document of the English-speaking race and you shall find the same spirit, the same way of action: its aim is always an arrangement, as if of business: no abstract setting forth of liberties, no pretense of grants of privilege or political rights, but always a formulation of limits and of methods, a regulation of the way governments shall act and individuals be dealt with. Take the first eight amendments to the Constitution of the United States as an example, and see in them the charter of liberties which the States insisted upon having added to the Constitution at the outset. The whole spirit and manner of the thing is exhibited in their businesslike phrases. "The right of the people to be secure in their persons, houses, papers, and effects, against unreasonable searches and seizures shall not be violated, and no warrants shall be issued but upon probable cause, supported by oath or affirmation, and particularly describing the places to be searched, and the persons or things to be seized," is the quiet language of the Fourth Amendment, denying to the government only unreasonable powers arbitrarily exercised. The words of the Fifth Article are equally businesslike and sensible: "No person shall be held to answer for a capital, or otherwise infamous crime, unless on the presentment or indictment of a grand jury, except in cases arising in the land or naval forces, or in the militia, when in actual service in time of war or public danger; nor shall any person be subject for the same offense to be twice put in jeopardy of life or limb; nor shall be compelled in any criminal case to be a witness against himself; nor be deprived of life, liberty, or property, without due process of law; nor shall private property be taken for public use, without just compensation." Every clause bears the same practical character. Such provisions make of the Constitution an agreement as feasible and as acceptable as Magna Carta. It is a body of distinct stipulations as to where the lines of privilege shall run, where individual rights shall begin and governmental rights stop, in the more critical dealings between rulers and citizens.

And the whole of constitutional history is similarly concerned with definition, with method, with machinery, as if principles were taken for granted and no one doubted that men should be free, their interests righteously adjusted to the powers of government, securely safeguarded against governments' possible encroachments. The question of machinery, of ways and means, is manifestly of capital importance in a constitutional system. Such a system is based upon a definite understanding between governors and governed. No constitutional government has been without explicit written statements of the terms of the understanding such as is contained in Magna Carta. But it is important that these terms should be definite and unmistakable, not merely in order that disputes concerning its meaning and content may be avoided, but also in order that it may be clear what steps should be taken to carry it out; and the means provided for maintaining it in practice are hardly less indispensable than its own definitions. That is the reason why English constitutional history has centered about the development of parliament.

Not until after the Revolution of 1688 was parliament looked upon as modern Englishmen look upon it, as chiefly interesting because of the laws it could make. Not until the eighteenth century had passed its middle term did it come to be what it is now, the maker and unmaker of ministries, the maker and unmaker of governments. For at least four of the six hundred years during which it has been an instrument of constitutional government it was looked upon merely as the "grand assize," the great session, of the nation, whose function was criticism and restraint, which came together to see that the terms upon which English life was understood to rest were being scrupulously respected by the king and his advisers. The thought grew vague enough at times; the nation once and again lost consciousness of what its parliament meant; the parliament itself sometimes forgot for generations together what its trust and duty was; but every critical turn in affairs brought the whole impulse and conception sharply to light again, and the great tradition was never lost.

We speak now always of 'legislatures,' of 'law-*making*' assemblies, are very impatient of prolonged debates, and sneer at parliamentary bodies which cannot get their 'business' done. We join with laughing zest in Mr. Carlyle's bitter gibe at "talking shops," at parliaments which spend their days in endless discussion rather than in diligent prosecution of what they came together to 'do.' And yet to hold such an attitude toward representative assemblies is utterly to forget their history and their first and capital purpose. They were meant to be talking shops. The name "parliament" is no accidental indication of their function. They were meant to be grand parleys with those who were conducting the country's business: parleys concerning laws, concerning administrative acts, concerning policies and plans at home and abroad, in order that nothing which contravened the common understanding should be let pass without comment or stricture, in order that measures should be insisted on which the nation needed, and measures resisted which the nation did not need or might take harm from. Their purpose was watchful criticism, talk that should bring to light the whole intention of the government and apprise those who conducted it of the real feeling and desire of the nation; and how well they performed that function many an uneasy monarch has testified, alike by word and act.

It was as far as possible from the original purpose of representative assemblies that they should *conduct* government. Government was of course to be conducted by the immemorial executive agencies to which Englishmen had grown accustomed, and parliaments were to support those agencies and supply them with money, and to assent to such laws as might be necessary to strengthen the government or regulate the affairs of the country, public or private. Their function was common counsel; their standard of action the ancient understandings of a constitutional system,—a system based on understandings, written or implicit in the experiences and principles of English life. They were expected to give their assent where those understandings were served, and to withhold it where they were disregarded. They were to voice the conscience of the nation in the presence of government and the exercise of authority.

To recall the history is to recall the fundamental conception of the whole process, and to understand our own institutions as they cannot be understood in any other way. It was only by a very slow and round-about development that representative assemblies—at any rate that the English representative assembly, which is the type of all the rest—came to possess or exercise the right to make laws. Many a generation went by before it was supposed that parliament had anything to do with the laws except to give its assent to them or withhold it when new enactments were submitted to it from the king. In the course of time it found only too often that changes in the law were submitted to it in vague general terms and then, after its assent had been given, were formulated and enforced in terms which gave them another scope and color; and such practices led the leaders of the Commons at last to insist that laws should be submitted to them in the full form and statement in which they were to be enforced. It was an easy step from that to the insistence that formulations which did not suit them should be changed,—an easy step to amendment; but it was a step they were long in taking, and even after they had taken it, they suffered the king's officers to formulate the amendment, and often found themselves again cheated, their real purpose defeated by the terms in which it was made. Even so, it was a long time before they undertook to draft 'bills' or proposals of their own, and a longer time still before it became settled practice to have the exact wording of every law submitted first to the debate and choice of parliament. To this day the legislation of parliament in all important matters comes to it on the proposal of the ministers of the crown and is formulated by the law officers of the government. Modern English ministries are in effect merely committees of the House of Commons, made and unmade as parties shift and majorities change; but parliament is still in all its larger aspects the grand assize of the nation, assembled not to originate business, but to apprise the government of what the nation wishes.

Our own legislatures were of the same character and origin. Their liberties and functions grew by similar processes, upon similar understandings, out of the precedents and practices of colonial laws and charters and the circumstances of the age and place. There is a passage in Burke which interprets their growth and character with perfect historical insight, as bodies which had grown, almost insensibly, upon the model of parliament itself. He uttered it as part of his defense of American self-government against the encroachment of parliament, and no one writing in a cooler age can improve upon its analysis.

It is plain that parliaments, that representative bodies, free to criticize not only but acting with independence, uttering the voice of those who are governed, and enjoying such authority as no king or president or officer of any kind may question or gainsay, constitute an indispensable part of the institutional make-up of a constitutional government. We sometimes attach a very artificial significance to the word 'institution.' Speaking in the terms of history, and particularly of political history, an institution is merely an established practice, an habitual method of dealing with the circumstances of life or the business of government. There may be firmly established institutions of which the law knows nothing. In casting about for a satisfactory way in which to nominate candidates for the office of President of the United States, for instance, our party leaders devised the national nominating convention, and it has become one of our institutions, though neither the constitution nor any statute knows anything of it. And so the growth of constitutional government has been the growth of institutions, of practices, of methods of perfecting the delicate business of maintaining an understanding between those who conduct the government and those who submit to it. The object of constitutional government is to bring the active, planning will of each part of the government into accord with the prevailing popular thought and need, and thus make it an impartial instrument of symmetrical national development; and to give to the operation of the government thus shaped under the influence of opinion and adjusted to the general interest both stability and an incorruptible efficacy. Whatever institutions, whatever practices serve these ends, are necessary to such a system: those which do not, or which serve it imperfectly, should be dispensed with or bettered. And it may be said that the history of constitutional government has been an experimental search for the best means by which to effect these nice adjustments.

The modern development of the functions of representative assemblies has been in many ways inconsistent with the real origins and purposes of the practices or institutions in which they had their rise and justification. We now regard them, not as bodies assembled to consult with the government in order to apprise it of the opinion of the nation with regard to what the government is planning or doing, not as bodies outside the government set to criticize, restrain, and guide it, but as themselves parts of the government, its originating, law-*making* parts. What used to be called the Government, we now speak of only as the 'Executive,' and regard as little more than an instrumentality for carrying into effect the laws which our representative assemblies originate. Our laws abound in the most minute administrative details, prescribe the duties of executive officers and the method by which statutes are to be put into practice with the utmost particularity, and all the reins of government seem to have fallen to those who were once only its censors. It is, of course, a necessary inference from even the most superficial analysis of constitutional government that under it those who administer the law and direct the policy of the nation in its field of action shall be strictly subject to the laws, must observe the prescribed methods and understandings of the system very precisely; but it is by no means a necessary inference that they shall be in leading strings and shall be reduced to be the mere ministerial agents of a representative assembly; and the inconveniences and anomalies of this new practice and conception in the use of assemblies will, many of them, become manifest enough in our subsequent examination of our government in its practical operations.

To inquire into such matters is to make intimate approach to the very essence of constitutional government; but we approach that essence still more intimately when we turn from the community, from the nation, and from the assembly which represents it, to the individual. No doubt a great deal of nonsense has been talked about the inalienable rights of the individual, and a great deal that was mere vague sentiment and pleasing speculation has been put forward as fundamental principle. The rights of man are easy to discourse of, may be very pleasingly magnified in the sentences of such constitutions as it used to satisfy the revolutionary ardor of French leaders to draw up and affect to put into operation; but they are infinitely hard to translate into practice. Such theories are never 'law,' no matter what the name or the formal authority of the document in which they are embodied. Only that is 'law' which can be executed, and the abstract rights of man are singularly difficult of execution. None the less, vague talk and ineffectual theory though there be, the individual is indisputably the original, the first fact of liberty. Nations are made up of individuals, and the dealings of government with individuals are the ultimate and perfect test of its constitutional character. A man is not free through representative assemblies, he is free in his own action, in his own dealings with the persons and powers about him, or he is not free at all. There is no such thing as corporate liberty. Liberty belongs to the individual, or it does not exist.

And so the instrumentalities through which individuals are afforded protection against the injustice or the unwarranted exactions of government are central to the whole structure of a constitutional system. From the very outset in modern constitutional history until now it has invariably been recognized as one of the essentials of constitutional government that the individual should be provided with some tribunal to which he could resort with the confident expectation that he should find justice there, —not only justice as against other individuals who had disregarded his rights or sought to disregard them, but also justice against the government itself, a perfect protection against all violations of law. Constitutional government is *par excellence* a government of law.

I am not repeating the famous sentence of the Massachusetts Bill of Rights, "to the end that this may be a government of laws and not of men." There never was such a government. Constitute them how you will, governments are always governments of men, and no part of any government is better than the men to whom that part is intrusted. The gauge of excellence is not the law under which officers act, but the conscience and intelligence with which they apply it, if they apply it at all. And the courts do not escape the rule. So far as the individual is concerned, a constitutional government is as good as its courts; no better, no worse. Its laws are only its professions. It keeps its promises, or does not keep them, in its courts. For the individual, therefore, who stands at the centre of every definition of liberty, the struggle for constitutional government is a struggle for good laws, indeed, but also for intelligent, independent, and impartial courts. Not only is it necessary that the people should be spoken for in the conduct of the government by an assembly truly representative of them; that only such laws should be made or should be suffered to remain in force as effect the best regulation of the national life; and that the administration should be subject to the laws. It is also necessary that there should be a judiciary endowed with substantial and independent powers and secure against all corrupting or perverting influences; secure, also, against the arbitrary authority of the administrative heads of the government.

Indeed there is a sense in which it may be said that the whole efficacy and reality of constitutional government resides in its courts. Our definition of liberty is that it is the best practicable adjustment between the powers of the government and the privileges of the individual; and liberty is the object of constitutional government. The ultimate and characteristic object of a constitutional system is not to effect the best possible adjustment between the government and the community, but the best possible adjustment between the government and the individual; for liberty is individual, not communal. Throughout English history, throughout all the processes which have given us constitutional government as the modern world knows it, those who strove to restrain or to moralize government have perceived that the whole reality of the change must find its expression in the opportunity of the individual to resort for the vindication of his rights to a tribunal which was neither government nor community, but an umpire and judge between them, or rather between government and the man himself, claiming rights to which he was entitled under the general understanding.

Nothing in connection with the development of constitutional government is more remarkable, nothing commends itself more to the understanding of those who perceive the real bases of human dignity and capacity, than the way in which it has exalted the individual, and not only exalted him, but at the same time thrown him upon his own resources, as if it honored him enough to release him from leading strings and trust him to see and seek his own rights. The theory of English and American law is that no man must look to have the government take care of him, but that every man must take care of himself, the government providing the means and making them as excellent as may be, in order that there may be no breach of the peace and that everything may be done, so far as possible, with decency and in order, but never itself taking the initiative, never of its own motion intervening, only standing ready to help when called on. Such an attitude presupposes both intelligence and independence of spirit on the part of the individual: such a system elicits intelligence and creates independence of spirit. The individual must seek his court and must know his remedy, and under such a compulsion he will undertake to do both. The stimulation of such requirements is all that he needs, in addition to his own impulses and desires, to give him the attitude and habit of a free man; and the government set over such men must look to see that it have authority for every act it ventures upon.

It further emphasizes this view and purpose of our law, that no peculiar dignity or sanctity attaches amongst us to any officer of government. The theory of our law is that an officer is an officer only so long as he acts within his powers; that when he transcends his authority he ceases to be an officer and is only a private individual, subject to be sued and punished for his offense. An officer who makes a false arrest without warrant is liable to civil suit for damages and to criminal prosecution for assault. He has stepped out of the ranks of public officers, represents nobody but himself, and is merely committing a private wrong. That is the explicit principle of American law not only, but of English law also: the American practice is derived from the English. It is a logical, matter-of-course inference of the constitutional system: representatives of government have no authority except such as they derive from the law, from the regulations agreed on between the government and those who are to be governed. Whoever disregards the limits of the law transgresses the very fundamental presumptions of the system and becomes merely a lawbreaker, enjoying no privilege or exemption. Such a principle in effect repeats the understanding of Runnymede: 'Here is this charter; sign it and observe it, and you are our king; refuse to sign it, violate or ignore it, and you are not our king, but a man without kingly authority who has done us wrong, and we are your enemies and shall seek redress.' It is the same understanding from the king at the top to the constable at the bottom.

It remains only to note what may be called the atmosphere of constitutional government. It is the atmosphere of opinion. Opinion is, of course, the atmosphere of every government, whatever its forms and powers: governments are contrasted with one another only by the degree and manner in which opinion affects them. There is nowhere any such thing as a literally absolute government. The veriest despot is a creature of circumstances, and the most important circumstance of all, whether he is conscious of adjusting himself to it or not, is the disposition of those about him to obey him or to defy him. Certain things are definitely expected of him: there are certain privileges which he must always respect, certain expectations of caste and of rank which he must always punctiliously regard. Above all there is the great body of habit, the habitual frame of the life in which his own people have been formed, which he would throw himself against in vain. The boundaries of his authority lie where he finds the limits of his subjects' willingness or ability to obey him. They cannot obey him if he seek to force upon them rules too strange to their habit: they will not know how, and their spirits will revolt. They will not obey him if he outrage them by too gross a violation of the understandings which they have come to regard as sacred and of the very essence of their life and happiness. The difference between a constitutional system and an unconstitutional is that in a constitutional system the requirements of opinion are clearly formulated and understood, while in an unconstitutional they are vague and conjectural. The unconstitutional ruler has to guess where his subjects will call a halt upon him, and experiment at the hazard of his throne and head; the constitutional ruler definitely knows the limits which he must not transgress and is safe in his authority so long as he does not overstep them.

But there is this radical difference between the opinion which limits the power of an unconstitutional ruler and that which limits the powers of a constitutional government: that the one is unorganized opinion, the other organized; the one hardly more than an impatient stir at any disturbance of tradition or of habit, the other a quick concert of thought, uttered by those who know how to guide both counsel and action. Indeed, there has seldom been in the case of a despotic government anything that really corresponded with what in constitutional government is known as public opinion. The wit who described the government of France as despotism tempered by epigram[2] was really formulating one of the approaches to constitutional government. When opinion spoken in the salon begins to be a definite organ of criticism, when criticism has become concerted and powerful enough and sufficiently mixed with the passion of action to serve from time to time as a modifying, guiding, and controlling force, the development of constitutional government has begun.

It is therefore peculiarly true of constitutional government that its atmosphere is opinion, the air from which it takes its breath and vigor. The underlying understandings of a constitutional system are modified from age to age by changes of life and circumstance and corresponding alterations of opinion. It does not remain fixed in any unchanging form, but grows with the growth and is altered with the change of the nation's needs and purposes. The constitution of England, the original and typical constitutional government of the world, is unwritten except for its statement of individual right and privilege in Magna Carta, in the Bill of Rights, and in the Petition of Right; is, in other words, only a body of very definite opinion, except for occasional definitions of statute here and there. Its substance is the thought and habit of the nation, its conscious expectations and preferences; and around even a written constitution there grows up a body of practices which have no formal recognition or sanction in the written law, which even modify the written stipulations of the system in many subtle ways and become the instrument of opinion in effecting a slow transformation. If it were not so, the written document would become too stiff a garment for the living thing.

---

2 "France was long a despotism tempered by epigrams." Thomas Carlyle, *History of the French Revolution*, Part I, Book I, Chapter 1.

It is in this sense that institutions are the creatures of opinion. Their breath and vigor goes out of them when they cease to be sustained by the conscious or habitual preference of the people whose practice has created them; and new institutions take their place when once that practice is altered. That is what gives dignity to citizenship among a free people. Every man's thought is part of the vital substance of its institutions. With the change of his thought, institutions themselves may change. That is what constitutes citizenship so responsible and solemn a thing. Every man in a free country is, as it were, put upon his honor to be the kind of man such a polity supposes its citizens to be: a man with his thought upon the general welfare, his interest consciously linked with the interests of his fellow-citizens, his sense of duty broadened to the scope of public affairs. Every generation in a free state realizes that the perpetuation of its institutions depends upon the thought and disposition of the generations which are to follow, and busies itself to hand the impulse and the conception on by careful processes of education, stamping its thought upon young men, seeking to make its own frame of mind permanent. Old phrases spring to new significance as one's thought clears in such matters. "Eternal vigilance is the price of liberty." The threadbare phrase seems new stuff when we wear it on our understandings. The vigilance of intelligently directed opinion is indeed the very soil of liberty and of all the enlightened institutions meant to sustain it. And that will always be the freest country in which enlightened opinion abounds, in which to plant the practices of government. It is of the essence of a constitutional system that its people should think straight, maintain a consistent purpose, look before and after, and make their lives the image of their thoughts.

We may summarize our view of constitutional government by saying that its ultimate and essential objects are:

1st. To bring the active and planning will of each part of the government into accord with the prevailing popular thought and need, in order that government may be the impartial instrument of a symmetrical national development;

2d. To give to the law thus formulated under the influence of opinion and adjusted to the general interest both stability and an incorruptible efficacy;

3d. To put into the hands of every individual, without favor or discrimination, the means of enforcing the understandings of the law alike with regard to himself and with regard to the operations of government, the means of challenging every illegal act that touches him.

And that, accordingly, the essential elements and institutions of a constitutional system are:—

1st. A more or less complete and particular formulation of the rights of individual liberty,—that is, the rights of the individual against the community or its government,—such as is contained in Magna Carta and in the Bills of Rights attached to our constitutions;

2d. An assembly, representative of the community or of the people, and not of the government: a body set to criticize, restrain, and control the government;

3d. A government or executive subject to the laws, and

4th. A judiciary with substantial and independent powers, secure against all corrupting or perverting influences; secure, also, against the arbitrary authority of the government itself.

II

THE PLACE OF THE UNITED STATES IN CONSTITUTIONAL DEVELOPMENT

It will greatly enrich our conception of what a constitutional government is to look a little farther into its history. The government of the United States came into existence at a very interesting turning-point in that history, and will lie very much more open to our analysis if we pause before we go farther to examine the circumstances of its origin. Historical excursions are sometimes tedious enough, but the matter we handle cannot be made vital until it is given its true historical setting.

Evidently, if a constitutional government is a government conducted on the basis of a definite understanding between those who administer it and those who obey it, there can be no constitutional government unless there be a community to sustain and develop it,—unless the nation, whose instrument it is, is conscious of common interest and can form common purposes. A people not conscious of any unity, inorganic, unthoughtful, without concert of action, can manifestly neither form nor sustain a constitutional system. The lethargy of an unawakened consciousness is upon them, the helplessness of unformed purpose. They can form no common judgment; they can conceive no common end; they can contrive no common measures. Nothing but a community can have a constitutional form of government, and if a nation has not become a community, it cannot have that sort of polity. It is necessary at the very outset of our analysis, therefore, that we should form a very definite conception of what a community is, and should ask ourselves very frankly whether the United States can be regarded as a community or not. Only in that way can we determine the place of the United States in constitutional development; and only practical historical tests will answer either the one question or the other.

The word 'community' is often upon our lips, but seldom receives any clear definition in our thoughts. If we should examine our implicit assumptions with regard to it, I suppose that we should agree in saying that no body of people could constitute a community in any true or practical sense who did not have a distinct consciousness of common ties and interests, a common manner and standard of life and conduct, and a practised habit of union and concerted action in whatever affected it as a whole. It is in this understanding of the term that we speak when we say that only a community can have a constitutional government. No body of people which is not clearly conscious of common interests and of common standards of life and happiness can come to any satisfactory agreement with its government, and no people which has not a habit of union and concerted action in regard to its affairs could secure itself against the breach of such an agreement if it existed. A people must have the impulse and must find the means to express itself in institutions if it is to have a constitutional system.

I should be at a loss to define what I mean by a common political consciousness, but fortunately it does not need definition. What it is is part of the imaginative conception of every one whose mind has traveled at all in the realms of history and of social experience. With every one of us it is an idea which is as definite as it is subtle and complex. We know that that body of persons is not a community along whose blood the same events do not send the same thrill, upon whose purposes and upon whose consciousness the same events do not make the same impression, and who are not capable, at every turn in their affairs, of forming resolutions and executing measures which will meet the exigency. You remember those fine sentences of De Tocqueville's with regard to the formation of our own government, in which he speaks with admiring wonder of the calm and self-reliant way in which the people of the colonies turned a critical eye upon themselves, detected, as if they looked not upon their own institutions but upon those of others, the serious defects of their political system, and remedied them "without having drawn a tear or a drop of blood from mankind." In proportion as they had a common consciousness with regard to their affairs, they were capable of handling them and of setting up a government which should last. The historical circumstances which explain the capacity of the colonists explain also the character of the government of the United States and make plain its place in constitutional development. How was the United States made a community? How far and in what matters was its consciousness as a community developed? How have its institutions responded to that development, and how do they now stand related to it? These are the questions whose answers may be expected to give us light upon our whole inquiry.

Looked at from the point of view of our present study, government may be said to have passed, roughly speaking, through four stages and forms of development: a first stage in which the government was master, the people veritable subjects; a second in which the government, ceasing to be master by virtue of sheer force and unquestioned authority, remained master by virtue of its insight and sagacity, its readiness and fitness to lead; a third in which both sorts of mastery failed it and it found itself face to face with leaders of the people who were bent upon controlling it, a period of deep agitation and full of the signs of change; and a fourth in which the leaders of the people themselves became the government, and the development was complete.

Government may be said to have been master both in the early Germanic feudal nation which occupied the European field after the break-up of the Roman Empire and in the developed feudal nation in which a monarch like Louis XIV could say with almost literal truth, *L'état c'est moi*; and also in the nations which have been subjugated by some military race or class, conquering them from without and retaining their hold upon them by organized force, as in China and Russia. Such governments represent always a stage of social development: the stage at which the people governed are conscious of no community of interest, no possible concert of action amongst them; do not feel themselves a single body or stir with any common purpose; have not formed the idea of an interest of their own opposed to the interest of the government, or, if they have begun vaguely to form it, know no means of making their separate wish known or effective: a people dumb and without knowledge of speech in such matters. A people may or may not linger at this stage. The nation which is most likely to linger until it stagnates is the caste nation, caught in a crust of custom which it is almost impossible to break or even to alter, unless some irresistible force from without break and destroy it, as the force of the western nations has so ruthlessly broken the ancient forms of Chinese life. The military nation is quite sure to change very rapidly: it is too full of stir and force to retain its first forms or stand still at one stage of development; and the monarch of the modern state to which the feudal state gave birth is more apt than another to attempt progress and development, as the kings of modern Europe did. The population which is ruled by a limited class who are its conquerors is apt, if we may judge by the case of Russia, to stand still until the polity rots.

The stagnation of peoples is very hard for us to think of in our modern western world, but it has none the less been the rule, not the exception, as Mr. Bagehot pointed out in that illuminating book, "Physics and Politics." If we reckon by numerical majorities, the rule has been stagnation; much the greater part of the population of the world has been caught fast in a crust of custom or in an iron net of military rule, and has known no political progress. Even those peoples who have struggled toward the light and sought emancipation from the trammels of too much government have moved with painful slowness toward their goal, so long as there were none of those quick means of concerting thought and action which have been supplied us in the telegraph, the railway, and the cheapened printing press. Without these instrumentalities it is to be doubted whether we could ever have spread a single free state over the spaces of a great continent, as we have done in America, where there were already people accustomed to do as they pleased and to act upon their own initiative. Concerted action does not come by impulse but by practice, by the slow schooling of experience, chiefly by the schooling of repeated failures. A common purpose can be formed only by the slow processes of common counsel, until our own day a thing infinitely tedious and difficult. Many a long age stretches between the moment when a nation begins to awaken to the consciousness that it has common ties and a common interest as against a too masterful and selfish government and the triumphant moment when it sees its own chosen leaders in actual control of its law and policy. The first stirrings of that consciousness change the face of affairs and usher in the second stage of development of which I have spoken; and from it governments that have sagacity enough to respond take their golden opportunity to lead.

It is then that government finds itself checked by the beginnings of independent action on the part of the nation, irregular and imperfectly organized it may be, but definite and significant enough to demand the consideration and often to modify the course of those who rule, lest government should fail of being obeyed and should jeopard civil order, if not its own authority and security. It was so in England in the time of Elizabeth. Parliaments had not yet obtained any place of command. They were consulted when the monarch pleased, and not oftener. Their counsels restrained, but did not govern. The will of the monarch was sometimes stronger than the understandings of the constitution. Opinion had not come to its full stature; authority still loomed large and imperative in every ordinary matter of state. But England was astir as she never had been before. In the old days she had been at the back of Europe; now she was at her front. The doors of the East had been closed by the conquests of the Turk; the barrier of his intolerant power was thrown across the old routes of trade out of Europe into the great Orient, and Europe had turned her face about to seek new outlets for her commerce: down the western coasts of Africa and so around the southern capes into the East again, and across the vast Atlantic to the new lands slowly rising to view over sea,—whether in fact a new world or only the old coasts of the East approached from another side mariners or geographers had not yet quite made up their minds. Columbus had turned his adventurous prows straight toward the heart of the seemingly limitless ocean whose mysteries no man before him had dared look into; and England herself, lying at the very gates of that sea, had been quick to send her own sailors in his wake. Englishmen of every rank and fortune began to turn to the sea for adventure and profit, and the sixteenth century saw the little kingdom wake to influences and ambitions she had never felt before. It was a mettlesome race Elizabeth found herself set to govern.

Whether she was conscious that they were not easy to rule and were likely to have minds of their own in matters of government it is not necessary to ask, because she was of the same mettle and spirit as they, a truly representative Englishman, inclined to lead her people in their own temper and quick to see their interests as they saw them. Mr. John Richard Green has said that in her dealings with foreign governments Elizabeth was one of the most accomplished liars of her day, but that she always dealt candidly and truthfully with her own subjects. It was not so much the circumspection of a wise ruler who wishes to retain the confidence of those upon whose obedience he counts for all the vigor of his policy as the instinctive sympathy and quick understanding that naturally exists between persons of the same purpose and breeding. England came to her full consciousness as a nation in that great day of enterprise and adventure, and Elizabeth was England's suitable embodiment. Her mastery was the mastery of natural leadership. Her instinctive knowledge of what was demanded of her shows in nothing better than in her treatment of the great seamen who explored the long coasts of the new world and lifted treasure from every Spanish fleet they could find. She gave them their commissions and asked no inconvenient questions. So long as they kept troth with her, came to her at her command, executed her purposes when she had need of them, paid reasonable tribute into her treasury, and made all rival seamen respect her power, she freely gave them leave as they wished. Never in any other age had English energy been so quickened and released: a great ruler made great subjects.

There were dark sides enough to the picture. There were phases of English life to which there is not here time to turn in which the royal authority showed sinister and without true insight into either the rights or the interests of the kingdom,—monopolies, illegal exactions, private favors, a thousand irregularities of power,—but that was nothing new; while it was a new thing to have a monarch who, at any rate in all large matters, understood her people and lent her sagacity to the task of leading and stimulating them. In the nick of time, when they most needed a leader, she gave them one in her own person,—a foolish woman but a great statesman.

We have another example of the same thing in a very different age in the leadership of Frederick the Great of Prussia. The Prussia of the middle of the eighteenth century was in almost no respect like the England of the middle of the sixteenth. Frederick, when he came to lead and develop Prussia, had but just put her together out of pieces swept under his single rule by the processes of war. Neither is there any close similarity between the characters of Frederick and Elizabeth. They resembled one another in character no more than any strong and masterful man who was born a statesman resembles any masterful woman born a statesman. But Frederick did for Prussia more than Elizabeth did for England. He first made it a compact and potentially powerful kingdom, and then himself called it into consciousness. Elizabeth gave expression in her own person and gifts to a new nation that had been born and would have been born whether she had lived to rule it or not; Frederick called his kingdom into life and gave it the leadership of an awakening; and he did so on the eve of the modern time, as peoples were everywhere beginning to awake, and so affords us an admirable example, as Elizabeth does, of what a government may do by way of leadership, in anticipation of the day when the people will find sympathetic leaders for themselves if their rulers fail to supply them.

Frederick probably did more for Prussia than she could have done for herself under leaders of her own choosing. He saw her and understood her as a whole. She was in a sense of his own making. He wished her to have internal development rather because he wished her to be strong among the states of Europe than because he wished to see her strength and prosperity increase as a statesman would in times when he was sure of peace; desired her economic enlargement chiefly because he wished his treasury to be full, his kingdom's resources sufficient for any long-drawn contest of arms that might be necessary with the rivals about him; and it must be said that he treated his subjects like servants rather than like citizens of a great state. But under all his purpose of aggrandizement and of international supremacy there lay a real sympathy with his people, a real insight into their interests and necessities, a real capacity to interpret and guide them. He was a leader as well as a master, and his rule gave Prussia such prestige as England had had in the times of the great Elizabeth. He led a new nation out on to the stage of Europe and made it ready for at any rate the initial stages of self-government, by giving it the self-consciousness and regard for its own interests which come of enterprise. A living people needs not a master but a leader.

Leaders like Frederick and Elizabeth are, of course, self-constituted, and the great statesmen whom such rulers draw into their counsels are, of course, of their own, not of the nation's, choosing. The nation is supplied with leaders, does not find them. It is too early for it to find them; it has not learned the way. Such a form and stage of government, the second on our list, represents a stage of political development, as the first of which I spoke represents a stage of social development. When a government is master and the people its unquestioned subjects, society is asleep, is unformed, inorganic, without self-consciousness, and without knowledge of its own interests and power. What is lacking is the birth of a national consciousness and self-knowledge. When the second stage comes the nation has become aware of itself, aware of the drift and significance of its affairs, aware in some degree of its rôle and ambition among the nations; but it has not yet learned to choose its own leaders. It has had the social development necessary to bring it to the threshold of fully developed constitutional arrangements, but not the political development. It has not yet learned how to express itself in men thrust forward out of its own ranks or how to form such common resolutions and contrive such common counsels as would give leaders of its own choice a definite program of action, even if it could choose them. Of course the England of the time of Elizabeth had already had a political development such as Prussia knew nothing of in Frederick's day. Her parliament lay ready to her hand, a true representative assembly, to be turned to any use of common counsel or concerted action she might wish; while Prussia had nothing but her king and a dependent bureaucracy which he had created. In England the full machinery of constitutional government as it were lay dormant, not put to its final uses because Elizabeth saved her people the trouble and by her own leadership postponed the final developments of constitutional government until the weak Stuarts who followed her should make the authority to which she had given such dignity and prestige at last ridiculous and intolerable.

Nations will pass from such a stage of political development by steady transition, change by change, into those arrangements whereby the freely chosen leaders of the people themselves at last assume control of the government, only if, while their hereditary rulers thus by natural genius lead them, a serviceable machinery of constitutional action exist or be formed by means of which the transition can be effected. This was the case in England, but not in Prussia. In England there were both parliament and a self-governing country gentry habituated to affairs. In Prussia there was nothing but a dependent bureaucracy neither derived from the people nor capable of independent initiative in their interest.

And yet, whether there be the requisite machinery at hand or not, an awakened modern nation cannot long stand still at the stage where its affairs are managed without its direct institutional participation and assent. Things cannot long stand still where a whole arrangement depends upon the temper and insight of rulers whose authority is independent of the people's choice, or upon an international situation and the social and economic condition of the country. National conditions are not often for long so simple or so comprehensible that a government not derived from the people can retain the sympathetic comprehension necessary to leadership. Moreover, the times which immediately followed the exceptional reigns of Frederick and

Elizabeth were times when deep common convictions began to stir amidst all ranks and kinds of men; the convictions of the great Protestant Reformation and of the fateful French Revolution, the two great epochs when plain men, who had hitherto taken little heed of affairs either in church or state, were aroused to know themselves and their rights, alike of conscience and of political recognition. Such awakenings of the minds and hearts of whole peoples produced leaders as of course. Great passions, when they run through a whole population, inevitably find a great spokesman. A people cannot remain dumb which is moved by profound impulses of conviction; and when spokesmen and leaders are found, effective concert of action seems to follow as naturally. Men spring together for common action under a common impulse which has taken hold upon their very natures, and governments presently find that they have those to reckon with who know not only what they want, but also the most effective means of making governments uncomfortable until they get it. Governments find themselves, in short, in the presence of *Agitation*, of systematic movements of opinion which do not merely flare up in spasmodic flame and then die down again, but burn with an accumulating ardor which can be checked and extinguished only by removing the grievances and abolishing the unacceptable institutions which are its fuel. Casual discontent can be allayed, but agitation fixed upon conviction cannot be. To fight it is merely to augment its force. It burns irrepressibly in every public assembly; quiet it there, and it gathers head at street corners; drive it thence, and it smoulders in private dwellings, in social gatherings, in every covert of talk, only to break forth more violently than ever because denied vent and air. It must be reckoned with, and to reckon with it is to set up a new understanding between governors and governed, to consent to new practices which are new institutions, to enter the fourth stage, which leads to the full development of constitutional rule.

The third stage of the matter, the stage of agitation, has often been a long one and a sad one. Governments have been very resourceful in parrying agitation, in diverting it, in seeming to yield to it and then cheating it of its objects, in tiring it out or evading it; and where men of conviction lack any permanent instrument, like the English parliament, upon which to centre their efforts, in which to find some unquestionable legal forum where to bring the pressure of their purposes constantly to bear on the government, agitation may often fail entirely for generations together, its flame smothered or scattered from age to age.

But the end, whether it come soon or late, is quite certain to be always the same. In one nation in one form, in another in another, but wherever conviction is awakened and serious purpose results from it, this at last happens: that the people's leaders will themselves take control of the government as they have done in England, in Switzerland, in America, in France, in Scandinavia, and in Italy, and as they will yet do in every other country whose polity fulfils the promise of the modern time.

We are so accustomed to agitation, to absolutely free, outspoken argument for change, to an unrestrained criticism of men and measures carried almost to the point of licence, that to us it seems a normal, harmless part of the familiar processes of popular government. We have learned that it is pent-up feelings that are dangerous, whispered purposes that are revolutionary, covert follies that warp and poison the mind; that the wisest thing to do with a fool is to encourage him to hire a hall and discourse to his fellow citizens. Nothing chills nonsense like exposure to the air; nothing dispels folly like its publication; nothing so eases the machine as the safety valve. Agitation is certainly of the essence of a constitutional system, but those who exercise authority under a non-constitutional system fear its impact with a constant dread and try by every possible means to check and kill it, partly no doubt because they know that agitation is dangerous to arrangements which are unreasonable, and non-constitutional rule is highly unreasonable in countries whose people can express such common thoughts and contrive such concert of action as make agitation formidable. But there is always another reason why rulers so circumstanced should instinctively fear agitation. Agitation is unquestionably very dangerous in countries where there are no institutions—no parliaments, councils, occasional assemblies even—in which opinion may legitimately and with the sanction of law transmute itself into action. Speech is not the only vent opinion needs; it needs also the satisfactions of action.

And action is very sobering to opinion. It is one thing to advocate reforms; it is quite another to formulate them. Many an ardent and burdensome reformer would be silenced and put to better thinking if he were obliged to express his reform in the exact words of a workable statute; and many a statute which amateurs may think eminently workable turns out impossible of execution. One of the things which is most instructive to the practical student of our own government is the tendency of our legislatures, both state and federal, to enact impracticable laws.

Our legislatures do not have to put their own enactments into execution. The chairmen of their committees may often be as absolute tyros in the actual business of government as the members of reform clubs whom they have contemptuously dubbed theorists; and their own theories of what ought to be done do not cease to be theories because expressed in documents introduced by an enacting clause. They sometimes escape the blame attaching to the failure of the laws they frame by adroitly putting it off on the executive officers of the government, representing them as not in sympathy with the enactment and disinclined to give it a full or honest trial in practice; but many a statute is still-born, and agitation which results in still-births is harmless. The agitators have had their way, and nothing has happened. Action has released the pent-up energy, and no harm has been done. But under non-constitutional forms of government no vent of action is supplied, and a sort of fury of helplessness may ensue whose mad issue may be the very destruction of government itself.

When the fourth and final stage of constitutional development is reached, when a people has gained so definite a consciousness of its own interests and of its own political force, has grown so accustomed to forming its own opinions and following its own leaders that it becomes natural and, indeed, inevitable, that its leaders should themselves take charge of the government and direct it, one or other of two forms of government may result: the parliamentary English form or the American form, which Mr. Bagehot has, not very happily, perhaps, called the "presidential." Under the parliamentary form of government the people's recognized leaders for the time being, that is, the leaders of the political party which for the time commands a majority in the popular house of parliament, are both heads of the executive and guides of the legislature. They both conduct government and suggest legislation. All the chief measures of a parliamentary session originate with them, and they are under the sobering necessity of putting into successful execution the laws they propose. Under our own system the people as a whole consciously take part in the choice of but one man, the President, and he is not expected to lead Congress, but only to assent to or dissent from the laws it seeks to enact and to put those which receive his signature or are passed over his veto into execution; while Congress is guided by men whom the nation may or may not have regarded as its leaders and who are preferred to places of leadership in the House and Senate by processes which those houses have themselves devised. The President may be of one party and the houses of Congress of the other. The executive and legislature are not necessarily united in counsel with us as they are in England.

Moreover, what is vastly more important in contrasting our system with others, we have not concentrated our constitutional arrangements in the federal government. We have multiplied our constitutional governments by the number of our states, and have set up in each commonwealth of a vast union of states a separate constitutional government to which is intrusted the regulation of all the ordinary relations of citizens to each other: their property rights, their family relations, their rights of contract, their relations as employer and employed, their suits at law, and their criminal liabilities. The federal government has only the regulation of those matters in which there is manifestly and of necessity a common interest, and for the rest constitutional government is put into commission among forty odd commonwealths.

Both arrangements, the partial separation of the executive from the legislature in the federal government and the parceling out of constitutional powers among the states, mark the historical stage alike of our own development and of the development of constitutional government on the other side of the water at which the government of the United States came into existence. In the state governments there is the same partial separation of legislature and executive that is characteristic of the federal government, because the constitutions of the states were formulated at the same time that the government of the Union was formulated. That is the characteristic they derive from the period in which they originated. The dispersion of constitutional powers among the states originated in circumstances peculiar to America. Switzerland, it is true, has a similar union and division; but though the results in Switzerland are very similar to the results in America, the circumstances of origin and formulation were very different in the two countries. Both peculiarities of our system yield upon analysis very interesting conclusions with regard to the nature and the characteristic processes of constitutional government.

The Constitution of the United States, as framed by the constitutional convention of 1787, was intended to be a copy of the government of England, with such changes as seemed to our own statesmen necessary to safeguard the people of America against the particular sorts of prerogative and power that had worked them harm in their dealings with the government of the mother country over sea. But the government of England was then in a process of transition from an older to a newer form of the constitutional series and had not advanced far enough in the transformation to disclose its real character. Even in our own day, when English ministries are acknowledged to be mere committees of the majority in the House of Commons, the king chooses the ministers. At least such is the legal fiction. But it is not so in fact. It is merely a form. He is obliged to select those of whom the majority in the House of Commons approves. Indeed, he merely calls on the leader of that majority to form a ministry and leaves it to him to say whom the other ministers shall be. He can follow his own judgment in the choice only in the very exceptional case where no one man looms conspicuously first among the leaders of the Commons and the majority in the House is not itself certain of its preference. But when the Constitution of the United States was framed, what is now a form was a reality. The choice of the king was a very real one. He as often as possible chose ministers to his own mind. It is true that ever since the Revolution of 1688 it had generally been necessary for him to select men whom the Commons would follow, against whom they would at least not revolt; but the suffrage for members of parliament was then so disposed that the king and a small group of peers could generally determine the majority in the House of Commons by one sort of influence or another. The king could even on occasion turn his pliant majority over from one minister to another of opposite views when the policy of the crown changed or yielded to pressure. And so the change that was steadily coming upon the whole composition of the government was obscured. The members of the constitutional convention of 1787 naturally enough thought of the king as the executive, a power separate from parliament not only but often in contest with it, and did not see that influences were already working throughout the system which were to transmute the ministry, so soon as the suffrage should be reformed and parliament should become truly representative of the nation, into a committee of the Commons of which the king should have formal appointment but not real choice, and which should itself constitute the working executive of the country, making choice, in the king's stead, of every step of regulation or policy. The President created by our Constitution was conceived upon the model of what it was thought the king should have been under the older practice of the English constitution, at the very time when English theory and practice alike were changing and direct party government by the legislative leaders of the people was actually in course of being set up. We were fixed fast, in respect of the presidential office, at the stage of constitutional development which England was leaving for forms simpler and still more advanced.

Our reasons for having a group of constitutional governments united in a federal constitutional system were not reasons of theory, but reasons of fact. The thirteen little commonwealths which had drawn together in confederation to fight out the war for independence had attained to a growth and character which had made veritable states of them. No merging of them as a single state under one government was possible or conceivable. It was a triumph of statesmanship to unite them by the bonds of a real federal state which was not a mere loosely joined confederation like that which had barely held together long enough to finish the war. A strong sense of community of interest had grown up among the colonies as they fought the French and Indians and struggled for independence; they were resolved to have a common life and stand together for common objects; were keenly aware that separately they could not survive the struggle for political existence which must certainly rise out of their own rivalries and the covetous attacks of foreign powers; and were determined that their common government should be at least strong enough to unite them firmly as a nation. But the catalogue of common interests, the list of powers they must for their own sakes concede to their common government, did not bulk very big in their thoughts. Their state governments were their chief governments, their everyday, essential, intimate, vital instruments of social order and political action. For a little while they looked upon the new federal organization as an experiment, and thought it likely it might not last. Men of first-rate capacity and high political ambition entered the service of their states readily enough, but looked askance upon offers of federal office. Only the extraordinary foresight and sagacity of the men who framed and advocated the federal constitution,—only the prevailing force of such men as Washington, and Hamilton, and Madison,—could have secured so compact and strong a central government in the face of the jealousy of local interests. The wonder was not that constitutional power remained "in commission" among the states, but that any central authority capable of rule and command had been got from the jealous politicians of the self-conscious little commonwealths.

That the states survived the union was no political accident. Their separateness did not consist in the mere casual circumstance that they had been settled at different times and their governments as colonies separately chartered by the English kings. Vital social and economic differences existed between them. They could not have been made a real political community by any single constitution, however broadly and wisely conceived, because they were not a community in fact. They were in many respects sharply contrasted in life and interest. Virginia was much more unlike Massachusetts than Massachusetts was unlike England. The Carolinas, with their lumber forests and their rice fields, felt themselves utterly unlike Virginia; and the Middle states, with their mixture of population out of many lands, were unlike both New England and the South. The Middle states, New York, New Jersey, and Pennsylvania, were, indeed, not mere transplantations out of the mother country; they had the mixture of peoples in them which was in the years to come to be characteristic of America. In them rather than in the communities east or south of them lay hidden the prophecy of what America was to be, and they in some subtle way felt the contrast between their own ways and purposes and those of their neighbors very keenly. Constitutional government is based upon common understandings, common interests, common impulses, common habits, and these each of the little commonwealths of the Union had; but in the federal state which they had devised in the Philadelphia convention these things did not yet exist except as regarded the matters of commerce, of coinage, of post-offices and post roads, of piracies and felonies on the high seas, of war and military defense, and of dealings with foreign governments of which so careful a catalogue had been made in the eighth section of the first article of the federal constitution. The states were not one community but many communities, and as such could not have had a single government; were under the necessity of having as many constitutional units as there were actual political divisions. The very complexity of the arrangement was of the essence of practical good sense and showed how true an instinct the leaders of that day had for successful constitutional method.

Our life has undergone radical changes since 1787, and almost every change has operated to draw the nation together, to give it the common consciousness, the common interests, the common standards of conduct, the habit of concerted action, which will eventually impart to it in many more respects the character of a single community. No student of constitutional development can have observed these vital processes without perceiving what their end and consequence will be. The copper threads of the telegraph run unbroken to every nook and corner of the great continent, like the nerves of a single body, transmitting thought and purpose with instant precision. Railways lie in every valley and stretch across every plain. Cheap newspapers make the news of every country-side the news of the nation. Industrial organization knows nothing of state lines, and commerce sweeps from state to state in currents which can hardly be traced for number and intricacy. Ideas, motives, standards of conduct, subtle items of interest, airs from out every region travel with the news, with the passenger on the express train, with the merchant's goods and the farmer's grain. Invisible shuttles of suggestion weave the thoughts and purposes of separate communities together, and a nation which will some day know itself a single community is a-making in the warp and woof of the fabric. The extraordinary way in which the powers of the federal government have been suffered to grow in recent years is evidence enough of the process.

It is a process which has gone forward with a noble dramatic, even epic, majesty, filling the whole stage of the continent with movement. Until 1890 we had always a frontier within the nation; until that year the makers of the census had always been able in drawing their maps to sketch a line somewhere between the older states and the Pacific which marked the front of organized settlement. A hundred years had gone by since the constitution was framed, and throughout all the century the same process of settlement had been going on which marked the first establishment of the colonies. The stages of development within the nation itself varied all the way from communities on the eastern coast which were at length hardly to be distinguished from European communities in their complexity, their variety, their pageantry of life to communities in the West more sharply contrasted with those in the East than Virginia from England in the seventeenth century. To travel from the Atlantic coast to the frontier was like viewing a colossal exhibit illustrative by actual life of all the processes that had made and were making the nation. Since 1890 there has been no traceable frontier; the processes have begun to be intensive rather than extensive. The processes which knit close and unite all fibres into one cloth are now everywhere visible to any one who will look beneath the surface.

It is familiar matter of history that it is this westward expansion, this constant projection of new communities into the West, this never ceasing spread and adaptation of our institutions and our modes of life, that has been the chief instrumentality in giving us national feeling, that has kept our eyes lifted to tasks which had manifest destiny in them, and could be compassed by no merely local agencies. It was the constant making of states that forced upon every generation of statesmen the question whether slavery should be extended or restricted in area until the Civil War answered it forever, and that controversy more than any other called the nation to consciousness and to action. Ours has been for the most part a very businesslike history. Our congressional annals have not been brightened by many picturesque incidents or quickened by many dramatic moments, but there is one debate to which every student turns with the feeling that in it lay the fire of the central dramatic force of all our history. In the debate between Mr. Hayne and Mr. Webster the whole feeling and consciousness of America was changed. Mr. Hayne had uttered, with singular eloquence and ringing force, the voice of a day that was passing away; Mr. Webster the voice of a day that had come and whose forces were to supersede all others. There is a sense in which it may almost be said that Mr. Webster that day called a nation into being. What he said has the immortal quality of words which almost create the thoughts they speak. The nation lay as it were unconscious of its unity and purpose, and he called it into full consciousness. It could never again be anything less than what he had said that it was. It is at such moments and in the mouths of such interpreters that nations spring from age to age in their development. And in our modern day influences less heated and dramatic than those of the days of the westward movement, influences that operate silent and unobserved in the economic and social changes that are working a great synthesis upon us, are carrying the nationalizing process steadily and irresistibly forward to the same great consummation.

But there are natural limits beyond which such a development cannot go, and our state governments are likely to become, not less, but more vital units in our system as the natural scope and limits of their powers are more clearly and permanently established. In a great political system like our own, spread abroad over the vast spaces of a various continent, the states are essential. We are now in the midst of changes whose sweep is so wide that we exaggerate their force and suppose that because they are not checked by state boundaries, and for the time even seem to obscure them, they will eventually obliterate them. We shall be surprised, when the changes are completed, to find how little they have altered our constitutional machinery. What they will alter very radically is our national consciousness, our perception of the interests we have in common, and of the principles upon which we must act in dealing with them. The change will be psychological rather than political, of the spirit of our action rather than of its method. Undoubtedly the sphere of our national government will be in many important particulars notably enlarged; but it will be in particulars and not in principle, by normal and legitimate alterations of the constitutional understanding and not by any reconstruction of the system.

Not only are the separate and independent powers of the states based upon real economic and social differences between section and section of an enormous country, differences which necessitate adaptations of law and of administrative policy such as only local authorities acting in real independence can intelligently effect; but the states are our great and permanent contribution to constitutional development. I call them a great contribution because they have given to the understandings upon which constitutional government is based an intimacy and detail, an adjustment to local circumstances, a national diversity, an immediate adaptation to the variety of the people themselves, such as a little country may perhaps dispense with but a great continent cannot. The development of the United States would have been as impossible without the state governments as the original establishment of our federal system would have been. They have furnished us with an ideal means of integrating a vast and various population, adapting law to changing and temporary conditions, modulating development, and permanently securing each item of progress. They have been an incomparable means of sensitive adjustment between popular thought and governmental method, and may yet afford the world itself the model of federation and liberty it may in God's providence come to seek. There can be no reasonable fear that our states will ever be less than they are, the normal constitutional machinery of our legal adjustment. As the federal government grows in scope and power it will grow, not to their curtailment, but only by way of supplementing them and by way of safeguarding those interests, from the first looked forward to by the makers of the Constitution, in which we shall consciously become a single community.

This is not a conclusion got out of sentiment or preference, but out of the necessary inferences of constitutional history. Constitutional government can exist only where there is actual community of interest and of purpose, and cannot, if it be also *self-government*, express the life of any body of people that does not constitute a veritable community. Are the United States a community? In some things, yes; in most things, no. How impossible it is to generalize about the United States! If a foreign acquaintance ask you a question about America, are you not obliged before replying to say, "Which part of America do you refer to?" It would be hard to frame any single generalization which would be true of the whole United States, whether it were social, economic, or political. It is a matter of despair to describe a typical American. Types vary from region to region, and even from state to state. America abounds in the vitality of variety and can be summed up in no formula either of description or of prophecy.

Moreover, she is a country not merely constitutionally governed, but also self-governed. To look upon her and comprehend her is to comprehend the distinction. Self-government is the last, the consummate stage of constitutional development. Peoples which are not yet highly developed, self-conscious communities can be constitutionally governed, as England was before she had got her full character and knowledge of herself, under monarchs who ruled her by their own will, checked but not governed by her parliament; but only communities can govern themselves and dispense with every form of absolute authority. There is profound truth in Sir Henry Maine's remark that the men who colonized America and made its governments, to the admiration of the world, could never have thus masterfully taken charge of their own affairs and combined stability with liberty in the process of absolute self-government if they had not sprung of a race habituated to submit to law and authority, if their fathers had not been the subjects of kings, if the stock of which they came had not served the long apprenticeship of political childhood during which law was law without choice of their own.[3] Self-government is not a mere form of institutions, to be had when desired, if only proper pains be taken. It is a form of character. It follows upon the long discipline which gives a people self-possession, self-mastery, the habit of order and peace and common counsel, and a reverence for law which will not fail when they themselves become the makers of law: the steadiness and

[3] The Editors have been unable to find any statement by Maine which corresponds exactly to what Wilson attributes to him. However, Wilson might have been summarizing and making logical inferences from views expressed by Maine in his *Popular Government* (London, 1885), especially in the concluding chapter, "The Constitution of the United States."

self-control of political maturity. And these things cannot be had without long discipline.

The distinction is of vital concern to us in respect of practical choices of policy which we must make, and make very soon. We have dependencies to deal with and must deal with them in the true spirit of our own institutions. We can give the Filipinos constitutional government, a government which they may count upon to be just, a government based upon some clear and equitable understanding, intended for their good and not for our aggrandizement; but we must ourselves for the present supply that government. It would, it is true, be an unprecedented operation, reversing the process of Runnymede, but America has before this shown the world enlightened processes of politics that were without precedent. It would have been within the choice of John to summon his barons to Runnymede and of his own initiative enter into a constitutional understanding with them; and it is within our choice to do a similar thing, at once wise and generous, in the government of the Philippine Islands. But we cannot give them self-government. Self-government is not a thing that can be 'given' to any people, because it is a form of character and not a form of constitution. No people can be 'given' the self-control of maturity. Only a long apprenticeship of obedience can secure them the precious possession, a thing no more to be bought than given. They cannot be presented with the character of a community, but it may confidently be hoped that they will become a community under the wholesome and salutary influences of just laws and a sympathetic administration; that they will after a while understand and master themselves, if in the meantime they are understood and served in good conscience by those set over them in authority.

We of all people in the world should know these fundamental things and should act upon them, if only to illustrate the mastery in politics which belongs to us of hereditary right. To ignore them would be not only to fail and fail miserably, but to fail ridiculously and belie ourselves. Having ourselves gained self-government by a definite process which can have no substitute, let us put the peoples dependent upon us in the right way to gain it also.

III

THE PRESIDENT OF THE UNITED STATES

It is difficult to describe any single part of a great governmental system without describing the whole of it. Governments are living things and operate as organic wholes. Moreover, governments have their natural evolution and are one thing in one age, another in another. The makers of the Constitution constructed the federal government upon a theory of checks and balances which was meant to limit the operation of each part and allow to no single part or organ of it a dominating force; but no government can be successfully conducted upon so mechanical a theory. Leadership and control must be lodged somewhere; the whole art of statesmanship is the art of bringing the several parts of government into effective coöperation for the accomplishment of particular common objects,—and party objects at that. Our study of each part of our federal system, if we are to discover our real government as it lives, must be made to disclose to us its operative coördination as a whole: its places of leadership, its method of action, how it operates, what checks it, what gives it energy and effect. Governments are what politicians make them, and it is easier to write of the President than of the presidency.

The government of the United States was constructed upon the Whig theory of political dynamics, which was a sort of unconscious copy of the Newtonian theory of the universe. In our own day, whenever we discuss the structure or development of anything, whether in nature or in society, we consciously or unconsciously follow Mr. Darwin; but before Mr. Darwin, they followed Newton. Some single law, like the law of gravitation, swung each system of thought and gave it its principle of unity. Every sun, every planet, every free body in the spaces of the heavens, the world itself, is kept in its place and reined to its course by the attraction of bodies that swing with equal order and precision about it, themselves governed by the nice poise and balance of forces which give the whole system of the universe its symmetry and perfect adjustment. The Whigs had tried to give England a similar constitution. They had had no wish to destroy the throne, no conscious desire to reduce the king to a mere figurehead, but had intended only to surround and offset him with a system of constitutional checks and balances which should regulate his otherwise arbitrary course and make it at least always calculable.

They had made no clear analysis of the matter in their own thoughts; it has not been the habit of English politicians, or indeed of English-speaking politicians on either side of the water, to be clear theorists. It was was left to a Frenchman to point out to the Whigs what they had done. They had striven to make

Parliament so influential in the making of laws and so authoritative in the criticism of the king's policy that the king could in no matter have his own way without their coöperation and assent, though they left him free, the while, if he chose, to interpose an absolute veto upon the acts of Parliament. They had striven to secure for the courts of law as great an independence as possible, so that they might be neither overawed by parliament nor coerced by the king. In brief, as Montesquieu pointed out to them in his lucid way, they had sought to balance executive, legislature, and judiciary off against one another by a series of checks and counterpoises, which Newton might readily have recognized as suggestive of the mechanism of the heavens.

The makers of our federal Constitution followed the scheme as they found it expounded in Montesquieu, followed it with genuine scientific enthusiasm. The admirable expositions of the *Federalist* read like thoughtful applications of Montesquieu to the political needs and circumstances of America. They are full of the theory of checks and balances. The President is balanced off against Congress, Congress against the President, and each against the courts. Our statesmen of the earlier generations quoted no one so often as Montesquieu, and they quoted him always as a scientific standard in the field of politics. Politics is turned into mechanics under his touch. The theory of gravitation is supreme.

The trouble with the theory is that government is not a machine, but a living thing. It falls, not under the theory of the universe, but under the theory of organic life. It is accountable to Darwin, not to Newton. It is modified by its environment, necessitated by its tasks, shaped to its functions by the sheer pressure of life. No living thing can have its organs offset against each other as checks, and live. On the contrary, its life is dependent upon their quick coöperation, their ready response to the commands of instinct or intelligence, their amicable community of purpose. Government is not a body of blind forces; it is a body of men, with highly differentiated functions, no doubt, in our modern day of specialization, but with a common task and purpose. Their coöperation is indispensable, their warfare fatal. There can be no successful government without leadership or without the intimate, almost instinctive, coördination of the organs of life and action. This is not theory, but fact, and displays its force as fact, whatever theories may be thrown across its track. Living political constitutions must be Darwinian in structure and in practice.

Fortunately, the definitions and prescriptions of our constitutional law, though conceived in the Newtonian spirit and upon the Newtonian principle, are sufficiently broad and elastic to allow for the play of life and circumstance. Though they were Whig theorists, the men who framed the federal Constitution were also practical statesmen with an experienced eye for affairs and a quick practical sagacity in respect of the actual structure of government, and they have given us a thoroughly workable model. If it had in fact been a machine governed by mechanically automatic balances, it would have had no history; but it was not, and its history has been rich with the influences and personalities of the men who have conducted it and made it a living reality. The government of the United States has had a vital and normal organic growth and has proved itself eminently adapted to express the changing temper and purposes of the American people from age to age.

That is the reason why it is easier to write of the President than of the presidency. The presidency has been one thing at one time, another at another, varying with the man who occupied the office and with the circumstances that surrounded him. One account must be given of the office during the period 1789 to 1825, when the government was getting its footing both at home and abroad, struggling for its place among the nations and its full credit among its own people; when English precedents and traditions were strongest; and when the men chosen for the office were men bred to leadership in a way that attracted to them the attention and confidence of the whole country. Another account must be given of it during Jackson's time, when an imperious man, bred not in deliberative assemblies or quiet councils, but in the field and upon a rough frontier, worked his own will upon affairs, with or without formal sanction of law, sustained by a clear undoubting conscience and the love of a people who had grown deeply impatient of the régime he had supplanted. Still another account must be given of it during the years 1836 to 1861, when domestic affairs of many debatable kinds absorbed the country, when Congress necessarily exercised the chief choices of policy, and when the Presidents who followed one another in office lacked the personal force and initiative to make for themselves a leading place in counsel. After that came the Civil War and Mr. Lincoln's unique task and achievement, when the executive seemed for a little while to become by sheer stress of circumstances the whole government, Congress merely voting supplies and assenting to necessary laws, as Parliament did in the time of the Tudors. From 1865 to 1898 domestic questions, legislative matters in repect of which Congress had naturally to make the initial choice, legislative leaders the chief decisions of policy, came once more to the front, and no President except Mr. Cleveland played a leading and decisive part in the quiet drama of our national life. Even Mr. Cleveland may be said to have owed his great rôle in affairs rather to his own native force and the confused politics of the time, than to any opportunity of leadership naturally afforded him by a system which had subordinated so many Presidents before him to Congress. The war with Spain again changed the balance of parts. Foreign questions became leading questions again, as they had been in the first days of the government, and in them the President was of necessity leader. Our new place in the affairs of the world has since that year of transformation kept him at the front of our government, where our own thoughts and the attention of men everywhere is centred upon him.

Both men and circumstances have created these contrasts in the administration and influence of the office of President. We have all been disciples of Montesquieu, but we have also been practical politicians. Mr. Bagehot once remarked that it was no proof of the excellence of the Constitution of the United States that the Americans had operated it with conspicuous success because the Americans could run any constitution successfully; and, while the compliment is altogether acceptable, it is certainly true that our practical sense is more noticeable than our theoretical consistency, and that, while we were once all constitutional lawyers, we are in these latter days apt to be very impatient of literal and dogmatic interpretations of constitutional principle.

The makers of the Constitution seem to have thought of the President as what the stricter Whig theorists wished the king to be: only the legal executive, the presiding and guiding authority in the application of law and the execution of policy. His veto upon legislation was only his 'check' on Congress,—was a power of restraint, not of guidance. He was empowered to prevent bad laws, but he was not to be given an opportunity to make good ones. As a matter of fact he has become very much more. He has become the leader of his party and the guide of the nation in political purpose, and therefore in legal action. The constitutional structure of the government has hampered and limited his action in these significant rôles, but it has not prevented it. The influence of the President has varied with the men who have been Presidents and with the circumstances of their times, but the tendency has been unmistakably disclosed, and springs out of the very nature of government itself. It is merely the proof that our government is a living, organic thing, and must, like every other government, work out the close synthesis of active parts which can exist only when leadership is lodged in some one man or group of men. You cannot compound a successful government out of antagonisms. Greatly as the practice and influence of Presidents has varied, there can be no mistaking the fact that we have grown more and more inclined from generation to generation to look to the President as the unifying force in our complex system, the leader both of his party and of the nation. To do so is not inconsistent with the actual provisions of the Constitution; it is only inconsistent with a very mechanical theory of its meaning and intention. The Constitution contains no theories. It is as practical a document as Magna Carta.

The rôle of party leader is forced upon the President by the method of his selection. The theory of the makers of the Constitution may have been that the presidential electors would exercise a real choice, but it is hard to understand how, as experienced politicians, they can have expected anything of the kind. They did not provide that the electors should meet as one body for consultation and make deliberate choice of a President and Vice-President, but that they should meet "in their respective states" and cast their ballots in separate groups, without the possibility of consulting and without the least likelihood of agreeing, unless some such means as have actually been used were employed to suggest and determine their choice beforehand. It was the practice at first to make party nominations for the presidency by congressional caucus. Since the Democratic upheaval of General Jackson's time nominating conventions have taken the place of congressional caucuses; and the choice of Presidents by party conventions has had some very interesting results.

We are apt to think of the choice of nominating conventions as somewhat haphazard. We know, or think that we know, how their action is sometimes determined, and the knowledge makes us very uneasy. We know that there is no debate in nominating conventions, no discussion of the merits of the respective candidates, at which the country can sit as audience and assess the wisdom of the final choice. If there is any talking to be done, aside from the formal addresses of the temporary and permanent chairmen and of those who present the platform and the names of the several aspirants for nomination, the assembly adjourns. The talking that is to decide the result must be done in private committee rooms and behind the closed doors of the headquarters of the several state delegations to the convention. The intervals between sessions are filled with a very feverish activity. Messengers run from one headquarters to another until the small hours of the morning. Conference follows conference in a way that is likely to bring newspaper correspondents to the verge of despair, it being next to impossible to put the rumors together into any coherent story of what is going on. Only at the rooms of the national committee of the party is there any clear knowledge of the situation as a whole; and the excitement of the members of the convention rises from session to session under the sheer pressure of uncertainty. The final majority is compounded no outsider and few members can tell how.

Many influences, too, play upon nominating conventions, which seem mere winds of feeling. They sit in great halls, with galleries into which crowd thousands of spectators from all parts of the country, but chiefly, of course, from the place at which the convention sits, and the feeling of the galleries is transmitted to the floor. The cheers of mere spectators echo the names of popular candidates, and every excitement on the floor is enhanced a hundred fold in the galleries. Sudden gusts of impulse are apt to change the whole feeling of the convention, and offset in a moment the most careful arrangements of managing politicians. It has come to be a commonly accepted opinion that if the Republican convention of 1860 had not met in Chicago, it would have nominated Mr. Seward and not Mr. Lincoln. Mr. Seward was the acknowledged leader of the new party; had been its most telling spokesman; had given its tenets definition and currency. Mr. Lincoln had not been brought within view of the country as a whole until the other day, when he had given Mr. Douglas so hard a fight to keep his seat in the Senate, and had but just now given currency among thoughtful men to the striking phrases of the searching speeches he had made in debate with his practised antagonist. But the convention met in Illinois, amidst throngs of Mr. Lincoln's ardent friends and advocates. His managers saw to it that the galleries were properly filled with men who would cheer every mention of his name until the hall was shaken. Every influence of the place worked for him and he was chosen.

Thoughtful critics of our political practices have not allowed the excellence of the choice to blind them to the danger of the method. They have known too many examples of what the galleries have done to supplement the efforts of managing politicians to feel safe in the presence of processes which seem rather those of intrigue and impulse than those of sober choice. They can cite instances, moreover, of sudden, unlooked-for excitements on the floor of such bodies which have swept them from the control of all sober influences and hastened them to choices which no truly deliberative assembly could ever have made. There is no training school for Presidents, unless, as some governors have wished, it be looked for in the governorships of states; and nominating conventions have confined themselves in their selections to no class, have demanded of aspirants no particular experience or knowledge of affairs. They have nominated lawyers without political experience, soldiers, editors of newspapers, newspaper correspondents, whom they pleased, without regard to their lack of contact with affairs. It would seem as if their choices were almost matters of chance.

In reality there is much more method, much more definite purpose, much more deliberate choice in the extraordinary process than there seems to be. The leading spirits of the national committee of each party could give an account of the matter which would put a very different face on it and make the methods of nominating conventions seem, for all the undoubted elements of chance there are in them, on the whole very manageable. Moreover, the party that expects to win may be counted on to make a much more conservative and thoughtful selection of a candidate than the party that merely hopes to win. The haphazard selections which seem to discredit the system are generally made by conventions of the party unaccustomed to success. Success brings sober calculation and a sense of responsibility.

And it must be remembered also that our political system is not so coördinated as to supply a training for presidential aspirants or even to make it absolutely necessary that they should have had extended experience in public affairs. Certainly the country has never thought of members of Congress as in any particular degree fitted for the presidency. Even the Vice President is not afforded an opportunity to learn the duties of the office. The men best prepared, no doubt, are those who have been governors of states or members of cabinets. And yet even they are chosen for their respective offices generally by reason of a kind of fitness and availability which does not necessarily argue in them the size and power that would fit them for the greater office. In our earlier practice cabinet officers were regarded as in the natural line of succession to the presidency. Mr. Jefferson had been in General Washington's cabinet, Mr. Madison in Mr. Jefferson's, Mr. Monroe in Mr. Madison's; and generally it was the Secretary of State who was taken. But those were days when English precedent was strong upon us, when cabinets were expected to be made up of the political leaders of the party in power; and from their ranks subsequent candidates for the presidency were most likely to be selected. The practice, as we look back to it, seems eminently sensible, and we wonder why it should have been so soon departed from and apparently forgotten. We wonder, too, why eminent senators have not sometimes been chosen; why members of the House have so seldom commanded the attention of nominating conventions; why public life has never offered itself in any definite way as a preparation for the presidential office.

If the matter be looked at a little more closely, it will be seen that the office of President, as we have used and developed it, really does not demand actual experience in affairs so much as particular qualities of mind and character which we are at least as likely to find outside the ranks of our public men as within them. What is it that a nominating convention wants in the man it is to present to the country for its suffrages? A man who will be and who will seem to the country in some sort an embodiment of the character and purpose it wishes its government to have,— a man who understands his own day and the needs of the country, and who has the personality and the initiative to enforce his views both upon the people and upon Congress. It may seem an odd way to get such a man. It is even possible that nominating conventions and those who guide them do not realize entirely what it is that they do. But in simple fact the convention picks out a party leader from the body of the nation. Not that it expects its nominee to direct the interior government of the party and to supplant its already accredited and experienced spokesmen in Congress and in its state and national committees; but it does of necessity expect him to represent it before public opinion and to stand before the country as its representative man, as a true type of what the country may expect of the party itself in purpose and principle. It cannot but be led by him in the campaign; if he be elected, it cannot but acquiesce in his leadership of the government itself. What the country will demand of the candidate will be, not that he be an astute politician, skilled and practised in affairs, but that he be a man such as it can trust, in character, in intention, in knowledge of its needs, in perception of the best means by which those needs may be met, in capacity to prevail by reason of his own weight and integrity. Sometimes the country believes in a party, but more often it believes in a man; and conventions have often shown the instinct to perceive which it is that the country needs in a particular presidential year, a mere representative partisan, a military hero, or some one who will genuinely speak for the country itself, whatever be his training and antecedents. It is in this sense that the President has the rôle of party leader thrust upon him by the very method by which he is chosen.

As legal executive, his constitutional aspect, the President cannot be thought of alone. He cannot execute laws. Their actual daily execution must be taken care of by the several executive departments and by the now innumerable body of federal officials throughout the country. In respect of the strictly executive duties of his office the President may be said to administer the presidency in conjunction with the members of his cabinet, like the chairman of a commission. He is even of necessity much less active in the actual carrying out of the law than are his colleagues and advisers. It is therefore becoming more and more true, as the business of the government becomes more and more complex and extended, that the President is becoming more and more a political and less and less an executive officer. His executive powers are in commission, while his political powers more and more centre and accumulate upon him and are in their very nature personal and inalienable.

Only the larger sort of executive questions are brought to him. Departments which run with easy routine and whose transactions bring few questions of general policy to the surface may proceed with their business for months and even years together without demanding his attention; and no department is in any sense under his direct charge. Cabinet meetings do not discuss detail: they are concerned only with the larger matters of policy or expediency which important business is constantly disclosing. There are no more hours in the President's day than in another man's. If he is indeed the executive, he must act almost entirely by delegation, and is in the hands of his colleagues. He is likely to be praised if things go well, and blamed if they go wrong; but his only real control is of the persons to whom he deputes the performance of executive duties. It is through no fault or neglect of his that the duties apparently assigned to him by the Constitution have come to be his less conspicuous, less important duties, and that duties apparently not assigned to him at all chiefly occupy his time and energy. The one set of duties it has proved practically impossible for him to perform; the other it has proved impossible for him to escape.

He cannot escape being the leader of his party except by incapacity and lack of personal force, because he is at once the choice of the party and of the nation. He is the party nominee, and the only party nominee for whom the whole nation votes. Members of the House and Senate are representatives of localities, are voted for only by sections of voters, or by local bodies of electors like the members of the state legislatures. There is no national party choice except that of President. No one else represents the people as a whole, exercising a national choice; and inasmuch as his strictly executive duties are in fact subordinated, so far at any rate as all detail is concerned, the President represents not so much the party's governing efficiency as its controlling ideals and principles. He is not so much part of its organization as its vital link of connection with the thinking nation. He can dominate his party by being spokesman for the real sentiment and purpose of the country, by giving direction to opinion, by giving the country at once the information and the statements of policy which will enable it to form its judgments alike of parties and of men.

For he is also the political leader of the nation, or has it in his choice to be. The nation as a whole has chosen him, and is conscious that it has no other political spokesman. His is the only national voice in affairs. Let him once win the admiration and confidence of the country, and no other single force can withstand him, no combination of forces will easily overpower him. His position takes the imagination of the country. He is the representative of no constituency, but of the whole people. When he speaks in his true character, he speaks for no special interest. If he rightly interpret the national thought and boldly insist upon it, he is irresistible; and the country never feels the zest of action so much as when its President is of such insight and calibre. Its instinct is for unified action, and it craves a single leader. It is for this reason that it will often prefer to choose a man rather than a party. A President whom it trusts can not only lead it, but form it to his own views.

It is the extraordinary isolation imposed upon the President by our system that makes the character and opportunity of his office so extraordinary. In him are centred both opinion and party. He may stand, if he will, a little outside party and insist as if it were upon the general opinion. It is with the instinctive feeling that it is upon occasion such a man that the country wants that nominating conventions will often nominate men who are not their acknowledged leaders, but only such men as the country would like to see lead both its parties. The President may also, if he will, stand within the party counsels and use the advantage of his power and personal force to control its actual programs. He may be both the leader of his party and the leader of the nation, or he may be one or the other. If he lead the nation, his party can hardly resist him. His office is anything he has the sagacity and force to make it.

That is the reason why it has been one thing at one time, another at another. The Presidents who have not made themselves leaders have lived no more truly on that account in the spirit of the Constitution than those whose force has told in the determination of law and policy. No doubt Andrew Jackson overstepped the bounds meant to be set to the authority of his office. It was certainly in direct contravention of the spirit of the Constitution that he should have refused to respect and execute decisions of the Supreme Court of the United States, and no serious student of our history can righteously condone what he did in such matters on the ground that his intentions were upright and his principles pure. But the Constitution of the United States is not a mere lawyers' document: it is a vehicle of life, and its spirit is always the spirit of the age. Its prescriptions are clear and we know what they are; a written document makes lawyers of us all, and our duty as citizens should make us conscientious lawyers, reading the text of the Constitution without subtlety or sophistication; but life is always your last and most authoritative critic.

Some of our Presidents have deliberately held themselves off from using the full power they might legitimately have used, because of conscientious scruples, because they were more theorists than statesmen. They have held the strict literary theory of the Constitution, the Whig theory, the Newtonian theory, and have acted as if they thought that Pennsylvania Avenue should have been even longer than it is; that there should be no intimate communication of any kind between the Capitol and the White House; that the President as a man was no more at liberty to lead the houses of Congress by persuasion than he was at liberty as President to dominate them by authority,—supposing that he had, what he has not, authority enough to dominate them. But the makers of the Constitution were not enacting Whig theory, they were not making laws with the expectation that, not the laws themselves, but their opinions, known by future historians to lie back of them, should govern the constitutional action of the country. They were statesmen, not pedants, and their laws are sufficient to keep us to the paths they set us upon. The President is at liberty, both in law and conscience, to be as big a man as he can. His capacity will set the limit; and if Congress be overborne by him, it will be no fault of the makers of the Constitution,—it will be from no lack of constitutional powers on its part, but only because the President has the nation behind him, and Congress has not. He has no means of compelling Congress except through public opinion.

That I say he has no means of compelling Congress will show what I mean, and that my meaning has no touch of radicalism or iconoclasm in it. There are illegitimate means by which the President may influence the action of Congress. He may bargain with members, not only with regard to appointments, but also with regard to legislative measures. He may use his local patronage to assist members to get or retain their seats. He may interpose his powerful influence, in one covert way or another, in contests for places in the Senate. He may also overbear Congress by arbitrary acts which ignore the laws or virtually override them. He may even substitute his own orders for acts of Congress which he wants but cannot get. Such things are not only deeply immoral, they are destructive of the fundamental understandings of constitutional government and, therefore, of constitutional government itself. They are sure, moreover, in a country of free public opinion, to bring their own punishment, to destroy both the fame and the power of the man who dares to practise them. No honorable man includes such agencies in a sober exposition of the Constitution or allows himself to think of them when he speaks of the influences of "life" which govern each generation's use and interpretation of that great instrument, our sovereign guide and the object of our deepest reverence. Nothing in a system like ours can be constitutional which is immoral or which touches the good faith of those who have sworn to obey the fundamental law. The reprobation of all good men will always overwhelm such influences with shame and failure. But the personal force of the President is perfectly constitutional to any extent to which he chooses to exercise it, and it is by the clear logic of our constitutional practice that he has become alike the leader of his party and the leader of the nation.

The political powers of the President are not quite so obvious in their scope and character when we consider his relations with

Congress as when we consider his relations to his party and to the nation. They need, therefore, a somewhat more critical examination. Leadership in government naturally belongs to its executive officers, who are daily in contact with practical conditions and exigencies and whose reputations alike for good judgment and for fidelity are at stake much more than are those of the members of the legislative body at every turn of the law's application. The law-making part of the government ought certainly to be very hospitable to the suggestions of the planning and acting part of it. Those Presidents who have felt themselves bound to adhere to the strict literary theory of the Constitution have scrupulously refrained from attempting to determine either the subjects or the character of legislation, except so far as they were obliged to decide for themselves, after Congress had acted, whether they should acquiesce in it or not. And yet the Constitution explicitly authorizes the President to recommend to Congress "such measures as he shall deem necessary and expedient," and it is not necessary to the integrity of even the literary theory of the Constitution to insist that such recommendations should be merely perfunctory. Certainly General Washington did not so regard them, and he stood much nearer the Whig theory than we do. A President's messages to Congress have no more weight or authority than their intrinsic reasonableness and importance give them: but that is their only constitutional limitation. The Constitution certainly does not forbid the President to back them up, as General Washington did, with such personal force and influence as he may possess. Some of our Presidents have felt the need, which unquestionably exists in our system, for some spokesman of the nation as a whole, in matters of legislation no less than in other matters, and have tried to supply Congress with the leadership of suggestion, backed by argument and by iteration and by every legitimate appeal to public opinion. Cabinet officers are shut out from Congress; the President himself has, by custom, no access to its floor; many long-established barriers of precedent, though not of law, hinder him from exercising any direct influence upon its deliberations; and yet he is undoubtedly the only spokesman of the whole people. They have again and again, as often as they were afforded the opportunity, manifested their satisfaction when he has boldly accepted the rôle of leader, to which the peculiar origin and character of his authority entitle him. The Constitution bids him speak, and times of stress and change must more and more thrust upon him the attitude of originator of policies.

His is the vital place of action in the system, whether he accept it as such or not, and the office is the measure of the man,—of his wisdom as well as of his force. His veto abundantly equips him to stay the hand of Congress when he will. It is seldom possible to pass a measure over his veto, and no President has hesitated to use the veto when his own judgment of the public good was seriously at issue with that of the houses. The veto has never been suffered to fall into even temporary disuse with us. In England it has ceased to exist, with the change in the character of the executive. There has been no veto since Anne's day, because ever since the reign of Anne the laws of England have been originated either by ministers who spoke the king's own will or by ministers whom the king did not dare gainsay; and in our own time the ministers who formulate the laws are themselves the executive of the nation; a veto would be a negative upon their own power. If bills pass of which they disapprove, they resign and give place to the leaders of those who approve them. The framers of the Constitution made in our President a more powerful, because a more isolated, king than the one they were imitating; and because the Constitution gave them their veto in such explicit terms, our Presidents have not hesitated to use it, even when it put their mere individual judgment against that of large majorities in both houses of Congress. And yet in the exercise of the power to suggest legislation, quite as explicitly conferred upon them by the Constitution, some of our Presidents have seemed to have a timid fear that they might offend some law of taste which had become a constitutional principle.

In one sense their messages to Congress have no more authority than the letters of any other citizen would have. Congress can heed or ignore them as it pleases; and there have been periods of our history when presidential messages were utterly without practical significance, perfunctory documents which few persons except the editors of newspapers took the trouble to read. But if the President has personal force and cares to exercise it, there is this tremendous difference between his messages and the views of any other citizen, either outside Congress or in it: that the whole country reads them and feels that the writer speaks with an authority and a responsibility which the people themselves have given him.

The history of our cabinets affords a striking illustration of the progress of the idea that the President is not merely the legal head but also the political leader of the nation. In the earlier days of the government it was customary for the President to fill his cabinet with the recognized leaders of his party. General Washington even tried the experiment which William of Orange tried at the very beginning of the era of cabinet government. He called to his aid the leaders of both political parties, associating Mr. Hamilton with Mr. Jefferson, on the theory that all views must be heard and considered in the conduct of the government. That was the day in which English precedent prevailed, and English cabinets were made up of the chief political characters of the day. But later years have witnessed a marked change in our practice, in this as in many other things. The old tradition was indeed slow in dying out. It persisted with considerable vitality at least until General Garfield's day, and may yet from time to time revive, for many functions of our cabinets justify it and make it desirable. But our later Presidents have apparently ceased to regard the cabinet as a council of party leaders such as the party they represent would have chosen. They look upon it rather as a body of personal advisers whom the President chooses from the ranks of those whom he personally trusts and prefers to look to for advice. Our recent Presidents have not sought their associates among those whom the fortunes of party contest have brought into prominence and influence, but have called their personal friends and business colleagues to cabinet positions, and men who have given proof of their efficiency in private, not in public, life,—bankers who had never had any place in the formal counsels of the party, eminent lawyers who had held aloof from politics, private secretaries who had shown an unusual sagacity and proficiency in handling public business; as if the President were himself alone the leader of his party, the members of his cabinet only his private advisers, at any rate advisers of his private choice. Mr. Cleveland may be said to have been the first President to make this conception of the cabinet prominent in his choices, and he did not do so until his second administration. Mr. Roosevelt has emphasized the idea.

Upon analysis it seems to mean this: the cabinet is an executive, not a political body. The President cannot himself be the actual executive; he must therefore find, to act in his stead, men of the best legal and business gifts, and depend upon them for the actual administration of the government in all its daily activities. If he seeks political advice of his executive colleagues, he seeks it because he relies upon their natural good sense and experienced judgment, upon their knowledge of the country and its business and social conditions, upon their sagacity as representative citizens of more than usual observation and discretion;

not because they are supposed to have had any very intimate contact with politics or to have made a profession of public affairs. He has chosen, not representative politicians, but eminent representative citizens, selecting them rather for their special fitness for the great business posts to which he has assigned them than for their political experience, and looking to them for advice in the actual conduct of the government rather than in the shaping of political policy. They are, in his view, not necessarily political officers at all.

It may with a great deal of plausibility be argued that the Constitution looks upon the President himself in the same way. It does not seem to make him a prime minister or the leader of the nation's counsels. Some Presidents are, therefore, and some are not. It depends upon the man and his gifts. He may be like his cabinet, or he may be more than his cabinet. His office is a mere vantage ground from which he may be sure that effective words of advice and timely efforts at reform will gain telling momentum. He has the ear of the nation as of course, and a great person may use such an advantage greatly. If he use the opportunity, he may take his cabinet into partnership or not, as he pleases; and so its character may vary with his. Self-reliant men will regard their cabinets as executive councils; men less self-reliant or more prudent will regard them as also political councils, and will wish to call into them men who have earned the confidence of their party. The character of the cabinet may be made a nice index of the theory of the presidential office, as well as of the President's theory of party government; but the one view is, so far as I can see, as constitutional as the other.

One of the greatest of the President's powers I have not yet spoken of at all: his control, which is very absolute, of the foreign relations of the nation. The initiative in foreign affairs, which the President possesses without any restriction whatever, is virtually the power to control them absolutely. The President cannot conclude a treaty with a foreign power without the consent of the Senate, but he may guide every step of diplomacy, and to guide diplomacy is to determine what treaties must be made, if the faith and prestige of the government are to be maintained. He need disclose no step of negotiation until it is complete, and when in any critical matter it is completed the government is virtually committed. Whatever its disinclination, the Senate may feel itself committed also.

I have not dwelt upon this power of the President, because it has been decisively influential in determining the character and influence of the office at only two periods in our history; at the very first, when the government was young and had so to use its incipient force as to win the respect of the nations into whose family it had thrust itself, and in our own day when the results of the Spanish War, the ownership of distant possessions, and many sharp struggles for foreign trade make it necessary that we should turn our best talents to the task of dealing firmly, wisely, and justly with political and commercial rivals. The President can never again be the mere domestic figure he has been throughout so large a part of our history. The nation has risen to the first rank in power and resources. The other nations of the world look askance upon her, half in envy, half in fear, and wonder with a deep anxiety what she will do with her vast strength. They receive the frank professions of men like Mr. John Hay, whom we wholly trusted, with a grain of salt, and doubt what we were sure of, their truthfulness and sincerity, suspecting a hidden design under every utterance he makes. Our President must always, henceforth, be one of the great powers of the world, whether he act greatly and wisely or not, and the best statesmen we can produce will be needed to fill the office of Secretary of State. We have but begun to see the presidential office in this light; but it is the light which will more and more beat upon it, and more and more determine its character and its effect upon the politics of the nation. We can never hide our President again as a mere domestic officer. We can never again see him the mere executive he was in the thirties and forties. He must stand always at the front of our affairs, and the office will be as big and as influential as the man who occupies it.

How is it possible to sum up the duties and influence of such an office in such a system in comprehensive terms which will cover all its changeful aspects? In the view of the makers of the Constitution the President was to be legal executive; perhaps the leader of the nation; certainly not the leader of the party, at any rate while in office. But by the operation of forces inherent in the very nature of government he has become all three, and by inevitable consequence the most heavily burdened officer in the world. No other man's day is so full as his, so full of the responsibilities which tax mind and conscience alike and demand an inexhaustible vitality. The mere task of making appointments to office, which the Constitution imposes upon the President, has come near to breaking some of our Presidents down, because it is a never-ending task in a civil service not yet put upon a professional footing, confused with short terms of office, always forming and dissolving. And in proportion as the President ventures to use his opportunity to lead opinion and act as spokesman of the people in affairs the people stand ready to overwhelm him by running to him with every question, great and small. They are as eager to have him settle a literary question as a political; hear him as acquiescently with regard to matters of special expert knowledge as with regard to public affairs, and call upon him to quiet all troubles by his personal intervention. Men of ordinary physique and discretion cannot be Presidents and live, if the strain be not somehow relieved. We shall be obliged always to be picking our chief magistrates from among wise and prudent athletes,—a small class.

The future development of the presidency, therefore, must certainly, one would confidently predict, run along such lines as the President's later relations with his cabinet suggest. General Washington, partly out of unaffected modesty, no doubt, but also out of the sure practical instinct which he possessed in so unusual a degree, set an example which few of his successors seem to have followed in any systematic manner. He made constant and intimate use of his colleagues in every matter that he handled, seeking their assistance and advice by letter when they were at a distance and he could not obtain it in person. It is well known to all close students of our history that his greater state papers, even those which seem in some peculiar and intimate sense his personal utterances, are full of the ideas and the very phrases of the men about him whom he most trusted. His rough drafts came back to him from Mr. Hamilton and Mr. Madison in great part rephrased and rewritten, in many passages reconceived and given a new color. He thought and acted always by the light of counsel, with a will and definite choice of his own, but through the instrumentality of other minds as well as his own. The duties and responsibilities laid upon the President by the Constitution can be changed only by constitutional amendment,—a thing too difficult to attempt except upon some greater necessity than the belief of an overburdened office, even though that office be the greatest in the land; and it is to be doubted whether the deliberate opinion of the country would consent to make of the President a less powerful officer than he is. He can secure his own relief without shirking any real responsibility. Appointments, for example, he can, if he will, make more and more upon the advice and choice of his executive colleagues; every matter of detail not only, but also every minor matter of counsel or of general policy, he can more and more depend upon his chosen advisers to determine; he need reserve for himself only the larger matters of counsel and that general oversight of the business of the government and of the persons who conduct it which is not possible without intimate daily consultations, indeed, but which is possible without attempting the intolerable burden of direct control. This is, no doubt, the idea of their functions which most Presidents have entertained and which most Presidents suppose themselves to have acted on; but we have reason to believe that most of our Presidents have taken their duties too literally and have attempted the impossible. But we can safely predict that as the multitude of the President's duties increases, as it must with the growth and widening activities of the nation itself, the incumbents of the great office will more and more come to feel that they are administering it in its truest purpose and with greatest effect by regarding themselves as less and less executive officers and more and more directors of affairs and leaders of the nation,— men of counsel and of the sort of action that makes for enlightenment.

IV

THE HOUSE OF REPRESENTATIVES

The President of the United States was intended by the makers of the Constitution to be a reformed and standardized king, after the Whig model; and Congress was meant to be a reformed and properly regulated parliament. But both President and Congress have broken from the mold and adapted themselves to circumstances, after a thoroughly American fashion,—partly because the king and Parliament which the convention of 1787 intended to copy, with modifications, had no real existence and were therefore largely theoretical, but chiefly because, even if they had existed at the moment the copy was made, they could not have been fixed in that transitional form by any law that the convention could have devised. They were sure to undergo rapid alteration in one direction or another, and each has taken its own course of change. It would be difficult now to believe that the American President and the English King, the American Congress and the English Parliament, were originally of the same model and intention if we did not clearly recollect the fact to be so.

It is the reaction of the several parts of government upon one another that gives each part its final form and character. It is useless to study any living structure of government anatomically, in its separate parts. Its character and significance come to light, as I have already several times insisted, only when we study it as an organic whole, living and acting from day to day. Our present study must at every stage be a study of the synthesis of power in the government on the one hand, and of the people's control of the government on the other; for there can be no power which is not synthetic, which does not operate with organic unity; and there can be no constitutional government where the organs of government are not constantly under the control of public opinion. We shall get our completest understanding of the House of Representatives, therefore, if we look at it from two points of view: from the point of view of its synthesis with the other parts of the Government, and from the point of view of its relations to opinion.

If you were to ask an Englishman to describe the government of England, he would of course include the Parliament in his description. Indeed, it is likely that he would have more to say of the House of Commons than of anything else. But if you were to speak to him of 'The Government,' he would not think of the House of Commons but only of the ministers, of what we should call the administration. I can make the part played by the House of Representatives in our system clearest by contrasting it with the English House of Commons, and in order to make that contrast carry its full significance it is necessary that we should bear these two meanings of the word government in mind and never confuse them. When I said in a previous lecture that it was not necessary for the full realization of constitutional government that representative assemblies should become a part of the 'Government,' I meant, of course, a part of the administrative organ of government, the organ that is looked to for initiative, which makes choice of policy and actually controls the life of the nation under the laws; and the significant difference between English and American political development is that in America Congress has become part of the Government, while in England Parliament has not. Parliament is still, as it was originally intended to be, the grand assize, or session, of the nation, to criticize and control the Government. It is not a council to administer it. It does not originate its own bills, except in minor matters which seem to spring out of public opinion or out of the special circumstances of particular interests, rather than out of the conduct of government. Every legislative proposition of capital importance comes to it from the ministers. The duties of the ministers are not merely executive: the ministers are the Government. They look to Parliament, not for commands what to do, but for support in their own programs, whether of legal change or of political policy.

What the House of Commons does, therefore, is not to act in any strictly originative way as the law-making body of the nation, but to make and unmake Governments, to prefer now one, and again another, committee of its leading members as its guides, not itself leading but choosing how it shall be led, insisting that the king make the leaders of its own choice the ministers of the crown. It is not the Government, but its leaders are. In the supreme act of insisting that they and no others shall be chosen by the crown for the executive posts of government it exhausts its originative force. Thereafter it follows and criticizes as of old.

Our Congress, on the contrary, does not make or unmake our Government. The people do that in their selection of a President. And because Congress cannot make or unmake the Government at its pleasure, it usually makes it a point of pride not to be led by the Government in what it regards as its proper and exclusive sphere, the making of laws. The making of laws is a very practical matter. It is not a mere enactment of opinions into commands. At least, it should not be. Neither should it be a means of forcing the favorite reforms of some members of the legislative body upon the nation, unless there is to be some direct and easy way of holding those members responsible for the untoward results of their intended reforms, should they fail to bring about the happy changes they were meant to effect. The practical side of law is its application. The Government, therefore, is the only possible body of experts with regard to the practicability and necessity of alterations in the law, and it is certainly a noteworthy outcome of our political development that the houses should have rejected the leadership of the Government in legislation. They stand alone among the legislatures of the world in having done so. It is in this sense that I speak when I say that the American Congress has become a part of the Government, and that the English Parliament never has. Our Congress freely and habitually originates law upon every subject upon its own initiative, plays a planning and devising part in the conduct of government, and is in many ways an administrative council acting in complete independence of those who are charged with actual administration. It even resents suggestions from administrative officers as impertinent invasions of its independence. It has in a thousand particulars taken charge of the Government, without assuming the responsibility of putting its leaders in to conduct it. A sharper contrast to the development of the English House of Commons, upon which it was modeled, could hardly be imagined. The House of Representatives has moved to the opposite pole both of theory and of action.

The Senate was, no doubt, meant to be a part of the Government. In the making of treaties with foreign governments and in the difficult and responsible business of appointments to office it was deliberately associated with the President as an administrative council, by the terms of the Constitution. But these are matters of consultation, in which it waits upon the executive. The Senate was not given the initiative in respect of them. It cannot originate treaties or make, or even suggest, appointments. It waits upon the initiative of the Government, as Parliament does, and has not departed from the original model. But in legislative matters proper its attitude is the same as the attitude of the House. House and Senate alike jealously guard their right to be their own guides in legislation, even when the laws they handle are clearly administrative in character and deal not with general matters but with the duties of the executive departments and the details of governmental business.

The development of our Congress thus affords a singular and instructive contradiction between theory and fact, which ought to interest practical politicians as much as it naturally interests historians. Congress and Parliament had the same origin. Our houses were conceived by the makers of the Constitution at a period when both Parliament and Congress were supposed to stand outside Government, its mentors and critics, holding aloof from it and yet determining its action, at any rate negatively, by what they consented to make legal or insisted upon making illegal. And yet our houses, developed under a theory of checks and balances which seemed intended to preserve that theory of separateness, have thrust themselves into the business of governing; while Parliament, frankly developed in these later years upon the theory of drawing the several parts of government together in close synthesis, has remained separate and still waits upon the Government for action.

By natural consequence, the organization of our legislative houses is entirely unlike that of Parliament. Having made up their minds to be indeed separate from the executive, to have a distinct life and an independent initiative, and to make themselves part of the Government upon a plan of their own, they have been obliged to create a suitable organization. The House of Representatives, being the more numerous body and in the nature of the case harder to organize as an originative and independent assembly, has effected the more thorough organization, and devotes itself to business with a precision and ease of method which the Senate has not attempted.

The House and Senate are naturally unlike. They are different both in constitution and character. They do not represent the same things. The House of Representatives is by intention the popular chamber, meant to represent the people by direct election through an extensive suffrage, while the Senate was designed to represent the states as political units, as the constituent members of the Union. The terms of membership in the two houses, moreover, are different. The two chambers were unquestionably intended to derive their authority from different sources and to speak with different voices in affairs; and however much they may have departed from their original characters in the changeful processes of our politics, they still present many sharp contrasts to one another, and must be described as playing, not the same, but very distinct and dissimilar rôles in affairs.

Perhaps the contrast between them is in certain respects even sharper and clearer now than in the earlier days of our history, when the House was smaller and its functions simpler. The House once debated; now it does not debate. It has not the time. There would be too many debaters, and there are too many subjects of debate. It is a business body, and it must get its business done. When the late Mr. [Thomas Brackett] Reed once, upon a well-known occasion, thanked God that the House was not a deliberate assembly, there was no doubt a dash of half-cynical humor in the remark, such as so often gave spice and biting force to what he said, but there was the sober earnest of a serious man of affairs, too. He knew the vast mass of business the House undertook to transact: that it had made itself a great organ of direction, and that it would be impossible for it to get through its calendars if it were to attempt to discuss in open house, instead of in its committee rooms, the measures it acted upon. The Senate has retained its early rules of procedure without material alteration. It is still a place of free and prolonged debate. It will not curtail the privilege of its members to say what they please, at whatever length. But the senators are comparatively few in number; they can afford the indulgence. The House cannot. The Senate may remain individualistic, atomistic, but the House must be organic, —an efficient instrument, not a talkative assembly.

A numerous body like the House of Representatives is naturally and of course unfit for organic, creative action through debate. Debate, indeed, is not a creative process. It is critical. It does not produce; it tests. A large assembly cannot form policies or formulate measures, and the House of Representatives is merely a large assembly, like any other public meeting in its unfitness for business. Like other public meetings, it must send committees out to formulate its resolves. It organizes itself, therefore, into committees,—not occasional committees, formed from time to time, but standing committees permanently charged with its business and given every prerogative of suggestion and explanation, in order that each piece of legislative business may be systematically attended to by a body small enough to digest and perfect it.

For each important subject of legislation there is a standing committee. There is, for example, a Committee on Appropriations, a Committee on Ways and Means, that is, on the sources and objects of taxation, a Committee on Banking and Currency, a Committee on Commerce, a Committee on Manufactures, a Committee on Agriculture, a Committee on Railways and Canals, a Committee on Rivers and Harbors, a Committee on the Merchant Marine and Fisheries, a Committee on the Judiciary, a Committee on Foreign Affairs, a Committee on Public Lands, a Committee on Land Claims, a Committee on War Claims, a Committee on Post Offices and Post Roads, a Committee on Military Affairs, a Committee on Naval Affairs, a Committee on Indian Affairs, a Committee on Education, a Committee on Labor,—the business likely to be brought to the attention of the House being thoroughly, indeed somewhat minutely, classified and the committees being some fifty-seven in number.

Every bill introduced must be sent to a committee. It would probably be impossible to think of any legitimate subject for legislation upon which a bill could be drawn up for whose consideration no standing committee has been provided. If a new subject should turn up, the House would no doubt presently create a new committee. The thousands of bills annually introuced are promptly distributed, therefore; go almost automatically to the several committees; and as automatically, it must be added, disappear. The measures reported to the House are measures which the committees formulate. They may find some member's bill suitable and acceptable, and report it substantially unchanged, or they may pull it about and alter it, or they may throw it aside altogether and frame a measure of their own, or they may do nothing, make no report at all. Few bills ever see the light again after being referred to a committee. The business of the House is what the committees choose to make it. What the House of Commons depends upon its committee, the Government, to do, the House depends upon its fifty-seven committees to do. The private member's bill has a little better chance, indeed, of being debated in the Commons than in the House of Representatives. The House of Commons does usually set aside one day a week for the consideration of private members' bills, when the Government is not pressed for time and does not insist upon using every day itself; and those members who are fortunate enough to draw first places in the makeup of the calendars for those days may have the pleasure of getting their proposals debated and voted upon. But in the House of Representatives there is only the very slender chance of getting the rules suspended, an irregularity which the businesslike chamber has grown very shy of permitting.

The very complexity and bulk of all this machinery is itself burdensome to the House. There are now more than half as many committees in the House as there are members in the Senate. It cannot itself choose so many committees; it cannot even follow so many. It therefore intrusts every appointment to the Speaker, and, when its business gets entangled amongst the multitude of committees and reports, follows a steering committee, which it calls the Committee on Rules. And the power of appointing the committees, which the House has conferred upon its Speaker, makes him the almost autocratic master of its actions.

In all legislative bodies except ours the presiding officer has only the powers and functions of a chairman. He is separate from parties and is looked to to be punctiliously impartial. He moderates and gives order to the course of debate, and is expected to administer without personal or party bias the accepted rules of its procedure. For political guidance all other representative assemblies depend on the Government, not upon committees which their presiding officer has created. But the processes of our parliamentary development have made the Speaker of our great House of Representatives and the Speakers of our State Legislatures party leaders in whom centres the control of all that they do. So far as the House of Representatives and its share in the public business is concerned, the Speaker is undisputed party leader.

Every one of the committees of the House the Speaker appoints. He not only allows himself to make them up with a view to the kind of legislation he wishes to see enacted; he is expected to make them up with such a view,—is expected to make them up as a party leader would. He is, it is true, a good deal hampered in the exercise of a free choice in their makeup by certain well-established understandings and precedents, of whose breach the older members of the House at any rate would be very jealous. Seniority of service has to be respected in assigning places on the more important committees, and the succession to certain of the chief chairmanships is well understood to go by definite rules of individual precedence and personal consideration. But it is always possible for the Speaker to determine the majority of his appointments in such a way as to give him that direct and continuing control of the actions of the House which he is now expected to exercise as the party leader of the majority. Even his own personal views upon particular public questions he does not hesitate to enforce in his appointments, so that the very majority he represents may be prevented from having an opportunity to vote upon measures it is known to desire because he has made up the committees which would report upon them in accordance with his own preferences in the matter. What the committees do not report the House cannot vote upon. Every bill that is introduced is assigned to a committee picked out by the Speaker's order, if there be any doubt about its character or reference. It is the Speaker's decision, also, that assigns the reports of the committees to the several calendars upon which the business of the House is allotted its time for consideration, and he may often choose whether the place allotted them shall be favorable or unfavorable, shall make it likely or unlikely that they will be reached at all.

Moreover, it has come about that by means of his prerogative of 'recognition' the Speaker is permitted to control debate to a very extraordinary degree. It is common parliamentary practice that no one can address an assembly until "recognized," that is, accorded the floor, by the presiding officer. The House of Representatives, feeling always pressed for time, even with regard to the consideration of the reports of its standing committees, which are numerous and amazingly active, restricts debate upon those reports within very narrow limits, and generally allots the greater part of the brief time allowed to any one report to the chairman of the reporting committee. Other members may get a few minutes of time allowed them by previous arrangement with the committee's chairman, and a list of those who are thus to be given an opportunity to speak generally lies on the Speaker's desk. These members the Speaker will "recognize," but no others, though they spring to their feet under his very nose in the open space in front of the seats,—unless, indeed, they have seen him beforehand and got his permission. No member who has not previously arranged the matter, either with the chairman of the committee or with the Speaker, need rise or seek to catch the Speaker's eye. And in the intervals of calendar business no one whose intention the Speaker has not been apprised of, unless indeed it be the leader on the floor of the one party or the other, may expect to be accorded the floor to make a motion. The Speaker may, if he choose, determine what proposals he will permit the House to hear.

The Committee on Rules has of recent years had a very singular and significant development of functions. Originally its duty was a very simple one: that of reporting to the House at the opening of each of its biennial sessions, when a new House assembles and a new organization is effected, the body of standing rules under which it was to act; for the House goes through the form of readopting its whole body of rules each time it reorganizes after fresh congressional elections. From session to session the rules were modified, now in one particular, again in another, on the recommendation of the committee; and any change in the rules at any time proposed is still referred to it for consideration and report. But now the committee is looked to, besides, for such temporary orders and programs of procedure as will enable the House to disentangle its business and get at the measures which the country expects it to dispose of or the needs of the Government make it necessary that it should not neglect. The party majority is well aware that, if it would keep its credit with the constituencies, it must not allow the miscellany of committee reports on its crowded calendars to stand in the way of matters which it is pledged to act upon. It looks to the Committee on Rules to sweep aside the ordinary routine of procedure whenever necessary, and bring in a schedule of action which will enable it to get at the main things it is interested in, or at any rate the things the party leaders think it most expedient it should dispose of. The committee has thus become a very important part of party machinery. It consists of five members, the Speaker himself, two other representatives of the majority, and two representatives of the minority. The majority members of course control its action; the representation of the minority is hardly more than formal; and the two members of the majority associated with the Speaker upon it are usually trusted lieutenants upon whom he can count for loyal support of his leadership. One self-confident Speaker smilingly described the committee as consisting of the Speaker and two assistants,—a pleasant way of saying that the committee was his instrument to govern the House. His direct control of the Committee on Rules rounds out his powers as autocrat of the popular chamber.

And yet the word autocrat has really no place in our political vocabulary, if we are to use words of reality and not words of extravagance. The extraordinary power of the Speaker is not personal. He is in no proper sense of the word an autocrat. He is the instrument, as well as the leader, of the majority in controlling the processes of the House. He is obeyed because the majority chooses to be governed thus. The rules are of its own making, and it can unmake them when it pleases. It can override the Speaker's decisions, too, and correct its presiding officer as every other assembly can. It has simply found it most convenient to put itself in the Speaker's hands, its object being efficiency, not debate.

And yet it is also an exaggeration to say that House bills go through as the committees propose practically without debate. Some measures it is clearly in the interest of the party no less than of the public to discuss with some fullness. Many financial measures in particular are debated with a good deal of thoroughness, and most matters that have already attracted public attention. Not everything is left to the operation of the rules, the chances of the calendar, and the dictation of the Speaker and his two assistants. The Committee on Rules may be counted on to arrange for debates upon important bills as well as for putting unimportant bills out of the way.

And standing over all is the party caucus, the outside conference of the members of the majority, to whose conclusions the Speaker himself is subject, and to which members can appeal whenever they think the Speaker too irresponsible, too arbitrary, too masterful, too little heedful of the opinions prevalent on the floor among the rank and file. The caucus is an established and much respected piece of party machinery, and what the party has not the organization to decide on the floor of the assembly itself it decides in this conference outside the House. Members who do not wish to be bound by decisions of the caucus can refuse to attend it; but that is a very serious breach of party discipline and may get the men who venture upon it the unpleasant reputation of disloyalty. Members who wish to maintain their standing in the party are expected to attend; and those who attend are expected to abide by the decisions of the conference. It is a thorough-going means of maintaining party unity. Caucuses are free conferences, where a man may say what he pleases; but they are held behind closed doors, and it is usually made a matter of honorable punctilio not to speak outside of the dissensions their debates may have disclosed.

It is thus that the House has made itself "efficient." Its ideal is the transaction of business. It is as much afraid of becoming a talking shop as Mr. Carlyle could have wished it to be. If it must talk, it talks in sections, in its committee rooms, not in public on the floor of the chamber itself. The committee rooms are private. No one has the right to enter them except by express permission of the committees themselves. Not infrequently committees do hold formal public hearings with regard to certain bills, inviting all whose interests are affected to be represented and present their views either for or against the proposed legislation. But such hearings are recognized as exceptional, not of right, and as a rule the public hears nothing of the arguments which have induced any committee to make its particular recommendations to the House. The formal explanations of the chairman of a committee, made upon the floor of the House, contain few of the elements of contested opinion which undoubtedly showed themselves plainly enough in the private conferences of the committee.

For each committee is a miniature House. The minority is accorded representation upon it in proportion to its numerical strength in the House. In every committee, therefore, there are men representing both party views, and it sometimes happens that the arguments of the minority members are very influential in shaping reports made upon measures concerning which no sharp party lines have been drawn. With regard to matters upon which the majority is known to have taken a definite position before the constituencies the majority members of a committee will of course insist upon having their own way. They are apt to be in frequent consultation with the Speaker about them. But with regard to measures on which no party issue has been made up they are willing on occasion to give a good deal of weight to the opinions of their minority colleagues. There is a very easy and amicable relation between majority and minority in the committees, and it will often happen that in committees which have to deal with highly technical matters, like manufactures or banking or naval construction or the regulation of judicial procedure, or with matters involved in precedent and to be understood only in the light of somewhat extended and intimate experience, like foreign affairs, members of the minority of long service in the House and of long familiarity with the subject-matter under discussion will in fact in no small degree guide and dominate the committees to which they have been assigned. Business is more like business, because less formal and less touched with party feeling, in the committee rooms than on the floor of the House.

The minority has its own party organization like that of the majority: its formally chosen leader for the floor, its caucus to secure common counsel. It is, indeed, usually less thoroughly disciplined than the majority, because it is in opposition, not in power, and can afford to allow its members freer play in choosing what they shall individually do and say. But its organization suffices to draw its forces together for common action when any matter of real party significance comes to the surface and the country expects it to put itself on record; and it is ready, at very short notice, to turn itself into an organization as complete and powerful as that of the majority, should the elections favor it and its leader become Speaker.

All lines of analysis come back to the Speaker, whether you speak of the organization or of the action and political power of the House. Such an organization, so systematized and so concentrated, has of course made the House of Representatives one of the most powerful pieces of our whole governmental machinery, and its Speaker, in whom its power is centered and summed up, has come to be regarded as the greatest figure in our complex system, next to the President himself. The whole powerful machinery of the great popular chamber is at his disposal, and all the country knows how effectually he can use it. Whatever may be the influence and importance of the Senate, its energies are not centered in any one man. There is no senator who sums up in himself the power of a great organ of government. The leaders of the Senate deal in all counsel with the other chamber with regard to legislative business with this single leader, this impersonation of the House. So do also the President and the members of the cabinet. As national leader of his party, the President must reckon always with the guide and master of the House, without whose approval and consent it is practically impossible to get any legislative measure adopted. Measures which are to prosper must have his countenance and support. Members of the cabinet must study his views and purposes, if they are to obtain the appropriations they desire or to see measures brought to a happy and successful issue which they deem necessary to the administration of their departments. One might sum up the active elements of our government as consisting of the

President, with all his sweep of powers; the Speaker of the House, with all that he represents as spokesman of the party majority in the popular chamber, with its singularly effective machinery at his disposal; and the talkative, debating Senate, guided no doubt by a few influential and trusted members, but a council, not an organization.

The House of Commons makes and unmakes governments. The House of Representatives makes and unmakes Speakers. As the originative capacity of the House of Commons is exhausted when it has produced a ministry, so the originative force of the House of Representatives is exhausted when it has made a Speaker. Neither does anything else, as a whole. For the rest, they follow and criticize: follow fifty-seven committees or one committee; criticize the Speaker and his committees or the ministers who have risen to a place of rule. A numerous assembly cannot do more.

In producing a single committee and securing for it the right to conduct the government, the House of Commons has, it must be admitted, done a more effective thing than the House of Representatives has done in producing an omnipotent Speaker and fifty-seven committees, and has obtained for itself much greater power. There is reason to believe that the House of Representatives sometimes finds its numerous committees a burden, and certainly they do not all serve it equally well. The average membership of its standing committees is twelve, so that the total number of committee places to be filled is six hundred and eighty-five. The total membership of the House is only three hundred and fifty-seven. There are, therefore, about two committee places for every member of the House. The appointments are not equally distributed, but every member is given some place. New members and members little thought of can be disposed of on committees which have little or nothing to do or whose work is light and formal: for the House keeps many committees on its list for which it has ceased to have any real or important use; but with any sort of equitable distribution of the Speaker's appointments it must always happen that many committees with very important work to do are made up of men of only average capacity and little experience in public affairs. The real leaders and masters of business are few and are soon disposed of by assignment to the two or three chief committees; and to assign a man to a committee is practically to silence him with regard to every matter of legislation except those referred to his committee. A Speaker must have a particularly clear vision of what the most important questions to come before that particular congress are, to be able to distribute the best men at his disposal in the best way and give the House effective service where it will most need it. The membership of most committees must be drawn from the rank and file. The House can use its best men for only a few things, and must make shift for the rest with the mediocre.

Standing alone, therefore, and undertaking to be sufficient unto itself in respect of everything it is authorized by the Constitution to handle, the House of Representatives is a much less powerful and influential body than it would have been, could it have had the luck of the House of Commons and got control of the Government itself. Independence in any organization is isolation; and isolation is weakness. You have no controlling authority; you have only the right to sell your favors, to exchange concession for concession, to come to an agreement by some compromise of views. You can never have more than a piece of your own way. It is, of course, a more important and influential thing to superintend a Government with supreme authority, as the House of Commons does, than to stand separate in a complex organization, play only an individual part, be only a piece of a balanced mechanism, as the House of Representatives is. It is an interesting conclusion in political dynamics that a body which stands jealously apart and avoids partnership of any intimate sort in the conduct of affairs, declines an opportunity to rule and gets only an opportunity to bargain. If it is strong enough to rule, partnership will bring it supremacy; if it is not strong enough to rule, it can make little out of compromises and bargains. It is hardly to be expected that, as the affairs of the nation grow more complex and interesting and difficult and require nicer adjustments of governmental power for their management, the House of Representatives will remain content with its present splendid isolation.

We are in love with efficiency and, as a practical nation, greatly admire the complete and thorough organization of the House, its preference for action and its impatience of talk: but if every part of our political machinery is to be organized for "business," where are counsel and criticism to come in? We never stood more in need of them than we do now. If our present representative assemblies are to be for action, we must let them go over in our thoughts to become outlying, detached parts of the executive, and must invent other assemblies for discussion. For public business cannot be transacted in a truly constitutional spirit without searching and constant discussion, unless we are mistaken in our analysis of constitutional government as government which is conducted in accordance with a clear understanding between those who administer it and those who obey it,—an understanding not only established by fundamental law, by charters and constitutions, but also accommodated to each day and generation by the criticisms and behests of representative assemblies whose business shall not be the actual discharge of governmental functions, but the maintenance of that nice balance between opinion and power which is of the very essence of the whole matter.

There is discussion and discussion. I suppose that we have come to think debate less necessary in our legislative assemblies than it may once have been because we have allowed ourselves to fancy that the action of government was sufficiently discussed and nicely enough squared with opinion by the news columns and editorials of our newspapers. But even if the chief newspapers were not owned by special interests; even if their utterances really spoke the general opinion of the communities in which they are printed, as very few of them now do, their discussion of affairs would not be of the kind that is necessary for the maintenance of constitutional government. There are many things to be said about the newspapers which will make this at once evident. For one thing, few men outside the big cities read more than one newspaper. Few men, therefore, ever get put before them in the newspapers they read more than one side of any question; and they generally decide for themselves beforehand which side that shall be, by their choice of a newspaper. But far more important than that is the little recognized fact that no number of separate discussions of a question, no matter how assembled, no matter from how many different points of view, from how many different papers or different sections of the country, constitute such a comparison of views as a responsible representative assembly can institute in its debates.

Discussions which are to lead to action must be combined, compounded, made up out of many elements, or else out of a few, by a process which can be thorough and trustworthy only when these several elements are, so to say, brought personally face to face, as living, contending forces embodied in men authorized to be the spokesmen of voters and speaking with a constant sense of being held responsible for what they say. Common counsel is not jumbled counsel. There is often common counsel in the committee rooms of the House, but there is never common counsel on the floor of the House itself. It goes without saying that the combined acts of a session are not a product of common counsel. They have been produced by a thousand agencies, not threshed out by one, and they have not been threshed out in the presence of the country, but behind closed doors.

It may sound a very subtle matter, but it is in fact intensely practical, and is worth looking into. It is because we do not look into it or understand it, though it lies at the very heart of our whole practice of government, that we sometimes allow ourselves to assume that the "initiative" and the "referendum," now so much talked of and so imperfectly understood, are a more thorough means of getting at public opinion than the processes of our representative assemblies. Many a radical program may get what will seem to be almost general approval if you listen only to those who know that they will not have to handle the perilous matter of action and to those who have merely formed an independent, that is, an isolated opinion, and have not entered into common counsel; but you will seldom find a deliberative assembly acting half so radically as its several members professed themselves ready to act before they came together into one place and talked the matter over and contrived statutes. It is not that they lose heart or prove unfaithful to the promises made on the stump. They have really for the first time laid their minds alongside other minds of different views, of different experience, of different prepossessions. They have seen the men with whom they differ, face to face, and have come to understand how honestly and with what force of genuine character and disinterested conviction, or with what convincing array of practical arguments opposite views may be held. They have learned more than any one man could beforehand have known. Common counsel is not aggregate counsel. It is not a sum in addition, counting heads. It is compounded out of many views in actual contact; is a living thing made out of the vital substance of many minds, many personalities, many experiences; and it can be made up only by the vital contacts of actual conference, only in face to face debate, only by word of mouth and the direct clash of mind with mind.

No doubt, as I have said, there is oftentimes genuine common counsel in the committee rooms of the House of Representatives; but the committee rooms are private and are so many that it would only confuse the nation to publish debates out of the whole body of them. One could not make his way through a Congressional Record like that. And yet the actual Congressional

Record is disappointing, because it seems to lack reality. The speeches it contains too often seem the mere speeches of parade; merely the formal dress array of arguments, so conned and formalized as not to seem like vital discussion at all, but only like things meant to have their effect by way of party justification or to make impressive reading for distant constituencies. In brief, the debate is not real hand to hand debate at all; and the people, finding things done they do not just know why or how in their legislative assemblies, indulge suspicions which deeply disturb them and make them unjust critics of the whole representative system. The process of legislation is not open and frank and obvious enough. Too much is hidden away in committee rooms. And anything hidden is suspected, no matter how honest it may be. The machinery of action is too complex to be easily understood. There are more excuses for suspecting covert influences than chances to comprehend what really takes place,—most of it in fact excellent, honest, practical, efficient enough.

It is very difficult for public opinion to judge such a body as the House of Representatives justly, because it is very difficult for it to judge it intelligently. If it cannot understand it, it will certainly be dissatisfied with it. Moreover, it is very difficult for a body which compounds its legislation by so miscellaneous a process as that of committees to bring itself into effective coöperation with the other parts of the government,—and synthesis, not antagonism, is the whole art of government, the whole art of power. I cannot imagine power as a thing negative, and not positive.

The matter is perfectly illustrated by the relations between the House and the Senate. They are not, it must be said, upon terms of very intimate and cordial coöperation. There is a subtle jealousy and antagonism between them, due to their desire to maintain their separateness and independence inviolate and be each a power to itself. When they come to a sharp difference of opinion upon any subject of legislation which really interests the people the advantage is sometimes with the one, sometimes with the other. The Senate has the advantage of being a public council, not a mere congeries of committees, and of setting forth its reasons in thorough debate; the House has the advantage of being regarded as the more truly representative chamber and of being more directly in touch with the general sentiment of the country. The House has also the advantage of being under thorough discipline and standing ready to do what it is told to do promptly when it becomes necessary to manœuvre for position in such a contest of wills. But what happens at last is proof of nothing, however the contest may end: it does not prove the popular sympathy of the House, if it win, nor the better counsel of the Senate, if it win. A conference committee is appointed by each house towards the very end of the session, the two committees meet and fight the differences of the houses out while business is hurrying to adjournment and a recess; and just as the session closes the two bodies hastily pass, without debate, a conference report which is a mere patchwork of compromises; or else reject the compromise and let the whole matter fall. There is no common leadership even when the majorities of the two houses are of the same political party. It is at best a haphazard method of compounding legislation, liable to suffer many singular accidents, and impossible for a busy people to understand when they occasionally look on with unwonted attention.

Such complications and subdivisions of machinery in the active and originative organs of the government result in its being in a very real sense leaderless. In the last lecture I spoke of the President as leader of his party and of the nation; but, though he clearly exercises such leadership, and exercises it with great effectiveness when he has the personal force for any originative rôle at all, he cannot be said to be the guide and leader of the Government as a whole. Our Government consists in part, as I have explained, of the House and Senate. It is in that respect contrasted with all other governments. And in each part of our subdivided Government there is a distinct arrangement with regard to leadership. The Senate submits to the guidance of a small group of senators, very jealous of the independence of the body they control. The House is under the command of its Speaker. The executive is in the hands of the President, whom the houses regard, when thinking of their own powers, as an outsider, and whose advice they are apt to look upon as the advice of a rival rather than of a colleague.

I suppose that when matters of legislation are under discussion the country is apt to think of the Speaker as the chief figure in Washington rather than the President,—at any rate in all ordinary seasons and under all ordinary Presidents. And yet, because he has the ear of the whole nation and is undoubtedly its chosen spokesman and representative, the President may place the House at a great disadvantage if he choose to appeal to the nation. It is this that makes the great difference between the Speaker and the President, whose figures you might come to regard as very nearly equal if you looked no farther than Washington city itself. The Speaker of the House is not in the habit of appealing to the nation. He would feel himself ridiculous if he did. It would probably make an unpleasant impression were the executive officer of one of the houses of Congress, himself merely the representative of a single constituency, to turn to the nation by some open appeal of speech or argument to decide between him and the President. It is a point of good taste with him, as well as of good politics, to say little, say that little in enigmatic phrases, and confine himself to his proper rôle of management. But the President may turn to the country when he will, with whatever arguments, whatever disclosures of plan, whatever explanations he pleases. Everybody will read what he says, particularly if there be any smack of contest in the air, while few will read what is said in the House where no one speaks for the whole body or for the nation; and if the nation happens to agree with the President, if he can win it to his view, the leadership is his whether the houses relish it or not. They are at a disadvantage and will probably have to yield.

The true significance of the matter, for any student of government who wishes to understand the life rather than the mere theory of what he studies, is that the greatest power lies with that part of the government which is in most direct communication with the nation itself,—as one would naturally expect under any constitutional system. The light this evident fact throws upon the House of Representatives is this: that it has greatly weakened itself as an organ of public opinion by yielding to the need it has felt itself under to play the rôle of an independent part of the government. In its effort to make itself an instrument of business, to perform its function of legislation without assistance or suggestion, to formulate its own bills, digest its own measures, originate its own policies, it has in effect silenced itself. The nation does not look to it for counsel; does not expect to understand its own affairs any better because of anything said or anything done in the House; has come to regard it as what it is, a piece of effective law-making machinery, but not a deliberative assembly in whose debates it may expect to find public questions clarified, disputed matters settled. The House seems to have missed what its average capacity and its undoubted integrity entitle it to, the chief privilege of giving counsel to the nation, the right to be its principal spokesman in affairs.

It is thus always a vital synthesis of parts that eludes us as we examine our constitutional system with its singular Newtonian equipoise of parts. But it is a study of persons and of forces of opinion, as in any other government. It is the actual temper and disposition of the two diverse chambers with which he deals that the President must study if he is to bring his party, as well as the opinion of the nation, to any program or measure of his own. The Senate and House must study one another and play a very difficult game of accommodation to maintain any workable agreement or coöperation in legislation. They are of different tempers and traditions; they are jealous of each other and yet are constrained to agree. No man can lay down any rule as to what will happen amidst so many and so powerful forces, which must coöperate and yet are independent of one another. Time and circumstance and wise management alone can secure union and energy among them. There is but one common solvent. The law of their union is public opinion. That and that alone can draw them together. That part of the government, therefore, which has the most direct access to opinion has the best chance of leadership and mastery; and at present that part is the President.

Each part of the government loses force and prestige in proportion as it ceases to give, and to give publicly, conclusive reasons for what it is doing and for what it is declining to do. The country in the long run is more interested to know that the right thing has been done and that it has been done wisely than to know merely that something has been done, hastily devised though well intended. There are seasons, it is true, when opinion, unduly excited, prefers action to counsel, but those are exceptional seasons among peoples trained to the thoughtfulness and self-control of constitutional action. Open counsel is of the essence of power, if the country's confidence is to be retained for any length of time. The most serious comment, therefore, upon the development of the House of Representatives is that in making itself an active part of the Government and falling into the silence of an effective, businesslike board of directors, it has forfeited the much higher office of gathering the common counsel of the nation and wielding the tremendous, the governing and sovereign, power of criticism. Criticism can make and unmake governments, but the conferences of committee rooms cannot. If the House must originate its own business and must be independent in action, it cannot be the voice of the nation.

V

THE SENATE

It is very difficult to form a just estimate of the Senate of the United States. No body has been more discussed; no body has been more misunderstood and traduced. There was a time when we were lavish in spending our praises upon it. We joined with our foreign critics and appreciators in speaking of the Senate as one of the most admirable, as it is certainly one of the most original, of our political institutions. In our own day we have been equally lavish of hostile criticism. We have suspected it of every malign purpose, fixed every unhandsome motive upon it, and at times almost cast it out of our confidence altogether.

The fact is that it is possible in your thought to make almost anything you please out of the Senate. It is a body variously compounded, made many-sided by containing many elements, and a critic may concentrate his attention upon one element at a time if he chooses, make the most of what is good and put the rest out of sight, or make more than the most of what is bad and ignore everything that does not chime with his thesis of evil. The Senate has, in fact, many contrasted characteristics, shows many faces, lends itself easily to no confident generalization. It differs very radically from the House of Representatives. The House is an organic unit; it has been at great pains to make itself so, and to become a working body under a single unifying discipline; while the Senate is not so much an organization as a body of individuals, retaining with singularly little modification the character it was originally intended to have.

As I have already said in a previous lecture, it is impossible to characterize the United States in any single generalization; and for that very reason it is impossible to sum up the Senate in any single phrase or summary description. For the Senate is as various as the country it represents. It represents the country, not the people: the country in its many diverse sections, not the population of the country, which tends to become uniform where it is concentrated.

Most of the leading figures among the active public men of the country are now to be found in the Senate, not in the House. This was not formerly the case. Before the House became an effective, non-debating organ of business, it shared quite equally with the Senate the leading politicians of the country; but it has not been so of recent years. Organization swallows men up, debate individualizes them, and men of strong character and active minds always prefer the position in which they will be freest to speak and act for themselves. The Senate has always been a favorite goal of ambition for our public men, but it has become more and more the place of their preference as the House has more and more surrendered to it the function of public counsel.

Of course, there are fewer senators than members of the House, and it is a more conspicuous thing to be one of a body of ninety than to be one of a body of three hundred and fifty-seven. Moreover, the tenure of a senator of the United States is three times as long as the tenure of a member of the House of Representatives, and every member of the Senate must feel it a considerable advantage that six years instead of two are given him in which to make his impression on the country. There is time to find out what he is about and to master a difficult task. Both the smaller membership of the Senate and the longer term of its members contribute to individualize the men who compose it and to give them an advantage and importance which members of the House do not often have, unless they rise to one of the three or four places of real power which crown the committee organization of the representative chamber.

And yet these are not the radical and fundamental differences between the House and the Senate. Size and tenure are after all matters of detail. They count, and count a good deal, in giving the Senate its character, but they do not go to the root of the difference between the two houses. What gives the Senate its real character and significance as an organ of constitutional government is the fact that it does not represent population, but regions of the country, the political units into which it has, by our singular constitutional process, been cut up. The Senate, therefore, represents the variety of the nation as the House does not. It does not draw its membership chiefly from those parts of the country where the population is most dense, but draws it in equal parts from every state and section.

It seems to me that those critics of our government—they are, I believe, without exception domestic critics—who criticize the principle upon which the Senate is made up on the ground that states having little wealth and small population have as many representatives in the Senate as the richest and most populous states of the Union, the newest and least developed as many as the oldest and most highly organized, entirely mistake the standard by which the Senate should be judged as an instrumentality of constitutional government in a system like ours.

They are entirely wrong in assuming, for one thing, that the newer, weaker, or more sparsely populated parts of the country have less of an economic stake in its general policy and development than the older states and those which have had a great industrial development. Their stake may not be equal in dollars and cents,—that, of course,—but it is probably greater in all that concerns opportunity and the chances of life. There is a sense in which the interest of the poor man in the prosperity of the country is greater than that of the rich man: he has no reserve, and his very life may depend upon it. The very life of an undeveloped community may depend upon what will cause a richer community mere temporary inconvenience or negligible distress. And yet even this, vital as it is to the validity of the usual criticisms of the make-up and character of the Senate, is in fact neither here nor there as compared with the essential point of the matter.

Neither is it of material consequence that some of the states represented in the Senate are not real communities, with distinct historical characteristics, a distinct social and economic character of their own, as most of the older states are. It is true that you have only to look at a map of the United States to see at a glance that many of the newer states of the Union are purely arbitrary creations, their boundaries established by the theodolite of the public surveyor. They are squares on a great checkerboard, elaborated into rectangular sections on broad plains where there are no natural boundaries to divide region from region; and these artificial squares, which Congress first laid off as the areas of territories, it has one by one converted into states, each of which sends two members to the Senate, just as Virginia and Massachusetts do, the history of whose boundaries and organization is a long history of constitutional struggle which gave them from the very outset characters and purposes of their own. Many a square western state, laid out by the public surveyor, has now a more homogeneous population and a more discernible individuality than some of her eastern sisters into whom a miscellaneous immigration has poured social chaos. And their very separateness of political organization insures them a development of their own.

Yet even that is not of material consequence. Even if every state of the Union were of artificial creation, not a natural community, but merely a region marked off to make a congressional district for elections to the Senate, the principle I am just now interested in pointing out as of capital importance in a system and country like ours would not be altered or affected. That is the principle that regions must be represented, irrespective of population, in a country physically as various as ours and therefore certain to exhibit a very great variety of social and economic and even political conditions. It is of the utmost importance that its parts as well as its people should be represented; and there can be no doubt in the mind of any one who really sees the Senate of the United States as it is that it represents the country, as distinct from the accumulated populations of the country, much more fully and much more truly than the House of Representatives does. The East and North are regions of concentration, regions of teeming population and highly developed industry,—the regions north of Mason and Dixon's Line and east of the Mississippi. It will not long be so. Cities are springing up in the South and beyond the Mississippi in the Middle West, on the Pacific coast, and upon the great lines of traffic that connect coast with coast, which will presently rival the cities of the East and of the old Northwest in magnitude and importance; and many a region hitherto but sparsely peopled is thickening apace with crowding settlers and an accumulating commerce. But for the present the South and West, if I may use those terms in the large, are not the centres of wealth or of population, and have a character unlike that of the marts of trade and industry; and there are more senators from the South and West than from the North and East. The House of Representatives tends more and more, with the concentration of population in certain regions, to represent particular interests and points of view, to be less catholic and more and more specialized in its view of national affairs. It represents chiefly the East and North. The Senate is its indispensable offset, and speaks always in its make-up of the size, the variety, the heterogeneity, the range and breadth of the country, which no community or group of communities can adequately represent. It cannot be represented by one sample or by a few samples; it can be represented only by many,—as many as it has parts.

It thus happens that there are in the Senate more representatives of the individual parts of the country than of the characteristic parts of it. At least that is true if I am right in assuming that the characteristic parts of America are those parts which are most highly developed, where population teems and great communities are quick with industry, where our life most displays its energy, its ardor of enterprise, its genius for material achievement. Other communities are no doubt more truly characteristic of America as she has been known in the processes of her making. Only modern visitors, visitors of our own day, have known her as industrial America, the leader of the world in all the processes, whether material or economic, which produce wealth and accumulate power, the land of manufactures and of vast cities. The older America is still represented by the South and West with their simpler life, their more scattered people, their fields of grain, their mines of metal, their little towns, their easier pace of intercourse, their work that does not crowd out companionship.

Certainly it is easier to represent a northern or eastern constituency in Congress than to represent a southern or western constituency. There is more individuality, man for man, in the West and South than in the East and North. How constantly we repeat each other's opinions and bow to each other's influence; how seldom we take leave to be ourselves and utter thoughts of our own genuine coinage, in regions where we are parts of a packed and thronging multitude! Rubbing shoulders every day with thousands of your fellow-citizens, putting your mind into contact with other minds at every encounter, you slowly have the individuality rubbed out of you by mere attrition and are worn down to a common pattern. Your opinion is everybody's opinion; my information is the common information current everywhere: your mind, like mine, like our neighbor's, is assaulted day and night with the multitudinous voices of clamorous talk, and a common atmosphere gives us a common habit and attitude. Only very unusual men can remain individual under such pressure of uniformity. It is uncomfortable to be singular in any habit, whether of action or of thought, where so many look on and make comment. Conformity is the easiest, plainest, safest way, and countless multitudes there be that walk in it. "Always be of the opinion of the person with whom you are conversing," was Dean Swift's advice to all who would win the repute of being sensible persons. And in crowded places of enterprise it is a very valuable asset of success to be thus reputed a man of sense. To conform opens the ways to promotion. It is the common and very uncomfortable fortune of men of original views to be greeted at every turn with a stare and a shrug of the shoulders, as Mr. Bagehot has said, and to be followed with the comment, "An excellent young man, sir, but unsafe, quite unsafe." Mr. Bagehot must certainly have known: he was himself most singularly original and seemed always to have had the freshness of youth about him.

The variety of the country, therefore, is better represented in the Senate than in the House, its variety of opinion as well as its variety of social and economic make-up,—its variety of opinion because [of] its variety of social and economic make-up. There are more opinions because there is more individuality in the uncrowded South and West than in the crowded East and North.

Each mind is there apt to have a greater, freer space about it, space in which to look around and form impressions of its own. No country ought ever to be judged from its seething centres. To be truly known, it must be known where it is quiet, in places where impulse is not instant, hot, insistent; where you can at least presume that opinion will next week be what it is to-day.

In those hot centres of trade and industry, where a man's business grips him like an unrelaxing hand of iron from morning to night and lies heavily upon him even while he sleeps, few men can be said to have any opinions at all. They may bury their heads for a few minutes in the morning paper at breakfast or as they hurry to their offices, may dwell with dull attention upon the afternoon paper as they go wearily home again or drowse after dinner; but what they get out of the papers they cannot call their opinions. They are not opinions, but merely a miscellany of mental reactions, never assorted, never digested, never made up into anything than can for the moment compare in reality and vitality with the energetic conceptions they put to use in their business. In small towns, in rural country-sides, around comfortable stoves in cross-road stores, wherever business shows as many intervals as transactions, where seasons of leisure alternate with seasons of activity, where large undertakings wait on slow, unhasting nature, where men are neighbors and know each other's quality, where politics is dwelt upon in slow talk with all the leisure and fond elaboration usually bestowed on gossip, where discussion is as constant a pastime as checkers, opinion is made up with an individual flavor and wears all the variety of individual points of view. And the Senate has more members from such regions than from those where opinion is made up by conglomeration and upon the moment, out of newspapers and not out of the contributions of individual minds. It represents the population of the country, not in its numbers, but in its variety; and it is of the utmost consequence that the country's variety should be represented as thoroughly as its mass.

The processes by which we have made states out of the territories of the United States have been seriously impaired once and again by mistakes which are the more to be deplored because they are apparently irremediable. Once make a state and you cannot unmake it. Once or twice Congress has admitted to the Union, in equal partnership with the older states, territories which not only did not have population enough to justify their admission, but which had no real prospect of gaining a population large and various enough to develop into compact and important communities with a character and purpose of their own,—communities already sufficiently represented in kind in the counsels of the country, and not constituted in a way which gave promise of political vitality. But such mistakes have been few, and many a state which at first seemed a premature and unjustifiable creation has been speedily lifted to a plane of real dignity and importance by the abounding forces of our national growth. It has been hard to make mistakes where populations throng forward so steadily and in such wholesome masses to occupy the free spaces of the continent. We have had to reclaim deserts to accommodate their multitude. And as each new-fledged state has come in, its two spokesmen in the Senate have added its voice to our counsels in a place where voices can still be individually heard.

The fact that the Senate has kept its original rules of debate and procedure substantially unchanged, is very significant. It is a place of individual voices. The suppression of any single voice would radically change its constitutional character; and, its character being changed, the individual voices of the country's several regions being silenced, there would no longer be any sufficient reason for its present constitution. If it were to follow the example of the House and make itself chiefly an efficient organ for the transaction of business, the critics who condemn it because it is unequally compounded upon any balanced reckoning of the wealth and numbers of the country would have not a little tenable ground to stand upon.

Another circumstance gives a senator of the United States an individual importance which the average member of the House of Representatives lacks. He comes into contact with a much greater variety of the public business. He is not a mere legislator. He is directly associated with the President in some of the most delicate and important functions of government. He is a member of a great executive council. He is brought into very confidential relations with the President in matters which oftentimes call for not a little discretion and for very prudent judgments,—judgments not to be drawn from public opinion, but only from official facts privately considered, not spoken of out of doors, belonging to intimate counsel and not to public debate. There is no better cure for thinking disparagingly of the Senate than a conference with men who belong to it, to find how various, how precise, how comprehensive their information about the affairs of the nation is; and to find, what is even more important, how fair, how discreet, how regardful of public interest they are in the opinions which they will express in your private ear.

The most reticent men in Washington are the members of the Supreme Court of the United States. It would of course be a great breach of professional honor on the part of any member of that Court to discuss any question involved in a pending case which the Court was considering or was about to consider; but his obligation of reticence goes much farther than that. Almost any piece of public policy that touches the individual, though it be never so indirectly, may sooner or later come before the Supreme Court for judicial examination. Every member of the Court, therefore, feels bound to keep his opinions upon such matters to himself. He will not discuss with you any but the most general public questions, holds discreetly silent with regard to every mooted matter of legal policy or construction. Men who know the proprieties never broach such matters with members of the Court. Senators feel a similar obligation of honor with regard to the matters in which they bear a confidential relation to the executive. They are not at liberty to state to you or even to their constituents at home the grounds for such action as they may have taken in executive sessions of the Senate until the whole matter is so long gone by that no possible harm or embarrassment can come of publicity with regard to it. Members of the House are not under such restraints. Nothing comes before the House of Representatives which it is not the right of every man in the United States to discuss if he will. No doubt members sometimes act upon private information from the White House or a department which they would feel it unwise to make generally known; but that seldom happens, and if the House talked at all, it might talk about anything it chose that it had information enough to understand.

It is no essential part of our present study to ask by what influences either members of the House or members of the Senate obtain their seats. That is a question concerning, not the form and purpose of our political institutions, but the moral character of the nation itself, the social influences which work in it for good or evil. But so much has been said in recent years about the methods by which seats in the Senate are secured, so much that is of evil report has been believed, that the question cannot be passed by without giving our whole inquiry the appearance of a lack of candor. And, after all, any serious loss of prestige it may suffer must greatly impair the Senate's power and influence, its usefulness as an instrument of constitutional government. It has become customary to speak of it as a rich man's club, and any writer who professes to adduce proofs that the corporate interests of the country, the great railroads and the greater trusts, have secured virtual control of it by putting into it men of their own choice, engaged in their behalf by one of influence or another to block any legislation likely to harm them, gains easy credence. Where there is so much smoke, must there not be a little fire? It is a question which touches the integrity of our whole constitutional system. It would be affectation to avoid it.

There are many opinions as to the way in which men obtain seats in the Senate; and I dare say that for every opinion there is a corresponding method,—not just the method suggested by the opinion, but sufficiently like it to give the opinion more than plausible color. There are many ways of getting into the Senate. There are some very bad ways; some ways that are neither bad nor good; and some very good ways. What it interests me most to observe with regard to the matter, in view of what I have just been saying of the make-up of the Senate and its general relation to the country, is that, so far as one may judge from rumor and from what appears in the public prints, the bad ways have been oftenest illustrated where population is thickest and in a few of the recently created states, which, because of their peculiar economic character, are dominated by a single interest or a single group of interests. They have not often been illustrated, to be more specific, in those normal western and southern states, which I have spoken of in contrast with the centres of population and industry as standing for the nation's variety, characteristic of its rich diversity alike of quality and of interest rather than of its accumulations of wealth and of material power.

The purchasing power of money in politics is chiefly exerted where there is most money. The selfish influence of great corporations is most often exhibited where they have their seats of control, at the financial centres of the country. The processes by which men procure places in the Senate have been most often under suspicion where men buy most things. One is forced to believe that there are some communities, even in the America which we love, where the dollar is god, where everything is estimated in money value, and where actual cash is paid for votes; and unquestionably there are other communities in which the highest political preferment has sometimes been bought, not by the direct use of money, but by means equally demoralizing,—perhaps more demoralizing because less obviously venal,—by a covert bartering of favors, unspoken promises, business opportunities offered and accepted without any sign given of aught but kindly interest and natural friendship. But the whole country knows the cases in which these things are suspected, and knows them to be few. No candid man who knows anything of the character and circumstances of the persons whose names he reads can look through the roll of the Senate and think for a moment that such influences predominate there.

In order to get a correct impression of the Senate, it is necessary that you extend your observation beyond particular sections of the country. One of the greatest disadvantages that public opinion labors under in the United States is that we have no national newspaper, no national organ of opinion. There is no newspaper in the United States which is not local, and narrowly local at that, both in the news which it prints and in the views which it expresses. Each paper makes such selections of general news as will interest the particular locality in which it is printed, and expresses such views of the nation's affairs as local interest or information suggest. If you read New York papers, you will have New York opinions; if you read Philadelphia papers, you will have Philadelphia opinions; if you read Chicago papers, you will have Chicago opinions; if you read San Francisco papers, you will have, not western, but merely San Franciscan, opinions. And if you read papers from all four cities, you will not get national opinion. Though the impressions they give you may sometimes seem to have the air of being national, you will find that they are after all local impressions, though made up out of national material. They bear the color of a place. I dare say the thing is inevitable in so big a country; but undoubtedly one of the reasons why we so habitually misjudge the Senate of the United States is that we have no national medium of intelligence, and the papers most widely read reflect not national, but local, conditions.

Indeed, one of the serious difficulties of politics in this country, whether you look at it from the point of view of the student or the point of view of the statesman, is its provincialism,—the general absence of national information and, by the same token, of national opinion. And one is forced to believe, reluctantly enough if he live in the East, that the East is the most provincial part of the Union,—a very serious matter, because most of our information and most of our opinion is printed in the East and transmitted thence. The East, being the oldest part of the country, having been for a long time the whole of it, having the oldest roots of history, the longest traditions of influence, the greatest wealth and hitherto an unquestioned command of the economic development of the whole country, shows as yet little intimate consciousness of the rest of it; is much less aware of other communities and other interests than its own than are other parts of the country. The chief reason why the President of the United States can concentrate in himself, if he choose, greater power and a more extended influence than any other person or any other group of persons connected with the government, is, as I have already several times pointed out, that all the country is curious about him and interested in him as our one national figure, eager to hear everything that emanates from him. His doings and sayings constitute the only sort of news that is invariably transmitted to every corner of the country and read with equal interest in every sort of neighborhood. He is the one person about whom a definite national opinion is formed and, therefore, the one person who can form opinion by his own direct influence and act upon the whole country at once.

It has, therefore, too often escaped the attention of the country as a whole that the large majority of the members of the Senate of the United States obtain their seats by perfectly legitimate methods, because the people whom they represent honestly prefer them as representatives; that the large majority of them are poor men who have little or nothing to live on besides their inadequate salaries; that the opinion and action of the Senate are for the most part determined by the influence of quiet men whom the country talks about very little and about whom it suspects nothing in the least questionable or dishonorable; and that the few notorious members whose reputations are most talked of generally play but a very obscure part in its business. In most of the states great corporations, great combinations of interest, have little to do with the choice of senators. Men go to the Senate who are in a very real sense the choice of the people, —or rather men to whom natural and genuine political leadership has come by reason of their personal force or of their services to their party,—men of the rank and file who have made their way to the top by political, not by commercial, means, and who enjoy a veritable popular support. There are one or two very influential members of the Senate who are also very rich men; but they are influential, not because of their riches, but because of their long and intelligent service, their complete experience in affairs, and the relations of intimate personal confidence which they have established with their fellow senators. You have but to make the most casual inquiries in Washington to ascertain that the men who are in fact most influential in the proceedings of the Senate are not the men most advertised in the newspapers, most conspicuous in the talk of the Capitol, not the men who talk most effectively for those far-off "galleries" which lie away from Washington, but small groups of quiet gentlemen seldom spoken of in the public prints, more thoughtful of their duties than of being generally talked about,—men who have not laid by fortunes, but who have been at the pains to grow rich in the esteem of the fellow citizens at home who know and support them.

One of the present difficulties lying in the way of maintaining a high grade of excellence in the Senate, as in the House, is that we do not pay our representatives in either house salaries large enough to command men of the best abilities, or even sufficiently to support those who accept seats in the houses, in the sort of domestic comfort and dignity we naturally expect them to maintain. Men of the highest ability do accept seats in the House and Senate, but they do so generally at a great sacrifice, find it exceedingly difficult to live in so expensive a place as Washington without a very teasing economy, and are usually forced at last to seek some remunerative employment in order to pay the debts they have almost inevitably accumulated in serving a country which economizes in the wrong items of its budget. If the Senate should ever come to deserve in fact the reputation of being a rich men's club, the true cause will be found rather in the salary account on our national budget than in the power of wealth to buy legislative seats. At its stands now, only rich men can afford, if they be in love with self-respecting ways of living, to accept an election in the Senate.

This, then, is the Senate, the House of individuals, a body of representative American men, representing the many elements of the nation's make-up, exhibiting the vitality of a various people, speaking for the several parts of a country of many parts and many interests, a whole and yet full of sharp social and political contrast; men much above the average in ability and in personal force; men connected in most cases by long service with the business of the government and accustomed to handle its affairs in all their range and variety; a body of counselors who act, if not always wisely or without personal and party bias, yet always with energy and without haste.

It is interesting to the looker-on in Washington to observe the unmistakable condescension with which the older members of the Senate regard the President of the United States. Dominate the affairs of the country though he may, he seems to them at most an ephemeral phenomenon. Even if he has continued in his office for the two terms which are the traditional limit of the President's service, he but overlaps a single senatorial term by two years, and a senator who has served several terms has already seen several Presidents come and go. His experience of affairs is much mellower than the President's can be; he looks at policies with a steadier vision than the President's; the continuity of the government lies in the keeping of the Senate more than in the keeping of the executive, even in respect of matters which are of the especial prerogative of the presidential office. A member of long standing in the Senate feels that he is the professional, the President an amateur.

I have dwelt at some length upon the character and the true constitutional purpose of the Senate because that character and purpose govern its whole organization and action. It is as different from the House in organization as in character and constitutional position. Its power is not concentrated in its presiding officer as the power of the House is. On the contrary, its presiding officer is of all its constituent parts the least significant. In mere fact, the Vice President of the United States is, in any analysis of the powers and activities of the Senate, practically negligible. Some occupants of that singular office have, it is true, made a considerable impression upon the Senate and have left distinct marks of their individuality upon its record, particularly in matters of procedure. Men of great natural force and unusual personality cannot spend four years in the chair of so serious and so busy an assembly without leaving some memory of their influence. But the Vice Presidents of the United States have, almost without exception, whatever their natural vigor or instinct of initiative, felt that their relation to the Senate was purely formal. The Vice President is not a member of the Senate. His duties are only the formal and altogether impartial duties of a presiding officer. His position seems to demand that he should take no part in party tactics and should hold carefully aloof from all parliamentary struggles for party advantage. Its very dignity seems to rob it of vitality in respect of the only duties assigned to it by the Constitution. And yet the president *pro tempore* of the Senate, the Vice President's substitute upon occasion, is a vital political figure. He is chosen by his party associates of the majority to play a real part in the business of the assembly. He holds office at the pleasure of the Senate and is in a much more intimate and sympathetic relation with the party he represents than the Vice President of the United States can be.

Once or twice it has looked as if the president *pro tempore* were likely to accumulate powers and prerogatives which might give his office a power and authority comparable with those of the Speaker of the House of Representatives. The Senate, like the House, prepares its business through the instrumentality of standing committees, and in 1828 it conferred upon its president *pro tempore* the authority to appoint its committees. But in 1833, for political reasons which it is not necessary to detail here, it again changed its rule and resumed to itself the right to constitute its committees by its own choice by ballot. Again in 1837 it turned to the president *pro tempore* for relief and conferred upon him the power of appointment, the balloting having proved very cumbersome and burdensome; but in 1845 circumstances again compelled it to withdraw the authority. Many considerations seem to render the president *pro tempore* unavailable for such functions. The statute of 1792 had put the president *pro tempore* of the Senate in the line of succession to the presidency of the United States in case of a vacancy, providing that if both President and Vice President should die or become disqualified, the president *pro tempore* of the Senate should assume the duties of the presidency. The Senate regarded its president *pro tempore*, therefore, as a necessary officer only in order that there should be no lapse in the office of President. It chose him only for the occasions when the Vice President was absent from his chair, and allowed his office to lapse again upon the Vice President's return. But a change in the law governing the succession to the presidency altered the whole character of the temporary office. In 1886 a new statute vested the succession in the heads of the executive departments, in an order of precedence determined by the dates at which their several offices had been created, and the president *pro tempore* of the Senate was omitted from the line of succession. Ten years before the Senate had decided that its president *pro tempore* need not be regarded as merely a temporary officer chosen from time to time upon the occasion of each absence of the Vice President from its sittings, and in 1890 it confirmed its decision in that respect and extended the tenure of this officer of its own choice indefinitely. He now holds at the pleasure of the Senate, takes the chair whenever the Vice President happens to be absent, and is superseded only by the election of some one else in his place. He is appointed to many important committees of the Senate like any ordinary member, is usually himself chairman of a leading committee, and is always sure to be one of the chief figures of his party on the floor. Upon a change of majority his office lapses and a successor is chosen from the new majority.

And yet, singularly enough, though he has grown in importance with the permanence of his office and has seemed once and again to be chosen as in some sense the leading representative of his party in the chamber, as the Speaker of the House is, he is not in fact in command in debate or in the direction of party tactics. The leader of the Senate is the chairman of the majority caucus. Each party in the Senate finds its real, its permanent, its effective organization in its caucus, and follows the leadership, in all important parliamentary battles, of the chairman of that caucus, its organization and its leadership alike resting upon arrangements quite outside the Constitution, for which there is no better and no other sanction than human nature.

The Senate, like the House, digests and manages its business through standing committees, and the appointment of those committees it has in large measure kept in its own hands. But the old method of actually choosing them by ballot it has not found it convenient or even possible to maintain. Its machinery for the selection of committees, as for other party purposes, is the caucus. The caucus of each party has its Committee on Committees, appointed by its chairman, subject to the ratification of the caucus itself, and charged with the important function of selecting its party's representatives on the standing committees. The majority caucus has, besides, its Steering Committee, similarly appointed, to which fall duties very like those of the Committee on Rules in the House.

The chairman of the majority caucus is much more nearly the counterpart of the Speaker of the House than is the president *pro tempore*. His influence is very great and very pervasive. Through the Committee on Committees and the Steering Committee, both of which he appoints subject to the confirmation of the caucus, he plays no small part in determining both the character and the handling of the business the Senate is called on to consider.

But the Senate is a deliberative assembly and is under no such discipline of silence and obedience to its committees as the House is. The duties of its committees are much more like those of ordinary old-fashioned committees such as are usually found in all parliamentary bodies, than are the duties of the House committees. They are by no means in complete control of the business of the Senate. A bill introduced by an individual senator may be put upon the calendar, debated, and voted upon without reference to a committee at all. The committees are an imperative convenience, and the greater part of the Senate's business is of course prepared by them; but they are not permitted to monopolize the floor, and the chamber is quick to recognize the right of its individual members to have their proposals considered directly, without committee intervention.

Moreover, the make-up of the committees of the Senate is determined much more strictly by seniority and by personal privilege and precedence than is the membership of the committees of the House, with much less regard to party lines and much more regard to personal and sectional considerations,—by equitable arrangement rather than by the personal choice or individual purpose of the caucus chairmen. The variety of the country is allowed to show itself in the constitution of its committees, as in its debates and its recognition of individual privilege among its members. An old-fashioned air of equality and democracy is still perceptible in the Senate, its popular reputation to the contrary notwithstanding,—something of the discipline of party whips and leaders, as must in any political assembly be inevitable, but much more of the air of debate, much less the air of rigidly organized business and mere efficiency, than in the popular chamber.

Indeed, the Senate is, *par excellence*, the chamber of debate and of individual privilege. Its discussions are often enough unprofitable, are too often marred by personal feeling and by exhibitions of private interest which taint its reputation and render the country uneasy and suspicious, but they are at least the only means the country has of clarifying public business for public comprehension.

When we turn to the question which is the central question of our whole study, the question of the coördination of the Senate with the other organs of the government and the synthesis of authority and power for common action, it at once becomes evident that such a body as I have described the Senate to be, must be very hard indeed to digest into any system. A coördination of wills, united movement under a common leadership, is of the very essence of every efficient form of government. The Senate has a very stiff will of its own, a pride of independent judgment, very admirable in itself, but not calculated to dispose it to prompt accommodation when it differs in its views and objects from the House or the President. Its very excellences stand in its way as an organ of coöperation: its slow deliberation, its tolerance of individual opinion, its confidence in the political judgment and experience of its own leaders, the feeling of permanency and stability which seems to lift it a little above the influences of the immediate day, the critical moment of decision. It looks upon the House of Representatives very much as it looks upon the President,—as an organ of opinion, indeed, and as a coördinate branch of the government of undoubted commission from the people, but as likely to change, a thing that, in its present character and disposition at least, is here to-day and gone to-morrow, to make room for new men and new moods.

The membership of the House is much less stable than the membership of the Senate. Not only is the term of a senator three times as long as the term of a member of the House, but members of the House are much less often reëlected than are members of the Senate. Most states are content to continue their senators in their seats for long periods together, but few congressional districts can be counted upon not to change their choice very frequently. Not only does the *personnel* of the House change rapidly and the *personnel* of the Senate change very slowly, but the party majority is much more often changed in the one than in the other. For a great many years now the leaders of our national parties have been obliged to think of the country as one thing when considered with a view to the make-up of the Senate, and another thing when considered with a view to the make-up of the House. Parties have often changed places in commanding the majority in the House during the last fifty years, but not often in the Senate. The people reckoned by states have usually preferred the Republican party; the people reckoned by numbers have turned in their choice of men and of parties first to the one party and then to the other, as men and programs have changed.

All this, of course, has its effect upon the temper of the Senate. It is less disturbed by elections than the House is, feels itself in great part sheltered from the winds of party contest, and is apt to look upon itself as the poise and makeweight of the whole system, which might swing into an erratic orb were it allowed to yield to the impulses of changing opinion too rapidly. And it is confirmed in this view of its functions by the character of its leaders. It must be said that the method by which leaders are made in the Senate is much more normal, much more in the course of nature, than the method by which they are made in the House. Nature intended that leaders should be self-selected, by proof given of their actual quality in the business in which they aspire to lead. And since leaders of the Senate are expected to lead in counsel, they are generally men proved by counsel, men of long training in public affairs who have been under inspection by their fellow members for many sessions together. The Senate is inclined to follow its veterans,—not necessarily its chief debaters, but the men who by long service have gained a full experience and, by many evidences of good sense and cool judgment, the entire confidence of their party associates, as guides who will not blunder. The leaders of the House win their places by service on the floor, no doubt, before being made Speakers, but they win them as masters of parliamentary tactics and as men of will and resource rather than as men of counsel; and they win them in a restless and changeful assembly few of whose members remain in the public service long enough to know any men's qualities intimately. The leaders the Senate prefers are almost of necessity its most conservative men,—men most likely to magnify the powers and prerogatives of the body they represent and to stickle for every privilege it possesses, not at all likely to look to the President for leadership or to yield to the House upon any radical difference of opinion or of purpose.

Particularly in its dealings with the President has the Senate shown its pride of independence, its desire to rule rather than to be merely consulted, its inclination to magnify its powers and in some sense preside over the policy of the government. There can be little doubt in the mind of any one who has carefully studied the plans and opinions of the Constitutional Convention of 1787 that the relations of the President and Senate were intended to be very much more intimate and confidential than they have been; that it was expected that the Senate would give the President its advice and consent in respect of appointments and treaties in the spirit of an executive council associated with him upon terms of confidential coöperation rather than in the spirit of an independent branch of the government, jealous lest he should in the least particular attempt to govern its judgment or infringe upon its prerogatives. The formality and stiffness, the attitude as if of rivalry and mutual distrust, which have marked the dealings of the President with the Senate, have shown a tendency to increase rather than to decrease as the years have gone by, and have undoubtedly at times very seriously embarrassed the action of the government in many difficult and important matters.

The Senate has shown itself particularly stiff and jealous in insisting upon exercising an independent judgment upon foreign affairs, and has done so so often that a sort of customary *modus vivendi* has grown up between the President and the Senate, as of rival powers. The Senate is expected in most instances to accept the President's appointments to office, and the President is expected to be very tolerant of the Senate's rejection of treaties, proposing but by no means disposing even in this chief field of his power. Advisers who are entirely independent of the official advised are in a position to be, not his advisers, but his masters; and when, as sometimes happens, the Senate is of one political party and the President of the other, its dictation may be based, not upon the merits of the question involved, but upon party antagonisms and calculations of advantage.

The President has not the same recourse when blocked by the Senate that he has when opposed by the House. When the House declines his counsel he may appeal to the nation, and if public opinion respond to his appeal the House may grow thoughtful of the next congressional elections and yield; but the Senate is not so immediately sensitive to opinion and is apt to grow, if anything, more stiff if pressure of that kind is brought to bear upon it.

But there is another course which the President may follow, and which one or two Presidents of unusual political sagacity have followed, with the satisfactory results that were to have been expected. He may himself be less stiff and offish, may himself act in the true spirit of the Constitution and establish intimate relations of confidence with the Senate on his own initiative, not carrying his plans to completion and then laying them in final form before the Senate to be accepted or rejected, but keeping himself in confidential communication with the leaders of the Senate while his plans are in course, when their advice will be of service to him and his information of the greatest service to them, in order that there may be veritable counsel and a real accommodation of views instead of a final challenge and contest. The policy which has made rivals of the President and Senate has shown itself in the President as often as in the Senate, and if the Constitution did indeed intend that the Senate should in such matters be an executive council it is not only the privilege of the President to treat it as such, it is also his best policy and his plain duty. As it is now, the President and Senate are apt to deal with each other with the formality and punctilio of powers united by no common tie except the vague common tie of public interest, but it is within their choice to change the whole temper of affairs in such matters and to exhibit the true spirit of the Constitution by coming into intimate relations of mutual confidence, by a change of attitude which can perhaps be effected more easily upon the initiative of the President than upon the initiative of the Senate.

It is manifestly the duty of statesmen, with whatever branch of the government they may be associated, to study in a very serious spirit of public service the right accommodation of parts in this complex system of ours, the accommodation which will give the government its best force and synthesis in the face of the difficult counsels and perplexing tasks of regulation with which it is face to face, and no one can play the leading part in such a matter with more influence or propriety than the President. If he have character, modesty, devotion, and insight as well as force, he can bring the contending elements of the system together into a great and efficient body of common counsel.

VI

THE COURTS

Our courts are the balance-wheel of our whole constitutional system; and ours is the only constitutional system so balanced and controlled. Other constitutional systems lack complete poise and certainty of operation because they lack the support and interpretation of authoritative, undisputable courts of law. It is clear beyond all need of exposition that for the definite maintenance of constitutional understandings it is indispensable, alike for the preservation of the liberty of the individual and for the preservation of the integrity of the powers of the government, that there should be some non-political forum in which those understandings can be impartially debated and determined. That forum our courts supply. There the individual may assert his rights; there the government must accept definition of its authority. There the individual may challenge the legality of governmental action and have it judged by the test of fundamental principles, and that test the government must abide; there the government can check the too aggressive self-assertion of the individual and establish its power upon lines which all can comprehend and heed. The constitutional powers of the courts constitute the ultimate safeguard alike of individual privilege and of governmental prerogative. It is in this sense that our judiciary is the balance-wheel of our entire system; it is meant to maintain that nice adjustment between individual rights and governmental powers which constitutes political liberty.

I am not now thinking of the courts as the lawyer thinks of them, as places of technical definition and business adjustment, where the rights of individuals as against one another are debated and determined; but as the citizen thinks of them, as his safeguard against a too arrogant and teasing use of power by the government, an instrument of politics,—of liberty. Constitutional government exists in its completeness and full reality only when the individual, only when every individual is regarded as a partner of the government in the conduct of the nation's life. The citizen is not individually represented in any assembly or in any regularly constituted part of the government itself. He cannot, except in the most extraordinary cases and with the utmost difficulty, bring his individual private affairs to the attention of Congress or of his state legislature, to the attention of the President of the United States or of the executive officer of his state; he would find himself balked of relief if he did by the laws under which they act and exercise their clearly specified powers. It is only in the courts that men are individuals in respect of their rights. Only in them can the individual citizen set up his private right and interest against the government by an appeal to the fundamental understandings upon which the government rests. In no other government but our own can he set them up even there against the government. He can everywhere set them up against other individuals who would invade his rights or who have imposed upon him, but not against the government. The government under every other constitutional system but our own is sovereign, unquestionable, to be restrained not by the courts but only by public opinion, only by the opinion of the nation acting through the representative chamber. We alone have given our courts power to restrain the government under which they themselves act and from which they themselves derive their authority.

And this is not merely because our constitutional understandings are explicitly set forth in written documents which the courts must regard as part of the body of law they are charged to maintain and interpret,—the chief and fundamental part to which all other parts must give way; for a very important part of the constitutional understandings upon which the English government rests is written in Magna Carta and in the great Bill of Rights, and yet the English courts have no authority to check the law-making organs of the government even though they override Magna Carta and the Bill of Rights in the statutes which they enact. No doubt the definitions of Magna Carta and of the Bill of Rights lie at the foundation of all government and of all individual privilege in England, and if any statute of doubtful interpretation were brought before an English court which seemed in contravention of rights clearly stated in those documents, the court would interpret it in accordance with the terms of those revered instruments of liberty; but if a statute should in plain terms ignore the definitions and restrictions even of Magna Carta and the Bill of Rights, I understand that the court would be obliged to enforce it. Parliament is sovereign and can do what it pleases. Only the opinion of the nation can check or restrain it. Only repeal can set an obnoxious statute aside. No government is more entirely governed by opinion than the government of England, but it is governed by the general opinion of the nation, not by the particular opinion of the courts.

This is not because the English courts have been less interested than our own to maintain individual rights and liberties or less liberal in their interpretation of individual privilege. No courts have been more liberal or more disposed to safeguard private privilege. The common law of England has, more than any other law, been a mirror of opinion and of social adjustment and has been made in its development to fit English life like a well-cut garment. Time out of mind English judges have liberalized and broadened it by reading into it good principle and enlightened opinion. There are some notable old cases in the English law reports in which the judges declare all principles of right reason and of humanity to be parts of the common law of England without precedent. But there is no fundamental law susceptible of interpretation by the courts which defines or limits the powers of Parliament. Magna Carta and the Bill of Rights define the rights of individuals as against the crown, but not as against Parliament, not as against those whom the nation has authorized to make its laws. Upon them no document which the courts can read or elucidate as law places any restraint. The courts must enforce whatever they enact. The powers of our law-making bodies are, on the contrary, very definitely defined and circumscribed in documents which are themselves part of the body of our law, and the decisions of the courts interpreting those documents set those law-making bodies their limits.

To us this power of the courts seems natural not only but of the essence of the whole system; but it is in fact extraordinary and has been looked upon by not a few of our foreign critics with unaffected amazement. And they have been the more amazed because they did not find this extraordinary power conferred upon our courts in any part or sentence of our fundamental law. "The judicial power of the United States," so run the quiet sentences of the Constitution, "shall be vested in one supreme Court and in such inferior Courts as the Congress may from time to time ordain and establish" and "shall extend to all Cases in Law and Equity arising under this Constitution, the Laws of the United States, and Treaties made or which shall be made under their Authority." It is only an inference drawn by the courts themselves that "the laws of the United States and treaties made under their authority" shall be tested by the Constitution and disallowed if they lie outside the field of power it has granted Congress and the President,—a very plain inference, no doubt, but only an inference: an inference made upon analogy, drawn out of historical circumstances and out of a definite theory as to the origin of our government.

There was never any sovereign government in America. The governments of the colonies were operated under charters granted by the English crown, and could legally exercise no powers which those charters did not confer. If they exceeded those powers, the king could annul their acts, and the king's courts could declare their charters forfeited. The same principle and practice still obtains with regard to the powers of the chartered English colonies. The constitution of Canada is "the British North America Act," an act of Parliament, federating the several provinces, giving each its legislature and its separate field of law, and setting over all the Governor and Parliament of the Dominion. Anything done either by the government of the provinces or by the government of the Dominion in excess or contravention of the terms of the British North America Act is null and void and can be so treated by the courts of the Dominion itself, though an appeal lies in all cases of such consequence to the Judicial Committee of the Privy Council in England, a court of the sovereign power. The sovereign power now set over us is the people. When the authority of the crown lapsed by revolution, they assumed it. For colonial charters they substituted their state constitutions, to which they presently added the Constitution of the United States. Their sovereign grant of power can no more be exceeded than can the grants of the sovereign king of the older day or the sovereign Parliament of our own time. Statutes must conform to the Constitution and are null and void if they do not. Our constitutions are comparable, say Professor Dicey and Mr. Bryce, to the charters of great corporations, our statutes to their by-laws, our treaties to their contracts. No by-law or contract made by them will be upheld by any court if in contravention or excess of their charter powers. Any English-speaking lawyer would have reasoned the matter out as we have reasoned it out.

None the less, plain inference though it be, this power of our courts renders our constitutional system unique. No other constitutional system has this balance and means of energy,—this means of energy for the individual citizen. The individual citizen among us can apply the checks of law to the government upon his own initiative, and they will respond to his touch as readily as to the touch of the greatest political officer of the system. More readily, indeed, for the courts will not hear abstract questions. Some concrete and tangible interest, involving the right of some particular individual or corporation, must be implicated, and implicated in some form which makes a legal inquiry and remedy both necessary and possible under the ordinary rules of suit and procedure. They will not take the question up otherwise, and an individual citizen is a more natural and usual party to such an inquiry than an officer of the government. An officer of the government cannot be a party to a suit in his official capacity except as he represents some claim or defense of the government itself. The rights of the individual touch the subject-matter of the law at a thousand points, and he may in mere controversy with his neighbor call in question rights which his neighbor professes to exercise under the authority of acts of Congress. No officer of the government need be or can be a party to such a suit; the court is adjudicating private rights and will not hesitate to set an act of Congress aside if it invade those rights in contravention or in excess of the powers granted Congress in the Constitution.

Only by slow and searching labor have the courts been able to keep our singularly complex system at its right poise and adjustment. It has required a long line of cases to thread its intricacies and afford the individual a complete administration of its safeguards. It is a system of many counterpoises and prescriptions. First, there are the restrictions placed upon our governments in respect of the powers they can use upon the individual. Congress can exercise no powers except those explicitly or by plain implication conferred upon it by the Constitution. And there are certain things which it is explicitly forbidden to do. "The privilege of a writ of Habeas Corpus shall not be suspended, unless when in Cases of Rebellion or Invasion public safety may require it. No Bill of Attainder or *ex post facto* Law shall be passed." The powers not granted to Congress remain with the states, but certain powers are denied the states by their own constitutions, some by the Constitution of the United States. "No State shall enter into any Treaty, Alliance, or Federation; grant Laws of Marque or Reprisal; coin money; emit Bills of Credit; make any Thing but gold and silver Coin a Tender in Payment of Debts; pass any Bill of Attainder, *ex post facto* Law or Law impairing the Obligation of Contracts, or grant any Title of Nobility," is the language of Section X of the first article of the Constitution. And added to the restrictions placed upon state and federal governments by the Constitution of the United States are the still more complex and numerous limitations imposed upon the states by their own constitutions. All these, from whatever constitution drawn, the courts must interpret and enforce. In respect of all of them the courts are instruments for the protection of the individual. Besides these definitions and restrictions, which partake of the nature of a Bill of Rights, our constitutions apportion power between the states and the federal government, and that apportionment the courts must assist to make definite and secure. They apportion powers also to the several parts of our state and federal governments, the executive, the legislature, and the courts themselves, and this apportionment also the courts must define and maintain.

It is thus that they are the balance-wheel of the whole system, taking the strain from every direction and seeking to maintain what any unchecked exercise of power might destroy. They are at once instruments of the individual against the government, of the government against the individual, of the several members of our political union against one another, and of the several parts of government in their legal synthesis and adjustment. No wonder De Tocqueville marveled at the "variety of information and excellence of discretion" expected of the American citizen by the constitutional system under which he lives. All these things he may sooner or later find himself obliged to call upon the courts to adjudicate and keep at their right balance for his sake, that the terms of his partnership with the government may be strictly and righteously observed.

It throws upon him a great responsibility and expects of him a constant and watchful independence. There is no one to look out for his rights but himself. He is not a ward of the government, but his own guardian. The law is not automatic; he must himself put it into operation, and he must show good cause why the courts should exert the great powers vested in them. They will not allow the validity of any statute or treaty or of any act of the government to be called lightly in question or drawn unnecessarily under discussion. He must show that, in order to determine definite, concrete rights of his own which are in dispute between himself and his opponent in litigation, it is necessary that the courts should answer the question he raises as to the validity of what the government has done or attempted; not drawing them on to an abstract thesis, but bringing them face to face with an actual question of law. If it lies in his direct way to do that, it makes no difference in what court he raises the question. It need not be the Supreme Court of the United States or the highest court of the state in which he brings suit. Any court can adjudicate the question of the constitutionality of the acts of the government, if it have jurisdiction over the general subject-matter of the case in which the question is raised. The dignity of the question does not alter the jurisdiction. Of course, constitutional questions of capital importance are very likely to be carried sooner or later to the Supreme Court by processes of appeal, but they may originate in any court of any grade and belong not to the extraordinary but to the ordinary processes of adjudication. It may fall in the way of any court in the ordinary administration of justice to compare by-laws with charters, statutes with constitutions, the subordinate parts of the law with the ultimate and fundamental parts, the acts of the government with their legal norms and standards.

The same jurisdiction would no doubt spring up in England were the rules of the British constitution to be reduced to writing and put upon the footing of Magna Carta, were the authority of Parliament to be limited and defined by charter as the authority of the crown has time out of mind been. For English legal practice is the same as American. American practice was derived from it. In England, as in America, the individual citizen is bidden take care of himself, not only against his neighbor but also, if he can, against the government. In England, as in America, an officer of the law ceases to be an officer of the law when he acts in excess of his authority. He may be fined or imprisoned or executed as any other man would be if he overstep the limits of his warrant and authority and do things which he has no right to do. He has no authority but that which is legal and for which he can show rightful warrant. But it is not so in any other country. In every other country an officer of the government is an officer whatever he may do, and cannot be haled before the ordinary courts. He will be restrained from doing illegal things, but only by his superiors, to whom injured persons must complain, or by special administrative tribunals provided for the purpose, before which the individual may cite him. No superior officer, no administrative court, will handle a complaint against him as an ordinary court would handle a suit or indictment. The offense charged will be looked at from the point of view of administrative officers, as a public indiscretion rather than as a private wrong; great latitude will be allowed an officer of the law if he profess to act in the public interest and cannot be shown to have acted in malice. The atmosphere of the inquiry is the atmosphere of authority, and the discipline applied will be the discipline of a corps, not the judgment of an ordinary court against a breaker of the law. Citizens are subjects, not partners of the government. It is against the whole spirit of our polity, on the contrary, that we should be running to the government with complaints. Our practice is built upon individual rights, and the individual is freely given the means to take care of himself in courts which are his own no less than they are the government's. The courts are meant to be the people's forum, open to all who wish the law determined.

It is of the deeper consequence that the courts should in fact be open to all, equally accessible and serviceable to every man. If it be true, as it is nowadays common to charge, that our courts are serviceable only to the rich, we should look to it, for in that case our system is impaired at its very heart; its poise and balance are gone. *Are* our courts as available for the poor as for the rich? It is not a question of impartiality or fairness, of disposition to hear the suit of the poor as readily and as attentively as the suit of the rich. Some inferior men are no doubt appointed to our federal bench; our state courts are many of them filled by processes of election which take account of the judge's political opinions and of his service to a political party rather than of his learning or of his rank among his fellow practitioners at the bar, and many men are chosen who are not suitable either in character or attainments; but the average integrity of the American bench is extraordinarily high. There are not many courts of which it can justly be said that a man will be denied his legal rights because he is poor or without influential connections. The question I raise is of another kind. Are not poor men in fact excluded from our courts by the cost and the length of their processes? The rich man can afford the cost of litigation; what is of more consequence, he can afford the delays of trial and appeal; he has a margin of resources which makes it possible for him to wait the months, it may be the years, during which the process of adjudication will drag on and during which the rights he is contesting will be suspended, the interests involved tied up. But the poor man can afford neither the one nor the other. He might afford the initial expense, if he could be secure against delays; but delays he cannot abide without ruin. I fear that it must be admitted that our present processes of adjudication lack both simplicity and promptness, that they are unnecessarily expensive, and that a rich litigant can almost always tire a poor one out and readily cheat him of his rights by simply leading him through an endless maze of appeals and technical delays.

If this be true, our very constitutional principle has fallen into dangerous disrepair, and our immediate duty is to amend and simplify our processes of justice. There is no guarantee of liberty under a system like ours, if the courts be not as accessible and as serviceable to the poor man as to the rich. Of course, they never can be so literally. The processes of justice must always, if they are to be thorough, be deliberate, not hurried, often elaborate, not always simple. Even if they were available to the poor man without any cost whatever in money, they must in any case cost him something in time and trouble; and the very poor, tied to their tasks in fear of momentary need, cannot spend time or attention on anything which does not earn them bread. But it were shame upon us if we could not bring our courts nearer to the poor man than they are now, and the most immediately necessary reform of our system lies in that direction. The individual of whatever grade or character must be afforded opportunity to take care of himself, whether against the power of his neighbor or against the power of the government.

I have spoken of the state and federal courts without discrimination. They are all branches of the people's forum. Constitutional questions may be determined by them all, of whatever grade, because individual rights must be adjudicated by them all. But it is interesting to observe the line that runs between state and federal jurisdictions. It affords a sort of insight into the character of our complex constitutional system which no other part of our study can afford. The political relations between the states and the federal government I shall consider in another lecture, and inasmuch as their political relations rest in large measure in a system like ours upon their legal relations, I will reserve also the greater part of what I have to say about the law of their union and separation until all parts of the picture may be put together in a single sketch. But some part of the matter lies immediately under our eyes here.

The tests of the federal Constitution can be applied in the state courts, and the tests of the state constitutions in the federal courts, but only in such a way as to make the federal courts the final judges of what the meaning and intent of the federal Constitution is, and the state courts the final judges and interpreters of what the state constitutions forbid or require. The Constitution of the United States makes the federal courts the forum for the trial, not only of cases arising under federal law, but also for the trial of suits between litigants who are citizens of different states and who have therefore no other common tribunal. Cases between citizens of different states need not be tried in the courts of the United States, if the litigants are content to submit them to the courts of the state in which the cause of action arose; but the federal courts are open to them; and if in such a case tried in them it should become necessary to interpret the provisions of a state constitution, the federal courts must of course attempt that interpretation as they would attempt any other question the case might bring under their examination. But they would feel themselves obliged to adopt the interpretation already put upon those provisions by the courts of the state whose constitution was under examination. Only when there were no decisions of the courts of the state upon the subject would they feel at liberty to follow their own reading and interpretation. The courts of the United States have not the right to impose upon litigants their own interpretations of the fundamental law of a state when that law in no way involves the jurisdiction or the authority of the federal government, and in the trial of ordinary cases between citizens of different states they must hold themselves to the administration of state laws as they are interpreted by the courts of the states in which they originated.

Similarly, the courts of the states are at liberty to determine cases which involve an interpretation of the Constitution of the United States. No question is foreign to them which belongs to a case regularly instituted before them; but they in their turn are bound to follow in such matters the decisions of the courts of the United States, so far as they may have covered the matter drawn in question. The courts of the United States must be the ultimate judges of the meaning and intent of federal law, as the courts of the states are of the principles of state law. A litigant in a state court may contend, for example, that some statute, or even some constitutional provision, of the state, under which his opponent is suing him or making defense, is inconsistent with the Constitution of the United States. If the court uphold him in this contention and treat the law which he challenges as null and void because inconsistent with federal law, there is an end of the matter. The court has upheld federal law against the law of the state,

and no appeal can be taken to a court of the United States,—
which could do no more. But if the court disallow the plea and
declare the state law valid notwithstanding its alleged conflict
with the law of the United States, the defeated litigant may take
an appeal to the courts of the United States; for with a federal
tribunal must lie the final determination of the conflict, lest the
state court might have been biased in favor of the law and
privilege of the state under whose authority it acted.

The significance of this principle of action is that the federal
government is, through its courts, in effect made the final judge
of its own powers. In no case can a conflict of authority between
it and the government of a state be finally decided against it by
a state court, by any court but its own, if the parties in interest
choose to appeal. The whole balance of our federal system, therefore, lies in the federal courts. It is inevitable that it should be so.
Our constitutional law could have no final certainty otherwise.
"This Constitution, and the Laws of the United States which are
made in Pursuance thereof; and all Treaties made, or which shall
be made, under the authority of the United States shall be the
supreme Law of the Land; and the Judges in every State shall be
bound thereby, any Thing in the Constitution or Laws of any State
to the Contrary notwithstanding": such is the definite, uncom-
promising language of the Constitution of the United States. No
one can doubt that it was necessary for the maintenance of the
system that the courts of the federal government should be the
arbiters of all questions of disputed jurisdiction or conflicting
authority. But of course such a principle constitutes the courts
of the United States the guardians of our whole legal development. With them must lie the final statesmanship of control.

For by according such powers to our courts we virtually vest
in them the statesmanship of control. The Constitution is not a
mere lawyers' document: it is, as I have more than once said,
the vehicle of a nation's life. No lawyer can read into a document
anything subsequent to its execution; but we have read into
the Constitution of the United States the whole expansion and
transformation of our national life that has followed its adoption.
We can say without the least disparagement or even criticism
of the Supreme Court of the United States that at its hands the
Constitution has received an adaptation and an elaboration which
would fill its framers of the simple days of 1787 with nothing less
than amazement. The explicitly granted powers of the Constitution are what they always were; but the powers drawn from it by
implication have grown and multiplied beyond all expectation,

and each generation of statesmen looks to the Supreme Court to supply the interpretation which will serve the needs of the day. It is a process necessary but full of peril. It is easier to form programs than to exercise a wise and moderate control, and the task of the courts calls for more poise, nicer discriminations of conscience, a steadier view of affairs, and a better knowledge of the principles of right action, than the task of Congress or of the President. Both the safety and the purity of our system depend on the wisdom and the good conscience of the Supreme Court. Expanded and adapted by interpretation the powers granted in the Constitution must be; but the manner and the motive of their expansion involve the integrity, and therefore the permanence, of our entire system of government.

By common consent the most notable and one of the most statesmanlike figures in our whole judicial history is the figure of John Marshall. No other name is comparable with his in fame or honor in this singular field of statesmanlike judicial control,— a field of our own marking out and creation, a statesmanship peculiar to our own annals. Marshall may be said to have created for us the principles of interpretation which have governed our national development. He created them like a great lawyer, master of the fundamental conceptions which have enlightened all great lawyers in the administration of law and have made it seem in their hands a system of life, not a mere body of technical rules; he created them also like a great statesman who sees his way as clearly without precedent as with it to those renderings of charter and statute which will vivify their spirit and enlarge their letter without straining a single tissue of the vital stuff of which they are made.

A thoughtful English judge has distinguished between those extensions of the meaning of law by interpretation which are the product of insight and conceived in the spirit of the law itself, and those which are the product of sheer will, of the mere determination that the law shall mean what it is convenient to have it mean. Marshall's interpretations were the products of insight. His learning was the learning of the seer, saturated with the spirit of the law, instinct with its principle of growth. No other method, no other principle has legitimate place in a system which depends for its very life upon its integrity, upon the candor and good conscience of its processes, upon keeping faith with its standards and its immemorial promises.

One of the most dramatic and interesting scenes in our history, the scene with which the imagination of the historian who is keenly alive to those processes of constitutional development which have made the nation and yet have threatened to unmake it is most engaged, is that enacted on the fourth of March, 1829, when Andrew Jackson, the sincere apostle of principles of action which were apt to make light of law, was sworn into office by John Marshall, the aged Chief Justice at whose hands the law of the nation had received alike its majesty and its liberal spirit of ordered progress. Jackson himself was not young. He had grown gray in having his own way, in acting upon principles he deemed right, whether they had the warrant of law or not;—no outlaw; on the contrary, a man of conscience and honor, but habituated to the principles of the frontier and of the field of battle, where action did not wait upon law but formed itself on the exigencies of the occasion. He took the oath of office in all solemnity and good faith, swearing "to the best of his ability to preserve, protect, and defend the Constitution of the United States." But he afterward explained, when he chose to ignore the decisions of the Supreme Court, uttered by Chief Justice Marshall in authoritative interpretation of the Constitution, that he had sworn to uphold and preserve it as he understood it, and would take no dictation as to its meaning from any source but his own intelligence and conscience. The two men were at the antipodes from one another both in principle and in character; had no common insight into the institutions of the country which they served; represented one the statesmanship of will and the other the statesmanship of control. General Jackson was a brave man, devoted to the performance of his duty with a genuine ardor of unselfish patriotism, and rendered services in his administration of the great office he held for which he must always be honored so long as the large interests of the nation are understood; but he was the sort of man who might very easily twist and destroy our whole constitutional system, were the courts robbed of their authority and the great balance-wheel of their power shaken from its gearings. One might moralize upon the picture of these two old men standing there face to face at Jackson's inauguration until he had expounded the very genius of our institutions. Marshall, putting the oath of office to Jackson, was repeating in quiet, modern form the transaction of Runnymede.

Some German critics of our constitutional system, trained in another school of politics and another school of law, have looked upon the powers of our courts as a dangerous anomaly. We have, they say, taken our courts out of their proper sphere and put them where courts do not belong, in the field of politics, where they are set as masters over Congress and the President by whom the policies of the nation are formed. But such criticisms ignore both the principle of constitutional government and the actual practice of our courts. They emanate from men for whom all law is the voice of government and who regard the government as the source of all law, who cannot conceive of a law set above government and to which it must conform. It must be admitted that such a law is not everywhere essential to the maintenance of constitutional government. The English nation restrains its king by written compact, but it has never restrained its Parliament. Parliament its law leaves supreme because Parliament is representative of the nation, and opinion is strong and concerted enough to restrain it without law and the assistance of the courts. But we faced a very singular task when we undertook to combine the one-time colonies of England in America into a constitutional federal state. There had been no time to form a national habit or accumulate precedents with regard to a common government. It was necessary to create it by law, to accommodate its various parts to one another by law, to define both its powers and the relations of the people to it by law. No other constitutional understanding was ever quite so detailed or so definite, no other constitutional understanding ever rested upon just such foundations of circumstance and purpose.

But we did not, with all our inventing, create anything abnormal or unnatural; and our continental critics mistake the actual practice of our courts in acting upon constitutional questions. They do not act as instruments of politics, but only as modest instruments of law, as any other courts would. A very superficial examination of the constitutional decisions of the Supreme Court of the United States will suffice to show how careful it has been to refrain from even the appearance of dictating to Congress or to the executive. It has sought to respect their authority and to give full scope to their discretion in every possible way, at every possible point, never setting its judgment or opinion against theirs in any case which admitted of reasonable doubt, never drawing political questions into discussion, but confining itself most scrupulously to its proper business of adjudicating individual rights, whether those rights arise under the Constitution or under statutes; and it has demanded that a very clear case be made out against any act of Congress said by the litigants before it to be unconstitutional, before it would venture to set aside what Congress had ordained. In no instance has it acted upon political grounds when setting aside an act of Congress, but always upon clearly defined legal grounds, because the act had been shown to be inconsistent with indisputable provisions of the fundamental charter of the government itself. There could be no alternative in the case of a government of limited and specified powers.

And there has never been any serious friction between Congress and the courts. Occasional irritation there has been, of course. Congressmen have sometimes, forgetting their constitutional principles, spoken in sharp and resentful criticism of the presumption of federal judges who have declared favorite pieces of legislation unconstitutional and refused to execute statutes by means of which politicians had hoped to store up credit to themselves or their party. Senators have shown a particular sensitiveness in the matter. There are many distinguished lawyers in the Senate whose opinion upon points of law ought no doubt to be regarded as individually quite as weighty and conclusive as that of a district or circuit judge of the United States who has declined to enforce acts which had passed under their scrutiny. Second-class lawyers, it has been said in heat, men who had themselves once been members of the House or Senate and who had there shown their inferiority in legal discussion, venture, when appointed to seats on the bench, to set aside the judgments of the very men who formerly worsted them in debate upon those very questions. But members of Congress must usually be patient under these crosses. They will often remember that it was upon their own recommendation that these very men, their one-time comrades, were appointed by the President; that the appointments passed the scrutiny of the Judiciary Committee of the Senate and were confirmed; and that the point of view of the lawyer in Congress is after all not always the point of view of the lawyer on the bench, whose concern is not with political considerations, but with the legal rights of the litigants before him and the exact maintenance of the terms of the law.

There are instances which they will recall which are full of instruction. Mr. Salmon P. Chase, when Secretary of the Treasury under Mr. Lincoln, advocated the issue of irredeemable paper currency in relief of the Treasury, and was largely instrumental in inducing Congress to pass the statutes which filled the country with "greenbacks," declaring it to be his opinion that such issues were legal under the powers granted Congress in the Constitution; but Mr. Salmon P. Chase, when afterward Chief Justice of the United States, joined with the majority of that great court in declaring the legal tender acts unconstitutional. The thing might happen with the most conscientious lawyer. It is one thing to have to decide a matter of that kind in connection with important business you are conducting, and it is quite another thing to have it to decide as a judge lifted above all personal interest in the matter and bidden take it upon its merits, not as an advocate but as an arbiter.

Undoubtedly federal judges may be mistaken and lawyers in Congress right, if the lawyers in Congress be of better stuff morally and intellectually than the judges they have recommended or allowed the President to appoint; but that simply points an old moral. No part of any government is any better than the men who administer it. A distinguished member of a well-known reform club once told me that after twenty years of hard work in trying to further the objects of good government to which the club had devoted itself, he had a very humiliating confession to make. Throughout all those years he had labored assiduously to get the laws of the State in which he lived modified and improved, and to have all practices of which his club disapproved in state or city governments made illegal by statute. Year after year he had gone to the capital of the state and pressed every legitimate influence he could command to induce the legislature to enact the desired laws, and once and again he had succeeded. But government did not seem to be reformed, whatever his success. Old practices went on unchecked, or took new forms, or eluded the processes of law. It was a long lesson, and he had very stubbornly refused to learn it, but he had learned it at last and was now ready to make his confession that after all he had been mistaken: the way to reform government was to elect good men to conduct it, and that was the whole matter. Good laws were desirable, but good men were indispensable, and could make even bad laws yield pure and righteous government.

Every government is a government of men, not of laws, and of course the courts of the United States are no wiser or better than the judges who constitute them. A series of bad appointments might easily make them inferior to every other branch of the government in their comprehension of constitutional principles, their perception of constitutional values. But that would be because the government had fallen into wrong hands, and would not invalidate the principle upon which our courts are constituted and empowered. It is an argument for electing the right men to the presidency and to the Senate, which confirms the President's appointments; it is not an argument for changing our constitutional arrangements. The constitutional powers of the courts are no less indispensable, no less central and essential to our whole system and conception of government, because they are sometimes unwise or unintelligent in their exercise of them.

Indeed, it is not easy to speak of this subject, so fundamental, so deeply significant, without pausing to point out the interesting interdependence of the several parts of our government and the many contingencies upon which their excellence and their integrity depend. The courts of the United States control the action of the other branches of the government in the interest of our fundamental constitutional understandings; and yet the courts of the United States are constituted by federal statute and by the President's appointment. The judicial power of the United States is vested "in one Supreme Court and in such inferior courts as Congress may from time to time ordain and establish"; only the Supreme Court exists by direct provision of the Constitution itself. Other courts Congress may establish or abolish, increase or decrease, assign to this jurisdiction or to that. The Constitution provides, indeed, that all judges of the United States shall hold their offices during good behavior, but Congress could readily overcome a hostile majority in any court or in any set of courts, even in the Supreme Court itself, by a sufficient increase in the number of judges and an adroit manipulation of jurisdictions, and could with the assistance of the President make them up to suit its own purposes. These two "coördinate" branches of the government, to which the courts speak in such authoritative fashion with regard to the powers they may and may not exercise under the Constitution,—namely, Congress and the executive,—may, in fact, if they choose, manipulate the courts to their own ends without formal violation of any provision of the fundamental law of the land. There has never been any serious fear that they would do anything of the kind, though an occasional appointment to the Supreme Court has made the country suspicious and uneasy. But it is well to keep the matter clearly before us, if only that we may remind ourselves of the only absolute safeguards of a constitutional system. They lie in the character, the independence, the resolution, the right purpose of the men who vote and who choose the public servants of whom the government is to consist. Any government can be corrupted, any government may fall into disrepair. It consists of men, and the men of whom it consists will be no better than the men who choose them. The courts are the people's forum; they are also the index of the government's and of the nation's character.

The weightiest import of the matter is seen only when it is remembered that the courts are the instruments of the nation's growth, and that the way in which they serve that use will have much to do with the integrity of every national process. If they determine what powers are to be exercised under the Constitution, they by the same token determine also the adequacy of the Constitution in respect of the needs and interests of the nation; our conscience in matters of law and our opportunity in matters of politics are in their hands. There is so much to justify the criticism of our German critics; but they have not put their fingers upon the right point of criticism. It is not true that in judging of what Congress or the President has done, our courts enter the natural field of discretion or of judgment which belongs to other branches of government,—a field in its nature political, where lie the choices of policy and of authority. That field they respectfully avoid, and confine themselves to the necessary conclusions drawn from written law. But it is true that their power is political; that if they had interpreted the Constitution in its strict letter, as some proposed, and not in its spirit, like the charter of a business corporation and not like the charter of a living government, the vehicle of a nation's life, it would have proved a strait-jacket, a means not of liberty and development, but of mere restriction and embarrassment. I have spoken of the statesmanship of control expected of our courts; but there is also the statesmanship of adaptation characteristic of all great systems of law since the days of the Roman prætor; and there can be no doubt that we have been singular among the nations in looking to our courts for that double function of statesmanship, for the means of growth as well as for the restraint of ordered method.

But our courts have stood the test, chiefly because John Marshall presided over their processes during the formative period of our national life. He was of the school and temper of Washington. He read constitutions in search of their spirit and purpose and understood them in the light of the conceptions under the influence of which they were framed. He saw in them not mere negations of power, but grants of power, and he reasoned from out the large political experience of the race as to what those grants meant, what they were intended to accomplish, not as a pedant but as a statesman, rather; and every generation of statesmen since his day have recognized the fact that it was he more than the men in Congress or in the President's chair who gave to our federal government its scope and power. The greatest statesmen are always those who attempt their tasks with imagination, with a large vision of things to come, but with the conscience of the lawyer, also, the knowledge that law must be built, not wrested, to their use and purpose. And so, whether by force of circumstance or by deliberate design, we have married legislation with adjudication and look for statesmanship in our courts.

No one can truly say that our courts have held us back or have ever exhibited a spirit of mere literalness and reaction. Many a series of cases has built the implications of the Constitution out to meet the needs and the changing circumstances of the nation's life. The process has seemed at times a little too facile. The courts have seemed upon occasion to seek in the law what they wished to find rather than what frank and legitimate inference would yield. Once and again they have been all too complacent in giving Congress leave to read its powers as best suited its convenience at a particular exigency in affairs. It is to be feared that they did so in connection with the many difficult questions which arose in regard to the settlements which followed upon the war between the states. But for the most part their method and their inferences have been conservative enough. The wonder is that they have kept so level a keel while serving a nation which has always insisted upon carrying so much sail.

When the Constitution was framed there were no railways, there was no telegraph, there was no telephone. The Supreme Court has read the power of Congress to establish post-offices and post-roads and to regulate commerce with foreign nations and among the several states to mean that it has jurisdiction over practically every matter connected with intercouse between the states. Railways are highways; telegraph and telephone lines are new forms of the post. The Constitution was not meant to hold the government back to the time of horses and wagons, the time when postboys carried every communication that passed from merchant to merchant, when trade had few long routes within the nation and did not venture in bulk beyond neighborhood transactions. The United States have clearly from generation to generation been taking on more and more of the characteristics of a community; more and more have their economic interests come to seem common interests; and the courts have rightly endeavored to make the Constitution a suitable instrument of the national life, extending to the things that are now common the rules that it established for similar things that were common at the beginning.

The real difficulty has been to draw the line where this process of expansion and adaptation ceases to be legitimate and becomes a mere act of will on the part of the government, served by the courts. The temptation to overstep the proper boundaries has been particularly great in interpreting the meaning of the words, "commerce among the several states." Manifestly, in a commercial nation almost every item of life directly or indirectly affects commerce, and our commerce is almost all of it on the grand scale. There is a vast deal of buying and selling, of course, within the boundaries of each state, but even the buying and selling which is done within a single state constitutes in our day but a part of that great movement of merchandise along lines of railway and watercourse which runs without limit and without regard to political jurisdiction. State commerce seems almost impossible to distinguish from interstate commerce. It has all come to seem part of what Congress may unquestionably regulate, though the makers of the Constitution may never have dreamed of anything like it and the tremendous interests which it affects. Which part of the complex thing may Congress regulate?

Clearly, any part of the actual movement of merchandise and persons from state to state. May it also regulate the conditions under which the merchandise is produced which is presently to become the subject-matter of interstate commerce? May it regulate the conditions of labor in field and factory? Clearly not, I should say; and I should think that any thoughtful lawyer who felt himself at liberty to be frank would agree with me. For that would be to destroy all lines of division between the field of state legislation and the field of federal legislation. Back of the conditions of labor in the field and in the factory lie all the intimate matters of morals and of domestic and business relationship which have always been recognized as the undisputed field of state law; and these conditions that lie back of labor may easily be shown to have their part in determining the character and efficiency of commerce between the states. If the federal power does not end with the regulation of the actual movements of trade, it ends nowhere, and the line between state and federal jurisdiction is obliterated. But this is not universally seen or admitted. It is, therefore, one of the things upon which the conscience of the nation must make test of itself, to see if it still retain that spirit of constitutional understanding which is the only ultimate prop and support of constitutional government. It is questions of this sort that show the true relation of our courts to our national character and our system of government.

The relation of the courts to opinion is a difficult matter to state, and as delicate as difficult; yet it lies directly in our path. I have pointed out in previous lectures that opinion was the great, indeed the only, coördinating force in our system; that the only thing that gave the President an opportunity to make good his leadership of his party and of the nation as against the resistance or the indifference of the House or Senate was his close and especial relation to opinion the nation over, and that, without some such leadership as opinion might sustain the President in exercising within the just limits of the law, our system would be checked of all movement, deprived of all practical synthesis by its complicated system of checks and counterpoises. What relation, then, are the courts to bear to opinion? The only answer that can be made is this: judges of necessity belong to their own generation. The atmosphere of opinion cannot be shut out of their court rooms. Its influence penetrates everywhere in every self-governed nation. What we should ask of our judges is that they prove themselves such men as can discriminate between the opinion of the moment and the opinion of the age, between the opinion which springs, a legitimate essence, from the enlightened judgment of men of thought and good conscience, and the opinion of desire, of self-interest, of impulse and impatience. What we should ask of ourselves is that we sustain the courts in the maintenance of the true balance between law and progress, and that we make it our desire to secure nothing which cannot be secured by the just and thoughtful processes which have made our system, so far, a model before all the world of the reign of law.

VII

THE STATES AND THE FEDERAL GOVERNMENT

THE question of the relation of the States to the federal government is the cardinal question of our constitutional system. At every turn of our national development we have been brought face to face with it, and no definition either of statesmen or of judges has ever quieted or decided it. It cannot, indeed, be settled by the opinion of any one generation, because it is a question of growth, and every successive stage of our political and economic development gives it a new aspect, makes it a new question. The general lines of definition which were to run between the powers granted to Congress and the powers reserved to the States the makers of the Constitution were able to draw with their characteristic foresight and lucidity; but the subject-matter of that definition is constantly changing, for it is the life of the nation itself. Our activities change alike their scope and their character with every generation. The old measures of the Constitution are every day to be filled with new grain as the varying crop of circumstances comes to maturity. It is clear enough that the general commercial interests, the general financial interests, the general economic interests of the country, were meant to be brought under the regulation of the federal government, which should act for all; and it is equally clear that what are the general commercial interests, what the general financial interests, what the general economic interests of the country, is a question of fact, to be determined by circumstances which change under our very eyes, and that, case by case, we are inevitably drawn on to include under the established definitions of the law matters new and unforeseen, which seem in their magnitude to give to the powers of Congress a sweep and vigor certainly never conceived possible by earlier generations of statesmen, sometimes almost revolutionary even in our own eyes. The subject-matter of this troublesome definition is the living body of affairs. To analyze it is to analyze the life of the nation.

It is difficult to discuss so critical and fundamental a question calmly and without party heat or bias when it has come once more, as it has now, to an acute stage. Just because it lies at the heart of our constitutional system to decide it wrongly is to alter the whole structure and operation of our government, for good or for evil, and one would wish never to see the passion of party touch it to distort it. A sobering sense of responsibility should fall upon every one who handles it. No man should argue it this way or that for party advantage. Desire to bring the impartial truth to light must, in such a case, be the first dictate alike of true statesmanship and of true patriotism. Every man should seek to think of it and to speak of it in the true spirit of the founders of the government and of all those who have spent their lives in the effort to confirm its just principles both in counsel and in action.

Almost every great internal crisis in our affairs has turned upon the question of state and federal rights. To take but two instances, it was the central subject-matter of the great controversy over tariff legislation which led to attempted nullification and of the still greater controversy over the extension of slavery which led to the war between the States; and those two controversies did more than any others in our history to determine the scope and character of the federal government.

The principle of the division of powers between state and federal governments is a very simple one when stated in its most general terms. It is that the legislatures of the States shall have control of all the general subject-matter of law, of private rights of every kind, of local interests, and of everything that directly concerns their people as communities,—free choice with regard to all matters of local regulation and development, and that Congress shall have control only of such matters as concern the peace and the commerce of the country as a whole. The opponents of the tariff of 1824 objected to the tariff system which Congress was so rapidly building up, that it went much beyond the simple and quite legitimate object of providing the federal government with revenue in such a way as to stimulate with too much disturbing the natural development of the industries of the country, and was unmistakably intended to guide and determine the whole trend of the nation's economic evolution, preferring the industries of one section of the country to those of another in its bestowal of protection and encouragement, and so depriving the States as self-governing communities of all free economic choice in the development of their resources. Congress persisted in its course; nullification failed as even so much as an effectual protest against the power of a government of which General Jackson was the head,—never so sure he was right as when he was opposed; and a critical matter, of lasting importance, was decided. The federal government was conceded the power to determine the economic opportunities of the States. It was suffered to become a general providence, to which each part of the country must look for its chance to make lucrative use of its material resources.

The slavery question, though it cut deeper into the social structure of a great section of the country and contained such heat as could not, when once given vent, be restrained from breaking into flame, as the tariff controversy had been, was, after all, a no more fundamental question, in its first essential form, than the question of the tariff. Could Congress exclude slavery from the territories of the United States and from newly formed States? If it could, manifestly the slavery system, once restricted in territory, would in time die of the strictures which bound it. Mr. Lincoln was quite right when he said that no nation could exist half slave and half free. But that was only by consequence. The immediate question was the power of Congress to determine the internal social and economic structure of society in the several States thereafter to be formed. It is not to my present purpose to trace the circumstances and influences which brought on the Civil War. The abolition of slavery by war, though natural, was not the necessary or logical *legal* consequence of the contention that Congress legitimately possessed the power which it had exercised in the constitution of the Northwest Territory and in the enactment of the Missouri Compromise. What happened before the momentous struggle was over came about by the mere logic of human nature, under stress of human passion. What concerns me in the present discussion is that here, again, as in the building up of a fostering tariff, what turned out to be a far-reaching change in the very conception of federal power had as its central point of controversy the question of the powers of the States as against the powers of the government at Washington. The whole spirit and action of the government were deeply altered in carrying that question one stage further towards a settlement.

And I am particularly interested to point out that here again, as in the tariff question, it was an inevitable controversy, springing, not out of theory, not out of the uneasy ambition of statesmen, but out of mere growth and imperious circumstance, out of the actual movement of affairs. Population was spreading over the great western areas of the country; new communities were forming, upon which lawyers could lay no binding prescriptions as to the life they should lead; new Territories were constantly to be organized, new States constantly to be admitted to the Union. A choice which every day assumed new forms was thrust upon Congress. Events gave it its variety, and Congress could not avoid the influences of opinion, which altered as circumstances changed, as it became more and more clear what the nation was to be. It was of the very stuff of daily business, forced upon Congress by the opinion of the country, to answer the inevitable question, What shall these new communities be allowed to do with themselves, what shall they be suffered to make of the nation? May Congress determine, or is it estopped by the reserved powers of the States? The choices of growth cannot be postponed, and they seem always to turn upon some definition of the powers of Congress, some new doubt as to where the powers of the States leave off and the powers of the federal government begin.

And now the question has come upon us anew. It is no longer sectional, but it is all the more subtle and intricate, all the less obvious and tangible in its elements, on that account. It involves, first or last, the whole economic movement of the age, and necessitates an analysis which has not yet been even seriously attempted. Which parts of the many sided processes of the nation's economic development shall be left to the regulation of the States, which parts shall be given over to the regulation of the federal government? I do not propound this as a mere question of choice, a mere question of statesmanship, but also as a question, a very fundamental question, of constitutional law. What, reading our Constitution in its true spirit, neither sticking in its letter nor yet forcing it arbitrarily to mean what we wish it to mean, shall be the answer of our generation, pressed upon by gigantic economic problems the solution of which may involve not only the prosperity but also the very integrity of the nation, to the old question of the distribution of powers between Congress and the States? For us, as for previous generations, it is a deeply critical question. The very stuff of all our political principles, of all our political experience, is involved in it. In this all too indistinctly marked field of right choice our statesmanship shall achieve new triumphs or come to calamitous shipwreck.

The old theory of the sovereignty of the States, which used so to engage our passions, has lost its vitality. The war between the States established at least this principle, that the federal government is, through its courts, the final judge of its own powers. Since that stern arbitrament it would be idle, in any practical argument, to ask by what law of abstract principle the federal government is bound and restrained. Its power is "to regulate commerce between the States," and the attempts now made during every session of Congress to carry the implications of that power beyond the utmost boundaries of reasonable and honest inference show that the only limits likely to be observed by politicians are those set by the good sense and conservative temper of the country.

The proposed federal legislation with regard to the regulation of child labor affords a striking example.[4] If the power to regulate commerce between the States can be stretched to include the

---

[4] Wilson here refers to a bill first introduced in the United States Senate by Albert J. Beveridge of Indiana on December 5, 1906. The culmination of steadily increasing agitation against the abuses of child labor since the 1890's, the measure was the first attempt to secure federal legislation on this subject. It prohibited any carrier from transporting in interstate commerce the products of any mine or factory that had not filed an affidavit that no children under fourteen were employed. Severe penalties were prescribed for violations, and enforcement was to be in the hands of federal district attorneys.

Although the bill had the support (later withdrawn) of the National Child Labor Committee, Beveridge failed to win its endorsement by the American Federation of Labor. Moreover, President Theodore Roosevelt refused to support it because he doubted its constitutionality and was unwilling to risk his prestige in what might be a losing fight in Congress. In his Annual Message to Congress in December 1906, Roosevelt only urged that Congress authorize an investigation by the Bureau of Labor into the conditions of labor of women and children and suggested the passage of a model child labor law for the District of Columbia. Congress authorized the investigation and enacted the District of Columbia bill in May 1908. However, the Beveridge national child labor bill never passed either house of Congress. For a thorough discussion of Beveridge's bill and the early history of child labor reform, see John Braeman, "Albert J. Beveridge and the First National Child Labor Bill," *Indiana Magazine of History*, LX (March 1964), 1-36. A briefer treatment appears in John Braeman, *Albert J. Beveridge: American Nationalist* (Chicago, 1971), pp. 112-21.

regulation of labor in mills and factories, it can be made to embrace every particular of the industrial organization and action of the country. The only limitations Congress would observe, should the Supreme Court assent to such obviously absurd extravagancies of interpretation, would be the limitations of opinion and of circumstance.

It is important, therefore, to look at the facts and to understand the real character of the political and economic materials of our own day very clearly and with a statesmanlike vision, as the makers of the Constitution understood the conditions they dealt with. If the jealousies of the colonies and of the little States which sprang out of them had not obliged the makers of the Constitution to leave the greater part of legal regulation in the hands of the States, it would have been wise, it would even have been necessary, to invent such a division of powers as was actually agreed upon. It is not, at bottom, a question of sovereignty or of any other political abstraction; it is a question of vitality. Uniform regulation of the economic conditions of a vast territory and a various people like the United States would be mischievous, if not impossible. The statesmanship which really attempts it is premature and unwise. Undoubtedly the recent economic development of the country, particularly the development of the last two decades, has obliterated many boundaries, made many interests national and common, which until our own day were separate and local; but the lines of these great changes we have not yet clearly traced or studiously enough considered. To distinguish them and provide for them is the task which is to test the statesmanship of our generation; and it is already plain that, great as they are, these new combinations of interest have not yet gone so far as to make the States mere units of local government. Not our legal conscience merely, but our practical interests as well, call upon us to discriminate and be careful, with the care of men who handle the vital stuff of a great constitutional government.

The United States are not a single, homogeneous community. In spite of a certain superficial sameness which seems to impart to Americans a common type and point of view, they still contain communities at almost every stage of development, illustrating in their social and economic structure almost every modern variety of interest and prejudice, following occupations of every kind, in climates of every sort that the temperate zone affords. This variety of fact and condition, these substantial economic and social contrasts, do not in all cases follow state lines. They are often contrasts between region and region rather than between State and State. But they are none the less real, and are in many instances permanent and ineradicable.

From the first the United States have been socially and economically divided into regions rather than into States. The New England States have always been in most respects of a piece; the southern States have had always more interest in common than points of contrast; and the Middle States were so similarly compounded even in the day of the erection of the government that they might without material inconvenience have been treated as a single economic and political unit. These first members of the Union did, indeed, have an intense historical individuality which made them easily distinguishable and rendered it impossible, had any one dreamed of it, to treat them as anything but what they were, actual communities, quick with a character and purpose of their own. Throughout the earlier process of our national expansion, States formed themselves, for the most part, upon geographical lines marked out by nature, within the limiting flood of great rivers or the lifted masses of great mountain chains, with here and there a mere parallel of latitude for frontier, but generally within plots of natural limit where those who set up homes felt some essential and obvious tie of political union draw them together. In later years, when States were to be created upon the great plains which stretched their fertile breadths upon the broad mid-surfaces of the continent, the lines chosen for boundaries were those which had been run by the theodolite of the public surveyor, and States began to be disposed upon the map like squares upon a great chessboard, where the human pieces of the future game of politics might come to be moved very much at will and no distinct economic, though many social, varieties were to be noted among neighbor commonwealths.

But, while division by survey instead of by life and historical circumstance no doubt created some artificial political divisions, with regard to which the old theories of separate political sovereignty seemed inapplicable enough, the contrasts between region and region were in no way affected; and resemblances were rendered no more striking than the differences which remained. We have been familiar from the first with groups of States united in interest and character; we have been familiar from the first, also, with groups of States contrasted by obvious differences of occupation and of development. These differences are almost as marked now as they ever were, and the vital growth of the nation depends upon our recognizing and providing for them. It will be checked and permanently embarrassed by ignoring them.

We are too apt to think that our American political system is distinguished by its central structure, by its President and Congress and courts, which the Constitution of the Union set up. As a matter of fact, it is distinguished by its local structure, by the extreme vitality of its parts. It would be an impossibility without its division of powers. From the first America has been a nation in the making. It has come to maturity by the stimulation of no central force or guidance, but by an abounding self-helping, self-sufficing energy in its parts, which severally brought themselves into existence and added themselves to the Union, pleasing first of all themselves in the framing of their laws and constitutions, not asking leave to exist and constitute themselves, but existing first and asking leave afterwards, self-originated, self-constituted, self-confident, self-sustaining, veritable communities, demanding only recognition. Communities develop, not by external but by internal forces. Else they do not live at all. Our commonwealths have not come into existence by invitation, like plants in a tended garden; they have sprung up of themselves, irrepressible, a sturdy, spontaneous product of the nature of men nurtured in a free air.

It is this spontaneity and variety, this independent and irrepressible life of its communities, that has given our system its extraordinary elasticity, which has preserved it from the paralysis which has sooner or later fallen upon every people who have looked to their central government to patronize and nurture them. It is this, also, which has made our political system so admirable an instrumentality of vital constitutional understandings. Throughout these lectures I have described constitutional government as that which is maintained upon the basis of an intimate understanding between those who conduct government and those who obey it. Nowhere has it been possible to maintain such understandings more successfully or with a nicer adjustment to every variety of circumstance than in the United States. The distribution of the chief powers of government among the States is the localization and specialization of constitutional understandings; and this elastic adaptation of constitutional processes to the various and changing conditions of a new country and a vast area has been the real cause of our political success.

The division of powers between the States and the federal government effected by our federal Constitution was the normal and natural division for this purpose. Under it the States possess all the ordinary legal choices that shape a people's life. Theirs is the whole of the ordinary field of law; the regulation of domestic relations and of the relations between employer and employe, the determination of property rights and of the validity and enforcement of contracts, the definition of crimes and their punishment, the definition of the many and subtle rights and obligations which lie outside the fields of property and contract, the establishment of the laws of incorporation and of the rules governing the conduct of every kind of business. The presumption insisted upon by the courts in every argument with regard to the powers of the federal government is that it has no power not explicitly granted it by the federal Constitution or reasonably to be inferred as the natural or necessary accompaniment of the powers there indisputably conveyed to it; but the presumption with regard to the powers of the States they have always held to be of exactly the opposite kind. It is that the States of course possess every power that government has ever anywhere exercised, except only those powers which their own constitutions or the Constitution of the United States explicitly or by plain inference withhold. They are the ordinary governments of the country; the federal government is its instrument only for particular purposes.

Congress is, indeed, the immediate government of the people. It does not govern the States, but acts directly upon individuals, as directly as the governments of the States themselves. It does not stand at a distance and look on,—to be ready for an occasional interference,—but is the immediate and familiar instrument of the people in everything that it undertakes, as if there were no States. The States do not stand between it and the people. It is as intimate as they in its contact with the affairs of the country's life. But the field of its action is distinct, restricted, definite.

We are not concerned in our present discussion with its powers as representative of the people in regulating the foreign affairs of the country. The discussion of the relation of the States to the federal government does not touch that field. About it there has never been doubt or debate. Neither is the power of the federal government to tax, or to regulate the military establishments of the country, any longer in dispute, even though the federal government use its power to tax to accomplish many an indirect object of economic stimulation or control which touches the independent industrial choices of the States very nearly. The one source from which all debatable federal powers of domestic regulation now spring is the power to regulate commerce between the States.

The chief object of the Union and of the revision of the Articles of Confederation which gave us our present federal Constitution was undoubtedly commercial regulation. It was not political but economic warfare between the States which threatened the existence of the new Union and made every prospect of national growth and independence doubtful,—the warfare of selfish commercial regulation. It was intended, accordingly, that the chief, one might almost say the only, domestic power of Congress in respect of the daily life of the people should be the power to regulate commerce.

It seemed a power susceptible of very simple definition at the first. Only in our own day of extraordinary variation from the older and simpler types of industry has it assumed aspects both new and without limit of variety. It is now no longer possible to frame any simple or comprehensive definition of "commerce." Above all is it difficult to distinguish the "commerce" which is confined within the boundaries of a single State and subject to its domestic regulation from that which passes from State to State and lies within the jurisdiction of Congress. The actual interchange of goods, which, strictly speaking, is commerce, within the narrow and specific meaning of the term, is now so married to their production under our great modern industrial combinations, organization and community of interest have so obscured the differences between the several parts of business which once it was easy to discriminate, that the power to regulate commerce subtly extends its borders every year into new fields of enterprise and pries into every matter of economic effort.

Added to this doubt and difficulty of analysis which makes it a constant matter of debate what the powers of Congress are is the growing dissatisfaction with the part the States are playing in the economic life of the day. They either let the pressing problems of the time alone and attempt no regulation at all, however loudly opinion and circumstance itself may call for it, or they try every half-considered remedy, embark upon a thousand experiments, and bring utter confusion upon the industry of the country by contradicting and offsetting each other's measures. No two States act alike. Manufacturers and carriers who serve commerce in many States find it impossible to obey the laws of all, and the enforcement of the laws of the States in all their variety threatens the country with a new war of conflicting regulations as serious as that which made the Philadelphia convention of 1787 necessary and gave us a new federal Constitution. This conflict of laws in matters which vitally interest the whole country, and in which no State or region can wisely stand apart to serve any peculiar interest of its own, constitutes the greatest political danger of our day. It is more apt and powerful than any other cause to bring upon us radical and ill-considered changes. It confuses our thinking upon essential matters and makes us hasty reformers out of mere impatience. We are in danger of acting before we clearly know what we want or comprehend the consequences of what we do,—in danger of altering the character of the government in order to escape a temporary inconvenience.

We are an industrial people. The development of the resources of the country, the command of the markets of the world, is for the time being more important in our eyes than any political theory or lawyer's discrimination of functions. We are intensely "practical," moreover, and insist that every obstacle, whether of law or fact, be swept out of the way. It is not the right temper for constitutional understandings. Too "practical" a purpose may give us a government such as we never should have chosen had we made the choice more thoughtfully and deliberately. We cannot afford to belie our reputation for political sagacity and self-possession by any such hasty processes as those into which such a temper of mere impatience seems likely to hurry us.

The remedy for ill-considered legislation by the States, the remedy alike for neglect and mistake on the part of their several governments, lies, not outside the States, but within them. The mistakes which they themselves correct will sink deeper into the consciousness of their people than the mistakes which Congress may rush in to correct for them, thrusting upon them what they have not learned to desire. They will either themselves learn their mistakes, by such intimate and domestic processes as will penetrate very deep and abide with them in convincing force, or else they will prove that what might have been a mistake for other States or regions of the country was no mistake for them, and the country will have been saved its wholesome variety. In no case will their failure to correct their own measures prove that the federal government might have forced wisdom upon them.

There is, however, something else that comes to the surface, and that explains not a little of our present dissatisfaction with state legislation upon matters of vital national importance. Their failure to correct their own processes may, in fact, prove that there is something radically wrong with the structure and operation of their governments,—that they have ceased to be sensitive and efficient instruments for the creation and realization of opinion,—the real function of constitutional governments.

It is better to learn the true political lesson than merely to improve business. There is something involved which is deeper than the mere question of the distribution of legislative powers within our federal system. We have come to the test of those intimate and detailed processes of self-government to which it was supposed that our principles and our experience had committed us. There are many evidences that we are losing confidence in our state legislatures, and yet it is evident that it is through them that we attempt all the more intimate measures of self-government. To lose faith in them is to lose faith in our very system of government, and that is a very serious matter. It is this loss of confidence in our local legislatures that had led our people to give so much heed to the radical suggestions of change made by those who advocate the use of the initiative and the referendum in our processes of legislation, the virtual abandonment of the representative principle, and the attempt to put into the hands of the voters themselves the power to initiate and negative laws,—in order to enable them to do for themselves what they have not been able to get satisfactorily done through the representatives they have hitherto chosen to act for them.

Such doubts and such consequent proposals of reform should make us look deeper into this question than we have hitherto looked. It may turn out, upon examination, that what we are really dissatisfied with is not the present distribution of powers between the state and federal authorities, but the character of our state governments. If they were really governments by the people, we should not be dissatisfied with them. We are impatient of state legislatures because they seem to us less representative of the thoughtful opinion of the country than Congress is. We know that our legislatures do not think alike, but we are not sure that our people do not think alike. If there is a real variety of opinion among our people in the several regions of the country, we would be poor lovers of democratic self-government were we to wish to see those differences overridden by the majorities of a central legislature. It is to be hoped that we still sufficiently understand the real processes of political life to know that a growing country must grow, that opinion such as government can be based upon develops by experience, not by authority, that a region forced is a region dissatisfied, and that spontaneous is better, more genuine, more permanent, than forced agreement.

The truth is that our state governments are, many of them, no longer truly representative governments. We are not, in fact, dissatisfied with local representative assemblies and the gov-

ernment which they impose; we are dissatisfied, rather, with
regulations imposed by commissions and assemblies which are
no longer representative. It is a large subject, of many debatable
parts, and I can only touch upon it here, but the fact is that
we have imposed an impossible task upon our voters, and that
because it is impossible, they do not perform it. It is impossible
for the voters of any busy community actually to pick out or in
any real sense choose the very large number of persons we call
upon them under our present state constitutions to elect. They
have neither the time nor the quick and easy means of coöperation which would enable them to make up the long lists of candidates for offices, local and national, upon which they are
expected to act. They must of necessity leave the selection to a
few persons who, from one motive or another, volunteer to
make a business of it. These are the political bosses and managers whom the people obey and affect to despise. It is unjust
to despise them. Under a system of innumerable nominations
they are indispensable. A system of so-called popular elections
like ours could not be operated successfully without them. But
it is true that by their constant and professional attention to
the business of nomination a real popular choice of candidates
is done away with entirely, and that our state officers and legislators are in effect appointed, not elected. The question at an
election is only which set of appointees shall be put into office,
those appointed by the managers and bosses of this party or of
that. It is this, whether our people are distinctly conscious of
it or not, which has so seriously impaired their confidence in the
state legislatures and which has made them look about for new
means by which to obtain a real choice in affairs.

Members of Congress are themselves voted for on the lists
which the local managers prepare, are themselves appointed to
their candidacy as the candidates for local functions are, but,
because they are relatively few in number, national attention is
more or less concentrated upon them. There is a more general interest in their selection, by which party managers are sure to be
somewhat checked and guided. After their election, moreover,
they become members of an assembly highly organized and
disciplined, and are under a very strict party responsibility in
which the personal force and character of the Speaker of the
House play a greater part than their own. The man by whom they
are led is scarcely less conspicuous as a national figure than the
President himself, and ordinary members are but wheels in a
great piece of machinery which is made sensitive to opinion in

ways which local managers in no sort control. The opinion of the whole country beats upon them. The country feels, therefore, that, however selected, they are in some sense more representative, more to be depended on to register the thoughtful judgments of the country itself, than the members of state legislatures are.

It is for this reason as much as for any other that the balance of powers between the States and the federal government now trembles at an unstable equilibrium, and we hesitate into which scale to throw the weight of our purpose and preference with regard to the legislation by which we shall attempt to thread the maze of our present economic needs and perplexities. It may turn out that what our state governments need is not to be sapped of their powers and subordinated to Congress, but to be reorganized along simpler lines which will make them real organs of popular opinion. A government must have organs; it cannot act inorganically, by masses. It must have a law-making body; it can no more make law through its voters than it can make law through its newspapers.

It would be fatal to our political vitality really to strip the States of their powers and transfer them to the federal government. It cannot be too often repeated that it has been the privilege of separate development secured to the several regions of the country by the Constitution, and not the privilege of separate development only, but also that other more fundamental privilege that lies back of it, the privilege of independent local opinion and individual conviction, which has given speed, facility, vigor, and certainty to the processes of our economic and political growth. To buy temporary ease and convenience for the performance of a few great tasks of the hour at the expense of that would be to pay too great a price and to cheat all generations for the sake of one.

Undoubtedly the powers of the federal government have grown, have even grown enormously, since the creation of the government; and they have grown for the most part without amendment of the Constitution. But they have grown in almost every instance by a process which must be regarded as perfectly normal and legitimate. The Constitution cannot be regarded as a mere legal document, to be read as a will or a contract would be. It must, of the necessity of the case, be a vehicle of life. As the life of the nation changes so must the interpretation of the document which contains it change, by a nice adjustment, determined, not by the original intention of those who drew the paper, but by the exigencies and the new aspects of life itself. Changes of fact and alterations of opinion bring in their train actual extensions of community of interest, actual additions to the catalogue of things which must be included under the general terms of the law. The commerce of great systems of railway is, of course, not the commerce of wagon roads, the only land commerce known in the days when the Constitution was drafted. The common interests of a nation bound together in thought and interest and action by the telegraph and the telephone, as well as by the rushing mails which every express train carries, have a scope and variety, an infinite multiplication and intricate interlacing of which a simpler day can have had no conception. Every general term of the Constitution has come to have a meaning as varied as the actual variety of the things which the country now shares in common.

The character of the process of constitutional adaptation depends first of all upon the wise or unwise choice of statesmen, but ultimately and chiefly upon the opinion and purpose of the courts. The chief instrumentality by which the law of the Constitution has been extended to cover the facts of national development has of course been judicial interpretation,—the decisions of the courts. The process of formal amendment of the Constitution was made so difficult by the provisions of the Constitution itself that it has seldom been feasible to use it; and the difficulty of formal amendment has undoubtedly made the courts more liberal, not to say more lax, in their interpretation than they would otherwise have been. The whole business of adaptation has been theirs, and they have undertaken it with open minds, sometimes even with boldness and a touch of audacity. But, though they have sometimes been lax, though they have sometimes yielded, it may be, to the pressure of popular agitation and of party interest, they have not often overstepped the bounds of legitimate extension. By legitimate extension I mean extension which does not change the character of the federal power, but only its items,—which does not make new kinds but only new particulars of power. Facts change and are taken care of, but principles do not change.

The members of courts are necessarily men of their own generation: we would not wish to have them men of another. Constitutional law, as well as statesmanship, must look forward, not backward, and, while we should wish the courts to be conservative, we should certainly be deeply uneasy were they to hold affairs back from their natural alteration. Change as well as stability may be conservative. Conservative change is conservative, not of prejudices, but of principles, of established purposes and conceptions, the only things which in government or in any other field of action can abide. Conservative progress is a process, not of revolution, but of modification. In our own case and in the matter now under discussion it consists in a slowly progressive modification and transfer of functions as between the States and the federal government along the lines of actual development, along the lines of actual and substantial alterations of interest and of that national consciousness which is the breath of all true amendment,—and not along lines of party or individual purpose, nor by way of desperate search for remedies for existing evils.

No doubt, courts must "make" law for their own day, must have the insight which adapts law to its uses, rather than its uses to it, must sometimes venture upon decisions which have a certain touch of statesmanlike initiative in them. We shall often find ourselves looking to them for strong and fearless opinions. But there are two kinds of "strong" opinions, as a distinguished English jurist long ago pointed out. There are those which are strong with the strength of insight and intelligence and those which are strong with the mere strength of will. The latter sort all judges who act with conscience, mindful of their oaths of office, should eschew as they would eschew the actual breaking of the law. That the federal courts should have such a conscience is essential to the integrity of our whole national action. Actual alterations of interest in the make-up of our national life, actual, unmistakable changes in our national consciousness, actual modifications in our national activities such as give a new aspect and significance to the well-known purposes of our fundamental law, should, of course, be taken up into decisions which add to the number of things of which the national government must take cognizance and attempt to control. That is a function of insight and intelligence. The courage it calls for on the part of the courts is the courage of conviction. But they are, on the other hand, called on to display the more noble courage which defends ancient convictions and established principle against the clamor, the class interests, and the changeful moods of parties. They should never permit themselves wilfully to seek to find in the phrases of the Constitution remedies for evils which the federal government was never intended to deal with.

Moral and social questions originally left to the several States for settlement can be drawn into the field of federal authority only at the expense of the self-dependence and efficiency of the several communities of which our complex body politic is made up. Paternal morals, morals enforced by the judgment and choices of the central authority at Washington, do not and cannot create vital habits or methods of life unless sustained by local opinion and purpose, local prejudice and convenience,— unless supported by local convenience and interest; and only communities capable of taking care of themselves will, taken together, constitute a nation capable of vital action and control. You cannot atrophy the parts without atrophying the whole. Deliberate adding to the powers of the federal government by sheer judicial authority, because the Supreme Court can no longer be withstood or contradicted in the States, both saps the legal morality upon which a sound constitutional system must rest, and deprives the federal structure as a whole of that vitality which has given the Supreme Court itself its increase of power. It is the alchemy of decay.

It would certainly mean that we had acquired a new political temper, never hitherto characteristic of us, that we had utterly lost confidence in what we set out to do, were we now to substitute abolition for reform,—were we by degrees to do away with our boasted system of self-government out of mere impatience and disgust, like those who got rid of an instrument they no longer knew how to use.

There are some hopeful signs that we may be about to return to the better way of a time when we knew how to restrict government and adapt it to our uses in accordance with principles we did not doubt, but adhered to with an ardent fervor which was the best evidence of youth and virility. We have long been painfully conscious that we have failed in the matter of city government. It is an age of cities, and if we cannot govern our cities, we cannot govern at all. For a little while we acted as if in despair. We began to strip our city governments of their powers and to transfer them to state commissions or back to the legislatures of the States, very much as we are now stripping the States of their powers and putting them in the hands of federal commissions. The attempt was made to put the police departments of some of our cities, for example, in the hands of state officers, and to put the granting of city franchises back into the hands of the central legislature of the State, in the hope, apparently, that a uniform regulation of such things by the opinion of the whole State might take the place of corrupt control by city politicians. But it did not take us long, fortunately, to see that we were moving in the wrong direction. We have now turned to the better way of reconsidering the whole question of the organization of city governments, and are likely within a generation to purify them by simplifying them, to moralize them by placing their government in the hands of a few persons who can really be selected by popular preference instead of by the private processes of nomination by party managers, and who, because few and conspicuous, can really be watched and held to a responsibility which they will honor because they cannot escape.

It is to be hoped that we shall presently have the same light dawn upon us with regard to our state governments, and, instead of upsetting an ancient system, hallowed by long use and deep devotion, revitalize it by reorganization. And that, not only because it is an old system long beloved, but also because we are certified by all political history of the fact that centralization is not vitalization. Moralization is by life, not by statute; by the interior impulse and experience of communities, not by fostering legislation which is merely the abstraction of an experience which may belong to a nation as a whole or to many parts of of it without having yet touched the thought of the rest anywhere to the quick. The object of our federal system is to bring the understandings of constitutional government home to the people of every part of the nation, to make them part of their consciousness as they go about their daily tasks. If we cannot successfully effect its adjustments by the nice local adaptations of our older practice, we have failed as constitutional statesmen.

VIII

PARTY GOVERNMENT IN THE UNITED STATES

In order to understand the organization and operation of parties in the United States, it is necessary to turn once more to the theory upon which our federal and, for that matter, our state governments, also, were constructed. They were, in their make-up, Whig inventions. At the time our national government was erected, the Whig party in England was engaged in a very notable struggle to curb and regulate the power of the Crown. The struggle had begun long before the revolution which cut our politics asunder from the politics of England, and that revolution itself was only an acute manifestation of the great forces which were at work among thoughtful Englishmen everywhere. The revolution which separated America from England was part of a great Whig contest with the Crown for constitutional liberties. The leaders of that revolution held Whig doctrine; the greater Whig statesmen on the other side of the water recognized them as their allies and gave them their outspoken sympathy, perceiving that they were but fighting a battle which must sooner or later be fought in England, whether with arms or with votes and the more pacific strategy of politics. Every historian now sees that the radical changes made in the government of England during the nineteenth century were quickened and given assurance of success by the changes which had preceded them in America; that the leaders of the American Revolution had but taken precedence of the Whigs at home in bringing government into a new and responsible relationship to the people who were its subjects.

The theory of the Whigs in England did not go the length of seeking to destroy the power of the throne. It probably would not have gone that length in America if the throne had been on this side of the water, a domestic instead of a separate and distant power. The men in the old country to whom the American revolutionists showed the way sought only to offset the Crown with other influences,—influences of opinion acting through a reformed and purified representative chamber, whose consent not only should be necessary to the enactment of law, but the advice of whose leaders the king should find it necessary to heed; and the influences of judicial opinion acting through stable and independent courts. It was, as I have already pointed out, this theory of checks and balances, which I have called the Newtonian theory of government, that prevailed in the convention which framed the Constitution of the United States,—which prevailed over the very different theory of Hamilton, that government was not a thing which you could afford to tie up in a nice poise, as if it were to be held at an inactive equilibrium, but a thing which must every day act with straightforward and unquestionable power, with definite purpose and consistent force, choosing its policies and making good its authority, like a single organism,—the theory which would have seemed to Darwin the theory of nature itself, the nature of men as well as the nature of animal organisms. Dominated by the immediate forces and aspirations of their own day, ruled in thought and action by the great contest in which they had found themselves engaged, to hold the royal power off from arbitrary interference with their interests and their liberties, they allowed themselves to become more interested in providing checks to government than in supplying it with energy and securing to it the necessary certainty and consistency of action. They set legislature off against executive, and the courts against both, separated the three in sphere and power, and yet made the agreement of all three necessary to the operation of the government. The boast of the writers in the *Federalist* was of the perfection with which the convention at Philadelphia had interpreted Whig theory and embodied Whig dynamics in the Constitution. Mr. Hamilton's theory, that government was an affair of coöperative and harmonious forces, and that the danger of coördinate and coequal powers such as the framers of the Constitution had set up was that they might at their will pull in opposite directions and hold the government at a deadlock which no constitutional force could overcome and yet many situations might render inconvenient, if not hazardous, the temper and circumstances of the time gave public men little inclination to heed. Checks and balances were then the orthodox gospel of government.

The most serious success of the convention in applying Whig theory to the government they were constructing was the complete separation of Congress and the executive which they effected. The English Whigs fought for long to oust the Crown from the power and intimate influence it had had in the House of Commons through its control of members' seats and its corrupting power of patronage: they succeeded only in placing the leaders of the Commons itself in executive authority in the stead of the Crown. The real executive authority of the English government is vested in the ministers of the day, who are in effect a committee of the House of Commons, and legislature and executive work together under a common party organization. The one is only an agency of the other: the ministers act for their party in the House. The separation of parliament and the Crown which the reformers of the early part of the last century finally succeeded in effecting was not, in fact, a separation of the legislature from the executive, but only a separation of the real from the nominal executive. They entirely succeeded in making the king a modern "constitutional" monarch,—a monarch, that is, who, notwithstanding the dignity with which he is still surrounded and the very considerable influence which he can still exercise by reason of his station, his personal force, should he happen to have any, and his intimate access to the counsels of the executive ministry, merely "reigns" and does not govern. His choice of advisers the House of Commons dictates. But our constitution-makers did their work during the earlier part of the struggle, when it seemed merely a contest to offset the authority of the king with effectual checks, and long before it had become evident that the outcome would be the substitution of an executive which represented the popular house for one which did not. Having a free hand and a clean sheet of paper upon which to write, there was nothing to hinder the complete realization of their ideal. They succeeded in actually separating legislature and executive.

It may be that circumstances rendered their success more complete than they had intended. There is no reason to believe that they meant actually to exclude the President and his advisers from all intimate personal consultation with the houses in session. No doubt the President and the members of his cabinet could with perfect legal propriety and without any breach of the spirit of the Constitution attend the sessions of either the House or the Senate and take part in their discussions, at any rate to the extent of answering questions and explaining any measures which the President might see fit to urge in the messages which the Constitution explicitly authorizes him to send to Congress. But after a few brief attempts to institute a practice of that kind, in the early days of General Washington's administration, actual usage established another habit in respect of the intercourse between the executive and Congress, and later days have shown the houses very jealous of any attempt to establish such an intimacy. Executive officers would be most unwelcome in the houses. Their doors are shut against them. Only the door of a committee room here and there opens to receive them, and they enter only when they are invited.

In what I have said in a previous lecture of the remarkable and, in some respects, unexpected development of the President's influence and functions, I have already pointed out one of the most interesting and significant results of this absolute application of early Whig theory to the practice of our government. Its result has been that, so far as the government itself is concerned, there is but one national voice in the country, and that is the voice of the President. His isolation has quite unexpectedly been his exaltation. The House represents localities, is made up of individuals whose interest is the interest of separate and scattered constituencies, who are drawn together, indeed, under a master, the Speaker, but who are controlled by no national force except that of their party, a force outside the government rather than within it. The Senate represents in its turn regions and interests distinguished by many conflicting and contrasted purposes, united only by exterior party organization and a party spirit not generated within the chamber itself. Only the President represents the country as a whole, and the President himself is coöperatively bound to the houses only by the machinery and discipline of party, not as a person and functionary, but as a member of an outside organization which exists quite independently of the executive and legislature.

It is extraordinary the influence the early Whig theory of political dynamics has had amongst us and the far-reaching consequences which have ensued from it. It is far from being a democratic theory. It is, on the contrary, a theory whose avowed object, at any rate as applied in America, was to keep government at a sort of mechanical equipoise by means of a standing amicable contest among its several organic parts, each of which it seeks to make representative of a special interest in the nation. It is particularly intended to prevent the will of the people as a whole from having at any moment an unobstructed sweep and ascendency. And yet in every step we have taken with the intention of making our governments more democratic, we have punctiliously kept to Whig mechanics. The process shows itself most distinctly and most systematically in the structure of our state governments. We have supposed that the way to make executive offices democratic in character and motive was to separate them in authority,—to prescribe each officer's duties by statute, however petty and naturally subordinate in kind those duties might be, to put it to the voter to elect him separately, and to make him responsible, not to any superior officer set over him, but only to the courts,—thus making him a law unto himself so far as any other official is concerned. So far have we carried the theory of checks and balances, the theory of the independence of the several organs of government.

The operation of the system is worth looking into more closely for a moment. Not very long ago a mob of unmasked men rescued a prisoner with whom they sympathized from the sheriff of a county in one of our States. The circumstances of the rescue made it very evident that the sheriff had made no serious attempt to prevent the rescue. He had had reason to expect it, and had provided no sufficient armed guard for his prisoner. The case was so flagrant that the governor of the State wrote the sheriff a sharp letter of reprimand, censuring him very justly for his neglect of duty. The sheriff replied in an open letter in which he curtly bade the governor mind his own business. The sheriff was, he said, a servant of his county, responsible to its voters and not to the governor. And his impertinence was the law itself. The governor had no more authority over him than the youngest citizen. He was responsible only to the people of his own county, from whose ranks the mob had come which had taken his prisoner away from him. He could have been brought to book only by indictment and trial,—indictment at the instance of a district attorney elected on the same "ticket" with himself, by a grand jury of men who had voted for him, and trial by a petit jury of his neighbors, whose sympathy with the rescue might be presumed from the circumstances. This is Whig dynamics in its *reductio ad particulam*. It is a species of government in solution.

It can be solidified and drawn to system only by the external authority of party, an organization outside the government and independent of it. Not being drawn together by any system provided in our constitutions, being laid apart, on the contrary, in a sort of jealous dispersion and analysis by Whig theory enacted into law, it has been necessary to keep the several parts of the government in some kind of workable combination by outside pressure, by the closely knit imperative discipline of party, a body that has no constitutional cleavages and is free to tie itself into legislative and executive functions alike by its systematic control of the *personnel* of all branches of the government.

Fortunately, the federal executive is not dispersed into its many elements as the executive of each of our States is. The dispersion of our state executives runs from top to bottom. The governor has no cabinet. The executive officers of state associated with him in administration are elected as he is. Each refers his authority to particular statutes or particular clauses of the state constitution. Each is responsible politically to his constituents, the voters of the State, and, legally, to the courts and their juries. But in the federal government the executive is at least in itself a unit. Every one subordinate to the President is appointed by him and responsible to him, both legally and politically. He can control the *personnel* and the action of the whole of the great "department" of government of which he is the head. The Whig doctrine is insisted on only with regard to dealings of the legislature with the executive, and of the legislature or the executive with the courts. The three great functions of government are not to be merged or even drawn into organic coöperation, but are to be balanced against one another in a safe counterpoise. They are interdependent but organically disassociated; must coöperate, and yet are subject to no common authority.

The way in which the several branches of the federal government have been separately organized and given efficiency in the discharge of their own functions has only emphasized their separation and jealous independence. The effective organization of the House under its committees and its powerful Speaker, the organization of the Senate under its steering committees, the consolidation of the executive under the authority of the President, only render it the more feasible and the more likely that these several parts of the government will act with an all too effective consciousness of their distinct individuality and dignity, their distinct claim to be separately considered and severally obeyed in the shaping and conduct of affairs. They are not to be driven, and there is no machinery of which the Constitution knows anything by which they can be led and combined.

It is for that reason that we have had such an extraordinary development of party authority in the United States and have developed outside the government itself so elaborate and effective an organization of parties. They are absolutely necessary to hold the things thus disconnected and dispersed together and give some coherence to the action of political forces. There are, as I have already explained in another connection, so many officers to be elected that even the preparation of lists of candidates is too complicated and laborious a business to be undertaken by men busy about other things. Some one must make a profession of attending to it, must give it system and method. A few candidates for a few conspicuous offices which interested everybody, the voters themselves might select in the intervals of private business; but a multitude of candidates for offices great and small they cannot choose; and after they are chosen and elected to office they are still a multitude, and there must be somebody to look after them in the discharge of their functions, somebody to observe them closely in action, in order that they may be assessed against the time when they are to be judged. Each has his own little legal domain; there is no interdependence amongst them, no interior organization to hold them together. There must, therefore, be an exterior organization, voluntarily formed and independent of the law, whose object it shall be to bind them together in some sort of harmony and coöperation. That exterior organization is the political party. The hierarchy of its officers must supply the place of a hierarchy of legally constituted officials.

Nowhere else is the mere maintenance of the machinery of government so complex and difficult a matter as in the United States. It is not as if there were but a single government to be maintained and officered. There are the innumerable offices of States, of counties, of townships, of cities, to be filled; and it is only by elections, by the filling of offices, that parties test and maintain their hold upon public opinion. Their control of the opinion of the nation inevitably depends upon their hold on the many localities of which it is made up. If they lose their grip upon the petty choices which affect the daily life of counties and cities and States, they will inevitably lose their grip upon the greater matters, also, of which the action of the nation is made up. Parties get their coherence and prestige, their rootage and solidity, their mastery over men and events, from their command of detail, their control of the little tides that eventually flood the great channels of national action. No one realizes more completely the interdependence of municipal, state, and federal elections than do the party managers. Their parties cannot be one thing for the one set of elections and another for the other; and the complexity of the politician's task consists in the fact that, though from his point of view interdependent and intimately connected, the constantly recurring elections of a system under which everybody is elected are variously scattered in time and place and object.

We have made many efforts to separate local and national elections in time in order to separate them in spirit. Many local questions upon which the voters of particular cities or counties or States are called upon to vote have no connection whatever either in principle or in object with the national questions upon which the choice of congressmen and of presidential electors should turn. It is ideally desirable that the voter should be left free to choose the candidates of one party in local elections and the candidates of the opposite party in national elections. It is undoubtedly desirable that he should go further and separate matters of local administration from his choice of party altogether, choosing his local representatives upon their merits as men without regard to their party affiliations. We have hopefully made a score of efforts to obtain "non-partisan" local political action. But such efforts always in the long run fail. Local parties cannot be one thing for one purpose and another for another without losing form and discipline altogether and becoming hopelessly fluid. Neither can parties form and re-form, now for this purpose and again for that, or be for one election one thing and for another another. Unless they can have local training and constant rehearsal of their parts, they will fail of coherent organization when they address themselves to the business of national elections. For national purposes they must regard themselves as parts of greater wholes, and it is impossible under such a system as our own that they should maintain their zest and interest in their business if their only objects are distant and general objects, without local rootage or illustration, centering in Congress and utterly disconnected with anything that they themselves handle. Local offices arc indispensable to party discipline as rewards of local fidelity, as the visible and tangible objects of those who devote their time and energy to party organization and undertake to see to it that the full strength of the party vote is put forth when the several local sections of the party are called upon to unite for national purposes. If national politics are not to become a mere game of haphazard amidst which parties can make no calculations whatever, systematic and disciplined connections between local and national affairs are imperative, and some instrument must be found to effect them. Whatever their faults and abuses, party machines are absolutely necessary under our existing electoral arrangements, and are necessary chiefly for keeping the several segments of parties together. No party manager could piece local majorities together and make up a national majority, if local majorities were mustered upon non-partisan grounds. No party manager can keep his lieutenants to their business who has not control of local nominations. His lieutenants do not expect national rewards: their vital rootage is the rootage of local opportunity.

Just because, therefore, there is nowhere else in the world so complex and various an electoral machinery as in the United States, nowhere else in the world is party machinery so elaborate or so necessary. It is important to keep this in mind. Otherwise, when we analyze party action, we shall fall into the too common error of thinking that we are analyzing disease. As a matter of fact, the whole thing is just as normal and natural as any other political development. The part that party has played in this country has been both necessary and beneficial, and if bosses and secret managers are often undesirable persons, playing their parts for their own benefit or glorification rather than for the public good, they are at least the natural fruits of the tree. It has borne fruit good and bad, sweet and bitter, wholesome and corrupt, but it is native to our air and practice and can be uprooted only by an entire change of system.

All the peculiarities of party government in the United States are due to the too literal application of Whig doctrine, to the infinite multiplication of elective offices. There are two things to be done for which we have supplied no adequate legal or constitutional machinery: there are thousands of officials to be chosen and there are many disconnected parts of government to be brought into coöperation. "It may be laid down as a political maxim that whatever assigns to the people a power which they

are naturally incapable of wielding takes it away from them."[5]
They have, under our Constitution and statutes, been assigned
the power of filling innumerable elective offices; they are incapable of wielding that power because they have neither the
time nor the necessary means of coöperative action; the power
has therefore been taken away from them, not by law but by
circumstances, and handed over to those who have the time and
the inclination to supply the necessary organization; and the
system of election has been transformed into a system of practically irresponsible appointment to office by private party managers,—irresponsible because our law has not yet been able to
devise any means of making it responsible. It may also be laid
down as a political maxim that when the several chief organs
of government are separated by organic law and offset against
each other in jealous seclusion, no common legal authority set
over them, no necessary community of interest subsisting
amongst them, no common origin or purpose dominating them,
they must of necessity, if united at all, be united by pressure
from without; and they must be united if government is to
proceed. They cannot remain checked and balanced against one
another; they must act, and act together. They must, therefore,
of their own will or of mere necessity obey an outside master.

Both sets of dispersions, the dispersion of offices and the
dispersion of functions and authorities, have coöperated to
produce our parties, and their organization. Through their
caucuses, their county conventions, their state conventions, their
national conventions, instead of through legislatures and
cabinets, they supply the indispensable means of agreement and
coöperation, and direct the government of the country both in
its policy and in its *personnel*. Their local managers make up the
long and variegated lists of candidates made necessary under our
would-be democratic practice; their caucuses and local conventions ratify the choice; their state and national conventions add
declarations of principle and determine party policy. Only in
the United States is party thus a distinct authority outside the
formal government, expressing its purposes through its own
separate and peculiar organs and permitted to dictate what Congress shall undertake and the national administration address
itself to. Under every other system of government which is
representative in character and which attempts to adjust the
action of government to the wishes and interests of the people,

[5] Henry Jones Ford, *The Rise and Growth of American Politics: A Sketch
of Constitutional Development* (New York, 1898), p. 299. Wilson relied heavily
on this work while writing this chapter.

the organization of parties is, in a sense, indistinguishable from the organs of the government itself. Party finds its organic lodgment in the national legislature and executive themselves. The several active parts of the government are closely united in organization for a common purpose, because they are under a common direction and themselves constitute the machinery of party control. Parties do not have to supply themselves with separate organs of their own outside the government and intended to dictate its policy, because such separate organs are unnecessary. The responsible organs of government are also the avowed organs of party. The action of opinion upon them is open and direct, not circuitous and secret.

It is interesting to observe that as a consequence the distinction we make between "politicians" and "statesmen" is peculiarly our own. In other countries where these words or their equivalents are used, the statesman differs from the politician only in capacity and in degree, and is distinguished as a public leader only in being a greater figure on the same stage, whereas with us politicians and statesmen differ in kind. A politician is a man who manages the organs of the party outside the open field of government, outside executive offices and legislative chambers, and who conveys the behests of party to those who hold the offices and make laws; while the statesman is the leader of public opinion, the immediate director (under the politicians) of executive or legislative policy, the diplomat, the recognized public servant. The politician, indeed, often holds public office and attempts the rôle of statesman as well, but, though the rôles may be combined, they are none the less sharply distinguishable. Party majorities which are actually in control of the whole legislative machinery, as party majorities in England are, determine party programs by the use of the government itself,—their leaders are at once "politicians" and "statesmen"; and, the function being public, the politician is more likely to be swallowed up in the statesman. But with us, who affect never to allow party majorities to get in complete control of governmental machinery if we can prevent it by constitutional obstacles, party programs are made up outside legislative chambers, by conventions constituted under the direction of independent politicians,—politicians, I mean, who are, at any rate in respect of that function, independent of the responsibilities of office and of public action; and these independent conventions, not charged with the responsibility of carrying out their programs, actually outline the policy of administrations and dictate the action of Congress, the irresponsible dictating to the responsible, and so, it may be, destroying the very responsibility itself. "The peculiarities of American party government are all due to this separation of party management from direct and immediate responsibility for the administration of the government."[6]

The satisfactions of power must be very great to attract so many men of unusual gifts to attempt the hazardous and little honored business of party management. We have made it necessary that we should have "bosses" and that they and their lieutenants should assign offices by appointment, but it is a very difficult and precarious business which they undertake. It is difficult and hazardous not only because it is irregular and only partially protected by law, but also because the people look askance at it and often with a sudden disgust turn upon it and break it up, for a little while rendering it impossible. The reason for these occasional outbursts of discontent and resentment is evident and substantial enough. They come when the people happen to realize that under existing party machinery they have virtually no control at all over nominations for office, and that, having no real control over the choice of candidates, they are cut off from exercising real representative self-government,— that they have been solemnly taking part in a farce. But their revolt is only fitful and upon occasion. Reform associations arise, committees of fifty or seventy or a hundred are formed to set matters right and put government back into the hands of the people, but it is always found that no one can successfully supplant the carefully devised machinery of professional politicians without taking the same pains that they take, without devoting to the business the time and the enthusiasm for details which they devote to it, or supplant the politicians themselves without forming rival organizations as competent as theirs to keep an eye on the whole complicated process of elections and platforms, without, in short, themselves becoming in their turn professional politicians. It is an odd operation of the Whig system that it should make such party organizations at once necessary and disreputable, and I should say that in view of the legal arrangements which we have deliberately made, the disrepute in which professional politicians are held, is in spirit highly unconstitutional.

There can be and there need be no national boss like the local bosses of States and cities, because federal patronage is not distributed by election. Local bosses commonly control the selection of members of Congress because the congressional districts are local, and members of Congress are voted for by local ticket;

6 *Ibid.*, p. 326.

but they cannot control federal appointments without the consent of the President. By the same token, the President can, if he chooses, become national boss by the use of his enormous patronage, doling out his local gifts of place to local party managers in return for support and coöperation in the guidance and control of his party. His patronage touches every community in the United States. He can often by its use disconcert and even master the local managers of his own party by combining the arts of the politician with the duties of the statesman, and he can go far towards establishing a complete personal domination. He can even break party lines asunder and draw together combinations of his own devising. It is against this that our national civil service laws have been wisely directed.

But what really restrains him is his conspicuous position and the fact that opinion will hold him responsible for his use of his patronage. Local bosses are often very obscure persons. To the vast majority of the voters they are entirely unknown, and it is their desire to be as little in evidence as possible. They are often not themselves office-holders at all, and there is no way in which by mere elective processes they can be held responsible. But the President's appointments are public, and he alone by constitutional assignment is responsible for them. Such open responsibility sobers and restrains even where principle is lacking. Many a man who does not scruple to make in private political arrangements which will serve his own purposes will be very careful to be judicious in every act for which he is known to be singly responsible. Responsible appointments are always better than irresponsible. Responsible appointments are appointments made under scrutiny; irresponsible appointments are those made by private persons in private.

The machinery of party rule is nominally representative. The several assemblies and conventions through which the parties operate are supposed to be made up of delegates chosen by the voters of the party, to speak for them with a certain knowledge of what they want and expect. But here again the action of the voters themselves is hardly more than nominal. The lists of delegates are made up by the party managers as freely in all ordinary circumstances as are the lists of the candidates in whose selection they concur. To add the duty of really selecting delegates to the duty of selecting men for office already laid upon our voters by law would be only to add to the impossibility of their task, and to their confusion if they attempted to perform it. When difficulties arise in the process, rival bodies of delegates can always be chosen, and then the managing committees who are in charge of the party's affairs—the county committee, the state committee, or the national committee—can dictate which of the contesting delegations shall be admitted, which shall have their credentials accepted. It is to this necessity we have been brought by farming the functions of government out to outside parties. We have made the task of the voter hopeless and therefore impossible.

And yet at the best the control which party exercises over government is uncertain. There can be, whether for the voter or for the managing politician himself, little more than a presumption that what party managers propose and promise will be done, for the separation of authority between the several organs of government itself still stands in the way. Government is still in solution, and nothing may come to crystallization. But we may congratulate ourselves that we have succeeded as well as we have in giving our politics unity and coherence. We should have drifted sadly, should much oftener have been made to guess what the course of our politics should be, had we not constructed this singular and, on the whole, efficient machinery by which we have in all ordinary seasons contrived to hold the *personnel* and the policy of our government together.

Moreover, there is another use which parties thus thoroughly organized and universally active have served among us which has been of supreme importance. It is clear that without them it would hardly have been possible for the voters of the country to be united in truly national judgments upon national questions. For a hundred years or more we have been a nation in the making, and it would be hard to exaggerate the importance of the nationalizing influence of our great political parties. Without them, in a country so various as ours, with communities at every stage of development, separated into parts by the sharpest economic contrasts and social differences, with local problems and conditions of their own which seemed to give them a separate interest very difficult to combine with any other, full of keen rivalries and here and there cut athwart by deep-rooted prejudices, national opinions, national judgments, could never have been formulated or enforced without the instrumentality of well-disciplined parties which extended their organization in a close network over the whole country, and which had always their desire for office and for the power which office brings to urge as their conclusive reason,—a reason which every voter could understand,—why there should be agreement in opinion and in program as between section and section, whatever the temptation to divide and act separately, as their conclusive argument against local interest and preference. If local and national politics had ever been for long successfully divorced, this would have been impossible.

Students of our politics have not always sufficiently recognized the extraordinary part political parties have played in making a national life which might otherwise have been loose and diverse almost to the point of being inorganic a thing of definite coherence and common purpose. There is a sense in which our parties may be said to have been our real body politic. Not the authority of Congress, not the leadership of the President, but the discipline and zest of parties, has held us together, has made it possible for us to form and to carry out national programs. It is not merely that the utmost economic diversity has marked the development of the different parts of the country, and that their consciousness of different and even rival and conflicting interests has rendered the sympathy between them imperfect, the likelihood of antagonism very great indeed. There have been social differences, also, quite as marked. These social differences were no doubt themselves founded in economic diversity, but they cut much deeper than mere economic diversity of itself could have cut and made real sympathy unnatural, spontaneous coöperation between the portions of the country which they had offset against one another extremely difficult, and, in the absence of party discipline, extremely unlikely. The social contrast between the North and South before the Civil War will occur to every one,—a contrast created, of course, by the existence of the slave system in the South and deepened and elaborated by many another influence, until the political partnership of the two regions became at last actually impossible. And yet there was no exclusive southern party, no exclusive northern party, until the war itself came. Until then each national party had a strong and loyal following both North and South, and seemed to be conscious of no sectional lines which need prevent cordial coöperation. The very interest which a section with peculiar needs and objects of its own had in maintaining its proportional influence in the direction of the policy of the general government, in order both to protect itself and to further such measures conceived in its own interest as it could induce the partners to concede, made it eager to escape actual political isolation and keep its representation in national party counsels.

And, though the contrast between the South with slavery and the other portions of the country without it was the sharpest and most dangerous contrast that our history has disclosed, many another crisis in our affairs has been accentuated by differences of interest and of point of view almost as great. The feeling of the communities beyond the Alleghanies towards the communities by the Atlantic seaboard throughout all the time when foreign powers owned the southern outlet of the great valley of the Mississippi; the feeling of the communities of the plains towards the communities to the eastward which seemed to grudge them their development and to prefer the interest of the manufacturer to the interest of the farmer; the feeling of the mining camps towards the regions of commerce and of all the old order which got their wealth but did not understand or regard their wishes in matters of local regulation and self-government; the circumstances in which Territories were set up and the heats in which States were forged,—these have been the difficulties and hazards of our national history, and it has been nothing less than a marvel how the network of parties has taken up and broken the restless strain of contest and jealousy, like an invisible network of kindly oil upon the disordered waters of the sea.

It is in this vital sense that our national parties have been our veritable body politic. The very compulsion of selfishness has made them serviceable; the very play of self-interest has made them effective. In organization was their strength. It brought them the rewards of local office, the command of patronage of many kinds, the detailed control of opinion, the subtle mastery of every force of growth and expansion. They strove for nothing so constantly or so watchfully as for the compact, coöperative organization and action which served to hold the nation in their hands.

But we have come within sight of the end of the merely nationalizing process. Contrasts between region and region become every year less obvious, conflicts of interest less acute and disturbing. Party organization is no longer needed for the mere rudimentary task of holding the machinery together or giving it the sustenance of some common object, some single coöperative motive. The time is at hand when we can with safety examine the network of party in its detail and change its structure without imperilling its strength. This thing that has served us so well might now master us if we left it irresponsible. We must see to it that it is made responsible.

I have already explained in what sense and for what very sufficient reasons it is irresponsible. Party organizations appoint our elective officers, and we do not elect them. The chief obstacle to their reform, the chief thing that has stood in the way of making them amenable to opinion, controllable by independent opposition, is the reverence with which we have come to regard them. By binding us together at moments of crisis they have won our affectionate fealty. Because the Republican party "saved the Union," a whole generation went by, in many parts of the country, before men who had acted with it in a time of crisis could believe it possible for any "gentleman" or patriot to break away from it or oppose it, whatever its policy and however remote from anything it had originally professed or undertaken. Because the Democratic party had stood for state rights and a power freely dispersed among the people, because it had tried to avoid war and preserve the old harmony of the sections, men of the same fervor of sympathy in other parts of the country deemed it equally incredible that any man of breeding or of principle could turn his back upon it or act with any other political organization. The feeling lasted until lines of party division became equally fixed and artificial. But with changing generations feelings change. We are coming now to look upon our parties once more as instruments for progressive action, as means for handling the affairs of a new age. Sentimental reminiscence is less dominant over us. We are ready to study new uses for our parties and to adapt them to new standards and principles.

The principle of change, if change there is to be, should spring out of this question: Have we had enough of the literal translation of Whig theory into practice, into constitutions? Are we ready to make our legislatures and our executives our real bodies politic, instead of our parties? If we are, we must think less of checks and balances and more of coördinated power, less of separation of functions and more of the synthesis of action. If we are, we must decrease the number and complexity of the things the voter is called upon to do; concentrate his attention upon a few men whom he can make responsible, a few objects upon which he can easily centre his purpose; make parties his instruments and not his masters by an utter simplification of the things he is expected to look to.

Every test of principle or of program returns to our original conception of constitutional government. Every study of party must turn about our purpose to have real representative institutions. Constitutional government can be vital only when it is refreshed at every turn of affairs by a new and cordial and easily attained understanding between those who govern and those who are governed. It can be maintained only by genuine common counsel; and genuine common counsel can be obtained only by genuine representative institutions. A people who know their minds and can get real representatives to express them are a self-governed people, the practised masters of constitutional government.

Book published by Columbia University Press, 1908.

A News Report

[March 26, 1908]

PRACTICAL ADDRESS

Given by President Wilson Before the
Law Club[1] Yesterday Afternoon.

At the first special meeting of the Law Club yesterday afternoon, to which underclassmen were admitted, President Wilson spoke on some of the practical questions which are being asked by men entering the legal profession.

He advised the prospective law student to enter a law school of high standard and take a three year course. He spoke against specializing in any one department at the beginning of a career, as this leads to a narrowing of the mind and the lawyer becomes a mere technical expert who runs more risk of failures than the man who has a general knowledge of the relations of the departments to one another. In selecting a location for practice he suggested that a small city of forty or fifty thousand inhabitants, in which the courts of the district sit, afforded a greater opportunity for establishing a reputation than a larger city.

President Wilson said that the law was full of tricks and intricacies, side doors and evasions which unscrupulous men take advantage of, at the risk of the penitentiary and the esteem of their fellow men. Honesty is needed among lawyers, for on them the whole state of civilization, and the candor and sincerity of the whole operation of the law depend.

In conclusion President Wilson said that the country was not only looking for men intellectually capable but morally trustworthy and that it was the honest, scholarly lawyer who would succeed.[2]

Printed in the *Daily Princetonian*, March 26, 1908.
  [1] The Law Club had been organized at a meeting held on January 7, 1908. Composed of undergraduates planning to study law, it was at first limited to seniors, but juniors were soon admitted to membership.
  [2] There is a brief WWhw outline of this talk bearing the composition date of March 24, 1908, in WP, DLC.

From John Lambert Cadwalader

My dear Mr. President,　　　　　　New York　27. March [1908]

I have seen Mrs. Sage. I think the matter is all right—and I am now in communication with de Forest to get a formal letter to be read at the Trustees meeting.[1]

I think we will be able to get over the question of exclusive occupancy, by arranging as suggested to supply other accommodation for Freshmen on the Campus to the extent that her building is used by other classes.

　　　　　　Faithfully yours,　John L. Cadwalader

ALS (WP, DLC).
　[1] Mrs. Sage's letter, dated April 7, 1908, is reproduced in the extract from the Minutes of the Board of Trustees printed at April 9, 1908.

From Moses J. Gries[1]

My dear Dr. Wilson,　　　　　　Cleveland　March 28, 1908

I was glad to receive your note, but extremely sorry to learn that you think you are unable to come to us this coming season. Your message at the Chamber of Commerce a short while ago[2] made so profound an impression on the men gathered there, that I should like to have you reach a larger general audience here in Cleveland.

As you go back and forth from Chicago to other points in the west, could you not make it possible to give us a date. Of course, though, we should need to know the exact date in advance. I wish you would reconsider and not give us a decided no.[3]

Reciprocating your kind regards,

　　　　　　Sincerely yours,　Moses J. Gries.

TLS (WP, DLC).
　[1] Rabbi of the Temple, E. 55th St. and Central Ave., Cleveland.
　[2] Wilson's address to the Cleveland Chamber of Commerce, "The Ideals of Public Life," is printed at Nov. 16, 1907, Vol. 17.
　[3] Insofar as the Editors know, Wilson never spoke at the Temple in Cleveland.

From James Hay Reed

Dear Dr. Wilson　　　　　　Pittsburgh.　March 30/08

I understand you are coming to Pittsburgh with the Pennsylvania people[1] and I do not know what change this may make in your arrangements but I want you to feel quite at liberty to do whatever is most convenient to you when in Pittsburgh. I should think the best thing for you would be to get away from the

crowd and rest quietly at our house during the afternoon & to stay
with us during the night and as the station is very near the house
you can take the train with them Saturday morning. I do not
think you will sleep much in the car in a side track. But I want
you to make the most convenient plans for yourself always understanding that the Reed house is yours for the occasion.

                                             Yours truly   J H Reed

ALS (WP, DLC).
¹ That is, when Wilson was to speak to the Western Association of Princeton
Clubs on May 2, 1908; the text of his address is printed at that date.

From Ralph Adams Cram

Dear Dr. Wilson: Boston, March 31, 1908.

    . . . I am sending you a copy of the report I propose to make to
the Sub-Committee on the site of the Graduate College.¹ It may
not be quite in order for me to submit this to you, but I feel that
you, more than anyone else, can advise me as to whether anything I have said, or any conclusions at which I have arrived,
are lacking in reasonableness. I am quite unable to disassociate
my architectural function from my greater interests in the
educational development of the University, and this confusion
of interests may, at times, lead me to speak of matters which
do not fall within my province. If I do this, you must correct me.
    I am sending this copy by post and shall bring the original
with me to Princeton for Wednesday, when, after the meeting of
the Committee on Grounds and Buildings, I shall hope to see
you, and if the report is all right, I will post it to Mr. Sheldon
from Princeton.   Very sincerely yours,   R A Cram.

TLS (WP, DLC). Enc.: R. A. Cram to E. W. Sheldon, March 30, 1908, TCL
(WP, DLC).
¹ This report, R. A. Cram to E. W. Sheldon, March 30, 1908, is printed as
an Enclosure with E. W. Sheldon to the Board of Trustees, April 9, 1908.
In his report, Cram suggested that the best site for the proposed Graduate
College was the area between Prospect and Seventy-Nine Hall.

To John Raleigh Mott

My dear Mr. Mott: Princeton, N. J.   April 1st, 1908.

    I would be most cordially willing to read the manuscript of
your lectures on Material for the Christian Ministry, if I could
find time to do so. I am sorry to say that April is so packed full
with engagements of every kind that it seems to me only too
possible that I might not find time to give the manuscript the

proper reading. If you could let me have it later, say about the first of May, I would certainly try to give it my careful consideration. The subject interests me very much and is of radical importance to us all, and I should very much like to be of any service to you I possibly can.[1]

With much regard,

Cordially yours,   Woodrow Wilson

TLS (J. R. Mott Coll., CtY-D).
  [1] See WW to J. R. Mott, May 1, 1908.

To Frank Arthur Vanderlip[1]

My dear Mr. Vanderlip: Princeton, N. J.   April 1st, 1908.

I take the liberty of supplementing our conversation of yesterday by sending you under another cover a report to our Board of Trustees on the Social Coordination of the University[2] and a copy of The Princeton Alumni Weekly containing an abstract of an address on the same subject which I made to the Princeton Alumni Association of Chicago.[3] If you should have time to read these papers, they will perhaps give you a more systematic idea of the things which are now so deeply concerning me than I was able to give you yesterday.

I enjoyed our conversation very much, and it set me thinking upon many interesting lines.

With much regard,

Sincerely yours,   Woodrow Wilson

TLS (F. A. Vanderlip Papers, NNC).
  [1] Vice-President of the National City Bank of New York and a trustee of the Carnegie Foundation for the Advancement of Teaching.
  [2] It is printed at June 6, 1907, Vol. 17.
  [3] Princeton Alumni Weekly, VIII (March 25, 1908), 402-405.

To John Robertson Dunlap

My dear Mr. Dunlap: Princeton, N. J.   April 1st, 1908.

I have been set thinking pretty hard by what I have seen in the papers about the expectation that Mr. Bryan will attend the Jefferson Dinner of the National Democratic Club on the thirteenth. If he attends, there can, I suppose, be no doubt that he will make an address.[1]

I can say with the utmost sincerity that I should have no feeling of jealousy of any kind that an address by Mr. Bryan, which would inevitably be the chief address of the occasion, should take precedence of one by myself in the public attention, but I do feel that Mr. Bryan's presence will entirely alter the character of the occasion and will render nugatory the plans which your committee had so wisely arranged with regard to the impression it was desired to make upon the country. I do not feel that anybody is to be criticized in the matter. These things come about in a most natural way. But I do feel very strongly that the plans for the dinner ought to be changed with a view to accommodating them to the new circumstances.

I should myself, I must frankly say, be put in a very awkward position by undertaking to deliver such an address as I had planned and looked forward to. I should be obliged to take a position extremely antagonistic to Mr. Bryan—I do not mean, of course, antagonistic to him personally, but antagonistic to all the loose notions which he puts forth as a party programme. This would give to the occasion a most inharmonious note, and I should feel that I was doing the National Democratic Club a distinct disservice should I introduce such a note. Inasmuch as it would be inevitable, I beg that you will very seriously consider the propriety of my withdrawing. I should do so without the least feeling of having been inconsiderately treated, indeed without any personal feeling whatever. I urge the suggestion solely upon the ground of the utter futility of my undertaking to do what I know you were expecting of me. I shall be all the more pleased if I should find that this suggestion relieves you from embarrassment, and I beg you to believe me when I most heartily assure you that it can be acted upon without my feeling in any way hurt or slighted. I know that you will understand the reasons, the good Democratic reasons, which lead me to feel that I have the right to ask to be excused.

With much regard and warm appreciation of your unfailing kindness, and also with cordial assurances to the committee of the club of my warm sympathy with their aims and desire to serve them in every possible way,

Sincerely yours,   [Woodrow Wilson]

CCL (RSB Coll., DLC).

[1] As the news report printed at April 14, 1908, reveals, Bryan was invited to attend the Jefferson dinner but not to speak. He declined to attend, and Wilson gave his speech as scheduled.

From Henry Smith Pritchett

My dear President Wilson: New York   April 2, 1908.

With this I enclose a communication from Mr. Carnegie,[1] in which he offers to the Foundation the sum of five millions of dollars to enable the state universities to be included in the scope of the Carnegie Foundation. As you know, I have preferred to see these retiring allowances for state institutions provided by the state. During the conferences of the past four months, however, it has become evident that the difficulties in the way of this are enormous (the legislatures of certain states prohibiting it). It has also become more and more clear that the division of American institutions of higher learning into two sharply divided groups—one comprised of tax-supported, the other of privately endowed universities and colleges—was very undesirable from every point of view. Under these circumstances, Mr. Carnegie's fine gift of an additional sum to include these institutions, provided their legislatures approve, seems the best solution of a difficult question. It seems to me clear that the trustees should accept this trust and administer it as in their best judgment the interests of education demand. I shall be glad to have at your earliest convenience your opinion in this matter. Please consider this matter confidential.

Yours sincerely,   Henry S. Pritchett

TLS (WP, DLC).
¹ A. Carnegie to H. S. Pritchett, March 31, 1908, mimeographed letter (WP, DLC).

An Abstract of an Address to the Traffic Club of Pittsburgh

[April 3, 1908]

THE GOVERNMENT AND BUSINESS.

In discussing the relation between government and business, Mr. Wilson said in part as follows: It is now no longer a question whether modern business operations, particularly upon the great scale upon which they are conducted by corporations, should be regulated by law. The question is only as to the best method of regulation, the method which will best accomplish the objects we have in view and at the same time least disturb the normal course of manufacture and of commercial interchanges. Our object is to secure absolute honesty and perfect fairness, but it is much easier to state the object than to reach it by legal process.

Business has in our day assumed many new aspects to which we find our older law inapplicable and which, therefore, render necessary a re-formulation of the law with regard to the matters in which it has grown old-fashioned. Business, moreover, has assumed a new size which has brought about an entirely new attitude of opinion towards it, has brought it in its larger combinations into a sort of competition with government itself and which has therefore rendered a new attitude of government towards it inevitable.

It is an unfortunate circumstance that this new adjustment of our law and policy should have to be undertaken amidst a spirit of party competition for popular favor. It is absolutely necessary, if the business of this counrty [country] is not to be brought into a serious embarrassment which can hardly be overcome within our generation, that the questions involved in the adjustment of law to new business conditions should be as much as possible divorced from party contest and treated in a dispassionate and businesslike manner. In this field, if in any, we certainly need expert advice, the advice not only of public-spirited business men, but also and more particularly of such lawyers as have had a nation wide experience in framing the business of our greater corporations and adjusting our greater enterprises to existing legal principle and statutory provision.

What is it that excites our alarm with regard to the present scope and power of corporations and makes new adjustments of the law necessary? In the first place, there is the very demoralizing manipulation of values in the field of both railway and industrial securities. This manipulation takes many forms. One of the most dangerous, and yet I should say one of the most manageable, is overcapitalization, where many properties are drawn together in a single combination offered for public sale at a price very much above their value not only, but with a virtually false representation of the assets and properties which lie in back of them. This is, of course, a form of fraud, and when the existing owners of the smaller concerns absorbed into a great combination are paid the purchase price which they demand they undoubtedly in many instances realize a great deal more than the property is worth. Other and more varied manipulations of value take place upon the various stock exchanges or at a conference of arrangements entered into by men who control large blocks of the various stocks involved. Combinations and arrangements are constantly netting to the persons who arrange them enormous unearned fortunes. This is unquestionably the evil of "predatory wealth" and, so far as I can see the only evil in which wealth, or rather the opportunity which wealth brings, can truly be said to be predatory. These manipulations of value have nothing to do with the essential worth of the properties involved not only, but they have nothing to do with the actual conduct of business. The business of a concern whose securities are recklessly or dishonestly manipulated may be perfectly sound, all its administrative processes efficient and honest, and yet it may be wrecked by the treatment to which its securities are subjected by men who are really in control of it and yet not nominally charged with the conduct of its affairs at all.

The other and very different thing which excites our alarm and makes new law necessary is connected with the actual conduct of the business of our greater corporations. It consists in all forms of unfair competition, all sorts of restraints of trade which are in their nature oppressive or inequitable. Many of our corporations have undoubtedly, after getting control of large areas of custom, crushed out local competitors by a local lowering of prices and the creation of other local conditions which made the existence of any similar concern within that area impossible. They have done this oftentimes with the active assistance of the railways, by means of special rates and special discriminations against the competitors whom they wished to crush. Such practices have brought upon all large combinations the suspicion of monopolistic purpose and have made it very difficult to distinguish between monopolies and legitimate combinations.

It is very evident that there is here no single body of practices to be dealt with. We have two things to correct: First, the manipulation of values; and Secondly, such an administration of the business of great corporations as will be essentially unfair and monopolistic in effect.

In seeking a remedy for existing evils we must realize that there are two methods of correction open to us and that the choice between the two is really a choice of principle as well as a choice of method. We can either pick out, under the guidance of experience, the particular transactions or classes of transactions which c[h]aracterize the practices which opinion condemns, or we can entrust the regulation of the larger sorts of business to nonjudicial governmental officials. In brief, we can attempt either a regulation by law administered through judicial tribunals, whether the existing courts or others to be created for the purpose; or a regulation by governmental officials to whom a wide range of judgment and discretion is accorded and to whom no fixed standards of legal determination are prescribed.

The regulation of business through governmental commissions exercising wide discretionary powers is the method we have so far adopted. This of course does not touch one of the radical abuses of the time, namely the manipulation of values. It touches only that very much more complicated side of the whole matter, the actual conduct of the business, a field in which mature experience and a very great range of knowledge is necessary for wise action. We have gone so far in the direction of putting regulation in the hands of governmental officials that some recent proposals look toward putting it absolutely within the choice of executive officers which corporations shall be regulated and which shall not, and the only means of enforcing the authority of officials and commissions which we have yet used consists in the imposing of very heavy fines upon the corporations themselves or with the actual withdrawal of their corporate powers.

To most thoughtful persons such methods of regulation seem both inequitable and futile. They are inequitable because they impose the penalties involved upon the stockholders of the coroporations [corporations], who are in most cases entirely without legal blame in the matter; and futile because they do not stop the practices for which the fines and penalties are imposed. Moreover, no one can reflect upon such methods without seeing that they are really a radical departure from the whole theory of English and American law as hitherto expounded by our statesmen and lawyers. They strike at business instead of transactions; they penalize bodies of persons instead of individuals, and they trend [tend] to accumulate discretionary power in the hands of the executive officers of the government. We certainly shall not be upon safe ground again until we can enforce individual responsibility for definite transactions and base the enforcement upon judicial determination by counts [courts] of law.

The fines imposed in most instances should be imposed upon the individuals responsible for the transactions complained of. Where fines are not adequate and the offense is in its nature criminal, imprisonment should invariably be the penalty, and the processes of proof and conviction should be simplified as to make the imposition of such a penalty feasible and practically invariable.

It is perfectly possible to pick out for legal restraints and regulation all the particular transactions and classes of transactions which embody the practices now demoralizing business in this country. It is perfectly feasible also by processes of legal definition to place the responsibilty for each kind of transaction upon individual officers or individual persons in fact responsible for them. It is perfectly practicable also to put the determination of offenses and penalties in the hands of judicial tribunals who shall administer not the processes of individual judgment but the processes of law. And until we can bring our practice to this basis, we shall be following a road which carries us directly away from all American principle and leads ultimately to the kind of power which American institutions are set up to prevent.[1]

T MS (WP, DLC).
[1] There is a WWhw outline of this address, dated April 3, 1908, in WP, DLC.

From Frank Frost Abbott

My dear President Wilson: Chicago, April 3, 1908

I have just received a letter from the Secretary of the Board of Trustees of this University informing me that my resignation has been accepted, and I am sending you this note to accept formally my election to the position at Princeton of which Dean Fine wrote me on January 21.

My friends in the classical department at Princeton have written me of the admirable plans which you are making to develop the graduate school, and I am looking forward with much interest to the prospect of helping to carry them out next autumn.

Very sincerely yours   Frank Frost Abbott

ALS (Trustees' Papers, UA, NjP).

From Ralph Adams Cram

Dear Dr. Wilson: Boston, April 4, 1908.

I am sending you today two very rough sketch plans[1] showing the working out of the Graduate School on the site I have taken the liberty of suggesting to the consideration of the Trustees in my report sent to Mr. Sheldon. These drawings are, as I say, rough and comparatively unstudied. The arrangement of grounds, paths, and all accessories must be considered as purely experimental and tentative. I have decided to send you two plans showing, first, the re-arrangement of the grounds of Prospect as they would work out were the Graduate School built on the site now in question and were the President's house removed to the recommended site; second, the same grounds, with the first construction of the Graduate School indicated only, the President's house and the grounds remaining as they are. If adequate gardens can be provided for the use of the Graduate School, without the removal of the President's house, I see no reason why this should not remain where it is for many years to come; in other words, if sufficient grounds can be assigned to the Graduate School, no change need be considered in the case of the President's house and grounds until it became necessary to increase the size of the Graduate School, even to an extent that could not be provided for by the assigning to this same school, for residential purposes, of '79 Hall.

If, in the opinion of the Trustees, this proposition is worth considering further, may I take the liberty of asking you to inform Mr. Bunn of this fact, requesting him to send me, at his earliest possible convenience, a section of the large scale map showing the location of all the trees of importance surrounding the President's house. This will be necessary, since it is obvious that the buildings of the Graduate School, if placed on this site, must be so disposed and planned that no trees of importance be sacrificed.

Very respectfully yours,   R A Cram.

TLS (WP, DLC).
¹ See E. W. Sheldon to the Board of Trustees, April 9, 1908, n. 6.

To Frank Frost Abbott

My dear Professor Abbott: [Princeton, N. J.]   April 6th, 1908.

Allow me to acknowledge with great appreciation your kind letter of April 3rd and to say again how deep my gratification is that you are coming to us in the autumn. I know that our Trustees will receive this letter of acceptance which lies before me, with the utmost satisfaction.

We are just about to undertake the reorganization of our Graduate Department on the lines indicated to you when you were here, and I hope sincerely that we can press our preparations to a satisfactory conclusion before Commencement, so as to be ready for next year.

With warm regard,
Sincerely yours,   [Woodrow Wilson]

CCL (WWP, UA, NjP).

To Ralph Adams Cram

My dear Mr. Cram: [Princeton, N. J.]   April 7th, 1908.

The Committee of the Board of Trustees on the Graduate School met yesterday and adopted the site which you suggested on the grounds of Prospect. They also resolved to recommend to the Board the subsequent modification of the grounds as you have suggested. I myself feel that this decison was somewhat premature and that there are many things to be considered before the radical changes suggested are actually made, but I shall hope to have more than one serious conference with you on the subject before any practical steps are taken.

The Dean of the Graduate School will seek an interview with you about the character and plans for the building. I know that I need not ask you to commit yourself in no way to him until you have seen me, because many important questions of a fundamental kind are involved.

I am asking Mr. Bunn to send you a section of the large map showing the location of all the trees of importance surrounding the President's house, as you request.

It was very delightful to see you the other day, and I feel that we are now getting deep into business which will bring us closer and closer together.

Always cordially and faithfully yours,

[Woodrow Wilson]

CCL (WWP, UA, NjP).

Edward Wright Sheldon to Francis Larkin, Jr.[1]

My dear Larkin: [New York]   April 7, 1908.

The Trustees of Princeton University have been engaged for several months in considering the site that should be selected for the Graduate College to be built with the proceeds of the residuary estate of the late Mrs. Swann. By the terms of the will the University was requested to consult fully with the executors with reference to the location and character of the building. The Committee on the Graduate School determined yesterday that the best available site was in the grounds of Prospect between '79 Hall and the President's house, and the Committee's report is to be submitted to the Board of Trustees at their meeting on Thursday. We have consulted with Mr. Bayard Stockton and Professor [William Milligan] Sloane, your two co-executors, and find I believe, that they approve this site. May I ask whether you also would regard it as an appropriate location? All of the Trustees with whom I have talked on the subject speak highly of the situation and I believe, myself, that it is the most dignified and satisfactory spot that could be found. I shall be glad to give you any further information upon the subject that you may desire.

Believe me, with kind regards,

Yours sincerely,   Edward W. Sheldon

TCL (Trustees' Papers, UA, NjP).
  ¹ Princeton 1879, lawyer of New York, and one of the executors of the Estate of Josephine Ward Thomson Swann.

A News Report About a Meeting of Princeton Alumni in New York

[April 8, 1908]

The new house of the Princeton Club of New York¹ again proved its utility and comfort when it was used on the evening of March 30th as a setting for the reunion of five classes on the novel plan devised by Edwin A. Dix '81. It will be recalled that this plan had its first trial a few years ago at the Hotel Astor, New York,² but in Princeton's own clubhouse its real attractiveness was even more markedly proved. The fact that class reunions are never held at Princeton in the same year with the other classes of the same college generation suggested this idea of getting together several classes of the same period. At the reunion on March 30th there were present almost one hundred men from '78, '79, '80, '81 and '82. They assembled in the foyer and lounging room of the club and then about 10 o'clock gathered in the large studio room at the top of the house, where there was plenty of opportunity for good college music and an interchange of courtesies between the classes. President Wilson was there,— not in his official capacity, but as a member of one of the classes. He was encouraged by '78 to make a few remarks unofficially as a one-time underclassman over whom they had had authority. There was also much singing and smoking accompanying a supper.

Printed in the *Princeton Alumni Weekly*, vm (April 8, 1908), 438; one editorial heading omitted.
  ¹ On February 15, 1907, the members of the Princeton Club of New York had voted to move from their club house at 72 East 34th Street, upon the expiration of the existing lease, to two newly leased residences at 119-121 East 21st Street, facing Gramercy Park. The two dwellings were joined together and remodeled. The new club house was opened with an informal gathering on March 26, 1908.
  ² See the news report printed at Nov. 19, 1904, Vol. 15.

To the Board of Trustees of Princeton University

Princeton, N. J.,   April 8, 1908.

At a meeting of the Committee on Honorary Degrees held this day it was voted to recommend to the Board

FOR THE HONORARY DEGREE OF LL.D.

MAHLON PITNEY, Chancellor of New Jersey.

HARRY AUGUSTUS GARFIELD, some time Professor of Politics in this University and President-elect of Williams College.

KOGORO TAKAHIRA, Baron of the Japanese Empire and Japanese Ambassador to the United States.

AND FOR THE HONORARY DEGREE OF D.D.

WILFORD LASH ROBBINS, Dean of the General Theological Seminary in New York.

JOHN CARRINGTON, Missionary in Siam and Translator of the Scriptures into Pali and Siamese.[1]

Respectfully submitted,   Woodrow Wilson
Chairman.

TRS (Trustees' Papers, UA, NjP).

[1] The trustees approved these recommendations on the following day.

Grover Cleveland to Moses Taylor Pyne

Lakewood, New Jersey   April 8, 1908

With heartfelt gratitude I congratulate my colleagues on the graduate school committee and also Princeton University upon the promise of a happy solution of a problem which has long sorely perplexed us. My only sorrow is that I have been deprived of personal participation in this reassuring outcome

Grover Cleveland

Hw copy of telegram (Trustees' Papers, UA, NjP).

Henry Burling Thompson *et al.* to the Board of Trustees of Princeton University

[April 8, 1908]

To the Trustees of Princeton University:

The undersigned committee, appointed by the President pursuant to a resolution of the Board adopted January 9, 1908, to confer with a committee of the alumni, consisting of the Messrs. Junius S. Morgan, George C. Fraser, Franklin Murphy, Jr., William W. Phillips and Charles B. Bostwick, regarding the correction and elimination of the evils connected with the upper class clubs, and to report to the Board at its April meeting, hereby respectfully report as follows:

Immediately upon our appointment we entered into conference with the alumni named above, whom we shall hereafter designate as the Graduates' Committee, and had several meetings with them. Having reached the conclusion that an efficient consideration of the subject involved in our appointment required an examination of club life from all available points of view, we visited Princeton both together and separately on various occasions, and conferred there, as well as elsewhere, with members of the faculty, graduates and undergraduates. By appointment we also met the Senior Council of the University,[1] and generally studied the club situation at Princeton, and also to some extent at Harvard and Yale. Two of our members went to Cambridge for that purpose.

As a result of our conferences with the Graduates' Committee they made to us a written report. This is hereto attached as Exhibit A, and embodies their views upon the origin and nature of the present defects in the club system, and certain remedial recommendations. Our own conclusions with reference to these recommendations, as well as upon the general subject, will be stated below.

By way of preface it seems proper to set forth what among the prevailing club conditions seem good and what seem to demand correction.

The assurance of proper food for the students would appear to be as logical an obligation of the governing body of an American university as providing adequate dormitory accommodation. But at Princeton no persistent effort to discharge that duty has yet been made. About thirty years ago, it will be remembered, while the undergraduates were thus left largely to their own devices, an attempt was made by a congenial group of students to secure under their own management as distinguished from that of a boarding house keeper, food of good quality and attractively served. The prompt success of this attempt gave it continuity and led to the permanent organization of the first upper class club. Eight years later a second club was formed. Eleven other clubs have since come into existence, and the thirteen organizations now embrace in their membership about three-quarters of the two upper classes.[2] These associations are still primarily eating clubs, and judged as such they do not, with the

[1] About this organization, formerly called the Senior Society, see n. 2 to Wilson's Annual Report printed at Dec. 14, 1905, Vol. 16.
[2] For a list of the clubs and the dates of their founding, see n. 1 to the report to the Board of Trustees printed at June 8, 1903, Vol. 14. Since that date, two additional clubs had been established: Terrace Club and Key and Seal Club, both founded in 1904.

exception of some undue cost in buildings and appointments, seem open to objection. The houses are orderly and well maintained, the food served is of good quality, no liquor is used and the house rules enforce discipline and a correct code of manners. The principal use of the clubs is at meal times, and as a rule the houses are empty of undergraduates by eight o'clock in the evening. There are no indications that the life of these institutions tends towards dissipation. On the contrary their atmosphere seems more likely to encourage morality, and in reality produces more satisfactory standards of conduct than exist among the two lower classes. As regards scholarship, while the proportion of honormen, that is, students gaining the first and second groups, is materially and perhaps naturally less among the larger body of club members than it is among non-club students, membership in the clubs does not seem to lower academic standing, nor to discourage study in itself. Upon the whole, having in mind the object of their being, the clubs impress us as creditable undergraduate organizations, and as conducive to the maintenance among their own members of a clean, manly and fairly studious life.

It is quite evident, however, that what are commonly called the extra-curriculum activities of the whole undergraduate body are exaggerated, both in inter-collegiate athletics and in the non-athletic organizations. Too much time is consumed in these at the necessary expense of the academic life, and too much money is spent on training tables and professional instructors at the necessary expense of academic ideals. What we need is a more general engagement in athletic exercises at home, and fewer contests by highly trained teams abroad. Moreover the inter-collegiate athletic schedules are increasing in number and size, the dramatic and musical clubs give more elaborate performances, the mere business of undergraduate organization is becoming more exacting. During the last academic year the various athletic teams, the Glee Club and the Triangle Club played outside of Princeton about seventy-five times. Eight years ago the total performances of those organizations at home and abroad did not exceed that number, and generally their activities seem to have doubled in that time. Last year the combined glee and instrumental clubs gave sixteen concerts, of which thirteen were out of town. This year the Triangle Club is advertised to give thirteen performances, of which nine are to be out of town. As about eighty students belong to the musical clubs, and about forty to the Triangle Club, it is easy to conceive what formidable demands the meetings, rehearsals and public performances make upon undergraduate time and effort. All told there are now more than eighty separate undergraduate organizations, and college life continues to increase in complication. But for all these tendencies we cannot see that the upper class clubs are primarily responsible. Similar tendencies prevail quite as noticeably at other colleges, and are indeed part of the greater importance of the young life of the country. All these undergraduate occupations, however, are within the control of the appropriate faculty committees, and we believe that some attempt at restraint should be gradually but firmly made.

But with all that may fairly be said in favor of the clubs, they have been the cause of academic evils which are no less serious in that they have grown up and flourish outside instead of within the club houses. These unfortunate results, which have been due primarily, in our opinion, to the rapid increase in the number of the clubs, are, first, the demoralizing struggle which engrosses the lower classmen to secure election to a club; secondly, their isolation from the upper classmen through the operation of an elaborate and highly technical inter-club treaty which creates artificial barriers between the classes;[3] thirdly, the discouragement of the higher scholarship among the lower classmen through their conviction that scholarship is valueless, and extracurriculum activities of paramount importance, in securing a club election; and, fourthly, the cutting off of the non-club upper classmen from the best social life of the University. Most of these evils have been recognized, and practical remedies for them sought, in the report of the Graduates' Committee. We will state and comment on these recommendations in order.

1. *That for the next few years, at least, permission for the organization of additional clubs be refused.*

We share the opinion that it is not desirable at present to create any new clubs. Indeed, we believe that there are already more clubs than would be needed if proper provision was made for the social requirements of the non-club members of the University. Nevertheless we doubt the theoretical fairness of an absolute prohibition of any new organization.

2. *That the existing inter-club treaty be abolished.*

While this is hardly a subject for action by the Board of Trustees, the proposition has our personal approval. The treaty

[3] About the inter-club treaty, see G. C. Fraser to H. B. Fine, March 18, 1907, n. 2, Vol. 17.

itself is essentially artificial and is largely disregarded. Whether strictly enforced or tacitly violated, it cannot but have a bad effect upon the college community.

3. *That the clubs, by mutual agreement, admit sophomores to active membership, beginning with a few at the opening of sophomore year, a few more in the following March and the remainder at the beginning of junior year.*

While this too is a matter of club regulation, and may require the test of time, it seems to us to give promise of benefit.

4. *That no pledge to membership in a club shall be exacted or recognized as obligatory for any purpose, and that every club member be privileged to resign from his organization and become a member of another club.*

We are not sure that this recommendation would have general acceptance. In any event, if adopted, it would require careful administration.

5. *That the faculty and the clubs encourage closer relations and a better understanding between their respective members.*

The wisdom of this is obvious but the methods of giving it effective application are not so clear.

6. *That steps be taken in co-operation with the undergraduates to promote the construction on some convenient site near the campus, of a University Club, whose membership shall be open to the three upper classes, the faculty, the Board of Trustees and the alumni.*

This recommendation is strongly urged by the Graduates' Committee and by the undergraduates, as well as by several members of the faculty, and is believed by them to have in it great promise of improving social conditions and restoring the old-time democratic life at Princeton. But after careful consideration and after studying in detail the interesting experiment presented by the Harvard Union,[4] we have not been convinced that this idea of a University Club would meet the difficulties of the situation, or would escape creating a fresh problem of its own. If it included a commons for the sophomore and non-club upper classmen, it would become essentially a large eating hall, with inevitable accessories which would tend

4 See n. 1 to Wilson's Supplementary Report to the Board of Trustees printed at Dec. 13, 1906, Vol. 16.

to repel rather than attract the college public. For a separate restaurant in which occasional meals might be served, there hardly seems a considerable University demand. To the extent that private offices of the building were visited at intervals by members of the various undergraduate organizations, we do not believe that general intercourse would be substantially promoted. It is, however, in the grill room, where men could gather in the late evening for something to eat and drink, that the advocates of the proposed club centre their hopes for the good fellowship and social improvement of the University. Here, too, our investigation indicates that no large proportion of the undergraduates regularly desire such an opportunity, but even if they did, we should doubt the wisdom of gratifying their desire. The limited success of the Harvard Union impresses us as due rather to its promotion of the occasional individual convenience of a much larger and more heterogeneous University body, than to any stimulation of general social intercourse. Without discussing the proposition at greater length, we cannot escape the conclusions that such a club would be costly and cumbrous in construction and maintenance, that on its utilitarian side it would meet no pressing need, and that it would be distinctly non-academic in tendency.

To facilitate dealing with all these questions affecting the clubs, we suggest that if the clubs are to be permanently maintained, some more definite and ready control over them should be established. This might perhaps take responsible form in an advisory committee composed of one graduate member of each club, which could deal authoritatively and directly both with the clubs themselves and with the University authorities in all matters affecting club welfare and club relations to University life. In this way discrimination between the clubs could be prevented and the general welfare promoted.

As a further step towards removing the present segregation of the sophomore class, we recommend the institution in University Hall of sophomore commons. Such commons for the freshmen have been in successful operation there for several years. After consideration of the question it is now believed practicable and comparatively inexpensive to convert the front part of University Hall into a similar commons for the sophomores, and in order that the work might be prosecuted in season for the ensuing year, we have as individuals given this step our informal but hearty approval. In carrying out the plan we suggest that without prohibiting natural table groups, the division of either sophomores or freshmen into separate clubs be discouraged, that the sitting rooms connected with the dining rooms of each class be used by the members of that class in common, and that as much general intercourse as possible among the members of each class be promoted. In addition to providing in this way for the sophomores, we are told that about two-thirds of the non-club upper classmen may also be accommodated in the same building, and we deem it wise that an effort to do this should be made. The experiment may throw light upon the best method of providing satisfactorily for these upper classmen.

This commons seems to promise at least a temporary and partial fulfilment of the obligation on the part of the University to provide proper food for the undergraduates. But we are not content with this achievement. If the way could be opened, we should advocate the construction on the campus of a college hall of appropriate and dignified architecture, administered by the undergraduates, in which a considerable number of the students and some members of the faculty might find good food served in attractive surroundings at moderate prices, and where the social life of a portion of the University might centre. Here the genuine atmosphere of our alma mater would be felt, and here the chosen visitor might share the intimate hospitality of a re-vivified Princeton. The establishment of such a hall would lend new attraction to college life and would tend to discourage the foundation of independent clubs by the undergraduates. Properly administered, it should add distinction as well as amenity to academic life.

So far as the foregoing conclusions can be translated into specific recommendations, they may be summarized as follows:

1. That the establishment of a University Club, as proposed by the Graduates' Committee, be for the present disapproved.

2. That the formation of new upper class clubs should not be encouraged.

3. That the upper class clubs should unite in appointing a duly authorized graduate committee to deal with themselves and with the University authorities in all matters affecting club life and club relations to the University.

4. That the faculty should be requested to consider and report to the Board of Trustees whether the trips of the athletic and

non-athletic organizations away from Princeton cannot be materially reduced in number.

5. That the establishment in University Hall of a commons for the entire sophomore class and for such of the upper classmen as can be accommodated be authorized, and that the matter be referred to the Committee on Grounds and Buildings, with power.

6. That the Committee on Grounds and Buildings be instructed to prepare and report, for the further consideration of the Board, tentative plans for college hall to be erected in immediate contiguity to some set of college dormitories, and to contain a dining room, a meeting room and a kitchen, adapted for the service of meals, and the social intercourse of about one hundred and fifty persons.

In conclusion we desire to express our high appreciation of the loyal and devoted spirit which has animated the members of the Graduates' Committee. They have given their time and effort generously to the solution of an important problem, and their assistance has been most valuable. Something of their spirit is reflected in the present attitude of the undergraduate members of clubs, and the time seems ripe for an abandonment of acrimonious discussion, and a hearty co-operation by all in the permanent betterment of social conditions in the University.

Dated, April 8, 1908.

> HENRY B. THOMPSON,　⎫
> EDWARD W. SHELDON,　⎬　*Committee.*
> ANDREW C. IMBRIE,　⎭

EXHIBIT A.

Messrs. HENRY B. THOMPSON, *Chairman,*　⎫　*A Sub-Committee*
　　EDWARD W. SHELDON and　　　　　　⎬　*of the Board of*
　　ANDREW C. IMBRIE.　　　　　　　　⎭　*Trustees of Princeton University.*

GENTLEMEN:

In accordance with the understanding reached at our recent conference with you, held pursuant to the request embodied in the resolution of the Board of Trustees of Princeton University adopted at its meeting on January 9, 1908, we beg to submit the following

REPORT AND RECOMMENDATIONS
RESPECTING
UNDERGRADUATE SOCIAL CONDITIONS
AT
PRINCETON UNIVERSITY.

PREFACE:

The preparation of this paper has been approached with diffidence and some trepidation; the inherent difficulty of the subject treated, the wide divergence in views of those competent to speak of conditions and the temper which has been engendered by their discussion, all combine to make the task difficult. What follows is not put forth as a panacea, nor is it pretended that the remedies proposed afford the only, or indeed a complete solution of the problems involved; on the contrary, it has been sought to present in concrete form for consideration and discussion, certain evils and possible remedies therefor which have become apparent and suggested themselves after careful thought and study of undergraduate conditions.

PRELIMINARY:

The growth of our universities and the changed scale of living generally have engendered social tendencies among undergraduates which are engaging the attention of thoughtful educators throughout the country.

The wide departure from conditions prevalent at Princeton fifteen years ago, has for some time been patent to alumni in touch with undergraduate affairs, and among them has been the subject of grave consideration and discussion. The report of President Wilson to the Board of Trustees at its meeting in June, 1907, and his remarks in presenting that report, both published in the *Alumini [Alumni] Weekly* of June 12, 1907, were read by Princeton men with deep interest, and made it evident to all that the undergraduate social life needed careful investigation with a view to formulating suitable remedies for such evils as might be found to exist.

Like many matters of common knowledge, it is not easy to define in a few words the difficulties in the present situation to be met and remedied. They are the outgrowth—doubtless the logical result—of conditions extraneous to the University, aided by circumstances over which both the university authorities and the alumni and undergraduates, had they appreciated the process of evolution, might have exercised control. They have now reached a point where not only the Board of Trustees, the faculty and the older body of alumni desire a change, but where the younger alumni and the undergraduates are in accord in demanding remedial measures.

THE EVILS:

Without attempting to detail these evils, or to emphasize them by citation of individual instances, it seems that the most important can be classified and summarized under the following heads:

1. The segregation of sophomores from other undergraduates;

2. The unfortunate position of upper classmen failing of election to any club;

3. The distraction of undergraduates from their academic pursuits at times of, and incident to club elections, and because of the social demands upon their time;

4. The under classmen's temptation to seek social advancement by choice of associates, tending toward snobbishness and incident extravagance.

THE CLUBS:

In the discussion of these evils, the upper class clubs have been made the prime feature, and criticism has been showered upon them to such extent that many firmly believe they are at the root of the trouble. As anyone familiar with the development of the university's social side must admit, these organizations are the logical consequence of the old eating club system. When there were only two or three clubs, none of the present difficulties existed; in those times it was a distinction to be a club member, and no reflection to be out. The increase in the number of clubs has changed this situation with deplorable results in many notable instances.

Whatever the cause of these difficulties, the remedy must be sought very largely in the proper direction of the clubs; it seems to us highly desirable that such remedy be along evolutionary lines, rather than destructive and reconstructive, so that the good in the past development will be retained and future progress be guided.

THE REMEDIES:

After most mature deliberation and very full discussion among ourselves and with members of the Board of Trustees and faculty, and with other alumni and representative undergraduates, we suggest as a basis of procedure the following:

1. That, for the next few years at least, permission for the organization of additional clubs be refused;

2. That the existing interclub treaty be abolished in its letter and spirit;

3. That the clubs, by mutual agreement, admit sophomores to their active membership, a few at a time, beginning at the opening of sophomore year; for example, that each club elect not to exceed six sophomores at the beginning of sophomore year, their elections to be immediately effective, not to exceed six other sophomores on or about the first of March in sophomore year, their elections to be likewise immediately effective, and that the balance of members from any class, to such number as each individual club may determine, be elected on or after the first of June in sophomore year, their elections to become effective not earlier than the opening of junior year;

4. That no pledge to membership in a club shall be exacted or recognized as obligatory for any purpose, and that every club member be privileged to resign from his organization and become a member of another club, provided he be in good standing in respect of dues and house charges with his original club, and that no resignation take effect until (say) at least thirty days after the same is presented in writing;

5. That the faculty and the clubs encourage closer relations and a better understanding between their respective members;

6. That steps be taken, in co-operation with the undergraduates, to promote the organization of a University Club whose membership shall be open to all members of the three upper classes, the faculty and Board of Trustees and alumni.

The abolition of the interclub treaty would, of itself, tend to break down the wall now existing between the sophomore and upper classes and promote a more rational intercourse between the members of these classes, while the admission of even a limited number of sophomores to the clubs would bring the members of the three upper classes into closer touch. The permission to club members of resigning their membership and joining other organizations, if a sentiment to such a course could be engendered, would do away with the possibility of any individual's being tied down to uncongenial surroundings and companionship because of a misconception at the time of his entering a club.

The University Club gives promise of affording a solution of many of the complexities, and aiding in the solution of others. It is our idea that such a club should be in no sense allied with the

University, but, on the contrary, be an independent organization, officered and managed by its members and that all candidates for admission should be passed upon in the usual way; that it should be simple in its construction, capable of economical operation and consequently charge such low dues as to open its membership to all; that it should be centrally located near the front campus and suitably equipped to afford headquarters for the University organizations (the Princetonian, Lit. and Tiger boards, the Glee and Triangle Clubs, etc.), as well as facilities for social intercourse and recreation; that it should contain dining rooms sufficient to accommodate such of its members as might desire to eat there, either occasionally or permanently, and furnish regular board at reasonable rates; that it should operate a grill room, open at appropriate hours, where light refreshments and beer (but no wine or spirits) would be served—in short, that everything should be done to make such club university in its scope and so attractive to the undergraduate, irrespective of his membership in any other social organization, that it would come to be the common meeting ground in leisure moments. Such a club would serve to give non-club members among the sophomore and upper classes a common place for their meals and diversion; to bring into closer touch members of different clubs and club members generally with non-club members, and to be the centre of all extra curriculum activities—in a word, to coordinate the social life of the undergraduates and so meet the first two of the evils listed above. By the same token it would exercise a levelling effect upon the whole undergraduate body where snobbishness, individual extravagance and exclusiveness would be rather frowned upon than encouraged. The fact that such an organization is favored by the undergraduates ensures their support, without which it would be doomed to failure.

The abolition of a fixed date for club elections and the admission of sophomores into clubs would do away with the excitement now characteristic of the ante-election period, remove the occasion for seeking advancement by cultivating paying acquaintances and, coupled with the University Club's furnishing the eating place for sophomores, put club elections once more in the hands of the upper classmen.

No mention has been made of freshmen, because under the present system they are satisfactorily provided for in their commons and beside tradition and past experience point to its being inadvisable to bring them into close intercourse with members of the three upper classes.

CONCLUSION:

The foregoing plan, while unavoidably involving some consideration of details, is seen at a glance to be susceptible of alteration, extension and amendment without materially affecting its general scope. To carry it out would effect a somewhat radical departure from the existing methods but in no sense involve anything revolutionary. It leans rather toward directing the future development of past evolution along more common sense, practical and healthy lines, than it does to the substitution of new conditions in lieu of a system which contains much that is good and around which centre traditions and, to many, fondly cherished associations which should not lightly be done away with.

Dated, New York, N. Y.,
  March 3, 1908.
    Respectfully submitted,
        J. S. MORGAN, '88.
        GEORGE C. FRASER, '93.
        FRANKLIN MURPHY, JR., '95.
        WILLIAM W. PHILLIPS, '95.
        C. B. BOSTWICK, '96.

Printed report (Trustees' Papers, UA, NjP).

Cyrus Fogg Brackett to the President and Board of Trustees of Princeton University

Gentlemen: Princeton, New Jersey. April 8, 1908.

I beg herewith to place in your hands my resignation of the "Henry Professorship of Physics" which was entrusted to me thirty five years ago. I desire that this resignation take effect at the close of the present academic year.

If I may occupy the house now assigned me, No. 4 Prospect avenue, I will continue to reside in Princeton where so many years of service have been spent.

My interest in the growth and work of the University is in no degree abated, and it may be that I will still be able to render some useful service in the future, as occasion shall arise, especially in connection with the new Physical Laboratory.

Again offering you my best thanks for the uniform confidence and support accorded me in the past I beg to remain as ever,
      Sincerely yours. C. F. Brackett.

TLS (Trustees' Papers, UA, NjP).

From Ralph Adams Cram

Dear Dr. Wilson: Boston, April 8, 1908.

I am just in receipt of your letter of April 7, and find it difficult to express my gratification at the action of the Committee of the Board of Trustees in the matter of the site for the proposed Graduate School. Since my last visit to Princeton, I have been studying this matter still more carefully and am increasingly convinced that this is unquestionably the proper site for the School.

You need have no fear that in case I am called in to consider more in detail the plans for this School that I shall act on the advice, or toward carrying out the desires of, one authority only. I think I realize as clearly as possible the complicated and difficult nature of this problem, but I am quite convinced that in the matter of plans, as satisfactory a working compromise is possible as has proved to be the case in the matter of the site.

It would be difficult to overestimate the fascination of this problem. I have little interest in schemes which present no difficulties of any kind, but the moment conflicting interests and apparently impossible conditions are to be met, every instinct in me rises to the occasion, and I find myself working out the problem with the absorbing interest that occurs in the case of a difficult game of chess, or would occur, were I a military man, in the solution of a complicated problem in strategy, or tactics.

I shall be only too delighted to meet the Dean and should like to arrange to come to Princeton immediately after Easter. We are to open the bids on '77 Hall[1] here in the Boston office at twelve o'clock Tuesday, April 21, and we are writing today to those particularly interested in this building to suggest that, if possible, we have a meeting in Princeton on Wednesday, the 22nd., to consider these estimates. I have accepted an invitation to dine with Mr. and Mrs. Cuyler the evening of Thursday, April 23, so I should have to be in Princeton either the 22nd., or the 24th. It would be more convenient for me if I could come there for the first of these two dates.

So far as the last paragraph in your letter is concerned, I can only say that I congratulate myself more and more every day on the extraordinary good fortune which has brought me into such intimate contact with yourself and the Trustees and Faculty of Princeton University.

Very sincerely yours,   R A Cram.

TLS (WP, DLC).
  [1] A dormitory being built by the Class of 1877, later named Campbell Hall. See H. B. Thompson to WW, Sept. 16, 1907, n. 3, Vol. 17.

Henry Burchard Fine to the Board of Trustees' Committee on Morals and Discipline

Gentlemen: Princeton University, April 9, 1908.

I beg to submit the following report:

Since my October report four students have been suspended for intoxication and one for false chapel registration. Two Freshmen have been finally dismissed, one for violating the Honor System, the other for sexual immorality. I have also two other serious cases of discipline to report.

The night of November 9th. three young ladies who were occupying a room in the Nassau Inn were subjected to a gross insult. Their room was on the second floor of the building, the window of which opens on the roof over the back part of the Postal Telegraph Office. On the same floor of the Nassau Apartment Building, adjoining the Nassau Inn on the East, is a room then occupied by three Sophomores, the windows of which also open on this roof. The young ladies had just retired for the night when someone came across the roof, opened their window, and called out to them to come across the roof. The intruder disappeared when the girls called for assistance to the father of one of them, who occupied the adjoining room. This gentleman made a formal complaint to the Dean on the following day, supplying evidence which pointed to two of the students occupying the room across the way. A full statement of this evidence and of the examination which followed is appended to this report.[1] It was not proved that either of these students was the person who opened the girls' window. But one of them was persistently untruthful when before the Committee. He was finally dismissed on the ground that he was persistently untruthful when examined by the Discipline Committee of the Faculty regarding an affair involving serious discipline. The other was disingenuous at the outset and then told us that he was so intoxicated that night that he had no knowledge of anything that may have occurred after he went to bed. This student had been suspended for drunkenness and disorderly conduct last June. He was finally dismissed on the ground that after having once been suspended for intoxication he should again have been intoxicated and should have attempted to conceal the fact from the Committee.

On the night of February 18th. a young woman of bad character came to Princeton from Trenton with three students and went with them to a room in '79 Hall, where she remained until

---

[1] This statement is missing.

discovered the following day by the College Proctor. A full account of the affair is also appended to this report.[2]

One of the students was a member of the Junior class in good standing. He was finally dismissed, on the ground that he had taken a woman of bad character to a college dormitory and had there spent the night with her.

Another of the students had just been dropped from the Sophomore class at the mid-year examinations. The Faculty voted that he be not allowed to return to college, on the ground that he had been party to the offense of harboring a woman of bad character in a college dormitory.

The third student, having twice been dropped from the Freshman class, was already finally separated from the University. The Faculty instructed the Dean to write to his parents that had he been a member of this University when the affair occurred he would have been finally dismissed on the ground that he was a party to the offense of harboring a woman of bad character in a college dormitory.

The number of men dropped at the end of first term because of failure in their studies was 75 as against 58 in February 1907, 71 in February 1906, 71 in February 1905 and 75 in February 1904.

They were distributed as follows among the several departments and classes:

	Seniors	Juniors	Sophomores	Freshmen	Specials of all Departments
A.B.	0	3	7	18	
B.S. & Litt.B.	1	1	9	4	
C.E.[3]	2	6	14	2	8
	3	10	30	24	8

The corresponding totals for last year were Seniors 5, Juniors 8, Sophomores 15, Freshmen 17, Specials 13. Hence the number of Upperclassmen dropped is the same as last year and the number of Specials 5 less than last year. On the other hand, twice as many Sophomores were dropped this year as last and 7 more Freshmen.

The Sophomore class, 1910, which now suffers the heaviest loss made an unusually good showing in the mid-year examina-

---

[2] This account is also missing.
[3] That is, Civil Engineer.

tions last year when the number of dropped Freshmen fell from 35 to 17. I find that the majority of the men now dropped from this class had either been dropped before or narrowly escaped coming under the dropping rule last year.

The most striking item in this years statistics is the number of Freshmen dropped from the A.B. Department as compared with the numbers dropped from the B.S. and C.E. Departments. Heretofore the Freshman loss has always been heavier in the B.S. and C.E. divisions of the class than in the A.B. divisions, but this year three times as many A.B. Freshmen were dropped as B.S. and C.E. Freshmen combined. This of course means what I had already learned from reports sent me during the term—the reports on which my warnings to students below passing in their term work are based—that last fall a larger number of weak and inadequately prepared students entered the Academic Department than either of the other departments. I may add that last fall 40 Freshmen were admitted on trial, of whom 13 were A.B. students, 8 B.S., and 19 C.E. All of the B.S. and C.E. students stood the trial successfully, but 7 of the 13 A.B. students were dropped.

On examining the record of Freshmen losses at the mid-year examinations for the past four years—the period in which the present plan of study has been in effect—I find that while the numbers change sometimes for the better and sometimes for the worse in the case of the A.B. and C.E. men, there has been a continual and rapid improvment in the showing made by the B.S.-Litt.B. men. Thus in the February examinations of the successive years 1905-1908 the numbers of B.S.-Litt.B. Freshmen dropped were 23, 14, 9, 5. This of course indicates a corresponding improvement in the preparation of the men entering the B.S.-Litt.B. course. I desire to call attention to this fact, not only because it is in itself interesting, but because of an important question which it suggests.

Our B.S.-Litt.B. students are those who enter without Greek, but with the wish to pursue a liberal course of study and to obtain a Bachelor's degree. Before the adoption of the present plan of study the entrance requirements to the B.S. (-Litt.B.) course were much lower than to the A.B. course and the B.S. (-Litt.B.) students were distinctly inferior to the A.B. students. But since the entrance requirements became at least as high for the B.S.-Litt.B. as for the A.B. course there has been a rapid improvement in the quality of the B.S.-Litt.B. men until this year a class has entered college in which the B.S.-Litt.B. division is fully as well prepared and as able as the A.B. division. I may add that there are now almost as many B.S.-Litt.B. men in this class as A.B. men.

Has not the time come, therefore, when it will be wise to extend to our B.S.-Litt.B. students the scholarship and remission of tuition privileges which are now enjoyed by our A.B. students exclusively? It is a fact often commented on here, at Yale, Harvard and elsewhere, that graduates of the large city high schools are on the average making better college records than graduates of the college preparatory schools. They are, on the whole, a more serious class of students and there is every reason why we should desire to increase the number of them at Princeton. But few of them can offer Greek at entrance, since Greek has practically dropped out of the high school curriculum; and most of them are men of limited means and therefore unable to avail themselves of our B.S.-Litt.B. course in which the payment of full tuition is required of all students. Moreover it is becoming true of boys of limited means in the college preparatory schools also, boys who have their own way to make in the world, that a course in which Greek is replaced by the Modern Languages and Science seems more attractive to them than one involving Greek—now that Greek is no longer regarded by people in general as indispensable to a liberal education. Of course a large percentage of such boys will prefer to attend universities where they can combine their college and professional studies. But I am satisfied that many more of them would come to Princeton if they could get the aid here which is offered them by other institutions, but which we confine to our A.B. students.

This seems to me a matter deserving of very serious consideration. There is a constant increase in the number of boys entering Princeton from families of wealth. To keep the tone of the place healthy and democratic, there should be a corresponding increase in the number coming from families of moderate means. Our present practice of restricting the scholarship and remission of tuition privilege to A.B. students stands in the way of this.[4]

In this connection it is interesting to note that there are 40 University Scholarships open to first and second group A.B.

[4] A special committee of the trustees consisting of William J. Magie, chairman, Moses Taylor Pyne, Simon J. McPherson, and Henry W. Green, was appointed on April 9, 1908, to consider the extension of scholarship and remission of tuition privileges. On June 8, 1908, the committee recommended that the benefit of all scholarships not specifically limited by the terms of their creation should be extended to B.S. and Litt.B. students, and the trustees so resolved. The committee also favored the extension of remission of tuition but suggested that, in view of the financial condition of the university, the matter be referred to the Committee on Finance. The Finance Committee recommended the extension of remission of tuition at the meeting of the Board of Trustees on June 14, 1909, and the trustees so voted.

students who have received remission of tuition. To judge from their first term's records only 25 men will qualify for these Scholarships next year.

Respectfully submitted,   H. B. Fine

TRS (Trustees' Papers, UA, NjP).

Edward Wright Sheldon to the Board of Trustees of Princeton University, with Enclosure

[New York]
April 9, 1908.

To the Trustees of Princeton University:

Pursuant to a resolution of the Board adopted January 9, 1908, the Committee on the Graduate School reports as follows regarding a site for the John R. Thomson Graduate College:

The inquiry thus committed to us has not been free from difficulty. We have investigated the subject at length and have given our best consideration to the various sites suggested. Among these, Merwick, the present seat of the Graduate School, was carefully weighed. Its great natural advantages and unusual beauty were appreciated, but a majority of our Committee deemed it unavailable for two reasons: first, because of its absolute physical detachment from the University campus and the consequent separation of the Graduate College as a visible and dominating influence of University life, and, secondly, because by the terms of Mrs. Swann's will the building was required, as we were advised, to be constructed upon the grounds of the University, that is, upon land included within the territorial unit commonly described as the campus.

Our next step was to investigate the availability for general building purposes of the large tract of land lying between the Pennsylvania Railroad on the west, the group of preceptors' houses on the east,[1] Prospect Avenue and Prospect on the north

[1] The "large tract of land" here referred to lay on both sides of Washington Road. As R. A. Cram indicates in the Enclosure printed with this document, the Graduate College would have been built either on one side of Washington Road or the other, had either site proved acceptable. The so-called preceptors' houses were a real estate development by a private organization of alumni and friends of the university known as the Prospect Company. The tract of some fifty acres purchased by the company about the beginning of 1907 lay to the east of the upperclass clubs on Prospect Avenue and ran down both sides of an extension of Princeton Avenue (the extension was soon renamed Broadmead) between Prospect Avenue and Lake Carnegie. The company ultimately erected twenty-two houses in English Tudor style, with from eight to twelve rooms each, on lots of 80 by 200 feet each. The houses were rented to faculty members at very moderate rates. The entire development was presented to the university in the 1920's. For a brief article, with an architect's drawing of the houses, see "The Prospect Houses," *Princeton Alumni Weekly*, VII (March 23, 1907), 399-402.

and Carnegie Lake on the south. A sub-committee, composed of the Chairman of this Committee, the President and one other member,[2] was appointed to conduct this investigation. Quite apart from the location of the Graduate College it was deemed essential that the possibility of using this important tract in the natural extension of the University should be studied. Mr. Rudolph Hering and Mr. George C. Whipple, consulting sanitary engineers of New York, were retained, and after personal and independent examination of the property, they made their separate reports which are hereto attached.[3] Subsequently, as set forth in Mr. Whipple's letter of March 30, 1908,[4] they conferred with our Professor Brackett. We commend these reports to the careful attention of the Board and ask for them such action as the importance of the subject may seem to demand.

Mr. R. A. Cram, the Supervising Architect of the University, then studied the question from the architectural point of view, and made a report, which is also hereto attached.[5] In completion of that report Mr. Cram has submitted the two annexed plans, marked respectively "Exhibit A." and "Exhibit B."[6]

As a result of our consideration of the entire subject we adopted on April 6, 1908, the following resolution:

"RESOLVED, That we recommend to the Board the site for the Thomson Graduate College proposed by Mr. Cram and shown on the plan marked 'Exhibit A.' hereto attached, with the understanding, (1), that there shall be reserved for the Graduate College and the President's house an area including the present grounds of Prospect and such land to the south as may be determined upon by this Committee after consultation with the Committe on Grounds and Buildings; and, (2), that there be a re-location of the President's house, as indicated on the plan marked 'Exhibit B.' hereto attached."

To bring about this solution of the problem, the initiative was heartily assumed by the President, and we appreciate keenly his thorough and self-forgetful effort in behalf of the University.

2 That is, Sheldon, Wilson, and Grover Cleveland.
3 R. Hering to G. Cleveland et al., March 26, 1908, TLS (Trustees' Papers, UA, NjP); and G. C. Whipple to G. Cleveland et al., March 24, 1908, TLS (Trustees' Papers, UA, NjP).
4 It is missing.
5 It is printed as the following document.
6 Exhibit A was a rough sketch placing the Graduate College between Seventy-Nine Hall and Prospect without moving the latter. Exhibit B, also a rough sketch, showed the arrangement if Prospect were moved. Both sketches are appended to Sheldon's report to the trustees.

During the final stage of our work, we were so unfortunate as to be deprived of the valuable assistance of our Chairman.[7] The keenness of his interest in the Graduate School and the profound ability of his judgment combine to intensify our regret at his enforced absence at this time. We are gratified to learn that the conclusion we have reached has his hearty concurrence.

We may add that in natural beauty and dignity of surroundings and in opportunity for future expansion, the site we have chosen seems to us to be the best available for the purpose; indeed it represents the choicest ground belonging to the University, and sets the highest possible standard for the development of the Graduate College.

Following the terms of our formal recommendation as above set forth, we submit for adoption by the Board the following proposed preamble and resolution:

WHEREAS, the late Josephine A. Thomson Swann by her last will and testament which was admitted to probate by the Surrogate of Mercer County, New Jersey, March 16, 1906, gave all her residuary estate to the Trustees of Princeton University in trust to devote the same or the proceeds thereof as soon as practicable to the erection and construction upon the grounds of the said University of a building to be known as "The John R. Thomson Graduate College of Princeton University," and in pursuance of such gift the University has received from the executors of the will various securities and property and the Trustees have since been engaged in selecting a proper site for such building and have consulted in relation thereto with the executors of the will, now it is

RESOLVED: That the site for the John R. Thomson Graduate College be fixed in the grounds of Prospect about midway between Seventy Nine Hall and the President's house, as shown on the plan of R. A. Cram, Supervising Architect of the University, which is attached as "Exhibit A." to the report of the Committee on the Graduate School dated April 9, 1908, it being understood, first, that there shall be reserved for the Graduate College and the President's house an area including the present grounds of Prospect and such land to the south as may be determined upon by the Committee on the Graduate College after consultation with the Committee on Grounds and Buildings; and, secondly, that

7 Grover Cleveland had been the original chairman of the sub-committee to select a site for the Graduate College. He was at this time in his terminal illness and died on June 24, 1908.

there be a re-location of the President's house as indicated on the plan of Mr. Cram marked "Exhibit B." and attached to such report.[8]

Respectfully submitted.

The Committee on the Graduate School,

By Edward W. Sheldon.

TRS (Trustees' Papers, UA, NjP).

[8] The Board of Trustees adopted this resolution on April 9, 1908.

E N C L O S U R E

Ralph Adams Cram to Edward Wright Sheldon

Dear Sir: Boston, March 30, 1908.

On Wednesday, March 25th, at the request of the Sub-Committee of the Committee of the Board of Trustees appointed to consider the site of the future Graduate School, I made a visit to Princeton and examined very carefully the sites referred to me for consideration.

As I understand the matter, I am, by reason of technical questions connected with the bequest, estopped from considering or referring to the site of the present Graduate School known as "Merwick." I may select solely the available sites either on the land which belonged to the University at the time of the bequest, or on property immediately adjoining such land and acquired by the University subsequent to this bequest. Specifically, I am asked to consider two sites south-east of the campus; one on the right of Washington Road, the other on the left.

It is to be assumed that I am at liberty to speak of the advantages of these, or any other sites, solely from the standpoint of their possible architectural qualities. It is, however, somewhat difficult to consider these, or any other sites, solely in this way. As you are aware, a very grave question exists bearing on the hygienic aspects of the case, and it would be impossible for me to deal with the subject in entire disregard of this hygienic problem; again, the question as to whether the Graduate School should be intimately associated with the Undergraduate departments, or should be isolated from them by a considerable space, must also be taken into consideration. I do not presume to speak authoritatively on either of these subjects; nevertheless, each is of such profound importance that it must be considered as modifying very materially anything I may say with regard to the several sites, viewed in the light of their architectural possibilities.

The site proposed on the right of Washington Road, which is, as I understand it, between the old sewer bed, now abandoned, and the new sewer bed, use of which has been granted to the Town of Princeton (though whether in perpetuity or not I am not advised) does not commend itself to me in any respect. Apart from the unfortunate juxtaposition of the old and the new sewer beds, the site seems to me without any distinction, lacking in distant views of any kind, and though actually on an elevation of perhaps 20 ft. above the level of Washington Road at this point, nevertheless giving the effect of being in a basin entirely shut in by high land and thick trees. I cannot but feel that it is important that the Graduate School should be not only of the highest type of architectural beauty, but that its surroundings of landscape and gardening should reach at least the high degree of perfection now obtained at Merwick. The site on the right fails, I believe, in all these respects, and lying, as it does, directly south of the main lines of view from the campus and at a much lower level would give the effect from the campus of a department isolated and depressed in a position of insignificance and unimportance. None of the criticisms noted above applies to the site at the left of Washington Road. Here, at no greater distance from the campus, we have a rounded hillock of considerable area, the elevation of which is greater than that of the site on the right, and which contains possibilities of landscape and gardening development second to none possessed by any portion of the grounds of Princeton University. This site is widely separated from the old and the new sewer beds, not only by distance, but by thick masses of intervening trees. Land which is almost a swamp intervenes between the campus and the site on the right, but on the left the intervening land is high, well drained and available for gardens or future buildings. From this hillock on the left a view of extreme beauty is obtained directly south between the semi-circle of trees, and a little judicious cutting would give, at all seasons of the year, an extremely beautiful view of a portion of the Lake, down to which the land slopes in a most effective manner. If built on this site, the Graduate School would immediately acquire dignity and impressiveness as seen both from any points on Washington Road, or from the campus, and the possibilities of effective and beautiful grounds and gardens are of the highest possible order.

I am of the opinion, however, that if built at this place a generous allowance should be made for the immediate construction of terraces, and gardens, and for tree planting. These accessories need not be carried very far at first, but very certainly brick or stone terraces to the south should be built, a masonry bridge constructed from Washington Street across the little brook, the grounds for a distance of 400' or 500' in all directions around the school should be laid out and a certain number of trees planted to provide for future shade and for the tying in of the new buildings to the landscape.

Granting the desirability of isolating the Graduate School from the Undergraduate departments, no better site than this is offered by any portion of the available grounds of the University.

May I take the liberty at this time of suggesting to the consideration of the Trustees another site, which, so far as I am advised, has not been brought to their attention. I have no desire to enter into a discussion of the question as to whether the Graduate School should, or should not be segregated in a position at some distance from the Undergraduate department. I am aware, however, that there are two definitely formulated ideas as to this subject. If the decision of the Trustees is in favour of an intimate association between the Undergraduate and Graduate departments, then it seems to me there is one site which is preeminently the one which should be devoted to the Graduate School.

I assume that it is admitted by all that if the Graduate and Undergraduate departments are to be closely associated, then it is imperative that the Graduate School should occupy a position of dignity and beauty. The sites still available which possess these qualities are so few in number that at first sight they may seem to be non-existent. I cannot feel this, and desire to suggest that one very perfect position is still subject to consideration. I refer to "Prospect." Now I am aware that this is, perhaps, preeminently the logical position for the President's house, and that the very extraordinary beauty of the grounds, trees and planting, might lead the Trustees to regard with disfavour any further encroachments on this property. I desire to submit, however, that the area now reserved for the President's house and grounds, in view of what seems to me the paramount necessity of coordinating the buildings of the University into an intimate group closely knit together, is larger than considerations of administration would justify, provided that this open area may be reduced in size in such a way as not to destroy its present unquestioned beauty.

If this land is carefully studied on the spot, it will be seen, I think, that that portion which lies to the east of the present carriage turn and between this and McCosh Walk, '79 Dormitory and the new Physical Laboratory, is the least beautiful or highly developed of the entire area. I venture to suggest, therefore, that this site be considered as a possible location for the Graduate School. This school might be so designed that it would consist of several courts, or quads, one of which would be entirely enclosed by buildings, while the others should be open, more or less, on different sides and so disposed as to permit the preservation of the greater number of the more beautiful trees now on the site. The first construction might be in the form of a quadrangle about 100 ft. x 150 ft. square, surrounded by buildings, and so placed that its easterly facade would be 75 ft. or 80 ft. from the west side of '79 Dormitory, its southerly side about 130 ft. from the north facade of the Physical Laboratory, while the westerly side would be a continuation in a right line of the west side of the Physical Laboratory. No important trees would be sacrificed by so using this portion of the site, and as the necessity for development of the Graduate School arose, living quarters might be obtained; first, by the turning over of '79 Dormitory to the Graduate School for residential purposes; second, by extending wings, or courts, of the first construction north toward McCosh Walk and west along McCosh Walk as far as the westerly end of McCosh Hall. The present residence for the President would remain where it is and would be 115 ft distant from the nearest portion of the Graduate School. Sometime in the future it may prove desirable to build a new residence for the President, which in style should correspond to the type of architecture so wisely determined upon by the Trustees as that which shall be maintained for all future buildings at Princeton. When this time arrived, the present residence might be entirely removed and a new building constructed near Brown Hall and occupying approximately the site now used as a rose garden. A house for the Dean of the Graduate School might then be built in a corresponding position to the east of the present site of the President's house and partially closing the vista between the Physical Laboratory and the proposed Graduate School. Were these changes effected and new wings for the Graduate School built along McCosh Walk, as indicated above, we should have a thoroughly united, architectural composition, opening out at the point where McCosh Walk and the road from Nassau Street meet near the westerly end of McCosh Hall, with a clear and extraordinarily beautiful view across the cleared site of the present house for the President away to the southerly horizon. This whole area, then, the present terraces and gardens of the President's house being retained intact, would become a great garden of the utmost beauty, which, with almost no changes whatever, except so far as paths are concerned, would become a garden comparable in area and beauty to those famous gardens associated with the different Oxford Colleges. South of the new house for the President, private gardens could easily be developed for the use of the President himself, while the beautifully wooded area remaining would become park-like gardens to be used in common by the President and by the occupants of the Graduate School, opened, possibly, to the public on certain days and under certain conditions.

I am aware that this suggestion may be considered revolutionary, but I cannot convince myself that it would result in any loss of beauty to Prospect as it now stands, indeed I believe that its beauty might be materially increased.

If, as I have said above, intimate association between the Graduate and Undergraduate departments is desirable, or even unobjectionable, then the site I have suggested is one of great strategic importance, since the Graduate School would then be in the most convenient possible position with regard to the laboratories, the recitation rooms of McCosh Hall, the Chapel, the Library and the Art Department.

Architecturally, the impressiveness of the University would be greatly increased by a development on these lines. As Supervising Architect, I am strongly impressed with the necessity of a building up and tying together of all the parts of the University, avoiding the old park idea, with isolated buildings dotted around in various points, and recurring to the scheme in vogue in Oxford and Cambridge since the XVth century, whereby the several parts are tied together into one consistent whole. Such a development as I have suggested would be directly in line with my idea of the desirable future growth of the University as an architectural entity, and I therefore venture to commend it to the consideration of the Trustees.

I am preparing several rough sketches showing how the school would work out on the site recommended above, and will submit these to you in a very few days.

Very respectfully yours,   R A Cram.

Supervising Architect.

TLS (Trustees' Papers, UA, NjP).

From the Minutes of the Board of Trustees
of Princeton University

[April 9, 1908]

The Trustees of Princeton University met in stated session in the Trustees' Room in the Chancellor Green Library, Princeton, New Jersey, at eleven o'clock on Thursday morning April 9, 1908.

The President of the University in the chair. . . .

CONSIDERATION OF REPORT OF COMMITTEE ON CONFERENCE
WITH ALUMNI POSTPONED

After a discussion of the report of the Committee, on motion of Dr. McPherson, seconded by Mr. Jones, the following resolution was adopted:

RESOLVED that the report of the Committee on Conference with Alumni be printed and placed in the hands of the members of the Board and that consideration of the report and the acceptance or rejection of its recommendations, except numbers 4 and 5, be postponed until the June meeting of the Board and that the Committee be continued.

ADOPTION OF RECOMMENDATIONS 4 AND 5 OF COMMITTEE
ON CONFERENCE WITH ALUMNI

On motion duly seconded recommendations 4 and 5 of the Committee on Conference with Alumni were adopted as follows:

That the faculty be requested to consider and report to the Board of Trustees whether the trips of the athletic and non-athletic organizations away from Princeton cannot be materially reduced in number.[1]

That the establishment in University Hall of a commons for the entire sophomore class and for such of the upper classmen as can be accommodated be authorized, and that the matter be referred to the Committee on Grounds and Buildings, with power.

REPORT OF COMMITTEE ON APPLICATION FOR
STATE APPROPRIATION

Mr. Pyne of the Committee to consider the question of appealing to the Legislature for financial assistance reported as follows:

The Committee appointed at the last meeting to consider the question of appealing to the Legislature of the State of New Jersey for financial assisance, after mature deliberation have concluded that it would be inadvisable at present to make such a request.

Respectfully submitted,

M. Taylor Pyne, Chairman. . . .

A GIFT FROM MRS. RUSSELL SAGE

Mr. Cadwalader presented the following letter from Mrs. Russell Sage:

To the Trustees of Princeton University:

Dear Sirs: New York, April 7th, 1908.

I have felt for some little time past that your University was perhaps lacking in suitable dormitory accommodations on your College campus for members of your Freshman Class, and, with the view of supplying such want if it exists, I have decided to make the following offer, viz:

I will donate to your University a sum not to exceed $250,000, for the purpose of erecting a dormitory building on the College campus, the primary use of which shall be for members of the Freshman Class. I can fully understand that, for various reasons, it would not be practicable to have a dormitory used exclusively for freshmen and this point could be easily covered by having it understood that to the extent the new dormitory be used for members of other classes like accommodation would be provided for freshmen in other dormitories.

If you should decide to accept my gift, I should wish to reserve the right to approve of the choice of architect and I should also wish to have the plans submitted for my approval before final adoption.

Yours very truly, (Signed) Margaret Olivia Sage.

THANKS TO MRS. SAGE

On motion of Mr. Cadwalader duly seconded the Board adopted the following vote of thanks to Mrs. Sage for her gift:

RESOLVED That the Trustees of Princeton University hereby accept the offer made by Mrs. Sage to provide funds for the erection of a dormitory on the college campus, primarily for the use of the freshman class, upon the terms and conditions prescribed by Mrs. Sage in her letter of April 7th.

FURTHER RESOLVED That this Board hereby tenders to Mrs. Sage its sincere thanks for her great liberality and expresses its satisfaction that the work of this University has commended itself to her interest and consideration.

FURTHER RESOLVED That the Grounds and Buildings Committee is hereby instructed to communicate at the proper time with Mrs. Sage as to the selection of an architect, and with reference to the plans and location of the new building.

"Minutes of the Trustees of Princeton University, April 1908-June 1913," bound minute book (UA, NjP).

¹ See the Princeton University Faculty Minutes printed at May 4 and June 5, 1908.

To Cyrus Fogg Brackett

[Princeton, N. J.]

My dear Professor Brackett: April 10th, 1908.

The Board accepted your resignation yesterday with the most profound and unaffected regret, and begged me to express to you their deep appreciation of your long and distinguished service in the University. I am expressing their feeling, therefore, as well as my own when I say that your services have been of the utmost value to the University, not only forming and stimulating your students, but also stimulating your colleagues and setting them by way of example a high standard of work and achievement. No other man, I venture to say, has contributed more than you have to that establishment of Princeton in the esteem of the country which was begun by the admirable work of Dr. McCosh, and I hope that it will be a source of pleasure to you that you take with you into retirement the warm admiration and affection of those with whom you have been associated.

The Board voted that your resignation should take effect at the end of the present fiscal year; that you should be requested to retain the title of Professor of Physics Emeritus; that you should retain the house which you occupy so long as the University has no immediate need of it; and that I should apply to the Carnegie Foundation for the Advancement of Teaching for the proper retiring allowance for you.

With warmest personal regard,
Always faithfully and sincerely yours,
[Woodrow Wilson]

CCL (WWP, UA, NjP).

To Henry Smith Pritchett

[Princeton, N. J.]

My dear President Pritchett: April 10th, 1908.

I wonder if you would think it burdensome to put on your mailing list the Trustees of Princeton University. I mean the several Trustees individually. They have professed a great deal of interest in the work of the Foundation and have asked me if it would be possible for them to obtain copies of your Annual Reports.

Quite unexpectedly, one of our older men felt obliged to tender his resignation at the meeting of our Board which occurred yesterday, the resignation to take effect at the close of the present academic year. This is Professor Cyrus F. Brackett, who has been the occupant of our Henry Professorship of Physics for thirty-five years, a man who has been singularly useful to the University throughout his connection with it. If you will be kind enough to have Mr. Bowman[1] send me the proper blanks, I will make an application for a retiring allowance for him. He is seventy-five, I am sorry to say, and not likely to be very long upon our rolls. I wish, by the way, that you would instruct me as to the proper way to estimate his salary as a basis of reckoning for a retiring allowance. He has received a salary plus a house free of rent, and it is our purpose to allow him to continue to occupy the house so long as the University has no immediate need of it. In such circumstances, should the rental of such a house be included in the amount I state as the amount of his salary for the past five years? I did include it in estimating the salary of Professor Packard, who has been treated in the same way, being allowed to occupy a house which stands on the college grounds, subject at any time to be removed to give place to other buildings. The house might prove a burden if it were not included in the reckoning.

Always cordially and sincerely yours,

[Woodrow Wilson]

CCL (WWP, UA, NjP).

[1] John Gabbert Bowman, Secretary of the Carnegie Foundation for the Advancement of Teaching, who later served as President of the State University of Iowa and as Chancellor of the University of Pittsburgh for many years.

To Henry James Forman[1]

My dear Mr. Forman: Princeton, N. J.   April 10th, 1908.

I wish very much that you could disobey Colonel Harvey's instructions. I do not feel that it is any longer true that I am being seriously considered as a possible recipient of the nomination at Denver this year,[2] and fear that Colonel Harvey is carrying his generous loyalty to an idea and a high purpose further than the situation makes necessary. I need not say how warmly I appreciate it all or how deeply grateful I am to have been considered worthy of the honor he has done me. I am merely giving expression to my feeling that the suggestion he so generously made is no longer one of the working elements of the political situation.

As for your question whom I would suggest to write an article for the North American Review if not Mr. Cleveland, I am entirely at a loss. I do not know anyone close enough to me to be able to write of me from intimate personal knowledge who would be likely to be an advocate of my candidacy, it happening that most of my closer associates are Republicans and not Democrats. I suppose that it would hardly be within your plan to have the article written by a Republican, though I know one or two Republicans who might *ex thesi* be willing to write it. Perhaps Mr. [William M.] Laffan of The Sun or Mr. Walter H. Page of The World's Work could suggest someone who would have the requisite political capacity to frame such an article properly.[3]

With much regard,

Sincerely yours, Woodrow Wilson

TLS (Berg Coll., NN).

[1] Associate Editor and General Manager of the *North American Review*.

[2] That is, the Democratic presidential nomination. The Democratic national convention was to meet in Denver on July 7, 1908.

[3] See H. J. Forman to WW, April 14, 1908, n. 1.

To Harry Augustus Garfield

My dear Garfield: Princeton, N. J. April 10th, 1908.

I have myself had a letter from Rowe[1] and have fixed Thursday afternoon, April 16th, as the date of an interview with him. My own predisposition towards [Henry Jones] Ford is so strong that I feel I should like to have all the light possible, but I will try to see you before Thursday so as to make sure that I calculate Rowe's personal equation properly and know how to estimate what he says.

Always affectionately yours, Woodrow Wilson

TLS (H. A. Garfield Papers, DLC).

[1] Leo Stanton Rowe, Professor and Head of the Department of Political Science, University of Pennsylvania, whose letter concerning a successor to Garfield as Professor of Politics at Princeton is missing.

From Harry Augustus Garfield

My dear Wilson: Princeton, N. J. April 10, 1908

I am sending a formal acceptance to Mr. McAlpin—but I wish to tell you personally of my very great appreciation of the honor the Trustees propose to bestow upon me. Highly as I shall prize the degree, the evidence of goodwill implied in its grant will always give me the greater satisfaction, & to receive it through you will give it a value it would not otherwise possess.

Very affectionately Yours,   H. A. Garfield.

ALS (WP, DLC).

A News Report

[April 11, 1908]

TENTH ANNUAL BANQUET

of the Daily Princetonian Board Held
Last Evening at the Princeton Inn.

The tenth annual banquet of THE DAILY PRINCETONIAN was held last evening at the Princeton Inn. The dinner was the largest ever given by the PRINCETONIAN, one hundred and thirty covers being laid. . . .

The banquet was concluded with an address by President Woodrow Wilson. He began by saying that he had found in his experience that where there is no interest among people, there is nothing for them to do. Expressing his passionate love for Princeton, President Wilson declared that Princeton is intended, if she would only use her power, for the conquest of the nation. A very serious age has come upon America, one sick with faulty thinking, and ignorance, which could but is not rescued by University graduates. The men who lead this nation lead it not because of their University training but because of their training in the hard school of life. The universities must take their choice as to whether they will learn knowledge which is knowledge. In conclusion, President Wilson appealed to the undergraduates to aid him in uplifting Princeton to a pivot of control in the affairs of America.

Printed in the *Daily Princetonian*, April 11, 1908.

From Henry Smith Pritchett

My dear President Wilson: New York   April 11, 1908.

Replying to yours of April 10, I am sending a supply of blanks for such use as you may have in the near future.

Professor Brackett has been so long at Princeton and has done such work there that his retirement is truly epoch-making. With regard to estimating his active salary, it is our custom to include in the active pay an allowance for the rental of a house which has been allowed, and this should be done in his case.[1]

I find that nine of the trustees of Princeton are now on our mailing list and I shall take great pleasure in seeing that the others are put on.

The executive committee at its meeting on Thursday did no further business than merely to call the trustees together.

Faithfully yours,   Henry S. Pritchett

TLS (WWP, UA, NjP).
[1] See H. S. Pritchett to WW, May 6, 1908.

From Cyrus Fogg Brackett

My dear sir: Princeton   April 11, 1908.

Allow me to thank you for your exceedingly kind and courteous letter informing me of the action by the Trustees touching my resignation of the "Henry Professorship of Physics."

I beg to assure you that my interest in the University will not diminish in the years to come so long as I may live to see it advance under your leadership.

Wishing you many years of success in your exacting labors and an abundance of strength to perform them I beg to remain, as ever,

Sincerely yours.   C. F. Brackett.

TLS (WP, DLC).

Edward Wright Sheldon to Charles Williston McAlpin, with Enclosure

My dear Sir: [New York]   April 13, 1908.

The enclosed letter dated April 11, 1908, from Mr. Francis Larkin, one of the executors of the will of the late Mrs. Swann, evidences his formal approval of the selection of the site for the Thomson Graduate College in the grounds of Prospect. To make the record clear I have attached to Mr. Larkin's letter a copy of the communication from me to which his is in answer.[1]

I had previously conferred with Professor Sloane upon this same subject and received an oral expression of his hearty approval of the site. Mr. [Bayard] Stockton has also, I am told, expressed the same conclusion to Mr. Pyne.

It seems to me of possible advantage for future reference if this letter and its enclosures were referred to in the margin of the report of the Graduate School Committee dated April 9th and filed with the records of the University.

Believe me,   Yours very truly,   Edward W. Sheldon.

1 It is missing.

E N C L O S U R E

Francis Larkin, Jr., to Edward Wright Sheldon

Dear Sheldon: Ossining, N. Y., April 11th, 1908.

Your letter relative to site for graduate collage [college] to be built with the proceeds of the residuary Estate of Mrs. Swann, deceased, was received. The location mentioned by you and approved by my co-executors is entirely satisfactory to me.

With kind regards,   Yours sincerely,   Francis Larkin

TLS (Trustees' Papers, UA, NjP).

From John Hessin Clarke[1]

My dear Sir: Cleveland, Ohio, April 13, 1908.

I had the pleasure and profitable experience of hearing the address which you delivered at the Cleveland Chamber of Commerce banquet last December,[2] and I was very much impressed by it.

I must say, however, that I did not appreciate the full importance of the point you made in your address as to the possibility of fixing legal responsibility for business abuses in a manner different from that which is now being so widely attempted until I read yesterday in the Railway Age an extract from your speech delivered in Pittsburg last week,[3] and which I recognized as in part at least very similar to the one delivered here.

I am especially struck with the paragraph:

"It is perfectly possible to pick out for legal restraints and regulation all the particular transactions and classes of transactions which embody the practices now demoralizing business in this country. It is perfectly feasible also by processes of legal definition to place the responsibility for each kind of transaction upon individual officers or individual persons in fact responsible for them. It is perfectly practicable also to put the determination of such offenses and penalties in the hands of judicial tribunals who shall administer not the processes of individual judgment but the processes of law. And until we can bring our practice to this basis we shall be following a road which carries us directly away from all American principle and leads ultimately to the kind of power which American institutions were set up to prevent."

I am writing to ask if you have in published form working out this suggestion more in detail. It strikes me, practicing lawyer as I am, as an extremely valuable and practical suggestion which is likely, however, not to receive the attention it deserves, especially from others than lawyers unless elaborated and perhaps illustrated by example.

If you have worked this out more fully in a published form I should like to know very much indeed where I can procure a copy of it. I am,

Very truly yours,   John H. Clarke

TLS (WP, DLC).
1 Prominent lawyer and civic leader in Cleveland, unsuccessful Democratic candidate for the United States Senate in 1903. At this time he was general counsel for the New York, Chicago & St. Louis Railroad Co. and attorney for many other corporations. Wilson appointed him to the Supreme Court in 1916.
2 The text of Wilson's speech is printed at Nov. 16, 1907, Vol. 17.
3 The abstract of Wilson's speech to the Traffic Club of Pittsburgh, printed at April 3, 1908, appeared in the *Railway Age*, XLV (April 10, 1908), 534-35.

A Press Release

[c. April 13, 1908]

LAW OR PERSONAL POWER

(Remarks of Mr. Woodrow Wilson at the National Democratic Club, New York, 13 April, 1908)

We hear a great deal of candidacies and programmes, but very little of principles. Parties seem almost to have gone to pieces and to have become indistinguishable, except in so far as men by habit call themselves by this party name or by that. Both parties have with like eagerness turned to the regulation of the business of the country, the restraint and regulation of the great business corporations, and vie with each other in the radical measures which they propose; but the measures of the one might be the measures of the other. They are virtually indistinguishable in principle, and the principle they have in common is a bad principle which, if carried far enough in its application, would inevitably change the whole character of our government. It is time we stopped, for a little, speaking of candidacies and undertook to test measures by principles.

The greater part of the business of the country has come into the hands of great corporations and trusts, and its new aspects unquestionably require adjustments and re-formulations of the law, which the courts have not had the power or the courage to make and which must therefore be made by legislation. The mere scale of business operations, moreover, has vastly increased. Comparatively small groups of men in control of great corporations wield a power and control over the wealth and the business operations of the country which makes them seem rivals of the government itself. Law must be strengthened and adapted to keep them in curb and to make them subservient to the general welfare. No one now advocates the old *laissez faire*; no one questions the necessity for a firm and comprehensive regulation of business operations in the interest of fair dealing, of a responsible exercise of power. We are all advocates of a firm and effective regulation, but those of us who are Democrats challenge the prevailing principles of regulation, the principles which the Republican party has introduced and carried to such radical lengths and which some Democrats, confused by the clamour of the hour, have too thoughtlessly and hastily espoused.

We have in fact turned from legal regulation to executive regulation. We have turned from law to personal power. It is that choice which as Democrats we challenge, and challenge with confidence, as opposed to every ancient principle of liberty and of just government. Have we given up law? Must we fall back on discretionary executive power? The government of the United States was established to get rid of arbitrary, that is, discretionary executive power. If we return to it, we abandon the very principles of our foundation, give up the English and American experiment and turn back to discredited models of government.

A mere casual examination of recent legislation will show that these statements are not based upon fancy or upon exaggeration, but upon the necessary character of the things we have been trying to do. Law which cannot define and discriminate the transactions which it is the purpose of the legislature to forbid is not ready to become law at all, and yet it is just that that our recent statutes enacted by way of regulating some of the most important enterprises of the country have failed to do. They have run in vague terms, lumping things permissible with things impermissible, interfering with business without analyzing it or carefully discriminating its good and bad features. And then when the results were unsatisfactory they have sought to lodge the power to discriminate, to permit and forbid, in the hands of commissions with very extensive discretionary powers, administrative in character, not judicial; for no process is judicial which does not rest upon definition, upon detailed and explicit provisions of known law. The Sherman Act was as clumsy as it has been ineffectual, and the remedy for it has been to lodge the power to discriminate between what it should have forbidden and what it should have permitted in the hands of bodies of commissioners appointed by the President.

The latest proposals are typical of all the rest. All combinations or agreements in restraint of trade had been forbidden by statute. But some agreements in restraint of trade, some sorts of pooling of rates by the railroads for instance, do not in fact operate to the detriment of the public or of trade itself, but are beneficial rather and to be desired in the interest alike of efficiency and economy. The law-makers, upon that discovery, are not invited by the reformers to attempt definitions of law which will discriminate between those agreements in restraint of trade which are innocent of monopolistic intent or effect and desirable in the interest of the community itself, from those which the vague original law was intended to prevent. They are urged, on the contrary, to put the whole matter in the hands of an executive officer. It is proposed to invite all corporations which wish to keep within the limits of the law to register with him and to submit all their contracts and arrangements to him for his sanction or disapproval, to let him make law by executive order.[1]

The principle underlying the laws which have here and there set up powerful public service commissions is the same. These commissions are authorized not to administer precise rules of law made clear in the definitions of statutes, but to order this, that, or the other alteration, addition or adjustment in the actual administration of the business of the corporations which they are set to supervise. It is true that these corporations are in a sense public servants: street railway companies, gas lighting companies, and the like. They use the public highways and enjoy public franchises of one kind or another and are engaged in kinds of business which can hardly be called private in character, but they are owned by private capital and operated for private profit. And yet their business is regulated, even in its chief administrative details, by public officers whose practical judgment is the standard of regulation, who are administering not rules of law but their own discretionary opinions. The law

[1] He was referring to proposals made by President Roosevelt in his Annual Message of December 3, 1907, about which see n. 1 to the news report printed at Dec. 30, 1907, Vol. 17.

attempts no definitions in respect of these undertakings: it puts them in the hands of public officers; and yet undertakes no responsibility for their success or bankruptcy.

If this is necessary, government by law has broken down, and personal government has been substituted. I for one do not believe that it is necessary. Neither do I believe that the American people have consciously made any such choice. They have been hastened by reformers who acted upon no principle whatever into measures the real character and consequence of which were not explained to them. When those measures are understood, the people of this country will turn from them and substitute law once more for personal power.

To all thoughtful persons, scrupulous of the ancient principles of our law, it is evident where this demoralization crept in. It is plain why the federal government has become the patron of the people instead of the arbiter of just and definite law. Our later tariff legislation has not been based upon the general welfare, but upon the patronage of special interests already strong, already very influential in politics. No one can examine the confused and illogical schedules of the present tariff without perceiving that it is really a mass of special favors piled together in a bill which was not seeking a symmetrical development of the industries of the country, such as Hamilton urged in his great Report on Manufactures upon which all tariff laws profess to be founded, but only to please every interest whose hostility was to be feared in the elections. A system of special favors is in its nature paternal. Its idea is not law but patronage, and, having created artificial conditions and produced thereby interests which in their time grew so large as to threaten to dominate the government itself by the very processes which produced the tariff, it is plain logic that this same patronizing government must play a further paternal role of special regulation, not by careful scientific definitions of law but by detailed variations of administrative process.

The opportunity of the Democratic party is the same all along the line: to return to government by law; to insist upon a tariff reconsidered in all its definitions, adjusted to the actual conditions of trade and manufacture, viewed, not interest by interest, but upon the broad basis of the country's needs and economies; to insist upon a currency, not based upon the sale of this, that or the other body or class of securities, but upon the actual assets and soundness of the banks of issue, redundancy checked by taxation, hazard offset by inspection for the enforcement of definite and uniform rules; to insist upon laws, whether of combination or of contract, of offensive or of defensive action, which shall be the same for the capitalist and for the laborer; to insist upon the precise fixing of responsibility on individuals; to insist in brief, everywhere upon definition, uniform, exact, enforceable. If there must be commissions, let them be, not executive instrumentalities having indefinite powers capable of domineering as well as regulating, but tribunals of easy and uniform process acting under precise terms of power in the enforcement of precise terms of regulation.

It is perfectly possible to pick out transactions one by one to which definitions and regulations of law can be applied. If it is not, then law is impossible. The process is indeed slow; it is a process of investigation and of experience of which ardent reformers are infinitely impatient: a process difficult to institute in a time of excitement and impatience for results like the present; but it is the only process of sound law-making. Moreover, it is perfectly possible to pick out responsible individuals and visit upon them the punshiments [punishments] of the law instead of checking business in order to eliminate undesirable practices. Sound government must ever be based upon definite law and individual responsibility. Corporate responsibility lacks vitality, corrects nobody. Corporations are creatures of the law; the law may exact of them any publicity of process it pleases, any analysis of their functions, any disclosure of their organization.

If juries have failed to convict indicted officials when the officers of the law have tried by indictment to correct corporate abuses, it has been because they were by no means sure that the persons indicted were really the responsible persons. Our lawmakers have made too little analysis of the things they wished to correct. Our law has not carefully enough discriminated real from nominal control, the masters from the servants. Many of the practices of our corporations which are most demoralizing, most against the public interest, most corrupt and most dangerous, were not originated by the official administrators of the corporation, the men actually in charge of its daily transactions, but by manipulators who owned or controlled the majority of their stock, who could change the officers of the corporation as they pleased, who wished to create this, that or the other impression on the stock market and who wished to get certain effects wrought on the balance sheet of the corporation reports. These were the real masters, with these rested the real responsibility. Has our law made any intelligent effort to find these men in its definitions of responsibility or in its imposition of penalties? It has known only fines, which fall upon innocent stockholders and guilty alike, and has left the real offenders unmolested in their practices.

The people of this country are not jealous of fortunes however great which have been built up by the honest development of great enterprises, which have been actually earned by business energy and sagacity; they are jealous only of speculative wealth, of the wealth which has been piled up by no effort at all but only by shrewd wits playing on the credulity of others, taking advantage of the weakness of others, trading in the necessities of others. This is "predatory wealth" and is found in stock markets, not in the administrative offices of great corporations where real business is conducted, real commodities made or exchanged. And what the law-maker has failed to perceive in recent years is that the charges made by corporations for their manufactured goods or for their services have been determined often times not by the desire of the corporation to charge more than what it sells is worth, but by the necessity it is under to earn dividends on watered stock or make good the terms of the sale of its plant at extravagant figures when it was made a part of some greater combination. Processes of over-capitalization are processes of fraud. The law should analyse and frustrate them. If it cannot, our situation will not be improved by putting the matter in the hands of some executive inquisitor. Our battle cry must be, "Back to the reign of law." The discretion of executive officers, whether you call them commissioners or not, is a mere quicksand upon which no nation can stand.

Only principles are constructive. No miscellaneous programme of measures formed by no principle, unified by no controlling purpose, can give life to a great national party and lift it above faction or futility. The principle to which the voters of this country should be called back now is the great constructive principle of the reign of law. The familiar Jeffersonian maxim that that government is the best which governs least, translated into the terms of modern experience, means that that government is best whose processes least expose the individual to arbitrary interference and the choices of governors, which makes him most secure of the regular and impartial administration of fixed and uniform rules, which makes no distinction between class and class, aims always at eliminating undesirable transactions rather than at setting up official interference with the management of business, and looks to individuals, not to the general public (such as investors) to bear the penalties of infraction. Law, and the government as umpire; not discretionary power, and the government as master, should be the programme of every man who loves liberty and the established character of the Republic.[2]

T MS (WP, DLC).
[2] There is a WWhw outline of this press release, dated April 13, 1908, in WP, DLC.

A News Report of an Address to the National Democratic Club

[April 14, 1908]

SILENT ON BRYAN AT JEFFERSON FEAST

But National Democratic Clubmen Cheer when Woodrow Wilson Mentions Gov. Johnson.

BRYAN DECLINED TO COME

The name of William J. Bryan was nowhere referred to by the speakers at the Jefferson Day dinner of the National Democratic Club at the Hotel Knickerbocker in Times Square last night, but the mention of Minnesota's candidate, Gov. [John Albert] Johnson, brought forth vigorous applause from the diners.

A return to the principles of Thomas Jefferson, a reign of law and not of individuals, and a thorough revision of the tariff, were three of the Democratic keynotes sounded by President Woodrow Wilson of Princeton University, who was the principal speaker. The other speakers were Senator [Furnifold McLendel] Simmons of North Carolina and Senator [Robert Latham] Owen of Oklahoma.

The dinner of itself was the greatest Democratic function of the kind the Democrats have held in this city for a long time, and President Wilson's speech seemed, to the majority of the diners, to be particularly appropriate to the occasion. It dwelt at length on the principles of the father of the Democratic Party. Mr. Wilson charged that the members of the party had forgotten the tenets of their faith. He attacked the Roosevelt administration in particular, though without mentioning his name, and he assailed government by the Republican Party in general, as the government of a party without any principles at all.

Government by commission was the topic to which the speaker devoted the greater part of his address. He spoke also of the relations of capital and labor, and considerably of the tariff and the great need of revision. He charged that this country was returning gradually to the form of government that it had rejected at the time it fought for its independence, and called on all true Democrats to return to real Jeffersonian ideals and fight for them even in the face of temporary defeat that they might eventually achieve permanent victory. He sounded a note of warning, too, to the corporation lawyers.

The dinner, which commemorated the 165th anniversary of the birth of Jefferson, was held in the large banquet hall of the Knickerbocker, which had been lavishly decorated for the occasion. . . . In the absence of President John Fox of the club, Warren W. Foster[1] presided.

This was the dinner to which, after much discussion, William J. Bryan was invited, though he was not asked to speak, and it was tacitly understood that he would be present only as a silent guest. Mr. Bryan declined the invitation, and it was remarked as significant that throughout the course of the dinner and the speechmaking that followed his name was not once mentioned. President Wilson, however, in the course of his address, spoke of Gov. Johnson of Minnesota, and instantly there was vigorous and enthusiastic applause. Mr. Wilson smiled.

"I paused," he said, "in the hope and expectancy that the mention of that name would bring forth applause."

Warren W. Foster spoke but briefly in introducing Dr. Wilson, stating, however, that never had the prospects of Democratic success in the country been brighter than at present. When Dr. Wilson rose to speak he was greeted with prolonged applause.

"I have come to the mortifying time of seeing both political parties in the hands of receivers," he said. "You know how you get in the hands of a receiver—you lose your principal. And, having gone into bankruptcy, some one—not yourself—must run the business. That is the present situation in both National parties. Individual receivers have been running our business and for the very reason that obtains in all similar matters. That is, we have lost our principles." . . .[2]

"The corporation lawyers of this country know what is going on; the legislators do not. I want to say to all corporation lawyers, 'If you would save the corporation, you will come out from cover and tell the legislators what is needed. You know what is needed; they don't. By telling them you will save the corporation. If you don't, you will have the mob at its doors in a decade.'

"I don't suppose you will do this. I just want the satisfaction, ten or fifteen years hence, of saying, 'I told you so.'"

In conclusion, Dr. Wilson said:

"There are signs that make one feel that the Democratic Party is going to pieces. I find a great many men who do not know which party they belong to because they cannot see any difference between them. This country is waiting for a party which will be brave enough to abide the slow processes of success and to say that they know that righteousness, that right judgment, that careful adjustments of law, that the firm processes of courts are the bases of human liberty; and that it will not despair of human liberty until it has itself departed from those historic and ancient bases."

Printed in the *New York Times*, April 14, 1908; some editorial headings omitted.
¹ Warren William Foster, Judge of the Court of General Sessions in New York since 1899.
² At this point the report quoted substantial portions of Wilson's press release.

From the Diary of William Starr Myers

Tuesday April 14 [1908]

... This evening our dept. gave a dinner at the "Inn" in honor of Garfield who leaves at the end of the year to become President of Williams College. Those present were President Wilson, Daniels, Paul van Dyke, Garfield, Coney, Adriance, Bogart, Corwin, Dawson, Elliott, McIlwaine, Meeker, Myers, Shipman, Spencer, Price, Pahlow, & Westcott. Daniels presided—& only two set speeches by Wilson & Garfield. Both splendid. "Woodrow" "opened his heart" in an unusually intimate manner. Garfield mentioned the fact that his father had said always give the Pres. of the U. S. the benefit of the doubt when any controversial question comes up,—he is the last man in the country to know the real truth of a matter in many cases, as all reports come to him with an official or political coloring. Afterwards we all sat around and told jokes for an hour or two—Woodrow leading. A most delightful & successful occasion.

Bound diary (W. S. Myers Papers, NjP).

From Henry James Forman

My dear President Wilson: New York. April 14, 1908.

Thank you for your letter of April 10th. I do indeed believe that you are a possible recipient of the nomination at Denver, and my only anxiety is to have your claims properly presented so far as concerns the *Review*. I tried to see Mr. Laffan, but, unfortunately, he is out of town. Do you think the [that] Mr. [Henry] Watterson would be a good man to ask for such an article? If he wrote it it would certainly add to the general attention the article would attract. If you think well of it, and will kindly telegraph me on receipt of this letter, I shall write to Mr. Watterson at once.[1]

With many thanks, I am,

Very sincerely yours,   Henry James Forman

TLS (WP, DLC).

[1] The *North American Review* planned to run in its June number a general article, "The Claims of the Candidates." The section on Wilson (*North American Review*, CLXXXVII [June 1908], 844-50) was written by Mayo Williamson Hazeltine, literary editor of the New York *Sun* since 1878.

To Henry Smith Pritchett

[Princeton, N. J.]

My dear President Pritchett: April 15, 1908.

I enclose herewith the application for a retiring allowance for Professor Brackett. His salary during the last five years has been $3000, and I am reckoning the house at $600, a conservative reckoning, since I find that there is not on the Treasurer's books any official memorandum of the rate at which it was to be reckoned as part of the salary.

Thank you for your letter of April 11th.

Always cordially yours,   [Woodrow Wilson]

CCL (WWP, UA, NjP).

From Cyrus Hall McCormick

My dear Woodrow: [Chicago] 16 April 1908

Mr. Farwell, President of the Trustees,[1] and Mr. Messer[2] would like to suggest the following topic for your address on the twenty-seventh: "The Contribution of the Association to the Life of the Nation."[3] It is our understanding that your thoughts run along the lines of the nation's problems, and we wish to give you liberty to speak broadly in any way that seems to you best, and our suggestion is that out of the above topic you can make anything that you please. The other speakers of the evening will deal with the subject more locally. Our suggestion is that your address should not be shorter than twenty minutes and not longer than thirty or thirty-five minutes, as there are four other speakers on the program.

If you wish any further analysis of the subject or any information which can be forwarded to you for your study on the train coming here, please telegraph me and I will send you some further information.

We are not planning any engagements for you except that we are inviting some friends to meet you at dinner on Sunday evening at our house. I am arranging your transportation to leave here on Tuesday afternoon at five-thirty, as you suggested. I am assuming that you are going to Princeton, and if you have any other plan, please advise me.

I am   Very sincerely yours,   Cyrus H. McCormick.

TCL (C. H. McCormick Papers, WHi).
1 John Villiers Farwell, President of the Board of Trustees of the Y.M.C.A. of Chicago.
2 Loring Wilbur Messer, General Secretary of the Y.M.C.A. of Chicago since 1888.
3 A news report of Wilson's address at the semi-centennial of the Chicago Y.M.C.A. is printed at April 28, 1908.

To Lucius Hopkins Miller

My dear Professor Miller: Princeton, N. J.   April 17th, 1908.

Thank you very sincerely for your kind letter of April 14th.[1] I have read the article with careful attention and do not see how any reasonable person could object to it. It seems to me to state the point of view of those who are studying the Bible and Christianity from the point of view of modern times, with moderation and good sense, and I hope that you will feel at liberty to publish it if you care to do so.[2]

I need not tell you that the ground of your scruple about publishing it at the present time has seemed to me most patriotic towards Princeton not only, but in every way most admirable, and I feel like rendering you my personal thanks for it.

With warm regard,

Faithfully yours,   Woodrow Wilson

TLS (Selected Corr. of L. H. Miller, NjP).
1 This letter is missing.
2 Miller did publish the article: "Modern Views of the Bible and of Religion," *South Atlantic Quarterly*, VII (Oct. 1908), 309-19.

From Ralph Adams Cram

Dear Dr. Wilson: Boston, April 18, 1908.

There seem to be some difficulties in arranging the time and place where I am to put before the Committee of the Class of '77 the estimates we are to receive on Tuesday next for the construction of '77 Dormitory. I hoped that this meeting might be in Princeton on Wednesday afternoon, but Mr. Pyne evidently wants it either Wednesday, or Thursday, in New York. I may have to change my date for Princeton to suit the wishes of the Class Committee, and I am writing you to be sure that either Wednesday, or Thursday will be convenient for you and for Dean West. I shall be there either one of these two days, probably Wednesday, but it may have to be Thursday, if Dean West is to be there.

I am coming on in response to your letter in which you told me that the Dean wanted to consult with me in the matter of the plans for the Graduate School, and of course I must be in Princeton whenever he is there, and when you are there also, as I wish to see you first. Monday is a holiday in this State, and if for any reason *either* Wednesday, or Thursday would not be available for you and for Dean West, may I not ask you to telegraph me Monday at my house, #52 Chestnut St., Boston. If I don't hear from you, I shall assume that I can see both you and the Dean either Wednesday, or Thursday, as the case may be.

Very truly yours,　R A Cram

TLS (WP, DLC).

To Cyrus Hall McCormick

My dear Cyrus:　　　　　　Princeton, N. J.　April 20th, 1908.

Thank you for your letter of the sixteenth. The topic suggested by the committee, namely, "The Contribution of the Association to the Life of the Nation," will suit excellently well for what I intend to say at the dinner on Monday night, the twenty-seventh, and I shall accordingly build upon it.

Thank you for the arrangements you have made for me. You are quite right in assuming that I am going to return directly home. I am looking forward with the greatest pleasure to seeing you again.

Always faithfully yours,　Woodrow Wilson

TLS (WP, DLC).

From Stephen Squires Palmer

Dear Doctor Wilson,　　　　　[New York]　April 23d, 1908

Pardon my seeming indifference in not sooner writing to you, and allow me to assure you that I deeply and fully appreciate the honor of being connected with Princeton and your own good self.[1]

I have given the entire subject matter much thought and careful consideration, and have very grave doubts as to my ability to fulfill your expectations. However, you and your associates think otherwise, and I have therefore notified the Secretary of the University of my acceptance.

I shall gladly do all that I possibly can to forward the best interests of the Grand Old Institution that possesses such great possibilities for so much that is good.

With assurances of my highest esteem,

I am—as always My dear Doctor

Faithfully yours   S S Palmer

ALS (WP, DLC).
[1] Palmer had been elected a Life Trustee at the meeting of the Board of Trustees on April 9, 1908.

From Simon John McPherson

My dear Dr. Wilson: [Lawrenceville, N. J.]   April 24, 1908

We desire very much to have representatives of leading colleges, and particularly of those to which we send boys from this school, to be present and address our boys during the coming school year. The addresses will need to be short, not more than forty minutes in length at the outside; probably thirty would be better.

Of course, our boys, like all those who expect to go to college, have an intense interest in the leading colleges and universities, and they would be delighted to hear leading representatives of them.

The days that are now vacant are all Wednesdays in October, and November 4th and the 25th; February 3d, 10th and the 17th; March 17th and the 24th; and all the Wednesdays in April. May I ask whether it would be possible for you to come to Lawrenceville on one of those dates to make an address to the boys on any subject that you may prefer yourself, and that you would regard as suitable in matter and style for boys ranging from fourteen to eighteen years of age and also, whether you will not be kind enough to state what honorarium would seem to you to be right for such a high service rendered to Lawrenceville?

The school is interested in yourself personally, as well as in your institution. Of course it would not be necessary to present the claims of your institution particularly, but rather to give the school the chance to hear you on any topic you would like to present.

Earnestly hoping that you can favor us yourself, or, if you cannot possibly come in person, that you can suggest a man who you think would be particularly happy in making an address to the boys,[1] I remain,

Sincerely yours,   S. J. McPherson

LPC of TLS (WC, NjP).
[1] See WW to S. J. McPherson, April 30, 1908.

An Outline of an Address

Chicago Y.M.C.A. Jubilee.   27 April, 1908.

Contribution of the Association to
The Life of the Nation.

What vitalizes a Nation? Force and Renewal.
   Self-elevation, self-purification, self-variation
The Y.M.C.A. has represented
   1) *Organized altruistic youth.*
      Youth conservative as to ideals, radical, or at least original, as to means and methods.
      Characteristics of a free society.
   2) *Purification at the source.*
   3) *Stimulation at the source.*
      Renewal by *volunteer effort,* enrichment by self-originitive forces, as against Socialism, *official origination,* which is impoverishment.
What is the sufficient motive of society?
      The Christ example operative *in the individual life. A government of men, not of laws.*

WWhw MS (WP, DLC).

A News Report of an Address in Chicago

[April 28, 1908]

Y.M.C.A. BANQUET CELEBRATION CLIMAX

Well Known Men From Many Parts of Country Eulogize
Fifty Years' Achievement on Part of
the Chicago Organization.

Sixteen days' jubilee, marking the semicentennial of the Chicago Young Men's Christian association, reached a climax of enthusiasm at the concluding citizens' banquet in the Congress hotel last night. . . .

Men whose connection with the Y.M.C.A. is of international importance paid eloquent tribute to fifty years' achievement on the part of the Chicago organization. Among the speakers were Woodrow Wilson, president of Princeton university, the Rt. Rev. Charles P. Anderson,[1] John V. Farwell, Jr., and Governor Charles S[amuel]. Deneen. Five hundred representative citizens of Chicago were gathered at the banquet tables and among the women who thronged the galleries of the banquet hall were many benefactresses of the Chicago association. . . .

Woodrow Wilson, president of Princeton university, the subject of whose address was "The Contribution of the Association to the Life of the Nation," declared that the Y.M.C.A. in America was turning young men away from socialism, "a new anxiety of which we have become conscious during the last decade."

President Wilson struck at socialism in the country in no uncertain terms, declaring it impossible to inculcate by government in a nation as a whole principles that Christ declared could be taught only to the individual.

Printed in the Chicago *Inter Ocean*, April 28, 1908; some editorial headings omitted.

[1] The Rt. Rev. Dr. Charles Palmerston Anderson, Protestant Episcopal Bishop of Chicago.

To Stephen Squires Palmer

My dear Mr. Palmer: [Princeton, N. J.]   April 30th, 1908.

I left home the very day your letter of April 23rd was written and got back only last night. I have just swung a circle the other end of which was Chicago.

I cannot tell you with what sincere gratification and thankfulness I learned of your decision to accept the election to the Board of Trustees. I never know how to tell men what I think of them, particularly when I greatly trust and admire them, and therefore I fear I have never been able to make you realize how much it will mean to me to be associated with you in the work of the Board. I feel that the Board is in many ways greatly strengthened by your addition to it and that your acceptance will prove one of the happy circumstances of my administration. I did not write to urge the acceptance of the election upon you because I always feel that matters of that kind are matters of considerable delicacy and that every man ought to be left to determine them for himself, but now that it is determined I have the very great pleasure of expressing my personal delight.

With warm regard and the deepest appreciation of your kind letter,

Always cordially and faithfully yours,

[Woodrow Wilson]

CCL (WWP, UA, NjP).

To Simon John McPherson

My dear Dr. McPherson: Princeton, N. J.   April 30th, 1908.

It will give me real pleasure to be one of the speakers in the series of addresses you are arranging for the Wednesdays of next year. It is a little difficult at this distance to choose a date, because I can never certainly foresee what my engagements in the autumn are to be, but I shall venture to choose Wednesday, November 4th, and shall look forward to the occasion with a great deal of pleasure.[1]

This is not one of the kind of addresses for which I should feel justified in receiving any fee at all.

With much regard,

Cordially and sincerely yours,   Woodrow Wilson

TLS (WC, NjP).
[1] The notes for Wilson's address at the Lawrenceville School on November 4, 1908, are printed at that date.

To John Prentiss Poe[1]

My dear Mr. Poe: Princeton, N. J.   April 30th, 1908.

I am greatly obliged to you for your kind letter of April 24th,[2] which came while I was absent in Chicago. I need not tell you what pleasure it would give me to accept the invitation of the Regents of the University of Maryland, if it were possible for me to do so, but ever since I became President here I have found it really impossible to accept Commencement invitations elsewhere, so constant and engrossing are my home engagements at that time. The only exception I have ever made I have made this year out of weakness for me [my] second daughter who is to graduate at the Woman's College [of Baltimore], where I have consented to speak on the third of June.[3] This engagement makes it all the more necessary that I should promise no other dates at that season.

I hope that you will express to your colleagues on the Board of Regents my very warm appreciation and unaffected regret.

With warmest regard,

Sincerely yours,   Woodrow Wilson

TLS (L. W. Smith Coll., Morristown National Historical Park).
    1 Princeton 1854; Dean of the School of Law and Regent of the University of Maryland.
    2 This letter is missing.
    3 A news report of this address is printed at June 4, 1908.

From Ralph Adams Cram

Dear Dr. Wilson: Boston, April 30, 1908.

When I was last in Princeton, Dean West expressed a desire to talk with me about the plans for the proposed Graduate School. I told him I thought I could come on for Wednesday, the 6th of May, and have just written him that I shall do so if this date is convenient for him. Of course, if any reason has developed which would make it undesirable for me to go into the matter more in detail with him at this time, you will not hesitate to let me know.

Mr. Goodhue[1] wishes very much to come to Princeton, for the purpose of meeting you and familiarizing himself with the University as an architectural and pictorial entity, and I told him that I thought it would be a good plan for him to come on with me next week. If you are not to be in Princeton on the 6th of May, I should be very glad if you would let me know, as in that case there would be less object in Mr. Goodhue's coming on at that time.

Very faithfully yours,   R A Cram.

TLS (WP, DLC).
    1 His partner, Bertram Grosvenor Goodhue.

To John Raleigh Mott

My dear Mr. Mott: Princeton, N. J.   May 1st, 1908.

I have read with real interest the manuscript of your lectures on the problem of securing able men for the ministry, and return the manuscript to you with my thorough approval. I do not see any point at which I should feel like suggesting an amendment of what you say, except that on pages 5 and 15 of the First lecture you seem to me to tread upon ground that it is worth while considering at least debatable.

I thoroughly believe in the widest activity for the church, but I have had the fear in recent years that the ministers of our churches, by becoming involved in all sorts of social activities (of course I use the word "social" in its widest sense), have too much diverted their attention from the effectual preaching of the

Word. The danger seems to me to be that individual churches will become great philanthropic societies instead of being what it seems to me they ought to be, organizations from which go forth the spiritual stimulation which should guide all philanthropic effort. Many of our modern pastors are so exceedingly busy with the affairs of the communities in which they live that they are not fountains of real spiritual refreshment to their people. The old-fashioned pastor had at least this advantage over the modern pastor, that he gave himself leisure for spiritual contemplation, meditated upon the real needs of the human heart, and associated himself intimately with the families and individual lives under his charge, making himself not the organizer of benevolent power but the spiritual source of it, as the spokesman of his master.

I know that you will take my meaning and understand that I am only suggesting that in the passages I have referred to it might be well, if your judgment was the same as mine, to emphasize this older side of the ministerial office and to guard against a misapprehension. I feel that we should emphasize the function of pastor and not dilute it into that of philanthropist. The intensive work of the pastor with his own people is surely the source of a community's power.

With warm regard and sincere appreciation of your wish to have my judgment upon these lectures,

Cordially and faithfully yours,   Woodrow Wilson

TLS (J. R. Mott Coll., CtY-D).

An Address in Pittsburgh to the Western Association of Princeton Clubs

[[May 2, 1908]]

Mr. Toastmaster[1] and Fellow-Princetonians: I am very much interested to see Pennsylvania turning toward the Democratic party. (Applause.) I am very delighted to have come here in Judge Gray's[2] train, and to enable you to see real representatives of the patriotism of this country. (Applause.) I understand your position perfectly. There are certain domestic reasons why you cannot be Democrats. (Applause.) You are not at liberty to act upon principle. (Applause.) I heard a story recently that you may not have heard, about socialism. Two Irishmen were talking

[1] Nathaniel Ewing, Princeton 1869.
[2] George Gray, Princeton 1859, Democratic United States Senator from Delaware, 1885-99, and judge of the United States Third Judicial Circuit since 1899, who also spoke.

together, and one of them prefessed [professed] himself a Socialist, and the other said,—"What is that?" He said,—"If I had two
cows, I would give you one." "You would?" he said. "If you had
two horses would you give me one?" "Yes." "If you had two pigs,
would you give me one?" "Yes." "If you had two goats, would you
give me one?" He said, "You go to hell; you know damn well
I have two goats." (Tremendous cheering and applause.)

Human nature erects many barriers to the progress of ideal
principles; and the ideal principles of Democracy have iron barriers erected in Pittsburgh. At the same time it shows a certain
liberal temper on your part that you should desire to hear the
chief Democratic orators of the country. (Laughter.) . . .

I believe that the time has come, gentlemen, when the universities of this country must use their influence. I say must, not
because of any moral policy, though I think the moral policy
exists; but the country is beginning to ask what they are for, and
the country has got to know within the next ten or fifteen years
what the universities it supports are for. And if the universities
do not give a satisfactory report, they will have to change their
character radically or go out of the business. And a satisfactory
report consists in the training they give the men who resort to
them for study. The report does not consist in what the presidents
of the universities go around and say. It does not consist of the
cheers that the alumni give. It does not consist of the admirable
gatherings which are brought together and the delightful times
they have. It consists in what the universities do to men under
their charge. That is the substantial and only report which
universities can make.

Now, there are two ideals of university life existing in this country; at least, there is one ideal existing and another struggling
for recognition. The one that exists is, that a university is a mode
of life, that a university is a place to which a young man goes
to subject himself to certain experiences and certain comradeships; that it is not a place devoted to any single or predominant
object, but a place where young men go to get together in order
to standardize themselves in respect to certain conceptions of
life and conduct. That is the prevailing ideal of university life in
this country, and I have had very serious men say to me that the
primary object of universities was not intellectual.

Now, the other ideal which is struggling for recognition (it
is modest now, but will be imperative presently) is the ideal
that universities exist first, last and at every turn for intellectual
objects. That ideal does not exclude the other. On the contrary,
it is the only substantial basis for the other. You can experience

the pleasures of life, the comradeships of life, the diversions of life, anywhere; but those comradeships will not be enriched, those pleasures will not be diversions, unless there is some substantial, consistent work in hand. You cannot have a diversion, unless you are turning to something for relief from the strain of serious occupation. The minute you make an object, a life object, of diversion, it ceases to be diversion and becomes profession. The central reason why the spirit of professionalism has touched at some points our university athletics, is that athletics have ceased to be a diversion and have become an object; and so long as they are objects, they will of necessity be professional. The spirit is professional. The spirit of the thing to which you devote yourself as a main object is of necessity the professional spirit. On the contrary, if men are devoted to those things which lift them into places of influence in the nation, if their ideal be that they are there to make themselves masters of a great social situation, then their bit of athletics will have a touch of wholesomeness which the pleasure of all gentlemen has. (Applause.)

There is no dignity in pleasure, if pleasure be the object of life. Life is a very serious undertaking. When you get to be fifty-one, you will know it. And it is serious, more serious for the youngster than for the man of mature age. The man of mature age either has arrived or has not arrived, and he knows where he is, at any rate. The game is settled for him. He has either found himself or he has not. But how does the youngster know whether he is going to find himself or not? If he knows nothing, he will not find himself. If he does not know his goal, he cannot run the race. He may start in the wrong direction. If he has not realized that it is then that he settles his tendencies, he has not realized that the real business of life is to pull himself together at the start. The man who does not get into the start is not in the race. He cannot overtake the running after the shot has been fired and the line is off.

And so it seems to me that this country is now looking to its universities with this question, "Are you teaching these young men that the business of life is work? Are you impregnating the atmosphere of the palce [place] with the conception that the business of life is work?"

Now, what do we reply? We say, "These young gentlemen are very much engaged about many things, very much engaged about many things." We have certain goads and whips. We say, "Gentlemen, there is a period at the end of January and the beginning of February when we determine" (not the question of scholarship but) "the question whether you may stay in this pleasant place or not." (Laughter.) And the relation which study bears to the life of the place to many men, to the majority of men, is that it is the means of remaining in the place. It is not the means of enjoying the place; it is not the means of experiencing the place: it is merely the means of keeping their grip on residence in the place. The question is, "Are we to be separated from these pleasant things, or not?" What pleasant things? Association with the great minds of all ages? No, we had not thought of that. Association with these young minds of the present age. We want all to be on the young level. We have not thought of those comradeships which are of old, which come out of the ancient days, which consist in all the old sayings that have made the world wise time out of mind. Those are not the comradeships we are thinking of; and yet, gentlemen, those are the only comradeships of the place which will make the other comradeships different from comradeships anywhere else. The only thing that differentiates, the only thing that should differentiate, the college man from other men is that the content of his fellowship is enriched beyond the content of the fellowship of any other class of men (applause); that he is a citizen of the world of mind, that he has been graduated into that great fraternity of men who know the significance of life and the tasks of their generation.

Until we can lift undergraduates to that conception by some kind of atmospheric saturation in our universities, we shall have condemned them to remain schoolboys until they come to that part of life where men will not permit them to put comradeship before work, but will say to them, "Here is the day's work. Do that; be judged by that; and after that you shall enjoy the comradeships, as you have proved yourself a man in the work hours of the day." Look around among your companionships. Are men happy in their comradeships of whom it has been adjudged that they have not succeeded; and has their success depended upon their excellence in social intercourse? It has depended on the day's work, and many a man not particularly agreeable in social intercourse stands head and shoulders above the "good fellow," and is bowed to as a man of power in the world.

Do we want power for our graduates, or do we simply want the amenities of life? For my part, if it be wrong to covet power, then, as King Henry said, "I am the most offending soul alive." I covet power, not for myself, but for that beloved body of men who go out from Princeton University and who should be the models and dependence of this great nation. (Applause.) A place of breathing in manliness! Yes, but manliness elevated by thoughtfulness; thoughtfulness enriched by knowledge; knowledge made human by belonging to a great body of brothers who are banded together for a common purpose—not the exaltation merely of the name of their Alma Mater, but the exaltation of the thought of their Alma Mater, of the principles of their Alma Mater, and of the great body of truth which endures through all ages, whether any nourishing nurse be found for it or not. (Applause.) This beloved nurse who nourishes us is without living milk, unless that milk be the ancient milk of established truth, unless learning enrich her blood, unless she be of that old spirit of thoughtfulness, of those persons who occasionally draw apart from the tumult of life, and forgetting party strife, and forgetting the moments of the day, listen to those established maxims of Princeton which steady the world at every stage of crises.

There never was a time when we were more confused with policies and more forgetful of principles than we are at this present moment in this beloved land. (Applause.) We are confused by programmes, and not one programme is made to square with any consistent body of principles. And, forgetting that America was built upon ideal foundations, we are going about to enrich ourselves in any kind of scramble to which order can be given by temporary methods and expediences. (Applause.)

Now I have devoted myself, so long as I have been President of Princeton, to preaching this thing, not only to Princeton men, but to college men everywhere; and I tell you without exaggeration that it has become a novel theme. Men congratulate me upon my courage in uttering what seems to me the utter commonplace of the history of education. When it has become courageous to say that a college is intended for intellectual objects, then what are we to say of the state of our colleges? If the interest has been so dispersed that we have forgotten the main interest, then it ought not to be courageous to recall men to that main interest. But every man who does not do it, ought to be ashamed of himself as a man who has forgotten what ought to be the fundamental of the thing in which he is engaged.

Now it is true, gentlemen, that a peculiar responsibility rests upon Princeton at this present moment, a peculiar responsibility, because, however you may explain it, the eyes of the academic world at this moment are upon Princeton, and we are expected to show the way to do this thing which every man connected with collegiate work in this country knows to be necessary; we are expected, we are challenged, to show the way, and it is the bounden duty of every Princeton man to give his serious thought to the question, "How, by what means, shall we serve the country, now that the country is turning its eyes to us with hope, with expectation, with confidence?" (Great applause.)

Printed in the *Princeton Alumni Weekly*, VIII (May 13, 1908), 520-22.

From the Minutes of the Princeton University Faculty

5 p.m.   May 4, 1908.

The Faculty met, the President presiding. The minutes of the meeting of April 6 were read and approved.

A remit from the Board of Trustees, recommending that the Faculty be requested to consider and report to the Board of Trustees whether the trips of the athletic and non-athletic organizations away from Princeton cannot be materially reduced in number, was received and referred to the Committee on Examinations and Standing. . . .[1]

"Minutes of the University Faculty of Princeton University Beginning in September, 1902 Ending June 1914," bound minute book (UA, NjP).
[1] For the report and action of the committee, see the Princeton University Faculty Minutes printed at June 5, 1908.

From Henry Burling Thompson

My Dear President Wilson: Wilmington, Del.   May 4th, 1908.

While we all regretted your absence at the meeting of the Grounds and Buildings Committee on Saturday, I believe that you will be in sympathy with all the work done at that meeting.

Mr. [Andrew Clerk] Imbrie's report on the Sophomore Commons,—which was very thorough and exhaustive,—was adopted, and a special Committee, consisting of Sheldon, Imbrie and myself, appointed to carry out the suggestions in the report.

The bids for the Biological Building[1] were opened,—Mr. Schroeder[2] being present,—and the contract will probably be awarded to Bishop & Company.[3] As the bid runs some $15,000.00 or $16,000.00 over the appropriation, Momo Pyne and I were appointed a special Committee to see Cleveland Dodge, and suggest that this amount be taken from the Endowment Fund,—of course, subject to his approval. This matter will be settled on Wednesday, the 6th instant.

The contract for the '77 Building was awarded to Matthews.[4] Our Committee do not consider it desirable that the work on this building shall be commenced until after Commencement.

Cram, Goodhue & Ferguson were appointed architects for the Graduate School.

On the suggestion of Mr. Cram, Frank Miles Day & Brother, of Philadelphia, were appointed architects for the Sage Dormitory, subject to the approval and acceptance of Mrs. Sage. The site which our Committee will recommend to the Board, for approval, will be part of the site of the new group of Dormitory buildings, facing on Nassau Street,—the Sage Building to be located on the new street between Blair Hall and Nassau Street.

Of course, Mr. Bunn's minutes will give you the entire proceedings, but I thought better to write you as above, as I was acting Chairman of the two Committees, in the absence of Mr. [Archibald Douglas] Russell.

Yours very sincerely,   Henry B Thompson

TLS (WP, DLC).
    [1] That is, the building to house the Departments of Biology and Geology, later named Guyot Hall.
    [2] James Langdon Schroeder of Parish and Schroeder, New York architects.
    [3] J. W. Bishop Co. of Worcester, Mass.
    [4] William R. Matthews, Princeton contractor.

To Moses Taylor Pyne

My dear Momo: [Princeton, N. J.]   May 5, 1908.

Here, I am sorry to say, is a supplementary list of apparatus needed by Professor Conklin. McClure has just handed it to me and, as you know, under our promises to Professor Conklin, there is no escaping from getting the things that he needs. McClure assures me that these things are indispensably necessary. I therefore send the list to you, with regrets that these things should accumulate.

I find that the appropriation of $1200 for the University Pulpit is exhausted. This is the first year that we have not been able to live within that appropriation. The reason we have failed to do so this year has been that it has proved impossible to get as often as usual the local preachers upon whom we have depended for gratuitous service. Dr. Henry van Dyke, for example, was not able to give us any Sundays at all, and Dr. Patton was not able to give us as many as usual. We are therefore short $250 (that is, five Sundays at $50 each). Will you authorize the Treasurer to extend the appropriation to that amount, or shall I try to get the

money from somebody outside, for example Mrs. Cyrus H. Mc-
Cormick, Sr.? I do not like to resort to this latter expedient now
that we have stopped miscellaneous requests, but if you think it
necessary, I will of course do so.

Always affectionately yours,   [Woodrow Wilson]

CCL (WWP, UA, NjP).

To Henry Jones Ford

My dear Mr. Ford: [Princeton, N. J.]   May 5th, 1908.

I fear that you have thought me discourteous in my failure to
reply to one or two of your letters, but the truth is that I did not
wish to reply until I had very thoroughly canvassed the situation
with regard to our plans in connection with the vacancy created
by Professor Garfield's resignation. I need not tell you that I
have never for a moment had any doubt that your intellectual
and scholarly qualifications for the place were as high as those
of any man in the country, but I have known that you had had
very little academic experience, and the conditions here are very
peculiar. It is necessary that a man who lectures to our classes
should have a particular kind of aptitude and command, and, to
speak frankly, I have been looking for someone whose experience
would make me clear upon that side of the question.

I know that in the circumstances, therefore, you will pardon
me for asking this question. Would you be willing, in case the
committee of the Trustees to which I must refer this matter
should deem it wise, to accept an appointment for a single year,
in order that both you and we could make a frank trial of the
desirability of continuing the arrangement?

I would not make this proposal, were I not sincerely anxious
to afford you the best possible opportunity to enter the ranks of
college teachers and carry forward the studies in which you have
already so greatly distinguished yourself and which seem to me
to promise such valuable and instructive results. I know that you
will reply to me in the same spirit of candor in which I have
written and will let me know your full mind in the matter.

With warm regard,

Sincerely yours,   [Woodrow Wilson]

CCL (WWP, UA, NjP).

From John Raleigh Mott

My dear President Wilson,   [New York]   May 5, 1908

I wish to thank you most sincerely and most heartily for the time and careful attention which you have so kindly devoted to my manuscript. I have considered the valuable suggestions which you have made and have been profited greatly by them.

I find myself in full and hearty agreement with the two points which you have emphasized with such force. I shall bear these in mind as I work over my manuscript to put it into final form. I can see from what you have said that I have taken too much for granted in neglecting to emphasize the primary and most important aspect of the work of the Christian minister. I am under deep obligation to you for calling my attention to this.

What you have been pleased to say about my work has come as a real encouragement. I shall keep you informed about the development of the book.[1]

With sincere regard, believe me,

Very faithfully yours,   [John R. Mott]

CCL (J. R. Mott Coll., CtY-D).
   [1] The book appeared as *The Future Leadership of the Church* (New York, 1908). There is a copy in the Wilson Library, DLC.

From Henry Jones Ford

My Dear Dr. Wilson: Baltimore, May 6, 1908.

I should not wish it otherwise than that the arrangement should be contingent upon my ability to give satisfactory service. I am quite willing to accept an appointment for a single year.[1]

You say the conditions of Princeton work are peculiar. Then, of course, nothing but actual trial will show whether I have the particular kind of aptitude and command that is required. I think, however, that I can say that I have this qualification—that I am able to command the alert interest and attention of my pupils. Both at the University of Pennsylvania and the Johns Hopkins University, it has been my practice to set down only the heads of the argument, and to keep the lecture on a conversational plane, admitting—and, indeed, encouraging—interruptions for purposes of inquiry into any pertinent matter. Sometimes points are raised that open lines of instructive discussion on thoughts and difficulties which have occurred to students. And, I notice that they are in no hurry to quit when the gong rings, although I have the period just before lunch.

My classes so far have been composed of seniors and postgraduates. The case of undergraduates may call for a different method. If I am honored with the appointment I shall make a visit to Princeton to examine the curriculum and to inform myself as to the situation and its requirements.

I am exceedingly grateful for the kind interest you have taken in me personally. I feel that the best requital I could make—the only one that you would probably care for—would be to display capacity to give aid of real value to Princeton in its work. I believe that I have such capacity and I am eager for the opportunity.

I am, with deep obligation,

Very sincerely yours   Henry J. Ford

ALS, (WP, DLC).

[1] At the end of his first year he was elected Professor of Politics on tenure and remained in this chair until his retirement in 1923.

From Henry Smith Pritchett

Dear Sir: New York   May 6, 1908.

I have the honor to inform you that, in accordance with your recommendation and in accordance with the rules of the Carnegie Foundation for the Advancement of Teaching, there was voted at a meeting of the executive committee on May 5 to Professor Cyrus Fogg Brackett an annual retiring salary of Two Thousand Four Hundred and Forty-Five Dollars. This will be paid to the treasurer of Princeton University, beginning at such time as Professor Brackett's active service may cease.

In conveying this information to Professor Brackett, I beg that you will at the same assure him of the very high estimate which the executive committee places upon his service to education and to science. In the department of science in which he has worked, the last thirty years have seen an enormous transformation and in this Professor Brackett has played a most honorable part. The committee hopes for him many years of health and prosperity.

Very sincerely yours,   Henry S. Pritchett

TLS, (WP, DLC).

From Henry Burling Thompson

Greenville, P. O. Delaware

Dear President Wilson: May 6th, 1908.

I have yours of the 5th instant.

The Committee on Grounds and Buildings have not adopted a site, but suggested a site, which site would have to be approved by the entire Board.

You speak of the possibility of Mrs. Sage being at Princeton within a week or two. One possible solution of the problem would be that you might induce Mrs. Sage to consider the entire group of buildings as the Sage Dormitory. While this would be a case of "crowding the mourners," it would be most desirable.

Yours very sincerely,   Henry B Thompson

TLS (WP, DLC).

From Moses Taylor Pyne

My dear Woodrow   New York   May 7/08

Referring to your favour of the 5th which I enclose I beg to say that the Finance Committee cannot appropriate any more money.

But I have seen Henry B Thompson who says he will send you, on request, $100 towards the Conklin expenditure. I shall do the same, which covers the $200 needed.

Cleve Dodge will give on request, $50.00 towards the University Pulpit. I shall do the same. The balance you must raise elsewhere.

Sincerely yours   M Taylor Pyne

ALS (WP, DLC).

To Nettie Fowler McCormick[1]

My dear Mrs. McCormick: Princeton, N. J.   May 8th, 1908.

I need not tell you that there is nothing I feel a greater delicacy in doing than asking for money, but the stringency of the times is such that we must turn hither and thither for even small sums to meet the necessities of the University, and I am writing to ask if you would be willing to contribute $150 to the University Pulpit fund. The University Pulpit is supplied by outside preachers from Sunday to Sunday, and we need that amount to complete the payments for the year for their services.

I sincerely hope you will not think me impertinent in making this request and that in the circumstances you will pardon my taking the liberty of doing so.

It was a great pleasure and privilege to see you when I was in Chicago, and I do not know when I have enjoyed more such a company as gathered about your lunch table. What Mr. Brockman[2] said about the success of the Young Men's Christian Association in China was to me more than interesting, it was thrilling.

With warm regard and appreciation,

Sincerely yours,   Woodrow Wilson

TLS ([Nancy] Nettie Fowler McCormick Papers, WHi).
    [1] Mrs. Cyrus Hall McCormick, Sr., businesswoman and philanthropist, especially active in the support of religious work and the Presbyterian Church.
    [2] Fletcher Sims Brockman, General Secretary of the National Committee of the Young Men's Christian Associations of China.

From Ralph Adams Cram

Dear Dr. Wilson: Boston, May 8, 1908.

This is positively one of the most unpleasant happenings of my life. Not having heard from you before I left for Princeton Tuesday, and remembering that you had said something about going to Pittsburg, I thought it probable that you were away. I arrived in Princeton late Wednesday afternoon, that is, about quarter past four. I brought Goodhue with me and [Frank Miles] Day happened to meet us at the Princeton Junction Station on his way to Princeton to look over the ground in anticipation of his having something to do there. Mr. Bunn met us at the Station and hustled us off to look over the coal bunkers. From there we went to his office, in order that I might explain to both Goodhue and Day the main lines of the general scheme, and while there I asked Mr. Bunn if you were away from Princeton. He replied that he was quite sure you were. He knew that you had been away and was under the impression that you would not return, if I understood him correctly, until Thursday afternoon. Goodhue, Day and I actually did walk up to Prospect and all around the house and I started to ring your bell and see if you actually were out of town, but decided I would not, as there seemed no reasonable chance that you were in Princeton. Wednesday night I dined at Merwick, and immediately after dinner Dr. [Howard Crosby] Butler and I tackled the question of the Graduate College and worked on it until one A.M. Thursday morning at 9.30 Dr.

Butler and Mr. Pyne appeared and from that hour until 5.30 we worked as I have never worked before over the sketch plans I had brought down. The only intermission was caused by a flying trip to Mr. [George Allison] Armour's house for luncheon.

You can see, I hope, how I got it into my head that you were away, but the fact that you actually were in Princeton and that I didn't even pay my respects to you fills me with actual dismay.

I think I now have a pretty clear idea as to the requirements of the Graduate College, at least so far as they can be put before me by Dr. West, Dr. Butler and Mr. Pyne. I understand that these three gentlemen have been made a Committee to report to the Committee on Grounds and Buildings the complete scheme of the proposed College, architectural and otherwise.

As a result of the time I spent in Princeton, I am convinced that the whole thing is straightening out after a fashion which will be satisfactory to everyone concerned. Several rather radical changes in the disposition of parts were tentatively determined upon yesterday, that is, these changes were agreed to by the members of the Committee of three, or, rather, they were suggested by them and accepted by myself, and they will form the basis for a new set of preliminary sketches, which, as soon as they are worked out, I shall bring to Princeton and submit to yourself for your consideration, criticism, and, if possible, approval. These changes were, roughly: throwing the great Hall to the south side of the quad, with the kitchens, etc. beneath facing the Physical Laboratory, and the omission of the easterly side of the comparatively small quadrangle I had originally suggested for the first construction.

I think the change in the position of the Hall will commend itself to you and I rather think the change in the quadrangle will also. You see the idea was that in order that the members of the Graduate College might have adequate grounds for their private use, grounds, that is, surrounded ultimately by their own buildings and not as open as the "Fellows' Garden," which will be equally the domain of the President, and taking into consideration the fact that '79 will ultimately be handed over to the Graduate College some time for the accommodation of the Graduate students, it might be well to consider the possibility of having one great quad, the easterly side of which should be formed of '79, though the first construction would be south, west and north wings in a kind of U shape, the easterly ends of the north and south wings projecting at first no farther toward '79 than the present line of the iron fence, which latter would be retained temporarily, in order to enclose the quad of the Graduate School.

I am under the impression that this will work out extremely well and the minute we have sketches in shape, they will be sent to you for your consideration, even before I bring the more finished sketches to Princeton in person.

I cannot begin to tell you what the giving of the Graduate College to my firm means to me personally and as a member of this firm. Nothing that has ever come our way in twenty years experience has been so interesting or so wonderful in its possibilities. I am also profoundly gratified at the action of the Committee on Grounds and Buildings in the matter of Mr. Day, and I look forward with the keenest anticipation to working with him on the Sage dormitories.

With renewed expressions of regret for the lamentable misunderstanding as to your whereabouts, I remain,

Very respectfully yours,   R A Cram.

P.S. Was the "pronunciamento" in the Alumni Weekly[1] all right? I wrote it hurriedly at Mr. Pyne[']s urgent request.   R. C.

TLS (WP, DLC).
[1] Ralph Adams Cram, "The Architectural Development of the University," *Princeton Alumni Weekly*, VIII (May 6, 1908), 504-506.

From the Diary of William Starr Myers

Friday May 8 [1908]

This evening Politics Club entertained by Paul van Dyke at his home. Subject—an open discussion on "The Policies of Roosevelt." Pres. Wilson was present and opened discussion by attacking Roosevelt, said his policies led to substitution of govt by commission, and executive discretion for govt by law. Woodrow stated that he was not a Jeffersonian Democrat because no one knew what kind of a Democrat Jefferson really was—that he agreed with him in this particular, that govt is a field for distrust, & he (W) distrusted Roosevelt's policies. A splendid discussion followed. Garfield gave his opinion last (strongly *pro*-Roosevelt) in a splendid spirit of calm, judicial reasonableness, & "Woodrow" then closed with one of his really masterful speeches—superb, although personally I do not agree with him. The final line-up was about as follows—"anti"-Roosevelt—5 (Wilson, van Dyke, Daniels, Coney, Dawson), "pro"—(10) Garfield,

Corwin, Bogart, Adriance, Elliott, Meeker, Spencer, Shipman, Iles, Myers, 1 (Price) divided in sentiment.[1]

[1] For another account of this meeting, see Edward S. Corwin, "Departmental Colleague," in William Starr Myers (ed.), *Woodrow Wilson: Some Princeton Memories* (Princeton, N. J., 1946), pp. 27-28.

To Henry Jones Ford

My dear Mr. Ford:　　　　　　Princeton, N. J.　May 9th, 1908.

Allow me to thank you for your letter of May 6th and to express my gratification that you find the suggestion I made in my last letter acceptable. It will give me pleasure, if it is agreeable to you, to propose to the Trustees of the University, at their meeting on the eighth of June, that you be invited to occupy our Chair of Politics for one year, at a salary of $3000. And I can assure you that I shall look forward with the greatest pleasure to having you in Princeton. I am sure we shall all feel the stimulation of your studies.

With much regard, Sincerely yours,　Woodrow Wilson

TCL (RSB Coll., DLC).

From Harry Augustus Garfield

My dear Wilson:　　　　　　Princeton, N. J.　May 12/08

I have seen Spencer & Shipman as you requested. Both are pleased to renew their engagements for the two years term.

Mr. Shipman stated that he was about to write you concerning an increase in salary; whereupon I told him of your regret that the financial condition made it impossible to advance him although you appreciated the merits of the request.

Upon my statement that I should be pleased to report to you his purpose to write, he said that in that case he would leave it to me & not trouble you. He will remain on the present salary.

Affectionately Yours,　H. A. Garfield.

ALS (WWP, UA, NjP).

From Henry Jones Ford

My dear Dr. Wilson:　　　　　　Baltimore, May 12, 1908

Many thanks for your kind letter. I shall be delighted to accept the position on the terms mentioned, and am greatly obliged and deeply grateful for your favor.

Would it be amiss if, previous to the action of the trustees, I should come in to Princeton to look over the field and get some information of the duties to be discharged? I have arranged to make a trip to Porto Rico in June, and the date of my departure from here is set for June 6th, which is prior to the meeting of the Trustees. In case the arrangement is consummated it would be an advantage to me to have some idea of details for consideration during the summer recess.

With cordial regard, I am,

Very sincerely yours   Henry J. Ford

ALS (WP, DLC).

To Ralph Adams Cram

My dear Mr. Cram: [Princeton, N. J.]   May 13th, 1908.

The mistake was a very natural one, and you may be sure that I am not in the least hurt. In the letter in which you spoke of coming, you simply said that if you did not hear that I was not to be here, you would carry out the plan, and that made me think it unnecessary to let you know that I should be. But pray dismiss the matter from your mind. It is absolutely all right.

I am intensely interested to know exactly what you are doing. Will you not be kind enough to tell me

(1) How many students would be accommodated in the Graduate School building under the modified plans?

(2) Whether Professor West and Mr. Butler spoke to you about the question of lodging servants in the building? I think that this should in no circumstances be done, considering the location of the building and the many consequences that it would involve.

(3) Whether it would not, under the plan you are now working on, be possible to put the ends of the building a little closer to Seventy-Nine Hall, in order to save more of the fine trees on this side of the building and to prevent making the quadrangle contemplated so large as to lose its cloistered effect when eventually worked out in connection with Seventy-Nine Hall? It would not be necessary to move it many feet in order to improve the whole situation of it so far as the surrounding grounds are concerned, very materially.

I am expecting to be in Boston on Friday, to attend a Princeton banquet,[1] but unhappily shall be there for only a few hours and shall be obliged to return on the midnight train. I wish I might see you, but after all these larger questions can be handled in part by correspondence. I cannot too much emphasize the fundamental importance of providing lodgings for as many men as possible in the Graduate School itself.

Always cordially and faithfully yours,

[Woodrow Wilson]

CCL (WWP, UA, NjP).

[1] Wilson was to speak to the Princeton Alumni Association of New England on May 15, 1908. The text of his address is printed at that date.

From Ralph Adams Cram

Dear Dr. Wilson:　　　　　　　　　　　　Boston, May 14, 1908.

I shall be able to send on either today or tomorrow to Dean West rough sketch plans showing the new arrangement we have worked out for the proposed Graduate College. If he can accept it in preference to the other arrangement with one very large quadrangle which was talked over the last time I was in Princeton, we shall then complete these preliminary sketches in presentable shape, and I shall bring them on to Princeton week after next in order to submit them to you, and, if possible, obtain your approval. You understand, of course, that these sketches go on to Dr. West now, for the reason that they are entirely different in arrangement to [from] the tentative scheme I agreed my firm should work out when I had my last conference with Dean West and Dr. Butler. I am wholly in sympathy with you as to the danger of getting too large a quadrangle and this modified scheme obviates this difficulty, but provides a great garden court opening to the west and separated from the present grounds of the President's house by a wall, or gates. Were the house to remain where it is, the resulting effect would be of much greater space to the east, while the results architecturally and from a pictorial standpoint would be immeasurably better than any scheme we have thus far worked out. The plan also saves more trees, which, as you say, is a most desirable thing, in fact my impression is that no more than four good trees in all would be sacrificed even were the Graduate College built in its complete and final form, with the wing reaching toward McCosh Walk and then turning west along the Walk. It really is quite miraculous the way the plan avoids the good trees. This scheme that we are working on now involves making '79 ultimately the east side of a complete and enclosed quadrangle 115 ft. wide and nearly 200 ft. long, while in addition to this we have the open forecourt toward McCosh Walk and the great garden court nearly 200 ft. square opening on the west toward the President's house.

As nearly as we can figure the thing out now, the proposed group of buildings would accommodate about 100 men, provided the chapel is ever built. If this were not constructed and the area turned over to residential purposes, we could get 20 or 30 more students. '79 Hall accommodates 48 men, so you would have about 150 bed-rooms in the whole Graduate College, that is, three units of 50 men each.

The question of lodging servants in the building is one which it hardly seems to me comes within my province. Is it not purely a question of administration? Structurally it is perfectly possible to accommodate all the servants in the building. The matter has no architectural bearing whatever and I am very anxious not to intrude myself into questions of pure administration which have no architectural or artistic aspect. I can quite understand the desire of the Graduate College authorities to keep their servants directly under their own eyes; on the other hand, I can see equally well the difficulties that might arise were this course followed out. As I say, however, it has no bearing on the architectural question and therefore hardly seems to come very explicitly within my province.

Of course it would be impossible to build accommodations at present for the full number of 100 students contemplated in the completed building, but the plans will work out so that we can stop anywhere as soon as estimates are received. It is just a question of how much money remains after we have built the great hall, breakfast room, commons room and library.

I am hoping against hope that you may get here tomorrow in season to run into the office for a moment. Of course you will not receive this letter until you return, but I am sending it on the chance that you may not be able to find time to come in on Friday.

Very respectfully yours,   R A Cram.

TLS (WP, DLC).

An Address to the Princeton Alumni Association of New England[1]

[[May 15, 1908]]

President Eliot has spoken of the variety amongst our leading institutions of learning,—not only of the variety which characterizes these three, but of the variety which is characteristic of the country at large. I believe it is entirely true that there is very con-

---

[1] Other speakers at this annual dinner meeting held in the Hotel Vendome in Boston on May 15, 1908, were Charles William Eliot, representing Harvard, and Samuel James Elder, who represented Yale.

siderable variety, but I must say that I wish there was a greater variety than there is. I believe that the most impoverishing habit that America has is the habit of imitation. I believe that the thing that limits the variety of success in America is that each kind of success is so ardently imitated; and imitation is not the process of variety or of strength. Not only that, but I believe that within each institution there is too little variety. The danger of every institution I know of, except perhaps Harvard, is that the processes of her life tend to reduce her undergraduates at any rate to a particular type, and, I think, tend to reduce men to certain standards of their own; so that it presently becomes possible to recognize a Yale man or a Princeton man or a man from this, that or the other particular institution.

I suppose that the fact that this is not in an equal degree true of Harvard is because of the variety of professional schools that center in Harvard, which are fed in large part, fortunately for her and fortunately for them, from the graduates of other institutions who come too late to be reduced to type and who therefore contribute to her considerable variety. But most undergraduate institutions have this standardizing tendency. Now for myself, I do not believe that the right intellectual processes should reduce men to similarity. I believe, on the contrary, that the natural operation of intellectual processes is to educe the variety there is in men, and that if they do not educe a considerable degree of variety, the nation is impoverished. For, while it is true that a democratic nation needs to discipline the minds of its voters and subject them to somewhat uniform processes of education, it is also true that the wholesome life of a democracy depends upon every man having his own opinion and speaking it individually and fearlessly.

The great trouble of America is uniformity of opinion in almost all processes of life—the fear of what the newspapers will say if we differ from our neighbors or differ from the majority. So long as that is the characteristic of the life of a nation, we of the universities in some degree err in not furnishing our men with the sort of individual impulse which comes from individual endeavor and individual achievement. It ought to be impossible for the men of real vitality of mind to let other people do their thinking for them; yet our tendency, as a nation, is to let the majority do our thinking for us.

The processes of politics are never wholly pure or wholesome unless they are dangerous and difficult for those who conduct them. So long as men go uncontradicted and uncriticized, they go undisciplined and undirected, and the oftener they are corrected, the better they will know their facts and their principles. I think the mere occupancy of the great offices of the country should exempt their occupants from personal criticism, but not from the most searching criticism of their principles and proposals, for it is only by that process that we should purify and clarify our politics. I am sometimes amused at the cry of congressmen that the President of the United States is encroaching upon their sphere. By what means is he thus encroaching? By getting the nation to agree with him rather than with them. (Laughter and applause.) I think that the powers of Congress will always be encroached upon if they cannot defend themselves in the forum of reason. If they cannot vindicate their own politics by their own utterances, then it is necessary for somebody else to speak for the nation. Let the field be free for everyone who has the prowess to enter it, but closed to every one whose stomach is not for the fight.

My moral is that the processes of our universities are processes of standardizing rather than intellectual processes of individualization. We hear a great deal said about the excessive addiction of our undergraduates to athletics, but I do not feel that the general body of undergraduates are too much addicted to them. I believe the degree to which they are addicted—the rank and file of them—is very wholesome indeed. I have not any jealousy of universal attention to athletics, if it be free from professionalism and other abuses. What I do regret is that there should have been added in college life to athletics a score of other very absorbing and exacting interests not connected with intellectual pursuits. To-day the real use of the passing of examinations to the average undergraduate is that it enables him to retain his connection with a delightful method of life. (Laughter.) The intellectual process is merely incidental so far as the college life is concerned; the intellectual processes of the university are incidental for the majority of undergraduates; and so long as that is true, the universities of this country are not vital parts of its life. Certainly the studies lend dignity and a picturesque background to the function of the teacher, but for my part, I do not care to be a background. (Laughter.) I do not mean that I want to be always at the front of the stage, but I certainly want to be a part of the plot, and at present I am not a part of the plot. They look at me as a sort of amiable lunatic. We must make some change in that respect or else we will lose our reason for existence.

The only method is for the universities to arrange their lives for the emphasizing of intellectual training—not only to put things into their minds, but to arouse their minds to understanding action. We must emancipate men's minds and give them a comradeship based on intellectual endeavor and intellectual enlightenment. We must challenge men to use their minds, and not merely to learn things. We must lead undergraduate life in such a way that it will not put us at a hopeless disadvantage among contending interests. We have not only come upon a strenuous age, but a more strenuous age is ahead of us. As the affairs of this nation thicken and become delicate and hazardous, full of all sorts of perplexing difficulties, it will be more and more necessary to supply the nation with men who can individualize themselves—more and more necessary for the universities to supply this country with those who can give a new meaning to a new age, and not simply stumble blindly and gregariously along old paths.

Printed in the *Princeton Alumni Weekly*, VIII (June 3, 1908), 568-69.

From James Edwards Wyckoff[1]

Dear Dr. Wilson, New York. May 18, 1908

In behalf of my brother Walter's family I want to convey to you our sincere thanks for the many kindnesses you have shown him in the past both before and during his last illness.[2]

I want also to express our appreciation of your thoughtfulness in representing the University at the funeral services and the interment.

These tributes of yourself and of Walter's many warm friends are a very comforting memory in this great sorrow.

I am, faithfully Yours J. Edwards Wyckoff

ALS (WP, DLC).

[1] Princeton 1889 and a lawyer of New York City.
[2] Walter Augustus Wyckoff, Princeton 1888, Assistant Professor of Political Economy at Princeton, died on May 15, 1908, at the home of Andrew F. West after a long illness stemming from an aneurism of the aorta.

A News Report

[May 19, 1908]

**LOVING CUP PRESENTED TO PROFESSOR BRACKETT
AT DINNER GIVEN IN HIS HONOR YESTERDAY EVENING.**

A dinner was tendered to Professor Cyrus F. Brackett last evening at the Princeton Inn in view of his resignation from the University Faculty, which was accepted on April 9 at the annual spring meeting of the Trustees of the University. The occasion of the banquet was the presentation to Professor Brackett of a loving cup, on which was engraved the inscription:

"TO CYRUS FOGG BRACKETT

FROM

COLLEAGUES AND FRIENDS

IN PRINCETON

May 18, 1908."

Dr. Brackett for thirty-five years has held the position of Henry Professor of Physics in the University.

Professor William Francis Magie '79 acted as toastmaster and the following toasts were responded to:

Professor William Francis Magie '79–"The Behavior of Heated Gas Under Pressure."

President Woodrow Wilson '79–"Mere Science."

Stephen S. Palmer–"Science and Sense."

Professor Leroy Wiley McCay–"Science Falsely So Called."

Ex-President Francis Landey Patton–"Physics and Metaphysics."

Dean Andrew Fleming West '74–"The Electric Fluid."

Professor Cyrus Fogg Brackett '79[1]–Response.

The menus at the banquet were in white, with untrimmed edges, and bore the inscription: "Dinner to Professor Cyrus F. Brackett at the Princeton Inn, Monday, May 18, 1908."

Printed in the *Daily Princetonian*, May 19, 1908.

[1] A misprint or an error. Brackett received the A.B. degree from Bowdoin College in 1859 and the M.D. degree from the same institution in 1863.

From Henry Burling Thompson

Dear President Wilson: Wilmington, Del.   May 20th, 1908.

Mr. Russell is anxious to set a date for the meeting of the Grounds and Buildings Committee. Will you kindly let him know a date that will be satisfactory to you, and he will then make his arrangements accordingly?

Mr. Cram writes me that he expects to be in Princeton on the 28th instant. This will be his last opportunity of seeing any of us before leaving on his summer vacation. It would seem most desirable if the questions of the architect and location of the Sage Building could be settled before Mr. Cram sails. The situation as I understand it to-day is as follows:

At our last meeting of the Grounds and Buildings Committee, Mr. Pyne reported that Mr. Henry DeForest was a little annoyed at our delay in suggesting an architect. The Committee authorized me to write to Mr. DeForest that Mr. Cram had recommended Mr. Day, and we approved of the recommendation,—of course, subject to Mrs. Sage's approval. As matters have turned out, I think it would have been better if this communication had gone through Mr. Cadwalader, but, in our anxiety to communicate at once with Mr. DeForest, I acted as above described. Mr. Goodhue, of the firm of Cram, Goodhue & Ferguson, some few days later, saw Mr. DeForest, and he said that Mrs. Sage had expressed some irritation from the fact that we had appointed an architect for her building, and that he had been at Princeton. Now, there was certainly no intention on our part to crowd the old lady, but we supposed we were acting in good faith and pushing the matter forward and meeting her wishes. I have written to Mr. Cadwalader, expressing the necessity of diplomacy as matters have developed; at the same time, saying that our Committee and Mr. Cram should consider any competition for this building most undesirable; in fact, I think it would be fatal at this stage. The type of building is already set for us, in Blair Hall, and Mr. Cram's desire was to secure an architect who would be conspicuously capable in carrying out this type. He has written me personally that he would prefer Mr. Day to any other man in the United States. While Mr. Day is a friend of mine, I have no personal interest in his securing the work, beyond the fact that I feel this group will be one of the most conspicuous on the campus, and it is most desirable that we should secure the best brains we can for it. I am very positive that the combination of Cram and Day will be able to maintain the high standard that has been set in the past by Cope & Stewardson.[1] Now, if you agree with me, I hope that you, with your powers of persuasion, will be able to convert Mrs. Sage to our point of view.

Cram's idea is to start this building opposite the new '77 Building, which would bring it up on the campus, and not back of University Hall.

Yours very sincerely,   Henry B Thompson

TLS (WP, DLC).
  [1] The distinguished architectural firm of Philadelphia which had originated the Collegiate Gothic style in the United States and had designed Blair Arch, Blair Hall, and Stafford Little Hall at Princeton.

From the Diary of William Starr Myers

Wed. May 20 [1908].

This evening departmental meeting at Nassau Club. "Woodrow" there, and had discussion of preceptorial system. He made, as usual, pregnant remarks as—our students too dependent in thought, look upon teachers as *authorities* rather than guides. A lecturer should make telling comparisons and stimulate hearers to thought, rather than describe or attempt to teach them.

To Henry Burling Thompson

My dear Mr. Thompson: Princeton, N. J.   May 21st, 1908.

Your letter of yesterday has just reached me. I am sincerely sorry that there should be any embarrassment about Mrs. Sage and the architect. I do not see, however, that there is any real ground for irritation on her part. I am expecting to spend a part of tomorrow in New York, and will try and see Mr. Cadwalader. If he thinks it wise, I will myself call on Mrs. Sage and do what I can to straighten the matter out. I shall certainly lend my aid in every way possible. I will report to you later what I have found it possible to do.

Always cordially and faithfully yours,

Woodrow Wilson

I should be free for a meeting at any time after June 3rd. except Sat. eve. the sixth.

TLS (H. B. Thompson Papers, NjP).

To Henry Lee Higginson[1]

My dear Major Higginson: Princeton, N. J.   May 21st, 1908.

I am sincerely obliged to you for your kind letter of May 19th.[2] The matter I was discussing at the Princeton dinner last week was one that concerns me very deeply, but I am sorry to say that I was not able to write out what I said, and there is therefore nothing that I can send you by way of a report of the speech. It is possible that the gentlemen in charge of the dinner had a stenographic report made of it and that they will send it to me for correction. Should they do so, I will take real pleasure in seeing that you get a copy of it. I should very much value your opinion concerning it.

I remember very well your generous suggestion that it might be possible for you to send the Boston Orchestra to Princeton,[3] and I can assure you that at any time it may be possible for you to do so we will be delighted to make the necessary arrangements.[4]

With cordial regard,

Sincerely yours,   Woodrow Wilson

TLS (H. L. Higginson Coll., MH-BA).
    1 Boston banker and philanthropist.
    2 It is missing.
    3 Higginson had founded the Boston Symphony Orchestra in 1881 and was its sole underwriter until 1918.
    4 Higginson did send the Boston Symphony Orchestra to Princeton for a concert in Alexander Hall on November 9, 1908. See WW to H. L. Higginson, Nov. 4, 1908.

From Ralph Adams Cram

Dear Dr. Wilson: Boston, May 21, 1908.

I have heard nothing from Dean West, or Dr. Butler since sending on the revised sketch plan for the Graduate College, except a telegram from the former, in which he expressed his surprise at the suggested change and stated that he would need time to consider the plans and consult about them. In any case, I shall come on to Princeton for Thursday, the 28th of May, when I shall meet Mr. Thompson and Mr. Pyne, as well as see Dean West and Dr. Butler. I sincerely hope that Mrs. Sage may be induced to make her decision with regard to the architect for her proposed dormitory before that date, or, at all events, before I leave for England. If she endorses Mr. Day, as I hope she may, I think he would like to come to England to study Oxford and Cambridge on the spot with me, particularly as it would appear to be impossible to start work on the Sage dormitories next Autumn, and he would therefore have plenty of time for a short trip to England.

                              Very truly yours,   R A Cram.

TLS (WP, DLC).

From Joseph McCarter Bowyer[1]

Dear Mr. Wilson: Washington, D. C.   May 22, 1908.

I have been very much interested in the various plans proposed for doing away with the bad points in the club system, and I should like to ask you whether the following scheme has been suggested to you.

It seems to me that the most obvious bad point at present is the wearing of hat bands. When I graduated in 1904, freshmen and sophomores were beginning to pay a great deal more attention and respect to an upper classman who wore a hat band of a popular club than they did to the upper classman who wore no hat band or wore one belonging to a less popular club. Then again, if an upper classman not in one of the clubs invited people to a football or baseball game, one of the first things to impress his friends would be the various colored hat bands, and when they found that he did not wear one they would come to the conclusion, probably not at all correct, that the persons wearing hat bands were better thought of throughout the college than he was. Of course it is useless to point out the evils of hat bands, for you know them very well. It does seem to me, however, that a college which boasts of its democracy should eliminate visible badges of class distinction.

If the money could be obtained, and I am afraid that is a very large "if" at the present time, why should a club house containing dining room, card rooms and library, etc. not be built and run for upper classmen not in the upper class clubs? I would suggest that it be given to them exclusively. If club men were allowed to eat there whenever they pleased, the importance of the club would be decreased. A fair amount could be charged for board and if the entire system proved satisfactory there appears to be no reason why the club should not be enlarged and all upper classmen fed there. The present upper class clubs could be used merely as clubs and not as eating places.

I think that almost all graduates of Princeton realize that the club system will get topheavy, if it is not that way already, and we all want to have some good system established before the effects are too apparent.

Sincerely yours,   Joseph M. Bowyer.

TLS (WP, DLC).
[1] Princeton 1904, patent and trade-mark lawyer in Washington.

To Joseph McCarter Bowyer

My dear Mr. Bowyer: Princeton, N. J.   May 23rd, 1908.

Thank you very much for your letter of May 22nd.

The suggestions you make have been a great deal discussed amongst us. I am afraid that the mere abolition of the club hatbands, while in itself a most desirable thing, would hardly accomplish much, because there would be always some means of distinguishing club-men from non-club-men in the social practices of the place.

As for a club for the men who do not get places in the Upperclass Clubs, those of us who have had the most experience here are convinced that it would not be desirable. It would in a still more marked way set the non-club men apart from the club-men, as a distant class especially provided for, and I know that the feeling of the non-club men is very strong against it. I doubt whether they would consent to patronize a club of that sort.

Moreover, the heart of the trouble is not in the evils incident to the clubs, but, to my mind, lies very much deeper. Any club system would result in absorbing the attention and energy of a large proportion of the best men in college. The reforms which I have most at heart are those which would lie toward obtaining the attention of the undergraduates for the more serious tasks of the University. So long as they are left to organize and conduct an elaborate social life of their own, their interest and energy will of course be absorbed in that, no matter how pure and unobjectionable that life may be, or free from snobbish qualities even. It will be their chief and most absorbing interest. My proposals have looked in another direction. I think it is perfectly feasible for the University to furnish to the whole body of undergraduates all the material appointments of their lives, places to eat with dignity and comfort and places in which they can assemble for general social intercourse, without the necessity of maintaining elaborate organizations which inevitably become rivals and center in themselves the social ambitions of the undergraduates. The students would be no less free than at present to form their own social groups and associations, and yet would be constantly associated as a body with the life of the University itself and in constant association with the men who were trying to give intellectual stimulation to the place. At present we have only a residuum, and a small residuum at that, of the attention of the undergraduates for the real tasks of the University, and that will remain the case so long as they center their thoughts and plans upon independent organizations which they must maintain and to which they must give prestige. This point is at the heart of my suggestion with regard to quads.

I hope that you will write to me most freely with regard to anything that occurs to you. I value such interest as you have shown most highly and appreciate your letter very much indeed.

Cordially and sincerely yours,   [Woodrow Wilson]

CCL (WWP, UA, NjP).

A Poem by Robert Bridges

[c. May 23, 1908]

"CULTURAL AND STRUCTURAL ENTITY."
Inscribed to the Supervising Architect

By Robert Bridges.

Well, Well! For a hundred and fifty years
    We've stumbled along in the dark;
We've soothed our souls with college cheers
    And made the campus a Park.
All wrong! The ancient American plan
    Benumbs and belittles the soul;
The buildings can never turn out a man
    Until they're a "cultural whole."
Old North and West must "articulate"—
    Tear down a structure or two!
Reunion and Blair should "interrelate"—
    So bother the beautiful view!
The President's house obstructs the way
    For a homogeneous whole;
Remove the blot and humbly pray
    To save your "structural" soul.
And jam the buildings into a heap,
    Wipe out the "vermicular walks,"
For Vistas and Views are nothing to keep,
    The Mass is the thing that talks.
The whole must neatly "coordinate"
    To lead in the cultural van;
Mere Beauty you must subordinate
    To the architectural plan.
Our Boys are back in the Ages Dark—
    They must live in a tenement block
And forget their dream of a beautiful Park
    And bravely endure the shock!
For we're going to Bostonize the place,
    And soon at Princeton you'll see,
With "dynamic force" and "logical" grace,
    The Harvard of New Jersee!

T MS (WP, DLC).

To Robert Bridges

My dear Bobby:　　　　　　Princeton, N. J.　May 25th, 1908.

Two members of the Committee of the Board on Grounds and Buildings, namely Momo Pyne and Harry Thompson, have seen the lines which you sent to The Alumni Weekly, inscribed to Mr. Cram, the Supervising Architect, and have come to me in a good deal of distress about them. They have asked me to undertake the very delicate task of asking you if you would be willing to reconsider or withdraw them. I know that you will be sure of the spirit and motive with which I comply with their request.

Mr. Cram's letter was, I am sorry to have to admit, a very foolish one indeed, and the thing that it seems most pertinent to say about it is that it conveyed an entirely false impression of the character and purpose of the man himself. Take, for example, the closing reference in your lines. There is no man in the United States whom I have heard more violently and contemptuously condemn Harvard or more heartily laugh at Boston than Mr. Cram himself. This will show you how singularly he has succeeded in conveying a false impression by what he wrote.[1]

I think that we all feel very keenly the things that may be said against some of the plans we have adopted for the development of the campus, but the point in my mind is that even in respect of the matters which are most criticized we are not departing radically from traditional lines, but are developing the campus in ways suggested by what has already been done and trying in every instance to leave open spaces large enough to preserve all the essential beauty and unity of the campus. We have devoted a great deal of thought to the matter and, as we have thought it out, it is far from revolutionary. It would embarrass the committee very seriously to have these lines of yours appear, because they are very witty, very telling, and would be signed by your name.

You know, of course, my dear Bobby, that I have not even a desire to ask you to limit your freedom in a matter of this kind. No one has or thinks that he has the right to ask you to withdraw the lines. The most that I wish to do is to call your attention to the misapprehension which I am sure has been created, and to ask if you will be willing yourself to withdraw them.

Always affectionately and faithfully yours,

Woodrow Wilson

TLS (WP, DLC).

[1] Cram's article (or letter, as Wilson called it), "The Architectural Development of the University," Princeton Alumni Weekly, VIII (May 6, 1908), 504-506, was prompted by a letter to the Editor of the Princeton Alumni Weekly,

(*ibid.*, April 29, 1908, p. 486) from Thomas Shields Clarke, Princeton 1882, a painter and sculptor living in Lenox, Massachusetts, and New York. Criticizing the choice of sites for the Graduate College, '77 Hall (later named Campbell Hall), and the Sage dormitory (later named Holder Hall), Clarke complained that these sites and other aspects of the architectural plan destroyed the open spaces of the campus and clustered buildings too close together. He requested an explanation from the Committee on Grounds and Buildings of the Board of Trustees.

In his article, cited above, Cram responded for the committee, arguing that the architectural plan had to be considered in its entirety and that criticism should not focus on "individual and isolated parts of a general, and consistent scheme." He further maintained that the desire to preserve open spaces was based on adherence to the "landscape-gardening theory"; that such an idea was a passing vogue and should not be pursued; and that Princeton's architectural development should follow lines of development emphasizing architectural symmetry and unity. While Cram's article vigorously defended the merits of his plan, it was also written in a patronizing and pompous tone, which is probably the reason why Wilson described it as "very foolish."

From John Lambert Cadwalader

My dear Mr. President: New York. May 25, 1908.

I have just talked to de Forest. He was not here on Friday or Saturday.

He says that the main difficulty with Mrs. Sage arose from the fact that she heard outside that somebody had been or was to be selected as an architect before she heard it directly, but that he will go and see her and straighten out the subject. He said he was satisfied that he could make it all right. I told him there were three or four architects bothering us. He said Mrs. Sage never had the faintest interest in any of them except one man who had built her Sag Harbor School,[1] but de Forest could not tell who that man is or where his office is.

I asked him also about Mrs. Sage going down to Princeton and explained that we would like to have her come and we thought it would interest her. He said she was going down to the exercises of the Sag Harbor School tomorrow to be gone the rest of the week; that if we *really* would like her to come down to Princeton he thought he could arrange it; that if she wanted him to do so he would go with her, and that he would either get her to do this or get a letter authorizing somebody to select the site.

All together, that is now, I think, on a good basis, and I hope to hear without delay that the matter is closed.

I am going to Boston tonight, but shall be here again on Wednesday.

Yours faithfully,   John L. Cadwalader

TLS (H. B. Thompson Papers, NjP).
[1] The Pierson High School, toward the construction of which Mrs. Sage gave $115,000. The cornerstone was laid in 1907. The architect was Augustus Nichols Allen.

To Robert Bridges

My dear Bobby: Princeton, N. J.   May 27th, 1908.

Thank you with all my heart. It really does relieve us of a serious embarrassment, and I feel the generosity of what you have done.[1]

As I said before, Cram's letter certainly deserved to be made fun of, and we all of us realize the criticisms to which the new plans seem to be open. No one realizes it more keenly than I do. I should be very much disturbed by the criticisms which have been elicited, were it not that I honestly think they are founded upon a misunderstanding and that as the plans are developed it will be seen that we are really not destroying the spacious beauty of the college grounds.

I was so sorry not to get hold of you again on Saturday. I suppose you are coming to the Yale game,[2] and if committee meetings of the Board make it possible, I shall certainly find you then.

Always affectionately yours,   Woodrow Wilson

TLS (WC, NjP).
[1] Bridges' letter is missing.
[2] Princeton won the second game of the annual three-game baseball series with Yale by a score of 3 to 2 at Princeton on June 6, 1908.

An Announcement

[May 28, 1908]

PRESIDENT WILSON

Will Address Last Meeting of Philadelphian
Society To-night.

President Wilson will address the regular meeting of the Philadelphian Society in Murray Hall at 7.15 o'clock to-night. This is the last mid-week meeting of the year.[1]

Printed in the *Daily Princetonian*, May 28, 1908.
[1] The *Daily Princetonian* did not print a report of this address.

From John Bates Clark[1]

Dear President Wilson,   New York   May 28, '08

I have been asked to write to you about a possible appointment to the vacancy created by the death of Professor Wyckoff; and though it jars a little to say anything about the successor of my friend, I cannot refuse to make the suggestion. Moreover you will see that the man in the case is not an ordinary candidate when I tell you that he is Professor Charles Lee Raper, of the University of North Carolina. He has held for some years the headship of the department of Economics in that university and he had more than one call to strong state universities elsewhere. Besides his doctor's thesis he has published a successful elementary treatise on Political Economy[2] and has become widely known and influential in the South. He is a captivating personality—a man of refinement and agreeable manners; and withal he has a record of unusual success as a teacher.

Cordially yours   John B. Clark

ALS (WWP, UA, NjP).

[1] Professor of Political Economy at Columbia University and an old friend of Wilson's.

[2] Raper's doctoral thesis was published as *North Carolina: A Royal Province, 1729-1775; The Executive and Legislature* (Chapel Hill, N. C., 1901). His elementary treatise on political economy was *The Principles of Wealth and Welfare: Economics for High Schools* (New York and London, 1906).

To John Bates Clark

My dear Professor Clark: Princeton, N. J.   May 29th, 1908.

Allow me to acknowledge the receipt of your letter of yesterday and to express my very sincere interest in what you tell me of Professor Roper.

The position which Professor Wyckoff filled was only that of Assistant Professor. It was a minor post, the rank and emolument of which we cannot advance at present, and therefore I have thought that the best way to fill it was to advance some one of the men in our preceptorial staff.

I am very much attracted by what you tell me of Professor Roper, and I wish very much that Princeton had a position to offer him which would be a real promotion from that which he now occupies.

With warm regard and appreciation,

Sincerely yours,   Woodrow Wilson

TLS (WC, NjP).

From Melancthon Williams Jacobus

My dear President Wilson: Hartford [Conn.]   31st May 1908

From correspondence with Mr. [David Benton] Jones and Mr. Garrett I gather that there is question in their minds, as there is in mine, whether the experiment of the Social Hall suggested in the final recommendation of the Conference Committee[1] will, after all, be beneficial to the Resident Quad idea.

It will be an experiment only; it will be launched under peculiar criticism from the Club men, who will do all in their power to discredit the general scheme of which it is supposed to be an expression.

Would it not be better to concentrate all our efforts on so disposing the Graduate Quad. as to show what can be done in the highest form of postgraduate University Social life, and so let the influence of the scheme, expressed in its most impressive (because postgraduate) form, work down upon the undergraduate body?

I think we are all ready to vote against the recommendation, if *you* approve of this action. But the only way we can get it voted down is by not showing too clearly that we are against it. The general feeling that the whole question should be allowed to be quiescent at present is the best way.

I know you are very busy; but if you have a moment to send me a word or two as to your views, there would be a consciousness on our part as to what we were doing in the meeting of the Board, that otherwise we could not have. I have small hope of getting a half hour's quiet talk with you next week, and so am writing you.

What a splendid address you gave at New Haven before the Phi Beta Kappas! I am hearing of it on many sides. This is the way to arouse the great sentiment by whose power you must finally win out.

Yours cordially   Melancthon W Jacobus

ALS (WP, DLC).
    [1] That is, the sixth recommendation of the report by H. B. Thompson *et al.* to the Board of Trustees of Princeton University, April 8, 1908.

To Frederic Yates

My dear Yates: Princeton, N. J.   June 1st, 1908.

Your letter[1] suggesting that I take the little cottage next you in bachelor form has just reached me this morning. I wish with all my heart I could do it, but it wouldn't pay. I must be foot loose in order to get the freedom to explore that I want, and I could not afford to pay for a house that I was not using practically constantly, though the temptation is sore.

Thank you with all our hearts for the dear letters that came this morning from you and Mrs. Yates.[2] I am looking forward with the greatest zest and pleasure to coming to you. I sail on the twentieth and shall reach Glasgow, I suppose, about the twenty-eighth, and when I get there, will know what I am going to do next and will write to you some details of my movements. I am afraid I must run up to see the Laird of Skibo,[3] and riding down from Glasgow to Rydal by wheel will probably be a round-about business, but my heart will lead me there as quickly as possible.

    With warm love from us all to you all,

Affectionately yours, Woodrow Wilson

TLS (F. Yates Coll., NjP).
  [1] F. Yates to WW, May 22, 1908, ALS (WP, DLC).
  [2] The letter from Emily Chapman Martin Yates is missing.
  [3] Andrew Carnegie.

To Cyrus Hall McCormick

My dear Cyrus: Princeton, N. J. June 1st, 1908.

    Thank you heartily for your letter of May 29th.[1] It is a real gratification to me to know that I was of some service in connection with the celebration of the Semicentennial of the Young Men's Christian Association, and I very much appreciate the cordial thanks that have come to me from the men most interested.

    I sincerely hope that you will be able to attend the Trustees' meeting and shall look forward as always with the greatest pleasure to seeing you again.

Always affectionately yours, Woodrow Wilson

TLS (WP, DLC).
  [1] It is missing.

To Melancthon Williams Jacobus

My dear Dr. Jacobus: [Princeton, N. J.] June 1st, 1908.

    Thank you most sincerely for your letter of yesterday. You express exactly my own feeling and conviction about the suggestion of Mr. Thompson's committee concerning an experimental beginning of something like a quad. I feel that such a beginning as is proposed would be abortive and that that would be more detrimental to the reforms we have at heart than anything else could be. I think that I will talk with Mr. Thompson and see if his committee would be willing to withdraw the suggestion for the present.

I cannot tell you what satisfaction your letters and your counsel give me.

In haste,

Cordially and faithfully yours,   [Woodrow Wilson]

CCL (RSB Coll., DLC).

From Ralph Adams Cram

My dear Dr. Wilson: Boston, June 1, 1908.

Some curious fatality seems to pursue me so far as meeting you in Princeton is concerned. I was bitterly disappointed at not finding you when I was there last week. Still, no particular question arose which demanded consideration. I have obtained from Dean West and Dr. Butler approval in principle of the last scheme for the Graduate College and Mr. Pyne has also endorsed it with all possible enthusiasm. I have reduced the great hall to 32 ft. in width and less than 100 ft. in length, and have explained to Dr. West why I have done so. I have talked to Dr. Butler about the installation of an organ in the hall, and he has agreed to take this matter up with Dean West. I have told Dr. Butler that I am personally out of sympathy with an innovation of this kind.

As the situation is now developed, the office here is going ahead with eighth scale plans, elevations and sections as a preliminary to the making of a large number of perspectives and a model, all of which will serve to show the effect of the proposed buildings and enable us to do our designing in perspective. I expect to find these plans and perspective sketches finished in pencil when I get back early in September. They will then be put into final form and as I understand it, serve as a basis for the report to the Committee on Grounds and Buildings which the sub-committee, consisting of Dean West, Dr. Butler and Mr. Pyne, is instructed to make. Of course details may be changed unlimitedly and undoubtedly will be changed during the Autumn, but I see no reason now why, if we are all agreed on the scheme, estimates should not be obtained early in the Spring and work begun as soon as weather conditions will permit.

I repeat, I was particularly worry [sorry] not to see you, in order to pay my respects and say au revoir before sailing, still I shall certainly hope to meet you in Oxford or Cambridge some time during the summer.

Very truly yours,   R A Cram

TLS (WP, DLC).

Harold Griffith Murray to Cleveland Hoadley Dodge

Sir: [New York]   June 1st, 1908.

The following is the Report of the Committee of Fifty of Princeton University to date, for the fiscal year ending July 31st, 1908.

The total income for the last fiscal year, ending July 31st, 1907, was $115,000, exclusive of interest on sums paid in to the endowment form of subscription; the pledges in the endowment form amounted to $605,125, of which $186,000 has been paid in; the balance, $419,125, drawing interest at 5% according to the terms of the pledge.

For the present fiscal year, ending July 31st, 1908, the pledges under the term form, and interest on unpaid pledges under the endowment form, amount to $103,959, $70,000 of which has been paid into the treasury of the University.

It is problematical, however, how much of the sums pledged we shall be able to collect, as this year has been an unusually difficult one in which to secure subscriptions and make collections. From August first until the middle of October the agitation over the Quads made it impossible for me to secure pledges of money, and from that time until the present, the financial depression[1] has not only caused many cancellations, but prevented my realizing on many promises made me. In addition, the Princeton Club of New York has been making an active canvass to raise $60,000 to defray the cost of the new Club House, and four or five classes, in addition to those mentioned in my last Annual Report, have decided to raise Class Memorial Funds. No stone, however, has been left unturned to raise as large an amount as possible. Every alumnus who is not a member of a class raising a Memorial Fund has either received a call or circular from me during the past year.

It will probably be gratifying to you to know that a general circular sent out last Fall begging for funds, at an expenditure of $500, produced in pledges $38,000.

The endowment fund during the present year has been increased to $639,125, and six of the alumni have made Princeton a beneficiary under their wills. The amounts mentioned in these wills aggregate some $700,000. These bequests are not included in any statement made in regard to moneys collected, as the wills might be changed or values depreciate. I only instance these cases to show that the work of the Committee is cumulative, nor capable of accurate financial measurement.

ALUMNI DORMITORY

The plan of erecting a dormitory at the South of Patton Hall and East of Brokaw Field, by various classes, under the plan pursued in the erection of Patton Hall, has made no material progress during the past year; the present financial condition making it impossible for the University to finance the plan. As the matter now stands two entries will be built by the principal of the alumni fund; one by the Class of '81; the tower by the Class of '84; and entries by '02, '03, '04, '06, and undoubtedly '07.

THE PRESS BUREAU

During the past year the Bulletin of the Committee of Fifty has been published regularly in the Alumni Weekly. The educational work done by this Bulletin I do not think can be overestimated.

The Press Bureau is sending out every week to 550 daily newspapers throughout the United States, items of interest relative to the University. From the number of these articles published and the editorial comments, I believe the Bureau is a decided success.

THE ALUMNI

My canvass to date shows that the following classes are contributing to special class funds: '77, '81, '87, '92, '94, '96, '98, '99, '00, '01, '02, '03, '04, and '06; in addition the classes of '73, '88, '90 and '05 are raising memorial funds; giving a total number exempt from my solicitation of 2570.

According to the last Alumni Directory, the total number of living alumni, including ex-members of classes, is 7190. To this I have added 54 names, and with the class of '06, which was not listed, we have a grand total of 7678 living alumni, exclusive of the class of '07, who have not yet been graduated long enough to list. The alumni have been disposed of by my canvass as follows:

Number exempt from solicitation	2570
Deceased	202
No address	230
Insane	24
Undesirable citizens	14
Contributors	630
Refused	1088
Repeated names in catalogue	6
Future promises	300
In country, to be reached by circular	2157
Not yet solicited, in various cities and towns	457
	7678

The financial depression has not made it advisable to travel in the interest of the Committee this year.

After careful figuring, I estimate that the alumni, during the past year, have given or pledged themselves over $200,000 a year annually to the various Princeton funds for the next year or two, of which the Committee of Fifty is receiving approximately $100,000, the balance being contributed to the support of Clubs, Class Memorials, etc. I believe, therefore, that as soon as some of the class memorials are paid up, and the social clubs are put on their feet, there will be no difficulty in having an income from this fund from the alumni alone of $150,000 a year, exclusive of interest account.

Respectfully,   H G Murray   Secretary.

TLS (Trustees' Papers, UA, NjP).
¹ The Panic of 1907, about which see C. H. Dodge to WW, March 28, 1907, n. 1, Vol. 17.

From John Lambert Cadwalader

My dear Mr. President: New York.   2 June, 1908.

Mrs. Sage has been away and de Forest has not yet disposed of the subject of the architect and the selection of a place for the building. He promises me, however, that he will do so the moment she comes to town. Whether he will do it before Thursday, when I am compelled to leave, I cannot say, but if not he told me he would make the arrangements with you. His address is,—Henry W. de Forest, 30 Broad Street, New York. I have no doubt he will straighten it out, and he agrees to do so.

I am exceedingly sorry that I cannot attend the Commencement & the Board Meeting and fulfill my duties in that respect, but for certain private reasons I am compelled to go away at this time, although it is very near the day for the meeting. I am very sorry indeed to be unable to attend.

Believe me, with my good wishes,

Faithfully yours,   John L. Cadwalader

TLS (WP, DLC).

Notes for a Commencement Address

Woman's College Baltimore   3 June, 1908.
The College and the Country

Let every college be judged by the graduates it sends forth.
1) *By their spirit.* Is it adjusted to the life and needs of the country and of the age? Are the men or women who come out of it specially fitted for the parts they are to play in the country's life: are the men more intelligently manly, the women more intelligently womanly? There is no avoiding the test
2) Not by their knowledge, which can never be complete, but *by their capacity*
3) *By their variety*, their suitability to be dispersed through the various body of the world's work with easy adaptability, —not set apart as a class. Danger of standardization, reduction to type.
4) *By their energy*, the manner and the persistency with which they attack their tasks.
Besides these tests there is the *characteristic* touch of the college
The touch of idealism, of enthusiasm, of intelligent hope, the courage and vision wh. are the real springs of achievement.
The mission of the college is to the mind, to enlighten it, and to the heart to give it reasonable hope.

WWhw MS (WP, DLC).

A News Report of a Commencement Address
at the Woman's College of Baltimore

[June 4, 1908]

GIRLS WIN DEGREES

Dr. Woodrow Wilson Speaks To Woman's
College Graduates.

In masterly language, President Woodrow Wilson, of Princeton University, spoke to the fair graduates of the Woman's College yesterday afternoon at the Lyric and told them that they should always preserve untarnished the ideals which they had received at college.

Mr. Wilson spoke clearly and forcefully, and his voice was so modulated that his audience listened as though spellbound through his address.

The auditorium was crowded with friends of the college, many of whom came from distant places. Seats were reserved for alumnae and undergraduates, who entered wearing cap and gown class by class. The class presidents acted as marshalls and each marshall bore her respective class banner. . . .

It is an interesting fact that President Wilson's daughter[1] was also a graduate.

President Wilson spoke without notes and with few gestures. His theme was, "College Work and College Administration," and he said, in part:

"This is a day in which it is generally thought that those most interested in their work think of the life that is before them; but that is a mistake. They are thinking of the life that is behind, of the days of comradeship, of close friendship, of days in which they realize they were being formed in character and in mind. It is a day when the world crowds in to view and to judge the college; consciously or unconsciously, it is a day of criticism.

"Every college must be judged by its graduates, not by its faculty. The purpose of a faculty may be excellent, but we judge by what it has accomplished and the graduates are this accomplishment. The Woman's College of Baltimore has already been judged by its graduates.

"There is an academic point of view. No man shut into a classroom can fail to feel that he is shut in to a point of view. In every book, in every classroom, life is simplified. No two lives run in the same order. Therefore, if the spirit of a student is narrowed to a book, it is a narrowed life. The graduate should feel that what he has learned is only transitory—his knowledge may be changed tomorrow by a new discovery.

"The spirit of the open eye, the open mind, is the spirit of the true college-bred man. He should feel not that he has learned, but that he has been put in the way to know how to learn.

"Not only spirit, but capacity, should mark the graduate. Every college graduate should have the ability to carry a process forward, should have infinite adaptation. No two have the same lives. Knowledge should sweeten life, should keep the flame of courage burning. Variety is the test. The college student is apt to be one of a type.

"The danger in a democratic country is that there is a certain penalty for one who has the courage to be different. A democratic country should have infinite variety of type. The trouble in a democratic country is that men who try to lead it don't know what a democratic country loves. Uniformity of opinion is insisted upon.

"There are two ways to give one's opinion—to speak it like a man with a fist, or to speak it in phrases like a man of the world. The life of college graduates has tended to reduce them to standards—they are expected to be a type."

Dr. Wilson cited something he had lately read as a new version of the ages of man, which were said to be not seven, but three.

"The first is when all plans are full of mischief and devilment —called innocence; the second when these plans are carried out —moral maturity; the third, in which all passed deeds are grieved over—dotage.

"The man who declines to be a type is the noblest. The man who will not sell his independence is the man who will rule in his small circle. There is need for variety. One must have courage, audacity even, to attempt and energy to persist. It is easy to attempt, but hard to go on to the goal.

"That he who does the best that lies in himself need not fear, should not be preached too much. The eye should not be upon itself, but upon the goal.

"If you do everything only to make a good character you will make a freak. Spend your time on your tasks; spend everything that is best in you; the very power you are spending will pile up in energy.

"The world is not depending on the colleges for men and women of energy. We are in a small minority. We are obliged by facts to be very modest in our claims. One thing we get in the college is idealism, a touch of imagination that gives us enthusiasm for higher things than we can ever attain ourselves.

"The great map of life has been turned out before you; you have a wider view; you have seen a vision not yet accomplished, a great destiny not yet fulfilled. It is by these feats that this college is to be judged."

Printed in the Baltimore *Sun*, June 4, 1908; some editorial headings omitted.

[1] Jessie Woodrow Wilson entered the Woman's College of Baltimore (now Goucher College) in September 1904 and was graduated on June 3, 1908. She was elected to Phi Beta Kappa and majored in English and German.

From the Minutes of the Princeton University Faculty

3 p.m. June 5, 1908.

The Faculty met, the President presiding . . . .

The Committee on Examinations and Standing, to which was referred the remit from the Board of Trustees relating to the out of town trips of the Athletic and Non Athletic organizations reported that it was their judgment that the matter would be better handled by the consideration of separate reports from the Committee on Out-Door Sports and the Committee on Non Athletic Organizations; and the Faculty having voted a reference of the matter to those Committees, a report was received from the Committee on Out Door Sports, and the recommendations therein contained were adopted as follows:

The Football, Baseball, and Track Athletic Teams to be permitted to arrange contests requiring not more than five days of absence for any one season, the Committee however retaining the right to grant such additional absences as may be necessary on account of unfor[e]seen contingencies.

The Gun Club to be permitted four days of absence, two in the autumn and two in the Spring.

The Minor Sports, Hockey, Basketball, Gymnastics, Swimming, Wrestling &c to have an allowance not exceeding three days.

The Committee on Non Athletic Organizations called attention to action already taken on April 6, 1908, on their recommendation and obtained leave to present a formal report as of the date of this meeting.[1]

[1] "On recommendation of the Committee on Non Athletic Organizations it was *Resolved* that the Triangle Club be not allowed to give more than two performances outside of Princeton during term time; the two performances permitted to be given in New York City on the afternoon and evening of the same day; and it was *Resolved* that the Musical Clubs be not allowed to give more than two performances outside of Princeton during term time." Minutes of the Princeton University Faculty, April 6, 1908.

From John Franklin Goucher[1]

My dear President Wilson: Baltimore, June 5th, 1908.

I want to thank you for the excellent service which you rendered the Woman's College in your address on Wednesday and for the courtesy which you and Mrs. Wilson showed the Institution by assisting us in receiving the friends of the College that evening, both of which are greatly appreciated.

I wish also to express my high appreciation of the influence exerted by your two daughters[2] while students in the Woman's College. Their thorough independence, delightful personality and uniform loyalty to the highest ideals of the College made them a charming and constructive influence. In fact, we are so pleased with the samples it would give us great pleasure if your third daughter would perpetuate in our student-body the delightful record which they have made.

Inclosed you will find an honorarium for the address.

Will you present my kindest regards to Mrs. Wilson and to your daughters, and permit me to wish that your Commencement Exercises may prove entirely satisfactory in every particular.

Cordially yours,   Jno. F. Goucher

TLS (WP, DLC).
  [1] President of the Woman's College of Baltimore, 1889-1908.
  [2] Margaret Wilson was a student at the Woman's College of Baltimore from 1903 to 1905, after which she began her professional musical studies with a year (1905-1906) of study of voice and piano at the Peabody Conservatory of Music in Baltimore.

A News Report

[June 6, 1908]

NEW PHYSICAL LABORATORY

Now Under Construction North of the Infirmary.

The new Physical Laboratory . . . is now being built on the ground lying between Seventy-Nine Hall, "Prospect" and the Infirmary. It was designed by Mr. H. G. [Henry Janeway] Hardenbergh, of New York. It is constructed of "Harvard" brick, slightly darker than that used in Seventy-Nine Hall, and of Indiana limestone; the roof being of gray slate. The building, which faces north, is in the shape of the letter H.

There are three floors, the combined area of which will be 85,000 square feet, a little under two acres. The construction is entirely fireproof, and it is believed that the greatest stability of walls and floors, which was especially desired, has been secured.

The entire upper floor of the building is given up to lecture and recitation rooms, and laboratories for upperclassmen; the main floor is devoted to the laboratory work of the Freshman and the various "honor" men, in order to provide for the development of the Physics Department in case the University should add a course in mechanical engineering. There will be five lecture rooms, one of which seats three hundred and sixty men; seven recitation rooms, a museum, library, chemical laboratory, electrical standards room, X-ray room, constant temperature rooms, liquid air plant, and twenty-eight rooms for professors and research students.

Each room in the building will have artificial ventilation, gas, water, heat, pressure and vacuum connections, air drying device and alternating and direct electric currents, ranging from two to five hundred volts pressure and up to one hundred amperes

Drawing of Wilson in 1908, by Frederic Yates

Margaret Wilson

Margaret Wilson and Jessie Woodrow Wilson

Ellen Axson Wilson and Eleanor Randolph Wilson

Margaret Randolph Axson

Ellen Axson Wilson

park, the park of Wasdale Hall, — mile after mile
of delicious Shaded lanes. When I emerged the light was
at just the right angle to render the huge, sheer
"Skrees" that descend precipitously from a great
height into the southern side of the unfathomable
lake doubly beautiful and impressive, striking
them as the setting sun strikes a level lawn.
Everywhere that the huge sliding pebbles have remained long enough stationary a slight, tender
verdure has begun to show itself, and in the
crevices and interspaces a rich turf. All of
this the level light disclosed like an atmosphere,
the more sparse and delicate verdure seeming
to hang like a gauze veil of tenderest green
across the harsher parts of the sheer face of
the frowning mountain, and every projecting
rock casting a long finger of shadow down upon
it, still further to soften it and touch it with
mystery. The Water lies with its head by Skafell, set about on all hands by sheer, majestic

Wilson's letter to Ellen Axson Wilson, July 23, 1908

Map of the Lake District of England

Palmer Physical Laboratory, shortly after completion, 1908

current. Finally, there will be a well-equipped machine shop for making and repairing apparatus.

Printed in the *Daily Princetonian*, June 6, 1908.

A Sermon

JUNE 7th, 1908.

BACCALAUREATE ADDRESS.

"Let no man deceive you: he that doeth righteousness is righteous, even as He is righteous."

YOUNG GENTLEMEN: You have come to the end of your college course and are about to see your life changed altogether, and it is generally supposed by those who do not know you that your thought is now intently and eagerly fixed upon the things to which you are about to devote yourselves in the work of the world. I, of course, know that it is not. These are the days of all others when your thoughts turn backward to the happy times that have made you comrades here, to your life as members and lovers of Princeton, and to the thousand little circumstances that have bound you together as classmates and friends. And these friends who have come to see you graduate, these men of other undergraduate days who throng back to their alma mater and fill the campus and streets with gay crowds that laugh themselves back into boyhood, do not bring the world with them. You are not yet even in the presence of the world in which you are to live. These Commencement visitors are not invaders, they are guests. They do not bring the thoughts of another world, they come to share the thoughts of yours. They are renewing the memories and the spirit of days gone by. They are yielding themselves to the temper and the ideals of the place. It is I who must do your thoughts and theirs violence, I who must ask you to turn your minds away from Princeton and look out upon scenes very different, very sharply contrasted with these. I must ask you to take your bearings for the start, not for the finish.

It matters very little what occupation or profession you are intending to enter, you are all going out into the same scene, to encounter the same circumstances and make a path for yourselves amidst the same conditions. It will be very confusing: it may be not a little disconcerting. The world in which you have lived hitherto has been a systematic and ordered world: a world of training, whether by your parents or by your teachers. The occupations you are about to enter upon will show no such order or connection. There is no common authority that can coördinate them: there is no common force that can control or shape them, except that very general, often whimsical, and always unsystematic authority which we call public opinion. The life of our own age shows no touch of system: it must be the despair of the logician, the delight of the critic and of the cynic. You must find your way amongst its confusing circumstances and conflicting standards by some compass of your own. You are your own sailing masters. Your manhood will be gauged by your own exercise of judgment, by your own display of discretion, your own discrimination between right and wrong. You must devise your own system of success. Whatever it is that you mean to do, you must, unless you mean to be a servant all your life, do it in your own way. And even if you are willing to remain all your days a servant, taking orders, you must choose whose servant you are willing to be, if you would retain your self-respect and enjoy the happiness of integrity.

There are two kinds of judgments to be acted upon in this world: practical judgments, as we call them, and moral judgments. Moral judgments are themselves very practical: a man cannot make a practice of ignoring morals in his choices and get any satisfaction out of life. And by the same token practical judgments are moral judgments. There are very few choices which do not involve moral considerations. And yet the distinction is an obvious and valid one. Success, in our own day in particular, involves many intensely practical questions, and there are choices to be made in which morality stands neither on the one side nor on the other. The most efficient way in which to organize any business or any practical undertaking; the most useful, economical and profitable processes of manufacture; the application of new discoveries to old problems of practical endeavor; the prevention and cure of disease, in so far as these are purely medical questions; the best kinds of knowledge to spread and the best means of spreading them; the most convenient and serviceable methods of banking; even the best means of legitimate advertising; every organization and facilitation of commerce: these will serve as examples, obvious examples, of questions, most of them of great range and complexity, upon which the best minds may spend themselves with profit both to themselves and to the world at large, without stopping to moralize; and many there be that study them. But I venture to say that these are not the difficult questions. The difficult questions of the day are moral questions.

The words of scripture I have chosen for the guidance and stimulation of our thought this morning are these: "Let no man deceive you: he that doeth righteousness is righteous, even as He is righteous" (that is, Christ). If you want to know the real difficulty of modern life, try to apply the utter simplicity of such a test as that to it. There is something terribly direct and simple about the moral standards of the Bible; and yet we do not in our hearts dissent from them. On the contrary, they alone satisfy us. They are tonic in their quality and quicken some native strength of judgment that is in us. We know that they belong with the strong pulse and the unhesitating courage that mean life and wholesome power, and the attitude we instinctively have towards them is not merely this, that we would like to find our way to their application, but that we acknowledge their compulsion and know that we must find it.

Who is he that doeth righteousness in our modern life? You know what that modern life is. You have not been closeted in school and college. You know, at least in some degree, what is going on about you. I shall not have to lay before you any elaborate picture of the world we now live in, as preface to my moral. Men do not choose their parts in life separately and individually in our day as they did in the days of our fathers. The men are becoming rare now who have businesses of their own, undertaken upon their own individual capital and built up and conducted independently upon their own responsibility. Professional men are rare who rise to the top of their professions without attaching themselves more or less intimately to institutions or corporations of some sort; doctors to hospitals, lawyers to great corporate undertakings, men of science to the great enterprises in which science is applied. Every affair of life takes on more and more the aspect and practice of wide organization; many men are drawn together in a common discipline and body; each man finds himself a small part of some great whole, whose operation is decided by votes taken about long tables in Directors' rooms, whose morals are composite morals, a compromise combination of what the material interests of the body dictate and what the enterprise of its managers suggests, the character of every man who participates being merged in the general compound. Each man concerned feels the range of his own choice to be very narrow and is forced to be content with seeing questions of conscience either ignored or administered by commission. It is a composite world, and its standards are for the time being sadly confused by its attempt to compound its morals with its material ambitions, to set up composite notions of righteousness and disperse virtue through the intricacies of an elaborate organization. Moral judgments have never been simple: they have always been complicated by a thousand circumstances which puzzle the will; but they have never been quite so difficult and complicated as they are now. The primary moral difficulty of every man immersed in modern business is to find himself, to make sure of his own range and necessities of choice, know where he is legitimately a fraction and where he must insist upon being an integer, whole and indivisible.

This is our peculiar and fundamental moral problem; where and how to separate the individual from the mass, lift the individual soul out of the confusion and distraction of modern societies, unions, brotherhoods, leagues, alliances, corporations, and trusts into some clear place of vision, where it may think and see apart, looking beyond the things of the day to the things that abide. "Let no man deceive you: he that doeth righteousness is righteous." And that is not the end of the matter, nor the whole of it. This thing that we call righteousness, this essential integrity of intention and of act, is not only the standard by which we shall ultimately be judged by others, by the world about us and the world that shall speak of us when we are gone: it is also the standard by which we shall judge ourselves, by which we shall get satisfaction or disappointment, the sweet or the bitter fruits of life, the energy that sets us free to assay the world or the subtle paralysis that ultimately ensues upon deceit and indirection. You will find that you cannot pool your consciences; you had better, then, not try to pool your morals. Keep your liberty in your morals and you can afford to live with your consciences.

I am not suggesting to you a mere philosophy of happiness. My point is not that if you are not righteous you will not be happy, though that is true enough. The point lies deeper than that. I am not sure that it is of the first importance that you should be happy. Many an unhappy man has been of deep service to the world and to himself, has guided his fellow-men and exalted his own life,—many a man, I mean, who has not had what he wanted, who has lost what he loved, who has struggled through pain and disappointment and heart-breaking strain, that he might stand erect and see the light. The captains of the world's thought and stern endeavor have not often been debonnair figures, taking life like a happy holiday, their tasks like easy sport. As often as not they have been wrought by agony of soul. Their joys have been in their triumphs over themselves.

And yet perhaps it is happiness that I would suggest as the reward of integrity and high endeavor after all, but a greater, nobler, more elemental happiness than that which men ordinarily pursue, the happiness of satisfied powers and fortified souls. Look into the matter a little more closely. What is righteousness? Why should we exalt it; why should we seek it; why should we break our fortunes for it and prefer it to a thousand other things we instinctively and deeply desire? You will find a definition of righteousness, a very specific description of the righteous man in the Fifteenth Psalm, and will find it very real as well as very beautiful: "He that walketh uprightly, and worketh righteousness, and speaketh the truth in his heart. He that backbiteth not with his tongue, nor doeth evil to his neighbor, nor taketh up a reproach against his neighbor. In whose eyes a vile person is contemned; but he honoreth them that fear the Lord. He that sweareth to his own hurt, and changeth not." Here is a very noble gentleman and a man who may be the bulwark of business and of the State. For "he that doeth these things," says the Psalmist, "shall never be moved." Righteousness is a thing of the heart and of the will as well as a thing of action. It is compounded of right thinking and right feeling; and the right action into which it issues is the fruit and consequence of these. It is a right attitude towards life, and its attitude is not an attitude of contemplation merely, but an attitude of action. The righteous soul is no critic, but an actor. He that "doeth righteousness" is he that enacteth it, he that gives it the reality of life and accomplishment.

It is a very specific standard and a very stern one. There is no compromising with it, nor evading it, nor obscuring it even. It must be lived up to or departed from; it cannot be put off with promises or placated with professions, and it is an individual, not a corporate, standard. At the bar where all things are determined with equity the man who departs from it compromises himself and no other. Morality is of necessity individual, not corporate. Men are bad, not societies. Wrong is conceived in the individual heart, not in boards and committees, and those who participate stain themselves with the same iniquity with which the author and originator of the wrong is blackened. This is the only doctrine that is true, and this is the only doctrine that will rectify and purify modern society. We shall find our reforms, not in law, but in conscience. Righteousness may indeed be facilitated by social arrangements, encouraged by law, but it must live in the individual soul and must proceed from it as from its source of energy.

Look about you with candid eye and you shall find that the malady of the age is lack of individual courage, lack of individual integrity of thought and action. We need not speak of other countries or sweep a whole age into our generalization. Let us confine our view to our own day and our own country. What is the law of life in America now? Is it that every man should form his own moral judgments and speak them fearlessly, that every man should seek to govern his own life and square it with his own independent moral judgments? Of course there never has been a time or a society in which the individuals emerged from the mass in noticeable multitudes and the air was quick with active independence. It has always been the exceptional individual here and there who asserted his own rights of conscience and took command of his own conduct. Does America today show a large or a small proportion of such men? That is our ultimate test of vitality.

> "A people is but the attempt of many
> To rise to the completer life of one,
> And those who live as models to the mass
> Are singly of more value than they all."[1]

Imitation is not for the strong, but for the weak; not for the individual, but for the mass. If imitation has become the law of our life, for the strong as well as for the weak, then we are indeed impoverished, and a time of decline is at hand. A democratic country, more than any other, needs for its enrichment, for its growth, for that variation which is life, men by the score, the hundred, the thousand, who have indomitable intellectual and moral initiative. It needs more than that: it needs men by the hundred thousand who will not submit to be put in the wrong, who will not sell their consciences, who will not run with the crowd out of craven fear and in despite of their convictions. And where shall we get such men if not from the colleges, if not from amongst you who know the truth, if you would but follow it? You have sold your birthright when you have sold your independence of moral judgment.

Every age has need to have righteousness preached to it, and this age is not worse than those which have preceded it. It is better. But it is to be doubted if it is clearer-sighted, if to its astonishing knowledge and its careful sanitary cleanliness it has added virtue and moral insight and the clear judgments of conscience in the same degree. And that is because by its complex business and social organization it has encouraged the individual to run to cover, to burrow into some private place of interior management, to sit comfortably at some minor function and hold his private conscience aloof from the tasks and practices of the organization to which he belongs. We have facilitated a very subtle process, the process by which the individual separates what he

---

[1] Robert Browning, *Luria, A Tragedy*, Act V, Lines 299-302.

calls his own life and conduct, his private character, from the life of the organization of which he forms a part, making himself a mere tool in the one thing and undertaking to be a moral agent only in the other. It will not do. No man is satisfied with the practice or holds his head very high in the presence of it, except by conscious histrionic effort. No man can cut his conscience into sections. Righteousness is of the individual heart, and the sound heart must have an inviolable integrity. If it be an age of organization, of intricate association, of business on the grand scale, of the temporary submergence of the individual and the consequent confusion of moral standards and codes of responsibility, there is all the more reason why every man should assert the rights of his own soul and recognize the compulsion of duty to find himself, to identify himself, to get a new release and liberty. I have called the present submergence of the individual temporary, because it can in the nature of the case be only temporary. The energy of all life, the energy of all business, lies in the individual. No one who knows human life as it is really supposes the action even of commerce or of manufacture to be in fact corporate. The counsel of many minds may give it form: the action of mind upon mind may modify and shape plans and purposes, but the impulse and conception come from individuals, and the minds that modify them are also the minds of individuals, every one of whom may, if he choose, act upon conscience as well as upon interest.

No doubt business looks impersonal; but it is not so. And even if it were so, what release of conscience would that bring us? We judge ourselves singly, die with the flavor of but one career on our palates, are laid away in our graves by neighbors who have known the man, not the corporation of which he formed a part. And why do I speak only of the end? Do we judge ourselves only on our death beds? Do our neighbors assess us only at our funerals? Is the daily conduct of life not a daily process of judgment, the assessment of satisfaction or deep disappointment? And is not the daily conduct of life a thing wholly of individual contribution? What laws of nature govern our moral lives, except the laws operative in our own wills? Let every man find himself and see to the integrity of his own soul. "Let no man deceive you: he that doeth righteousness is righteous." And you are not to be deceived about yourselves any more than you are to be deceived about other men: only when you do righteousness are you righteous. It is a stern code, but it is the only sufficient one; and its stern definiteness makes many things clear.

Moreover, it is the code and principle which have lain at the heart of all history. Collectiveism has always to be moralized by individualism. The church was purified by the Protestant Reformation, by the most radical of all assertions of the freedom of the individual soul, its right to determine its own responsibility and establish its own spiritual connections. The too much concentrated, the too inclusive and burdensome power of the State has always, when men have ventured to create it, in the long run been rectified by the revolt of the individual. It has always been the conscience of the individual that has kept the citadels of the church and made good the triumphs of liberty and political progress. Men who judged and acted for themselves have always been the rulers and arbiters of their time. And now once again comes the old challenge, renewed in new circumstances, in a new age which is our own and which we alone can understand and rectify.

The tendencies of our minds, the tendencies of our age, have affected alike our standards and our conduct. We have grown very "practical." We have seen the life about us and the life of which we form a part take on a certain organization in which men were, so to say, pooled and compounded, and enormous material energy, unexampled business efficiency have been the result. We have stood amazed, with a sort of childish delight, at the work of our own hands. Success upon the grand scale has meant power upon a scale unprecedented, the power of the individual and the power of the nation. The eyes of all the world have been turned upon us in uneasy wonder and admiration, with a touch of fear as well as of amazement. We have said, "Behold, it is a good thing. Look at its tremendous efficiency. It is the glory of America, of the practical American genius, the colossal success which has crowned all the rest that preceded it. What if the individual is submerged? That is the inevitable result of the system. It may be moralized, that is controlled, as a whole by law, but it would break down under the too great self-assertion of the individual." The moralist, not infatuated by the gross material results, can only reply: "Then it will inevitably break down." The individual conscience has never in any age been successfully digested into the mass. It is insusceptible of absorption. It will reassert itself and the system will undergo radical transformation, a transformation as complete as may be necessary in order to release the individual and give him his liberty again. It is tedious that history should be obliged to repeat the process so often, but it will repeat it as often as necessary. Our present cynicism will not last, is not lasting. The tendency to be "practical" will not conquer the tendency to be moral. The great awakening we have just had to the moral aspects of so much of modern business is but the beginning of change. The moralist will dictate both to the lawyer and to the man of business.

It is a strange and interesting thing that in this very age in which we have become so intensely "practical" we have grown also exceedingly sentimental. And yet perhaps it was natural enough. Moral sentiment was driven out of the practical field; it therefore took refuge where it could, outside the field of business, amidst that fringe of habits and practices which had little or nothing to do with the work of the world. The moral sentiments are very robust and splendid forces when they work upon the real stuff of life, but when they potter about amongst private habits, when they attempt the rôle of mere sympathy and succour, excusing the criminal, petting the degenerate, and trying to save the individual by mere corporate protection, putting him in a nursery in which he can do nothing to please himself, they are in danger of becoming very ridiculous and very dangerous. Thoughtful philanthropy, manly and sensible help to those who have fallen either into vice or into misfortune, we all believe in with all our hearts, but not sentimental excuses for those who have done wrong. We all understand how much the individual is moulded by his environment, but we know also that he will not be rescued by the mere change of his environment and that, if the proper challenge be given his will, he can override his environment. The moral tonic of personal responsibility will save him. Mere sympathy will not.

There is no more subtle dissolvent of morals than sentimentality; and there is no more hopeless method of seeking to moralize an age than beginning at the edges. Go straight to the point. Put every individual, great and small, upon a stern probation. Let him not escape your judgment because he is unfortunate and well-meaning. Be just. Distinguish what is really unrighteous from what is not really unrighteous. Go to Christ for the abiding standards of moral judgment. Be sure that you allow the individual his real liberty to live truly and serve loyally. Do not impose your private judgments upon him; but within the limits of Christian justice judge inflexibly. Let standards be standards, not sliding scales that follow your sympathies. Judge men according to their essential character, but demand that they have some essential character to be judged, and be not time-servers.

After all, it is a search for standards. The interior meaning of the text of scripture upon which I have founded this last discourse of mine to you is that every man is deceived who supposes that he is righteous when his righteousness is not the righteousness of Christ. "Let no man deceive you: he that doeth righteousness is righteous, even as He is righteous,"—he who is the model for the mass and "singly of more value than they all." We go many a long way 'roundabout to moralize the world, while the true way is very direct. There all the while has stood the figure of Christ, exquisite in its simplicity, indisputable in its example, not insistent, thundering no command, simply lifted up, like the serpent in the wilderness, to draw all who will look upon him unto himself. All true righteousness is a search after Christ. We know this: it is no matter of argument here.

Let us start, then, with the open eyes of men who see the truth. The object of all university teaching is to see the truth and bring it to acceptance. That illuminating verse which I quoted from the Fifteenth Psalm is a perfect description of the true university teacher: "He that speaketh the truth *in his heart*," he whose whole nature is cleared for the action of truth. And you are university-taught only if that is the spirit and intention with which you go forth to the work of the world. It is a confused stage, but you need not lose your head. You, of all men, are inexcusable if you do lose it. You know the difference between right and wrong, between what is honorable and what is dishonorable, between what stands square with conscience and what lies athwart its standards. Go out and honor yourselves and Princeton and the standards of Christ by enacting righteousness in the field of affairs; by refusing to put your conscience at the service of any man, of any corporation; by playing a part, at whatever temporary cost; which will not cost you your individual liberty and integrity.

GENTLEMEN OF THE GRADUATING CLASS: It would be an intolerable pain to see you leave this place, if we did not think that you would be heedful of the great lesson I have tried this morning to expound to you. Let me say again what I said at the outset: that it is my duty today to draw your thoughts away from the past, from the college days upon which they are dwelling so fondly and from which you draw such a sweet store of fruitful memories. I am obliged to ask you to look the other way, to look forward to where you are going to make another life for yourselves, and to put this question to you: What sort of Princeton men are you going to be outside Princeton? You have received the stamp now. To what documents of life are you going to affix it? You have spent the four years comrades, enjoying a sort of corporate strength and mutual support, governed by the traditions of the place and by the standards of years of preparation and hope. Henceforth you are to have much less support from others and from fixed traditions. You are to be individuals, cast upon your own separate resources. How do you mean to justify the past by the actions of the future?

I do not ask these questions in doubt or misgiving. I ask them in confident hope. But I must ask them in the same breath in which I speak of the very deep affection we have felt for you and of the regret with which we see you go. You have been our partners through interesting and significant years. You perhaps do not realize how conscious we have been of the partnership, of our dependence upon you for the spirit and success of the work we have tried to do, or how conscious we have been of your several characteristics and of your influence upon the life of the place; but we have been your comrades, and we bid you godspeed as those who feel the breaking up of a little family, the severing of a very vital tie. We count upon you to be men such as all just and righteous persons love. We shall look to see you make virtue a thing of action, not of sentiment merely, upon the field of life, and to see Princeton justified in your lives.[2]

T MS (WP, DLC).
[2] There is an undated WWhw and WWsh outline of this address and a WWsh draft, dated May 26, 1908, in WP, DLC.

From the Minutes of the Board of Trustees of Princeton University

[June 8, 1908]

The Trustees of Princeton University met in stated session in the Trustees' Room in the Chancellor Green Library, Princeton, New Jersey, at eleven o'clock on Monday morning, June 8, 1908.

. . .

CONSIDERATION OF REPORT OF COMMITTEE ON CONFERENCE WITH ALUMNI DEFERRED

After a discussion of the report of the Committee on Conference with the Alumni, on motion of Mr. Jones seconded by Mr. Stewart, it was

RESOLVED that the consideration of the Report of the Committee on Conference with the Alumni be deferred and that the report be published.[1]

[1] It was printed in the *Princeton Alumni Weekly*, VIII (June 10, 1908), 585-91.

A News Report

[June 10, 1908]

ALUMNI LUNCHEON.

Excellent Speeches Delivered by Representatives
of Many Classes.

The annual Alumni Luncheon was held in the Gymnasium at 1 o'clock yesterday afternoon. Covers were laid for seven hundred and fifty guests. The Honorable James R. MacFarlane, '78[1] presided, introducing President Wilson as the first speaker. Judge MacFarlane expressed the implicit confidence of the alumni that Princeton is safe in the hands of President Wilson, who has won a high place in the regard of all by his intellectual force and splendid personality. He said in part:

Among the matters of interest to alumni at this time, we naturally are desirous of learning what gifts have been made to the University during the past year.

The keynote of President Wilson's speech was the intellectual supremacy toward which Princeton is striving and its natural advance which has contributed so greatly toward this end. It has been a year rich in gifts, but it is invidious to pick out individuals, whose love to Princeton should not be measured by what they give. Two gifts, however, are too notable to escape mention. The first is that of a thoughtful public-spirited woman, Mrs. Russell Sage, who has donated the new Freshman dormitory; while the second is that of the laboratories, which will prove splendid additions to the resources of the University. We make these buildings beautiful that they may worthily house the men who work in them.

Another fact which is becoming noticeable is that the ambitious younger men and the scholarly men are turning to Princeton, not for what she says but for what they know she is. In Princeton there is an ancient accumulation of moral force, which has always been to her advantage. In no other college has there always been such insight into the future, and such perception of the signs of the times as at Princeton. These are not now the signs of peace but of an age disturbed with change. America must eschew childish hope and must put her faith in men who know the facts. Colleges commend themselves according as they produce serious and thoughtful men as there is no room for excuses in the modern world. What the world needs, and what it is the effort of colleges to produce are men endowed with sober purpose, serious endeavor and consciousness of responsibility.

The main duty of those who are working for the welfare of Princeton is to strengthen the graduate department, so that Princeton will take her part in producing master minds. The obligation of a university is to broaden the fields of universal knowledge and for this Princeton is well fitted through her universal power of character and mind. America needs nothing so much as thoughtful knowledge and self-possession. University men who lend themselves to hysterical movements should be stricken from the rolls of their Alma Mater.[2]

Printed in the *Daily Princetonian*, June 10, 1908.
[1] James Rieman MacFarlane, Princeton 1878, judge of the Court of Common Pleas, Pittsburgh.
[2] There is a WWhw outline of this address, dated June 9, 1908, in WP, DLC.

From Cleveland Hoadley Dodge

Dear Woodrow: New York   June 10, 1908.

I hope that you are not entirely used up by the hard work of Commencement and am very glad that you are getting away so soon.

I of course do not want to press you at all to come with us on the yacht during August,[1] but will leave is entirely to your inclinations, although it is needless to say that we will be perfectly delighted to have you. Whether you come or not will make no difference with our arrangements, and if you wish to communicate with me on the other side, my address will be C/o A. W. Finch, 16 Leadenhall street, London.

Hoping I may have a glimpse of you before you sail,
                      Ever faithfully yours,   C. H. Dodge

TLS (WP, DLC).
[1] Dodge planned to charter a yacht in England for a trip through the fiords of Norway.

From Norman Mattoon Thomas[1]

My dear Dr. Wilson: New York City.   June 11, 1908.

Of course this letter requires no answer. It is from a young graduate who is still so enthusiastic about the joys of Princeton that he feels like giving thanks.

I never saw a more beautiful place than Princeton this June, nor one dearer by reason of many ties. Every day I live I am more thankful that I am a Princeton man. My only regret is that I graduated in the Dark Ages before the preceptorial system and other good things of the present!

I trust that you will not think me over bold in writing this letter to tell you, not only of my love for Princeton, but of the deep sense of gratitude that I in common with all Princeton men, young and old, feel that we owe to you for your wonderful services to Princeton.

Respectfully yours,   Norman M Thomas   1905.

ALS (WP, DLC).

[1] At this time Thomas had just begun his work at Christ Church House in New York where he worked during his studies at Union Theological Seminary, begun during the autumn of 1908. Thomas had also recently returned from a trip around the world which lasted from July 1907 to March 1908. Earlier, following his graduation, he had worked at the Spring Street Church and Neighborhood House in New York.

From David Benton Jones

My dear Doctor   Lake Forest, Illinois   June 12 1908

I do not need to tell you of my deep appreciation of what you said at your luncheon to The Trustees at Princeton. This note is not for that purpose. The unexpected incident gave me no time to consider the wisdom of telling those men the reasons for the transformation in Princeton's position and purposes in the past five years. I have wanted to do so for some time and at the luncheon it was the only thing I had on my mind. I said over some words while pondering & concluded the situation did not warrant my telling them what most of them do not seem to be able to see.

I am unwilling however to let the incident pass without saying now what I wanted to say then and that is that the only thing that makes work on the Princeton Board attractive and worthwhile in my opinion is your effort to reestablish it as a seat of learning. When the revolt against present conditions sets in, what you are now saying & doing will be recognized and rewarded.

With careful handling Mr. Palmer will be with you on all matters of moment. He is now most friendly and I have no doubt you can keep him so. His Laboratory and the work to be done in it are certain to play a large part in his life. I am confident he will follow the needs of the situation in a very sympathetic spirit.

I shall watch the progress of your work with the same interest and enjoyment as I have felt in it since you took charge a few years ago.   Very Sincerely   David B. Jones.

ALS (WP, DLC).

To Malcolm MacLaren[1]

My dear Mr. MacLaren: [Princeton, N. J.]   June 13th, 1908.

It is with the greatest pleasure that I learn from [William Francis] Magie that you are willing to join us here and take charge of the instruction in the Electrical Engineering School.

Not having been able to be certain of your acceptance of the appointment, I did not feel justified in taking your name to the Board, but I did obtain the full and hearty approval of the Committee of the Board on the Curriculum, the committee through whom nominations are reported, and I did also get the direct authority of the Finance Committee for the financial arrangements. Your name will be presented to the Board at its October meeting for formal election. In the circumstances, I feel that it is perfectly safe to send you this formal invitation to join the faculty and to assume charge of the School of Electrical Engineering, with the title of Professor of Electrical Engineering.

Pray let me say again how sincerely glad I am that you have seen your way clear to accept this appointment and how happily I look forward to our association with you.

With warm regard,
Cordially and sincerely yours,   [Woodrow Wilson]

CCL (WWP, UA, NjP).
[1] Princeton A.B., 1890; E.E., 1892; A.M., 1893; at this time an electrical engineer at the Pittsburgh works of the Westinghouse Electric and Manufacturing Co.

To Cleveland Hoadley Dodge

My dear Cleve: Princeton, N. J.   June 18th, 1908.

I was in New York yesterday and tried hard to find time to drop in and have a minute with you, but it proved impossible because I had to rush back by the three o'clock train to preside at the transaction of some important faculty business.

I need not tell you how warmly I appreciate your kind wish that I should join you on your yacht, and it is particularly generous of you to hold the matter open for me. Of course you understand that the only thing that holds me back from accepting the invitation with delight is my knowledge that, whether we talk of them or not, we would in our mere presence remind each other of very important and troublesome Princeton problems.

I have found the past year go very hard with me. I feel, as you know, blocked in plans upon which I feel the successful administration of the University, both as a teaching body and as a wholesome society, depends, and for which I can find no substitute, and in these circumstances it has been a struggle with me all the year to keep in any sort of spirits. I must try, as you must, to divest my mind of the matter altogether at least for the summer, and my affection for you is too strong to make me willing to put any burden upon your thought, even by my presence. Inasmuch as I am the person chiefly concerned and chiefly responsible, being with me could not but remind you of these matters.

I am expecting to play the tramp in the most irresponsible and delightful manner, and I know of no place where I can so lose consciousness of the ordinary occupations of my life as in the region of England in which I expect to linger longest.

I hope with all my heart that you will have a perfectly refreshing and delightful summer, and in all circumstances I shall always be,   Your devoted friend,   Woodrow Wilson

TLS (WC, NjP).

From Malcolm MacLaren

My dear President Wilson: Pittsburgh Pa.   June 18th 1908.

Your very cordial letter has been received and it gives me great pleasure to confirm the acceptance of this offer which I have already given informally through Mr Magie.

While I have considerable hesitation in taking up the work which has been carried on so ably by Dr. Brackett, I feel that it will be a great privilege to enter into the University as Proffessor of Electrical Engineering and I am looking forward with much pleasure to getting into the Princeton life again.

I expect to spend a few days in Princeton within the next week or ten days and trust I may see you at that time.

Thanking you for your very warm welcome and good wishes
          Very sincerely yours   Malcolm MacLaren

ALS (WWP, UA, NjP).

From Cleveland Hoadley Dodge

Dear Woodrow: New York. June 19, 1908.

Thanks for your perfectly delightful letter of the 18th. I fully appreciate all you say, but if, at the last moment, you should get a little tired of tramping and have a longing for the fjords of Norway, you have my address in London, and a bunk is always ready for you, and if you come, I will guarantee not to mention Princeton to you, and to give you the time of your life.

Trusting that in any event you will have a most delightful summer,   Yours affectionately,   C H Dodge

TLS (WP, DLC).

From William Henry Roberts[1]

My dear Sir: Philadelphia, Pa.,   June 19th, 1908.

Yours of May the 20th came to hand while I was absent at the General Assembly. It gives me pleasure now to state that the General Assembly appointed you as one of the Delegates to the Ninth Council of the Alliance of the Presbyterian and Reformed Churches throughout the world, to be held in New York City at the end of September or at the beginning of October, 1909. The principal sessions of the Council will be held in the Fifth Avenue Presbyterian Church, and also in the Collegiate Reformed Church, 5th Ave. and 48th St.

It will be a body representative of all the Presbyterian Churches of the five Continents. The movement originated in 1870, under the guiding hand of such men as James McCosh, Howard Crosby,[2] William Adams,[3] etc. You will not be required to be in constant attendance. I certainly hope that you will be able to accept the appointment.[4] The Council will continue in session about eight days.

With high regards,   Yours very truly,   W. H. Roberts.

TLS (WP, DLC).
    [1] Stated Clerk of the General Assembly of the Presbyterian Church in the U.S.A. since 1884 and, since 1888, American secretary of the Alliance of the Reformed Churches throughout the World Holding the Presbyterian System.
    [2] The Reverend Dr. Howard Crosby (1826-1891) was a prominent Presbyterian clergyman who served as minister of the Fourth Avenue Presbyterian Church of New York from 1863 until his death. He was an organizer of the Y.M.C.A. of New York and its second president and held the position of Chancellor of the University of the City of New York (now New York University) from 1870 to 1881. He also founded the Society for the Prevention of Crime. In 1873 he was Moderator of the General Assembly of the Presbyterian Church in the U.S.A., and at the Assembly's meeting that year the Reverend Dr. James McCosh delivered an address which sparked the creation of the Alliance of the Reformed Churches throughout the World. Crosby, McCosh, and the Reverend Dr. Edwin Hatfield made up the committee which organized the new ecumenical organization. It held its first meeting in Edinburgh on July 3, 1877. Its foremost leaders were McCosh and the Reverend Dr. William Garden Blaikie of the Free Church College, Edinburgh.
    [3] The Reverend Dr. William Adams (1807-1880), first a Congregational and later a Presbyterian minister, was one of the founders of Union Theological Seminary in 1836 and served as its president from 1874 to 1880. From 1834 to 1853 he was minister of the Central Presbyterian Church in New York, and in 1853, with a majority of his congregation, he founded the Madison Square

Presbyterian Church in New York. After 1837 he was a leader of the New School Presbyterians but labored strenuously for reunion, serving as chairman of the New School Committee on Conference until 1870, when the Old and New Schools were reunited.

4 Wilson accepted election as a delegate to the Alliance meeting in New York in 1909 and did attend its sessions. See W. H. Roberts to WW, Feb. 17, 1909, n. 2.

To Ellen Axson Wilson

My precious darling,   [New York]   20 June, 1908

We are off.¹ I send you this as another kiss, with all my heart in it. I love you, I *love* you, I *love* you, and yearn for you beyond words. Oh, if you were but with me!

McAlpin and Jack Hibben were down to see me off. I am well and all right, but desperately lonely and deeply in love with you.

With unbounded love for all   Your own   Woodrow

ALS (WC, NjP).
¹ He was about to sail for Scotland aboard S. S. *California* of the Anchor Line.

From Owen Willans Richardson

Dear President Wilson,   Princeton N. J.   24 June 1908

I made several attempts to get into communication with you over the telephone before your departure but was unfortunate in not being able to do so.

I wished to explain to you why I felt compelled to vote in favour of the resolution which was submitted to you by the Department of Physics as I felt that you might possibly have misunderstood my action. As I still feel that this may be the case I am taking the liberty of doing so now.

I did not know any thing about the business under consideration until I reached the meeting which was convened, as I was informed, to consider some matters relating to the new laboratory. The meeting was informed that you proposed to create two new offices in the physics department, a general Director and a Director of Research, that you had suggested two names, which were not mentioned for some time, for these positions and desired to obtain the opinion of the department as to the wisdom of the arrangement. There seemed to be a general and lively opposition to the plan and the proposal that was ultimately submitted to you was immediately proposed and seconded. I opposed the motion on various grounds, the most cogent being that I was given to understand that you had intended to consult me, among others, about the question and had not yet done so and that I did not feel justified in supporting the motion until I had more first hand information about the proposals under discussion. I was informed that there were no means of doing this and for the department subsequently to consider the matter as you were going away the next day, intended to make the appointments before going and were very busy anyhow. As a matter of fact you did not leave till the next day but one. I was informed that the resolution would not be taken to you unless it were passed unanimously. I argued my case off and on for more than an hour altogether I think and during that time have no recollection of having received any support from any one in the department. I was then informed that I had been selected for the Research Position and McClenahan for the other. As I understand it I was in this position. If I did not vote for the motion I elected myself to a position which none of my colleagues desired either me or, presumably, anyone else to hold whereas if I did vote for it I merely gave you time for a fuller consideration of the question, which seemed necessary in view of the attitude taken by the department. Under the circumstances I felt that I had no option but to vote for the motion.

My opinion of the general character of the scheme is that it is an excellent one. I believe that such an arrangement would greatly promote the efficiency of the department. In fact I believe that some such arrangement is absolutely necessary to save the department from the evils of the democratic form of government into which it has fallen.

I am inclined to agree with the opinion, which some have expressed, that the positions ought to be created in the first instance by the Board of Trustees. Whether the appointments are actually made by the President alone, or by the Board of Trustees on the recommendation of the President, does not seem to me to be an important matter; but I am convinced that they ought not to be made by the department of physics by election out of its members. It seems to me that such officers to be effective must hold their authority from outside the department.

I need hardly say that it has been my ambition ever since I came to Princeton to fill the position which you did me the honour of selecting me for.

After thinking about the opposition which occurred at the meeting of the department I am certain a great deal of it was an indirect effect of the trouble about the department of electrical engineering, which is now blowing over, I think. The bulk of the rest would be removed if the positions were created by the Board of Trustees; and if any remain over I feel certain that it is a small

matter compared with the troubles ahead if some such arrangement is not carried out. I feel also that it will be much easier to
make changes of the kind contemplated before we enter the new
building than afterwards.

In writing this I do not desire that you should trouble to reply
to the points I have raised. My only wish has been that you should
not misunderstand my position. I think the matter itself can be
safely left over till your return.

I expect you are now earning a well deserved rest under the
shadow of Loughrigg Fell. I wish I were. With best wishes for a
happy vacation, I am

Yours very truly,   O. W. Richardson.

ALS (WP, DLC).

From Walter Hudson Watkins[1]

Dear Dr. Wilson: Chattanooga, Tenn.   June 24, 1908.

As Secretary of the Princeton Alumni Association of Tennessee
it is my pleasure to extend to you the sincere request of our Association that you come to Tennessee again next October to be
present at our annual meeting, which meeting will be held this
year in Nashville, Tennessee. As heretofore, we will be much
pleased to fix the date of the meeting to suit your convenience,
and feel that our meeting will not be a success unless you do us
the honor of being present. We would appreciate it very much
indeed if you will let us know as soon as possible what date would
be suitable for you in order that we might have opportunity of
advising all the members of our Association at the earliest possible moment the date of our meeting, and also in order that we
might be able to send out circular letters to the Alumni of the
University outside of the State of Tennessee who would desire to
be present at our annual meeting.

The writer regrets exceedingly that he failed to see you in
Princeton during Commencement Week in order that the matter
of the meeting this year might be discussed with you. Your Secretary advised the writer that he could see you on Friday after
commencement, but my plans had been made to go to New York
on Thursday and therefore it was impossible to see you on Friday.

Kindly let us hear from you at your earliest convenience, advising us just what week in October would be suitable and convenient for you to be with us in Nashville and we will fix our
annual meeting accordingly.[2]

With kindest regards from our Association and from the writer, I beg to remain

Yours very sincerely,   W. H. Watkins   Secretary.

TLS (WP, DLC) with WWhw mem. on recto: "Mem.–The last week in October. W.W."

¹ Princeton 1900, member of the law firm of Watkins and Thompson of Chattanooga.

² There is later correspondence about this proposed visit; as it turned out, Wilson was unable to go on account of illness.

To Ellen Axson Wilson

My sweet, my precious darling,   S.S. California, 26 June, '08

This letter cannot begin its journey to you until two days after we land; the swaying and quivering of the ship make it harder than usual for me to control my pen, and the effort makes me a bit dizzy; but I *cannot* refrain from talking to you at least a *little* to-day. I *must* ease my heart with words. I do not know when I have so longed for you, so tenderly and passionately, or with so keen a consciousness of my utter dependence upon you, as I have since I left you on Saturday. You are my heart's home and its very life. I am your *lover*, my darling, in as deep and all-inclusive a sense as ever the word was used, and, oh, *how* I love you! My happiness depends directly upon the degree in which you comprehend and accept my love for what it is, in spite of all my frailties and absurdities, as they must seem to you. It is the strongest, noblest, dearest force of my life. All these slow days through I have felt, almost like a physical pain, my lack of you, have longed for the sound of your dear voice, the touch of your hand, some slightest token of you. Knowing that I could not carry it on my wheel with me, I brought no photograph of you with me, and now I miss it poignantly. What would I not give for one! If I had it, I would cover it with kisses! Ah, Nellie, my *precious* Nellie, I love you, I *love* you, I *love* you, with the whole passion of my heart,– and fairly dread the summer without you. No doubt things will go better with me when I land and am in action, but for the present it seems to me as if I must turn about and go back to you at once. I wish they¹ would nominate me for *some*thing, with anybody, that I might be obliged to go back. I might see you *some*times even in the midst of a campaign, where as *now*,–alas! My sweetheart, my sweetheart! Do you love me? Are you sure?

We have had a singularly favourable passage, so far,–a little fog, but for the most part fair and pleasant weather and quiet

¹ The Democratic national convention.

seas; and I have found many pleasant persons on board, though none of first-rate interest. I have slept, slept, slept, morning, afternoon and night, some twelve or fourteen out of every twenty-four hours, and am beginning to feel thoroughly rested. But I have slept, partly, in order to forget how sad and lonely I was without the dear one to whom I owe everything that is sweet and worth having in the world. This turns out to be a slow boat, slower than the *Caledonian*,[2] and we shall not get in until early Monday morning—a passage of nearly nine days, instead of eight. For once I am impatient to land and to have the distraction of a strange country—not as strange to me now as it once was, but still strange enough to be fascinating. What with going to see Mr. Carnegie and lingering somewhere while the Democratic convention sits, in order that Stock. may be able to reach me directly by cable, it will probably be the twelfth of July before I am on the road and headed for the Lakes; but I shall try to find some means of diversion, and every day my love for my darling will be my chief thought, my chief joy, my chief disturbance!

27 June

I have been unusually well throughout the voyage, my darling. I have not only slept a great deal, and so felt more and more rested and refreshed from day to day; I have also exercised systematically, by *running* every day. The quiet, unoccupied deck just outside my stateroom has afforded a clear, secluded course, and there I have run morning and afternoon. It has been delightful exercise, much less monotonous and much more invigorating than walking. I never knew such quiet seas or so much bright weather on this course, and I shall begin my vacation on shore feeling quite fit for anything. We are expecting to reach Moville to-morrow (Sunday) about noon, Glasgow late the same evening or at some unearthly hour Monday morning. As we near the end of the voyage plans begin to form in my head. I shall stay in Glasgow long enough to uncrate my wheel and get it ready for the road and long enough to get my first mail forwarded from London; then I shall go to Edinburgh and make that my headquarters until after the Democratic convention, staying there while the convention is actually sitting in order that Stockton may, if necessary, reach me directly by cable. In between there will be time to visit Skibo. I do not know where it is; whether nearer Glasgow or Edinburgh but that will not matter in little Scotland, since I can go there by rail. I shall not attempt that part of my programme on my bicycle.

2 Actually, the *Caledonia*, on which the Wilson family had sailed to Great Britain in 1906.

To-night (Saturday) comes the inevitable concert, and I am to preside. I shall make the duties of the chair as light and nominal as possible, but I cannot escape *some* opening "remarks." I have come to know a good many of the passengers very well, and shall not feel quite as shy as if they were entire strangers.

Monday, 29 June.

We reached our dock here about midnight last night, my darling, and by 7.30 this morning I was at my hotel. Like the creature of habit I am, I have come to the Grand Hotel, the hotel I came to twelve years ago, when I first came over alone for a bicycle trip, and here I sit in the writing room where I then laboriously wrote my first letter to you with my left hand![3] The moment I entered the room the whole thing came over me again, with startling vividness; and, with that, every other detail of the trip, for I have not stopped at this hotel since and so nothing has intervened here to blur or supplant those first associations. I remember how we parted in New York, how you went to the 23rd. St. car with me and there left me, of course without a parting kiss; how I watched your dear figure as long as I could see it, with an intolerable lump in my throat. I remember the dress you had on as if I had seen it yesterday. And then the novel voyage and all that followed! There is no dear Mr. Woods[4] this time, alas! sitting here with me in the writing room, and I am desperately lonely. I love you more now than I did then,—with a deeper, tenderer knowledge of what you are and of all that you mean to me. I miss you more now than I did then. The landing, I am sorry to say, has not revived me a bit in spirits: I would give every prospect of the summer for a day, *to-day*, with you! And it's not fatigue that has lowered my spirits. I am not tired. I am rested—more rested than I have been in a *long* time, and feel fit for anything, physically, but fit for nothing in spirits. Darling, will you be very generous to me and make love to me in your letters this summer—if you feel like it?[5] I never needed your love more. I long for it as if for air to breathe,—and yet I never had cause for greater thankfulness or (barring Quad. complications and consequences) content than now. There can be but one explanation: *I love you* with all my heart and am yours inevitably!

---

[3] Because he had suffered a small stroke in late 1907, about which see M. T. Pyne to WW, Dec. 6, 1907, n. 1, Vol. 17.

[4] Charles Albert Woods of Marion, S. C., whom Wilson had met on S.S. *Ethiopia* en route to Great Britain in 1896.

[5] All her letters to Wilson during this trip are missing.

Of course the news of Mr. Cleveland's death[6] met us at Moville, the Irish landing port. I was greatly shocked and astonished. When I saw Mrs. Cleveland the previous Friday she was unusually cheerful about him and expressed with some touch of confidence the hope that she would be able to take him to Tamworth.[7] I am writing to Mrs. Cleveland. I do not think that my knowledge of how he failed and disappointed us during the past few years, and particularly since he allowed himself to be made West's dupe and tool, will long obscure my admiration for his great qualities and his singularly fine career. For the moment my feeling is, of course, coloured by my recollection of recent months, and it seems to me that, for the maintenance of his reputation, his death was not untimely. The degree and the manner in which some of his early moral weaknesses had returned might soon have become generally known. How the doctors did fool us (at Princeton) and keep us in ignorance of the serious organic troubles they now tell us of!

I sent my "Charcos"[8] cable this morning, and, inasmuch as your time is five hours earlier than ours here, I am hoping that it may reach you before you go out this morning. Remember, sweetheart, that there are two European mails every week now. They go on Wednesdays and Saturdays, I think. They do from this side, though I am advised to post this to-day to make sure of catching the Wednesday boat at Southampton. I am *so* eager to hear of your arrival at Lyme:[9] that you are all well— you not too tired out by the preparations at home and the settling in Lyme; that you are comfortable and content at Miss Griswold's; that you like Mr. Dumond;[10] and that everything is turning out

---

[6] Cleveland had died on June 24, 1908, of heart failure following complications of pulmonary thrombosis and edema. He had also been suffering from severe gastric attacks and rheumatic gout.

[7] That is, to their summer home in Tamworth, N. H.

[8] "Charcos" was a code word devised by Mrs. Wilson during her trip to Italy in the spring of 1904 to be used in cablegrams. It meant "All quite well, lodgings satisfactory, and everything going smoothly and happily." See EAW to WW, March 26, 1904, Vol. 15.

[9] She, her daughters, and her sister, Margaret Axson, had left on June 22 for Old Lyme, Conn., to stay at Florence Griswold's boardinghouse for artists and their families.

[10] Frank Vincent DuMond (1865-1951) began his artistic career in 1884 as an illustrator for the New York *Daily Graphic*; two years later he joined the staff of *Harper's Weekly*. He studied painting in Paris under Gustave Rodolphe Boulanger, Jules Joseph Lefebvre, and Benjamin Jean Joseph Constant. During the 1890's and early 1900's DuMond's paintings won several prizes, including the third class medal, Paris Salon, 1890; the Gold Medal, Boston, 1892; the Gold Medal, Atlanta Exposition, 1895; two Silver Medals, Buffalo Exposition, 1901; and the Silver Medal, St. Louis Exposition, 1904.

At this time, DuMond was teaching at the Art Students' League in New York and conducting a summer school in Old Lyme in which Mrs. Wilson and Eleanor Wilson were enrolled. DuMond urged his students to shun "personal" art and take their inspiration from nature.

to your mind. Please omit no detail. I shall be hungry for everything.

I have tired my hand out by adding this sheet to my notes
to Stock. and Mrs. Cleveland (Stock. on a piece of business I
forgot). I would *like* to go on all day just to be, at least in that
degree, with my darling, but this is all I can do now without
risking an ache in my arm. Give my dearest love to our precious
girls and to dear Madge. God bless you, my own darling, and
teach me how, in some worthy way, to satisfy you as

Your own   Woodrow

ALS (WC, NjP).

Notes for an After-Dinner Speech

Entertainment, 27 June, 1908

(*Presiding*)

S.S. California.

Had hoped that some *responsible* person would have been chosen
   to preside.

A comfortable and happy voyage

The older and better traditions of ocean travel realized on this
   line—Natural association.

   No sharpers—no senseless swells, devoting themselves to ex-
      pense regardless of pleasure

   Plenty of Scotsmen, of rich and individual flavour

   My own relations to Scotsmen—an Irish strain—How I was
      picked out *on principle*.

Our relations to the tasks of our governments

   Travel and diplomacy. International understandings. The
      unity of Eng.-speaking peoples

   American danger—isolation and provincialism

The programme

WWhw MS (WP, DLC).

From Willard Evans Hoyt[1]

My dear Sir: Williamstown, Mass.   June 27, 1908

The ceremonies attending the induction of Dr. Harry Augustus
Garfield into the office of President of Williams College will take
place at Williamstown on Wednesday, October 7, 1908. A
formal invitation will be sent to you later. It is the unanimous
desire of the corporation to confer upon you on that occasion the

honorary degree of Doctor of Laws and I shall be greatly obliged to you if you will inform me at your earliest convenience whether you will be present and accept the degree.[2]

Very respectfully yours,   Willard E. Hoyt

TLS (WP, DLC).
[1] Secretary and Treasurer of Williams College.
[2] The citation is printed at Oct. 7, 1908.

A Statement

Mr. Cleveland.   [c. June 29, 1908]

In Mr. Cleveland's death the country suffers a very serious loss. Just because he had come at last to be rightly judged, he had reached the ideal part of his life when what he was and what he said were a constant reminder to the country of the significance to it of a great man and a great career. He was listened to as no other private citizen in the country was and all his counsels made for righteousness and good government and wholesome public sentiment. Those who were near him and who were permitted to know him intimately during the closing years of his life think chiefly of their personal loss and of the great gap his death leaves in an important academic community; but it seems almost an impertinence to think of his death in that way. He belonged to no single community. He was a great man and had served the country greatly. His death deprives a nation of a great influence; he steadied and lifted it and kept it in mind of high standards and permanent principles of conduct.[1]

Woodrow Wilson

Transcript of WWsh MS (WP, DLC).
[1] The Editors have been unable to find this statement in any contemporary publication.

Three Letters to Ellen Axson Wilson

My darling, darling Sweetheart,   Glasgow, 1 July, 1908.

The man to whom I entrusted my card to the British Linen Co. at Londonderry, instructing them to send my first letters here, must have forgotten to post it as he promised, for I have waited here three days and no letters, though I *know* that the European mail which left New York four days after I did has come in. It makes me desperately forlorn, for, besides putting my wheel together and making a few purchases, there has been *nothing* to do here *but* wait for letters (Alas, for my dear brown cape which you dislike so! I wish with all my heart I had it. There's not a cape to be had in Glasgow that does not weigh at least four pounds! They are made for "motorists" only now, and not for the poor forgotten bicyclist!) I went to the galleries, of course, which I had not visited before, and saw, as well as the glass which covered it would allow, Whistler's wonderful Carlyle (how could that absurd Mephistopheles do such grave and masterly things?) But everything put together has not made the waiting seem anything but very long, and I find myself a good deal depressed to-night (Wednesday) by my disappointment about the letters. It has been twelve days since I knew *any*thing about my dear ones! Are they well, I wonder, and happy? I shall not wait any longer, but shall start out on my wheel to-morrow morning. I find that Skibo is most inaccessible, in the far northern Highlands, and that it would be practically impossible for me to pay Mr. Carnegie any kind of a visit and get away in time to get in touch with Stock. during the convention (the seventh to the tenth). To go up there after the tenth would be to miss all the good July weather in the Lake District and condemn myself to the August rains, which would be silly. To-morrow, therefore, I shall start out on my wheel for Edinburgh by way of Stirling, which I never saw except in a thick mist, and round by the East Coast of the Firth, crossing to the western side as low down (i.e. as near the Firth) as I can find a bridge or ferry. There are unusually big manoeuvres "on" just now for the home squadrons of the British navy and more than three hundred war vessels are in, or on their way to, the Firth of Forth. My old zest for things of the sea returns at thought of what I may see! After the tenth I shall take wheel for the Lakes. I do not mean to travel by train at all if I can help it. After I get to Grasmere I will write to Mr. Carnegie and try to arrange for a visit in the latter part of August, when there is nothing else to do. It will be better than to take him by surprise, anyhow. Ah, dearest, I hardly dare let myself think about you, I long for you so intolerably and am *so* anxious for some word from you. Do you love me and want me? How it would ease my heart if I could put into words the love, compounded of everything dear in the world, that I feel for you, my beloved, my incomparable darling!

Stirling, 2 July, 1908.

Well, here I am in Stirling. It is, it turns out, only twenty-six miles from Glasgow, but I took six hours (!) to do the distance, and am *very* tired. It is eight years since my legs attempted labour of this kind, and my knees, in particular, ache quite resentfully. But I am not going to take the road again till day after to-morrow and shall have two nights' rest before setting out again. One thing that has made me more tired than I would otherwise have been is that the day has been as hot as an American summer day, and not a breath of air astir. I had to put Glasgow full twenty miles behind me before I got altogether beyond the influences of her pall of smoke. As I rode through her streets in the still air of the morning I could not see a city block's distance through the haze of smoke ahead of me. There were no clouds in the sky and yet the sun hardly tinged the smoke with yellow. The whole city—the houses as well as the people—looked blear-eyed and unnatural. I should have thought myself in a depressing dream but for the very real pungent odour in my nostrils and the sense almost of suffocation. Not till I got near Stirling did nature begin to resume her natural appearance; but I realized and enjoyed the exquisite beauty of the country I passed through as I neared the town in spite of the heat and my fatigue. For one thing, it was down hill the last three or four miles and I was coasting merrily with my free wheel. I think the most beautiful fields of all, in their exquisite verdure and peace, were those upon which the battle of Bannockburn was fought. They have no memory of war! I never really *saw* Stirling before. Not only was there a veil of mist over it the only other time I was here, but no one ever really *sees* any place from a railway train! It is almost as impressive as the rock of Edinburgh. It rises so boldly and yet so serenely from the green fields and the long curve of the river. Being alone, I could imagine what I pleased, with nothing but the quiet fields about me, and the whole region seemed a place of romance, as if I were a boy again. By the way, I did not fully realize how literally and entirely alone I am till I turned my back upon too familiar Glasgow and rode out into a new world by myself. In '96 I had the dear Woods with me and in '99 Stock.—now, for the first time, in my old age, when I am sombre and *capable* of loneliness, I am alone, absolutely! Never mind, I shall make my own acquaintance, and may be the better man for it! The only thing I have learned as yet is the depth and intensity and almost tragical strength (tragical *tenderness*, if there be such a thing) of my love for you. I know I do not give you satisfactory proof of it, my darling, but it is there as the greatest deepest force of my life. Try to believe it and realize it and accept it with a *little* joy! Love unbounded to the precious three and to dear Madge. I am perfectly

well and already fast resting. I must post this this evening to be sure of the Saturday steamer. It carries you the whole heart of
Your own   Woodrow

No letters before I left Glasgow. I must wait now till I reach Edinburgh!

My precious darling,   6 July, 1908—Edinburgh.

My! but this is a strain on the heart, this waiting for letters, for news of my beloved! It is sixteen days since I sailed, eight since I landed, and no letters yet! I ought not to have expected or even hoped for any yet, but somehow I did. The least calculation shows me unreasonable,—but, then, love always is unreasonable. You went to Lyme on Monday, of course, the twenty-second and *could* not have had time to get a letter off by one of the Wednesday (24th) steamers; and letters which started on the following Saturday, the 27th, could hardly by this time have gone to London, been redirected, and come on to Edinburgh. Perhaps I shall not even get one to-morrow, alas!

I have been here since Saturday afternoon. My ride from Stirling was through beautiful country which I had never seen before and in many ways I enjoyed it greatly. But in one way I did not. Early in the day the knee I hurt on the steamer on the voyage down to Bermuda[1] began to hurt me and soon developed a good deal of pain as well as a most inconvenient degree of weakness. I had to take the day's journey by very slow and easy stages, and have been a good deal worried lest the knee should seriously interfere with my cherished plans. But, after all, that is an unreasonable fear. I have not ridden *far* on a wheel for years, and since my attack of phlebitis[2] not at all. It is not at all strange that that leg should at the outset and before it hardened to the job show weakness, and, if I were put on the witness stand under oath I could not swear that the pain in the knee was in the same ligaments that were strained in my awkward fall on the *Bermudian*. I should have to admit that it was a bit farther forward and a bit farther down. Furthermore, it has passed away, with rest, and does not pain me at all in walking even when it does on the wheel!

I shall, as I said, be here till the Democratic convention has adjourned, which will probably be the end of the week, unless Mr. Bryan handles *his* convention more expeditiously than Mr.

1 See WW to EAW, Feb. 4, 1908, Vol. 17.
2 See WW to R. Bridges, Dec. 9, 1904, n. 1, Vol. 15.

Roosevelt handled his,—and I do not see how that would be possible. I must admit that I feel a bit silly waiting on the possibility of the impossible happening. I am here with absolutely nothing to do but that—no doubt in one of the most interesting and enjoyable cities in his Majesty's kingdom but, none the less, with nothing to do! The only thing that reassures me a bit (i.e. makes me think myself not altogether a fool for taking the impossible possibility so seriously) is that Colonel Harvey has gone out to Denver. I take pains to get a copy of the Paris edition of the *New York Herald* every day; and it contains *some* news of what is going on. The papers here, of course, contain nothing—except deaths, heat records, and railway disasters. What on earth Colonel Harvey has gone for, except his own amusement, I cannot imagine. There is evidently not a ghost of a chance of defeating Bryan—but since Col. H. *is* there I might as well be here.

I am suffering a severe discipline of silence! I do not know when I have been so long silent before. I have had only one talk in a week—with an acquaintance I happened on here in the hotel —a man I met at the table of the little hotel at Keene Valley the only meal I took there,—the evening I walked in to see Henry van Dyke.[3] Another acquaintance has just arrived, but I am not likely to have much conversation with him. I met him face to face at the door of the hotel just before I came up to my room to write this letter and he cut me dead,—not for the first time. It is one James Mark Baldwin![4] Isn't that hard luck? But a hotel is a big place, and the encounters need not be many. So much silence has had the same effect upon me that, you remember, I have so often said that long abstinence from writing has. That makes me feel, after a while, as if, probably, I *could* not write: this makes me feel as if, probably, I could not talk. Writing to you is as much like easy talk as any written words could be (I mean of course, in my own consciousness), and it actually feels odd to be making connected remarks—and very delightful, particularly to you, my darling, my darling! If I could rely on my pen hand and arm as I used to, I should certainly send you reams of talk, for the relief both of my heart, which yearns for you as it never did before, and of this burdensome silence!

I have leisure, and fortunately the curiosity as well, to see things in and near Edinburgh I never saw before. To-day I went to see St. Mary's cathedral, the Episcopal cathedral, Sir. G. G.

---

[3] When the Wilsons vacationed at St. Hubert's, Essex County, New York.
[4] Stuart Professor of Psychology at Princeton, 1893-1903; at this time Professor of Philosophy and Psychology at the Johns Hopkins.

Scott's masterpiece, erected in 1874-'79, and was delighted, especially with the interior. It is a noble church, two hundred and sixty feet long, and consistently, and, I must say, most beautifully Early English throughout. You know I have sometimes said, to your great disgust, that I did not especially care for the Early English; but I must say that this modern architect has used it delightfully. Perhaps it is because he has none of those arches which are too broad for their height that I was delighted. I wish you could see it. But nothing, big or little, happens to me these lonely days that does not produce some longing wish about you!

Then, besides seeing the permanent collection of pictures in the National Gallery again, I went to see the annual Exhibition of the National Society of Scottish Artists. But it was *very* poor. There were perhaps half a dozen landscapes, most of them quite small, which were the real thing and drew me back to them; but as a whole, the collection was most disappointing and made an impression of *weakness*.

7 July, '08

To-day, Heaven be praised, your letter came. It has so changed the whole face of things that I will now admit that I was desperately blue, and just about to cable—something absurd. Your handwriting, my sweet one, is *beautiful*: I never saw anything I so doted on as the mere writing on the envelope when I saw it waiting for me on the table downstairs. Ah, dear one, *what* a comfort to have news of you: to know that you are well, that the foot continues to improve, that you are all well and comfortably lodged and happy! As you love me, tell me every detail of what you do or think or plan. I want you, I *want* you, I *want* you, and nothing less than love letters and details about yourself can keep me in even tolerable spirits. Give immeasurable love to the dear girlies and to Madge. As for yourself, you may have all you want, nothing less than the adoration of

Your own   Woodrow

My precious darling,   Edinburgh, 8 July, 1908.

I am rich and happy to-day! Another letter from you has come,—written four days after the one that came yesterday; and its contents delights me. What in particular made me happy was Mr. Dumond's criticisms of your work. *Of course* he saw the beauty of them, but I am so glad my darling should be so encouraged, on authority which she will respect. I read what you repeated from him again and again, with delight. It is high praise, my sweet one, from such a man. Oh, I am *so* glad to have you so heartened at the start. Of course you knew yourself what progress you had made since you were in Lyme last.[1] And you *learn* so astonishingly fast under instruction. It is delightful to think what increasing pleasure and satisfaction your painting will give you as your command of your medium grows. God bless you!

This is just a supplementary note, to go by the same post as yesterday's letter,—to tell you how happy your letter has made me with *all* its good news of the prompt pleasure you are all getting out of Lyme. I love you all beyond words—and my precious, precious wife with the whole power of my nature. You are so inexpressibly sweet and dear and fine! I love you, *love* you, *love* you, and am altogether

Your own   Woodrow

ALS (WC, NjP).
  [1] In 1905, when the Wilsons spent the summer at Boxwood in Old Lyme.

To Owen Willans Richardson

My dear Mr. Richardson,   Edinburgh, 8 July, 1908

Allow me to thank you most sincerely for your letter of the twenty-fourth of June, which reached me here this morning. I appreciate very highly your desire to explain to me your vote in the meeting of the Department, though I beg to assure you that I had not misunderstood it. Professor Fine, who perfectly understood your position and agreed with your judgment in the matter, repeated to me the substance of a conversation he had had with you and made your views very clear to me. I think that you could not have acted otherwise than you did in the circumstances.

I do not feel as certain as you do that the democratic plan proposed in the resolutions adopted by the Department will work badly. There is a unanimous desire in the Department that you should act as director of research; and I do not think that you will find your colleagues disposed to hamper you with rules or to curtail your freedom and authority. I told Professor Magie and Professor Trowbridge, the committee who visited me for the Department, that I did not feel at liberty to decline a request so presented, though I considered the plan suggested by the Department inferior to the plan I had, with the acquiescence and approval of Professor Magie, myself proposed; that I would consent to its being tried, and hold the Department responsible for results. The little flurry of feeling about the reorganization of the Electrical Engineering School had, of course, complicated matters, and made it seem just as well not to insist now on a plan for the time being, at any rate, unacceptable to the majority of the men in Physics. I shall watch the progress of affairs very carefully and shall hope to have an early conference with you in the Autumn.

It would be very delightful to look forward to seeing Mrs. Richardson and you again at the Lakes. I am about to start thither on my wheel. With warmest regards to you both,

Cordially and faithfully Yours,   Woodrow Wilson

ALS (WC, NjP).

From Andrew Fleming West

My dear Wilson: Princeton, N. J., July 9, 1908.

You may recall the fact that I brought up the importance of securing additional money for a Fellowship for 1908-1909 for Mr. Henry B. VanHoesen[1] at the meeting of the Trustees Committee on the Graduate School held just before Commencement. Only two hundred dollars was left of the appropriation of the Trustees for Fellowships and no additional money could be secured at Commencement. Mr. [George Allison] Armour, however, promised to give one hundred and fifty dollars in case the other one hundred and fifty could be secured to make a total of five hundred dollars. Rudolf Schirmer[2] has promised the other hundred and fifty. I have therefore gone ahead and sent word to VanHoesen, who is in Germany, informing him that a special fellowship has been secured. As the matter was favorably received by you and the Trustees' Committee when it was presented, and as the approval of the Classical Department may be confidently expected, and as, moreover, it is summer vacation and "time is of the essence," I trust you will sanction what I have done.

Mr. Cleveland's death was wholly unexpected until the afternoon of the day before he passed away. The intense heat and the weakness of his heart gave the finishing stroke. The burial was simple and most impressive. Never have I seen Princeton so utterly silent, and never have I seen a great throng of people so quietly reverent as was the great crowd that filled the streets on the way to the cemetery.

I hope you are getting a good rest and diversion and that your summer will be in every way delightful.

Ever sincerely yours,   Andrew F. West

TLS (WP, DLC).
    [1] Henry Bartlett Van Hoesen, who was graduated from Hobart College in 1905 and received the A.M. degree from Princeton in 1906 and the Ph.D. in 1912. At this time he was pursuing classical studies at the University of Munich.
    [2] Rudolph Edward Schirmer, Princeton 1880, president of the music publishing firm of G. Schirmer, Inc., of New York.

To Ellen Axson Wilson

My precious darling,   Edinburgh, 10 July, 1908

How slow and silly the Democrats are at Denver! Even Edinburgh grows tiresome if you are *obliged* to stay in it, with nothing in particular to do. There isn't even a play on here that I care to see,—and I have no shopping to do, except for the cape. Ah, madam, the extravagance you have got me into! The beauty of that dear ugly cape, now, alas! at home, is that it is rain-proof and yet *not* rubber, but very light cloth. They have nothing ready-made now in rain-proof cloth, except heavy and elaborate wraps for motorists. They have forgotten that there is such a thing as cycling; and the long and short of it all is, that I have been obliged to have a cape made *for three guineas*,—and all your fault, my dear one! By the way, I have been on the roads only two days as yet, and not on roads very much frequented by motors, I dare say, but a good many have passed me, and on the whole they have not been more annoying than they were to us when we walked at Rydal. I find I do not dread them at all when I am actually a-wheel, but am only bored by them.

Until Wednesday the weather had been singularly clear and suitable for out-of-door exercise, except for one or two days of excessive heat (the day I rode from Glasgow to Stirling was the hottest on record for thirty years!—some 83°), but on Wednesday a decided change set in and we have been having a good deal of rain. It has made no great difference to me except to make the days seem a little longer. I have taken to serious reading! I saw a review in one of the papers of a volume, just published, of lectures on English Constitutional History which Professor Maitland delivered in 1888,[1] and I at once made for a bookshop to buy it. I was somehow suddenly hungry for just that—something solid and suggestive in my own neglected garden. Maitland is never dull, but I could have relished even a very dull book, if not written by a fool! I tried a novel, but it was no go. My *mind* was hungry. I am only sorry that I cannot lug Maitland's volume about on my wheel. It is too heavy. I must read it in pieces as I from time to time catch up with or get back to my trunk. The only book I brought with me was the Oxford Book of English verse. Jack Hibben brought a novel, "The Postscript,"[2] down to the steamer for me, but so far I have not been able to read it! The Oxford Book, on the contrary, has been a great companion and solace to me. I have even read some *new* poems in it–I mean poems I had not read before–though my habit is to read the familiar ones over and over again. I find that I *must* keep my attention fixed on something all the while, to keep Princeton discouragements out, and to prevent myself from examining old wounds so curiously as to open them again. I hope it will not be so all summer! I find I am a little dreading the dear Lake District,–dreading its loneliness–its emptiness of what made it so sweet to me two years ago–its associations with my darling and my home. Ah, my sweet one, you are absolutely indispensable to me. By whatever compass of thought I steer I find the needle in me swinging around to you, to whom I belong, without whom I cannot think of or understand or guide myself. I have thought again and again since I received your last dear letter, my darling, the second, of Mr. Dumond's initial criticism of your work,–thought of it with such happiness and relief, because of the encouragement, the very great encouragement, it gave you at the start. The heartiness of his praise was what gave it its chief value. How delightful it is to think of the interest and happiness, my sweetheart, you are to get out of your work in the years to come, now that at last you feel that you are beginning to get a real command of your material! I was in the art gallery here again yesterday, and it happened to be one of the days when art students are admitted, to copy. They were making, as usual, what seemed to me an odd selection of things to copy, but I must say that the copies I looked at were much better than usual. One man, whose work was not noticeably better than that of the rest, seemed to think himself quite beyond all tyros, and was instructing the woman near him in the most condescending way. I do not know why I write to you of these commonplaces except for the luxury of feeling that I am talking to you and getting the sense of nearness and intimacy which that brings. For the past week and more a great international Conference of Congregationalists has been sitting here, and I must say that I was a good deal impressed by the papers and discussions at the only session I attended. Last Sunday nearly all the churches in the city opened their pulpits to these strangers. I went to a special service for the Conference in the afternoon at St. Giles and was not at all pleased with the sermon, which was preached by a fellow countryman of ours whom I found I was supposed to know all about but knew nothing about —except that his utterance did bewray him a New Englander— beyond a peradventure. In the morning I had gone, as I supposed, to the church where, the morning papers announced, Dr. Twitchell, of Hartford,[3] was to preach; but I had got into the wrong building, and heard a dear Scotsman preach a much better sermon than Dr. Twitchell ever preached in his life—one of the best sermons I ever heard. I constructed my next baccalaureate on the spot. I have not the least idea what the man's name was, but he put the very meat of life into the unlikely text, "If a man compel thee to go with him a mile, go with him twain." My text is to be, "We are unprofitable servants; we have done that which was our duty to do."[4] I think I need not tell you what my theme will become in showing that the text is no paradox. I would like to begin it at once.

But what I most want to do is to make love to you, my precious darling. I wish I could for once put into words the tenderness that is in my heart for you and the enthusiasm of love! You are so delightful to think about,—so fine, so unspeakably sweet, so capable, and capable in such a lovable way, so interesting, so natural, the charm of perfect womanhood in everything that you do. I saw your face as clearly as if you had actually been within touch of my lips the other night in a dream. It has come to me again and again of late, but this time it was so real, so vivid, so dear, that it brought me wide awake and I could have cried with longing for you. My darling, my darling! may God keep you and bring you to my arms again! I am perfectly well. Give a heartful of love to each of the darling girls for me and to Madge, and keep for yourself a love deeper than words from

Your own   Woodrow

ALS (WC, NjP).

[1] Frederic William Maitland, *The Constitutional History of England* (Cambridge, Eng., 1908).

[2] By Eleanor Stuart, pen name of Eleanor Stuart Patterson (Mrs. Harris Robbins) Childs. *The Postscript* was published in New York in 1908.

[3] The Reverend Dr. Joseph Hopkins Twichell, pastor of the Asylum Hill Congregational Church in Hartford, Conn., since 1865.

[4] That was indeed the text he used for his baccalaureate sermon in 1909. It is printed at June 13, 1909, Vol. 19.

From William Douglas Mackenzie

My dear Dr. Wilson: Hartford, Conn., July 10th, 1908.

It is too bad to follow you across the ocean and even into the Lake region, where I trust your soul is enjoying summertime amid the dales and the lakes. But I am under a necessity to approach you as soon as possible. This Seminary has entered upon its seventy-fifth year, and we are planning to hold a somewhat elaborate celebration next May, when the Seventy-fifth Anniversary exercises will take place. On that occasion we hope to have the recognition and assistance of various eminent men, and among others our hearts very earnestly desire to have you with us. We hope you will consent to give the Commencement address on Wednesday morning, May 26th, 1909. As you know, our classes are small, but our eyes are on the future and we believe that a message from you regarding the ministry and its claims on the best young brains of America will do much to help ours and many other institutions. There are few men whose voice on this topic will carry more conviction and persuade more college men than yours. I need not say that, apart from all institutional reasons, it will be a joy to Jacobus and myself to see you here and to have the very great assistance which you can render to us on an occasion of so much importance to ourselves and to our central life work.

Please give my warmest regards to Mrs. Wilson. I trust that your whole family are in first-class health, and that you yourself are enjoying complete relaxation of spirit.

Yours ever sincerely,   W. Douglas Mackenzie

TLS (WP, DLC).

From Melancthon Williams Jacobus

Private

My dear President Wilson: Hartford [Conn.]   12 July 1908

I dislike greatly to intrude University matters upon you while you are enjoying the rest of your needed vacation; but the death of Mr. Cleveland introduces a new complication into the already rather strained situation of vacancies on the Board, and I think it behooves us to be wise in what we plan to do.

You, of course, have already heard from this side of the water concerning the matter but I wish you should hear also of the proposition which came to me through correspondence from

Mr. Thompson[.] To my mind it is a most significant suggestion—all the more so because it was so unexpected

Soon after Mr. Cleveland died I wrote Harry, asking what he would think of nominating Judge Gray of Delaware in Mr. Cleveland's place. It impressed me as a nomination in kind with the vacancy to be filled—and as an alumnus I felt we would be reasonably sure of an active interest in the University's affairs. Harry's reply, however, disclosed the fact that Judge Gray could not spare time to do much with the business of the Board and, at the same time, suggested as a substitute the name of Mr. David Jones' brother, Thomas.

The suggestion was a surprise to me and a grateful one, for it showed that such "deliberation" as was being given to the subject was in the direction of a strong man and one who on the question of the University's social conditions entertains views most sympathetic with his brother's.

At the same time I find myself confused. Should Thomas Jones be elected, it is not likely that his brother would ever be nominated—even to Alumni membership on the Board, and the worth and value of the services he has already rendered to Princeton in the Corporation make such an outlook most unpleasant. The question thus which remains is whether the election of one of the brothers now is preferable to the election of the other later on.

Personally I move in the direction of securing the one now—even though he be untried in the problems which confront us and his coming dispose of the other one's coming back. We need strong men on the Board at all times but never more than now—and Bayard Henry's ominous move in the direction of snap nominations makes imperative the guarding of the election of the best men. If such a chance be offered us now, we must take it.

So far I have not written anyone in the matter—nor have I heard from anyone, apart from Harry Thompson. I have written you first and expressed my views, in the hope that you will correct them where a better course opens up to us. If, however, you agree with them, would it not be well to move as early as possible to secure the result?

Pardon me for my intrusion; but I have felt we should not let a new situation, such as has been created by Mr. Cleveland's death, go neglected—especially when the whole question of new members is at present embarrassingly complicated

    With kindest regards

            Yours cordially   Melancthon W. Jacobus

ALS (WP, DLC).

Two Letters to Ellen Axson Wilson

My precious, precious darling,   Carlisle, 13 July, 1908

Here I am in Carlisle, on my way to the Lakes, and waiting for possible letters from home. I shall not wait beyond to-morrow forenoon (Tuesday). My next stages are, Penrith, Keswick, Grasmere. I hope to be in Grasmere on Thursday, early enough to look up the Yates that day. The whole distance is only about 50 miles and I ought to do it in a couple of days, even at my slow pace.

I did not ride all the way from Edinburgh on my wheel, or I should not have been here so soon (the distance is one hundred miles.) The weather has been very unsettled recently, and is still so. There are frequent showers, not only, but it is likely at any moment to set in to rain several hours. I thought it most sensible, therefore, to get over the country I was least interested in by train, and so, on Saturday, travelled in orthodox fashion down to Lockerbie (about seventy-five miles). Lockerbie *seemed* much further than that because I travelled in the same (3rd class) compartment with five other grown persons (women) and six small children, at every stage of uncontrolableness! And that for two solid hours! It is only six miles north of Ecclefechan, for which place I set out, after lunch, on my wheel. But, alas! six miles! I had gone but three of them when it came on to rain—oh, such a gentle, deceptive rain, so thin, so translucent, so full of promise that it was only a shower. For almost half an hour I lingered under a friendly spreading tree—smiled at covertly by wet passers by, my new cape covering both me and my wheel, waited just long enough for the road to get thoroughly wet and sloppy, and then saw the hopelessness of the case and pushed on. I wish you could have seen me when I alighted at the door of the Bush Hotel in bleak little Ecclefechan! My *cape* was all right, oh yes; but what had not taken place *under* it. My bicycle has no mud-guards over the wheels, as the English bicycles have, and all the wetness of the road was thrown up on me and on the bicycle itself at every revolution of the succulent things! The wheel and its rider both looked as if they had been plunged in a mud bath. The very seat under me was streaked with mud. What a time I did have cleaning the machine the next morning before church! I had dry underclothes in the little carryall on my wheel, and for the rest had to make shift with some unspeakable garments lent me by mine host till mine should be dried and brushed. The rain kept on and I stayed all night—comfortably enough, despite the musty smell of the bed-clothes, which would, I am afraid, have kept my fastidious little wife awake all night. I must say the host and hostess of the little inn were most kind and attentive. Like so many Scottish people of their class they had not a little education and some tincture of letters. Mine host took me to the sitting room and put in my hands the latest volumes of Carlyle's Letters (edited by Alexander Carlyle),[1] which I noticed had been sent him by the publisher, Mr. John Lane, and I spent a very cheerful evening over them—for Carlyle is a much more cheery and agreeable companion in these letters than in Froude,[2] for example. I dwelt on the earlier letters chiefly,—with my natural inability to *skip*,—and found them charming, every page irradiated with some flash of his singular genius for *perceiving*, either a person or a thing. On Sunday morning (yesterday) I went to church. It was communion Sunday and the church was full—a congregation of solid, self-respecting folk amongst whom I, with my blue shirt, blue tie, and cycling shorts, felt vulgar and common. (They did not give me a seat among the communicants nor utter any invitation from the pulpit.) The service was quaint and unfamiliar in many respects, but very touching and solemn. The seven elders (an eighth lay dying and was prayed for in very beautiful phrases) sat on the däis in front of the pulpit with the preacher and were a most impressive looking body of men, the very incarnation of plain, handsome trustworthiness, men you could tie to, and who believed and looked what they professed. The church was fuller of men than I have seen any mixed congregation in America—and almost every seat in the body of the church was occupied. I was put on one side, and felt like a little boy or some uninitiated yokel looking on.

What a bleak, unhome-like little town it is,—and the house where Carlyle was born stands in the bleakest, unloveliest part of it! It was pitiful to see his grave untended, by its grim, brown headstone,—inscribed to other members of the family as well as

---

1 Either Alexander Carlyle (ed.), *New Letters of Thomas Carlyle* (2 vols., London and New York, 1904), or Alexander Carlyle (ed.), *The Love Letters of Thomas Carlyle and Jane Welsh* (2 vols., London and New York, 1909). The latter volumes were not published until March 18, 1909, but it is possible that Wilson saw advance copies.

2 James Anthony Froude published four separate works on Carlyle. Wilson was perhaps referring to Thomas Carlyle, *Reminiscences* (New York, 1881), which Froude edited. This is the only volume by Froude dealing with Carlyle in the Wilson Library in the Library of Congress. However, it is possible that Wilson was referring to Froude's massive biography of Carlyle, published as *Thomas Carlyle: A History of the First Forty Years of His Life* (2 vols., London, 1882), and *Thomas Carlyle: A History of His Life in London, 1834-1881* (2 vols., London, 1884). Froude also published a memoir, *My Relations with Carlyle* (London, 1903).

to him—and in the midst of as bleak, unkempt a churchyard as you will anywhere see, apparently unused now, and with no touch of beauty anywhere but on the face of the sweet, open hills that flank it about. The village lies in the lap of a beautiful valley which is unlovely only in the drear little town itself. A yard beyond the streets and you are in country as sweet, though of course not as majestic, as that about Ambleside.

I rode into Carlisle yesterday afternoon and here I have rested all day. I slept last night, by the way, about eleven hours, —as I slept on the boat coming over. I think that this time I have at least found the locality of the house, under the castle walls, in which dear mother was born. The town must have changed a great deal in these eighty years (?) and I have little to go by, but I feel pretty sure of the general locality. There are only two places where houses *could* stand with their gardens running behind them to the castle wall, as she used to tell me theirs did. Uncle James [Woodrow], she remembered, used to play hand-ball against the wall of the castle itself, at the back of their garden. I visited the cathedral here to-day for the first time. The choir is a really noble example of Early English and Decorated,— the east window a glorious thing in line and the upper part full of rich old glass. Of the Norman nave only two bays (which the Scots were once kind enough to leave standing) remain, as im-pressive almost as the pillars and bays of Durham, but a mere torso now.

My hotel, the Crown and Mitre, stands on the market square, where all sorts of chance crowds collect, and it was most amus-ing to see a socialistic propagandist yesterday addressing his little audience within twenty feet of a religious meeting whose singing periodically drowned his voice out entirely. Meetings came and went, so to say, all evening. I don't know how many more there may have been before I got here at five o'clock in the afternoon!

I have just rec'd (14 July—Tuesday morning) your sweet, sweet letters of the first and sixth, and how I did devour them! I think a letter every day would not satisfy me, I am so hungry for you and my thoughts are so busy with you all day long. I think of you with a tenderness and a longing which are almost painful. But you are *mine*, are you not, my sweet one. The eager loving words with which your letters close make me thrill every time I read them—and I read them over and over again—make me thrill with joy and thankfulness. Your dear, abiding charm is in them always. I could almost cry for a single embrace and kiss.

I love you with all my heart and am altogether yours—. I never knew it better than I know it now. Love without measure to all.

Your own   Woodrow

Off to-day to Penrith

My own precious darling,   Grasmere, 16 July, 1908.

I had a happy day yesterday, getting to Grasmere and Rydal and seeing our dear friends. Finding my muscles rather soft for the business of steady wheeling, I had not expected to reach Grasmere until to-day. I had meant to take the eighteen miles from Carlisle to Penrith on Tuesday, the eighteen from Penrith to Keswick on Wednesday, and the remaining fourteen to Grasmere and Rydal to-day. But I was too eager to get on to the dear lakes to content myself with that leisurely schedule after I once got started. Tuesday was a delicious "fair" day: I finished the 18 miles to Penrith very comfortably before lunch and, after an hour for the meal and a little rest, pushed on for Keswick, which I reached about five o'clock, the whole thirty-six miles behind me. I was very tired, but very happy, too, and not *over*-fatigued. A good dinner & a long night's rest put me all right again—and a little before ten yesterday morning I was trudging up the mile-long hill out of Keswick in great spirits. By twelve, after a really glorious ride, I was in Grasmere. The usual cold lunch was ready,[1] and, as soon as I could bathe and get some dry under-clothes on (the wheeling, of course, throws me into a profuse perspiration, and has already, Heaven be praised, reduced my belt measurement), I sat down to it. After lunch I went to a shop at a little distance on an errand, and on the way back to the Rothay was waylaid by—whom do you suppose?—Alf. Hayes.[2] I had walked past his lodgings and he had spied me as I walked by the window. He took me into a very cosey room where his wife, his mother, and his father[3] were at lunch, and there we sat and chatted for half an hour. Then I set off straightway by the Nab Scar path to Rydal. Ah, my dear, my dear, what a walk it was! Every foot of it was eloquent of you—and of all my dear ones. At every turn I came upon some tree or nook or sweet outlook that you had admired and loved. I could almost hear your dear voice at my elbow and feel the touch of your dear hand on

[1] He was staying at the Rothay Hotel in Grasmere.
[2] Alfred Hayes, Jr., Princeton 1895; LL.B., Columbia, 1898; Professor of Law at Cornell since 1907.
[3] Christine Grace Robertson Hayes, Mary Miles Van Valzah Hayes, and Alfred Hayes, Sr., respectively.

my arm: "Oh, Woodrow, isn't this exquisite!" I had to hurry, almost stumbling, on to keep the welling emotion down. I was *very* lonely and very *homesick*; and yet it was a sort of happiness, too. I felt you so near me; so many sweet memories thronged my thought; I was so conscious of your love—your dear, intimate love, which to me is the very breath of life,—and of your charm, —so aware of your presence and of your thought, my dear, incomparable little wife! And then I found the Yates! All the bleak newness had gone from the spot already. Instead of piles of loose stone and all the ugly rubbish the masons and carpenters had accumulated on it when we saw it, was a very nest of flowers and a thriving plantation of pretty shrubs about as fresh a plot of terraced greensward and as attractive a cottage as you would find in a day's walk, even hereabouts,—a charming spot, altogether, with a glorious outlook. I had not written. The time of my arrival had been too uncertain to the end, and I rather wanted to take the dear souls by surprise, too. I knocked at the door, Mrs. Yates opened it, and we faced one another with delight. She almost embraced me. Yates himself was in the garden up the hillside, putting in some lettuce, and, before my greetings with Mrs. Yates were over, I had him, too, by the hand. Mrs. Yates drew us both into the house, one arm about her husband, the other for a moment about me. They had grown a little anxious, wondering where I was, for they knew the date at which my steamer should have arrived (I had forgotten that they had the dates). Mary[4] was at school, taking the last examination of the term; but came in a little later, hardly changed a bit, except for a somewhat more mature beauty and a little less of the awkwardness of a half-grown girl. It was, I suppose, about four o'clock when I reached the cottage. I did not leave until ten, taking both tea and supper with them, and a great talk we had. About six it came on to rain (it had been fine till then). Yates trudged in, in spite of it, to send my cable[5] off to you, my darling, merely to say "Grasmere" and let you know that I had got to this dear, familiar place; and I had to walk back in it at bed-time. You know it does not get really dark and I came, of course, by the road, taking the slight cut-off afforded by "Moderate Reform,"[6] by de Selincourt's[7] house (I could see every familiar land-

[4] Their daughter.
[5] It is missing.
[6] A road, so named, according to legend, by Dr. Thomas Arnold.
[7] Ernest de Selincourt (1870-1943), prominent English scholar, literary critic, and educator. Educated at Dulwich College and University College, Oxford, De Selincourt became Lecturer in English Language and Literature in University College in 1896 and University Lecturer at Oxford in 1899. In 1908 he was beginning his distinguished career at the University of Birmingham, first as

mark dimly, and felt strangely forlorn and yet strangely at home!). I did not get wet at all except about my feet and ankles, for I had my own cape, which is rather long, and the dear Yates had tied a rubber cape of their own about my waist like a skirt. It was a strange walk. I fancy I know now how a man, long absent from the places he had known and loved, feels when he returns to find friends, indeed, but the dear ones of his own home gone! The Yates have not changed at all, except that Mrs. Yates is now *quite* well and a good deal heavier—where ladies especially object to filling out. Her figure is not so trim, but she looks *so* much stronger, and they are all thriving so happily, in their own Bohemian fashion, in their new cottage, in which they have at last found a real home exactly to their mind. They have space enough now to be tidy in, and the whole setting and environment some [seem] so much better to sustain their self-respect. The cottage is really entirely charming. The other half of it is occupied now, by a retired army officer, graduated from long service in India. He and his wife are the only members of his little household—and her they have not seen yet. Yates said, gently, that she was "slightly deranged" because of some terrible shock or fright she had received in India,—her husband has never been able to learn from her exactly what! Is not that infinitely pathetic in all that it implies. The only news of old acquaintance that I gleaned was, that Mr. Peterson[8] has at last received a permanent appointment to a curacy in one of the suburbs of Carlisle (he is quite well and fit again) and that Mrs. Wordsworth[9] is going to be ousted by her landlord from Loughrigg cottage next year, at the expiration of her lease, and is at her wits' end to find another house within easy reach of her daughter.[10] The cottage is owned, you may remember, by [John] Tolson, the draper, in Ambleside. He means to alter it a bit and occupy it himself. You can imagine what a stew the old lady is in!

But we talked chiefly of ourselves. There was nothing they did not want to know, in their ardent affection for every one

---

Professor of English Language and Literature, then as Dean of the Faculty in 1919, and finally as Vice-Principal from 1931 to 1935. As a scholar, De Selincourt edited authoritative editions of poetry by John Keats, William and Dorothy Wordsworth, and Edmund Spenser; he was also the author of books on literary criticism. Frederic Yates painted a portrait of De Selincourt which now hangs at the University of Birmingham.

[8] Magnus Fraser Peterson, former curate of the Church of St. Mary Virgin in Ambleside, now curate of St. Michael All Angels Church in Stanwix, near Carlisle.

[9] Adelaide Troutbeck (Mrs. Henry Curwen) Wordsworth.

[10] Violet Wordsworth (Mrs. John Fisher Jones) Wordsworth. On his marriage to Violet Wordsworth, Jones was authorized by Royal Licence to adopt the surname of Wordsworth.

of you. It choked me a bit at times to talk too much in detail of you and the sweet daughters and Madge: my own love and longing were too strong, my own lack of you too acute. It was a delight and yet a sharp, stabbing pain, too, to dwell, with them on detailed recollections of that happy, happy, summer. Ah, my loved one, you are life itself to me. I belong to you, every fibre. It is going to be sweet to linger here, after I get used to the loneliness and live down, if I can, the homesickness, because *every*thing is associated with you and makes me feel so near to you,—as if I were alone, at an inn, in Princeton. God bless you and keep you! Love unmeasured to all.

Your own   Woodrow

I will write to Bunn about the floor.

ALS (WC, NjP).

To Jessie Woodrow Wilson

Grasmere, 17 July, 1908

Thank you with all my heart, my sweet Jessie, for your letter.[1] It was most welcome. It was handed to me just as I was mounting my bicycle to leave Carlisle and I had the pleasure of reading it by the wayside as I rested on a long breezy hill. It makes me very happy that you are all finding so many interesting and amusing things to do, and that Lyme bids fair to be a place of real pleasure and refreshment. Be sure to give my love to all old friends there.

All day yesterday it rained here in that hopeless way you remember, the hills most of the while blotted out by the mists that came down on them, and I was kept in-doors until after dinner in the evening. About the middle of the afternoon Alf. Hayes came in and we had a long, lively, interesting, somewhat controversial conversation on various legal and political subjects (he is now a professor in the law school at Cornell). Then in the evening, when the rain held up a bit, I went in and sat with them in their lodgings. I am to dine with them tonight;—they go on Monday. They are very pleasant people, and Alf's mind has a great deal in it that interests me. I wished very much all day for an interesting book that is in my trunk, but, alas! my trunk, though sent forward from Carlisle on Tuesday, hasn't got here yet (Friday). I filled out the day very well, though, with the writing of letters (slow work for me now and needing plenty of free time!).

This afternoon I am going to take tea, along with the Yates, at Rydal Mount, to meet a nephew of the poet (William Wordsworth, John's son, who was for a long time at the head of a college in India; but now lives in retirement at Capri) and a grandson of Coleridge's,[2] whose exact name and pedigree I can't give. The Yates represent the Wordsworths of Rydal[3] as very anxious to make amends in some way for the letter the old lady[4] wrote mama. They are very attentive to the Yates. Mama will remember that the old lady very promptly repented of her discourtesy.[5]

I saw one of the Simpsons[6] on the road to-day, on her bicycle —the one who is *always* on her bicycle; and shall have to call there very soon. Then there is Mr. Roby, the elderly scholar once of Oxford,[7] to whom Sir William Mather gave me a letter—or, rather, whom he sent to call on me. He lives just a little way behind the Simpsons, on the road to Easedale Tarn. I shall have to call on him;—and on Miss Arnold[8] at Fox How. Miss Mason[9] is off on a vacation in Italy.

The weather is exceeding "showery" and uncertain to-day, in a very fitful temper; but I shall have to be patient with it and resume the habits of the place. It was one thing to be patient around our own dear fireside at Rydal, with the dear ones I love best in all the world about me or within call, and quite another thing all by myself in a hotel!

Give unbounded love to dear Margaret and Nellie and Madge, and keep as much as you want for yourself, from

Your loving   Father

ALS (WP, DLC).

[1] This and all other letters from his daughters during this trip are missing.

[2] Ernest Hartley Coleridge, who edited *Letters of Samuel Taylor Coleridge* (2 vols., London, 1895); *Anima Poetae from the Unpublished Note-books of Samuel Taylor Coleridge* (London, 1895); and the authoritative *The Complete Poetical Works of Samuel Taylor Coleridge* (Oxford, 1912).

[3] Mr. and Mrs. John Fisher Jones Wordsworth.

[4] Adelaide Troutbeck (Mrs. Henry Curwen) Wordsworth, the mother of Mrs. J. F. J. Wordsworth. The letter is missing. She had complained about damage to Loughrigg Cottage when the Wilsons rented it in 1906.

[5] Adelaide T. Wordsworth to WW, Dec. 18, 1906, ALS (WP, DLC).

[6] Eleanor, Catherine, or Gertrude Simpson, daughters of Harriette Abby Simpson, widow of the Rev. William Frederick Simpson, who had died in 1892.

[7] Wilson was mistaken. Henry John Roby spent his entire academic career at Cambridge and the University of London. An educator and scholar, Roby was known for his work on Latin grammar and Roman law. He also served as a member of Parliament from 1890 to 1895.

[8] Frances Bunsen Trevenen Arnold, a sister of Matthew Arnold. The Wilsons had met her in 1906.

[9] Charlotte Maria Shaw Mason, the founder and proprietress of The House of Education at Scale How, near Ambleside. The House of Education was a training school for teachers, governesses, and other women who would have the educational charge of young children. Miss Mason was also the founder of the Parents' National Educational Union (of Great Britain), an organization devoted to the study of the principles of education, and was widely known as a lecturer and the author of many textbooks as well as books on educational theory and practice.

From Daniel Merriman[1]

My dear Sir,   Intervale, N. H.   July 18, 1908.

As chairman of the Committee of arrangements of the Trustees of Williams College for the induction into office, as President of the College, of Dr. Harry A. Garfield, Oct. 7th, allow me to say that it is the very earnest desire of the Committee that you should be present and make a short address at the formal exercies [exercises], as the representative of other colleges and institutions. Your relations with the President Elect make it peculiarly fitting that you should perform this service, and I trust that our desire may find a response in your own inclination.

As we need to make our plans in advance, an early reply to this invitation will greatly oblige the Committee as well as[2]

Yours very faithfully   Daniel Merriman.

ALS (WP, DLC) with WWhw notation: "Ans. 8/5/'08."
[1] Pastor and pastor emeritus of the Central Congregational Church of Worcester, Mass., since 1878 and a trustee of Williams College, 1895-1912. He was also a trustee of Worcester Polytechnic Institute and President and Director of the Worcester Art Museum.
[2] Wilson's reply is missing; however, the text of his address at Garfield's inauguration is printed at Oct. 7, 1908.

To Ellen Axson Wilson

My precious darling,   Broughton-in-Furness, 20 July, 1908

I am on my way to Wast Water. I have given you my history up to Saturday, when I took tea with the Wordsworths at Rydal Mount, to meet Mr. William Wordsworth (he must be the son of John, the poet's nephew,[1] for John, the brother, died in 1805. He merely spoke of "my father, John") and Mr. Ernest Coleridge. They were both very likeable, Mr. Coleridge very jolly,—quite "a good fellow." Mr. W. was full of reminiscences of the old age of his "aunt Dorothy,"[2]—some of them very amusing. Yates is doing a chalk drawing of Mr. Rawnsley,[3] the poor gentleman who can't walk, you remember, who lives at Rothay Holme,

[1] He was correct.
[2] Wordsworth's sister, Dorothy.
[3] Willingham Franklin Rawnsley, elder brother of Hardwicke Drummond Rawnsley (further identified in WW to EAW, July 27, 1908, n. 7). W. F. Rawnsley, born in 1845, had attended Corpus Christi College, Oxford, and was graduated in 1869. He was an Assistant Master at the Uppingham School from 1871 to 1878 and seems to have had no full-time occupation thereafter, although he served at one time as Justice of the Peace for the County of Southampton. He was a friend of Alfred Lord Tennyson until the poet's death in 1892. W. F. Rawnsley was also the author of several books on travel and English literature. In the *Uppingham School Roll, 1824-1913* (London, 1914), p. 34, he is listed with two residence addresses: "The Manor House, Shamley Green, Guildford, and Loughrigg Holme, Ambleside."

beyond Mr. Gordon Wordsworth's,[4]—and is doing it to admiration. He now does the chalk drawings in full colour, and has made *strides* of improvement. He has done one of Mrs. Yates which is really extra[or]dinarily beautiful,—which, I mean, gives her beauty at its best and with delightful interpretation, not only, but is itself a beautiful work of art; and also one of Mary [Yates] which is now at an exhibition but the photograph of which makes me sure that the original is the very child herself. It is really wonderful. He *insists* that he is to do me again,—a new drawing, I mean,—and began on Sunday (yesterday) morning. I sat for him for nearly two hours and he got it blocked in entirely to his own satisfaction. I cannot yet form any idea of what it is to look like. But I told him we must take rainy days. The fine weather set in again on Saturday. Yesterday was a perfectly glorious day. In the afternoon (Yates having gone off to work at Mr. Rawnsley again) I took tea with the Simpsons, who made the most particular inquiries after all of you and were most delightful. I quite lost my heart to Mrs. Simpson. She received me like an old friend, and was very natural and very sweet, as well as most interesting. De Selincourt and his sister[5] were there,—not at all offish or stiff and really very attractive at his ease. Mrs. S. had learned that I was at the Rothay and had written me a nice note asking me to come. This morning came in fine again and I took to the road (a bit sad because there were no letters, and I've had none for a week), feeling very "fit." I rode to Coniston, taking the road over Red Bank,—you remember it, where the Loughrigg terrace walk comes out on to the road to Grasmere at the top of a series of sharp hills, and where there is a seat on a very high bank. My, what hills they are to push a wheel up! I could not take my bicycle up the easier assent [ascent] of the woodland path we used to follow because of the queer gates. The ride, by the way, took me by Silver How. The place has been bought, and is, alas! now out of our reach. How I did, and do want it! It looks more attractive than ever now that it is occupied and cared for. The ride to Coniston was eight miles, —hills, hills, hills,—nothing but hills. I had never seen Coniston Water. It is very beautiful, with a broad, peaceful beauty that is very attractive; but it is so much less beautiful, it seems to me, than the lakes we love,—has so much more commonplace, less distinctive a charm. At Coniston I took train for this quaint little town, which I had never heard of before. It lies near the

[4] Gordon Graham Wordsworth, a grandson of the poet and son of the poet's namesake.
[5] Theodora de Selincourt.

mouth of the Duddon, and de Selincourt had urged me to get off here and go up the valley of the Duddon. I did so this afternoon, and was richly rewarded. It is exquisite and has every kind of beauty,—a singular variety. The valley has several sections, made by its several turns, each at its own characteristic angle to the mountains which flank and top it, and the mountains themselves stand about it in the utmost variety of form. One especially fascinated me. It is like a much larger and more stately Wansfell. You know how broad and gracious the slopes of dear Wansfell are,—like some great nourishing breast, it always seemed to me. Well, this mountain, Ulpha Fell, I think, has infinitely wide and rich expanses of green slope, sweeping up from the wooded spaces of the valley, about the stream, in curves of exquisite beauty. One wonders at the sustained *drawing*, no mistake anywhere! The Duddon itself is much wilder than the dear Rothay, but not so romantic, it seems to me, brawling thro.' a very rocky bed like that of the Rothay near Pelter Bridge and often flanked by dry broad shingles of hugh [huge] pebbles much less pretty than green banks. I am so sorry that I am not familiar with the series of Duddon sonnets.[6] The sweet valley would probably have meant much more to me. I did not know until last night that I was coming here,—too late to get a Wordsworth and read the sonnets. I at any rate saw the whole valley with fresh eyes, and on a perfectly glorious afternoon. I sleep here to-night and then go a little further on, on the railway,—to Drigg,—to get access to the valley in which Wast Water lies. It is only from this western side that it can be got at without terrible climbing which would have had to be done without my bicycle and at the cost of great fatigue. I am *very* tired to-night,—but not too tired. It was a climb all the way up the valley (8 miles); but I got back by six and had a bath and some supper,—and it refreshes me to sit here a[nd] talk to you, my darling. I have enjoyed getting into *new* places that do not too poignantly remind me of you. I have not yet been able to go as far as Pelter Bridge or to pass the cottage,[7]—I mean I have not yet had the courage to do so. Neither have I been near Ambleside. Miss Arnold has heard of my being in the District and has expressed to several persons her desire to see me, so that I must go "under Loughrigg" soon,—but, oh, how my heart *aches* for my dear ones, and how much sharper the pain will be there! I never in my life longed for *you*, my sweet,

6 He was referring to *The River Duddon*, a series of thirty-four sonnets by William Wordsworth.

7 That is, Loughrigg Cottage, where they had lived during the summer of 1906.

sweet darling, as I do now or realized more entirely all that you mean to me,—everything that sustains and enriches life. You have only to believe in and trust me, darling, and *all* will come right,—what you do not understand included. I know my heart now, if I ever did, *and it belongs to you.* God give you the gracious strength to be patient with ⟨you⟩ me! "Emotional love,"—ah, dearest, that was a cutting and cruel judgment and utterly false; but as natural as false; but I never blamed you for it or wondered at it.[8] I only understood—only saw the thing as you see it and as it is *not*,—and suffered,—am suffering still, ah, how deeply!— but with access of love, constant access of love. My darling! I have never been worthy of you,—but I love you with all my poor, mixed, inexplicable nature,—with everything fine and tender in me. Suffering and thinking over here by myself, *I know it!* Love without measure to our darlings and to dear Madge. I am so relieved and happy that Lyme is turning out a success. When does Stock join you?

> Always and altogether   Your own   Woodrow

ALS (WC, NjP).
[8] He was probably referring to a remark that Mrs. Wilson had made about Wilson's feeling for Mary Allen Hulbert Peck.

From George Brinton McClellan[1]

My dear President Wilson,   Essex Co. N. Y.   July 21/08

Your letter of July 3 gave me very great pleasure.[2] I not only value your letter, as coming from you, but I appreciate your thoughtfulness, for I know how difficult it is, when travelling, to spare the time to write. Words such as yours make me feel that my friends have realized the difficulty under which I labored, & sympathize with me.[3]

The political situation from a Democratic point of view is not all it should be or might be. How different our prospects would have been had we you for our candidate. You would have appealed to North & South with equal force, you would have brought the party back to the faith of the God of our fathers, & wandering Democrats back to the party, & you would have been elected. I often wish that I might, when at Princeton, have an occasional talk with you, on the Democratic faith that you & I hold, for that seems in these days to be going out of fashion. But I know how busy you are. I can't help thinking that the pendulum will swing back again before very long, so that we who profess & call ourselves Democrats of "the old fashion" can again hold up our heads. My wife joins me in best wishes for your holiday & safe return. I am

Yours very truly   Geo B McClellan

ALS (WP, DLC).
1 Princeton 1886, former congressman and, at this time, Mayor of New York.
2 Wilson's letter is missing in McClellan's papers.
3 Wilson had undoubtedly congratulated McClellan on the recently announced results of a drawn out battle over the mayoralty election of 1905, which McClellan won over his chief opponent, William Randolph Hearst, by some 3,400 votes. Hearst immediately contested the election and in his newspaper, the *New York American*, began referring to McClellan as "the Fraud Mayor." Hearst's friends managed to obtain passage by the New York legislature of a recount bill permitting Hearst to go before any state Supreme Court justice and demand a recount. McClellan fought this bill to the New York Court of Appeals, which declared it unconstitutional. Hearst then turned directly to the courts. After long litigation the case came to trial in a *quo warranto* suit brought by the Attorney General and was tried under John S. Lambert, Supreme Court justice for the eighth judicial district. The jury rendered a verdict on June 30, 1908, declaring McClellan duly and legally elected with no evidence found to sustain the charge of fraud. A news report in the *New York Times*, July 1, 1908, carried a detailed statement by McClellan in which he reviewed his long fight to defend his office.

To Andrew Fleming West

Rothay Hotel, Grasmere.

My dear Professor West,   23 July, 1908.

I hope you will pardon a very laconic reply to your important letter. Two attacks of neuritis in my right arm have made writing slow and painful to me.

You have done perfectly right about Van Hoesen. I congratulate you on having secured the money, and hope he will come back to us.

Mr. Cleveland's death was a great shock to me, and I shall never cease to regret that I could not be present to pay him my last respects. Certainly a very great man is gone. Thank you for what you tell me of the impressive funeral.

Faithfully yours,   Woodrow Wilson

ALS (UA, NjP).

To Ellen Axson Wilson

My precious darling,   Grasmere, 23 July, '08.

I am back from my little trip. I had glorious weather throughout and a delightful, refreshing time. I feel quite exhilarated by it. Wast Water was all that I expected,—and that is saying a great deal. The weather was almost *too* clear. I would rather have seen the place under heavy breaking clouds: it would have been, I dare say, even more grand and awesome for being also sombre. When I saw it on Tuesday there was hardly a cloud in the sky, except for a white veil which Skafell [Sca Fell] kept almost all day wound about its head, or, rather, its neck, quite in the English fashion, almost every woman you meet having a white boa on her shoulders as the most conspicuous part of her costume. I rode out on to the shores of the Water (the northern shore) from thick woods, almost suddenly: I had been riding through a wooded park, the park of Wasdale Hall,—mile after mile of delicious shaded lanes. When I emerged the light was at just the right angle to render the huge, sheer "skrees" that descend precipitously from a great height into the southern side of the unfathomable lake doubly beautiful and impressive, striking them as the setting sun strikes a level lawn. Everywhere that the huge sliding pebbles have remained long enough stationary a slight, tender verdure has begun to show itself, and in the crevises and interspaces a rich turf. All of this the level light disclosed like an atmosphere, the more sparse and delicate verdure seeming to hang like a gauze veil of tenderest green across the harsher parts of the severe face of the frowning mountain, and every projecting rock casting a long finger of shadow down upon it, still further to soften it and touch it with mystery. The Water lies with its head by Skafell, set about on all hands by sheer, majestic peaks and everywhere, except at its foot, where Wasdale Hall lies, at the most perfect point of observation, is wildness, the wildness of open heath like that of the Scottish highlands and of bracken-covered hills. I loved it all and lingered, in a sort of fascination. I rode out another bleaker way, and brought away a perfect impression. Then I spent the night in a sordid inn at Egremont and yesterday morning wound my way through noisy, smoky mining towns to the road which took me to Ennerdale and another noble lake, lying very placid and remote amidst mountains not unlike those which stand about Thirlmere but at Ennerdale they stand closer, more impressive, wilder. From Ennerdale I rode to Cockermouth and there took the train to Keswick—at Keswick the coach (my bicycle and all) to Grasmere, where I arrived at just this time (6.15 P.M.) last evening (Wednesday). This morning I spent with the Yates, or, rather, from eleven this morning to three this afternoon,—taking their nondescript midday meal with them, to our mutual satisfaction. They are a great solace and joy to me, bless their hearts! I found quite a formidable pile of letters waiting for me here,—business letters which had come either through Close or direct from men who knew my address, and since I got back here to the hotel (where I have a convenient little writing table in my room) I have been getting off my mind answers to about half of them,—slow work with a pen! And, oh, the dear letters awaiting me from you, my darling, and from Nell and Jess! I had had no letters from home for ten days and was very, very hungry at heart! Your two letters were in sweet contrast to one another, —the one being written just before you got my first letter from this side and the other just after you had received two. Ah, my darling, my darling! What a charming lover, what a sweet, sweet wife you are. The difference in the tone of the the two letters, the evident love and delight with which you had read my letters, thrilled me with happiness,—completed the refreshment and invigoration I had taken from my trip, made my heart sing all evening and all night. It is *so* delightful that you should think of me so, as you work, my pet, and it is so sweet to have our correspondence thus at last established in its completeness,—word answering to word, thought to thought. I could have cried out with longing when I read that second dear letter, of brooding, tender love, I wanted so to take you in my arms and have you as my own again, kissing you till you had no breath but mine! I love you, I *love* you, I *love* you. Everything that is fine in me enjoys you with an exquisite enjoyment,—every perception I have rises up and calls you blessed, my *darling* wife. Your love is like life to me. I feel as if I suffocated when I fancy that it wanes or is clouded by what you think of me. Tell dear Nell and Jess. that I cannot write by this post,—my hand will not stand it,—but I bless them for their delightful letters. I deeply enjoyed every word of them. They contain just what I want, flavoured exactly to my taste with Jessie and Nellie themselves! I will answer just as soon as I can,—as soon as my hand recuperates! I have no more long trips in mind. I shall take rides from here, but generally only for the day or over one night at a time. For the rest, I shall linger here,—let Yates draw me to his heart's content (in another light, which does not strain my eyes),—and amuse myself in all the ways that became dear and familiar to me two years ago. The loneliness which saddened me during the first weeks has of course gone, now that I have the Yates and other friends at hand, and even the poignant consciousness, and conscious lack, of you and the dear children which which [*sic*] is constantly at my heart here is *so* much sweeter than being where I would *not* have you vividly before me all the while. These places are just so much the dearer to me because they are all, in all lights and weathers, associated with you. I love them *in connection with you* and in some subtle sense *because* of you. Because it is sweet to think of you,—infinitely sweet even when I cannot have you, —it is sweet to be here. I have not *yet* been over Pelter Bridge or by the cottage, but I must go presently, because I must go as soon as possible to see Miss Arnold. I dare say I shall have a good deal of calling and tea drinking to do (though the Yates vote unanimously that I need not call on old Mrs. Wordsworth. Mrs. Yates thought it was a great stroke of courteous diplomacy on my part to ask after Mrs. Wordsworth when I took tea at Rydal Mount the other afternoon and thought the daughter very much pleased because I did so! That was indeed an easy way to do a courtesy). I am very well, and, in spite of a little intrusion of business through the letters I have just had to answer, am feeling quite in my Bermuda humour,—as if social duties which in the midst of work would annoy or burden me were now, with my mind at leisure and my time free, a normal and enjoyable thing,—perhaps the real business of life, as poor Hinton[1] used to think. And it is an essential part of this frame of mind that my thoughts have grown so at ease about you and the children —that I know the experiment of "Miss Florence's" such a success, the situation so different from what it was at Boxwood,—your teacher so capable and direct in his method of helping,—and the outcome for you so certain and satisfactory in my mind. After all, the whole thing centres in you whom I love. Love without measure to all and for you, my beloved, the deep and tender devotion of

Your own   Woodrow

ALS (WC, NjP).
[1] Charles Howard Hinton, Instructor in Mathematics at Princeton, 1893-97, who had died in 1906.

To William Douglas Mackenzie

My dear Dr. Mackenzie,   Grasmere,   24 July, 1908
I find it impossible to say No to your kind letter of the tenth. I accept with very genuine misgivings, doubting my capacity for so important a task, but with the hope that I may be of a little service to you by speaking out of deep conviction. I deeply appreciate the honour the Seminary does me in this invitation.[1]
I am having a very refreshing vacation and am very well.
With warmest regard and the hope that you are hearing the best news from the West[2]
Cordially and faithfully Yours,   Woodrow Wilson

ALS (W. D. Mackenzie Papers, CtIIC).
1 Wilson's address, "The Present Task of the Ministry," is printed at May 26, 1909, Vol. 19.
2 This statement is mysterious to the Editors.

To Ellen Axson Wilson

My precious darling,   Grasmere, 27 July, '08

I spent the greater part of yesterday (some six hours) with the Yates, as I wrote dear Nell, and I read them two passages from your letter of the fifteenth, which I had just received: the one about Mr. Howe and his solid, realistic, saleable cattle,[1] and the one about the little tragedy of the telephoned cable message, G-r-a-s-m-e-r-e [.] Yates pricked up his ears at the name of Howe. They were fellow students, in the same atelier, it seems, in Paris, —and the young Howe, as Yates describes him, was father to the man,—his eye always for the direct means of practical success, and never a moment of aesthetic or artistic feeling. It seems that Yates frankly broke with him when pressed for a reason why he did not come and see him: "It's always Howe, Howe, Howe, the whole time I'm with you," he told him, "and I do not get any enjoyment out of it." Said without heat but quite in character! Do you not *feel*, on the telling of the story, the natural and inevitable antipathy of the two men? The feeling of that old interview came over Yates again, as he told of it, and his mouth went up tight into his moustache as, you remember, it does when he is warm with a thing,—the nostrils wide and taking the air audibly! The new drawing of my phiz. is getting on very successfully, I think. The mouth is still his difficulty, but even that is softening and coming into harmony with the eyes, which are very calm and thoughtful. Did he say, in his letter to you the other day, whether he was going to send you the drawing itself or only a photograph of it? I don't know which he will do—but I imagine the more generous of the two, as usual.[2]

To-day he has gone to London, to meet Mary's (American) god-mother,[3] who has, I think, been on a journey around the world, and is just passing through England a little belated, without time enough to come up here before her steamer for America sails. He will be back again *next* Monday. I have no particular

1 William Henry Howe of New York, especially known as a painter of cattle.
2 The Editors have been unable to discover the location of the original of this colored pastel drawing of Wilson. A contemporary photograph of the original is reproduced in the illustrations section of this volume.
3 Mrs. Jeannie W. Dougherty, who had taught in the Philippines and had met Yates in San Francisco.

plans for the week, but feel a little freer in his absence. He is, unconsciously, of course, very exacting, as you know, about the sittings, and the sittings are very confining and a little fatiguing, but, the whole thing being something conceived out of his affection and generosity, I do not feel at liberty either to resist or to make the least show of any kind of impatience. I think he can finish in a sitting or two now when he gets back and goes at it with a fresh eye. Meanwhile I can take short (comparatively short) rides and walks and attend to my widening acquaintance. The man I met at the Simpsons and whose name and identity I got no clue to, is a Judge Pennington,[4] who holds a judicial appointment in Africa somewhere (I have yet to ascertain exactly where). I had another talk with him the other day and found him very lively and interesting—though he does not compare with my judicial friend in Bermuda,[5] who affects me in his own (in *our* own) field very much as Professor [Josiah] Royce does,—as a walking, sentient mind, agog about everything and not to be resisted or put off or mystified or left half answered in its inquiries. I am to dine with Judge Pennington on Friday evening, to help entertain a medical friend he is expecting "up." The rushbearing[6] comes on Saturday, and I am to take tea, just before it, with the Simpsons,—to meet Canon Rawnsley,[7] alas! whom I have been studiously avoiding. We are all praying for good weather, though quite aware that Saturday will be the first day of August and that Providence does not usually arrange August that way. All the *rest* of this week, however, is July, and perhaps August will hold off beginning until a week of its own! Last Saturday it rained practically all day. Mrs. Yates had gone in to Windermere, to attend a conference concerning the Westmoreland (Musical) Festival, in which, of course, she takes a lively and, I dare say, leading interest, and Mr. Yates was busy at Mr. William [Willingham] Rawnsley's, finishing his portrait,—so Mary and I lunched with Miss Arnold. Yates had "promoted" the invitation in some daring way of his own, which made me a little uncomfortable, but I knew that Miss Arnold really wanted to see me. She was very interesting, as usual,

[4] The only Pennington in Africa listed in the *Colonial Office Lists* for this period was Arthur Reginald Pennington, who became Attorney-General for Southern Nigeria in 1910.

[5] Henry Cowper Gollan, Chief Justice of Bermuda.

[6] "An annual ceremony in northern districts of carrying rushes and garlands to the church and strewing the floor or decorating the walls with them." *The Shorter Oxford Universal Dictionary on Historical Principles*, 3rd edn. (Oxford, 1955), p. 1771.

[7] The Reverend Hardwicke Drummond Rawnsley, vicar of Crosthwaite, Keswick and Rural Dean since 1883; Honorary Canon of Carlisle. Author of many books of poetry and travel literature.

and I enjoyed myself very much indeed. Mary said hardly a word,—just looked serene and wholesome and took everything in. She is still a child in feeling and attitude, but is developing into a splendid woman. She improves, by the way, in her work and her last group is distinctly more beautiful and more mature in method than those we saw two years ago. She does not seem to have done much work: her school work occupies most of her time, and she is distinguishing herself at that, also.

I am entirely rested from my Duddon-Wast Water-Ennerdale trip, and do not think I can long refrain from taking the road again. It has the greatest fascination for me. On Friday afternoon I for the first time rode into Ambleside, crossing Pelter Bridge, going by the dear familiar way under Loughrigg, past the cottage and Fox Howe, over Rothay Bridge, and so into the village. Of course on Saturday Mary and I walked part of the same way. It would be quite impossible for me to describe my feelings! No walk in Princeton, not even the road from our gate to our door at Prospect, could have been more familiar to me than was every foot of that way, or could have stirred deeper feelings, more varied or vivid memories. I hurried a bit; I did not *wish* to stop at any one point. I did not scrutinize the cottage: I only glanced at it. It seemed as if I did not have to *look* at anything. A singular warmth came into my veins,—such as has always come into them when I was conscious of *you*,— the warmth of comradeship and solace and love and close sympathy,—the warmth of a sort of permanent romance, the source of all my happiness,—the warmth of being your lover in every fibre of me, in every drop of my blood! In the midst of my acute loneliness, I was intensely happy. It was as if I had ridden into your atmosphere, the atmosphere of home and love and comfort and pleasure and I was *intensely* happy. The two trees in the Aitchesons'[8] which you painted, with a glimpse of the cottage, the tree projecting from the bank further down, by the old, tumble-down barn,—*every*thing flashed upon my *inward* eye as I rode past like a gleam of the dear light in your own eyes when you look at me without doubt and in utter love! Ah, it was sweet and precious! I had dreaded it and it turned out a delight! A very *sober* delight, as every delight must be into which the most intimate and sacred and elevating influences and memories of one's life are distilled, but a delight second only to seeing you and holding you in my arms and telling you, between kisses, the mere truth of my whole experience, that you

[8] The home of Jane Aitchison, a widow who lived at Field Foot, Rydal, and was a close friend of Mrs. Yates.

are my *life*! *What* a sweet summer that was! I shall not be satisfied until it is repeated. De Selincourt's house can be had next summer, I believe, at a lower rent than the cottage. Would there be too much hill for you to live on "Moderate Reform"? It would be a very proper road for *my* residence, considering my principles.

I have not heard an item of American news,—I have hardly seen a newspaper,—since the Democratic convention adjourned. Please tell me of anything significant that may occur. I do not wish to be wholly ignorant, and there's no use searching the English papers for what is not in them. And, please, my pet, tell me *everything* about your painting. You cannot imagine how hungry I am for intimate and detailed, as well as general and, so to say, external news of you. I am so eager to hear absolutely everything about your experiences in your painting and your lessons,—just *what* you are painting, and where; just what Mr. Dumond says of your work, either in praise or criticism. I long for touch of your daily life,—such as I *try* to give you. You can do it better than I can. Your letters are charming in every touch. Mrs. Yates read me your last to her, and I enjoyed it like a good book. I love you, I love you,—passionately and with my whole heart. Love beyond measure to all the dear ones, whom I love more and more, it seems to me, including, of course dear Madge, and for yourself, my darling absolutely all you want from

Your own   Woodrow

ALS (WC, NjP).

From Henry Burling Thompson

Dear President Wilson: Wilmington, Del.   July 28th, 1908.

I received some two weeks ago a letter from Henry deForest, stating that Mrs. Sage had approved of Frank Miles Day & Brother as architects for the new building. On the strength of this letter I have spent part of one day at Princeton with Mr. Day, showing him the proposed site, giving him an idea of the type of dormitories now in vogue, and showing him the interior arrangement and finish. About all that Mr. Day can hope to do between now and your return home is sketching a ground plan and a possible pencil elevation.

I thought best, in view of conditions as I see them, to start him this far,—believing it would meet with your approval.

Trusting that all of the above will be satisfactory,—I am

very sincerely yours,   Henry B Thompson

TLS (WP, DLC).

To Ellen Axson Wilson

My precious darling,   Grasmere, 30 July, 1908.

The good news,—the invariable good news,—from Lyme makes me so happy—gives me such peace and content about my dear ones! It *is* wonderful about the foot, and deeply, deeply delightful. I am *so* thankful and happy about it. It was a particular ground of anxiety with me. If it had not got better, if it had not got *well*,—it would have been a very serious hindrance to your work, and *might* have prevented it altogether, *with the class*, besides being a source of actual and constant suffering to you. I was very much worried about it. And that you should be in all ways as well as you ever were in your life, brown and ruddy and vigourous, fairly makes my heart sing. *My darling!* I am *so* glad! It *makes* a holiday for me,—a holiday from worry and stress,— just to hear these things! And what shall I say of myself? *Have* I been so thoughtless and stupid as not to mention my knee again, I wonder, after quite unnecessarily setting you worrying about it? It has given me scarcely a twinge since that first threat, and is now as sound as a bell. Forgive me if I have not told you this before. The fact is, I, too, am as well as I ever was in my life. The Simpsons say that there is a *wonderful* change in my appearance since they first saw me two years ago,—that I look several years younger as well as incomparably more vigourous. And of course I feel so. The walks that used to fatigue me very much then now scarcely fatigue me at all. The hills I remembered as very formidable now seem much less steep and much shorter, surprising me as I go up them at an almost unslackened pace and am not thrown out of breath. I took my favourite walk yesterday,—up Kirkstone Pass, three miles of hill in steady, almost unbroken ascent, and down through the incomparable Troutbeck valley to Windermere, ten miles altogether (riding back on the coach from Windermere) without the least distress and with a delightful feeling of 'fitness.' I took lunch next door to the little cottage in Troutbeck which we did not buy,[1]—at the Mortal Man Inn,—and was sorry we had not bought. It is a *dear* cottage and an adorable situation!

Next to the good news about your health, my darling, I rejoiced most in your report that you were 'not so discouraged' about your painting. Of course I know that there was no real ground for discouragement, but, if you thought there was, there might as well be in fact, so far as the effect on you was concerned,—and the report you give in your last letter of the definite help Mr.

1 See WW to EAW, Aug. 24, 1906, n. 1, Vol. 16.

Dumond has given you and the improvement he has noted in your work in respect of the qualities wherein he had thought it lacking, gave me the keenest pleasure,—for I know what it will mean to you,—with how much more heart your work will go. I am so glad that Mr. Dumond is proving so interesting and serviceable a teacher. In brief I'm glad and happy about you all! Yesterday when I was in Windermere I went in to see the exhibition of the work of the Lake painters which is being given there this year, and in which Yates, after keeping out for a year, is again taking part. I must say I thought it better than the exhibition in Edinburgh of the Scottish artists, though of course smaller. It contains some very beautiful things, according to my taste, and I cannot say that Yates's work was the best. There was none better than his, but there was some which seemed to me quite as good,—except that the oil portrait which was among his pictures (of a Dr. Hamilton[2]) was conspicuously the best thing in the room,—a really very remarkable piece of painting, as real as a living man.

Thank the dear girlies for their letters, which are *so* dear and so interesting, and tell dear Margaret that she shall be answered next. How delightful it is that they are all finding so many enjoyable occupations and amusements. If I could feel sure of the climate and that you would all return to Princeton as refreshed physically as you seem to be likely to be mentally, I would be deeply content, and would dismiss you—the lot of you—from my mind! Tell the dear girlies that I will write to them as fast as this slow and lame hand of mine can manage.

I was *so* annoyed yesterday at having to spend *fifteen shillings* on a cablegram, in reply to this from Princeton: "City of Pittsburgh celebrates one hundred fiftieth anniversary last week September. Committee most urgent in wishing you to address great gathering Sunday twenty-seventh; theme connected with good citizenship or civil righteousness. McAlpin." On the 27 of Sept. I must be on my way to Denver! When I was in Bermuda a New York banker who is one of the Executive Committee-men of the American Bankers Association made me promise to address the annual convention of the Association in Sept. It is the kind of thing I like to do; but he then thought that the Association would meet in Chicago.[3] Since I got here Close has forwarded me a letter saying that it is to meet in Denver. I am to speak on the 30th. And on the 7th of Oct. I shall be due at Garfield's inauguration at Williamstown! By the way, they have

2 The local physician who lived at Windermere with his daughters.
3 See L. E. Pierson to WW, March 2, 1908.

not (as yet, at any rate) asked me to speak, but only to receive an honorary LL D.,—which will be my eighth. I hope they will not ask me to make an address: it will be so much more delightful to be there with a free mind.

I am getting a good deal *engaged* here, socially. To-night I am to dine, as I think I have told you, with Judge Pennington, my new South African acquaintance; to-morrow night with Mr. Roby whom I so elaborately *missed* meeting two years ago; and to-morrow afternoon, before the rush-bearing, I am to take tea with the Simpsons. The Simpsons are proving a great pleasure to me. I called the other evening and had a delightful time. Their reserve is steadily thawing out and they are showing themselves more and more friendly. For one thing, they are directing me to all the places worth seeing near here, and are guides of just the right taste and intelligence: guides such as the *mind* desires, instinctively knowing what I would enjoy seeing. Next week they will probably get up a little expedition to a fascinating spot down towards Furness Abbey, including de Selincourt and me in the party. I am looking forward to it with real pleasure.

American friends and acquaintances are at last beginning to turn up. I have twice caught sight of Professor Crawford and his family, of Middletown,[4] here in Grasmere, in circumstances which made it impossible for me to catch them, and I am sure they are lodging here somewhere, but I have not yet been able to find where. When I rode back from Windermere, after my Troutbeck walk, I found on the coach with me a Mr. Wells and his family, from Wilkes-Barré[5] whom I know. He is a Princeton man, I think of Jack Hibben's class, and his family is most attractive. They have taken lodgings here, and I am hoping to see some of them. I think I shall enjoy them, if the dear Yates will let me off long enough at a time! How sweet and affectionate they are,—and how unconscious! I find that it is here just as it is in Bermuda, with me: social engagements do not bore me. They seem more like the natural occupations of the day. At home they are interruptions, and are *added* to the hard work of the day.

Ah, my sweet one, how perfect it w'd be if *you* were here! My heart dwells on you all the days through, with a constant longing. My *mind* is at ease and is content about you: you are having a

---

4 Morris Barker Crawford, Professor of Physics at Wesleyan University and a colleague of Wilson's while he taught at that institution; his wife, Caroline Rice Crawford; and their two children—Frederick North, and Margaret.

5 Henry Hunter Welles, Jr., Princeton 1882, who was traveling in England with his wife, Caroline McMurty Welles, and their three children—Katharine Ryerson, Henry Hunter III, and Charlotte Rose. Welles was engaged in managing family properties and developing suburban real estate in the Wilkes-Barre area. He was a classmate of John Grier Hibben.

better time at Lyme than you would have with me; but my heart
is sick for you, and is not comforted by thinking of you! You
are *so* sweet, so *desirable*! I want and need you so! My heart
knows no permanent cheer without you. I love you with all my
heart, and desire you with every taste and longing there is in
me. My love, my love!

Kiss all the dear girls for me (Madge always included) and
give them whole-hearted messages of devoted love; and keep for
yourself, my darling one, love beyond all words or measure from
                                          Your own   Woodrow

ALS (WC, NjP).

The *Nation's* Review of *Constitutional Government in the United States*

[July 30, 1908]

The eight lectures that make up President Woodrow Wilson's
"Constitutional Government in the United States" (Columbia
University Press), are a suggestive, but not very profound, examination of certain aspects of the American system, viewed
primarily as an attempt at self-government in a country of
diverse local circumstance. President Wilson naturally finds our
greatest and most permanent contribution to be the States, since
in them we have at once the greatest variety of interests and the
most striking success in political adaptation. In the Federal field,
the President alone represents the whole people, while the House
represents its population masses, and the Senate its local spirit
and diversity. The author's defence of the personal and political
attitude of the Senate, however, is singularly insufficient, while
the implication that the House, in sacrificing discussion and
leadership to efficient organization, has really become an efficient
legislative body, will hardly bear the test of thorough examination. There are strong words on behalf of the courts, and a pretty
obvious rapping of President Roosevelt for his treatment of them.
As for the boss and the machine, no cleaner bill of health for
their essential activities has lately come under our eye. It is
certainly matter of regret that, with such keen insight and so
much literary skill, the distinguished author should have held his
plough with so light a hand.

Printed in the New York *Nation*, LXXXVII (July 30, 1908), 94.

To Charles Williston McAlpin

My dear McAlpin,   Grasmere.   31 July, 1908.

Your cablegram reached me yesterday, and I answered it at once,—I hope intelligibly. I am to address the American Bankers Association in Denver on the 30th of Sept., and have promised to reach Denver the preceding day, the 29th; and that makes it clearly impossible that I should speak in Pittsburgh on the 27th. I am sincerely sorry to disappoint them, but why did they wait so long? I must have been a second thought!

I am having a *very* restful and enjoyable time. This is my headquarters. I make frequent sallies into different parts of the District, either afoot or on my wheel, and am sufficiently acquainted hereabouts to have a very pleasant, and sufficiently large circle of friends, who keep my mind and spirits alive. I am very well, and feel very far away, in everything but heart, from affairs Princetonian.

I hope that you are taking care of yourself and that Mrs. McAlpin and you are having an enjoyable vacation. I wish I had a strong enough pen hand to write you a long letter.

Please give my very warm regards to Mrs. McAlpin, and believe me always

Most affectionately Yours,   Woodrow Wilson

ALS (photostat in RSB Coll., DLC).

To Stockton Axson

My dear Stock.,   Grasmere.   31 July, 1908

Thank you for your letters:[1] they have been just what I wanted, and it was a great pleasure to hear from you. I am sorry you had to worry about the Vice Presidency.[2] It was an amusing convention and a diverting outcome, taken all together. Mr. Kern[3] is, I should judge, a most appropriate running mate for the great Inevitable. I am glad I am to be witness of only part of the campaign!

I am very well and am having as quiet and restful a time as my heart could desire—amongst *very* agreeable people,—the most enjoyable being, of course, the Yates. I am forming a little circle of acquaintances here whom I enjoy very much indeed, and am taking to teas as kindly as I did in Bermuda. I make trips on my wheel often enough to keep in form, and in between times take long walks over these adorable hills. Last week I explored the *sea* side of the District, going to the Duddon Valley, which is

exquisite, to Wast Water, which is sheerly grand, and to Ennerdale which has the quiet, remote beauty of a nun. Thence to
Cockermouth and back by Keswick.

Don't stay in Princeton *too* long

With much love

Affectionately Yours,   Woodrow Wilson

ALS (WC, NjP).
[1] They are missing.
[2] A mysterious reference.
[3] John Worth Kern of Indiana, Bryan's running mate in 1908. He had been
twice defeated for the governorship of his state, just as Bryan had been twice
defeated for the presidency—hence Wilson's remark.

From the Diary of Mary Yates

July 31 [1908]

. . . At tea, Dr. W[ilson] spoke of the distaste most people have
for Americans, & said how the latter are characterised by self
consciousness wh. makes them often objectionable but yet makes
them pleasant & forbearing in a crowd, or inconvenience when
an Englishman growls & doesn't help matters. He told of a
coloured cook they had who needed winding up about every three
weeks; then he would go down & artificially get into a raving bad
temper. She wd. be frightened, & for a week after wd. be superb,
the next one, fair, & the next abominable again. It is the only way
to deal with colored servants. Once when he & Mrs. W. were first
married & in lodgings the cook came up & began to row her
mistress. Dr. W. flew at her & she retired & revenged herself
(knowing him to be a southerner) by muttering as she worked,
"slavedriver!" Thence to the social position of educated negroes.
A man with a very comfortable relation between himself & his
darkies, said, when one asked if he'd seen the President, "No, &
I don't much want to see a man who has asked a black man to eat
with him."[1] The darky answered "Misser Roosevelt, he don' know
niggers like we know 'em!" Another darky at a white man's dinner table was asked if he ever ate with them down south, "Oh,
no, they're gentlefolks there!" Individually many negroes are
splendid, but they are exceptions. Dr. W. thought it an unwise
piece of bravado in President R. to put that negro over white
wholesale traders—too much for them to stand.[2] And intermarriage would degrade the white nations, for in Africa the blacks
were the only race who did not rise. Our greatest civilization
came from Egypt, ∴ its not the climate. The Chinese rose to a
certain point, & stayed there, but not so the negroes. Social intercourse would bring about intermarriage.

Hw bound diary (F. Yates Coll., NjP).

1 He referred to President Roosevelt's entertainment of Booker T. Washington at dinner in the White House on October 16, 1901, about which see Willard B. Gatewood, Jr., *Theodore Roosevelt and the Art of Controversy* (Baton Rouge, La., 1970), pp. 32-61.

2 He referred to Roosevelt's appointment of Dr. William Demos Crum as Collector of the Port of Charleston, S. C. Roosevelt originally sent Crum's name to the Senate for confirmation on December 31, 1902, but the upper house did not confirm him until January 6, 1905. Meanwhile, Crum held the post under a series of recess appointments. For an account of this affair and its repercussions in the South and the nation at large, see *ibid.*, pp. 90-134.

To Ellen Axson Wilson

My precious darling,   Grasmere, 3 Aug., 1908.

I am rich and fortunate this morning: I have a letter from you and a letter from dear Jessie,—both post-marked "New London," —I wonder why? It makes me *so* happy to get these dear letters. They are so full of love and sweet thoughts and content and good news of health and enjoyment. I am *so* glad you all went to Lyme, and to "Miss Florence's." It was just the right thing to do, and all my thoughts of you are so peaceful. Much, and constantly as I long for you,—sometimes as if I simply could not endure the need and the lack,—I cannot find it in my heart to wish, for you, that you were here! Lovely as this place is, dear as the Yates are, you are better off and surer of refreshment and renewal doing what you are, enjoying what you are, and (perhaps, alas!) away from me. I do not say this with the least touch of *any* feeling you would not like me to have, my beloved darling, but only with a wistful realization of the trouble I give you! I know that you would scold me for saying this, if you were here and had a chance, and that you never in your life *felt* me a trouble in any way, much and deeply as I have distressed you. I only know that I am glad to have you have a vacation from my selfishnesses and subtle exactions, and that I especially rejoice in your present vacation, your chance to make a step forward in your art, your days of interesting occupation and diversion, as different as possible from the occupation and the *absence* of diversion of your winters. And I know what my heart holds for you as I never knew it before. My days are spent, in thought and feeling, with you. My very loneliness during the first weeks of our separation I knew to be a loneliness not for company, but *for you*. It always comes when I am away from you. I am naturally a lonely spirit. It was the spirit of isolation and loneliness in me that was exorcised by the blessing of my marriage to you, the most loyal and marriageable, the most truly womanly darling in the world. Whenever I am away from you for any length of time it comes back upon me. When I am actually *with* other persons whom I enjoy, the *consciousness* of it often leaves me; to come back again when I am alone. But, thank God, it no longer rules, or can rule, my life. If ever a woman's love and union with her husband was tried and proved, yours is. God has been singularly good to me, and you, my incomparable darling, have been generous beyond words! You have blessed me with the deepest, truest love that ever a woman gave a man! Ah, how I love you, and how unutterably I long for you. If only I could just for a moment every morning look into your eyes and hear your voice and touch your lips, I should find the days so much brighter and sweeter! I am not complaining—*you* understand—it is only that my heart would *crack* if I did not tell you how much *and in what way* I love you. I need you so: you are so utterly indispensable to me!

I have everything here *except* you to make me content. The weather is uncommonly fine; friends multiply and are very kind and thoughtful; I am comfortable in my lodgings and satisfied with what each day brings me, whether of action or inaction; I am conscious of growing every day more normal both in nerve and muscle, and, consequently, in mind also. My vacation is bringing me solid profit, and each added day there is usury from it. The little dinner at Judge Pennington's on Friday night was very pleasant,—an intelligent Scottish university man, the local doctor,[1] and a youngster of engaging words and appearance being the other guests,—the conversation both gay and serious, and the little house quite fascinating. On Saturday night, at Mr. Roby's, the guests were two of the Simpsons, Mr. and Mrs. de Selincourt,[2] and an American, whose name I did not retain, who has become a don at Merton College.[3] Mr. Roby is certainly very genial and charming, as the [George McLean] Harpers reported, but is as yet quite inscrutable to me,—a most whimsical person whose serious foundations of opinion I cannot yet discriminate from his playful assertions and comments. I shall look into him further. Yesterday at church we had a sermon from the Bishop of S. Dakota,[4]—a very manly, helpful sort of discourse, quite suitable

[1] That is, Dr. Hamilton.

[2] Ernest de Selincourt and Ethel Shawcross de Selincourt.

[3] Wilson was certainly confused. There was no Fellow at Merton College, Oxford, in 1908 or 1909 who was not British-born.

[4] The Protestant Episcopal Bishop of South Dakota at this time was William Hobart Hare. However, Hare was over seventy years old, in poor health, had undergone a very serious surgical operation in 1907, and had but a year to live. His biographer specifically mentions his being in Rapid City, South Dakota, on June 15, 1908, and makes no mention of a trip abroad during the remainder of his life. The preacher Wilson heard was probably Frederick Foote Johnson, appointed "Bishop Assistant to the Bishop of South Dakota" in 1905. A

as coming from a missionary bishop,—and he is an exceedingly satisfactory person to look up,—a man, and a very handsome man, every inch. The Episcopal church certainly knows how to pick out its western generals, if I may judge by the specimens I have seen. After church Mrs. Simpson drew me with her little group to The Wray and kept me to lunch in the kindest, most informal, friendly way. I enjoyed them very much. After lunch Mrs. Simpson got down a book and read a portion of it, *à propos* of something we had been speaking of, most charmingly. It was a legend of Esk and Wasdale valleys and included a good deal of comment and conversation in dialect wh. came off her tongue most musically and delightfully. When I left The Wray I walked over to Rydal, by Nab Scar (and, for once, it *was* hot, *piping* hot!) and spent the rest of the afternoon, till seven, with Mrs. Yates and Mary (Sunday dinner at my hotel is at 8)[.] I have been over to see them almost every day since Mr. Yates went to London, of course. To-day *they* went to London,—to be gone, probably, for the rest of the week. It was the only way that they could manage to see the god-mother. She could not make time to come up here before her steamer. Then, after dinner, I went around to call on the Wells, of whom I spoke in my last letter, at their lodgings. Altogether, I talked, during the day, some eight hours! And yet it did not wear me out: it rather refreshed me. This week, the Yates being away, I think I shall try, if the weather holds fair, to see Cartmel Priory and Hawes Water. I cannot much longer keep away from the open road or forego the freedom of the tramp; but there are not many more expeditions which will keep me away over-night. Most of the places I still want to visit can be visited between breakfast and dinner in this snug little District—with a bicycle to quicken the pace. *What* an enchanting country it is! To see any part of it is only to want to see it again,—is only to want to linger and *live* with it, and the charm of the most familiar parts grows and is confirmed from moment to moment,—till it seems quite *impossible* to turn your back on it. It will take a great deal of rain to drive me away! Mr. Close has been very good to me so far. Not *many* business letters have invaded my leisure, and I have had the utmost possible command of my time. To write to *you* is one of my sweetest *enjoyments*, and I extend it to what I have found to be the limit of my hand's endurance. I take a fresh, whole morning for each letter,

---

photograph of Johnson in the biography of Hare reveals him to be a tall, hand-some man such as Wilson described. See Mark Antony DeWolfe Howe, *The Life and Labors of Bishop Hare: Apostle to the Sioux* (New York, 1914), pp. 390-400.

so as not to drive the poor member too hard,—and a delightful morning it is. I sit at my window to write, and, as each coach or char-a-banc arrives and draws up at the door of the hotel, I stop to observe the passengers for a moment of rest, and then turn to my darling again,—the thought quite uninterrupted. Generally I have one of your own sweet letters beside me, to look into,—reading, particularly, the words of love again and again, and reminding myself of each part of its contents, so that I may carry very definite thoughts of what you are doing. These are exceedingly interesting items of gossip about Mr. Metcalf and the rest in this morning's letter. Miss Ludington[5] certainly puts you on the inside of things. It seems to me nothing short of ridiculous and outrageous that Mrs. Robinson[6] and the others should have demanded of Miss Griswold the dismissal of the Metcalfs[7] *after* he had so finely righted both his relationship with his wife and his own conduct and character. How pharasaical and contemptible! *That's* what disgusts a man with conventional morals and tempts him to utter revolt! This is Bank Holiday, and crowds of "trippers" are pouring through; the roads are alive with walking parties; lunches are to be provided without number; and there is a general bustle and stir, in the midst of genuinely American heat. I would have walked off into the hills somewhere if it had not been so hot,—to escape the crowds. I hope Mrs. Yates and Mary are not being too much distressed by them. By the way, Mr. Yates has left the drawing hanging on the wall of the cottage and it is, even now, admirable,—really incomparably better than the one at home,—the expression serene and natural. I am sure that you are going to like it.

I am going to send a letter to dear Nellie by this post. The letters the dear girlies are writing me are a source of great comfort and delight to me. Their love for me touches and surprises me as much as it delights me, and their dear assurances of it will constitute one of the brightest memories of the summer. Give them and Madge dearest love from me. I love *you*, my darling, with all the passion of my whole heart and am altogether

Your own   Woodrow

ALS (WC, NjP).

[5] Katharine Ludington, another art student and Miss Griswold's cousin. She was later one of the founders of the League of Women Voters and president of the Connecticut League for many years.

[6] Lois Ball Robinson, wife of the artist, William S. Robinson. They lived in New York.

[7] Willard Leroy Metcalf and Henriette McCrea Metcalf of New York. Metcalf was one of the leading American artists of his time.

To Andrew Carnegie

My dear Mr. Carnegie,   Grasmere.   4 August, 1908.

I am on this side of the water for my vacation, and cannot return feeling that I have had all the pleasure available if I do not, before sailing, pay my respects to you.

I am expecting to sail from Glasgow on the fifth of September, and am wondering if it would be possible for me to find you at Skibo some time towards the end of August if I were to come that way for the purpose of looking in upon you. I should feel it a privilege if I might have only a glimpse of you before I go.

I know how you must have been distressed by the death of Mr. Cleveland. To us at Princeton it seems a special loss of a great man, not only, but also of a friend and counsellor.

Pray present my regards to Mrs. Carnegie[1] and believe me
With warmest regard,
Faithfully and cordially Yours,   Woodrow Wilson

ALS (A. Carnegie Papers, DLC).
  [1] Louise Whitfield Carnegie.

To Jessie Woodrow Wilson

My precious Jessie,   Grasmere.   4 August, 1908

You and Margaret and Nellie are *very* sweet and thoughtful and generous to me, and your letters have made me *very* happy. I wish I could write as interesting letters in return. But you know how *I* spend my days here, if left to myself,—and just now I *am* left entirely to myself, the Yates *all* being in London. I watch people, and the more I have to watch the more complete my content. You remember the joke on me about "the Queen's bench,"—and, as I have said several times in my letters, the seat from which I write, at my bed-room window is just a more elevated Queen's bench. I reviewed the rushbearing procession from it to great advantage, and from it I can look almost directly into the faces of the passengers on the coaches. They come in, almost in procession, every morning and afternoon both from Windermere (bound for Keswick) and from Keswick (bound for Windermere) and sometimes stand several abreast right underneath my window, displaying travelling human nature in all its varieties,—and by no means always in its brightest holiday humour. Perhaps the most interesting persons of all are the drivers. I see them so often that I have come to know their characters quite well, and they are very individual, and yet very amusing in their habit of doing and saying just the same things from day to day, like ourselves at a reception. If I could successfully put into words some of the impressions made upon me by persons I meet,—for instance at Mrs. Simpson's,—I dare say it might be really interesting,—but, unfortunately, they are so vague as to escape expression. There is a vague impression I get from practically every English person I meet, for example, of the general English attitude towards America and Americans which I should *very* much like to formulate, but it is too fleeting and volatile. It is not exactly an attitude of condescension, but it is an attitude of tolerant curiosity: as if they would *like* to know what Americans are like and what they think and how they talk and act and feel about the ordinary things of existence, but are not *very* keen about it,—do not regard it as *very* interesting, and would, on the whole, rather talk to their own kind and about their own things. It is as if their normal intense self-concentration were, through an impulse partly of kindliness, partly of curiosity, adjourned that they may for a moment notice this stranger who, orbitless, has swum into their ken. I do not like it, for it makes talking to them seem too little like genuine human intercourse to be thoroughly worth while. With an American I can really grapple:—which, perhaps, proves nothing except that I am as provincial as they are! I love you, dear, with all my heart and all that you are makes me very happy. Deepest love to all from

Your devoted   Father

ALS (WP, DLC).

To Andrew Carnegie

My dear Mr. Carnegie,   Grasmere.   7 August, 1908

Thank you most cordially for your kind telegram.[1] I find myself bound by various engagements with friends here for the rest of this week; but I hope to go north the first of next week. I shall expect to go from Inverness by the train which leaves there at 9.50 A.M., on Wednesday next, the twelfth of August, and to reach Bonar Bridge at 11.52.

It is very gracious of you to make such hospitable arrangements. I hope that you will let me know if Wednesday should prove an inconvenient day for me to come. I am, I am sorry to say, entirely alone. I know what pleasure it would give Mrs. Wilson to visit Skibo, were she with me.

With warm regard,

Sincerely Yours,   Woodrow Wilson

ALS (A. Carnegie Coll., NN).
    1 It is missing.

To Ellen Axson Wilson

My own darling,   Grasmere, 9 Aug., 1908.

I am rich and happy this morning, and staying away from church to say so,—because I am to 'sit' again this afternoon for the inexorable and very charming Frederick Yates, and am to start early to-morrow morning for Scotland. Of that anon. For the moment, and as the real *text* of my letter (this being Sunday!) I can speak only of the *four* letters I got this morning from Lyme, Connecticut,—one from my *darling*, and one from each of my adorable daughters, whom I love with all my heart and whose letters interest and delight me so. It is a red letter day for me and my heart sings with all the sweet, sustaining love these dear letters have brought me. They were better for me than any sermon I could hear at St. Oswald's, Grasmere.

The trip to Scotland is to see Mr. Carnegie. It turns out that (for him) this is the convenient time for me to go. It's a long journey, but I shall break it twice, rather than spend a night in a Scottish railway carriage. I shall sleep to-morrow night in Edinburgh, and Tuesday night at Inverness. I shall reach Skibo about noon on Wednesday. Mr. Carnegie was *very* cordial in his reply to my letter asking him when it would be convenient for me to visit him, and *may* insist upon my staying some time; but I shall try to get away on Saturday and be back in this blessed District by Monday, the 17th. So much travelling is involved in this programme (which means spending Thursday and Friday at Skibo) and I am so entirely without means of judging what use I shall be expected to make of my time while I am there that I *may* not be able to get any letter written to send by the week-end mail. I will if it is possible, you may be sure, but please do not be anxious or disappointed if no letter follows this for a week. I need not say that I do not want to go. We are having, and have all along had, perfect weather. Even August has withheld its rains and smiled in the most fascinating manner. And there's no telling what humour the heavens will be in when I get back at the end of another ten days. But I shall at least have the Scottish visit off my mind and be free to enjoy the blessed peace and beauty of this dear land for the remaining two weeks and a half of my stay on this side the sea. I do not mean to stir from the District till I am obliged to get my wheel to Glasgow to be crated for the homeward voyage! We *must* come here for another summer,—all of us!

Friday I spent with the Marburg's,[1]—very delightfully, as it turned out. He is a *very* thoughtful man, quite out of the usual type of millionaires, and Mrs. Marburg is a sweet little southerner, with a delectable tongue in her head, and a houseful of sweet, natural children. I rode over to Briery Close, the place they have had for several seasons (they have been coming here almost every summer for fifteen years, and are real lovers of the District) on my wheel about eleven o'clock and had a delightful chat with him on matters big and little, grave and gay, sitting on his terrace and looking off across the head of the lake to the noble Langdales, lying in transparent mist, till lunch time. After a delightful lunch,—at a table fairly loaded with flowers,—followed by coffee and fruit on the terrace, we took the only automobile ride I have ever enjoyed. Their chauf[f]eur *was* their coachman, and drives with a coachman's care and sense. They like and insist upon a sensible pace,—every other motor going their way passes them, with a whirl and a flaunt,—and their car is delightfully comfortable. We rode over to Keswick and had tea at a cosey inn, with beautiful gardens, beyond the town at the upper end of Derwent Water. The afternoon was exquisite,—the *most* beautiful of all the beautiful afternoons that have made the summer a delight,—and the lights on the hills, as the road turned first this way and then that amidst the shifting panorama of fields and fells, fairly took one's breath with a sort of rapture. They left me here at the door of the Rothay (an "under-coachman" having ridden my wheel back) and I was quite happy with the refreshment of good company and the enchantment of lovely scenery. They are still trying to make me go and stay with them, —but, much as I like them, I cannot give them my freedom. It is the foundation of all my enjoyment for the nonce. If I cannot have you, I will have nobody. I should not be so free to live with you in imagination in anyone else's household,—and that, when I am free to be alone in these hills, I can do till I am deeply blessed and altogether happy!

Yesterday I took a bicycle trip into the fells with the Simpsons. The party consisted of the two Simpsons whom the girls first met on the road, Mr. de Selincourt and a Miss Hadow,[2] his guest, on a tandem wheel, Oliver de Selincourt, his oldest boy, and myself. They all ride at a moderate pace and walk up the hills, as I do! We rode over Dunmail Raise (or, rather, walked up this side and

---

[1] Theodore Marburg and Fannie Grainger Marburg of Baltimore. He was the heir to a tobacco fortune, a gentleman scholar and publicist, and a civic leader in Baltimore.

[2] Grace Eleanor Hadow, Tutor in English at Lady Margaret Hall, Oxford.

rode down the other) and along a charming road I had never taken before on the west side of Thirlmere (the main coach road is on the east side) to the other end of the lake, and then, leaving our wheels under a wall, climbed Shoulthwaite Fell to Shoulthwaite Rock, a noble point, commanding a wide view and bearing traces of having been fortified,—by the very ancient Britons,— Canon Rawnsley and others prefer to think by the still earlier Fell Folk, who are pre-historic. Quite certainly *some*body at one time fortified it. The traces of trenches and at least earthworks are quite evident and also the foundations of small buildings nearby. The Rock is seldom visited, and is now soft, in all its beautiful outlines (for it is beautiful) with heather at the most perfect stage of bloom. Each member of the party had taken lunch with them (as light and simple as possible) and we sat under the shadow of the Rock, by a little beck, and pic-niced, —each eating his or her own lunch and offering nothing, except chocolate or cake! It was very surprising and amusing and English (I suppose). Then we clambered to a still higher crag ("Raven Crag") from which we could see *every*thing from Ambleside almost to Keswick, and sat till the sacred hour of the English day approached,—the hour for tea. For that we resorted to an interesting farm house about a quarter of a mile from the foot of the Fell, and fared sumptuously on good tea, excellent bread and butter, and black currant jam. We rode back at the most beautiful hour of the afternoon. It was a really delightful day. Stiffness has worn off entirely now between me and the Simpsons, and even between me and Mr. de Selincourt; and Miss Hadow, the other member of the party, proved very interesting and attractive. She and her brother have edited, it seems, an anthology of old English ballads which is considered a very scholarly and creditable piece of work.[3] It came out that she had taught, a single year, at Bryn Mawr, and had the same opinion of Miss [Martha Carey] Thomas that—*every*body who knows her *must* have. It was interesting to see the change her face underwent when I asked her what she thought of Miss Thomas. Her lips and nostrils alike grew taut and tense and unutterable things came into her eyes. She is very spirited, and had evidently 'had it out' with Miss T. I enjoyed her very much. Indeed, I enjoyed them all. Talk went freely and naturally and lightly, and there was no constraint of any kind. I had a little dreaded the day,— a whole day is a considerable test of companionability and a picnic is a very intimate affair when the party is small,—but it

[3] Grace Eleanor Hadow and William Henry Hadow, *The Oxford Treasury of English Literature* (3 vols., Oxford, 1906-1908).

turned out a day of pleasure from beginning to end. Even Oliver, though he dreamily rode all over the road, with an incalculable wobble, once and again almost over-turning one or the other of us, and was on the whole less suited for company than most English boys, was a dear little chap at bottom and not *much* in the way! His father would have heard and responded to my many interesting observations much better had his mind not been quite so preoccupied with the erratic youngster. I wish Mrs. de Selincourt had been with us. She seems to be worth knowing. I did not get a chance to talk to her at Mr. Roby's dinner.

The news your letters bring me of Barry Duffield's[4] insanity is, of course, not unexpected but is none the less infinitely sad and distressing. I have the profoundest sympathy for all concerned. Do you think, my dear one, that you could write his mother a letter of sympathy? You could do it so sweetly, and I am sure it would be a real comfort to her.

You ask the exact dates of my return voyage. I am to sail, on the *Caledonia*, on the 5th of September, and should, I suppose, reach New York on the evening of Sunday, the 13th, or the morning of Monday, the 14th. The Caledonia is the same boat we crossed on two years ago. She is an eight-day boat; but she does not really get to sea before afternoon (the passengers leaving Glasgow by train about ten in the morning) and has a difference of time of five hours against her going westward, so I doubt if I can *count* on getting in before Monday, the 14th.

I love you, my precious one, with all my heart. Your love is *so* sweet and delightful to me,—is my very breath of life and happiness. I bless you for it every moment of my days. Love without measure to all.   Your own   Woodrow

ALS (WC, NjP).
    4 George Barry Duffield, Princeton 1904, son of John Fletcher Duffield, Princeton 1876, and Margaret Wall Duffield of 45 Nassau Street, Princeton. Young Duffield had taught at the Syrian Protestant College in Beirut, 1904-1906, and had most recently been an assistant to the Secretary of Princeton University. He eventually recovered and went on to a career as an educator in Colorado and New Mexico.

To Edgar Odell Lovett

Caledonian Hotel, Inverness.

My dear Lovett,   11 August, 1908

It was a great pleasure to get your letter.[1] We must by all means find each other. I am on my way just now to make a brief visit at a private house; but I hope and expect to be at the Rothay Hotel, Grasmere, Westmoreland, England, from about the 17th till the 2nd of September. Do not you and Mrs. Lovett want to see the English Lakes? Grasmere is at the heart of them.

Thank you also for the information about your visit to Mr. Proctor.[2] I am very much indebted to you for seeing him.[3]

I hope that Mrs. Lovett[4] and you are well and enjoying your trip to the full.

With warmest regard to you both,

Cordially and faithfully Yours,   Woodrow Wilson

ALS (E. O. Lovett Papers, TxHR).
    [1] It is missing.
    [2] William Cooper Procter, Princeton 1883, President of the Procter and Gamble Co., soap manufacturers of Cincinnati.
    [3] The purpose of Lovett's visit to Procter is unknown.
    [4] Mary Ellen Hale Lovett.

From Melancthon Williams Jacobus

Hartford, Conn.,
August 11th, 1908

My dear President Wilson:

I was greatly rejoiced to learn, through Dr. Mackenzie before his departure for his vacation, that you had consented to deliver the graduation address at our Seventy-fifth Anniversary Commencement next year, and I am writing at once to convey to you an invitation to be our guest during your visit. We have just succeeded in moving into our new home, and have fair promise of being able to care for our friends with some degree of comfort.

I thank you for your letter which came to me the other day,[1] in answer to my inquiry about a possible candidate for the Trustee vacancy caused by Mr. Cleveland's death. I sincerely hope that Mr. [Thomas Davies] Jones may be put in nomination and elected. I only wish I knew just how much to do and not to do in advocating his selection. If you have any suggestions in this direction, I shall be glad to carry them out, for I feel most earnestly that every strong man we can now secure will be of growing advantage to us as the time ripens to the adoption of the policies to which we are logically committed. . . .

I trust that you will not tire yourself in making any attempt to answer this letter. I only want to keep you informed of such things as have come to my knowledge, and I could not resist the temptation of being early with my invitation for next June.

With kindest regards,

Yours very sincerely,   Melancthon W. Jacobus

TLS (WP, DLC) with WWhw notation: "Ans. 8/21/08."
    [1] It is missing.

To Ellen Axson Wilson

My own darling,   Skibo, 13 August, 1908

I have run away for a few words with you: I hope they will catch the Saturday steamer. I reached here yesterday in time for lunch. It's a long, a very long journey,—for a 'small' island, and I broke it twice rather than take it all in one dose. I slept Monday night in Edinburgh and Tuesday night in Inverness, after a railway ride of six hours each day, and had to add two more hours yesterday,—making fourteen hours altogether on the train. Breaking the journey as I did, I managed to arrive fresh for my duties as guest at Skibo. This immense house is full of interesting people, and the meals are a bit like *table d'hote*. The only ones I think you would know are Mr. and Mrs. Whitelaw Reid, the American ambassador and his wife,[1] who also arrived yesterday. Mr. Reid is a very tiresome person, in my opinion, but has *some* lucid intervals, and has now many interesting things to talk about. Yesterday afternoon I went out fishing with Mr. Carnegie and one of his guests, acting as boatman and taking the fish in in a little net as they were brought to the surface; and all day to-day I have been out on the firth with a majority of the guests in a little steam yacht,—a very pleasant company and a refreshing cruise. I am writing these lines in the few minutes available before dressing for dinner. I am perfectly well, am behaving properly, so far as I can judge, think of you all the time with homesick longing, and shall breathe a sigh of relief when I am free again and can ease my heart with a real letter to my darling. Love to all and for yourself the heart of

Your own   Woodrow

ALS (WC, NjP).
[1] Elizabeth Mills Reid.

From Walter Hudson Watkins

My dear Dr. Wilson: Chattanooga, Tenn. Aug. 13, 1908.

I am in receipt of your esteemed favor of July 24th, written from England, and in reply beg to advise you that it would suit us exactly to have our annual meeting of the Tennessee Alumni Association during the last week of October.

I note with much pleasure that you will be able to be with us during this week, and it would suit our plans perfectly for you to leave Princeton on Wednesday, October 28th, and be with us in Nashville the following Friday, Saturday and Sunday. This would give you the opportunity to be present at your Tuesday lecture, and we are not so selfish as to wish to deprive your students of the pleasure of receiving the Tuesday lecture heretofore mentioned.

We have hopes that this year's reunion will be both pleasant and profitable and will further advertise in Tennessee the fact that Princeton University stands at the very top of the Universities of this country. I am making endeavors now to have with us at the reunion some of the staunch supporters of the University from Chicago, St. Louis and Louisville, and I hope to be successful in getting to Nashville a very representative body of Princeton men.

I will write you again when you have returned from abroad and send you an outline of the schedule you can rely upon to get to Nashville no later than Friday morning. We will certainly count on your being with us, and do not feel that our meeting would be a success unless you could be with us, especially since you have heretofore been kind enough to discommode yourself by being present at our three former annual meetings.

With very kind regards from myself and my mother and father,[1] I beg to remain

Yours very truly,   Walter H. Watkins

TLS (WP, DLC).

[1] Edmund Watkins and Idelette Christian Dial Watkins. Edmund Watkins was a lawyer in Chattanooga.

To Ellen Axson Wilson

My precious darling,   Edinburgh, 16 Aug., '08

Here I am in Edinburgh again, on my way back from Skibo to Grasmere,—and very eager I am to get back! I do not know that it is worth while to attempt in a letter to describe the visit,— it can be so much better done with the little touches of conversation. They have a perfect stream of visitors at Skibo: I should think that a season of it would utterly wear poor Mrs. Carnegie out. The Castle is like a luxurious hotel. Some twenty or twenty-five persons sit down to every meal. Guests are received, for the most part (if—say—of less than Cabinet rank) by the servants; shown to their rooms; and received by the host and hostess when all assemble for the next meal. The list of guests while I was there was, so far as I can recall it: Lord Morley (i.e. Mr. John Morley translated to the House of Lords, and an old goose for accepting the translation!); Ambassador and Mrs. Whitelaw Reid; the Baroness von Suttner,[1] (a very fat Austrian lady whom Mr. Carnegie introduced as having won the Nobel prize [in 1905] for the best book written in promotion of international peace,[2] and whom I had to escort as far as Perth yesterday—with the incidental inconvenience that she rode first class and I third!); a Mr. Moscheles,[3] a portrait painter, etc., etc., once a familiar friend of Du Maurier's[4] and one of those persons born to have and to write Reminiscences;[5] Mr. Shaw,[6] the present Lord Advocate for Scotland in the Cabinet,—a jolly good fellow and my favourite in the list,—and Mrs. Shaw,[7] a sweet Scottish lady with no conversation to speak of; a young Englishman named Herndon, who was generally out shooting (for I reached Skibo the very day the shooting season opened) and whose identity I could not establish, even by inquiry; Mr. "Tom." Miller,[8] a life-long chum of Mr. Carnegie's and a most docile creature; Mr. Reid's son, Ogden, a Yale man just through with his bar examinations;[9] and a Mr. Sam'l Dennis, his wife[10] (very pretty and entertaining), and their young son and daughter,[11]— the son a Junior in Princeton. Mr. Dennis is the son of an old friend[12] of Mr. Carnegie's. There was everything to do that you

[1] Bertha Felicie Sophie Kinsky von Suttner, widow of Freiherr Arthur Gundaccar von Suttner.

[2] The book was her novel, *Die Waffen Nieder!* (Berlin, 1889), the most popular of her numerous works of fiction and non-fiction, which was widely circulated in an authorized English translation by T. Holmes, *Lay Down Your Arms: The Autobiography of Martha Von Tilling* (London, 1892). It graphically portrayed the impact of the Austro-Prussian and Franco-Prussian wars on various members of one family and their friends and quickly became extremely popular among pacifist groups. Among her other peace activities, the Baroness founded the Austrian Peace Society in 1891 and founded and edited from 1892 to 1899 a magazine also called *Die Waffen Nieder!*, which became the organ of the International Peace Bureau in Bern. Before her marriage in 1876, she had been for a brief time secretary to Alfred Nobel and remained his life-long friend and correspondent. She seems to have had some influence on his decision to establish the peace prize.

[3] Felix Moscheles, artist and writer of London and godson of Felix Mendelssohn-Bartholdy.

[4] George du Maurier.

[5] Felix Moscheles, *In Bohemia with Du Maurier. The First of a Series of Reminiscences . . .* (London, 1896) and *Fragments of an Autobiography* (London, 1899).

[6] Thomas Shaw, also M.P. from Hawick District since 1892.

[7] Elsie Forrest Shaw.

[8] Thomas Noble Miller, a friend of Andrew Carnegie's since the latter's arrival in Allegheny, Pennsylvania, in 1848. A long-time business associate as well, Miller had been responsible for bringing the young Carnegie into the iron manufacturing business.

[9] Ogden Mills Reid, B.A., Yale, 1904; LL.B., Yale Law School, 1907.

[10] Samuel Shepard Dennis and Eliza Thomas Dennis of Morristown, New Jersey. Dennis devoted his time to the management of the family estate and was a director of numerous corporations.

[11] James Shepard Dennis 2d, Princeton 1910, and Dorothy Dennis.

[12] Alfred Lewis Dennis (1817-90), businessman of Newark, New Jersey, who founded the family fortune largely through investments in Newark real estate and New Jersey railroads.

can think of: hunting, fishing, golfing, sailing, swimming (in the most beautiful swimming pool I ever saw,—the water tempered to about 70°), driving, motoring, billiards, tennis, croquet; and there was perfect freedom to do as you pleased. Wednesday afternoon I managed the boat for Mr. Miller and Mr. Carnegie while they fished; Thursday morning and afternoon I was with a party on a small steam yacht; Friday morning I followed the players over the golf course; Friday afternoon I went with a big party in a motor carry-all to inspect the kitchen gardens of the tenants on the estate who had been competing for a prize; Saturday I came away. The estate is some twenty miles long and, on a[n] average, about six miles broad, and includes a whole town in its sweep,—or, rather, a large village. The evenings were spent in dining, talking, playing whist or billiards (I naturally chose the latter), or reading,—by those who had nerves steady enough for it. It was an interesting experience, of which I shall have many things to tell you not suitable to be written down. My opinion of my host, in particular, had better be reserved for the modulations of the voice, rather than of the pen. Mrs. Carnegie is *very* sweet and true, and sent you every cordial message. I like and admire her extremely. I was, of course, very glad to see Mr. Morley (as I will take the liberty of calling him still,[)] and enjoyed what I heard of his talk very much. He came only twenty-four hours before I left. What he said had that flavour of sincerity and simplicity which I so love in the best English men, and was expressed as you would imagine he would express it,—with an elegance natural to a real man of letters and a deliberation (such as I greatly admire but have not) characteristic of a man who thinks both before and while he speaks. I was a good deal shocked to find him old and bent and a bit feeble. Mrs. Carnegie said she was herself shocked by the evidences of how much he had broken since she last saw him,—only a year ago, I think. He is over seventy and is Secretary of State for India,—a post of the heaviest labour and, just now, in particular, of the gravest anxiety. To be Secretary of State for India is like being all the ministers at once for that vast and restless and in large part incomprehensible empire, and it is telling on him seriously. I imagine, too, that the whole Liberal ministry is just now, besides, on the anxious bench. Opinion here is not on the whole, I should say, sustaining them. The Lord Advocate does not seem to take it very hard. He is as jolly, as genuine, as humorous a Scotsman as I would care to meet. We took a great fancy to one another, and I sincerely hope that I shall run across him again,—though I do not care to have converse with his wife again throughout a whole dinner! I am glad to be away and free again, and am eager to get back to the little Rothay Hotel and the more simple friends at the dear Lakes. I am tired and in a humour to be entirely my own master again.

Grasmere, 18 Aug., '08

My wish is fulfilled: I am back in sweet Grasmere, though I have not yet seen the friends. I went from Edinburgh to Carlisle Sunday afternoon and remained there till 1.40 yesterday afternoon (Monday), in order to see Mr. Peterson, who is now, as I think I told you (tho. I did not know it when I first passed though Carlisle on my way down here) curate of the parish of Stanwix, a suburb, practically a part, of Carlisle. I started out right after breakfast to find him. I did not know his address, so I went straight to the parish church, St. Michael's, and there he was in the vestry room, and mighty glad to see me,—as well as I could judge the emotions of a *very* shy and undemonstrative man. He took me at once to his house. Mrs. Peterson and the boys were going away to Cheshire by a noon train, so I went down to the station with them all and then took him to lunch with me at my hotel. It was all very natural and enjoyable. We had a jolly good talk, and carried our friendship and understanding, I think, a stage forward. He looks *perfectly* well and strong, and is vastly improved in appearance since we saw him that night at dinner. He gave me, by the way, a photograph of Yates's drawing of him,—a capital thing, though a little too *smooth*, there being in fact very few angles in Peterson's face,—a very singular and, for the artist, I should think, a very difficult face, with (as it were) *suppressed* expression. He is *very* fine and interesting and true. The little visit did me good.

And then when I got here, in time for dinner, I found your sweet, sweet letters (for I had had none sent after me and had been a long week without), and letters from dear Margaret and Jessie, as well as, alas! business letters a few, against answering which I rebel. Your letters, my beloved one, are sweet beyond all words, and bring me such deep content with their news of peace and pleasure and satisfactory work and good health! How thankful I am,—and obliged to dear Jessie for telling me *she* thought dear mother was *rather pining for me*! You still are provokingly silent about the details of your work and of your own days. When *shall* I be able to teach you to talk about yourself,— the only theme that engages *all* my powers of enjoyment? I read between the lines that you are making very substantial and satisfactory progress,—I am sure of that,—but I ought to read it *in* the lines. *My darling!* What would I not give to have you in my arms again, where I could tell you in sweet intimacy all my heart contains of love and devotion. You are unspeakably dear to me, and precious beyond words. I could not live without you: I cannot think of myself without you. You are *the* indispensable thing in my life. I wish you knew how often and with what feelings I read the dear words of tenderness and love in your letters! They seem to put life and hope into me. There is a sense in which it may be said that I keep alive on them when I am away from you. There are times when I am *with* you, as I am sure you know, when I grow faint and all life and hope seem to go out of me because you seem to grow a bit distant, to draw off a bit in feeling, and to look at me as I am,—not as the man whom you uncritically love and who loves you, his dear wife and sweet companion, with passionate devotion,—but as a fellow full of unlovable faults and grievous weaknesses whom you are yet bound by some blind compulsion of your heart to love and endure,—and revive only when your heart breaks bounds again and comes running back to me! In just the same way, the intervals between your letters, between their words of love, are for me like periods of suspended animation, and I live again only when I read the sweet words of love once more. My precious darling! You are infinitely sweet and generous and loving. Like a true woman, you let your heart override your judgments! God bless you and keep you! I love you as you would have me love you. You are all the world to me: my pride, my solace, my joy, my link with all things high and pure and noble, —the informing blessing of my career. I would have been nothing noble without you! Love to the darling girlies and to dear Madge.

Your own   Woodrow

ALS (WC, NjP).

From John Van Antwerp MacMurray

Dear Dr. Wilson,   Bangkok, Siam   August 17th, 1908.

It has been on my mind for some time to answer your letter of March 9th. . . . The difficult part of my assignment here has been the feeling of losing touch with friends & interests at home. It is unaccountably harder to write, in proportion to the distance; & I have found myself drifting, in spite of myself, from the familiar associations. I want to get back to Princeton, where so much has happened in the past year that I feel, in my most confident mood, like a fairly well-informed stranger. The items that get printed give so little indication of the spirit behind the bare facts. The paragraph in your letter, about the reform you propose in the social system of the University, gave me a better conception of the real question, than all that the "Alumni Weekly" has published. Admitting the possibility of a fair opposition to your plan, it seems to me that the attitude actually taken by the opposition is not fair; & in its unfairness it gives the final proof of the inadequacy & futility of the present social system. There must be a reform in that; & while, for my part, I should like to see that reform accomplished by the least revolutionary means possible, I feel as you do that no less radical plan is likely to effect the change. And I most devoutly hope that you can succeed in the reform before Princeton has lost its distinctive character.

You have had, I hope, a refreshing & invigorating summer in Scotland, & can now carry on your work with your highest efficiency. That really is the best that one could wish you—the opportunity to do your best work.

Please convey my regards & good wishes to Mrs. Wilson & to Miss Axson & Mr. Axson; & believe me

Yours, most sincerely,   John V. A. MacMurray.

ALS (WP, DLC).

From Magnus Fraser Peterson

Dear Dr. Woodrow Wilson,   Carlisle. Aug. 17. 1908.

I send the copy of the photographic reproduction of Yates' drawing which you were so kind as to accept.[1]

I cannot express to you my appreciation of your great kindness in coming to see me, nor my enjoyment in your visit. Mrs. Peterson wished me to say how sorry she was that she had to go away as she did. It would have been so great a pleasure for her to have spent the whole time of your too brief visit, in your company.

In an age in which so much of the conventional talk of life seems to be a strenuous endeavour to avoid all points of contact, it is a happiness as real as it is rare to meet "spirit with spirit" in such conversation as you always bring with you. The memory of the hours that we have spent together will ever remain with me as a joy and an inspiration.

In case we should not meet again before you leave for America, may I ask you to convey to Mrs. Wilson & the others our warmest remembrances and our sincere hope that some future year will bring a reunion in the dear old Lake country.

Believe me, Yours very faithfully   M. Fraser Peterson

ALS (WP, DLC).
1 This enclosure is missing.

To Louise Whitfield Carnegie

My dear Mrs. Carnegie,   Grasmere, 18 August, 1908

I escorted the Baroness von Suttner as far as Perth, where she took a sleeping carriage, and reached my own destination here, after breaking the journey twice for a night's rest, quite fresh and unfatigued.

I left Skibo with the utmost reluctance and brought away with me altogether delightful and refreshing memories of one of the most enjoyable visits I ever made anywhere. Your hospitality is certainly of a most delicious flavor, and I appreciated so much the opportunity of seeing you and Mr. Carnegie on this side of the water. It is pleasant to think that you, too, return to America, and that I may again have the pleasure of seeing you both next winter.

Please give Mr. Carnegie my warmest regards and thanks for all his kindness, and believe me

Gratefully and Sincerely Yours,   Woodrow Wilson

ALS (A. Carnegie Coll., NN).

Four Letters to Ellen Axson Wilson

My precious darling,   Grasmere, 20 Aug., 1908

It delights me to think that there are only four mail steamers after the one that carries this,—no, only *three*,—before I myself go, instead of a letter, and take my beloved little wife in my arms and tell her, between kisses, what is in my heart about her: *look* at her to see with my own eyes how she has fared and how she is; see the dear girlies,—and the summer's work, about which I have heard so little; and feast on all the sweet talk and 'catching up' that will follow! Ah, how I long for it all! How unbearable it is becoming to be separated from my darling, my mate and comfort! To-day is "Sports Day" here. The little village is as full of people and motors and confusion as Princeton will be in November when the game with Yale is played. I did not go to see the Sports. I know they must be as slow and tedious to watch as the 'track games' at Princeton. I see the crowds as well from my window, and there is no *social* reason why I should go. The people would be strangers to me, and I would be as lonely as possible amidst the impossible Britishers, who so *exaggerate* not seeing you or finding you superfluous. I even went over to Ambleside for lunch, to escape the noise and confusion, and I am writing this just after my return,—and just before it is time to go to the hospitable Simpsons' for tea. There will, of course, be a great jamb [jam] there; I am going only because they are so kind and *want* me to be there. Then, later in the evening, I am going up to take supper with the de Selincourts. Mr. de Selincourt seems to have taken quite a fancy to me and is, with me, really *very* natural and genial and attractive, though *not* talkative and still a little hard to find out, to run from cover. I have still a *very* vague notion of his essential *table of contents*. It requires a life time to know an Englishman thoroughly. I shall never have time enough on this side the water to attain the slow intimacy. The women seem to me a *little* bit less difficult to get in touch with. I have just met one who is truly delightful, and whom it distresses me you cannot know. I found her sitting on the Yates' tiny piazza when I got back from Scotland. Mr. Yates had been away, while I was at Skibo, to fetch her from her home near Manchester. She is a beautiful woman of (I should say) about sixty-five, *truly* beautiful, without any allowance made for age, with singular vivacity of eye and mouth of exquisite lines, at once firm and tender, showing a spirit which can neither be broken nor hardened; and with a *mind*, withal, a delightful mind, which came out to meet mine with charming grace and frankness. We had a *good* time together, and Mr. Yates could hardly drag me away for another 'sitting' upstairs under his skylight. Mrs. Kirkman—for such was the lady's name—is the wife of a Manchester barrister and is an old friend of the Yates.[1] I hope she will stay a long time! The portrait, by the way, is finished. It is to be sent at once to London to be photographed by some expert who does reproductions for the art magazines,— for our old friend *The Studio*, for example.[2] Mr. [Herbert] Bell, the Ambleside photographer, no longer satisfies the exacting

[1] Christina Kirkman. Her husband was probably William Wright Kirkman, solicitor, of Taylor, Kirkman and Co., Manchester.

[2] An article on Yates, with seven reproductions of his portraits and landscapes, appeared in *The* (London) *Studio*, XLV (1909), 202-209. However, the reproductions did not include one of the drawing of Wilson.

Yates,—who demands the best whenever he can get it,—and quite rightly, too. I *hope* it will please you, my sweetheart. I[t] does me very much. It is really a remarkably fine piece of work, —far superior to the other drawing and to the painting. For one thing, it is done in as full colour as if it were done in oils,— with all my summer's tan and glow on my face, and is the picture of a very healthy specimen,—a good record of what wheeling and the dear Lakes do for me. The colour, indeed, needs the toning down of the glass which is to go over it. It has none of the pained look of the other drawing and none of the drawn and peaked look of the painting. I told both Mr. and Mrs. Yates how grateful you had been for their letters and how much you had enjoyed them. I hope you have written to them in reply. I shall have a hard time making up reasons and excuses if you have not!

That break means tea at the Simpsons'. I write so slowly that many events of the day are apt to occur between the beginning and the end of a letter! It was very pleasant, though very English. I was one of the few persons there who were not of the neighbourhood circle, and was looked at with a curiosity which, so far as appeared, was unmixed with interest. But Mrs. Simpson is an ideal hostess; noticed whenever I was out of action; and introduced me to a number of persons who, when once launched, were easy enough to navigate. There is, I must say, a singular absence of grace and beauty among the women at such gatherings. The Simpsons keep open house on Rushbearing and Sports and all similar days, and one may take it for granted, I dare say, that he sees a picked set of samples, on such as [an] afternoon as this, on their lawn. If so, there are very few pretty women in these counties. The crowds have swarmed under my window all day, and I have scanned them almost in vain for women worth looking at! The weather has been as fair as possible. Indeed all summer it has been bright and perfect for out-of-door pleasures,—except for the dust,—which to-day is almost intolerable on the roads. I think there have been less than four days of rain since I got here five weeks ago. It was the same in Scotland,—sunshine and fine airs all the season. The Spring was uncommonly wet here, as it was with us, and all the raining was over before I landed. The barns are simply packed with hay and the farmers for once almost content and without grievance. Perhaps the dryest season in many years may account for the dearth of pretty women! By the way, one of the best looking women I have seen to-day was [Annie] "O'Conner," our whilom cook at Loughrigg Cottage. I caught sight of her standing in a door by the roadside in Ambleside,—at this end of the village, just as you enter it,—and she recognized me at the same moment. I was on a char-a-banc. She waved her hand to me quite beamingly and seemed delighted to see me again, and I must say she looked very handsome indeed. Was she not about to be married when we left, two years ago?

I suppose by this time our dear Jessie is in Maryland on her mission.[3] I am glad she has been made "fit" for her labours by such a season of out-door sports and pleasures, and hope that she will really enjoy, without strain, what she has to do. I have quite forgotten the dates of her engagement. Will she be back at home when I get there? I shall be sorely disappointed if she is not. I think I have told you my plans in detail. I shall remain here until the second of September. On that day (which is a Wednesday) I shall go to Glasgow, reaching there before evening. I have to go ahead of sailing time in order to get my bicycle crated and on board by Friday afternoon, before the *Caledonia* drops down the river, where we join her, by train to Grenock, the next morning. I have two days less than two more weeks here, therefore. I wonder, my darling, if it is possible if you want me and home as much as I want you, who *are* home for me? It seems incredible you should. My heart fairly aches with its lack of you! It has been *so* long away from you! Your letters are sweet, *very* sweet. I close every one of them with a heart and mind full of joy and thankfulness because of you. You are *so* dear and lovely, and your letters are so redolent of your adorable self. But they are not you! I cannot talk to them: I cannot *exchange* thoughts with them. To kiss them is a cold business! One hour of you would be better than all of them put together, dear as they are, and satisfactory! I fancy it's different with my letters. I dare say they are much more satisfactory than I am. I am a rather fine fellow in my letters and can sometimes manage to show myself in words as I really am; while in action I am very trying, even when I *think* I am true to love in everything I do. Thank God, my darling generally understands and makes allowances and is generous beyond all reason! I am coming back to you, my Eileen, singularly well, and I hope that, being more normal, I shall be less trying. You *darling*! Your love is very wonderful and very precious. You are the most perfect lover that ever lived! It is delightful to sit here at my window, with a perfect hurly-burly below in the road and hustling crowds seeking vehicles in which to get away, and talk with you,—feel myself *with* you and with you alone. The

[3] The object of her "mission" is unknown to the Editors.

bustle and noise do not distract me in the least. I have a delicious sense of privacy and of being alone with the dear lady I love in a place apart which *no* one can invade. Bless you, my beloved one, and keep you safe and well! My deep love to the dear girlies and to Madge. I am always and altogether

Your own   Woodrow.

My precious darling,   Grasmere, 23 August, '08

I have just come from church and must have a little chat with you before I go to the Yates for the afternoon. There is very little to tell about since my last letter. On Friday I spent the day with the Marburgs, whom I like extremely, and met at lunch there Dr. and Mrs. Osler,[1] who were touring in a motor car and were at the Low Wood Inn nearby for a short stay. They were very interesting and attractive. Of course I had long known and often enjoyed Dr. Osler, but Mrs. Osler I had never met before,—an unusually handsome woman with a great deal of gracious individuality. Dr. Osler is full of fun and was the life of the occasion. After lunch Mr. Marburg took me over to Applethwaite, in Troutbeck valley, too [to] see the sheep-dog trials. It was most interesting. We stood on one breezy hill and watched the dogs and sheep on an opposite hill which sloped towards us. It was one of the most glorious days I have ever seen even in this wonderland of sweet hills and the magic of sun and shadow. The clouds in this sky certainly have a dramatic instinct, and on Friday afternoon, after a night and forenoon of rain, they played their parts with really thrilling effect. The scene before us was Troutbeck valley. We were on its southern slopes, where we could look up into the pile of mountains at the top of its wonderful amphitheatre, by Kirkstone, and across to the exquisite slopes where Troutbeck village lies. I could hardly take my eyes from the scene about me to watch the dog trials. Its beauty took my breath and every moment some new movement of light across the slopes or on the distant tops would give it a new aspect of majesty or of soft, winning beauty. I quite forgot that I was sitting close by a singularly pretty and charming young woman, the Marburgs' French governess, a quite enchanting young person! Then, after the trials, we went to tea at a house nearby from whose lawns the whole

[1] William Osler and Grace Revere Gross Osler. Osler was at this time Regius Professor of Medicine at Oxford University. He had been Professor of the Principles and Practice of Medicine at The Johns Hopkins University, 1889-1905.

wonder of the day was seen at its best:—in one direction the whole poetry and grace of Troutbeck, and, in the other the distant majesty of the Langdales,—the lights so softened and disposed that each distance had its own appropriate value and its own far-away mystery,—the house itself one of the most beautiful in its broad and quiet lines that I have ever seen, and set in delicious gardens made perfectly to compose with the scene about them and full of every lovable flower and graceful plant. It was an afternoon I shall long remember. Even the people at the tea did not mar it! I stopped for dinner with the Marburgs, and he brought me home, at half-past nine, in his comfortable motor-car. I have really delightful conversations with Marburg, —conversations which rouse and exercise my mind without fatiguing it.

Yesterday I went early in the forenoon to the Yates, and stayed until four in the afternoon, again enjoying Mrs. Kirkman, of whom I spoke in my last letter. She leaves, I am sorry to say, to-morrow. The new drawing had not yet been sent to the photographer's and the dear artist comparing me with it (on the wall behind me) as we sat at lunch, discovered something else he wished to do to it: so, after the meal, we went upstairs and did it. Then he signed it, and it *is* finished! At four I left there to make a call on Miss Arnold, whom I had not called on since Mary Yates and I lunched with her. The call was a *very* pleasant and interesting one, as usual, *and*, as usual, the talk was very much interfered with by tea, and *all* sorts of things to hand about! It seems that the *Times* of last Wednesday had a long article on American colleges, from an American correspondent (at least a correspondent in America), with editorial comment; and that the writer has a good deal to say about my arrested plans.[2] It is not critical, but expository; but the implications are clearly against fraternities and clubs and in favour of reforms which will do what the quadrangles would. I will, of course, bring the paper home with me for you to read.

In the evening I went to hear a "Suffragette" speak—to a very unmannerly crowd,—in front of the Red Lion,—in what Grasmere calls "Red Lion Square." She was a very clever, well-informed young woman from Australia (where she *has* a vote) and put the men down who interrupted her very effectually, if without feminine delicacy. She skipped all the difficult parts of the argument—consciously or unconsciously, I could not

[2] "A Year Amongst Americans. X. Colleges and Democracy. (From An Occasional Correspondent.)," London *Times*, Aug. 19, 1908. An editorial entitled "American Colleges," commenting upon the article, appeared in the same issue.

tell which—and made very effective use of the parts which did not require proof,—and was, altogether, an excellent speaker, able to meet, I should say, any audience. The scene was very amusing, though it was an exhibition of the brutal bad manners of an English crowd, and it was very annoying to any one who wished to hear what the woman had to say to have a constant tooting of horns and jeering and ringing of dinner bells going on in the outskirts of the crowd. The woman kept her temper and got in many a good thrust at the disturbers and interrupters.

24 August, 1908

After writing yesterday I went over to Rydal, walking by the 'radical reform' road (as was suitable after attending a Suffragette meeting the night before), and spent the afternoon and evening, until nearly nine, with the Yates. This time Yates was doing a drawing of Mrs. Kirkman, the fascinating old lady, and I was set to my old duty of reading poetry aloud while he drew. I read from a book of sonnets, from Lucas's "Open Road" collection,[3] and, finally, when we had gone down-stairs and Yates was preparing supper, from Sill.[4] Mrs. Kirkman is keenly appreciative of all good things in that kind and it was the same *sort* of pleasure to read to her that it is to read to you. I can read much better to her than I can to Mrs. Yates, whose mind, for all her loveliness, has the quite hopeless New England limitations.[5] She understands poetry with a singular literalness and a deep curiosity about all immaterial points,—points, I mean, immaterial to the essential spiritual meaning and verbal felicity of the poem. It is the inevitable prying *smartness* of that seed-dry mind which the mental soil and climate of New England has produced. She almost prefers a Yankee joke to a vision of insight,—partly because she understands the one and does not quite fathom the other. But I dislike even to *seem* to criticise the dear lady, she is *so* sweet and affectionate to me. I cannot help being sorry that Mrs. Kirkman left this morning,—and she must have left in the pouring rain, for our good weather is, I fear, breaking up. That here much regarded prophet, "the glass," is not speaking hopefully. But, for the present, we are having what is better than *whole* good days, namely, half good days, glorious afternoons following upon rainy mornings. Even this afternoon will, I think,

---

[3] Edward Verrall Lucas, *The Open Road. A Little Book for Wayfarers* (London, 1899). A "new and enlarged edition" appeared in 1905.
[4] Edward Rowland Sill (1841-87), American poet and essayist. There are four volumes of his collected poetry and prose in the Wilson Library, DLC.
[5] Mrs. Yates was born in New Haven, Conn., in 1855.

be fine, though it is, while I write, rather consistently "showery," and, if it is fine, Mrs. Simpson and I are going to walk out to a Mrs. Marshall's, beyond Skelwith Bridge, to tea. Mrs. Marshall is a bright old lady who seemed to take quite a fancy to me at the tea at Mrs. Simpson's after the Sports. It was then that she bade Mrs. Simpson bring me out to her on Monday. I have no objection. I shall enjoy the walk with Mrs. Simpson and Mrs. Marshall is very much alive and very interesting to talk to.[6]

I am so much pleased & interested, my loved one, to learn from Margaret's letter, received this morning, that you now have a *studio*. Why, madam, may I ask, did I not get this interesting news from *you*? I would like, for my happiness, to know *every*thing that you do or think or feel,—and I am *so* glad that you now have room and the necessary conveniences for your work. How much there will be to talk over when I get home, and *how* delightful it will be to talk it over! And to see your sketches and go over with you the work and the lessons of the summer! Ah, how impatient I am to get at it,—with my darling *close* by my side, her dear voice in my ear! The nearer the sweet time comes the more impatient I grow! Only about three weeks from to-day before my steamer should be at her pier in New York! My love, my love! How passionately I long for you, how deeply I need you, how inexpressibly sweet it will be to be beside you again *at home*. I have forgotten when you said you meant to be in Princeton again, but I vaguely remember that you were to be there before me. I am glad that the Lyme exhibition comes the *first* week in September: I dare say you will go home immediately after that. I hope with all my heart that all things will continue to go happily with you to the very end. Margaret speaks of herself in her letter as "decidedly under the weather." I hope that was only a passing thing. Thank my blessed girlies for their sweet letters: a lovely one came from Nell, too, this morning, just as sweet as it could be, and, with dear Margaret's and yours, made me feel very rich and as content as I can be away from you all. I love you, my pet, my precious Eileen, with an intense and eager love. You are all the world to me. God bless you and keep you! Love to the sweet girlies and to dear Madge. Your own Woodrow

[6] The Editors have been unable further to identify her.

My precious Love, Grasmere, 27 Aug., 1908

My next, and last, letter I shall address to Princeton, for fear it should reach Lyme after you had left for home. Ah, how

sweet the very words are to me,—*my last letter* and *home*! The
weather here has become quite autumnal: all last night the
wind and rain beat upon my window with a voice like that of
late November. I could almost fancy myself at sea and on the
homeward voyage. The rains have kept me within doors the
last few days and I have done nothing except call on one of
Mr. Yates' friends, a Mr. Badley,[1] got once to the Yates themselves, and begin a walk from which I had to retreat on a char-a-
banc in the rain over Red Bank. Yesterday afternoon Yates
looked in on me, on his way to a reception at Mr. Roby's in
the pouring rain. It was the first time he had seen me in my
tiny room here at the Rothay. He was so much struck and amused
by my quaint little canopied bed that he made the enclosed sketch
for you.[2] The figure is supposed to be me, sitting on my trunk,
talking to him, and the scratches on the door by the bed are
meant to represent a coat hanging there. A more detailed sketch
of me would hardly have been proper. I was half undressed,
about to crawl into bed for a rainy-day snooze, which I had the
luxury of enjoying for two hours and more after he left, getting
up only in time to dress for a half-past seven dinner. After dinner I read [Du Maurier's] "Peter Ibbetson," borrowed of Mary
Yates, till bed-time (it's queer and dreary enough for a howling,
inclement night) and then went to sleep again as promptly as if
I had not slept a wink in the afternoon. I've had a sweet treat
this week in letters from *all* my dear ones at Lyme and feel *very*
near you all. You are *all so* sweet and generous to me, your letters a perfect tonic and delight. Kiss the precious girlies for
their dear love letters. I will not try, with my reluctant and difficult hand, to write to them again. The *ability* to write letters to
those I love intensely begins to leave me these last days before
sailing. My mind refuses any longer to satisfy itself in that way.
I can only send messages of deepest love and long, long, long
for the home-going! Your own letters, my my [*sic*] incomparable
darling, are too sweet and precious for words! The exquisite
little love passages in them thrill me with what is, for me, life
itself. I think it is sweeter and more life-giving to be loved when
one does not deserve it and feels himself a kind of trial to his
lover, than it would be to enjoy love that one might feel he had
earned; but I know very well that that is no excuse for continuing
to be unworthy of it. I cannot tell you, my lovely Eileen,—because
there do not seem to be any words which prose can employ for
the purpose,—how deeply, intensely I reverence and admire and
adore you, or what a passionate delight, as of my whole nature,
it stirs in me to know that I have your love and that you have

given your exquisite life of purity and devotion and every high womanly thing to me. The whole excellence and beauty of my life centres in you. It often seems to me that there is *nothing* fine or noble in me apart from you. Everything that is best in me has gone into my love, my deep, true, passionate love, for you. I cannot say it often or strongly enough. I wish it might be written on my tombstone when I am buried! I know it sometimes seems to you sentimental talk, but to me it is the one indisputable reality of my life. And, as the sweet days approach again when I shall see you, shall hold you close in my arms, and *know* that you are mine, it seems to me as if my love for you was all that I am conscious of. I can think of nothing else for long at a time, can desire nothing else,—grow uneasy and impatient, and would start to-morrow if I could! My darling, my darling! God keep you and recompense you for all you have been to me and to all who love you!

I have no plans for the few days that remain of my stay here: they will, I fear, be, of necessity, filled chiefly with calls, saying good-bye to the kind people who have made the summer so pleasant for me; but the very calling will involve a good deal of walking through this blessed countryside and will, on that account, if no other, have its compensations and joys. How I do love this place, and all its healing grace to me! I am quite well, of course, and hope that I shall come back to you in a condition which will seem to you to render me 'fit' for anything. Unbounded love to all, and for you the very heart of

Your own   Woodrow

Thank you, with all my heart, for the details about your work. My dear, dear pet! I understand.

[1] John Haden Badley, founder and headmaster of the Bedales School in Petersfield, 1893-1935. Badley became well known as a writer on and practitioner of progressive education, and his school was the first permanently successful co-educational boarding school in England. See W. A. C. Stewart and W. P. McCann, *The Educational Innovators* (2 vols., London and New York, 1968), II, 13-17, 270-281, and *passim*.
[2] This enclosure is missing.

My darling,   Grasmere, 30 Aug., '08

This will go by Wednesday's post, and by Saturday's I will go myself! Ah, how happy I shall be to take the place of my letters and go to you. How I have missed and needed you all summer! How constantly, day by day, I have had to fight sadness because I did not have you as my close companion. God bless you for your sweet letters and the cheer and comfort they have brought me. You are adorable,—the perfect wife and lover, and my heart is sick with the separation. I could not endure it much longer. I don't care what happens to me if only you love me, if only I can be with you as your lover and husband. God grant I shall find you well and happy! The weather has continued "showery," *very* showery, but I have gone about, notwithstanding, as I used to, two years ago, and have taken no harm from the wettings I have got. Whom should I see on a coach under my window on Friday but Miss Bella Owen and Mrs. Legh Reid.[1] They were here only the ten minutes of the coach's stop and hastened to see the graves in the churchyard and look within the church itself, as all passers through do, but I was with them while they did that, and am afraid they saw and took in the less because of their interest in meeting me. Miss Bella, however, had been here once before, for a week's stay. It was very delightful to get this glimpse of home folks. It refreshed and excited me. I have made several interesting new acquaintances: e.g., a Mr. Badley, a school-master, whom Yates insisted I should know, and who proved worth knowing,—a genuine, tonic sort of man, with an out-of-doors mind, I mean a mind that seemed conscious of the world as a whole and not narrowed to the view of books, as well as a mind in love with out-of-doors and fresh with stimulating exercise; and a Rev. Mr. Jones,[2] a vital young rector to whom the Simpsons introduced me, the son of a delightful old lady[3] who lives next to Scale How, Miss Mason's school, and is one of the personages of Ambleside. Two of the Simpsons, he, and I took a walk, between showers, yesterday afternoon, to see a characteristic old farmhouse, the oldest about here, and to see a cottage or two that are for sale. There is a *very* attractive little house, well built and delightfully situated, on the former site of Michael's house (of the poem)[4] and called "Michael's Fold" (the actual fold is in the fells just above it) which can be had for £1000,—a large kitchen and two rooms, suitable for dining and sitting room, below stairs, and above four bed rooms, a bathroom and a little storeroom on the second floor and three good servants' rooms on the third, besides a little storeroom downstairs and a supplementary kitchen or laundry. The rooms downstairs are about the size of the dining room at Loughrigg Cottage and the bedrooms average about the same. The views in three directions, down upon Grasmere village and lake, across into Easedale, and northward through Dunmail Raise, are charming, especially from the upper windows. There is a good out-house or two, a little paddock, and a sweet bit of garden.

Since beginning this letter,—indeed, in the middle of one of the sentences,—Lovett came in upon me, and has been with me most of the day. He had telegraphed to know whether he could see me for another talk. He travelled most of the night up from London, reached Windermere a little before five this morning, and was driven over in a hired rig. We walked over Loughrigg terrace and around under Loughrigg to Ambleside, took lunch there, and walked back by the road in time (four o'clock) for him to take his rig again for Windermere, which he was to leave at 5.45 for Liverpool. From there they are going, to-morrow, to Dublin, and from Ireland to Norway. We saw the valley at its loveliest,—at least *I* did. I am not sure he took anything in very consciously, so absorbed was he in the questions he had come to discuss. I drove with him as far as Rydal on his way back to Windermere, and spent a couple of hours with the Yates before coming back to dinner and to you, my precious darling. It has been an interesting day and I am very little fatigued, notwithstanding strenuous talking and ten miles of walking. The simple fact is, I am strong and fit and know you will be satisfied with the way I look. I *hope* my darling has not overdone this summer, standing in the sun and keeping stretched to her work all the while. It would make me very sad to find her unrefreshed and a bit worn out by her 'vacation'! Two dear letters came this morning, posted the twenty-first, a lovely one from my darling Nell and a dear, dear one from you, —so that I am content,—and happy beyond all words that *I am going home*. With love unspeakable

Your own Woodrow.

ALS (WC, NjP).
    [1] Isabella Sheldon Owen, of 10 Mercer Street, Princeton; and Mrs. Reid, the wife of Legh Wilbur Reid, Professor of Mathematics at Haverford College.
    [2] The Reverend Herbert Gresford Jones, Vicar of St. John's, Keswick, 1904-1906; at this time Vicar of Bradford.
    [3] Margaret Cropper (Mrs. William) Jones.
    [4] William Wordsworth, "Michael. A Pastoral Poem."

Frederic Yates to Ellen Axson Wilson

Dear Mrs. Wilson,   Rydal, Ambleside.   2nd Sept. 1908.

I am sending you by the Doctor this morning a tube of orange madder. I will be glad when you receive the portrait that you will write and tell me what your family think of it—pros and cons.

He goes away today and there will be a mighty vacuum in Rydal—he has been a part of our summer—that is, that when next summer comes we shall tag on to it the memory of this one. He was like a boy last night in his light heartedness. You wouldn't think he ever had a care—it has done him good to come over—and he returns with a new grip of things. He came with his heart rather heavy—told us at once—it seemed to do him good to unburden it to us. I think there is no pain like the disloyalty of a man that one has trusted through a life time.[1] Well, he has gone back home with renewed vigour and love of a whole neighborhood. We finished up last night at the Heards,[2]—and Peterson was there—the whole evening having that kind of sensation when we four dined at the Petersons the last night you were together in Rydal. It left quite a bloom on things—and that is just what one feels about last night—Addio!

Fred Yates.

ALS (WP, DLC).
[1] He was undoubtedly referring to John Grier Hibben.
[2] The Reverend Dr. William Augustus Heard and Elizabeth Burt Heard. He was Headmaster of Fettes College, Edinburgh, a position which he had held since 1890.

To Frederic Yates

S.S. Caledonia [Greenock, Scotland],

My dear Yates,   5 Sept., 1908.

Your note reached the hotel too late for me to answer it there. My chief argument was briefly this, that women, whether by nature or circumstances, draw their conclusions about public affairs from logical reason, whereas safe and wise conclusions in such affairs can be drawn only from *experience*,—experience of the world,—such as women have not had and cannot have unless drawn entirely into the open and safe-guarded in no way. Married women could never *get* the necessary experience unless the present constitution of the family and the present division of duties as between husband and wife is to be absolutely altered.

It is a pleasure to have a chance to send you all another message of deep affection. You have made the summer very happy for me, and my love for you all is greatly enhanced.

I am quite well, and the ship is off.

Gratefully and affectionately Yours,   Woodrow Wilson

ALS (F. Yates Coll., NjP).

Notes for an After-Dinner Speech

Entertainment 11 Sept., 1908

S.S. Caledonia

Presiding)

Pleasure in acting as *impresario* in so amiable a function,—when fellow passengers put themselves at one another's disposal for entertainment. A Scots-Irishman

Proceedings of the previous meeting

Presiding officer's function only langoppe [lagniappe]

The good feeling between England and America

   Same political mission (even Am. Rev.)

   Same language (?)

   Intercourse ("Can't hate a man I know")

      The Smoking Room a clearing house.

         My stories exhausted there

   American danger—isolation

The programme

WWhw MS (WP, DLC).

From Melancthon Williams Jacobus

Hartford, Conn.,

My dear President Wilson: September 11th, 1908.

. . . I have heard nothing further either from Mr. Thompson or any one else concerning the possible candidacy of Mr. Thomas Jones for the Cleveland vacancy on the Board, but I have in mind to write both Mr. David Jones and Mr. Stephen Palmer in whose interest in the matter and best judgment I think I have the utmost confidence.

I wish to plan to be in Princeton for some days previous to the next meeting of the Board. If there is anything you feel as worth while suggesting in the situation either by letter now or personally then, I shall be only too glad to do all I can to secure a successful issue.

   With kind regards,

      Yours very sincerely,   Melancthon W. Jacobus

TLS (WP, DLC).

To Harry Augustus Garfield

My dear Garfield: Princeton, N. J. September 14th, 1908.

I got back from my vacation only yesterday, and hasten to take up your kind letter of August 28th.[1]

Mrs. Wilson and I are really very much distressed about the complication which has arisen because of Mrs. Hun's[2] invitation to us to stay with her. Of course, we would rather stay with you and it really would be a great disappointment to me if we cannot. I know how little it will be possible to see of you on such busy days in any case, but, being in the house with you, I might see a little more than I would otherwise have the opportunity to see. I do not know how to handle the matter. I should say that the merest intimation on your part to Mrs. Hun that there were official reasons why it was desirable that I should be your guest during the celebration would settle the matter without any real feeling on her part. I feel that she would misunderstand it and be very much hurt if the suggestion came from either Mrs. Wilson or me, and if you feel that even such an intimation on your part would be a mistake of taste, I really see nothing for it but for us to go to Mrs. Hun's.

Of course, I do not for a moment mean that it would not be delightful to stay with Mrs. Hun, but I am sure I need not explain that side of the matter to you. It is merely my very warm affection for you which makes me feel that it would be really distressing to be in Williamstown and not be with you.

I hope that you have had some real vacation and that you are approaching the beginning of your new work refreshed and vigorous. I have thought of you a great many times this summer and shall always link my thoughts with yours in whatever you do.

With warm affection,

Faithfully yours, Woodrow Wilson

TLS (H. A. Garfield Papers, DLC).

[1] It is missing.

[2] Caroline Gale (Mrs. Edward Reynolds) Hun, the widowed mother of John Gale Hun, Preceptor in Mathematics at Princeton. Mrs. Hun maintained a residence at 23 South St., Williamstown, Mass.

From Benjamin Franklin Trueblood[1]

Dear Sir: Boston, Sept. 19, 1908.

We have received your contribution of one dollar to make you a member for one year of the American Peace Society.

It gives us great pleasure to have the privilege of enrolling you on our list of members, and to know that we have your sympathy and active support in the work which the Society is doing in trying to educate public opinion in right ideas as to peace and war, and in promoting friendship and unity among the nations and the settlement of all international controversies by pacific means.

You will receive regularly hereafter the "Advocate of Peace," the monthly organ of the Society.

With much appreciation of your interest and co-operation,
Yours very sincerely,   Benjamin F. Trueblood

TLS (WP, DLC). Enc.: membership card in the American Peace Society dated Sept. 19, 1908.
¹ General Secretary of the American Peace Society since 1892.

To Charles Scribner

Princeton, N. J.
My dear Mr. Scribner: September 22nd, 1908.

It is with genuine regret that I find that October 16th is already promised. It is on that day that Haverford College celebrates the Seventy-fifth Anniversary of its foundation, and I promised as long ago as last spring to be present throughout the celebration and to deliver one of the addresses.

It would be very pleasant indeed to speak before the Friday Evening Club of Morristown and still more delightful to be your guest. I am indeed sorry that it cannot be. My calendar for October is already fuller than I know how to justify, in view of my duties at home.

I sincerely hope that you had a refreshing vacation in the summer.

Cordially and faithfully yours,   Woodrow Wilson

TLS (Charles Scribner's Sons Archives, NjP).

From Walter Hudson Watkins

Dear Sir: Chattanooga, Tenn.   Sept. 23, 1908.

Since writing you some few weeks ago while you were abroad, asking whether or not it would be convenient for you to be in Nashville on Friday and Saturday, October 30th and 31st, I have had no letter from you and am awaiting a reply before I make up my announcement cards to be sent to various Southern Alumni, seeking to get a large attendance at our fourth annual meeting. I would be very much pleased if you would write me at your earliest convenience, advising me that it will be suitable for you to be with us in Nashville on the above dates. In conformity with your request heretofore made, we have put the meeting at the end of the week in order that you might hold your Tuesday lectures. You could leave Princeton some time Wednesday afternoon and easily reach Nashville by Friday morning. We are counting on you to be with us, and do not feel that our meeting would be in any wise a success if you should fail us, so I trust that I will hear from you in the next few days, stating definitely that you can be with us on the desired dates.

With warmest regards from the writer and all of my family, I am

Yours most sincerely,   Walter H. Watkins

TLS (WP, DLC).

A News Report

[Sept. 25, 1908]

OPENING EXERCISES

The one hundred and sixty-second college year was formally opened in Marquand Chapel yesterday afternoon by the usual exercises. The procession of the Trustees and the University Faculty which formed in Nassau Hall, entered the chapel shortly after three o'clock.

The exercises were opened by President Wilson with a short prayer, which was followed by another brief prayer by Dr. DeWitt of the Seminary.

President Wilson had a cordial welcome for all, both old and new members of the University, but strove to impress on the latter especially, that the real spirit of the University is the spirit of learning. He emphasized the point that school is a place of routine work and tasks, while college is a place of subjects—a school of men.

A University, he declared, must exist for University purposes. University life, minus intellectual endeavor would be without flavor.

He closed by saying that although Princeton was not an ancient University, yet it was old enough to be connected with the whole national existence and traditions of America, by means of the men it had produced whose stamp on the nation's life will be a guarantee of the honest purpose of Princeton and its governing body.[1]

The exercises were then closed with a benediction by President Wilson.

Printed in the *Daily Princetonian*, Sept. 25, 1908; one editorial heading omitted.
[1] There is a WWhw outline of these remarks, dated Sept. 23, 1908, in WP, DLC.

To Frederic Yates

My dear Yates: Princeton, N. J.   September 25th, 1908.

I feel like a dog, not having written to you before, but I think that even you can have no conception of how constantly and in what a multitude things grip me after I get back to this home of my business.

I got home perfectly well, after a comfortable voyage with sufficiently interesting fellow-passengers, and found the dear little company who had summered at Lyme just as well and happy as possible. They had come home several days ahead of me, so that the house was all beautiful and in order and I could fall right into the old home life again without any break. They have all plied me with questions about Mrs. Yates and you and Mary, and have spoken again and again the love for you for you [*sic*] all which I am sure they would wish me to convey. I am almost alone in the house today, since this is the season of autumn shopping and the ladies are constantly either in New York or Philadelphia.

They are all perfectly delighted with the drawing. They think it wholly admirable, and their gratitude is as great as their delight. We have not yet had an opportunity to have the picture framed, but you may be sure it got here in perfect order because I carried it in my own hand from Grassmere to Princeton and guarded it at every turn.

It is delightful to hear of your visit to Ullswater and of the pleasure and refreshment it gave you. I am so glad that you should have had this outing and this contact with delightful people.

Your letter of the fifteenth[1] came this morning after Ellen had started away for Philadelphia, but I know that she will wish me to say that she joins me in sending you all a heart full of love. The girls also send their most loving greetings.

Always faithfully and affectionately yours,
Woodrow Wilson

TLS (F. Yates Coll., NjP).
[1] F. Yates to WW, Sept. 15, 1908, ALS (WP, DLC).

To Melancthon Williams Jacobus

[Princeton, N. J.]

My dear Dr. Jacobus: September 25th, 1908.

I am back in harness again and was very much pleased indeed to get your letter of September 11th. I have been fortunate enough to have an opportunity to talk, within the last two or three days, with both Cyrus McCormick, who came East to put his son[1] in college, and Henry B. Thompson, and I spoke to both of them about Mr. Thomas Jones. Mr. McCormick was, I think, the first to suggest that selection, and he feels that the only difficulty about it is the possible feeling of Mr. David Jones. He promised to do his best to find out for me through an intimate friend of the Jones's just how the matter would strike them, so that we could go forward without any fear of hurting our loyal friend's feelings. I also spoke to Mr. Thompson about it, who is, as you know, most anxious to have that choice made and who seemed to feel quite confident that Mr. Thomas Jones could easily be elected.

I am delighted to hear that you are expecting to be here a few days before the meeting of the Board. I do not now know of any business which would make it necessary to call an extra meeting of the Curriculum Committee, so that we shall be free to talk about what we please. I start for Denver tomorrow, to address the National Bankers Association, and immediately upon my return from Denver I shall have to run up to Williamstown to attend Garfield's inauguration, but I hope to be back in Princeton by the ninth of October.

I find that my vacation has refreshed me very much, and I sincerely hope that Mrs. Jacobus and you and the children have come through the summer with rest and satisfaction, notwithstanding the moving into a new house. I am delighted to hear that you are at last in possession.

Always cordially and faithfully yours,

[Woodrow Wilson]

CCL (RSB Coll., DLC).
[1] Cyrus McCormick, Princeton 1912.

To Mary Allen Hulbert Peck

My dear Mrs. Peck,   Denver, Colo., 30 Sept. 1908

I was so rushed by a multitude of duties before leaving home that I was grossly negligent of my duty, and my privilege, to write to you about the time of our arrival on the fifth.[1] Please accept my very sincere apologies. I trust this will reach you in time.

We are expecting to leave New York on the afternoon of the fifth, by the "Pittsfield Express," at 3.26. I have no schedule by me here, but trust that you will need to know only the leaving time.

Mrs. Wilson and I are looking forward with the greatest pleasure to our visit, and I trust that it will not be inconvenient to you if we come back to you, from Williamstown, on the eighth, when I am to address the Young Man's League.[2]

With warmest regard and appreciation,

Cordially Yours,   Woodrow Wilson

ALS (WP, DLC).
[1] The Wilsons were planning to visit Mrs. Peck at her home in Pittsfield, Mass.
[2] A news report of Wilson's address to the Men's League of the First Congregational Church of Pittsfield is printed at Oct. 9, 1908.

An Address in Denver to the American Bankers' Association

[[Sept. 30, 1908]]

THE BANKER AND THE NATION

Mr. President and Gentlemen of the American Bankers' Association:

I would not properly represent my feeling upon this occasion if I were not first to express my very deep appreciation of the courtesy and of the honor of the invitation to address this Association. I hope I may take it for granted that there will in listening to me be a certain element of refreshment for you, for I am not a banker, and I am, in fact, in that attitude of impartiality with regard to banks which must belong to a man living upon a salary. I was once asked to address the New York State Bankers' Association on the subject of the "Elasticity of the Currency,"[1] and I said that I took it for granted that I was summoned as an impartial witness, because experimentally I knew nothing of the elasticity of the currency. (Laughter.)

I want to assure you at the outset, gentlemen, that I am not here with the least idea that I can instruct you with regard to anything concerning banking. I am here with the hope that we may by conference together a little better understand the relationship that we sustain to the country as a whole. I want, in brief, to remind the bankers, as I would remind myself, of our social

[1] See the news report printed at Dec. 19, 1902, Vol. 14.

and political functions, no matter what business we are engaged in.

It therefore becomes a necessary introduction to what I want to say to you to remind you of the extraordinary awakening which has characterized recent years in this country with regard to the moral obligations involved in business. There has, as I think you will agree with me, been a very extraordinary awakening of the public conscience, and of the private conscience as well. I believe a great many business men have themselves, individually, become conscious of the fact that they have pushed legitimate undertakings to illegitimate lengths, and that, thinking too much of their rivals and too little of their consciences, they have done things which they now regret. And this reawakening and rejuvenescence of our consciences is one of the most hopeful signs of the times. (Applause.)

Now, I know that a great deal of exaggeration has been indulged in with regard to the illegitimate methods of business, but I believe every one of us who examines his conscience will not care to dwell too much upon those exaggerations; because we are all aware that in our eagerness to build up our material power in this country we have forgotten some very sacred old-fashioned considerations.

You know that modern business is so complicated that the individual is in a large degree lost in the organization of it, and that, therefore, because we cannot always ourselves find out individual responsibilities, we are the more inclined to relieve ourselves from an examination of the question, what our consciences usually demand that we should do. We have taken refuge, we have taken covert, in the organization to which we belong and have excused ourselves from asking old-fashioned questions as to right and wrong.

That this is a general condition does not mean that there has been a general demoralization, for the significant circumstance of our time is that we have only to bring the moral issues forward for an instant to get universal recognition of them and response to them, not only on the part of those who fail to agree, but also on the part of those whose achievements are affected by the impeachment. I believe that the moral conscience of this country is still sound and is still to be depended upon. (Applause.) The trouble with us is not that we have been wilfully wrong, but that we have been sleeping and are now awake. So, it seems to me that we can discuss matters of this sort without incriminating either each other or ourselves, and that it is very desirable to see what has happened.

It is very dangerous to uncover the anatomy of the social structure, because the moment you insert the dissecting knife you begin to look upon the living thing, not as a body, but as a cadaver; and you forget that these processes of dissection stop the wholesome courses of the blood. But the one thing that we cannot excuse ourselves from is facing and handling the facts; and the fact is that the dissecting knife has been inserted, that the cadaver is upon the table; and that we might as well stop to understand its anatomy. (Applause.)

The chief thing to which our attention is called is the sharp contrast—some persons say between classes, but I think it is more accurate to say between interests—which has been disclosed in this country. It is not a contrast between organized capital merely, on the one hand, and organized labor on the other, though that is a brief and easy and erroneous way of stating it; but it is a contrast between organized capital on the one side and the general masses of the people and the movements of business throughout the country, on the other.

There is a general feeling in this country that there is a difference between the general interest and the interests recognized by those who handle capital. I do not need to tell you that this contrast does not in thoughtful minds exist, even among those who handle capital, even among those who handle it on the grand scale, because it is the part even of selfish calculation to know that no interest can hurt the country as a whole and serve itself; that our prosperity as individuals and as corporations is dependent upon the prosperity of the country; and that a country checked in the courses of its life is a country which will not yield to individual or to corporation the best results. (Applause.) We all of us know that there are these intimate connections of life, these absolute dependencies of one interest upon another; but, whether we are conscious of that or not, we are obliged to swing around face to face with the facts and to realize that most of the subjects that we are now discussing are necessary to be discussed because it is not generally thought that that interdependence is recognized.

What is the result? The result is a great body of programs which we assemble under the general name Socialism. Now, I would speak with considerable respect of Socialism as a theory. The abstract theories of Socialism are not easily to be distinguished from the abstract principles of Democracy. The idea and object of the thoughtful Socialist is to protect every man, to give him the best opportunity, and to serve him in such ways as will be in the general interest and in the interest of nobody in particular. That is the object of Socialism. But that is the object of Democracy too. The trouble with Socialism is not what it desires, but the method by which it proposes to reach what it desires. (Applause.)

I think it can be said without unfairness, by those who have really studied this matter, that the programs of Socialism are either very vague or entirely impracticable. They are necessarily very vague in promises which would bring on the millennium. They are necessarily impracticable whenever they propose by any general scheme to change the present operations of human nature. The one thing which it is impracticable to deal with by way of rapid change through the medium of legislation is that something that is implanted in every one of us upon which we fall back by way of excuse and denominate human nature. Every one is chuck full of it.

Now it is all very well for me to stand here and say that the programs of Socialism are not practical, but the interesting thing is that it does not make any difference whether I think so or not. The only way I can stop the programs of Socialism, the only way you can stop them from being attempted, is not by denial, not by disproof, not by any negative process whatever, but by proposing a better program. (Applause.) It is a case—in the vulgar—of "put up or shut up." If you don't believe in Socialism, do you believe in existing conditions? If you don't believe in existing conditions, how are you going to remedy them? You will be heard upon that question in the great court of public opinion, but you will be heard on nothing else. It is all very easy to destroy two or three programs by criticism, but it is a very difficult matter indeed to set up a rival program which can itself not be as easily destroyed.

Now, what I want to call your attention to is this, that the present situation can be analyzed in this way: In the first place, there is on the one hand (you may call it the public imagination or you may allow it to be the fact) the great power of accumulated capital; and there is, on the other hand, the great body of the people. Accumulated capital in great bodies has never, in our day or in any other day, been in the hands of a relatively large number of persons; they always constitute a minority, and a small minority as compared with the whole. There is, then, on the one hand, a comparatively small minority holding the enormous power of capital—the greatest, the most readily wielded, the most powerful factor of our day and generation— and there is, on the other hand, the great body of men engaged in industry and trying to live from day to day.

It is all very well for those of us who live where our life affords the opportunity to read history and to recall the precedents of past generations to speak calmly of the situation; but all that the busy man can recall is his own experiences and what his father has told him. Now, in our experience, in the experience of this generation, in the experience of the generations to which our fathers belonged, no American, no Englishman, has had any reason to fear the government. We have, in our day, forgotten what it is to fear the government. I venture to predict that we will find out again; but for the present we have forgotten what it is to fear the power concentrated in the government, because we have not yet allowed power to be too much concentrated in government in our day. But we have learned to fear—the great majority of us—the power accumulated in the hands of those who control the capital of the country. And what is taking place now is, that, in order to escape the power of capital, the people are tempted to throw themselves into the arms of government; and this country, which was the first to find a practicable means of escape from the exaggerated power of government, is apparently now about to go back upon the path upon which it was the pioneer and upon the successful pursuit of which it led the other nations of the world. It will require cool heads and sober judgment to escape throwing ourselves into one gulf in order to escape being overwhelmed in the other. (Applause.)

And the next thing that I want to call your attention to is, that in [the] view of the country, and as a matter of fact, the special, and as it is often thought the exclusive, instrument of accumulated capital is the bank. The bank is the most jealously regarded and the least liked instrument of business in this country. I don't envy you the situation. (Laughter.) I am glad to be out of it. But wherever I go I perceive that to be the case—and I go to a great many places and hear a great many things,—a good many things which knowledge might correct; but knowledge is a slow beast. You know that very clever perverter of maxims, Mr. Oliver Herbert,[2] has provided those engaged in education with the proverb: "You can lead an ass to knowledge but you can't make him think."[3] (Laughter.) You can lead as many persons to knowledge that you choose, but you cannot make them think; and even if you do make them think, the only things they can effectually think about are the concrete objects with which their lives bring them into direct contact.

[2] Oliver Brooke Herford, author and illustrator of many humorous books.
[3] The quotation appears in Ethel Watts Mumford, Oliver B. Herford, and Addison Mizner, *The Entirely New Cynic's Calendar of Revised Wisdom 1905* (San Francisco, 1904).

The banks of this country are remote from the people and the people regard them as not belonging to them but as belonging to some power hostile to them. Now that is the fact, gentlemen. I am not arguing whether it is reasonable or not. I think it is unreasonable; but I am stating the fact as every man observing without prepossession must acknowledge it to be in this country. The bank is regarded by the average man in the United States as the exclusive, peculiar instrumentality of the men who are doing business upon a great scale, and who are at present negligent of the general interest and intent upon their own.

Now, what are we going to do about it? I know, and you know, that the banker is just as desirous of touching the general resources of the country as he is of touching the larger resources of it. I know, of course, that the banks have turned away from their old-time modesty and reserve and have now gone out into advertising and that they are drumming the country up and down for business and sending out the most attractive, even if deceptive circulars. (Laughter.) I know that the bankers of this country, in other words, are in a certain way falling over themselves and each other to get into communication with the general body of people in this country. But they have not managed to make that impression; they have not managed to make it anywhere that I know of. I have talked to a great many bankers. It has been my privilege to know a great many and to learn a great deal from them. They are a body of men engaged in a particular expert business and having an extraordinary hold upon a certain body of information pertinent to their business; but I hope I will not be regarded as impertinent if I say that they do not seem to me to be very successful in explaining to the public that it is to the interest of the public that bankers should prosper, as it is to their own interest. (Applause.) They know what they are about, but they are not gifted with the power of explaining it very lucidly to the average man.

I have asked the most simple questions of bankers, upon the presumption that I was a man of ordinary understanding, and I often have not understood a word of their reply. I once asked a banker what speculating on a margin was, and I don't know yet. (Laughter.) They talk in technical terms which among academic men is a sure proof of limited knowledge; though I don't think it is in this case. In the business in which I am engaged if a man cannot explain his own subject in the ordinary terms of the dictionary, we assume that he does not know what he is talking about. (Laughter.) Most bankers talk in the same sort of language that a colleague of mine used one day. I met him when evidently he was in deep thought and I said, "What's up?" He said, "I have subsumed Hegel under a concept." (Laughter.) I said, "My dear fellow, have you got him about you?" He was using, unconsciously, because they were the terms of his own thought, the peculiar language of his own studies. They happened to have been my own studies and I knew what he was talking about, but I was very fortunate in that.

Now, how are the bankers of this country going to get in connection with the minds of this country? That word had a *d* in it,—the "minds" of this country, not the "mines." (Laughter and applause.) I have been told (though, because of an infirmity which prevents my remembering figures, I don't remember) the number of banks in this country and I know that it is very large indeed; but I know that the number of communities in this country is very much larger. I know that a friend of mine rode through seven counties of one of the older States of the Union without being able to find any place where he could get a $20 bill changed. I know that I myself spent a whole summer in that same State when it was necessary for me to send any bill exceeding $5 in denomination by express to a bank fifty miles distant in order to get it changed. This was a thriving agricultural community where men have plenty of the things that money is supposed to be obtainable for, but where they were necessarily reduced almost to the processes of barter because they could not get any cash at all. Not because there wasn't cash enough in the country,—it wasn't the inelasticity of the currency, it was the inaccessibility of the currency. And in that community,—do you wonder at it?—they believed in the free coinage of silver; and were all of them convinced that somebody, presumably in Wall Street, was hoarding the money of the country. Before the summer was over I began to wonder if they were not right (laughter), because at the very center of a great State nobody saw any money from one week's end to the other.

You now see how my theme brings me back to a very intimate connection with Mr. Walker's theme.[4] Mr. Walker seemed nervous lest you should not like him. I am not in the least nervous about that. I am not in the banking business. I am in a

[4] Byron Edmund Walker, President of the Canadian Bank of Commerce of Toronto, had spoken immediately before Wilson on the subject, "Abnormal Features of American Banking." He especially criticized the chaotic and inelastic American currency system and the lack of a centralized system of large banks with many branches in the various localities of the country. His speech is printed in *Proceedings of the Thirty-Fourth Annual Convention of the American Bankers' Association* . . . (New York, 1908), pp. 207-26.

business which makes it unnecessary that I should care whether I am popular with anybody or not. (Laughter.) Therefore I tell you frankly that I should like to convince you, but it shall not make me unhappy if I do not; because I am trying to deal with the facts and the facts are quite independent of your agreement. The point I want to make by constant reiteration is this: If you would save your credit—I don't mean your commercial credit, but your credit in the opinion of the country— if you would save your credit in the face of opinion, you must get into connection with the general body of the people of this country by serving them intimately; you must put the resources of the country at the disposal of every plain man to exactly the extent to which his credit is good (applause); you must not oblige him to go to a distant city and get a difficult introduction and produce handsome securities in order to establish his credit. You must have agents who will know in the several localities the men who are to be trusted by reason of their character as well as by reason of the securities they can put up, by reason of their established success in the occupations they have been following; you must extend your credit to these men, offer it to them, before you will gain their confidence and dissipate the prejudices which exist against you; and that can be done only by a system of inexpensive branch banks. (Applause.)

I am not here to advocate the establishment of branch banks or argue in favor of anything which you understand better than I do. But I have this to say, and to say with great confidence: that if a system of branch banks, very simply and inexpensively managed and not necessarily open every day in the week, could be established which would put the resources of the rich banks of the country at the disposal of whole countrysides to whose merchants and farmers only a restricted and local credit is now open, the attitude of plain men everywhere towards the banks and banking would be changed utterly within less than a generation. You know that you are looking out for investments; that even the colossal enterprises of our time do not supply you with safe investments enough for the money that comes in to you; and that banks here, there, and everywhere are tempted, as a consequence, to place money in speculative enterprises, and even themselves to promote questionable ventures in finance at a fearful and wholly unjustifiable risk in order to get the usury they wish from their resources. You sit only where these things are spoken of and big returns coveted. There would be plenty of investments if you carried your money to the people of the country at large and had agents in hundreds of villages who knew the men in their neighborhoods who could be trusted with loans and who would make profitable use of them. Your money, moreover, would quicken and fertilize the country, and that other result would follow which I think you will agree with me is not least important in my argument: the average voter would learn that the money of the country was not being hoarded; that it was at the disposal of any honest man who could use it; and that to strike at the banks was to strike at the general convenience and the general prosperity. I do not know what the arguments against branch banks are; but these I know from observation to be the arguments for them; and very weighty arguments they seem to me to be.

I do not care what your program of intimate association with people is, but there must be some program of intimate association; there must be voluntary association or there will be involuntary association, and the involuntary association will be ignorantly conceived, whereas the voluntary association can be naturally conceived.

This is what I mean by the social and political function of the banker. The banker is not only obliged in a country governed by opinion to do banking upon wise principles, but he is obliged to make the right impression on the people of the country. I do not mean by chicanery; I do not mean by anything unsound and unsafe, for that would not be serving the people; but I mean that by whatever sound means are available it is your business to make the right impression and convey the right instruction to the people of this country. And only you can do it; I cannot do it for you; no one else can do it for you. We laymen do not know what we are talking about when we get into the technicalities of banking. When we explain the technicalities of banking in terms which we understand some banker comes along and says: "Oh, nothing of the kind," and so we are discountenanced and are supposed to be merely advocating bankers because we have some interest in some bank. The college president, in particular, is often under the suspicion of wanting to tap some great body of wealth and therefore of being under the temptation to defend somebody who is in possession or control of a great body of wealth. Well, I have never been conscious of that temptation; I am sure I have never yielded to it because I have the strange conviction that the way for a college to get money is to attend to business and be worth the money. (Applause.)

So I say that it is your function, it is your duty, it is for you the command of mere prudence and safety that you should put the resources of this country at the disposal of the common man everywhere.

What have you done by your banking system? The local bank is built up by local resources. Only the local resources for the most part can be called upon for local advantages. Every community is as poor as its own resources. You cannot get the riches of the country in order to make it rich until it gets rich enough to establish a bank. It cannot get credit in the money centers until there accumulates enough capital to make it partially independent of that credit. You have set this country a task of developing in the most difficult and most improbable way. Do you suppose the country is not going to become aware of that? It is aware of it.

Gentlemen, we live in an age of extraordinary change; in a very interesting time of awakening, in a period of reconstruction and readjustment, when everything is being questioned and even old foundations are threatened with change. I know that the impression that that makes upon most men is that it is an age of extraordinary danger. It is an age of extraordinary danger only for the coward and the recreant. Every man with red blood in his veins and with a conscience under his jacket knows that it is an age of extraordinary opportunity and that the extraordinary opportunity takes this form: It is the business of every man who can lead anybody to lead in the direction of the public welfare. It is the duty and the opportunity of those who control wealth to pay less attention to the business of making particular individuals rich and more attention to the business of making the country rich. (Applause.) It is the business of the banker to constitute himself a statesman; for every man in a free country ought within his own little sphere to be as much of a statesman as he can be. One of the finest tributes ever paid to the American people was paid by M. de Tocqueville, who said that under our Constitution there was an extraordinary challenge to the intelligence, the discretion, the wisdom, the prudence, and the public spirit of every citizen, and that only in proportion as men answered this challenge in the spirit in which it was given could institutions like those of the United States flourish and remain upon those high planes of opportunity and achievement which we promised ourselves at the outset of our national history.

A time of danger! It is a time of wonderful opportunity. Do you recall that splendid speech made by Prince Henry at the Battle of Agincourt when he invited every man who had no stomach for the fight to go home and leave only those who wanted to serve England and who would feel it an honor to serve her, saying that there would come a time when men would tell of St. Crispin's Day, and every man descended from that little company would show the emblems of that fight and say, "My grandsire fought on St. Crispin's Day with Henry of Plantagenet"? So, gentlemen, there will come a time when the annals of this country will be ennobled by the names of the men who at this time of change and of opportunity rose above their selfish and personal interests and constituted themselves statesmanlike servants of the country. (Prolonged applause.)[5]

Printed in *Proceedings of the Thirty-Fourth Annual Convention of the American Bankers' Association* . . . (New York, 1908), pp. 226-35.
    [5] There is a WWhw outline of this address, with the composition dates of Aug. 7 and Sept. 21, 1908, and a WWsh draft of an abstract in WP, DLC. There is also a typed copy, dated Sept. 21, 1908, of the abstract in WC, NjP. The text of the abstract was printed in the *Congressional Record*, 62nd Cong., 2nd Sess., Vol. 48, Appendix, pp. 502-503.

From Melancthon Williams Jacobus

My dear President Wilson: Brookline, Mass., Sept. 30 1908

Your notes of 25th & 26th inst were forwarded to me here, where I am taking a few days off before the Seminary year opens.

I am returning to Hartford today & will have the notices for the Curriculum Com. meeting sent out at once.

I trust Cyrus McCormick will be able to approach the Jones-trusteeship persuasively. If in either of the brothers minds is lodged the idea that this is intended to head off any possible return of our friend[1] to the Board, the case is permanently closed with both of them. He should make it clear that the proposition originated with those who could not be charged with such a motive, and that [our] intent in the selection of his brother was the continuing in the Board of the influences which he himself had exerted & which his declination of reelection threatened to that degree to weaken.

If there is anything I can do in the situation to help things out, I shall be only too glad to do it.

The enclosed editorial from Mondays "Herald" will interest you. It shows an appreciation of the kind of work you are doing for Princeton.[2]   Yours cordially,   M W Jacobus

ALS (WP, DLC).
    [1] That is, David Benton Jones.
    [2] It was a clipping of an editorial, "The Human Touch," Boston *Herald*, Sept. 28, 1908, about the importance of the personal factor in education. It said, among other things, that "the contact of personality with personality, the touch of

a mature, disciplined, human soul upon the growing, aspiring and achieving soul of youth" was the "secret today of the renewed prosperity of Princeton."

From Cleveland Hoadley Dodge

Dear "Tommy"   New York   Sept 30th [1908]

Your beautiful letter has touched me deeply and is a real comfort and help.[1]

I appreciate your warm sympathy more than I can tell you and want to thank you heartily for writing

I am very glad that you had such a good change this summer & trust that you have come back thoroughly rested & braced up.

Hoping to see you soon   Yr's sincerely   C. H. Dodge

ALS (WP, DLC).
[1] Dodge had just suffered a nervous breakdown and was replying to a missing letter of sympathy from Wilson.

From Zephaniah Charles Felt[1]

My dear Wilson,   Denver, Colo., 8 PM 10/1 1908

I am sorry not to see you again. I have been trying to locate you but have been unable to do so, and as you are leaving Denver tonight I probably shall not have the pleasure. I would like to tell you in better words than in my haste last evening I was able to do how proud we Princeton fellows are of you and the impression you made here. I have talked with many bankers and they all agree that your words will make them do some tall thinking about themselves and their methods. I sat in the Iowa section and in front of me was a banker who had to turn to me at intervals during your address to relieve himself of his growing enthusiasm. At the close he said to me "I have always been a strong Republican, but by Jove if the Democrats nominate Wilson for President, I'll surely vote for him." I don't write thus to flatter, but I know how we all appreciate well earned compliments, so I pass these on to you with my best wishes for a safe journey back to dear old Princeton and for a college year that shall be ever more successful than any of the past. Believe me dear Wilson

Ever yr friend   Zeph. Chas. Felt

ALS (WP, DLC).
[1] Wilson's classmate, at this time a real estate broker in Denver.

From George Brinton McClellan

My dear President Wilson: New York   Oct. 1, 1908.
    Let me congratulate you most heartily on your Denver speech. What you said was greatly needed and must do great good.
    Please don't bother to acknowledge the receipt of this, for I hope that I shall see you before long.
    I am, with kind regards,
                                Yours very truly,   Geo B McClellan
TLS (WP, DLC).

An Announcement and News Item
                                                [Oct. 6, 1908]

PRINCETON'S PRESIDENT BEFORE A LOCAL CLUB

    The Men's League of the First Congregational Church is issuing invitations to a meeting to be held in the parlors Thursday evening at 8 o'clock. President Woodrow Wilson L.L.D., of Princeton university, will be the speaker of the evening. . . .
    During his stay in this city Dr. Wilson is being entertained by Mr. and Mrs. Thomas D. Peck, East street. He spoke before the Wednesday morning club at the Athenaeum today on the present political conditions in the United States.

Printed in the Pittsfield, Mass., *Berkshire Evening Eagle*, Oct. 6, 1908.

From Henry Ferguson[1]

                                                Concord, N. H.
My dear President Wilson,   October 6th, 1908.
    You were kind enough last winter when we missed one another so hopelessly in Bermuda, to raise my hopes that another year you would be able to come to us at our Anniversary.
    It will be held this year on the 3rd of June, and I assure you that it would give us the greatest pleasure if it were possible for you to arrange your time in such a way as to spare us that day.
    We are getting to be in closer and closer connection with Princeton, and I am sure that it would be a very great pleasure to all our boys who are thinking of going to you, if they could see you at the School, and I should particularly enjoy having you see the School, and appreciate what we are trying to do.
    I shall hope to see you tomorrow at President Garfield's inauguration, but at that busy time I can hardly expect to have any conversation with a person, who will be so much in the foreground as you naturally will be.

Hoping that you will be able to give us this time,[2] which I appreciate is a good deal of a request, I am

Yours very sincerely,   Henry Ferguson.

TLS (WP, DLC).
[1] Rector of St. Paul's School, Concord, N. H., since 1906.
[2] See WW to H. Ferguson, Oct. 12, 1908.

An Address at the Inauguration of
Harry Augustus Garfield as President of Williams College

[[Oct. 7, 1908]]

Mr. President: I esteem it a real privilege that I was invited to stand here and bid you welcome to that singular fraternity to which college presidents belong. I think that you would deem it, and all who know the circumstances would deem it, an affectation on my part if I did not express, first of all, the personal feeling which is uppermost in my heart at this moment. I know, of course, that one element in choosing me to perform this service was the delightful personal relationship which had existed between you and us at Princeton; otherwise there are men representing older institutions and of longer experience who would have been entitled to stand in my place.

Perhaps a public occasion is not ordinarily a suitable occasion for expressing personal friendship and personal confidence; but perhaps, also, it will be an act of authentication of you to the gentlemen who have so trusted you with this high office to say what you have been at Princeton. I know that you have been honored by us on another occasion, and that you have won many friends by your experience at Princeton; but I want to say that Princeton is rendered poor by your leaving, that Princeton has profited by your counsels, by your signal equipoise of character, and by the marked proofs of your deep-seated kindliness and wholesomeness of nature, and that any institution is singularly fortunate to get so strong a leader and so wise a counsellor as yourself.

I think that the choice of a man like yourself, trained not merely in academic circles, but trained also in the broader circle of business and the world, has a singular significance at the present time. For, sir, it is important that college administration should receive more than a touch of statesmanship. It is that touch which you may be expected to give to the administration of this conspicuous and distinguished institution. For the college is now bound, in times of confused counsel, to supply the country not merely with men, in the ordinary popular sense of that word, not merely with strong individualities, not merely with wholesome natures,—natures rendered wholesome by the purifying influences of counsel,—but also with men who can think, men who can interpret, men who can perceive, men who have something more than skill and aptitude and knowledge, men who look beneath the surface of affairs and know the genesis of affairs and can forecast—as much as it is given to men to forecast—the future of affairs, men who are ready to serve the country with something more than skill and knowledge, men who have a great surplus of energy and of understanding to spend in the service of the country, men whose attention is not wholly centred upon making their own living, but is spent also upon the very exigent matter of lifting all the counsels of the country to a higher plane and place and opportunity of vision.

And so the function of the college is changing with the character and necessities of the times. I believe that we have centred our thoughts too much upon matters of curriculum; that we have centred our thoughts too much upon serving the individual student who came to us and too little upon serving the country through the instrumentality of that individual student; and that it is just as important to concentrate our attention upon the spirit of the college in respect to learning and the service of the country, and upon the organization of the life of the college, as it is to centre it upon the curriculum itself. The curriculum is a means of enabling the college faculty to promote a spirit and to perfect an organization which shall carry the students forward to better things; and therefore it is as important to draw the college together in its several parts and unite them in a common undertaking as it is to give instruction in the classroom and see to it that the students understand the difference between truth and error; because if the student does not draw near to the professor because of deference to him, there is coming a time when the professor will not draw near to the student because of deference to him.

The student's attention is so much absorbed by the affairs of what he calls his life that the teacher gets only the residuum and balance of his intellect. There is coming a time when we must draw these elements together, and, subordinating neither, unite them both upon an equality, so that the life and the learning and the attention will all be indistinguishable, and there will be no contest, but our very pleasures shall give accent and salt and flavor to our intellectual ambitions. For the object of the university is singly and entirely intellectual. The object of sport, the object of social pleasure, is relief from the strain of work; but pleasure is not pleasure, and any diversion is professional, if it be not simply a relief from the main object of college ambition.

It is this conception which, it seems to me, you, coming from a varied experience, having touched the world at many points and known men of many kinds,—it is this that you will seek, and this which you, perhaps better than any one else, will be instrumental in accomplishing. I congratulate you upon the opportunity, and for my colleagues of all the colleges of the country I congratulate Williams College upon her choice of a man.[1]

Printed in Williams College, *The Induction of Harry Augustus Garfield, LL.D. into the Office of President* . . . (Cambridge, Mass., n.d.), pp. 22-26.
[1] There is a WWhw outline of this address, dated Oct. 7, 1908, in WP, DLC.

A Citation of Wilson for an Honorary Degree

[[Oct. 7, 1908]]

WOODROW WILSON, graduate of Princeton College; President of Princeton University since 1902.

The date of the founding of Princeton College would seem to indicate that a fair expanse of what is popularly known as history must lie between it and this celebration, but when the modern passion for marking epochs shall attack it, a clearly dividing line will be drawn in 1902. The historian of this latter epoch will not fail to signalize a new departure in university, or rather college, education, which is working a revolution in the undergraduate life of Princeton. It may be too soon to predict with confidence the entire effect of this departure known as the preceptorial system, that is being watched with keen interest by the college world, but "it has already produced more and better work: it has begun to make reading men, and it has brought teachers and pupils into intimate relations of mutual interest and confidence: it already shows interesting results in the new attitude of the undergraduates, in the increased ability to study, and in the intelligence of approach and facility in work."[1]

To have won even a reluctant consent, to have secured the means for the trial of a scheme involving such enormous outlay, as surely marks a new epoch, as it bears witness to serene faith, constructive imagination, and creative genius.

Printed in Williams College, *The Induction of Harry Augustus Garfield, LL.D. into the Office of President* . . . (Cambridge, Mass., n.d.), pp. 74-75.
[1] This quotation is a condensation of several passages from Wilson's Annual Report to the Board of Trustees of Princeton University printed at Dec. 13, 1906, Vol. 16.

From Mary Livingston Gilbert Hinsdale[1]

Pittsfield, Massachusetts.
Dear Dr. Wilson: October 8th, 1908.

I am forced to believe that the Wednesday Morning Club is a most un-American organization, for it awoke on Wednesday, on Thursday, and again on Friday mornings with the same thrill and stimulation which it received during your address on Tuesday.

Surely it was most gracious in you to come and pay us the unusual and very gratifying tribute of a talk on politics.

Could you have heard the enthusiastic words of appreciation after your lecture you would feel fully repaid.

I, myself seem very American for I have begun energetically what I can not finish,—to thank you adequately for your courtesy to the Club.   Very sincerely,   Mary L. Hinsdale

TCL (WC, NjP).
1 Secretary of the Wednesday Morning Club of Pittsfield, Mass., prominent in charitable and civic affairs. Her husband, James Henry Hinsdale, was a retired woolen manufacturer.

A News Report of an Address in Pittsfield, Massachusetts

[Oct. 9, 1908]

PRESIDENT WILSON SAYS WE CAN'T TELL POLITICAL PARTIES APART WITHOUT LOOKING AT THE LABEL—CANDIDATES RETICENT AS TO "PRINCIPLES."

Of some men it is said:
"It is not so much what they say, but the way they say it."
Of others:
"What they say is fine, but their delivery is poor."
Of President Woodrow Wilson of Princeton, who addressed a company of 150 representative citizens at the First Congregational parish house last night, it can truthfully be said:
"It isn't only what he says, but the way he says it."
In what follows an attempt is made to body forth some of the ideas expressed by the head of this great university. Any attempt to portray the matchless manner of the man would be futile.
He is the medium height, has a fine, strong, smooth face, wears eyeglasses and smiles easily. Every sentence he utters is as clean-cut as the facets on a diamond. Every sentiment is couched in language that is forceful and effective. Many of his word-figures are arrayed in robes of wondrous beauty.

Rev. Dr. W[illiam]. V. W. Davis, pastor of the church, presided and told of meeting Dr. Wilson in England one summer and of the warm friendship formed at that time. While Dr. Davis had enjoyed many of Dr. Woodrow's books, he had enjoyed the man immensely more.

It so chanced, said President Wilson, in opening, that he was to pass through Pittsfield, and simultaneously there came an invitation to speak here. He always welcomed the opportunity not so much to make an address as to meet men and discuss with them the great problems of our time. His subject on this occasion was "Public Affairs and Private Responsibility."

Here are some thoughts from the admirable address which consumed just an hour. When the speaker finished the long continued applause indicated that not a man in the attentive audience was weary, but on the contrary wanted him to proceed:

"He must have a bad conscience who devotes himself to private affairs to the exclusion of public concerns."

Here was the keynote. Dr. Wilson said that in Denver recently he addressed the bankers' association, and felt that he had said there many useless things. He held it to be difficult to tell these men what they should do in order to transact their business with the greatest degree of efficiency. It is for us to turn out what is fair and square. We should acquire knowledge of the anatomy of things.

"The present conflict in this country is not a contest between capital and labor. It is a contest between those few men in whose hands the wealth of the land is concentrated, and the rest of us. Most men, it will be admitted, are honest, sincere. The tendency, however, is to devote attention to their immediate concerns and disregard the welfare and happiness of other men.

"It is dangerous to concentrate moral forces upon self. The way to do right is to do in the best way possible duty as it is perceived. Character will take care of itself.

"It is bad business to concentrate energy exclusively upon private enterprise. The lawyer is a bad adviser who concentrates all his energies and thought upon one feature of a large corporation by whom he is employed. Rather should he attempt to ascertain what relation one part bears to the other parts and the relation the whole sustains to the other affairs of life.

"There is in the sense in which I speak, no such thing as private responsibility. Our responsibility is to all. Every bit of credit that is due to this country comes from perception of duty and does not depend upon the excellence of our institutions.

"The nation is constantly calling upon men who are able to talk. It is necessary however painful it may be.

"It is a good thing not to eulogize and to say the things that please, but we must excite interest in others by discussion and disagreement. We must work for co-operation.

"Many men make a distinction between their life at home and their business down street. It is a false distinction. We know men who are the most delightful husbands and fathers and good friends, whose conduct in these relations square with every standard of honor and excellence, but who in business are tricky men—men who adjourn their consciences when they go into their offices.

"It is a demoralizing maxim that business is business. By that we imply that every method, no matter how questionable, is permissible and right.

"Everything that man does, dreams, hopes for, executes, dreads, seeks, is a part of his life. Friends, there is not a moment when we can truthfully say 'we are not living our life.' We are living it every minute, at home, in the office, everywhere.

"There is danger that the life of the nation will fall below the level of the individual.

"If there is a place where we must adjourn our morals, that place should be in what we call the private life. It is better to be unfaithful to a few people than to a considerable number of people. I do not say we can afford to adjourn our morals in either case. I simply assert that we can better afford to adjourn them in private life.

"Yes, there are so many men who are good in their private lives who are unwise in public affairs and purposes. Men who are saints in private life may be poor leaders. I have known some men so stiff in their individuality, that they refused to join any party or organization. They cannot tolerate the thought of being part of an aggregate. They break up every committee of which they become a member. They disturb. They are impractical men, cranks—sometimes reformers. There are two kinds of reformers— untimely reformers and timely reformers. The function of the former is one of irritation. He dies leaving behind him a series of interrogation points. We begin to think. We conclude that what he said and did had in it elements of the practical. We take hold of his ideas. We didn't consider his ideas worthy at the time they were offered, but now we exclaim 'He has upset us. He has pointed the way. Let's get to work.' He was the drop of acid that irritated and caused us to take notice and to participate in affairs. It is all a part of the adjustment and the readjustment."

Alluding to Benjamin Kidd's book which offered a solution of all social ills,[1] Dr. Wilson said that

"As I am 51 and have therefore reached the age of discretion, I do not hesitate to say that I do not know of a single generalization that is true of a half dozen men. I do not know of a single affirmative generalization that is true of America. I have said that when asked for an opinion abroad.

"Force and renewal are the two elements in the nation. I am reminded of the story of the colored preacher in Tennessee who went aside and prayed long and earnestly for power. When he had finished one of the brethren said to him: 'You ought not to pray for power. You ought to pray for ideas.'

"We have forgotten to fear government. We look upon it as a new power to correct abuses. Time was when it was feared and dreaded as a mighty, deterring, awful force in the affairs of men. What we should do and what we must do is to walk the median line that lies between the two extremes of capital and government. One needs to be checked as much as the other. It was revolt, the exercise of force that made men of us. It is supineness, acquiescence, that make children of us. We are too prone to take things for granted and let them go.

"What we need is the renewal of the general principle, the renewal of right.

"I believe in governmental regulation, but it should not be carried to excess. Capital must get a return. Government does not have to get a return and so can go as far as it likes.

"We pay no attention to the men whom we send to the legislature. We go to the polls. We see the names on our ticket. If we don't happen to be angry with the man named, we vote for him. If we are angry with him we look over the list that the other fellows have prepared and if we find there the name of a man with whom we are not angry we vote for him. We don't seem to care. The real evil would come if we found that unfit men had been chosen and we didn't care then!

"When I see men agreeable I feel that they are not the best men. When they agree with everything you say, they are not good citizens[.] After perfect agreement comes supineness. The American government originated in the biggest kick on record. When I look at the flag I think of it as strips of parchment. The blue represents the principles that have been the guiding stars through all the years. The red represents the blood that has been shed that those principles might be confirmed.

[1] Benjamin Kidd, *Social Evolution* (London and New York, 1894). There is a copy of this book in the Wilson Library, DLC.

"I take the ground that when we criticize the government we are doing the only thing that is American.

"I know men who have covered over with concrete the springs that are within them, but when this covering is lifted we find there is water there. We see it sparkling, clear and radiant. I have sat with men who are regarded as the most hard-fisted business men in the country—sat with them until the small hours of the morning. As they began to feel the softening influence of the quiet of those early morning hours, suddenly their ideal began to make itself manifest. Perhaps it came back as a memory from childhood's days. Such is the source oftentimes of the renewal of the ideal."

Printed in the Pittsfield, Mass., *Berkshire Evening Eagle*, Oct. 9, 1908; some editorial headings omitted.

Henry Burling Thompson to Cyrus Hall McCormick

[Wilmington, Del.]
My Dear McCormick: October 9th, 1908.

I have received your letter of the 3d instant, with regard to the election of the under classmen to the upper class clubs by sections instead of as individuals.

Our report to the Board took cognizance of this condition, and there were two recommendations that we considered would ameliorate the evil,—recommendation No. 5, as to Sophomore Commons, which the Board adopted; and recommendation No. 3,—"That the upper class clubs should unite in appointing a duly authorized graduate committee to deal with themselves and the University authorities in all matters affecting club life and club relations to the University."

The installation of the Sophomore Commons I believe will be a success, as the class are now living as a class, and are not living in separate sets of groups. The latter condition was one of the great sources of evil on the very question that you bring up.

Now, with regard to our report,—recommendation No. 3, which I quoted above, has been strongly opposed by President Wilson and the so-called "quad" men. Their reason for disapproving is that they believe it puts the Univers[i]ty stamp of approval on the club system and renders the clubs more permanent.

I have talked this matter over with Wilson within the past ten days, and have tried to prove to him that the appointment of such a committee is necessary; and I propose to try to prove to the members of the Board its necessity.

The Board cannot deal with these matters of club detail, but a well-chosen graduate committee, with authority, could deal with such matters intelligently.

The treatment of our report by the Board has been a source of regret to me. Between the extreme "anti-quad" men, who object to Sections Nos. 1 and 6, and the extreme "quad" men, who object to Sections Nos. 3 and 6, it seems likely to me that the report stands a fair show of being pigeon-holed.

I know that the report is not a cure-all, but I believe, if the Board are willing to accept it as it has been presented, it unquestionably will be a move in the right direction. It is the beginning of a progressive movement for reform; but the extremists of both parties apparently are willing to leave present conditions untouched.

I am sorry that you will not be present at our Board meeting, for your letter unquestionably indicates that you see the necessity for some action at this time.

I am— yours sincerely, Henry B Thompson

TLS (Thompson Letterpress Books, NjP).

To Edwin Grant Conklin

Princeton, N. J.

My dear Professor Conklin: October 10th, 1908.

I write to ask if you will not be kind enough to accept appointment as Chairman of the Department of Biology. I know that this appointment will be most acceptable to all of your colleagues in the Department, and it particularly pleases me to look forward to the relations which it will establish between you and myself.

With much regard,

Sincerely yours, Woodrow Wilson

TLS (E. G. Conklin Papers, NjP).

From Robert Randolph Henderson

My dear Woodrow, Cumberland, Md. Oct. 10th 1908

Upon my return I found your kind note.[1] Nothing in your manner had struck me as at all lacking in cordiality. If there had been anything it would not have occurred to me to attribute it to anything but preoccupation with some of the many cares you have to bear.

I hope none of the dear old crowd will ever suspect any other member of any change in the feeling that has bound us so closely together.

We had a most delightful motor trip of two weeks, without accident or delay.

With kindest regards for Mrs. Wilson and the young ladies I am as ever

Affectionately yrs   Robert R. Henderson

ALS (WP, DLC).
[1] It is missing.

The Outlook's Review of Constitutional Government in the United States

[Oct. 10, 1908]

Professor Woodrow Wilson's book on "Constitutional Government in the United States," though less detailed, less legal, less scholastic, and possibly less scholarly than Professor Stimson's,[1] is broader, more philosophical, more vital, animated by a clearer perception of actual conditions, less constricted by reference to the letter of the law. To Dr. Wilson the Nation is a living, growing organization, and the Constitution is a body of principles not to restrict but to guide and direct that growth. The actual functions of the President, of the Senate, and of the House of Representatives have all undergone great changes since the Constitution was written, just as the body of Presidential Electors no longer fulfills the function allotted to it by the Constitution. That body still exists, but it does not really elect the President, it only registers and makes legal the action of the people in electing him. There is nothing in the Constitution of the United States which confers on the Supreme Court of the United States power to declare a law unconstitutional and therefore null and void, and that power was contemptuously denied by Andrew Jackson; but, in spite of that denial, it has come to be exercised by the Supreme Court and is acquiesced in and confirmed by the people. Similar changes have taken place in the functions and the practical working authority of the President and of Congress. The President as the one representative of the Nation, elected by all the people, not by the State as are the Senators, nor by the Districts as are the Representatives, is, if he chooses to make himself so, the leader of all the people, and more and more is coming to have the initiative in legislation. While thus the President is acquiring increased National power as the voice of the Nation, the House of

Representatives is losing National power because it is ceasing to be the voice of the Nation. It is making itself instead a business organization for the purpose of framing legislation which has been initiated elsewhere. "In making itself an active part of the Government and falling into the silence of an effective, business-like board of directors, it has forfeited the much higher office of gathering the common counsel of the nation and wielding the tremendous, the governing and sovereign, power of criticism." Whether it can recover the power which it has largely lost, Dr. Wilson does not discuss. We may add, however, that the attempt to lessen the power of the Speaker, to remove the desks from the House and commit the business work of the House to the Committee Rooms, and to re-establish freedom of debate on the House floor, are all parts of a half-conscious endeavor to recover the power to speak for the Nation which during the last half-century it has so largely lost. The Senate ought to be the Great Council of the Nation, the President's advisers. It ought to bring to him from the different sections of the Nation knowledge respecting the various currents of public opinion which it is impossible that he should personally possess, and so guide him in his own executive actions and co-operate with him in shaping the policy of the Nation, especially in international affairs. But this power of counsel and co-operation it has often sacrificed. "The Senate has shown itself particularly stiff and jealous in insisting upon exercising an independent judgment upon foreign affairs, and has done so so often that a sort of customary *modus vivendi* has grown up between the President and the Senate, as of rival powers." How the ideal relationship of fellowship in counsel between the President and Senate may be re-established Dr. Wilson does not discuss. But we may add that this relationship cannot, in our judgment, be re-established unless some of the absurd traditional rules of the Senate are abolished, the oligarchic power given to a little body in the Senate is taken from it, and the power of Senatorial committees to stifle all debate in the Senate on measures referred to such committees is destroyed; and such co-operation between the President and the Senate will be greatly facilitated by taking the election of Senators from the State Legislatures and giving it to the people of the State. We have seen nothing on the Constitution of the United States which seems to us more suggestive, and more really and fundamentally valuable, than this volume of Woodrow Wilson's, since the volumes—similar in spirit though different in character and purpose—of de Tocqueville and of James Bryce.

Printed in the New York *Outlook*, xc (Oct. 10, 1908), 313-14.

[1] Wilson's book was reviewed together with three others: Frederic Jesup Stimson, *The Law of the Federal and State Constitutions of the United States* . . . (Boston, 1908); F. J. Stimson, *The American Constitution: The National Powers, the Rights of the States, the Liberties of the People* (New York, 1908); and Franklin Pierce, *Federal Usurpation* (New York, 1908).

To Mary Allen Hulbert Peck

My dear Mrs. Peck,   Princeton, 12 Oct., 1908.

We look back with the keenest pleasure to our delightful visit to Pittsfield. I did not realize until the train had actually left the station that I was very tired. The trip to Pittsfield and Williamstown came, as I told you, on the heels of a trip on which I had hurried to Denver and back within the brief space of eight days, making three speeches as part of my programme, and it was natural that at last I should feel the results of hurry and excitement. So soon as the train got under way and I was no longer sustained by pleasure and movement from one interesting thing to another, I fell into a heavy sleep from which I did not wake for three hours. I felt as if I had been drugged, and pulled myself together in a sort of daze at New York, feeling the whole world unreal. I have felt dull and heavy and out of spirits ever since. A man with such nerves ought not to run about making speeches and attending functions, ought he? And I think intense pleasure tires me more than anything else.

We have settled down to our usual quiet routine again. On Monday and Tuesday mornings I lead chapel at five minutes before nine, lecture from ten minutes after nine till ten, and then devote the rest of the day to my correspondence and the quite unclassifiable variety of university business. I am obliged to put this letter together in the infrequent intervals between calls, as I sit in my office, exposed to every sort of interruption.

I have taken the liberty of sending you by post to-day another photograph of myself,—or, rather, a photograph of a drawing of myself,—to take the place of the likeness you have, which Mrs. Wilson pronounces very poor and says I ought never to have sent. We think that the drawing from which this photograph is taken is much the best "counterfeit presentment" of me we have had. It should be. It was drawn, with generous enthusiasm, by a genuine artist who knows me and who relished the task because he truly loves me. I hope that you will like it and think it worth keeping.

I am paying the penalty for having been so long away from home at a critical period of the university year. The University had been open only two days when I started for Denver, so that when I got back from Pittsfield on Friday there was everything to be done that ought to have been done during the first two weeks of the term, and the business of the Board of Trustees, which is to meet this week, to be got ready, besides,—committees without number to be attended, and all looking to me for exact information and carefully considered advice. Even Mrs. Wilson is involved, because she has to get ready to entertain the whole Board, of twenty-five, at lunch, engaging waiters and playing caterer. You can imagine the scene. Mrs. Wilson is the only woman at the long table, and is taken in to lunch by the senior trustee present, generally some old gentleman who is *very* dull to talk to and who makes the whole thing a burden to the poor lady.[1] The slow, elderly members gather at her end of the table, held together by a certain natural affinity, while the younger and livelier ones sit at my end,—most of them former college mates of mine, and as ready for lively talk and jest and badinage as they were thirty years ago. When the lunch is over (the business meeting comes before lunch) and we have smoked and I am rid of them, I go off for a lonely walk into the country, or through the lanes and by-ways of the little town and try to forget and clear my head for a little while of all we have discussed.

I began this letter on the day whose date it bears, but am finishing it on Tuesday evening, after spending the greater part of the day at a meeting of our finance committee in New York. The Board meets on Thursday, and on Friday Ellen and I are to go away to another college function. Haverford College, a stout little Quaker institution of high repute is to celebrate its one hundred and,—no, I am mistaken,—its seventy-fifth anniversary. I am to make one of several addresses at the formal exercises and am, besides, to 'make a few remarks' at the inevitable dinner. I do not know what I can scrape together to say,—I shall have to carry it all off with that "matchless manner" of mine spoken of in the paper you were kind enough to send me. How diverting that characterization was! I did not know myself! By the way, Miss Hinsdale did a very unusual and pretty thing on behalf of the ladies of the Wednesday Morning Club. She sent me a box of American beauty roses, with the very graceful and delightful note which I enclose,[2] that you may see how *very* well your Secretary does things. I was very much gratified indeed.

It is very delightful to me to have had an opportunity to see Pittsfield and to know your surroundings there as well as in Bermuda, and I am deeply pleased that my dear Jessie is to have a chance to know you. I *hope* you will think her lovely as we do, and I am sure she will think you wholly lovely as we do. Ellen and I will long look back upon our visit to you as to one of the happiest little expeditions we have made together. Jessie will write you from Boston at what time to expect her.

Please thank Mr. Peck for all his thoughtful kindness and give him, as well as Mrs. Allen,[3] your daughter and son,[4] our warmest regards.

Gratefully and faithfully Yours,   Woodrow Wilson

ALS (WP, DLC).
[1] The Senior Trustee at this time was John Aikman Stewart.
[2] This enclosure is missing.
[3] Anjenett Holcomb (Mrs. Charles Sterling) Allen.
[4] Her stepdaughter, Harriet Peck, and Allen Schoolcraft Hulbert.

To Henry Ferguson

Princeton, N. J.
My dear Dr. Ferguson: October 12th, 1908.

Referring to your kind letter of October 6th and our all too short conversation at Williamstown, allow me to say that it will give me pleasure to be present at your next anniversary on the third of June, 1909. I would be very much obliged if you would express to me very frankly your preference as to the kind of address I should deliver on that occasion. I shall look forward to it with a great deal of interest and pleasure.

With much regard,

Sincerely yours,   Woodrow Wilson

TCL (RSB Coll., DLC).

From Henry Ferguson

Concord, N. H.
My dear President Wilson,   October 14th 1908.

I am very much obliged to you for your kind letter of October 12th received this morning. It will give us the greatest pleasure to have you with us as our guest at the Rectory, and as one of the speakers at our luncheon on the third of June.

I am very anxious that you should see the School, and know what we are trying to do here, and the Anniversary gives a good opportunity to meet a good many of our prominent alumni, who come back at that time.

I should like you to be the speaker at the luncheon on some such subject as the Transition from School to College, and the worthy openings for a boy's ambition at college,—and Princeton especially. They are much too apt to think only of athletics, and it is hard to make them realize that there are other openings, even for those who are not scholars.[1]

Thanking you very much for your kindness, I remain

Yours very sincerely,   Henry Ferguson

TLS (WP, DLC).
    [1] Wilson spoke on the relationship between intellectual life and extracurricular activities in schools and colleges. A news report of his address is printed at June 3, 1909, Vol. 19.

Two Resolutions

[c. Oct. 14, 1908]

RESOLVED, That in the death of the Hon. Grover Cleveland the Board of Trustees of Princeton University feel that the University has suffered an especial and very great loss;

That it recognized in him, not only one of the greatest and most conscientious public servants this country has had, whose counsel the whole country will be the poorer for lacking, but also a counsellor in university affairs whose influence was always thrown on the side of what he deemed to be the highest interests of the institution, and who devoted himself to its service with the same thoughtful and painstaking attention to duty that characterized him as an officer of the State and a custodian of the honour, integrity, and prosperity of the nation;

And that the board feel also that in losing him it loses from its membership a faithful friend and wholly admirable man, whose death leaves a gap it will be impossible to fill.

◊

RESOLVED, That the Board express its deep sense of obligation to Mr. Stephen S. Palmer for his great generosity in providing for the University a physical laboratory which is in every way suitable to the needs of the University not only but which is also probably the most complete and most admirably fitted laboratory of its kind in the country, and that it express also its especial appreciation of the peculiarly liberal manner in which he has met all the expenses attending its construction and preparation for use, including even the grading of the ground about it, and the constant personal attention he has given to its perfect completion in every detail.[1]

T MS (Trustees' Papers, UA, NjP).
    [1] Both of the foregoing resolutions drafted by Wilson were adopted and spread on the minutes of the Board of Trustees for the meeting on October 15, 1908.

A Report and a Recommendation

[Oct. 15, 1908]

REPORT OF THE COMMITTEE ON PLAN AND SCOPE.[1]

To the Committee of Fifty of Princeton University:

Your Committee on Plan and Scope submits the following report:

If the Committee of Fifty is to become an effective organization for the purpose of increasing the endowment of the University, it is necessary to make of it something more than a mere collection agency. The solicitation of funds, no matter for what purpose, is quite as distasteful to those who must ask for the money as to those who are expected to give it. Such work is rarely, if ever, carried on with enthusiasm over an extended period by any body of volunteers.

But if the scope of the Committee of Fifty can be enlarged, somewhat after the manner suggested in this report, the work will be so varied and interesting, and membership in the Committee will be of such distinction as to lead the members to coöperate with more energy than has hitherto been shown in the difficult task of providing funds for the current expenses of Princeton.

There have been, and are still, two serious obstacles to the effective work of the Committee of Fifty. The first is found in many appeals made to the alumni by various quasi-official bodies for purposes often proper enough in themselves but of relative unimportance when contrasted with the pressing needs of the University itself. Few alumni are in a position to judge of the comparative merits of these varied appeals; so that most graduates have naturally failed to accord to the work of the Committee of Fifty the recognition to which it is fairly entitled. Under the plan we are about to propose, the alumni will presently understand that this Committee is the established medium through which the Trustees make public the vital needs of Princeton.

The only other organization which is now canvassing the alumni at large for subscriptions to meet the current expenses of the University, is the Alumni Fund. We are told that there will be a meeting of the Trustees of the Alumni Fund in the fall for the purpose of acting upon the suggestion made by your Committee on Plan and Scope that the work hitherto carried on by the Alumni Fund shall henceforth be conducted by the Committee of Fifty. We have satisfactory assurances that this suggestion will be favorably considered.

---

[1] Appointed at a meeting of the Committee of Fifty on May 13, 1908, to propose a plan for the reorganization and revitalization of that group.

While it is essential to merge with the work of the Committee of Fifty, that of all other committees making general appeals to Princeton graduates, we must give the heartiest encouragement to the several class committees engaged in securing contributions for class memorials. The success of many of these committees in awakening a substantial Princeton interest in the great majority of their class-mates, is a striking example of what the Committee of Fifty may do if properly organized and its work systematically undertaken.

The second obstacle to the effective work of this Committee is our present method of asking for money. It is impossible to arouse enthusiasm by urging men to help ward off an impending deficit. A comparatively few men have contributed from a sense of duty or because they have been approached by some one whom they do not like to refuse. But the great body of small contributors have not responded with anything like the spirit with which so many of them have subscribed to their class memorials. We have ample proof that the majority of Princeton graduates, if appealed to in the right way, will cheerfully join with classmates in the common purpose of providing the University with funds for specific objects, particularly if credit for the gift is publicly given.

What we propose in this report is to modify the existing method of appealing for funds, so that each individual contributor may feel that his gift is to be devoted to some definite purpose, rather than to be merged in a general fund to meet the unspecified expenses of the University.

To accomplish this end your Committee recommends that the Trustees of the University be requested to submit to the alumni, through the Committee of Fifty, at the beginning of each fiscal year, a list of the several purposes for which specific funds will be needed during the ensuing year, and for which there may be no adequate endowment. From such a list it will be possible for individuals, or alumni associations, or classes not otherwise committed to the raising of memorials, to select the particular object for which they desire to contribute.

For example, in the event of a class choosing to devote its funds during a certain year to the maintenance of a particular professorship or of a particular preceptorship, the name of the professor or preceptor would be printed in the University Catalogue, as for instance: "The Class of 1892 Professor of Classics," or "The Class of 1900 Preceptor in English."

(As a matter of convenience it might be well, under this plan, arbitrarily to compute professorships at the uniform rate of

$3,500 a year, and preceptorships at the uniform rate of $2,000 a year.)

Every effort should be made to persuade a class, having once undertaken to support (let us say) a professorship, to continue its gifts for the same purpose from year to year. It is not impossible to hope that some classes, through the sustained interest of a majority of their members, may eventually be able to endow their professorships; and thus by degrees to establish perpetual memorials. In this way Princeton may encourage many of her graduates to share, according to their means, in the upbuilding of her endowment, whereas, under our present method, they are discouraged by the size and apparent hopelessness of the problem.

Such a plan as we have here suggested would carry out the original purpose of the Committee of Fifty to obtain funds for pressing University needs not otherwise provided for, while leaving it with the Board of Trustees to say from year to year, what these needs may be.

In order that this plan may be made practically effective, we must enlarge the scope of the Committee of Fifty, so that it may sustain a position of dignity and importance in all matters which interest the alumni. Thus only will the Committee be enabled to discharge its financial obligations to the University for which purpose we are primarily brought together. We propose such an organization of the Committee that it may supply the alumni with authoritative information upon University affairs, and become the recognized medium through which alumni sentiment may properly be expressed; that it may provide a means of communication between graduates and undergraduates; that it may spread the influence of Princeton among the preparatory schools from which it is particularly desired to draw new students; that it may maintain a discriminating Press Bureau; that it may encourage effective class organization, stimulate the efforts of local alumni associations and aid in the formation of new associations.

The name, "The Committee of Fifty," has no special significance with relation to Princeton or to the functions of this organization. Moreover, it is suggestive of countless civic and philanthropic associations in various parts of the country, usually gathered for purposes of reform. Your Committee therefore suggests "THE GRADUATE COUNCIL" as a name significant of the broader activities of the Committee of Fifty, when reorganized as here proposed.

We recommend the following plan for "The Graduate Council":

1. *Membership*. The Graduate Council shall be composed of one representative from each of the thirty-five classes last graduated, and fifteen members at large.

2. *Election of Members*. A nominating committee chosen from members of the Graduate Council, shall present each year to the Trustees of the University at their stated meeting in October, the names of seven class representatives and three members at large, for election as members of the Graduate Council, to serve for five years.

3. *Meetings*. There shall be two stated meetings each year; one in October and one in April.

4. *Vacancies*. A member who shall be absent from two consecutive stated meetings shall thereupon cease to be a member unless excused by the Council. The Trustees of the University at any stated meeting may fill vacancies in the Graduate Council when properly nominated by the Nominating Committee.

5. *Officers*. The officers shall be a Chairman and a Secretary, who will be elected by the Council at the stated meeting in October of each year.

6. *Sub-Committees*. There shall be six sub-committees appointed by the Chairman at the October meeting to serve for one year. Vacancies in Committees may be filled at any time by appointment of the Chairman. It is recommended that every member of the Graduate Council shall serve on a sub-committee.

A. *A Committee on Finance*. It shall be the duty of this committee to lay before the several class or alumni organizations desiring to contribute to the University, the several purposes for which funds are needed and to report to the Graduate Council for transmission to the Board of Trustees, information as to what specific purposes the contributions of the said organizations are to be devoted and for which they are to be given credit in the University Catalogue. To perform such other duties as may be delegated to them from time to time, by the Alumni Council.

B. *A Committee on Class Records and Organization*. The purpose of this Committee is to encourage efficient class organization and to coöperate with the Secretary of the Alumni in the preparation of the alumni directories.

C. *A Committee on Publicity*. The purpose of this Committee is to coöperate with the Secretary of the Graduate Council in the maintenance of an efficient Press Bureau.

D. *A Committee on Preparatory Schools.* It shall be the function of this Committee to obtain information with regard to the sources from which the University is drawing its students, and to use every proper means to spread the influence of Princeton among the schools from which it is especially desired to draw new students.

E. *A Committee on Alumni Associations.* It shall be the duty of this Committee to gather information regarding the character of work undertaken by the alumni associations in order that, if possible, the work may be improved; that inactive associations may be stimulated to become more efficient, and that associations situated in neighboring localities may be encouraged to work in harmony for the best interests of the University.

F. *A Committee on Athletics.* It is suggested that the five members of the present Graduate Athletic Advisory Committee shall be elected members at large of the Graduate Council, and shall compose this sub-committee on athletics. This will provide a proper medium through which the graduates may be authoritatively informed regarding the athletic interests of the undergraduates. The inclusion of the Athletic Advisory Committee within the Graduate Council is in line with our expressed purpose to bring into closer organic relation the many college interests which engage the attention of Princeton alumni.

In preparing this report your Committee has earnestly desired to suggest a plan which would invite the coöperation of our ablest and most influential alumni in the difficult task of creating an adequate endowment for Princeton. But we have also hoped that in a practical way we might so organize our varied graduate activities that the splendid loyalty and enthusiasm of Princeton men may be directed into those channels which shall best promote the welfare of our University.

> Respectfully submitted,   C. C. CUYLER '79,
> JOHN G. HIBBEN '82,
> WILLIAM F. TIMLOW '86,
> GLENN FORD MCKINNEY '91,
> CHARLES W. HALSEY '98,
> JOSEPH R. TRUESDALE '04,
> ANDREW C. IMBRIE '95,
> Chairman.
> H. G. Murray '93,
> Secretary.[2]

Printed report (WP, DLC).

[2] For the Board of Trustees' action and subsequent developments, see the report printed at Jan. 13, 1909.

Henry Burchard Fine to the Board of Trustees' Committee on Morals and Discipline

Gentlemen: PRINCETON UNIVERSITY, OCTOBER 15, 1908.

I beg to submit the following report:

The night of April 18th. (in the spring recess) three students were taking an automobile ride through the streets of Trenton with three women of questionable character when the machine skidded and killed a passerby. The Coroner's jury held that the accident was due to the condition of the street and not to reckless driving. For the offense of associating with the women as they were doing the Faculty suspended the three students for one year.

Since my last report was submitted three students have been suspended for intoxication.

Shortly before Commencement the Freshmen were told that if they were to have the customary Freshman Parade it must be with the understanding that any member of the class would be suspended who on the day of the parade was intoxicated or was seen to visit a place where liquor is sold. I am glad to be able to say that so far as I know—and the saloons were watched—no member of the class attempted to obtain anything to drink that day. The parade was as free from objectionable features as it had been the year before.

This fall the Faculty voted to do away with the parade in masquerade which the Seniors have been accustomed to hold on the day of the Sophomore-Freshman base-ball game. The parade has in recent years been the occasion of intoxication and unseemly conduct. Happily the sentiment of the great majority of the class was in sympathy with the attitude of the Faculty and our action was accepted without any show of resentment.

It is a matter for congratulation that within the past two years we have succeeded in abolishing keg parties, the drinking incident to the Freshman parade, and the unseemly Senior parade.

Respectfully submitted,   H. B. Fine
Dean of the Faculty.

TRS (Trustees' Papers, UA, NjP).

From the Minutes of the Board of Trustees
of Princeton University

[Oct. 15, 1908]

The Trustees of Princeton University met in stated session in the Trustees' Room in the Chancellor Green Library, Princeton, New Jersey, at ten minutes after eleven o'clock on Thursday morning, October 15, 1908.

The President of the University in the chair. . . .

Mr. Thompson moved the adoption of the recommendations contained in the report of the Committee on Conference with Alumni. After discussion, on motion of Mr. Sheldon the first recommendation "That the establishment of a University Club, as proposed by the Graduate Committee, be for the present disapproved" was adopted.

Dr. McPherson moved that the second recommendation "That the formation of New Upper Class Clubs should not be encouraged" be laid on the table. The motion was lost.

Dr. McPherson then moved to amend the recommendation by the addition of the words "within the next two years" but the amendment was not seconded.

Mr. John A. Stewart moved the previous question. A vote was taken and the original recommendation was adopted by a vote of eleven to seven.

The third recommendation "That the upper class clubs should unite in appointing a duly authorized graduate committee to deal with themselves and with the University authorities in all matters affecting club life and club relations to the University" was adopted unanimously.

After a discussion of the sixth recommendation "That the Committee on Grounds and Buildings be instructed to prepare and report, for the further consideration of the Board, tentative plans for a college hall to be erected in immediate contiguity to some set of college dormitories, and to contain a dining room, a meeting room and a kitchen, adapted for the service of meals, and the social intercourse of about one hundred and fifty persons" and after the recommendation had been amended by striking out the words "to be erected in immediate contiguity to some set of college dormitories, and" the words "of about one hundred and fifty persons" it was, on motion of Dr. Jacobus, voted to lay the recommendation on the table. . . .

On motion of Mr. Russell, seconded by Mr. Thompson, it was
RESOLVED, That at the request of the donors of the Biological and Geological building it be named ARNOLD GUYOT HALL.

An Address at the Seventy-Fifth Anniversary of Haverford College

[[Oct. 16, 1908]]

President Sharpless, Ladies and Gentlemen:

A revolutionist[1] should bring you a better voice in which to proclaim his revolution than I have brought you this afternoon; but in this hall of convenient size, perhaps I can make myself audible on some of the subjects which have interested me most in recent years.

It is really a great privilege to be allowed to speak of matters which seem essential to the life of colleges, to an audience composed of men who can judge whether I speak the truth or not. And it seemed to me a particularly appropriate occasion upon which to speak of some matters of reform which do not directly concern Haverford, because she has in many respects been an honorable example to the contrary (Voices: "Hear! hear!") I believe that Haverford should receive our homage because of the conservative manner in which she has preserved the simplicity and homogeneity of her life. The wholeness of her life, the direct contact between those who teach and those who are taught, the democratic unity of the community, and many other things for which we know she stands, are among her honorable distinctions.

For it seems to me that in recent years the life of our colleges has become so heterogeneous that it is impossible to get the best results out of it. You know that one of the things that is confusing us in our statesmanship with regard to the affairs of the nation is the heterogeneity and complexity of our modern national life. We are not so much in doubt as to our moral standards as we are with respect to the application of those standards in very difficult and complicated cases; for the country is no longer a congeries of families, no longer a body of men; it is a body of complex corporate organizations in which the individual is largely lost, and in which, therefore, the old commands of the law, addressed to individuals, are hardly susceptible of application. The individual has run to cover; and in the complexities of modern life it is very difficult to discover so much as his trail. (Laughter.)

We are not in doubt what we wish to have done; but we are sadly in doubt how, having made only an imperfect analysis of our modern life, we are to accomplish what we desire. We are

[1] President Sharpless had introduced Wilson by referring to his innovations at Princeton as "perhaps revolutionary in their effects upon collegiate life in America."

attempting to reform a society which we have only partially analyzed and imperfectly understood; so that there is a contest among the best minds in this country as to whether certain things are good or evil. There is a contest amongst honest, thinking men as to whether the trust, for example, is, or is not, an evil. We know that trusts harbor men who do the nation deep wrong, but that is another question; and the real perplexity of our thought is to discover these individuals and bring them out of the cover of their association with other men at directors' tables and elsewhere, and set them before the tribunal of the nation's judgment.

And this same complexity—which is due to a thousand material circumstances, which have led to a thousand corresponding social circumstances—has spread to our schools and our colleges, spreading by natural process out of the life and experience of the nation itself. If you go into a modern school, or a modern college, and ask them to lay a program before you of what they are doing, it is like a catalogue of everything that concerns modern life. They are not doing anything in particular; they are doing everything in general. And it is very much in general; for, doing everything in general, they have not time to do anything in particular. So that they are touching the life of the nation here, there, elsewhere, everywhere, in the attempt to make a program as various as the life of the nation itself. A program this, highly proper to a university; because a university is the place where men must get their expert knowledge and that final touch of particular preparation and special skill which will fit them for the immediate tasks of a practical world. A university is a school for those who have their eyes turned directly either to research, or to teaching, or to the higher sorts of the applications of science to modern industry and to all the material undertakings of the age. The university must have the variety of the nation.

But reaching down from the university, and particularly from the German university, through the college into the schools, we have made this same diversity to prevail among the colleges and the schools. And in these places, hitherto means [meant] for discipline, hitherto meant for discovering whether men have minds or not, hitherto meant for a common discipline which would produce types of thinking and types of moral attitude, we are seeking the diversity, the multiplicity, the scattered purposes, of the university itself. In the university we don't allow the individual student to scatter his attention—the individual studies two or three things; but in the school and in the college the individual scatters, and attempts to study everything; we make it impossible to produce uniform results, not only, but impossible to find a method of discipline.

We have come to an age of absolutely dispersed standards, of an absolutely anatomized and analyzed system of instruction; and it is necessary that we should begin for the school and for the college, as we should begin for the nation, a very determined and studious attempt at synthesis. We must know what we would be at; and then we must discover the organization best adapted to accomplish that thing.

We do not yet know what we would be at; if we did, we would not ask an entering freshman what he wants; we would tell him what he ought to have. (Applause, and a voice: "Good!"). The wisdom, the ordering, the success, of the modern college course largely depends upon the intelligence of the entering class. Now I don't think, for my part (belonging to the teaching part of the university), that the university should have as its standard of intelligence the intelligence of the men who are just beginning to come under its discipline and influence. I don't care to put myself at the disposal even of my dear friends of the freshman class at Princeton. I think that unless, as I approach the age of fifty-two, I know better what these young gentlemen should have than they know, one of them—the best of them, I hope—should take my place. (Laughter.) The parts are singularly and ridiculously reversed; because we have not attempted any synthesis, and don't know what we would be at.

Now, why is synthesis difficult? It is not difficult to get a body of thoughtful men together in a room and make a program of study which will be better than the programs of study in most of our colleges; it would be very difficult to make a worse in some of them. I mean, by a worse, not in respect of its contents, but in respect of the relations of the subjects to each other and the portions considered essential, and the portions considered non-essential, or the portions considered more essential than others. That is what I mean by a program: a program for a course of study made up of the most excellent parts of the body of knowledge placed in their right order, and assigned to the most capable scholars to be taught. Until you have such a scheme you have not got a course or a program of study. I say it is not difficult to get thoughtful men together and make out a reasonably consistent and intelligent course of study; but when you have made the course of study, then you have to go out and capture your students.

For what are your students doing? Your students are doing

everything except paying serious attention to their studies. And they are not doing it because they are averse from study; they are not doing it, I believe, because they are unconscious of the beauty and desirability of study. They are doing it because there are so many other interesting things to be done in the college to which they go that, really, they haven't the time to be interested in study. And the things that they do are, in themselves, innocent and worth doing. The point is not that they are doing vicious things, not that they are doing things that lead to mere idleness; not that they are doing things that are unworthy of cultured and even of ambitious young men; but that, because the things they are doing are excellent, because they are interesting, because they are very well suited to engage the attention of honorable men, they engage their attention entirely and their instructors get the residuum. (Laughter.) College life has swallowed up the college curriculum, and has swallowed it whole, without digestion. (Laughter.)

In order to insert knowledge, you must really get the attention of those whom you are addressing; and unless you get that attention you can do nothing. You cannot get it unless you see to it that their minds are sufficiently disengaged from other things to be free to turn to you.

Now look at the modern college! You cannot count the number of organizations that exist in the larger college. There are not only athletic organizations. We have been getting excited about the wrong thing. It is not athletics that absorbs the attention of the average undergraduate. Athletics absorb the attention of the members of the athletic teams, to an unnecessary and to a demoralizing extent; but they do not absorb the attention of the average undergraduate very seriously. He goes out to see the practice, and he cheers the team; but he ought to be out of doors that long; and if he has not the ambition to exercise himself, it is just as well to cheer others on in their exercise. I see no harm in that. It improves the lung power and it draws undergraduates together in a certain disposition of spirited co-operation. (A voice: "That's good!") I am not in the least jealous of that. It is not the athletic organizations that are engrossing their attention, though they do engross the attention of very many capable young gentlemen who are some-time to be the heads of corporations; but there are scores of other organizations which do engross it; particularly social organizations, musical organizations, dramatic organizations, organizations to play chess, organizations to play whist, organizations to swim, organizations to do everything you can imagine; and the more capable, the more energetic, the more popular sort of man, has so many of his energies drawn upon by the necessity to organize his fellow-students in these ways that he has not time for his studies.

I had one of our most capable undergraduates say to me once that he didn't have time to take the mental science fellowship that season because he had to run the college (laughter); the point was, that though the lad was talking in jest, the thing was very nearly literally true. He was a fellow of extraordinary administrative capacity, and the whole undergraduate body did look to him for the suggestions which were to organize them for this, that, and the other thing that they wanted to do; and many a boy in school nowadays chooses his college by the tests of the number of interesting things there are to do there which have nothing to do with study. I don't blame him. I have no doubt that if I were at his age and in his place I would do just the same thing. But I want to ask college presidents if it is their ambition to be presidents of country clubs? (Laughter and applause.) Country clubs are very admirable things; but their presidencies do not afford careers; an ambitious gentleman must have something else to do beside that.

Now our colleges are not yet country clubs; and I do not think that the one college that I know most of, is at present in any danger of becoming one. But I am aware that in many a college the faculty happens to be in this ungracious position; it says to these young gentlemen placed under its care, "You must study;" and presently does drop them wholesole [wholesale] because they will not. Then they study; and if they are asked and pressed for a reason why they study, it is not because of the loveliness and desirability of knowledge, but because they want to stay in the place to enjoy its life. The price of the life is the successful passing of examinations.

Now, gentlemen, what is knowledge that is not itself an expression of life? How shall we ever produce men who will add to the intellectual force of this nation until we have turned away from this idea that college is merely, or chiefly, a delightful and desirable place in which to live, to that other ideal—older, more sacred, more beautiful, more vital—that it is a place in which to awaken the energies of the mind—to all those conceptions which lift men and nations to higher planes of living?

Then, when that spirit begins to obtain, the colleges of this country will so throb with life that men won't ask themselves whether they ought to send their sons to these places, any more than they will ask themselves whether, if they want electric power, they had better make connections with dynamos. They will then know that power is stored in such places, and that their sons may be treated like storage batteries and filled with that power.

But that power is not now there, except for individuals. There do come individuals one by one, sometimes, fortunately, by hundreds, to those places: boys with serious eyes in their heads, boys dreaming of things that lie beyond graduation, boys who have been thoughtful of life, who have pored upon great biographies and conceived great purposes and seen visions; and they segregate themselves and go through such schools as men set apart for a great undertaking; but they do not leaven the mass. For my part I don't want to be a taskmaster; I don't want to compel likable, lovable, youngsters to study because I say they must. I crave the privilege of showing them how beautiful a thing it is; the privilege of living with them and asking them if there is any flavor in my mind and in the minds of my colleagues, in the minds of those who represent life's study, that is to their taste, whether this is the flavor and the impulse they desire. I want a part in their life; and the only way in which the colleges in this country can be lifted out of their present heterogeneity into some fateful unity is by an organization which will make a common life, from top to bottom, for students and professors.

Now I am not going to lay out a program, or any special favorite plan of my own, by which that can be done; but I tell you, with the utmost confidence, that that is the only way in which the colleges of this country will be made real powers in the nation—a common organization, of which the faculty shall be just as intimate and vital a part as the undergraduates themselves; in which sport will be sport and not an occupation; in which diversions will be diversions and not the object of life; in which all the things that relieve the strain of work will be reliefs from work and not from other, similar occupations; and all of life shall be permeated with the consciousness that these men are members of a great community devoted to things which touch the highest ideals of the life, of the individual, and of the country.

You cannot get the spirit of learning transmitted through a non-conducting medium; and the modern organization of college life is a non-conducting medium for a score of reasons which you know just as well as I do; I do not have to expound them. It is a non-conducting medium; and you are wasting your power in trying to make a non-conducting medium conduct. If you believe in the real laws of spiritual transmission, first connect the veins and the vertebrae of your college life: you would then see the blood transmitted. Until you have done that, it will be impossible. We are now awakening to the fact that our college success does not depend chiefly either upon the excellence of our course of study, or the excellence of our body of instructors; it depends upon the character of the college life. If these excellent things are to be received the organization must be of one kind; if they are not to be received it must be of the present kind. Our task is a task of reconceiving and reorganizing the life of the American college. (Applause.)[2]

Printed in *Haverford College Bulletin*, VII (April 1909), 8-17.
[2] There is a WWhw outline and a typed outline, both dated Oct. 16, 1908; and a WWsh draft and transcript of an earlier version of this address in WP, DLC. The text printed here is from a stenographic report.

From Walter Hudson Watkins

Dear Sir: Chattanooga, Tenn. Oct. 16, 1908.

I have just received a letter from Mr. Gilbert F. Close, written under date of October 12th, in which he advises that it is your plan now to leave Princeton on Wednesday afternoon, and arrive in Nashville via the L. & N. at 8:35 P. M. on Thursday. We will therefore arrange to meet you on Thursday evening at the station unless we hear from you, indicating a change in your plans.

We are very glad indded [indeed] that you have arranged to be with us all day Friday. Everything is progressing satisfactorily and we are hopeful of having a successful reunion.

With kind regards, I am
                    Yours very truly,   Walter H. Watkins

TLS (WP, DLC). Enc.: printed program of the fourth annual meeting of the Princeton Alumni Association of Tennessee.

An Interview

[Oct. 17, 1908]

PRINCETON "FRATS" GET A REPRIEVE

President Woodrow Wilson Declares Report That Class Clubs and Societies Are to Be Abolished This Year Is Premature.

"The report that the authorities of Princeton have decided to abolish upper class clubs and fraternities in the present academic year[1] is premature and incorrect. We hope to bring about this change in time, but nothing definite has yet been accomplished."

This was the statement made by President Woodrow Wilson, of Princeton, yesterday, when asked to confirm the reports to the effect that the exclusive clubs and fraternities of the college would be ousted by the university authorities. President Wilson was seen at the ceremonies on the campus of the Haverford College grounds.

"I saw the report in one of the morning papers," he said, "but you will notice that the wording of the article is rather ambiguous. Reference is made to 'the first step' taken by the trustees at this week's meeting, but that does not mean by any means that the final word has been said on the subject. I fancy that the undergraduates will have to be allowed to present their side of the question before anything definite is accomplished."

Printed in the *Philadelphia Press*, Oct. 17, 1908.

1 Wilson referred to a news report which appeared in the *New York Herald*, Oct. 16, 1908, under the very misleading headline "Princeton Ousts the Class Clubs." The report itself was a straightforward summary of the action concerning the clubs taken at the meeting of the Princeton Board of Trustees on October 15, 1908. However, it was perhaps too brief to be fully intelligible to anyone not familiar with the details of the club controversy.

To the Editor of the *Daily Princetonian*

[Dear Sir:]   [Princeton, N. J., Oct. 17, 1908]

I drop you a line to say that the alleged interview with me, printed in this morning's Philadelphia Press, is an absolute fabrication. I had an interview with a representative of that paper, but said to him nothing even remotely resembling what he reports me to have said.

With much regard,

Sincerely yours,   Woodrow Wilson.

Printed in the *Daily Princetonian*, Oct. 19, 1908.

To Mary Allen Hulbert Peck

My dear Mrs. Peck   Princeton, 19 Oct., 1908

I had a very interesting visit to Haverford. Mrs. Wilson went with me; we stayed with old friends, who once lived in Princeton, —very congenial southerners;[1] and we had two enjoyable days amidst beautiful surroundings. The college exercises, too, had a certain touch of novelty and variety, because Haverford is a Quaker college where a great deal of genuine simplicity has been preserved, amidst surroundings marked by all the solid comfort and quiet beauty which are also characteristic of the canny Friends. The Haverford College grounds (covering some two hundred and twenty-five acres of land for which well-to-do Philadelphians would be willing to pay any price, set down, as it is, in exquisite variety of surface, within nine miles of the sacred city and in the midst of the most beautiful suburban region in America) are famous for their stately sweep of soft lawns and their fine groves of old trees, placed three life-times ago by an English master of park and garden arrangement; and the simple little pageant we saw there was even more favoured by setting and the stateliness of nature than were the processions at Williamstown. I was treated with real humanity. Besides the one speech I was scheduled for, I was not asked to do anything that I did not want to do; and so I had a really "good time,"—as good, at least, as the heavy cold I carried with me permitted me to have. Mrs. Wilson was taken on a long motor ride,—from which I, as usual, excused myself, perhaps selfishly,—and enjoyed it enthusiastically. Though we once lived for three years at Bryn Mawr, only a mile away, she had never before had a chance to see so much, so many nooks and corners, of that beautiful neighbourhood, which is kept almost as well as many of the more frequented parts of England. While she rode I wrote,—chiefly notes correcting an absolutely fabricated interview with me which had appeared in the Philadelphia *Press*. My cold stills [still] has its grip upon me, keeping me feeling half ill and *very* much in the depths of "the blues." I am a person, I am afraid, who observes no sort of moderation in anything, and when I *do* have the blues I go in for having them with great thoroughness and fairly touching bottom. All the while I am properly ashamed of myself,—admit that I have the deepest and best reasons possible for being proud and satisfied and happy,—if it were decent and permissible to be proud and wholesome to be satisfied and feasible to be happy with a heart that covets the world,—but reasoning has nothing to do with the matter so long as one feels ill and wretched. Sanity can come only when the organs return in a proper temper to their regular business. They are slowly returning and all will be well in time. Fortunately, I do not have to go away from home this week, but can work in a quiet routine which makes recovery quite certain. Next week the Princeton alumni of Tennessee hold their annual reunion, and I must be with them three days, Thursday, Friday, and Saturday, in Nashville. My brother lives in Nashville, and that lightens the burden of the business a little.

Wednesday, Oct. 21.

I began this letter on Monday,—only to be interrupted and the next day, after lecturing to my class, to be forced to bed by the cold I had been fighting for more than a week. I am still in bed as I write, and am still very wretched, but I am taking good care of myself and making slow but sure progress towards recovery. My stiff thumb, which makes writing in the ordinary posture very difficult, seems to make it well-nigh impossible on my back; but I *must* try to scratch off at least a line or two to tell you how much I have enjoyed and blessed you for the delightful letter I received from you to-day,[2] and to say again how happy it makes me to have our dear Jessie with you. I know she is having a lovely time, and I envy her with all my heart. The other girls were so tied up with engagements of every kind that it was really impossible for them to come to-day without gross discourtesy to others and some actual neglect of appointed duties. We were all deeply disappointed.

I will take the liberty of writing again and meantime must apologise for this poor letter written out of a very thick head.

With warm regards to all

Your devoted friend   Woodrow Wilson

ALS (WP, DLC).
[1] The Legh Wilbur Reids.
[2] It is missing.

To Horatio Whitridge Turner[1]

My dear Mr. Turner: Princeton, N. J.   October 19th, 1908.

I am sorry to find myself so tied up with a cold and engagements this week that I fear it would not be prudent for me to attempt to address the Municipal Club,[2] but if it would suit the convenience of the club for me to address it on the evening of Monday, October 26th, I will do so with pleasure.[3] Engagements are multiplying upon me so fast that it will be difficult for me to find any other early date.

With much regard,

Sincerely yours,   Woodrow Wilson

TLS (received from Horatio W. Turner).
[1] A member of the Class of 1909 at Princeton.
[2] An undergraduate organization, founded in 1905, devoted to the discussion of problems of the cities. The Municipal Club was a member of the National Municipal League.
[3] As it turned out, Wilson spoke to the Municipal Club on December 2, 1908. A news report of his address is printed at Dec. 3, 1908.

From Josephine Perry Morgan

Princeton, New Jersey

My dear Mr. Wilson: October 22d, 1908

I have been the medium of such a happy and eventful transaction today—and the day seemed so fitting—that I write to tell you of it. Mrs. McCosh has consented today to have her portrait painted by Mr. John W[hite]. Alexander, as a gift from him to the University, and to be hung in the Infirmary.[1] It is Mrs. McCosh's request that the portrait now hanging in the Infirmary shall be removed. I feel sure all of her friends will rejoice to have so poor a portrayal of her beautiful character done away with! I am sorry to hear that you have been ill, and I shall hope to see you before very long to tell you more in detail of this beautiful gift. I am very sincerely Josephine P. Morgan.

ALS (WP, DLC).
[1] It hangs in the lobby of the Isabella McCosh Infirmary of Princeton University.

From Walter Hines Page

My dear Mr. Wilson: New York October 22, 1908.

I thank you for your prompt kindness in enabling me to read your address,[1] and I wish to publish it in the World's Work very much.

But, in its present form, it would not carry far. It is very much more condensed and, if you will permit me to use the word, more professional than it is your habit to make your speeches. I fancy indeed that this is only the gist of what you said.

To reach a large, miscellaneous audience such as I serve, which is an audience of laymen, it would be necessary to have the theme hammered out, put more into the speech of the people and less into an academic mould and an academic vocabulary.

I wonder if you could get the time some day soon to make this change of its shape and of its method of expression. If you cam [can], I wish very much to use it.[2]

With all good wishes,

Very heartily yours, Walter H. Page

TLS (WP, DLC).
[1] To the American Bankers' Association on September 30, 1908. Wilson had sent Page a copy of the abstract of his address.
[2] Wilson's reply is missing, but he did not revise the abstract for publication. However, Page did print several quotations from the abstract in an editorial, "Banks Closer to the People," *World's Work*, XVII (Nov. 1908), 10856-57.

From Robert Morris McKinney[1]

Dear Sir: Chicago, October 23, 1908.

I want to express to you my appreciation of the splendid address which you delivered before the American Bankers Association recently, at Denver. It was especially pleasing to me for the reason that it touched upon a matter which has for some time seemed to me of the utmost importance. I refer particularly to that portion of your address where you say "Men in our day, in England and America, have almost forgotten what it is to fear government, but they have found out what it is to fear the power of capital . . . and we have forgotten what the power of government means and have found out what the power of capital means, so we do not fear government and are not jealous of political power." There is no question in my mind but that the present tendency to refer so large a variety of matters to the law making powers for correction is fraught with grave menace to the liberties of the people, and it is very reassuring to find that the subject is being given earnest thought by men of large affairs, especially by those who have under their direction the educational training of the young men who in future years are to shape the destiny of our country. I sincerely hope this may not be the last we shall hear from you along this special line.

Thanking you again for my share in the pleasure and profit afforded by your address,

Yours very truly   R. M. McKinney

TLS (WP, DLC).
[1] Cashier of the National Bank of the Republic in Chicago.

To Mary Allen Hulbert Peck

My dear Mrs. Peck,   Princeton. 25 October, 1908.

I am sorry I should have seemed to withhold important news from you,—but it was only *seemed*; for there was none. The newspaper men are always capable of inventing a sensation and their reports of the recent action of our Board of Trustees are a case in point. I am not pressing the Board, for the present, to "back me up," and their action the other day was on the report of a committee appointed to suggest a *modus vivendi* while we are waiting, at an unstable equilibrium, to make up our minds upon more fundamental undertakings. In brief, nothing of significance has happened, and all things stand as they were. I would have written you this before if I had known the false impressions would reach you, and if I had not been on my back, in a frame of mind and body unfit for human inter-course. I have been in bed for four days, with as wretched, *radical* a cold as ever I had, and would not be up now if friends, the [Frank A.] Vanderlips of N. Y., had not come to spend the week-end with us. I am writing now while they are at church (at the college chapel). The day is of uncertain temper and it did not seem prudent for me to go out-of-doors quite yet,—so exceeding prudent am I induced to be. Courtesy comes sometimes at a certain cost. Because I talked so much (confusing quantity with quality) last evening, I coughed most of the night, and am aware of being a bit the worse for wear now; but it was worth while to be forced out of bed by *some* compulsion. I had gone fairly stale, and felt as remote and ancient as the seventeenth century lying there read[ing] Pepys's Diary volume after volume, with amusement and interest but without edification! An age one would certainly *not* have wished to live in: many persons of many kinds, but how few noble and worth the love that seems the very essence of all that is worth living for,—no heroism, no unselfish devotion, no conceiving of visions or witnessing of dreams come true!

Our dear Jessie came home very well and very happy,—full of enthusiasm for her new friends in Pittsfield. I wish you could have seen her sweet frank eyes shine as she exclaimed how *per-fectly* charming you were and how she *loved* you. Even a doting parent would be satisfied if you loved and admired her as much as she loved and admired you. And the presents you gave her were certainly beautiful and characteristically generous. Her mother and she were exclaiming over them and trying them on for many happy minutes together,—admiring your taste no less than your generosity.

And now you plunge into the burdensome work of getting ready to vacate your home and transport all your necessary goods to Bermuda! Will you think me presuming if I express the hope that you will be very prudent and not overwork yourself? I have formed the impression that you throw yourself into work with the same ardour and eager interest with which you do everything else, but that your strength is by no means proportioned to your energy, and I should fear the effect of this biggest of all your movings on your health, if you were to work at it without meas-ure or restraint.

I have just had the pleasure of a visit from your son. It took me completely by surprise. I did not know that he was anywhere near this part of the world,—and the sight of him raised the sudden hope in my thought that you or some other member of the family might be near at hand and that I was to have the pleasure of seeing more of the delightful Pittsfield circle we have learned to love. He had come over from Trenton in a motor car with young Roebling.[1] It is cruelly hard luck that I am confined to the house by this wretched cold and cannot show him about my beloved Princeton,—and the rest of the family are all out. He is looking very well, and seemed to be enjoying his outing.

My cold has, by its ugly persistence, thrown me out of my regular routine and reckoning in many things. It is not likely now that I will go to Tennessee the latter part of this week as I had intended. A long journey and much speaking would probably be the height of impertinence toward Providence. I shall have to send one of my colleagues in my stead.[2] Not that I am not making noticeable progress toward being rid of my cold; but it is slow progress and I shall have to be patient and careful.

I cannot tell you what a privilege it is to hear from you, and to know that you are generously willing that I should keep in touch with you by correspondence. Your letters are truly delightful. You put yourself—your own individual flavour and delightful force—into your letters in an extraordinary degree, which makes me deeply your debtor, but makes me despair of ever evening the score between us. I have neither the delightful individuality nor the art of quickening written words as you do, —as if they were spoken, and the very tones of your voice in them! I feel selfish to be so greatly and so manifestly the gainer in the exchange,—but I am grateful in proportion to my deep debt and enjoyment. Mrs. Wilson, Madge Axson, and Jessie all bid me send you their warm love. Please give our warm regards to all your household, and believe me in all things

Your devoted friend   Woodrow Wilson

ALS (WP, DLC).
[1] Perhaps Siegfried Roebling (born 1890), son of John Augustus Roebling 2nd, of the famous engineering and industrial family of Trenton, N. J.
[2] He sent Dean Andrew F. West.

From Moses Taylor Pyne

My dear Woodrow   [Princeton, N. J.] Oct. 25/08

Cleve has written me asking if you had as yet appointed a Committee on Plan and Scope as directed by the Board at the October meeting. It should be done at once.

I trust that you will not feel obliged to go to Tennessee. Your cold ought to be sufficient excuse, and I trust that you will pardon me for reminding you

(a) That you are today Princeton's best asset,

(b) That you have no right to reduce the value of that asset by careless handling of yourself.

(c) That we need you now more than ever. We must clean up the finances this winter and you can be of more benefit to Princeton in the near future by keeping yourself in good health, by getting closer to the work here and by helping us in our financial campaign.

This letter requires no answer.

Yours ever   M Taylor Pyne

ALS (WP, DLC).

To Robert Morris McKinney

Princeton, N. J.

My dear Mr. McKinney: October 26th, 1908.

I very warmly appreciate your kind letter of October 23rd. I enjoyed very greatly the opportunity of addressing the Bankers' Convention in Denver and have been very much gratified by the kind way in which the address was received. I have the matter to which you refer very much at heart and shall take every occasion that offers to urge it. It heartens me very much to receive such a letter as yours.

Very sincerely yours,   Woodrow Wilson

TLS (Berg Coll., NN).

Henry Burling Thompson to
Melancthon Williams Jacobus

Dear Jacobus: [Wilmington, Del.]   October 26th, 1908.

I saw both Stephen Palmer and Harry Fine in Princeton on Saturday, and discussed the question which is now before our Committee on Curriculum.[1]

Fine seemed a little discouraged at the result of his first conversation with Wilson. He finds him hard to pin down, as he keeps shifting the argument. Fine proposes to see him again this week, and if nothing can be done, will then communicate with you; and the Committee will then have to decide what their plan of action will be for our next meeting with Wilson. I sincerely hope that Fine will be able to carry his point without calling on us, but if he does not, then, I feel that our Committee must assume the responsibility of making a recommendation to the Board on the lines discussed.

I have been entirely clear in my own mind for the past two years of the necessity of doing just what we are discussing, but in view of the fact that there has been so much before us, that has been disquieting, I have been patiently waiting for what I considered a fitting opportunity to bring the matter up before the Committee.

There is no question that our School of Science or Department of Science, needs a head, and certainly some of the departments need a decided bracing up to render them efficient for the future. We are not getting best results to-day; and this condition of affairs is on my conscience, and has weighed heavily on it for some time.

The plan that we have outlined is reasonable and feasible, and, I am sure, will prove efficient.

I do not think it necessary to recite details to you to prove my argument, but I could flood you with evidence to prove my position, if necessary.

Yours very sincerely,   Henry B Thompson

TLS (Thompson Letterpress Books, NjP).
[1] That is, the establishment of the new office of Dean of the Departments of Science, with Henry Burchard Fine as the first incumbent.

From Harvey Edward Fisk[1]

Dear Doctor Wilson,   Elberon, N. J.   Oct. 27th 1908

I have an impression that the instruction in Physics is way over the heads of the boys. I feel at liberty to write you because by your advice I had Harvey[2] prepare in German and let his Physics wait until he could take it up at Princeton. The course is I believe too theoretical for a beginner class. I hope you will pardon my writing, but just look into the matter in your own way. Harvey has not said a word to me and does not know that I am writing. I have reasons to believe that I am right in my criticism.

I feel sure you will take this suggestion as it is meant simply as a hint to look into the matter.[3]

With kind regards, believe me
Yours sincerely,   Harvey E. Fisk

ALS (WWP, UA, NjP).
[1] Princeton 1877, banker of New York.

2 Harvey Edward Fisk, Jr., survived the freshman physics course to graduate with the Class of 1912.

3 See W. F. Magie to WW, Nov. 7, 1908, and WW to H. E. Fisk, Nov. 11, 1908.

To Josephine Perry Morgan

My dear Mrs. Morgan, [Princeton, N. J.] 28 October, 1908.

I know that you will understand my delay in acknowledging your kind note of the twenty-second. I was in bed (being punished for defying a savage cold) when it came, and only to-day am I down stairs to stay. Heretofore I have dressed and come down only to meet important committees or to see guests who had been invited to come to us from out of town.

It was very kind of you to write me so promptly the delightful news that Mr. Alexander is going to paint a portrait of our dear Mrs. McCosh. God send he may have the genius and insight to paint a spirit! It is futile to regret that it could not have been done when she had the full beauty of her prime; and those of us who know her will be able to see in whatever Mr. Alexander paints the dear lady we so deeply love and reverence. It is for the sake of those who come after us that I pray the artist may be given some special gift of insight and interpretation[.]

With warm appreciation and regard,

Sincerely Yours, Woodrow Wilson

ALS (Isabella McCosh Infirmary, Princeton University).

To Stephen Squires Palmer

My dear Mr. Palmer: [Princeton, N. J.] October 28, 1908.

Mr. Henry B. Thompson of our Board of Trustees was kind enough to inspect the Laboratory of Physics, as you suggested, and has reported to me its completion with the exception of certain items of which he has made a list. I take the liberty of enclosing this list of exceptions in order that you may satisfy yourself that it is correct.

It gives me great pleasure, as the result of Mr. Thompson's report, to accept the laboratory in the name of the University and to assure you of the very great satisfaction with which we assume control of it. It seems to me in every way the best laboratory of its kind in the country, perhaps in the world, and I am sure that every year of use will enhance our appreciation of it.

With warmest regard,

Sincerely yours, [Woodrow Wilson]

CCL (WWP, UA, NjP).

From Melancthon Williams Jacobus

Private

My dear President Wilson:

Hartford [Conn.]
28 October 1908

Since my return from the Trustees meeting I have been laid up with a rheumatic attack which has disclosed such a low state of nervous vitality that I am in for a siege of resting for some weeks yet

But I must get out of my mind the vital interests at Princeton & write to ask whether favorable reply has been received from Mr Jones as to his acceptance of election to the Board.[1] If such reply has come, I think we can congratulate ourselves on another strong friend for the best interests of the University.

In any event I would like to ask what vacancies still remain and what we can do before the next meeting of the Board to get strong candidates placed before the important members of the Board for their approval. We are forced now to go at elections this way and we must make the most of our necessity.

I hope an extra Curriculum Committee meeting will not be called soon; for I am anxious to be present when it is convened & I am not yet out of bed.

In your consultation with Dean Fine can you two not work out some general scheme which will involve reorganizing the relation to your Presidential authority of the present Deanship of the Graduate School? You may think it best to pass it over at present —for we have large schemes in view as to the residential quad. development of the Graduate College, where no "niggers in woodpiles" need be feared—but it would be well to give the problem earnest thought. . . .

With kindest regards,
Yours cordially   Melancthon W. Jacobus

ALS (WP, DLC).
   [1] Although his letter of acceptance is missing, Thomas D. Jones had accepted election as a member of the Board of Trustees.

From Stephen Squires Palmer

My dear Dr. Wilson: New York   October 29, 1908.

I am greatly obliged for your good letter of 28th instant accepting the Laboratory on behalf of the University.

As to the exceptions, as noted in the list which you were so good as to send me, much of the work has been finished and we are pushing the balance as rapidly as possible. So soon as it is completed we shall ask Mr. Thompson to inspect same and if he is satisfied that everything has been properly done to so advise you.

I expect to receive from Professor McClenahan on Friday or Saturday of this week a complete list of what equipment is still needed, which I shall at once close for.

It is my earnest desire to have everything pertaining to construction and equipment completed as quickly as possible, and I am bending my efforts to that end.

Very truly yours,   S S Palmer

TLS (WP, DLC).

The Independent's Review of Constitutional Government in the United States

[Oct. 29, 1908]

Many years since Dr. Woodrow Wilson published a book on "Congressional Government," in which he described the method of Congressional legislation by committee. His present book* shows an advance from the more technical method that he then followed, and he deals free hand with the broad subject of "Constitutional Government in the United States." His chapters have much of the life of the spoken word; indeed, they were lectures, and stimulating ones, before Columbia University.

From his initial question, "What is Constitutional Government?" thru his discussion of its various phases in President, Congress and courts, and in the inter-relation of State and nation, to his remarkable review of the present condition of "Party Government in the United States," he maintains the simple and often neglected proposition that the government of the country is of vital importance to the citizens and is vitally affected by them. The relation of the various branches of the Government to the people is always in view. The word "academic" is to be applied to no part of the book.

Usually Dr. Wilson is optimistic and he loves to find in the relation of State to nation an example of the federation of the world, but he has no fear of obliteration of State lines. Now and again he puts in a nutshell and answers a question that fills volumes of discussion. Of the Philippine Islands he says, "Self-government is not a thing that can be given to any people, because it is a form of character and not a form of constitution."

* *Constitutional Government in the United States.* By Woodrow Wilson, Ph.D., LL.D. New York: Macmillan Co. $1.50.

The perennial accusation that justice is not as accessible to the poor man as to the rich (indeed, nature seems as unable as society to treat all men equally, tho granting them equal rights) is stated at length, but a solution of the difficulty, if indeed there really be a governmental difficulty in it, Dr. Wilson does not give, but leaves it with somewhat destructive criticism. He decries also the too practical tendency of our legislation that leads to the makeshift escape from temporary inconvenience. He deals also with the experimental legislation we have had as to cities, that we fear has been thrust upon us by unprecedented conditions.

The real worth of the book, and for this we hope it may be widespread, is that it often answers the cry for law to correct this or that iniquity. "Moralization," he says, "is by life and not by statute"; and then in his chapter on party government, in which he shows anew the necessity for party government and for politicians and even for political methods as we generally know them, he gives a really splendid challenge to political activity.

Dr. Wilson's lectures are clearly intended for the thoughtful citizen not necessarily learned in the law—a popular treatise.

Printed in the New York *Independent*, LXV (Oct. 29, 1908), 1001.

To Mary Allen Hulbert Peck

My dear Mrs. Peck,   Princeton, 2 Nov., 1908.

I am happy to say that my cold is so nearly well that I am doing full work again without distress and regard myself as again in 'full and regular standing' among my colleagues. That means, unhappily, only a scrap of time here and there when the letters one *wants* to write can be written. There seems to be no measure or limit to college work: we must be at it from the time we leave the breakfast table until we go to bed at night: our only relaxation and indulgence is that there are little pauses here and there in the hurried movement of the day when we can *think* of our best friends and *wish* for a sight of them, for an opportunity to open our minds and hearts to them, and can for a few delightful moments at a time use at least the cold medium of pen, ink, and paper to put our minds alongside theirs.

How few those pauses are is illustrated by the fact that I wrote thus far on Monday and it is *now* Wednesday! But that only makes them the more precious! I will not grumble if only they will come now and then!

Since beginning this letter another discipline has fallen on me: my poor teeth, which I have systematically neglected for eight years, have at last risen in their resentment to strike me, and have smitten me hip and thigh! I have been to my dentist and have suffered what I had supposed was reserved for a later stage of my existence! And the end is not yet. The aching intermission which I am now enjoying (?) is only a sort of purgatory, an intermediate stage, from which I shall again plunge into torture. It all comes with the day's work, no doubt. Life is no holiday, and it does not make it any more bearable (besides making it much less dignified) to make wry faces. I would only like to remark that having three several roots pulled from one and the same cavity makes one think unspeakable things,—especially one who will not condescend to take gas and who is, therefore, free to think, during the performance. Pardon me for speaking of it. I suppose it is a recognized privilege of friendship that one may show his weaker, even his weakest, side to the friends who will best understand and most deeply sympathize. That is the delightful mystery and solace of friendship and affection, that one can abandon all reckonings of what is worth speaking of and what is not, speak of trifles as freely as of big things of lasting importance, and be sure at every turn of a complete understanding and sympathy. The truth is, that there are no more big things in a college president's day than in another man's, and there's no use in his posing and pretending that his life is not made up of trifles,—made or marred by them. There is nothing new or entertaining to say about my daily round of duties, and I might as well indulge myself and ask leave to say, what interests me as deeply as if it concerned only myself and not the whole country, namely, that the results of yesterday's voting[1] confirm the Republican party more deeply than ever in the possession of a power they have grossly misused and render it almost impossible to organize a successful party of opposition within less than another generation,—unless men as unlike Mr. Bryan as principle is unlike expediency will devote themselves to gaining influence and control as if to a daily business, as Mr. Bryan has done. He has devoted himself to creating and maintaining an immense personal influence,—and to nothing else, for 'causes' with him have been means to an end,—for the last twelve years; and even now no one can supplant him who will not

[1] The Republican, William Howard Taft, defeated the Democratic candidate, William Jennings Bryan, for the presidency, 7,675,320 to 6,412,294 popular votes. The Republicans also retained control of both houses of Congress by large majorities.

deliberately enter the lists against him and do the like,—with this immense difference, that he must devote himself to principles, to ideas, to definite programmes and not to personal preferment, —that he must be a man with a cause, not a candidacy. It's a desperate situation,—for what man of that kind will be willing to risk the appearance of personal ambition? If someone only would, how gladly I would help him! Two years from now I can retire on a Carnegie pension of $4000. I have $2000 of my own. I shall not willingly wait more than two years for the Princeton trustees to do what it is their bounden duty to do with regard to the reform of university life. At the end of that time I would be glad to lend my pen and voice and all my thought and energy to anyone who purposed a genuine rationalization and rehabilitation of the Democratic party on lines of principle and statesmanship! I know what you, in your partiality, will say: 'Why not take the initiative yourself, and yourself build up a leadership which will be effective?' Because I do not judge myself as partially as you judge me. I am willing to do *this*: I am willing to *seem* to take the initiative, to seem to venture upon the field alone and of my own motion, and then yield the field, with the best will in the world, to some one of the rivals who would certainly be drawn out by my action. The man who *first* adventures will be the one misunderstood and most easily discredited by the forces of jealousy which would be gathered against him, and if that sacrifice is necessary I am not unwilling to offer myself for it. Certainly I do not want the presidency! The more closely I see it the less I covet it. The 'sacrifice' would be a release from what no prudent man, who loved even his physical life, could conceivably desire!—But how I talk! Here is another of the selfish indulgences of friendship! I would not dare write thus to any one who knew me less well. To any but an intimate friend, already understanding me and knowing how to assess me, what I have written would seem a piece of insufferable egotism,—whereas the simple fact is that I do not deem myself the man, but was born political and chafe like a dog in leash that I must sit here in academic seclusion and not run the game to cover. The fray would be delightful, and would be free from all the polite restraints of academic controversy! One could say what he really thought and make the fight a fight!

I am very anxious to hear your plans. When are you now purposing to sail for Bermuda? May I know the date so that, if possible, I may be at the wharf to say good-bye? It would be a melancholy pleasure.

Mrs. Wilson joins me in warm regards to Mrs. Allen, Mr. Peck, Miss Harriet, and Mr. Hulbert,[2] and I am

Your devoted friend   Woodrow Wilson

ALS (WP, DLC).
 [2] Her mother, Anjenett Holcomb (Mrs. Charles Sterling) Allen; her husband, Thomas Dowse Peck; her stepdaughter, Harriet Peck; and her son, Allen School-craft Hulbert.

A Memorandum[1]

Memorandum.   November 3rd, 1908.

THE DEAN OF SCIENTIFIC STUDIES

I. Shall be charged with the duty of consulting with the several scientific departments and advising the President of the University with regard to instruction in the mathematical and physical sciences.

II. Shall have administrative oversight, under the President of the University, of the organization, development, and conduct of all work in applied science.

III. In respect of all special appropriations and endowments for maintenance or equipment in the several departments of scientific instruction, it shall be his duty, after consultation with the departments concerned, to advise the President of the University how the funds may be best expended to secure the greatest usefulness, efficiency and economy.[2]

T MS (WP, DLC).
 [1] This draft of a by-law of the Board of Trustees is a revision of a draft submitted by Henry B. Fine, Hw MS entitled "Dean of the Departments of Science" (WP, DLC).
 [2] For the by-law finally approved by the Board of Trustees, see the Committee on the Curriculum to the Board of Trustees, Jan. 13, 1909.

From John Lambert Cadwalader

My dear Mr. President,   [New York]   November 3, 1908.

I was sorry to miss your visit the other day—I came back from Europe a week too late—to my regret, and I have had a very bad time in trying to catch up.

I do not know the condition of Mrs. Sage's matter[1]—or or [sic] whether it is on a satisfactory basis. If not, and you desire me to do anything, let me know. I think I should say to you in confidence that I have determined not to be a candidate for election as alumni Trustee, at the next election.[2] I have been elected &

reelected since the beginning, and I am of opinion that the office should not be a permanent one—as the number of Trustees is small. Jones and I came to this conclusion some time since. I need not say how grateful I am for the kindness and consideration I have received at your hands and from the entire Board— and my retirement shall, in no respect, lessen my interest in Princeton, & all that concerns it. I shall be glad if you will come here—any night when you are to be in town.

Yours faithfully—   John L. Cadwalader

ALS (WP, DLC).
    [1] That is, plans for the dormitory, later named Holder Hall, being financed by Mrs. Sage.
    [2] He announced this intention in J. L. Cadwalader to C. W. McAlpin, Nov. 28, 1908, *Princeton Alumni Weekly*, IX (Dec. 9, 1908), 165.

To Henry Lee Higginson

Princeton, N. J.

My dear Major Higginson: November 4th, 1908.

I warmly appreciate your kind letter of the first of November.[1] We are looking forward to the concert of the orchestra with the greatest pleasure. We have but a little audience here, but they are all music lovers and I am sure will appreciate the very great treat which is in store for them.[2] We feel very grateful to you for your generous kindness in this matter.[3]

With warm regards,

Sincerely yours,   Woodrow Wilson

TLS (H. L. Higginson Coll., MH-BA).
    [1] It is missing.
    [2] For a report of the concert by the Boston Symphony Orchestra, see the *Daily Princetonian*, Nov. 10, 1908.
    [3] About Higginson's sponsorship of the concert, see WW to H. L. Higginson, May 21, 1908.

Notes for a Talk at the Lawrenceville School

Lawrenceville Scholl [School], 4 Nov. 1908.

What Kind of Citizens Shall We Be?

A question even boys cannot shun.
    1. Clean men, "models for the mass."
    2. Thoughtful of duty.
    3. Regardful of the public interest,—which *now* means the rights and feelings of others.

4. Studious of our national history,—not a book subject, but a subject of life and reality.
5. Preferring men, not merely for what they are, but also for what they represent and for *whom* they represent.

Why go to college, unless upon a principle?

3 Nov., 1908[1]

WWhw MS (WP, DLC).
[1] Wilson's composition date. No report of this address appeared in the school paper, *The Lawrence*.

From John Lambert Cadwalader

My dear Mr. President: New York, 5 November, 1908.

My letter appears to have crossed yours.

Mrs. Sage is not in New York, but is at Lawrence, Long Island, where I have addressed your letter and have had it posted. I am quite sure she cannot attend any meeting from the country; it is possible that when she gets to town she may be able to do so.

I saw Robert de Forest last night (his brother,[1] with whom I had the principal conversation, is now ill), and explained the circumstances to him. He said send the letter by all means, but he doubted whether Mrs. Sage could attend, although she would like to get the letter, in any event. He added that he would see her within a day or so and would urge her, if it could be done reasonably, to comply with your suggestion. If she goes, I will try and go, and I told de Forest that we would arrange to have him go. I doubt, however, whether she goes, and the next best thing is to have her say she cannot go and invite you to go ahead without her.   Yours faithfully,   John L. Cadwalader

TLS (WP, DLC).
[1] That is, Henry Wheeler de Forest.

From Joseph R. Wilson, Jr.

My dear brother: Nashville, Tenn. 11-5-'08.

It is needless for me to say that I was disappointed because of your inability to visit us this fall and doubly so because your trip was prevented by sickness. When your letter reached Nashville announcing your coming, I was away from home representing the Banner in the night rider district of West Tennessee where the times for a while were very war-like.[1] I reached home just in time to receive your second letter stating that you could not come. I do hope that you have by now recovered from your sickness.

I met and enjoyed Dr. West who attended the Princeton alumni meetings here. I saw him at a smoker given in his honor and also at the annual banquet last Saturday night. I was much pleased with him. He is apparently an able man and is certainly a most delightful gentleman.

Perhaps you do not realize it, but your letter last week stating that you were coming to Nashville, was the first time I had heard from you since your visit to us last fall, more than a year ago now. I have partially kept up with your most important movements through the press reports, accidentally learning in this way of your trip abroad last summer.

Since I last saw you I have had rather an eventful life in connection with my newspaper work. I have been all over the state as a special campaign correspondent for the Banner[2] and have made many delightful friendships and acquired considerable valuable experience thereby. This work occupied me for more than two months during the spring and early summer. This gave me a state wide acquaintance and reputation, although, of course, those who differed from me politically took occasion at times to say rather harsh things. This mattered little to me, however, I realizing that this was only one of the things that must come to a man in public life, especially political life. Nothing was said, I am glad to say, that was in the least degree a reflection on my integrity. This was very wearing upon me and as soon after the trip as possible I took a rest of two weeks at Monteagle and in Clarksville, the benefit of railroad passes for us three making this possible without additional cost to me.

Then followed a season of varied other work, much of which claimed my entire time at the desk in the office and added all the more to my experience and acquaintanceship with the newspaper field in its various phases. After this was a period of "war correspondence" in the night rider district where the otherwise strenuous work from early morning until past midnight each day with drives of as much as forty miles across country in between for good measure, was made all the more interesting by the fact that a clash between the troops and the lawless element was constantly feared. I came out of this, however, with a whole skin and became again engaged in the activity of campaign work and the handling of complicated election returns.

With all of this I have kept my health and God has been good to Kate and Alice by keeping them well, too.

Please let us try to write at least semi-annually after this, thus hearing from each other twice as often as we now do.

Much love from us three to you and yours.

Your affectionate brother, Joseph.

TLS (WP, DLC).

[1] For a discussion of the tobacco night riders of Kentucky and Tennessee, see R. H. Fitzhugh to WW, March 4, 1908, n. 1. However, J. R. Wilson, Jr., here apparently refers to an affair which seems to have had little direct connection with the tobacco night riders. The incident arose out of a lengthy controversy over hunting, fishing, and grazing privileges on and around Reelfoot Lake in Obion and Lake counties in western Tennessee. The residents of the area claimed these rights from time immemorial, while the West Tennessee Land Company, which owned most of the land surrounding the lake, insisted that the rights were theirs by purchase. On the night of October 19, 1908, a band of masked men seized two lawyers representing the company at their hotel near the lake and carried them off into the countryside. One of the lawyers was shot to death after being hanged from a tree. The other managed to escape. The Governor of Tennessee called out the militia, and numerous sheriff's posses were formed. By mid-November, all suspects in the crime had been captured. The leaders were convicted, but the judgments were ultimately reversed on appeal and the defendants released. See James O. Nall, *The Tobacco Night Riders of Kentucky and Tennessee, 1905-1909* (Louisville, Ky., 1939), pp. 143-45, which argues that the night riders had no connection with the Reelfoot Lake affair. However, Hillsman Taylor, "The Night Riders of West Tennessee," *The West Tennessee Historical Society Papers*, VI (1952), 77-86, maintains that tobacco night riders were responsible for the Reelfoot Lake incident.

[2] J. R. Wilson, Jr., here refers to the bitterly contested Democratic primary campaign between incumbent Governor Malcolm Rice Patterson and former United States Senator Edward Ward Carmack for the governorship of Tennessee from April to June 1908. The principal issue was prohibition, with Patterson favoring the local option system then in operation in Tennessee and Carmack demanding state-wide prohibition. Patterson defeated Carmack in the primary election by some 7,000 votes. Carmack continued the fight for prohibition, most notably in his role as editor of the newly founded Nashville *Tennessean*. Feeling continued to run high into the autumn of 1908, and on November 9, 1908, Carmack was shot to death on a main street of Nashville by two partisans of Governor Patterson offended by editorials written by Carmack. Carmack became a martyr to the cause of prohibition, and the Tennessee legislature adopted a state-wide prohibition law in January 1909 and subsequently passed it over Governor Patterson's veto. See Eric Russell Lacy, "Tennessee Teetotalism: Social Forces and the Politics of Progressivism," *Tennessee Historical Quarterly*, XXIV (Fall 1965), 219-40; Arthur S. Link, "Democratic Politics and the Presidential Campaign of 1912 in Tennessee," *The Higher Realism of Woodrow Wilson and Other Essays* (Nashville, Tenn., 1971), 172-99; and especially Paul E. Isaac, *Prohibition and Politics: Turbulent Decades in Tennessee, 1885-1920* (Knoxville, Tenn., 1965), pp. 137-66.

News Reports of Two Addresses in Jersey City

[Nov. 6, 1908]

UNIVERSITY CLUB HEARD PRES. WILSON

Guest of Honor at Reception There Last Night.

President Woodrow Wilson, of Princeton University, was the guest of honor at a smoker and reception given by the University Club at its headquarters in Hasbrouck Hall.[1] In speaking to the members of the club and to the college men of the city in general, Mr. Wilson said in part:

"What the country needs in the present day is the man who does things. Theorizing and preaching do well enough in their way, but there is something beyond these things.

"The ordinary man of affairs is content to expatiate on the grievous condition of men and things of the day. He will criticize and correct, but he seldom offers a remedy for those things which he deprecates. The state of the nation is bad, he says, morality and decency in the wane and the body politic in a grievous condition, but when you ask him why he does not play a part in correcting them he can not answer you. He is ready and willing to tear down but he is not constructive, he can not build up. I say it is the duty of every man with the welfare of the times and of his fellows at heart to take some active part in the uplifting and betterment of their state. Men should get out and perform but shrinks from doing.

"For instance men will criticise the laws of the country but they will not attempt to change them. So when you find an individual who will tell you of these things do not let him get away. Pin him down and make him do something. Make him sit down and write a statute if he thinks the present one is not all that it should be. In the parlance of the street make him 'put up or shut up.'

In speaking of things political Mr. Wilson [commented upon] the orthodoxy of the parties of the present day saying they are distinguishable by name rather than doctrine. "Individuality of thought as well as of action is a necessary adjunct of improved conditions and blind subserviency to a pat standard is neither desirable nor helpful. The party man should be such because the predictions [predilection] of his party appeal to his better judgment and belief and not because perforce there are but two great parties to choose and he choose[s] at random."

Mr. Wilson also spoke of the relations of the affairs of the individual to the affairs of the community at large and said that the times are such that the people have a right to know just how each man is conducting his business. "Of a necessity," he declared, "in these days there should be a public declaration of intention. Each man is an integral part of civilization and as such his fellows have a right to know what he is doing and how he is doing it. They may be bettered by by [sic] such knowledge and he may be bettered by the thought that others know of his procedure. Business and private existence are not separated by any wide chasm, but are interrelated and should not be considered one without the other."

During his stay in this city Mr. Wilson was the guest of George G. Tennant.[2]

1 On November 5, 1908.
2 George Grant Tennant, lawyer and President of the Board of Education of Jersey City.

◇

DR. WILSON AT JERSEY CITY HIGH SCHOOL

President Woodrow Wilson of Princeton University addressed the pupils of the Jersey City High School this morning, being the first of a number of heads of leading educational institutions of the country who during the coming winter will speak before the pupils of the school on the relation between the college and the public school. Dr. Wilson gave a notable address, which was listened to with the greatest interest by the pupils and several hundred visitors. In the course of his remarks he was time and again interrupted by appreciative applause.

President of the Board of Education George G. Tennant, Mayor [Henry Otto] Wittpenn and many of the leading educators of the city were on the platform with Dr. Wilson. In addition there was a committee from the University Club and also a committee of citizens. As a special tribute to their guest of honor the pupils of the High School, as Dr. Wilson was introduced, sang "Old Nassau," the Princeton anthem, which was admirably rendered. Dr. Wilson said in part:

"It is a unique but very great pleasure for me to talk before such an audience as this, composed as it is of the very bone and gristle of the country's future strength. One of the things that men coming to middle life would like to impart to you is a realization of the chastening effect of experience.

"The pathos of the situation has often appealed to me that I cannot impart to you from my experience anything that will keep you from being just as great a fool as I was at your age. Had I then known what I know now I am sure I would know more now and have been better than I have been.

"One of the mistakes young people make in these times, and in this connection, is to think that we older people who are charged with their direction along the lines of education, make them study for our own delectation. This is not so. There is no pleasure in merely driving a young mind. The ones who are deriving or at least should derive pleasure from their studies are the ones who enter upon those studies with zest and enthusiasm, who study because they like it and because they feel that by it their minds will be developed and broadened for the work they have to do in the world. If you don't and won't study it is your own funeral and yours alone. Societies will very willingly and quite automatically attend to the obsequies.

"There is one thing that young people do not seem to realize and that is the necessity of doing things with force and precision. Hit the mark with your efforts. When I was a young man there was one piece of advice that my father gave me that I have never forgotten. He told me when I was shooting at a mark not to use birdshot which might touch the bulls' eye but would also pepper the whole countryside as well. 'Use a rifle,' he told me, 'and hit the bulls' eye and nothing else.' For directed and concentrated effort achieves the best results.

"The records of Princeton University have shown this year that but 18 per cent of the entering came from the public High Schools, such as this great one of yours, leaving a great majority to come from private institutions. This proportion is not as it should be, for the private schools contain but a small and selected part of our citizenship. The section from the public schools represents the great rank and file of our nation, and I want to see our colleges benefited and vitalized by the increment of blood and gristle from the very backbone of our civilization.

"High School and college educations are closely connected in that one leads directly into the other and is really a part of it. But an education is not merely knowledge. The educated person is not one who has great mass of miscellaneous information and learning. It is the person who has learned how to control his mind effectively, who has been really educated.

"Young people often question the utility of certain studies, such as Greek, seeing no direct returns to be derived from them. Why do they practice in the gymnasium? They do not expect to go through such motions later in life, but they do hope to so toughen the fibres of their muscles that their muscles will be able to respond to future demands. The analogy is complete, for the object of education is to put the mind in such agile shape that it may attack any task with a reasonable prospect of accomplishing it.

"If I can leave with you some glimpse of that greater land beyond the horizon toward which scholars are striving in the hope that they may find new fields, some new freedom of the mind, I shall have been well repaid for my coming here. I would, if I could, awaken in you some perception of that great beyond that you too might join with others in that field of discovery and join with zest."

Printed in the Jersey City *Evening Journal*, Nov. 6, 1908; some editorial headings omitted.

From Henry Burling Thompson

[Wilmington, Del.]

Dear President Wilson: November 6th, 1908.

I have had inquiries from two club representatives with regard to the third resolution of our report which was adopted by the Board at its last meeting; viz, the appointment of a Graduate Committee representing the various clubs.

I have been asked whether a formal notice is to be sent to each club, asking them to appoint a representative; and whether the Board had appointed a Committee with whom they could confer; also, could they confer with our present Committee, which, as I understand it, has not yet been discharged by the Board.

I have been unable to answer any of these questions,—assuming that, while our Committee had not yet been discharged, we had no authority to act in the matter.

Will you please let me know how I should answer these inquiries?

Yours very sincerely,   Henry B Thompson

TLS (Thompson Letterpress Books, NjP).

From William Francis Magie

My dear Wilson,   Princeton, New Jersey, Nov. 7. 1908

After reading Mr. Fisk's letter and looking into the matter I am prepared to tell you that there is nothing in his strictures worthy of notice. The textbook used with the Freshman class in the School of Science is a very elementary one, written for use in High Schools.[1] The students give half their hours to simple practical work illustrating the principles taught them, & from the little experience I had with them lately in the laboratory, they seemed to have the principles well in their minds. Professor McClenahan probably supplements the book with lectures in which the elementary theory of some subjects is developed beyond what is found in the book, but I know he does not give

anything that college students should not be expected to understand. The course is based on an elementary outline of the
subject and is somewhat modified and advanced to suit College
students. I am sure we would all agree that anything less
"theoretical" would be unworthy of our students, and inconsistent with our desire to make our first courses in physics illustrate scientific method as well as present the main facts of the
science.

The examination test is a good one, and our Freshman course
in physics does not yield a disporportionately large number of
conditions; about from 10 to 15 per cent of the class.

I am   Yours sincerely   W. F. Magie

ALS (WWP, UA, NjP).
¹ It was Robert Andrews Millikan and Henry Gordon Gale, *A First Course
in Physics* (Boston and New York, 1906).

To Andrew Fleming West

Princeton, N. J.
My dear Professor West: November 9th, 1908.

May I impose upon you the duty of replying to the enclosed
invitation to the President and Faculty of Princeton University,
in a letter which, at the same time that it regrets our inability
to be represented at the inauguration of Dr. Hill,¹ extends to the
University of Missouri the warm congratulations of Princeton?
I know how well you can do this and I hope that you will not
think that I am imposing upon you by asking you to do it.

Very sincerely yours,   Woodrow Wilson

TLS (UA, NjP).
¹ Albert Ross Hill, who was inaugurated as President of the University of
Missouri on December 11, 1908.

From Moses Taylor Pyne

My dear Woodrow: New York   November 10th, 1908.

The Treasurer has received two cheques of $5,000 each from
Charles A. Munn¹ and from Mrs. Henry N. Munn,² to establish
the O. D. Munn Fellowship in Electrical Engineering.³

The Treasurer has also received from James Speyer,⁴ Esq.,
No. 24 Pine Street, the sum of $10,000 to found the Gordon Mac-
donald Fellowship.⁵ I enclose copy of the letter he wrote to Mr.
Duffield.⁶

I think it would be advisable for you to write both to Mr. Speyer and to Charley Munn, thanking them personally for these gifts.   Yours very sincerely,   M Taylor Pyne

TLS (WP, DLC).
1 Charles Allen Munn, Princeton 1881, publisher and co-editor of *Scientific American*.
2 Ann Elder (Mrs. Henry Norcross) Munn, sister-in-law of Charles Allen Munn and mother of Orson Desaix Munn, Princeton 1906.
3 The fellowship was a memorial to Orson Desaix Munn (1824-1907), father of Charles Allen Munn and for many years publisher and co-editor of *Scientific American*.
4 Member of the Speyer family of international bankers; senior partner of the New York banking firm of Speyer & Co.
5 Founded by James Speyer in memory of his friend and partner in Speyer & Co., Gordon MacDonald, who had died on August 14, 1908. The fellowship was not assigned to any specific department.
6 J. Speyer to H. G. Duffield, Nov. 9, 1908, CCL (WP, DLC).

From Catherine Hunter[1]

[Lawrence, L. I.]
My dear President Wilson,   November tenth [1908].

Mrs. Sage has received a very attractive invitation to visit you at Princeton which it would give her pleasure to accept, if that were possible. It is not practicable for her, however, to visit Princeton at the present time, and she will have to put off all consideration of leaving home until she has again established herself in the city.

Mrs. Sage thanks you and Mrs. Wilson warmly for this kind courtesy towards her, and is sorry to be obliged to say that she cannot accept it now. With her very kind regards, I am
                    Sincerely yours,   Catherine Hunter

ALS (WP, DLC).
1 Secretary to Mrs. Russell Sage.

To Harvey Edward Fisk

My dear Mr. Fisk: [Princeton, N. J.]   November 11th, 1908.

Allow me to acknowledge with appreciation the receipt of your letter of October 27th. I made it the occasion of an inquiry into the instruction in Physics, because it seemed to me very important that I should assure myself of the character of that instruction, after the intimation which your letter conveyed.

Of course such inquiries are delicate and difficult. I have myself no opportunity to hear the instruction given, and, under the established etiquette of university life, it would be considered very strange if I made an occasion.

I have done what I could by way of inquiry and have learned that the text book used with the freshman class is a very elementary one, written for use in High Schools. The students give half their hours to simple practical work illustrating the principles taught them, and it was the testimony of those whom I made inquiry that they seemed to have the principles very well in mind. Professor McClenahan, I believe, supplements the book with lectures in which the elementany [elementary] theory of some topics is developed beyond the point to which the exposition is carried in the text book, but he does not in his lectures give anything that college students might not be expected readily to understand. The course is based on an elementary outline of the subject and is only a little modified and advanced. Anything less theoretical would hardly be worthy of our students and would seem to our instructors inconsistent with our desire to make our first courses in Physics illustrate scientific method as well as the main facts of the science.

Judged by the examination test, the success of the course would seem to be fair. The number of freshmen conditioned in the Physics examinations is not disproportionately large, being only about from 10 to 15 per cent of the class usually. I think, therefore, that probably the difficulties lie in the subject itself, but I should be very much obliged to you, if you have any detailed or specific criticisms to make, to have you state them very frankly indeed. I feel that your criticism is entirely legitimate, and I am sure that we wish to be guided by intelligent impressions about the matter as muc[h] as the nature of the subject would permit us to be guided.

With warm regards,

Sincerely yours,   [Woodrow Wilson]

CCL (WWP, UA, NjP).

To Charles Allen Munn

[Princeton, N. J.]
My dear Mr. Munn: November 11th, 1908.

Allow me to express again, not only for the Board of Trustees of the University but for myself personally, the warm appreciation we all feel for the generous gift of $10,000 to the University, in which Mrs. Henry N. Munn and you have joined to establish the O. D. Munn Fellowship in Electrical Engineering. I cannot help feeling that we are on the eve of a very considerable development at Princeton on the side of Applied Science, and a gift like this comes at just the right moment to give impetus to our plans and to encourage us in the hope that they can be successfully carried out. Their execution is, of course, chiefly a matter of money, but it is also a matter of deliberate plan, and I feel that the wish to act in that direction will presently bring about the desired consummation.

I have told you personally, I know, what I think of this very generous gift, but I wished to give myself the pleasure of expressing again in a more formal and official way the high appreciation we all feel of this very admirable and useful gift to the University.

With warmest regard,

Always faithfully yours,   [Woodrow Wilson]

CCL (WWP, UA, NjP).

To Horatio Whitridge Turner

Princeton, N. J.

My dear Mr. Turner: November 11th, 1908.

Thank you very much for your letter of November 10th. I will take pleasure in addressing the Municipal Government Club and am only sorry that I could not fulfill my last promise to it.

I am to be away from home next Wednesday evening and the Wednesday evening following, but I am free for Wednesday evening, December 2nd, and if that date would be agreeable to the club, I will take pleasure in addressing it at that time.[1]

With much regard,

Sincerely yours,   Woodrow Wilson

TLS (received from Horatio W. Turner).
[1] As has been noted, Wilson spoke to the Municipal Club on December 2, 1908, and a report of his address is printed at December 3, 1908.

To Melancthon Williams Jacobus

Princeton, N. J.

My dear Dr. Jacobus: November 11th, 1908.

I have been prevented by all sorts of distracting engagements from replying to your kind letter of the 28th of October.

It was very distressing to learn that you had been laid up with a rheumatic attack. I trust that it has long since passed.

There are now still two vacancies in the life membership of the Board of Trustees, if Mr. James W[addel]. Alexander's place is considered vacant; only one place if it is not.[1] I feel very strongly that the one place now certainly vacant should, if possible, be filled by a clergyman, and for my part, as you know, I am very anxious that (inasmuch as for the present it seems unwise to push the name of Dr. Mackenzie, whom I desire more than any other man in the country) the choice should fall upon some minister of the Southern connection, and the man who seems the most available as well as fully suited in character and principles is the Rev. Dr. [Harris Elliott] Kirk of the Franklin Street Church of Baltimore. I have spoken with several of the clerical members of the Board concerning him, as you know, but shall make an effort before the next Board meeting to see them all and find just how they feel.

With regard to the other matter of Mr. Alexander's place, you know how things have ebbed and flowed and how awkward it has been to get any agreement with regard to what was to be done or how the matter was to be regarded. For my own part, I think the place should be considered vacant,[2] but that a resignation should be obtained for the sake of not having it appear in our records that there was anything irregular in Mr. Alexander's retirement. And if this place is considered vacant, my own present judgment is that it should be filled by some man who can be of very material assistance to the University, some man like Mr. George W[albridge]. Perkins,[3] for example, or Mr. Frank A. Vanderlip. I know, however, that the thought of men like Mr. John A. Stewart turns to some person of large public influence, like Mr. Cleveland, if such a man could be found. I have heard no name of the kind suggested.

We are very seriously taking up the matter of the University relationships with the Dean of the Graduate School. . . .

With warmest regard, and tha [the] hope that you are long since relieved of your rheumatism,

Cordially and faithfully yours,   [Woodrow Wilson]

CCL (RSB Coll., DLC).
  [1] It was the vacancy created by the death of Grover Cleveland.
  [2] Because Alexander had failed to attend meetings of the Board of Trustees since his resignation from the presidency of the Equitable Life Assurance Society in June 1905. About the circumstances of his resignation, see W. Wilson, G. Cleveland, and W. J. Magie to J. J. McCook and C. B. Alexander, Dec. 29, 1905, n. 1, Vol. 16.
  [3] Partner in the banking firm of J. P. Morgan & Co. and organizer of many great corporations.

An Address at the Hotchkiss School

[[Nov. 12, 1908]]

THE MEANING OF A COLLEGE EDUCATION

Mr. Buehler,[1] *Young Gentlemen, Ladies and Gentlemen:*

It seems like bringing coals to Newcastle to come to commend to you a college education; and I want to say at the very outset that I would, if possible, relieve myself of the suspicion of trying to commend any particular college to your attention. There are many colleges equally desirable and all colleges are equally undesirable.

The theme I come to speak of is the theme of education in general, for it seems to me that it is part of one's public duty, as a citizen, to ask one's self the question, very frankly indeed, whether one means to take a college education or not.

You know it has become a little unfashionable to suppose that the object of a college is to educate. It has become a little unusual to insist that the main object of a college is intellectual. I cannot imagine any other reason for a college existing except to make the men who resort to it intellectual men,—men who know the enjoyment and the luxury of using their minds, if they happen to have any.

Of course, there are some men who go to college who haven't any minds. They are in the position of a man I heard spoken of the other day whose head was referred to in conversation. "Head," exclaimed someone, "That's not a head; that's just a knot the Almighty put there to keep him from raveling out." (Laughter.)

And I have known persons as singularly constituted. But it is a genuine luxury to use your own mind, if you happen to have one; and it is not only a luxury, it is a duty.

I am not one of those who suppose that men are attracted by having easy paths shown to them. Men who are men are attracted by the difficult things, and only the men who attempt difficult things are ever distinguishable from the common mass. There is a sense in which I really pity a boy who looks forward to inheriting wealth; because it is no longer a distinction in this country to be rich, and to be rich, unless you be something else, is to be condemned to insignificance. An English writer[2] once said, "If you wish me to consider you witty, I must really trouble you to make a jest." If you wish me to consider that you amount to something, I must really trouble you to do something; and in

[1] The Rev. Huber Gray Buehler, Headmaster of Hotchkiss School.
[2] The Editors have been unable to identify him.

this complicated age in which we live in America, it isn't easy to do something. It is very, very difficult indeed for a man to raise his head even an inch above the level of heads that stretches the continent over, and to become noticeable for any particular individual contribution which he may have made to the national life or the life of the community in which he lives.

The object of schools and colleges is not to put sense into men's heads, but to enable those who choose to do so to pick themselves out for the achievements of life. Any man who really achieves anything picks himself out. He is not elected by anybody else to be distinguished; he is chosen by himself to be distinguished; or else condemned by himself to be insignificant. Colleges, like schools, are the open door upon which is written, "Here is the Portal to Opportunity for Those Who Know How to Use It." Opportunity is of no consequence, of no significance, to those who do not know how to use it.

What I want to point out to you, therefore, in order that those of you who are going to college—and I dare say all of you are going to college—shall ask yourselves whether it shall be worth while or not, is this: It is not worth while to go to college and spend your time and your parents' money if you do not mean business. It is not worth while; it is a fraud on somebody; and every conscientious boy ought to ask himself the question very soberly: "Is it worth my while? Is it worth the while of the persons who are educating and supporting me, for me to go to college?"

There is a sense in which it is almost necessary, in a free country, that every boy should go to school; not necessarily to the schools of this grade, which carry you beyond the elementary education, but to some school. It is very necessary that the population of a free country should have an elementary schooling, and it is very desirable that everybody should have more than an elementary schooling, a schooling which carries them to the point to which you are carried, for example, at graduation at a school like this.

But there is a difference between the school training and the college training. The school training, if I may put it so, is a means of showing you the tools of the mind, and their use; of showing you those things which it is absolutely necessary for you to know how to do with your mind, if you would understand anything beyond the rudiments of life, or have any skill lifted above the skill of the unskilled laborer,—those things which it is necessary to learn in order that you may be released from the actual dangers of ignorance; from the actual awkwardness of not knowing how to use your mind; from the actual blindness of not knowing how to see, to discriminate and distinguish knowledge from ignorance. It is just as fatal for a young person not to know how to use his mind as it is for a carpenter not to know how to use his tools. And in school, since the stage of study is not advanced enough to carry men beyond that point, the whole object and purpose is to insure a training which will enable you to know what the mind is for and what the main means are for using it.

I suppose that some of you are touched with what seems to me the heresy of our own day; that heresy which leads everybody to ask about the practical utility of each particular study, What is the use of this or of that? What is generally meant by that question is, "What is the direct use that I can make of this in a money-making occupation?"

There is, by the way, a singular exception universally made to that question. I have never known anybody to ask that question with regard to mathematics; and yet it is perfectly obvious that mathematics is a purely abstract study, after you carry it past the main elementary stages and subjects, and that there isn't one man in ten thousand who uses anything higher than arithmetic in his business. Did you ever hear of anybody using algebra in his business? You have heard of men,—I am not now, of course, speaking of the professions, like engineering, where mathematics is a part of the whole process of reckoning,—but in the whole range of commercial undertaking, did you ever hear of anybody using algebra and geometry? Did you ever hear of anybody, excepting an engineer, making any money out of algebra and geometry? Everybody admits that mathematics is, of course a practical study. Nobody asks the question about mathematics that everybody asks about Greek.

You know that a very distinguished person once said that you might as well teach a youngster Choctaw as Greek, and the obvious reply was made that you couldn't argue the question with a man who didn't know the difference between Choctaw and Greek. One of the essential differences happens to be that Choctaw does not contain a literature and Greek does; Greek contains the fine essence of the most substantial thinking in the world, and all subsequent intellectual effort has been lifted upon the broad surface of that great stream of thought. The man who does not dip in that is neglecting the sources and merely tapping the streams.

Those were some of the things that could be said by way of preferring Greek to Choctaw, and yet there is a universal indictment against Greek as something that is not practical.

Now, I do not hold any particular brief for the study of Greek, but I want to illustrate by this the general object of education, which is not information. I have known some men singularly well informed and absolutely uneducated. I have known some men singularly uninformed and perfectly educated. For by an educated man I mean a man who uses his mind as a source of illumination and as an instrument of precision,—a man who, when he goes for an object, does not shoot with birdshot and hit the whole countryside besides, but shoots with a rifle, and is vexed with himself if he does not center the mark; the man who has his mind in such shape that he can do anything with it, and oblige it to do anything that he pleases.

Why do you go into the gymnasium? Do you expect to do the double trapeze with your partner in business? Do you expect to make a guy of yourself by doing any of the things in your office that you do in the gymnasium? Do you expect to make money or advance yourself in a profession by anything that you ever saw done in a gymnasium? Certainly not. What you are trying to do in the gymnasium is to get your muscles in such shape, and the red corpuscles of your blood so enriched that you can do anything with your body afterwards that you want to do, make it carry any burden that life brings upon you. You are keeping yourself physically fit in order that you may be fit for the things which are not physical, for the real strains of life which are upon the spirit, not upon the body. The real vexations of life are the things that are invisible, not the things that are visible and tangible, and the man who cannot stand up under his sorrows, under his trials, is the man whom the world will crush. He will be the better able to stand up under those trials if his body is fit, if his mind is clear, if he has read something of the experience of the race and does not suppose that Providence is putting this upon him as a peculiar punishment in which he stands apart and singular. The object of education is to acquaint you with the experiences and the processes of the mind and to put you in the saddle in respect to the use of your own faculties.

Now, when you come out of school the question is, What part of the world do you expect to be made free of, if the real object of a college education is to make you students of the world of thought? After you have got past the school period, then, if you please, you may go on to be released into the field of free study; not free in the sense that somebody doesn't pick the way out for you to a greater or less extent, but free in this sense, that the new studies are part of the map of life which you are expected to pore upon, in order that you may use these tools of the mind with which you have become acquainted in your schooldays, and begin to have that attitude towards thinking and towards knowledge which a man should have who is no longer in leading strings to any one, who is no longer a lad, but has come into some of the privileges of thoughtful manhood.

You are released, in respect of the studies of the college, from that merely disciplinary stage which is necessary at school and are competent to stand upon your own feet and think your own thoughts and choose, to a certain extent, your own road, sure that you are fit for that freedom.

Moreover, a college life is more than half way to that thing which we call The World. We do a great deal of artificial thinking when we suppose that at school we are not in the world already. As a matter of fact I suppose that statistics would bear me out in saying that the average college graduate is half through the world in respect of age; and for many a college graduate there is only a little bit of the journey beyond. Not many have many years stretching ahead of them. If they have not touched the world by that time they are singularly remote from ordinary human experience.

It is rather an unwholesome idea, it seems to me, to tell youngsters that they are not in the world. You are in the world. You aren't in the world on your own hook, it may be; you are not thrown out into the contest of life to sink or swim, as you may be able; you are not under the necessity, most of you, of making your own living and providing for others, carrying those burdens which will certainly come upon most of you in later years; but you are in the world, being fortified by circumstances, and if you do not keep your eyes open there is no point at which they will be suddenly freed from the scales you have kept upon them, the scales of inexperience and the failure to observe. There is no door that I know of, anywhere, which issues straight and suddenly upon the world.

Now, an interesting thing about the college and the university is that it is a great deal more than half way to that place of freedom and experience where you will be thrown upon your own responsibility. For the real test of the college is that after that is entered upon you are on your own responsibility.

I have had a great many interesting experiences in my connection with the administration of colleges. There used to be a time, for example, when I was much softer hearted than I am now. I used to be a member of the committee of our faculty which was called the "Committee on Discipline," a very unpleasant committee to belong to because it brings you into contact with all the ugly side of the college; and I used to have the notion that if a fellow had good stuff in him it was worth while not to be too hard on him, to urge the faculty to mitigate the ordinary punishment, to, as the general phrase goes, give him another chance. Again and again I exerted my utmost influence to get youngsters excused from the full penalty for what they had done, and I have to say, with great regret, that I was never rewarded by amendment on their part. Not in a single instance. I at last came to the realization of the fact that the only way to save a lad is to make him lie in the bed that he has made for himself. First make sure that he made it; that he chose that thing; and then make him digest that thing, whether it agrees with him or not. Then there is a chance that he will pull himself together; there is a probability that he will pull himself together. But if you excuse him, then life will look to him like a thing where the natural consequence does not ensue; where there is no certainty of nature taking her own course in the moral world as well as in the physical world, and where he will begin to hope against all experience that he will be excused for his delinquencies when it come to the world of business and to the world where great enterprises hang upon the absolute fidelity of those who are entrusted with every part of them.

So that the college should be no field of indulgence; it is a field of absolute individual responsibility. That is what we call the world itself. So that you will see that a college is a place and a process of maturing. Persons are just like fruit, they will or will not mellow, according to their soundness. They will or will not mature, according to their intrinsic soundness and wholesomeness. And the process of college life is a process of maturing; it is a release of the faculties, a release of the character to find its natural laws.

One of the interesting things that we observe in college is that, though we do not come into contact with the undergraduates—there are too many of them—nevertheless we manage to know, in many instances, more about them than their own mothers and fathers know. There is in the family a sort of atmosphere which dominates you, to which you conform; and you do not need to have it pointed out to you that young gentlemen are often one thing at home and another thing when away from home. You have been away from home and you have been at home with them, and you know that there is a sort of compulsion of feeling in the home which does not exist elsewhere, and that therefore you can often best find the real character of one of your companions away from his home. That is not an indictment of the home. On the contrary, the power of the home is judged by its power to extend its atmosphere.

I have said again and again that I am perfectly sure that I was kept from certain vicious practices when I was an undergraduate, not by any principle, not by any integrity, that was native to me, but by the subtle consciousness that it would be incredible to certain dear people at home that I should do that thing, and that if I did that thing I could never look those two dear people in the eyes again. That was the compulsion, and when that compulsion works, and those eyes follow one all down the walk of life, steadiness is absolutely assured. It is like all the sweet influences of old generations, of men of honor, women of Christian virtue, following you and keeping hold of you, and making you feel the strong, pure courses of the blood that connect generation with generation of honorable men and women. So that this thing that you feel at home you ought to feel all the time. But the test whether you feel it all the time, and whether you are of the true stuff that makes homes, is the way in which you behave out of the home, and the testing ground, the trying-out ground, is the college where you are not watched, where you are left to seek your own levels, where you can choose your own companions; where you can go to the bad just as soon and just as quickly as you please. That is the process of maturing.

But the real thing that you ought to think about in looking forward to college is this: Do you now feel or do you wish to feel *the spirit of scholarship*? I do not mean, Do you want to be scholars? Nobody can make scholars in four years. You are not in the least danger of being a scholar by the time you are graduated from a university. It takes a lifetime to be a scholar, and most men do not manage it by the time their funeral occurs. (Laughter.)

That is not the point. Not, Do you wish to become scholars? but, Do you find an acceptable flavor in the *spirit* of scholarship? What is the spirit of scholarship? In the first place it is a desire to know and to comprehend. It is a spirit also of tolerance. It is the spirit which perceives that there may be other sides to questions than those which we have been in the habit of entertaining and assuming to be the truth with regard to them.

Not only that, but there is in it the eagerness which comes with the desire of discovery. Have you ever thought of the map of knowledge? Have you ever thought that the history of it has been like the history of the settlement of America, for instance,—of the settlement of all countries to which men with knowledge and enterprise have gone, generation after generation, century after century? Here on the edges of the coast we see the great well-known ports of entry, our settled and known regions, and then beyond is the great hinterland, the undiscovered country. The mapping of the world of knowledge is all the while going forward. Where? In quiet studies where men write books; in laboratories where men pore the night through over obscure experiments; in places where invisible things are sought out. In such places are these fine lines on the map of knowledge traced little by little; and there breathes in the nostrils of the men making those quiet inquiries just the same sort of spirit that breathes in any discoverer, in any adventurer. Their pulse may not actually move faster in their veins; but the pulse of their minds beats like that of men who are on some romantic quest which has led again and again forward from generation to generation, from adventure to adventure. They have not climbed the hill that has taken them slowly up the incline because of any impulse except the impulse of the mind; and every step of liberation, whether of political liberty or moral liberty, has been first a step of knowledge. Steadily the mists of prejudice, the mists of superstition, which have hampered and clogged and delayed the race, have been slowly cleared away by the purer airs of knowledge and of real spiritual insight, so that men might not be afraid of their shadows any more, or afraid of their gods any more.

Men have come to understand themselves and the universe, to move with erect frames and undaunted spirits alike in the physical world and in the world of thought; are not afraid of the thing that may turn up around the corner. They with a free heart prosecute their inquiries. This is the progress of the world. This is what has made it necessary that there should be schools, and that upon schools should be built universities, and that men should spend their days crying to their fellows: "Come on, come on, the country is yet undiscovered in which the race shall be lifted to its final levels of achievement and of happiness."

Have you ever fallen in love with the spirit of knowledge? Have you ever desired to be made free of the citizenship of the world of thought and of ideas? If you have not, you have never dreamed the dream of the true college man.

Young gentlemen, we have gone recently through a period, lasting several generations, during which it has slowly come about—to judge by my own observation, rapidly come about—that schoolboys have come to think of college as a delightful mode of life, and have ceased to think of it as a mode of learning. The consequence is that colleges have fallen into a certain disrepute among wise men in this country. One of the things I am told by every man of achievement who deals with college men is that the first thing that he has to teach them is how to work; that they have lost the conception of what it is to do a full and honest day's work. If that is true, then the colleges are entirely discredited; for they are no longer serviceable. This is not a world of play; it is a world of work, and if you don't learn how to work in college, you have learned nothing, absolutely nothing serviceable to the world.

There is an indirect way of inducing men to work. Life at college is so delightful that you can make a certain number of men work for the privilege of staying there. I very much suspect that with most undergraduates the real compulsion to pass the examinations is not a desire to learn anything but a desire to stay in a place where they have delightful companionships and where they are doing a great many interesting things. They do not wish to be separated from those companionships or divorced from these interesting things. What they come for is college life; that is what interests them. The rest does not interest them.

Every time that a college lecturer stands up before a college class he has a task that is very much more difficult than standing up before a general audience anywhere else. He has to capture their attention. In the middle of the football season I always feel that I have to spend the first fifteen minutes getting the latest football scores out of the heads of my class, so that I can have their attention for the subject of jurisprudence. (Laughter.) I have to work by every device that is in me to divest their minds of the thing which stands there as a block to everything that I am trying to get into their heads. I cannot make them understand one principle of the subject that I am talking about until I stop their thinking about the relative merits of certain halfbacks. (Laughter.)

Now, that is working under a considerable handicap, and I, for my part, believe that until we can remedy that, it is not particularly worth while to teach in a college. Colleges situated outside of great cities are getting so attractive in their lives that they are getting to resemble a very superior kind of country club, and I have made up my mind that I have no ambition to be president of a country club. (Laughter.) I might consent incidentally to be president of a country club, but it does not constitute an interesting career, and there are other things that I can think of that I would rather do, and spend my time upon.

I have made up my mind that I won't be president of a country club, and that the young gentlemen who think they are at a country club when they are at college will have to be divested of that impression. In other words, the college must now assert itself and make every man who attends it understand that his first, chief object is to get the spirit and love of knowledge; and that, if he cannot get that, he had better apply himself to something else.

You know that some persons amongst us think that the object of an education, or rather of school and college life, is to produce character. Well, I certainly would not object to its producing character, but there is only one way that I know of in which character can be produced. Character cannot be deliberately produced. Anybody who goes to work to produce a good character in himself will produce nothing but a prig. But anybody who will studiously attend to duty will produce a character. Character is a by-product, and it is nothing but a by-product. You cannot produce it by intending to produce it, and you inevitably produce it by attending to your duty.

Some years ago the faculty of Princeton very unwisely permitted a very attractive evangelist to come to the University and hold meetings, just two weeks before the mid-year examination, and a great many young gentlemen, with the highest motives, went around every night and tried to drum up a big attendance for him. One night they came upon a door that was securely fastened and on the outside was this placard, "I am a Christian and studying for examination." (Laughter.) What I want to commend to your attention is that that is a perfectly logical sequence of ideas. The particular thing which a Christian would be doing, two weeks before examinations, would be studying for examination, and that is the only thing that a Christian would be doing at that period of the year; he would be deepening his Christianity and establishing his character by doing it.

A gentleman came to me just after the entrance examinations one year and said he was very sorry to hear that young So-and-so of such a school had not got in. "Yes," I said, "I am sorry, too." "Don't you think," he says, "you are making a mistake in not admitting him? He is one of the finest fellows in school. His influence was always for good things, and he was a leader and is a boy of unusual capacity and character." "Yes," I said, "so I was told; but he did not pass the entrance examination."

"Oh, but," he said, "I don't think you understand–," and he went all through the boy's virtues again. I said: "I beg your pardon, it is you who don't understand. *He did not pass the entrance examinations.* Now," I said, "if the Angel Gabriel were to apply for admission to Princeton University he would have to pass the entrance examination." (Laughter and applause.) Because if he could not pass that he would be wasting his time there, and would inevitably get dropped at midyear. It would be, to admit any boy under those circumstances, a fraud on his parents. We have no right to admit boys when we know that they are not ready to be admitted.

And the only test we have–it is a crude test, it is a very unsatisfactory test in some ways–is by asking questions. If you cannot answer the questions, that proves that, so far as we can ascertain, you are not prepared to enter. I know there are some boys who know and cannot say; at least, I theoretically know it, I have never met them. (Laughter.) I generally find that if you really knew the thing you could say it in some intelligible form. You might not say it in the most elegant language, but you could say it so that somebody who spoke your language would understand.

Crude test though it be, examination is a necessary test; and it is the test of many things. It is a test of character as well as a test of knowledge; and it is a prophecy of a career.

It is an absolute weakness and absurdity to admit men to college who do not have some pulse of sincerity in them in respect to the matters for which they have been commended. I sometimes wish that it weren't fashionable to go to college, that it weren't taken for granted that gentlemen of a certain class in society would send their sons to college. I wish that only those came who had a definite purpose and knew what they wanted.

The task of those who administer the colleges of this country is, for the next generation, to prevent young men from going to college who do not intend to use them as colleges. Perhaps most of you are old enough to get in before the difficulties are made insuperable. (Laughter.) But there are some small boys now, let us say, five years of age, who I foresee are going to get into college with very sober thoughts. Because there is a general awakening to the fact that there is an undesirable vacant interval in the lives of most young men. They work under the compulsion of one school system or another up to a certain point, then they go to college and don't work, then they go to professional school and work harder than they ever worked in their lives.

Society will not long tolerate this condition of affairs. It is going to say we cannot afford to have the fibre of our young men made pulp, and then convert it into fibre again, because it won't be a good fibre after it has been pulp. We don't want any pulp period. We don't want any period of the relaxation of effort. We want young men to stretch themselves upon some task that will give them command of themselves and of their circumstances in the years which ensue.

And this is not, need not be, a process of pain. It is normally a process of pleasure. I, for one, would not condescend to be a taskmaster; I would not condescend to put the whip to the backs of young men and drive them through a process which was intolerable to them; but I know just as well as I know that I have lived and teach these things, that the moment a man is introduced into this liberty and opportunity it fills life with a new and novel pleasure.

For the only way in which to have amusement is to have it as a relief from work. When you make amusement an object it becomes an occupation. The only way to have diversion is to have it as a release from something and not as a thing sought for its own sake. The only way to enjoy conversation with your friends is to have something to talk about. The only way in which you can know who your real friend is, is by having something in your mind and requiring of him that he should have something in his, and then matching minds with him, and seeing whether they be of the same strength and taste and caliber or not.

That is the reason many a man is disappointed in his classmates after they get out into the struggle of life. He finds they aren't of the stuff he supposed them to be of, that when he tested them as boys there was nothing in them.

All the comradeships which have rewarded me, or rewarded any man in middle life, or any woman either, are the comradeships which have been the comradeships of the spirit and of the mind, where you found thoughts, impulses, purposes like your own springing up in a like soil, through a like yearning for the light, with a like impulse and yearning. Those are the friendships which are cemented for all eternity, because they are the friendships of the stuff that is immaterial and not of that which is material.

The meaning of college, therefore, is the enrichment of life; the enjoyment of life; the lifting of life to those levels which are the levels not of toil merely, but of privilege and pleasure. (Long applause.)

Printed in Woodrow Wilson, *The Meaning of a College Education, An Address* (n.p., n.d.); editorial sub-headings omitted.

From Henry Burling Thompson

Greenville P. O. Delaware
Dear President Wilson: November 12th, 1908.

I have yours of the 11th instant,[1] with reference to the Graduate Club Committee, and my understanding of the matter is exactly as you have put it.

Our Committee did not contemplate the appointment of a Committee from the Board of Trustees to confer with the Graduate Committee. Any conferences, under the resolution, would naturally be with the Faculty. A possible exception to this might be some extraordinary condition arising which would render necessary the appointment of a temporary Committee of the Board of Trustees.

The only question at issue, as I understand it, is the notice to the Clubs of our resolution. How and when are the Clubs to be notified of the resolution adopted?

After such notice has been served, and after the Clubs have appointed their Committee, then, as above stated, I assume future negotiations will be with the Faculty and not with the Trustees.

Yours very sincerely,   Henry B Thompson

TLS (WP, DLC).
[1] It is missing in the H. B. Thompson Papers, NjP.

From Harry Clarkson Westervelt[1]

E[ast]. E[nd]. Pittsburgh, Pa.
My dear Dr. Wilson: November 12th 1908

In thanking you for your cordial reply to my recent letter,[2] allow me to say that no announcement which the Association[3] has made for many years has been received with such universal expression of satisfaction and pleasure as that of your promised presence at our Anniversary service,[4] and am sure that were the audience room twice the size it is, we would still lack space: The fact that many are to be shut out of the meeting that night emboldens me to pass along to you a most urgent appeal which the men have been keeping before me for the last two weeks: It is the custom on Sunday afternoons to have a meeting for *men* only (at 4 O'C) and as many men can be at this meeting who will be unable to attend the evening service—it is the great desire that you meet the men alone at this time: Is it asking too much that you attend this service and give the men a short informal talk on some gospel subject of your own selection? Believe me—I would not even suggest the matter to you did I not know so well the great pleasure it will give and the good it is sure to do; You will not be burdened with any of the details of the service, and your convenience and comfort will be carefully planned for.

Should the suggestion meet with your approval, I will be grateful if you will so advise me by *telegram* (my expense) that special announcement may be made Sunday—and if you care to suggest a *topic* it will lend added interest.

I sincerely trust that you may see your way clear to grant us this favor,[5] but I wish you to feel beyond question that our feeling toward you is so cordial and our sense of obligation so great because of what you have already promised us, that should it seem wise to you to deny this request our only feeling will be of disappointment—wholly uncritical.

Very sincerely yours,   H. C. Westervelt

TLS (WP, DLC).
[1] Physician of Pittsburgh.
[2] It is missing.
[3] The East Liberty branch of the Y.M.C.A.
[4] That is, the thirty-fourth anniversary of the East Liberty branch of the Y.M.C.A. on November 22, 1908. A news report of Wilson's address on that occasion is printed at Nov. 23, 1908.
[5] Wilson did give the second address. A news report of it is printed at Nov. 23, 1908.

From Margaret Olivia Slocum Sage

My dear Mr. Wilson,   Lawrence, L. I.   Nov. 13th, 1908

Yours of November 2nd was received.

In consequence of my town house not being in order, I am detained here. Until I return to New York, it will not be convenient to visit Princeton, on any date you appoint.

I have felt that your judgment, and the Trustees' will be sufficient, regarding the site of the new dormitory and that the work may not be delayed while waiting for me.

Sincerely yours,   M. Olivia Sage

ALS (WP, DLC).

From Huber Gray Buehler

Lakeville, Connecticut

My dear President Wilson,   November 13, 1908

In sending you the enclosed check to cover the expenses of your recent visit to the Hotchkiss School, I wish again to express my deep appreciation of the service which you rendered us, and to thank you in behalf of all the boys and masters. Your address made a profound impression, in spite of its "narrow mindedness." One of the older masters remarks this morning that it "was the best thing that ever happened"; and the younger masters, living with the boys in the dormitories, tell me that they never knew the boys to be so enthusiastic over a serious address.

Mrs. Buehler[1] and I, and our friends, greatly enjoyed the privilege of meeting you in our home, and I earnestly hope that sometime we can arrange for another visit from you to the Hotchkiss School.

With kindest regards,

Very gratefully yours,   H. G. Buehler

TLS (WP, DLC).
[1] Roberta Wolf Buehler.

A News Report of a Speech in New York
to the City History Club

[Nov. 14, 1908]

CROWD AT THE BAZAAR

Mr. Carnegie and President Wilson Speak—
Many Attractions.

Artists, writers, patriots, fashionable women, Indians, Dutch girls in the quaintest of caps, Colonial girls, actresses pouring tea, Andrew Carnegie talking about the disadvantages of city life for children, flowers, music, a jumble of pretty things clamoring to be bought, a fragment of Christopher Columbus's bones in a gold and crystal cross; these are a few of the impressions the visitors brought away from the crush that signalized the opening of the bazaar of the City History Club at the Hotel Plaza yesterday.

Woodrow Wilson, president of Princeton University, made the chief address at the historical conference with which the bazaar opened. Mrs. Robert Abbe,[1] who presided, said it was a little unusual to mix bazaars and historical conferences. "But," she said, "our city history classes are going on all over the city, and we can't get people to go and see how they work. People will come to bazaars, and while you're here we're going to show you a sample class and tell you about the work."

A score or so of East Side lads—working boys all of them—composed the class. They read minutes, elected a new member, and came forward and read essays about New York's Fire Department with pretty fair grammar and deportment, considering that the eyes of the bazaar were upon them.

President Wilson talked about "the civic revival." The people are waking up, he said, but the heaviness of sleep is still upon them, and they hardly know what they ought to do in the way of changing things, but they know they ought to do something. He gave a word of sympathy to the business man, "who has awakened to the knowledge that some of his methods in acquiring his fortune have been against the public welfare. He knows it, but he knows business, and around him are great bodies of men who don't know business, wildly running after unconsidered nostrums."

The moral awakening, the speaker said, must be individual. "It will do no good to sit down and beg omnipotent government, 'Come, appoint commissions, manage the business we don't [know] how to manage ourselves, moralize us.' We must moralize ourselves and spread the contagion. But to moralize ourselves we must know ourselves, and to moralize the state we must know the state—its past, its history—and that is why clubs like the City History Club are so good a thing."[2]

Printed in the *New York Tribune*, Nov. 14, 1908.
[1] Catharine Amory Palmer Abbe, President of the City History Club of New York and wife of the distinguished surgeon, Robert Abbe.
[2] There is a WWhw outline of this address with the composition date of Oct. [Nov.] 12, 1908, in WP, DLC.

To Henry Burling Thompson

Princeton, N. J.
My dear Mr. Thompson: November 14th, 1908.

Thank you for your letter of the 12th. I think that I will myself formulate a brief circular letter to the clubs, explaining the object of the Trustees' action and notifying them of the desire of the Trustees that a graduate committee representing the clubs as corporate bodies should be named, to await any conference that might be found necessary upon matters affecting the clubs and the University. That seems to me the simplest solution of a rather puzzling question.

Always cordially and faithfully yours,

Woodrow Wilson

TLS (H. B. Thompson Papers, NjP).

From Frank Miles Day and Brother

Dear Dr. Wilson: Philada.   November 14th, 1908.

The drawings made for submission to Mrs. Sage are now ready. Mr. Henry B. Thompson saw them yesterday and asked us to inform you that we would bring them to Princeton at any time to go over the matter with you. Mr. Thompson suggests that we should stand in readiness to meet you in Princeton at the time of Mrs. Sage's visit, if you should deem it wise to have us present to make any explanation.

The drawings that are now ready consist of

1st. The general block plan which you saw but in which slight modifications have been made to bring it into harmony with the instructions of the Committee.

2nd. The several elevations of the building which were submitted to you.

3rd. A new set of elevations of the four sides of Mrs. Sage's building made at the same scale and in the same manner as the Nassau St. front already presented.

4th. A plan of each of the three stories of Mrs. Sage's building.

5th. A perspective of University Tower and of portions of the adjoining buildings as seen from the great Quad., the drawing being rendered in water color.

Mr. Thompson seemed greatly pleased with all these drawings, especially with the water color perspective of the Tower. He thought it desirable that we should make another perspective of a larger size of the great tower and the entrance to the quadrangle as seen from Nassau St. This we are undertaking at once but it will probably not be ready for a week or ten days. If the appointment with Mrs. Sage were made for an early date, we might present the drawing before it is entirely finished but it is perhaps not essential that it should be ready then. At any rate, we will advance it as rapidly as possible.

The only engagements which Mr. Frank Miles Day has at the present time which would prevent him from coming to Princeton, are a meeting in New York November 30th, December 1st and 2nd and the convention of the American Institute of Architects in Washington which will probably occupy the week beginning Dec. 14th.

Very truly yours,   Frank Miles Day & Brother

TLS (WWP, UA, NjP).

From Melancthon Williams Jacobus

Hartford [Conn.],
My dear President Wilson: 15th Novr. 1908

Unfortunately I am still in bed. It's a case of run down nerves rather than rheumatism—though either is bad enough & this means slow getting back to the liberty of work. But all this will go to show how especially welcome your letter was; for as I have been lying here Princeton has been much in my thinking.

I imagine that with Mr. Alexander's suspended vacancy we will have to be patient until things take the course which you indicate & which I believe most of the Board think desirable. As to the clerical vacancy I have been for a long while anxious for Princeton to have a Southern point of contact & I am sure Dr Kirk will be a most helpful acquisition to the Corporation. I suppose after all I am the obstacle in Dr. MacKenzie's way. To have him elected would be considered too much Hartford by the other Seminary trustees & perhaps too much my sort of a man by some of the other men around the table. Perhaps some day they will see things differently. As to the men you named for Mr. Alexander's possible place, I am sure they would be a great help from the financial point of view & it does seem as though we needed that sort of help pretty badly just now. The information you gave me as to the present & the coming deficit is especially ominous as it undoubtedly is so largely due to our preceptorial expenditures. If this should be pressed home upon us, do you believe it could be possible in any way to reduce the number of preceptors without endangering the system? This of course we must never let go, as long as we have a word to say. What it has gained for Princeton is too grand to abandon & yet I suppose reductions will have to be all along the line & particularly at the point of salaries, inasmuch as friends do not seem to be making up the deficit. . . .

As to Mr. Stewart's desire for a man of large public reputation I have thought since last summer of George Gray of Delaware though Harry Thompson says he does not have the time which would make it possible for him to attend to the business of the Board, and, of course, that sort of a man would be of no help to us—in fact would be of hurt to us in proportion to his reputation.

Should the choice happen to come upon Mr. Perkins or Mr. Vanderlip, have you any knowledge of how they stand on the educational & social questions which are so vital now to Princeton? If I remember rightly you said something of Mr. Vanderlip's interesting himself to get Mr. Carnegie interested in the proposition you recently placed before him.[1] We certainly must get a strong man in this vacancy when the time comes.

You have of course seen the enclosed clipping regarding the proposed Cleveland memorial.[2] It is good that it comes to Princeton, though I wish there were some way it could be made of direct benefit to the Graduate School, or to the University at least. I imagine however that popular subscriptions cannot be secured for anything except some external & tangible object to be looked at along the Highway or in the Public Place. If Mr. Carnegie would only materialize his admiration for Mr. Cleveland by a great gift to the University!

I am glad to know you are taking up the matter of the Graduate Deanship. I suppose you are also conferring with Fine about the Scientific Deanship. I do hope you will be able to come to some agreement with him by which, under your authority as President, you can relieve yourself as far as possible of the burdens & responsibilities of administration[.] Your opportunity—through your magnificent hold upon men in public address, to get your ideas before the educational world is so splendid that I would do everything I could to give myself freedom of time & thought to spread them & make them tell. If your vision of what Princeton can be is to be realized, it will be by what you can do this way: for the thinking public has got to be educated, and no man can do that as you can do it. Give Fine the authority (under your Presidential rights), if he will take the burden & do you keep the freedom & the time to carry on with the public the great service upon which you have entered for American education.

With kindest regards,

Yours most cordially   Melancthon W. Jacobus

ALS (WP, DLC).

1 That is, that Carnegie give the money to implement Wilson's quadrangle plan.

2 An unidentified, undated clipping about the organization of the Cleveland Monument Association under the chairmanship of John Fairfield Dryden of Newark, United States Senator from New Jersey, 1902-1907, and founder and President of the Prudential Insurance Co. of America.

To Moses Taylor Pyne

My dear Momo: [Princeton, N. J.]   November 16th, 1908.

I know that you will want to know what has happened about Mrs. Sage. I pushed my invitation as fast as possible, but find that Mrs. Sage's town house is in the hands of workmen, so that she cannot return to it for several weeks, and that she is still at her country home at the far end of Long Island. She has written me a very courteous note in which she begs that we will feel at liberty to go forward with our plans without waiting for her visit to Princeton, and I am in correspondence with Thompson and Mr. Day with regard to a meeting to consider the plans.

I am going to take the liberty of calling you up on the telephone as soon as possible and arrange for a talk about the numerous matters we ought to talk over and to which you have called my attention in several notes.

Always faithfully yours,   [Woodrow Wilson]

CCL (WWP, UA, NjP).

To Melancthon Williams Jacobus

[Princeton, N. J.]
My dear Dr. Jacobus: November 16th, 1908.

It was a real grief to me to learn that you are not yet free from your attack, and I beg that you will take care of yourself with the utmost prudence. It would be a very sad thing to have you get up too soon and still further delay your liberty, and, as you know, your freedom to be about and to give counsel is in my view very essential to the University. I trust that you are not actually suffering and that you are making real progress.

I know that you would have been gratified by a conversation I had yesterday with Mr. Palmer. He spoke of the long talk he had had with you after the last meeting of the Board and expressed the greatest admiration for you and the greatest confidence in your judgment.

I feel just as you do about the Cleveland memorial. I doubt whether it would be possible to start anything in the nature of a general popular subscription in our direction, and it might be misunderstood if we tried to do so, but I think it would do no harm to see Senator Dryden, who is acting as Chairman of the Committee, and see whether persons interested in the University cannot join in the movement without interfering with the plans of this particular committee, and secure something for the University itself. Mr. Bayard Henry, who is always watchful in matters of this sort, came in to see me on Saturday and made that suggestion.

Fine and I have been in frequent consultation since the meeting of the Board, about the new deanship, and I think we shall have no trouble in coming to an agreement. I very much appreciate your interest in the matter and your counsel. If your illness brings me long letters like this, I have just received, I cannot find it in my heart to regret it as entirely as I otherwise would.

With warmest regard,

Always faithfully yours,   [Woodrow Wilson]

CCL (RSB Coll., DLC).

To Henry Burling Thompson

Princeton, N. J.

My dear Mr. Thompson: November 16th, 1908.

I have a letter from Mr. Day apprising me of the readiness of the drawings for the Sage Dormitory.

I am at last able to report about the invitation to Mrs. Sage. Her town house is in the hands of workmen and will not be ready for her re-occupation for some weeks to come, so that she is still at her summer home at the other end of Long Island. She has, therefore, declined our invitation, but very kindly leaves the matter of pushing the plans forward to our own judgment and discretion.

If you will be kind enough to put the correspondence for a conference in motion, I shall be very glad to hold myself available for any free date I have in the near future. At present my free dates are the 19th, 20th, 21st, 23rd and 24th of November, the 3rd and 5th of December. I can go further, if none of these dates is available to the other men concerned. I have left out the 30th of November and the 1st and 2nd of December as dates when Mr. Day cannot come. If you wish me to, I can notify Mr. Russell in any way you think best.

Always faithfully yours,   Woodrow Wilson

TLS (H. B. Thompson Papers, NjP).

From James Speyer

My dear President Wilson: New York, Nov. 16th, 1908

I am very much obliged to you for your kind letter of Nov. 11th,[1] and am glad that my little gift, (and the conditions under which I made it,) meets with your approval.

I also wish to thank you particularly for your personal expression of esteem, which is much appreciated by me.

Sincerely yours,   James Speyer.

TLS (WP, DLC).
[1] It is missing.

From Catharine Amory Palmer Abbe

My dear Mr. Wilson   [New York]   Nov 17th 1908

Every moment since you spoke for us I have wanted to write and thank you both for coming, and for what you said, it was all so helpful and truthful. I regret however more than I know how to express that we did not have a stenographer on hand to have taken down word for word all you said, as I should so like to make a tract for use in the City History Club. It would do us all good to read your words over again and again till we should know them by heart. They made our work seem so vital, and inspired me anew. You will be glad to know that the Bazaar was a great success from every point of view, most of all in starting new thought in our direction. Believe me I can never forget what you have done for us.

Most sincerely yours   Catharine A. B. Abbe.

ALS (WP, DLC).

From Horatio Nelson Davis[1]

                              [St. Louis]   November seventeenth,
Dear Sir: Nineteen hundred and eight.

We regret exceedingly that you will be unable to address the League at its meeting in December. The Executive Board at its meeting on Friday requested me to extend to you an invitation to be the guest of honor at our Annual Meeting in March and to deliver an address on some municipal subject at that time. While the date of the Annual Meeting is fixed for the second Tuesday in March it can be changed to some other day in that month to suit your convenience.

The Civic League is committed to the policy of intelligent, continuous and persistent discussion of municipal questions as a most permanent solution of the problem of the city and an address by you on that occasion will aid materially in that direction.

We hope you will be able to accept the invitation for the Annual Meeting in March.[2]

Respectfully yours,   H. N. Davis

TLS (WP, DLC).

[1] Princeton 1873, President of the Smith & Davis Manufacturing Co., which made furniture, and a member of the board of directors of several St. Louis corporations. He was also President of the Civic League of St. Louis and one of the founders of the Princeton Club of that city.

[2] Wilson did indeed accept the invitation. The text of his address is printed at March 9, 1909, Vol. 19.

From Charles Scribner's Sons

Dear Sir: New York, Nov. 17th, 1908.

We are in receipt of your favor of the 16th inst., and have forwarded, as per your instructions, to Mrs. T. D. Peck, "Shoreby," Paget West, Bermuda copies of the books ordered.

Thanking you for your favor, we remain,

Very truly yours,   Charles Scribner's Sons. J H

TLS (WP, DLC).

To Howard McClenahan

[Princeton, N. J.]

My dear Professor McClenahan: November 19th, 1908.

I need not tell you that I have given very serious thought to the subject matter of the conversation I had with you and Professor MacLaren the other day, and I have, moreover, tried to think it out with due consideration to all the feelings involved.

My thinking carries me always to the conclusion that in the list of the faculty of the Electrical Engineering School[1] Professor MacLaren's name should come first, and that upon the ground which I stated to you and to him the other day.[2] It seems to me an administrative question and, considered upon administrative grounds I can see no other legitimate conclusion.

I am very sorry to be unable to meet your wishes in the matter, and it distresses me very much that this decision will give you pain.[3] I beg you to believe that in my mind there is no possible cause for chagrin on your part and that I would, if I could, meet your wishes in every particular. I cannot imagine anything of this kind affecting the esteem in which you are held or the position which has been accorded you.

 With much regard,

Sincerely yours, [Woodrow Wilson]

CCL (WWP, UA, NjP).
 [1] That is, in the university catalogue.
 [2] Because MacLaren had charge of instruction in the School of Electrical Engineering.
 [3] McClenahan had presumably argued with some feeling that his name should come first on the masthead of the School of Electrical Engineering because he had seniority as a professor over MacLaren.

To Malcolm MacLaren

[Princeton, N. J.]

My dear Professor MacLaren: November 19th, 1908.

 Careful consideration of the matter has not altered the conclusion I stated to you and Professor McClenahan the other day. It seems to me clear that your name should come first in the list of the faculty of the School of Electrical Engineering, and I cannot believe that this decision can work Professor McClenahan any real harm. I should be distressed if it did.[1]

 With much regard,

Sincerely yours, [Woodrow Wilson]

CCL (WWP, UA, NjP).
 [1] MacLaren was listed first, McClenahan second in the catalogue for 1909-10.

A News Report of a Religious Talk

[Nov. 20, 1908]

"MEDITATION."

President Wilson Delivers an Impressive Address
on Its Relation to Impersonal Ambition.

 President Wilson delivered an eloquent and interesting address before the mid-week meeting of the Philadelphian Society last evening. His subject, "Meditation," was developed from the second and third verses of the first Psalm.

 The President said that this is not a time when meditation is prevalent. True meditation is the result of letting one's thoughts dwell in private on things which are of permanent and not merely passing interest. It does not come from mere musing, nor is a real meditator the man who sits by the fire, and lets his thoughts drift along on pleasant things which slip away with the generation.

Meditation day and night on the law of God is a quiet conscious effort to adjust ourselves to its majestic and almost irresistible course. The man who conforms his thoughts to the will of God, is sure to find spiritual refreshment.

There are times when men's lives are at their best, and everyone should be prepared for the season of fruitage, and should not let the sap ebb, but keep it ever on the flow. Men immersed in some selfish enterprise and in a narrow circle of self-interest inevitably dry up and fail to produce lasting results.

The man who goes through adversity with up-lifted countenance will inevitably prosper, just as our Lord stimulated others to spiritual endeavor, because of the way He bore His burdens. The real achievements of this world come from the men who pursue their undertakings impersonally.

As an example of work done impersonally and without reward for a long time, the President referred to President Eliot, of Harvard, who only realized the fruitage of forty years of effort in the last fifteen years of his service.[1] Many of the sources of his strong administration at Cambridge were in his serene and undisturbed religious faith.

The speaker closed by asserting that meditation gives one sanity of judgment, poise, and connection with the permanent forces of the moral universe, and he urged his hearers to give themselves opportunity for meditation and to make personal desires secondary to their ideals of doing right.[2]

Printed in the *Daily Princetonian*, Nov. 20, 1908.

[1] The announcement of the resignation of Charles William Eliot from the presidency of Harvard University, to take effect on May 19, 1909, upon the completion of forty years of service as president, had been made public on November 4, 1908.

[2] For this talk, Wilson used the notes printed at April 4, 1895, Vol. 9.

From Frank Thilly[1]

Ithaca, N. Y.

My dear President Wilson: November Twentieth [1908].

I have just learned that there will be a meeting of Presidents at Cornell University[2] during the first week in January. I sincerely hope that you will be present at this meeting and will give Mrs. Thilly and me the pleasure of entertaining you in our home. May we not also express the hope that Mrs. Wilson will accompany you?

With cordial greetings to Mrs. Wilson and yourself, in which Mrs. Thilly[3] joins, I am

Very sincerely yours,   Frank Thilly

ALS (WP, DLC).

¹ Former Stuart Professor of Psychology at Princeton, at this time Professor of Philosophy at Cornell.

² That is, at the meeting of the Association of American Universities.

³ Jessie Matthews Thilly.

To the Editor of the *Princeton Alumni Weekly*

My Dear Sir: Princeton, N. J., November 21st, 1908.

I have taken the liberty of calling the attention of the editors of The Princeton Tiger[1] to an advertisement in their last issue,[2] which is apt to lead to some misapprehension. But inasmuch as their publication is only from month to month, I beg to say through your columns that Mrs. Wilson Woodrow, the author of The Silver Butterfly there advertised,[3] is no relation of Mrs. Wilson's or mine.[4]

Very truly yours,   Woodrow Wilson.

Printed in the *Princeton Alumni Weekly*, IX (Nov. 25, 1908), 137.

¹ This letter, in a slightly different form, was printed on page three of the December issue of *The Princeton Tiger*. It read: "In the current number of The Tiger an advertisement is printed which is calculated to create the impression that Mrs. Wilson Woodrow, the author of 'The Silver Butterfly,' is in some way connected with Princeton. I beg to say that she is not in any way related either to Mrs. Wilson or to myself. Very truly yours, Woodrow Wilson."

² The following full-page advertisement appeared on page sixty-eight of the October 1908 issue:

Princeton, Attention
Mrs. Wilson Woodrow's New Book
"The Silver Butterfly"
The Bobbs-Merrill Company, Publishers.

³ Nancy Mann Waddel Woodrow, divorced wife of Wilson's first cousin, James Wilson Woodrow.

⁴ The same letter appeared in the *Daily Princetonian*, Nov. 23, 1908.

Two News Reports of Addresses in Pittsburgh

[Nov. 23, 1908]

DR. WILSON ADDRESSES Y.M.C.A.

"Success and How to Attain It" was the subject of an address by Woodrow Wilson, LL.D., president of Princeton university, yesterday afternoon before the East Liberty Y.M.C.A. The prominence of the speaker attracted large numbers to the meeting, and long before 4 o'clock the auditorium was crowded to the doors.

The speaker brought out strongly the important qualities a man must cultivate to be successful in whatever he undertakes to do, illustrating his points with interesting anecdotes of real life. He made the statement that a man who devotes his attention and time to cultivating a noble character is a failure—instead of accomplishing his end he becomes an egotist and a prig. The following of what he deemed duty, he declared, formed character.

Printed in the *Pittsburg Post*, Nov. 23, 1908.

◊

DR. WOODROW WILSON SAYS REAL RADICALS ARE MEN OF MIDDLE AGE

Princeton's President at East End Y.M.C.A.
Thinks Young Men are Conservative.

ANNIVERSARY SERVICES

"The Contribution of the Young Men's Christian Association to the Life of the Nation" was the topic of an address delivered by Rev. Dr. Woodrow Wilson, president of Princeton University, at the thirty-fourth anniversary services of the East Liberty Branch, Young Men's Christian Association, last night. Pastors of four East End churches took part in the exercises, a liberal offering was raised for the support of the institution and every seat in the large auditorium and balcony was filled. Dr. Wilson said in part:

Force and renewal constitute the vitality of a nation. Force does not exhaust but is renewed, like a spring. I am not confining myself to material force, as many nations have depended on material force and have been destroyed. The vital nation is one which constantly renews self-preservation. The nation which is the largest in force is the one which has the largest variety of forces, not one of specialists, but one having specialists in many lines.

I think of the Young Men's Christian Association as an altruistic force devoted to objects common. Some get the impression that young men are radical, but they are the most conservative. Real radicals are men of middle age who have gone wrong. The cynical man who has led a life of disappointment is the radical man, and such men will combine forces for the destruction of society. The impression I get of young men is that they are radical in method and aim to accomplish old things in a new way. They ask many questions, but go back of the surface and they are conservatives.

In the Young Men's Christian Association we get re-incarnation of the ideals of the Bible. The organization is the best contributor to the process of self-purification.

The only nation that can exist is one of men and not of laws. It takes good men to enforce the laws.

Printed in the *Pittsburg Dispatch*, Nov. 23, 1908.

From Arthur Twining Hadley

[New Haven, Conn.]
My dear Mr. Wilson: November 24th, 1908.

I have heard with great pleasure that the New Haven Chamber of Commerce is asking you to speak at its dinner on December seventh. If things are in such shape that you feel you can accept the invitation, I shall feel tenfold greater pleasure—not only for the sake of the meeting itself, but for the chance that it will give me of seeing you personally.

The Chamber of Commerce of New Haven is an ancient and honorable organization, of which I have been for many years a member. Its dinners are better and its speeches more interesting than those of almost any similar body that I have had the pleasure of knowing. Its president, Mr. H. C. Warren, who extends to you the invitation,[1] is a man with whom I have had the pleasantest relations, both in business and personally; and I am glad to have this letter of mine serve as a sort of a note of introduction for him.

Faithfully yours, [Arthur T. Hadley]

TL (Hadley Letterbooks, Archives, CtY).
[1] Herbert Cleveland Warren, President of the Merchants' National Bank of New Haven and President of the New Haven Chamber of Commerce, 1907-1908. His letter of invitation is missing.

A News Report

[Nov. 25, 1908]

SITE SELECTED

For the Sage Dormitory for Freshmen. General
Plan of the Building.

The plans for the Russell Sage Freshman Dormitory, which have been under consideration all Fall, have now been decided upon in the main, although some minor details have still to be arranged before the final draught of the plans can be made public. The architect is Mr. Frank Miles Day, of Boston. The exact position of the building about which there has been doubt until lately, was finally settled upon at a meeting of the committee in charge, held last Friday. The structure will be in the form of an L, with the main part parallel to, and about seventy feet to the rear of '77 Hall, and with a wing jutting out toward Nassau Street, and at right angles with it. The entries will be located on the sides of the building which face '77 Hall and Alexander Hall. It will be of gothic architecture, similar to that of Blair, Little, and '77 Halls, and like them, will be of two stories in height with a few rooms on a third story under the eaves. The building will cost $250,000, and will accommodate about one hundred and ten Freshmen. There will be a drive running between '77 Hall and Sage Hall, which will form a continuation of the drive in the rear of Alexander Hall.

Printed in the *Daily Princetonian*, Nov. 25, 1908.

From Rudolph Grossman[1]

My dear Professor: New York, Nov 25th 1908

In connection with the Temple of which I am the Rabbi, I have an association of young men and women which has existed for over ten years, and whose purpose is to spread culture, education and a higher sense of religious and civic duty among the Jewish youth. One of the means we employ for the fulfillment of this purpose is a series of lectures given by men of high position, and national reputation, which are delivered in my Temple: having a seating capacity of over 1800; and those who have in previous years addressed us have spoken before audiences that have taxed the Temple capacity to its fullest.

I am arranging such a series for this season and take the liberty of most cordially inviting you to be one of our speakers. Could you honor us with your presence and your words of counsel on any week-day evening, of your own selection in the months of December to May 1909?

Any subject you may choose would be acceptable to us. Your fellow citizens of the Jewish faith would welcome your coming to us with deep gratitude and I can assure you of both a large and a highly appreciative audience.

Anticipating the pleasure of your acceptance[2] and assuring you of my high esteem, I am, dear sir

Very sincerely Yours   Rudolph Grossman

P.S. I need not state that we shall cheerfully meet any expenses that may be incurred.

ALS (WP, DLC).
  [1] Rabbi Rudolph Grossman, D.D., of Temple Rodeph Sholom in New York.

2 Wilson accepted; a news report of his address is printed at March 19, 1909, Vol. 19.

Gilbert Fairchild Close to Arthur Twining Hadley

Princeton, N. J.
My dear President Hadley: November 26th, 1908.

President Wilson has been away from home all this week, with the exception of a few hours yesterday afternoon, and has been obliged to leave again for Toledo, Ohio, where he is to deliver an address tomorrow night. He did not have time to write to you personally and has therefore asked me to thank you sincerely for your kind letter of the 24th, and to say how very sorry he is to find that he is prevented by an imperative engagement from accepting the attractive invitation of the New Haven Chamber of Commerce for the evening of December 7th. It would have given him very great pleasure to come to New Haven, if it had been possible.

Sincerely yours,   Gilbert F. Close

TLS (A. T. Hadley Papers, Archives, CtY).

An Announcement and News Report

[Nov. 27, 1908]

TOLEDO WILL BE GIVEN A BOOST

Toledo will be given a great boost at the first general meeting of the Chamber of Commerce, to be held in the Valentine theatre tonight, and the hundreds of citizens who have reserved seats for the occasion will doubtless be greatly instructed and entertained by the address by Professor Woodrow Wilson, president of Princeton university, whose topic will be The Business Man and the Community. . . .

Two boxes have been reserved for Princeton alumni, while at least 100 prominent business and professional men will occupy the stage. Practically all of the seats in the pit and balcony have been reserved.

Dr. Wilson arrived in Toledo yesterday and is a guest at the Hotel Secor. He was received by a committee of Princeton men, who made arrangements to entertain the distinguished educator at luncheon in the Secor at 1:20 this afterno[o]n. A half dozen visiting Princeton men were at the luncheon and will hear Dr. Wilson tonight.

Printed in the *Toledo Blade*, Nov. 27, 1908; one editorial heading omitted.

From Charles Duke Atkins[1]

Philadelphia.

My dear President Wilson: November 27th, 1908.

On some Friday or Saturday afternoon preferably in March, the American Society will hold its nineteenth Annual Meeting in Witherspoon Hall. It would be esteemed a great privilege if you would consent to deliver for us the annual address on this occasion. The Meeting is held at 3 o'clock and a large, cultivated and appreciative audience can be promised. The subject might most appropriately be one concerning books and culture but we could, I have no doubt, adopt your preference. As honorarium, the Society has usually paid for the annual address a fee of $60 but in this, too, we should like to meet your wishes.

Since your last lecture before us in 1902,[2] the Society has increased in numbers from less than 250 at that time to some 1000 members at the present, an endowment fund has been acquired and the work has steadily grown in extent and influence. Through nearly 100 Centres we are carrying cultural influences to thousands of persons in all walks of life. The list of speakers at similar meetings in the past include Mr. Richard Watson Gilder, Prof. Bliss Perry, Mr. Herbert Putnam,[3] Prof. Shaw, of Oxford,[4] Dr. Hamilton W. Mabie,[5] etc.

Will you be so good as to consider the matter and, if possible, send us a favorable reply.[6] The exact date is not important and could be made to suit your convenience.

Respectfully and hopefully yours,   Charles D. Atkins.

TLS (WP, DLC). Enc.: printed advertisement entitled *University Extension.* (*Comments from Letters.*).

[1] Secretary and Director of the American Society for the Extension of University Teaching.

[2] He meant Wilson's lecture series, "Great Leaders of Political Thought," which Wilson delivered in Philadelphia from January 9 through February 13, 1901, about which see the news item printed at Jan. 12, 1901, Vol. 12.

[3] Librarian of Congress since 1899.

[4] William Hudson Shaw, formerly Fellow of Balliol College, Oxford, at this time rector of Alderley.

[5] Hamilton Wright Mabie, Associate Editor of the New York *Outlook* and author of several books on literature, nature, and travel.

[6] He accepted the invitation; a news report of his address is printed at March 13, 1909, Vol. 19.

Henry Burling Thompson to
Melancthon Williams Jacobus

[Wilmington, Del.]

My Dear Jacobus: November 27th, 1908.

I have read your letter of the 26th instant[1] with much interest; and am glad to know that you have written to Wilson and that you have received a reply from him which does not impress you as unfavorable.

When in Princeton last Saturday, I spent an hour with Fine, and went over this question somewhat in detail, and he recited conditions to me as they were at that time. I came to the conclusion that Fine's interviews had been satisfactory, and that the President will be inclined to take the Committee's view of this matter at our next meeting.

I sincerely hope that the President will be willing to turn over the burden of the minor details as we want it.

I should consider any controversy on this subject would be most unfortunate, for I am a great believer in Wilson's personality, and, unquestionably, he is doing magnificent work in his presentation to the public of the Princeton work, but it is necessary he should be made to see that details suffer unless they have a closer supervision than he is giving.

With regard to Dr. Kirk, of Baltimore, I have already given my approval to Wilson on this possible nomination. There is no question that Dr. MacKenzie's candidacy is handicapped from the fact that it brings two men from one institution. Personally, I have always been willing to vote for him, but there is a strong opposition in the Board, which would make it unwise to push his name.   Yours very sincerely,   Henry B Thompson

TLS (Thompson Letterpress Books, NjP).
[1] This letter is missing in the H. B. Thompson Papers, NjP.

A News Report of an Address to the Toledo
Chamber of Commerce

[Nov. 28, 1908]

WILSON SCORES MODERN METHODS OF BUSINESS

Before an immense audience at the Valentine theater, the Chamber of Commerce on Friday night publicly inaugurated its work when President Woodrow Wilson, of Princeton, explained the relationship between "The Business Man and The Community."

President W[illiam]. L. Milner[1] gave a brief outline of the work of the Chamber of Commerce in this, its first year of existence.

In his opening remarks President Wilson said a remarkable civic awakening had taken place in the last ten years in this country, and he declared it to be an awakening full of happy augury if thoughtful citizens everywhere bestir themselves to make use of it for the betterment of their communities.

During his address President Wilson said:

"Some demoralizing old business standards have already been discredited. For example, the old maxim that 'Business is business' is in ill repute. It was never a handsome saying. It meant business is not morality, is not public spirit, is not regard for others, but an eye for the main chance and every man looking out for himself and only for himself.

"There is still life and validity to that other old saying that competition is the life of trade. From the consumer's point of view it surely is. But on the principle that business is business, men came to justify themselves in killing competition, and they killed it by its own processes.

"I don't believe that the age through which we have just passed has been one of dishonesty. Dishonesty is a part of our human life and we always have and always will have dishonest men among us.

"The majority of the men who have been benefiting themselves and the corporations with which they were connected in recent years by doing everything they could do in restraint of trade and of competition, were no doubt perfectly honest men, according to the standards accepted in business circles, when business was done on a smaller scale.

"Many corporations otherwise perfectly honest in their business methods, habitually paid money into the treasuries of local political parties to be let alone by city councils and of [by] state political machines.

"In the same way they made large subscriptions to the national party, which was most likely to secure them in the many direct and indirect benefits and advantages which they derived from a protective tariff.

"There can never be any valid justification for using the taxing power of government for the benefit of the few or for anything less than the national interest.

"Business men have come to realize that no man can afford to be as small as his business; that the environment he makes for himself will make him big or little; that the community in which he lives is his place of expression, his place of stimulation and his atmosphere.

"No people has got its strength from being taken care of or coached by its government. A country is made great by the affection of its people, their voluntary exertions in its behalf. Toledo is to be most heartily congratulated upon its instinctive right action in giving such evidence of its own conscious participation in the general civic awakening."[2]

Following the address members of the Princeton alumni, occupying boxes at the theater, gave their college yell. The theater was beautifully decorated in the Princeton and King Wamba[3] colors.

Printed in the *Toledo News-Bee,* Nov. 28, 1908; some editorial headings omitted.
[1] President of the Toledo Chamber of Commerce, 1908-1909, and of Toledo's large mercantile establishment bearing his name, "W. L. Milner Co."
[2] An abstract of this address is printed as an addendum in this volume.
[3] The colors of a carnival to be sponsored by the Toledo Chamber of Commerce.

To Frank Thilly

Princeton, N. J.
My dear Professor Thilly: November 30th, 1908.

I warmly appreciate your kind letter of the 20th and would have answered it long ago, had I not been out of town for some ten days.

I am not at all certain that I can attend the meeting of the Association of American Universities in January, but I shall certainly do so if possible, and it will give me the greatest pleasure, should I be able to come, to be your guest.[1] Please thank Mrs. Thilly very warmly for thinking of me in this way.

I am sorry that I have to leave the matter thus in the air. I hope that it will not cause you inconvenience for me to do so.

We often speak of you both with the greatest interest and with many delightful recollections.

Cordially and sincerely yours,   Woodrow Wilson

TLS (Wilson-Thilly Corr., NIC).
[1] As it turned out, Wilson did not attend; Dean Fine and William Francis Magie represented Princeton at the meeting.

A Tribute to Charles William Eliot

[Dec. 1908]

The work of very few men has been so impressive as that of President Eliot; and there are two things about it which particularly interest me.

First, its disclosure of the man. The way in which President Eliot attacked the tasks set him and carried to completion the plans which he formed has revealed a character and power which are themselves deeply interesting as showing the real process of individual influence. He has not hurried, but he has never given way. He has shown infinite patience, but it was not patience in which the steady pressure of his purpose was withdrawn; it has been the patience, rather, of calm persistency, the patience which makes each day add its inch of advance. And so he has seemed to walk amidst difficulties and animosities and adverse influences like an irresistible force. The impression this has made of greatness and of insight would not have been so strong, had not the measurement of the achievement been so long in time, but, having been made upon an ample scale of time, it has been deep and lasting.

Second, its steady broadening from a single field to many fields of public usefulness. The steadfastness of the man, his love of work, his clear knowledge of what he was about, his ardor to bring things to a better form and purpose has, at any rate throughout all the later part of his career, made him a part of many important affairs, has arrested the attention of the country, has given him influence in public affairs of the widest range and consequence, and has won him recognition as one of the chief citizens and ornaments of the country, a man who has performed his duty on a great scale with no niggardly expenditure either of thought or action.

Woodrow Wilson.

Printed in the *Harvard Monthly*, XLVII (Dec. 1908), 89-90.

To Frank Arthur Vanderlip

Princeton, N. J.

My dear Mr. Vanderlip: December 2nd, 1908.

I very warmly appreciate the kind invitation brought me this morning by your letter of yesterday[1] and wish with all my heart that it were possible for me to accept it, but I feel in honor bound to reserve Mondays and Tuesdays for my college teaching. I do so little of it that I do not feel at liberty to neglect that little for any social pleasure or any engagement which is not clearly a duty. One of my two lectures comes early on Tuesday morning at an hour which makes it impossible for me to get back from New York in time to meet my class.

I know that you will appreciate the force of these reasons and will understand that I am declining only under a clear compulsion of duty an invitation which is delightfully attractive.

Always cordially and faithfully yours,

Woodrow Wilson

TLS (F. A. Vanderlip Papers, NNC).
[1] It is missing.

From George Butler Storer[1]

[Toledo, Ohio]   December Second,
Dear Mr. Wilson: Nineteen Hundred Eight.

I am in receipt of your letter of the 30th, and am very glad to know that you had a comfortable trip home.

I am sure it would please you to hear the complimentary remarks made concerning your address and our meeting. Many of the older and substantial citizens have said to me that never in the history of Toledo has there been held a meeting which has done so much to bring the best elements here together, and with one voice they are enthusiastic in praise of your address.

If you come again, and we hope you may many times, you will need a very much larger hall than the Valentine Theater.

We of the Chamber of Commerce are very grateful, indeed, to you for all you have done, and feel that the check for $62.22, which we enclose, is very inadequate compensation.

Mr. Milner and Mr. Libbey[2] desire me to extend to you their warm regards, in which I am pleased to join.

Sincerely yours,   Geo. B. Storer

TLS (WP, DLC).
[1] Secretary of the Toledo Chamber of Commerce.
[2] Edward Drummond Libbey, organizer and President of the Libbey Glass Co. and the Owens Bottle Machine Co. of Toledo, and Vice-President of the Macbeth Evans Glass Co. of Pittsburgh.

A News Report of an Address in Princeton

[Dec. 3, 1908]

"CITY GOVERNMENT."

President Wilson's Address Before the Municipal Club
of Vital Interest to All Americans.

President Wilson's address before the meeting of the Municipal Club last night, on the subject of City Government, was one of exceptional interest.

City government in America, President Wilson said, is the worst in any civilized country in the world, and this is due to two facts, that our method is formed on the wrong analogy of state and federal government, and that we are obliged to vote for too many officers.

State government is formed on a system of checks and balances, and state government has existed fairly well, since it is not obliged to cope with very important or live issues. But this system when applied to city government is seen to be radically wrong, since city affairs are so near to us all that any defect in their management is clearly apparent. A government should not be a mechanism, but an organism, and nothing can live if its organs are set to check one another. Yet we have this system in our city government. To eradicate this defect we must have a complete change. We must have a strongly centralized body, which will act directly through its various departments, and to which the blame for any mismanagement can be laid.

Then under the present method of election, we are compelled to vote a ticket varying in length from twenty-five to one hundred or more names. And where there are so many people to be nominated, somebody must make a business of nominating them and so the political machines have become necessities in our public life. Consequently men are nominated and elected of whom the voters know nothing, who are responsible to nobody, and act accordingly. To be sure, reform parties have several times formed a ticket and had their nominees elected, but due to their very nature they soon dissolve and the political bosses again have their way. But if there was only one man to be nominated in a district, it would be easy to select a man fitted for the place and to influence others into voting for him.

The need of a city government is to have a unified body, for only a unified body can be efficient. One man cannot possibly know every detail of a complicated business, and it would be manifestly unfair to hold him personally responsible for any defects in its management. A centralized body, however, acting through its several departments, could satisfactorily perform all the tasks of government and would be directly responsible to the people. This is the model of every successful city government, and the model of every unsuccessful one is exactly the opposite.

It will take generations to effect this change, and would necessitate a great personal sacrifice on the part of the reformers, but the final result would justify every effort. In conclusion, President Wilson made a strong plea for students and educated men to take up this question of municipal government and work for a more unified concentrated system.

Printed in the *Daily Princetonian*, Dec. 3, 1908.

From Walter Lee McCorkle[1]

My dear Brother Wilson: [New York]   December 4th, 1908.

Dr. John A. Wyeth, the President of the Southern Society, called upon me again this autumn to arrange the details of our annual banquet to be held at the Waldorf on the evening of December 9th and although I begged hard to be relieved of the work I was unable to overcome his insistence that I should take care of the detail, which he seemed to feel would be well cared for in my hands.

The Executive Committee was delighted to learn, through the Chairman of the Committee on Speakers, Mr. Marion J. Verdery,[2] that we would be honored with your presence on this occasion and we do hope that nothing will interfere with your coming.

The purpose of this note is to state that I have reserved a room at the Waldorf for yourself and Mrs. Wilson, which room will be assigned to you upon your arrival if you will call for it.

I will thank you to advise me whether Mrs. Wilson will accompany you to the City on Wednesday next if you have not already advised Dr. Wyeth to that effect.

I hope you have entirely recovered your good health and that nothing will interfere with your giving to us your views upon "Conservatism, True and False" on Wednesday evening next.[3]

Believe me to be with kindest regards,

Fraternally and sincerely yours,   Walter L. McCorkle

TLS (WP, DLC).

[1] A Wall Street lawyer who was chairman of the dinner committee of the New York Southern Society.

[2] Marion Jackson Verdery, at this time secretary and superintendent of the New York Stock Exchange Building Co., a member of the Southern Society's Executive Committee, and chairman of the society's Speakers Committee.

[3] The text of Wilson's address is printed at Dec. 9, 1908.

From Horatio Nelson Davis

                                [St. Louis]   December fourth,
My dear Sir: Nineteen hundred and eight.

We are greatly pleased to receive your kind acceptance to deliver an address before the Civic League at the Annual Meeting on March 9, 1909. The members of the organization and the citizens in general will listen with keen interest to what you have to say on municipal matters.

The time is an especially opportune one in view of the city election in April which promises to be a hard struggle in both parties between the forces for and against reform.

An invitation will be extended to all Princeton men to attend the dinner.

I have asked the Secretary of the League to send you a set of our publications.[1] These will indicate to you the work which we are trying to do in St. Louis.

Again expressing to you our real pleasure in anticipation of your address in March, I am,

Yours very truly,   H. N. Davis

TLS (WP, DLC).
[1] They are missing.

From John Lee Tildsley[1]

My dear President: New York, Dec. 4, 1908.

The High School Teachers Association of New York City has taken for its year's work the consideration of the course of study in the high schools of New York City with a view to its possible revision. A special committee is on work on this question and the general quarterly meetings of the association are being devoted to the discussion of various phases of the subject. At the first meeting of the year, Professor Franklin H. Giddings of Columbia spoke to us on "The Aim and Scope of the Public High School in the City of New York." The address is being issued in pamphlet form and I will send you a copy.

At the next meeting in January, we wish to continue the discussion of this general subject and the teachers are very desirious that you should address them. I know that your engagements are many and that the notice is short but you would greatly aid public education in New York City if you should address us. The meeting will be held on Saturday morning, preferably January 16th, but possibly January 9th, at 11 O'clock.[2]

I have felt for some time that two of the dangers that confront us in education are, first, the substitution of the acquisition of information for the development of power to think as an aim of education; secondly, in the emphasis laid upon methods of teaching, especially in this city, there is a constant tendency to underrate the personal element in teaching. To me, good teaching is primarily the projection of a rich personality.

You probably know the charge is constantly made against high school training that it is not suited to the needs of the present day and there is therefore a demand for industrial training. With this demand I have some sympathy, but I fear lest in our desire to make education practical, we fail to train the boy to think. Very little of our training today fits our boys to grapple with a problem and solve it. For our boys and girls, "denken ist schwer." I have an impression that some of your recent addresses have been along this line. In what I have said can you not find a suggestion for a talk which will help us to solve this problem of what is the right high school training for the boys and girls of New York City and will you not give us such a talk?

You have never spoken to the high schools teachers of this city of whom there are eleven hundred and I believe there are few ways in which you could do more for Princeton than by addressing the teachers of the twenty-seven thousand high school pupils of this City. I am constantly asked by them about the working of the preceptorial system at Princeton. Every one is seeking a school and college where the boy works of himself and is not allowed to be merely a sponge. I am urging this strongly upon you. Pardon my zeal for I feel I am working both for the High schools and for Princeton in so doing.

You may be interested to know that I expect to be elected next week to the principalship of the De Witt Clinton High School of this City, a school of two thousand boys and eighty-five teachers, so that these problems of secondary education will be for me still more pressing.

Very truly yours,   John L. Tildsley.

TLS (WP, DLC).
[1] Princeton 1893, Ph.D., University of Halle, 1898, who was teaching economics at the High School of Commerce and serving as President of the High School Teachers Association of New York City. However, within a matter of days he assumed his new position as Principal of De Witt Clinton High School. See J. L. Tildsley to WW, Dec. 11, 1908.
[2] Wilson spoke on January 9, 1909. His address is printed at that date.

From G. Fred Ege[1]

Dear Dr Wilson: Jersey City, N. J., December 8, 1908.

At a meeting of the Board of Education held Nov. 24, 1908 the following resolutions were adopted:

The Board of Education takes pleasure in recording its recognition of the honor which Doctor Woodrow Wilson, President of Princeton University, conferred upon the pupils of the High

School and the Board of Education by his visit to the High School on November 6, and its high appreciation of the scholarly and inspiring address which Dr. Wilson delivered on that occasion.

The Board of Education hereby extends to Doctor Wilson its sincere thanks for the favor which he has shown directly to the High School, and in general to all the schools of the city, and the Secretary of the Board is requested to send a copy of these resolutions to Dr. Wilson.

Very truly yours,   Fred Ege

TLS (WP, DLC).
1 Secretary of the Board of Education of Jersey City.

An Address to the New York Southern Society

[[Dec. 9, 1908]]

CONSERVATISM: TRUE AND FALSE

The campaign is over but it was not a campaign which settled anything. Each party offered to the people in its platform a miscellaneous body of policies drawn together by no discernible principle and intended to command immediate attention rather than to form the basis of consistent co-operative action on the part of those who are most concerned to find for the country a programme which will be a real solution of existing difficulties and a real guide for the future. No one can feel that that campaign settled anything or that its issues were satisfactorily concluded. Indeed, there is no clear indication that the country considered it a settlement of anything, except of the question who should be President of the United States.

Such a campaign, therefore, must have set men thinking very seriously of the future of parties and of the whole question of consistent and intelligible party programme. Men cannot long be united in strong and co-operative bodies unless they are united upon principle, unless they have set before themselves some certain goal and have formed some definite idea of the course they shall take to reach that goal. It is inevitable, therefore, that we should follow up the campaign which has just closed with a great deal of conference upon political programmes and party organization. We are conscious of a sort of dissolution of parties, of a confusion of issues, of singular intersection of opinion and interminglings of impulse, and of a notable absence of leadership, not of leadership of the political organizations to which we happen to belong, but of leadership of the constructive thought and purpose of the country.

There can be no mistaking the uneasiness of thoughtful men in the presence of such circumstances, or the universal desire that there should be some action upon definite principle, some set of conceptions susceptible of uniting men upon a higher basis than the mere basis of expediency. And the principles desired are not principles which look backward, but principles which look forward. It is futile to talk of a "return" to anything, a return to any past stage of party action, to any past body of measures, to any set of formulas invented for an earlier time and another set of circumstances. It is necessary that we should recognize very clearly that the problems of our own day cannot be squared to the measures of any day which has preceded it. Our economic conditions are such as have been unknown hitherto. The problems of our law are conditioned by a new variety of circumstances, a new face of affairs, a new set of fundamental conditions, and it is necessary that whatever programmes we devise should be programmes which face forward and can be projected into the future. It is useless to look over our shoulders and regard with regret the men and the policies and the ideals of a time irrevocably gone by. We cannot hark back: we must hark forward.

This is not to say that any sound principle of action is out of date or has been discredited. It is merely to say that we must translate principles that are sound into the language and measures of the day.

Not only are the circumstances of our time new circumstances, whether in the field of economic or of political conditions, but they are peculiarly new in America because the great combinations of capital and of labor and the new complexities of economic organization and of enterprise which have been set up in America have been set up under conditions quite different from those which obtain elsewhere, because of the still inexhaustible and no doubt in part still undiscovered resources of this great continent. Perhaps it will never again be possible as it has been during the past generation to pile up wealth with extraordinary rapidity in this country and to enrich the commerce of the world with unlimited supplies of ore and coal, but it will for a long time be true that America more than any other country is a place in which the development of resources and their use will proceed upon a very great scale and at a very rapid pace. Our conditions must for long remain less settled, and therefore less controllable, less calculable, less predictable than those of older countries whose resources are known and whose methods of exploitation are measurably established. America will, therefore, continue to be a scene of changeful conditions for at least another generation, and it will throughout that generation be more difficult in America than elsewhere to adjust action to definite principle in the field of politics and of enterprise. The temptations to irregular action will be greater and the difficulties of controlling it much more complex than elsewhere.

It is for this reason that it has been so easy to make the voters of this country impatient of any form of conservatism. The problems to be met are so great and perplexing that we have been in a temper to approach them boldly and with very radical proposals, and we have been easily rendered impatient of any who have cried a warning to us or who have tried to draw us back to slower, safer and better tested processes. There is a false conservatism which justifies impatience in our existing circumstances, namely, that sort of conservatism which proposes a return to old measures and expedients intended for other circumstances or to old formulas now in large part emptied of their meaning. For example, the old formula "tariff for revenue only" has a barren sound to our ears in existing circumstances, because the tariff as we now know it is not a system of taxation; it is rather a vast body of economic expedients which have been used, under the guise of taxation, for the purpose of building up various industries, great and small, and enriching the nation as a body of individuals rather than as a government. It would be perfectly futile to propose out of hand a tariff for revenue only, because you cannot get out of a system except by systematic effort and adjustment, and the point to determine at present is not, How may we best secure the necessary revenue for the maintenance and conduct of our government by means of duties on imports, but How shall we adjust our duties on imports to the present real circumstances of the nation and the present interests of our economic development as a whole. Let the one example serve for many. What we want is not a set of issues which will sound like echoes of circumstances which no longer exist, but a set of issues arising out of and intended for the present.

The conservatism which should be sharply distinguished from this false and bastard conservatism, which is merely reactionary, is the conservatism which seeks a return to old and well recognized principles, but a return to them in such a way as will give them a new interpretation and a new meaning for the time we live in. The true conservatism consists in re-examining old principles, seeking such a reformulation of them as will adapt them to the circumstances of a new time. There is no danger that the tested principles of government which we have derived from the long experience of our race will be discredited, if we understand their present application. They will be discredited only by applying them in some inadequate or pedantic way. The true way to keep our principles is to keep our heads; is not to be confused by new circumstances, but to see how and where they square with the principles by which we are trying to be guided.

Let me take a few examples. Let my first example be drawn again from the question of the tariff, which after all is central to half the questions which now perplex us in regard to the reform of our economic structure and processes. The principle for which we should seek a new interpretation and application is this: That the power of government to tax ought never to be used to confer privileges upon individuals or groups of individuals, but should be used always and only to secure general benefits, the benefit of the tax-payers as a whole or of the nation as an organism.

This general benefit and development was the object sought by our policy of protective tariff as it was originally conceived by Alexander Hamilton, and all valid arguments for that system are simply reiterations of his argument in his masterly Report of [on] Manufactures. But there came a time, and it came very early in the history of our actual tariff legislation, when the adjustment of import duties became a matter of contest and bargain, of give and take, amongst the various interests which sought its advantages. The tariff of 1828 was called the Tariff of Abominations, because it was thought not to be made in the general interest but to be a miscellaneous piling together of the various duties which manufacturers of different kinds desired. Tariffs of more recent date have been touched with the same disfigurement alike of symmetry and of principle. We need not stop to inquire when and where the line was crossed. Suffice it to say that it is the present general conviction that our more recent tariff legislation has been a doling out of privileges on the part of the government and that certain protected interests have been built up with no particular regard to the interests of the nation as a whole.

When privileges have been created, governmental oversight and regulation are necessary. Those who act upon privilege or enjoy any artificial advantage must be controlled. Those who act upon right need not be. Half our present difficulties arise from the fact that privileged interests have threatened to become too strong for the general interest, and that therefore the government has had to step in to restrain those who enjoyed the very privilege which it itself had granted. Reform, therefore, must come, not in the shape of a new adjustment of interests, but in the shape of a reconsideration of the general policy of the government in these matters which shall square it with the general interest. And this reform must proceed without injustice and with as little injury as possible. It must proceed, also, gradually and with a due regard to a maintenance of economic stability. But it must proceed fearlessly and it must proceed upon the principle, not that all protection is to be withdrawn, but that all protection is to be adjusted to the general interest and withdrawn from the field of the granting of special privileges and advantages.

Take another principle which true conservatism demands should be revived and retranslated into the terms of our present life. The control of the government should be exercised by processes of law and not by administrative discretion. This does not necessarily mean that the control of the government should be exercised only through the courts as we have known them, that is, only through the formal, elaborate, and somewhat tedious judicial processes which we have come to think of as characteristic of judicial action. The government may act less formally, more summarily, through commissions, without the violation of any fundamental principle of liberty, provided only the action of the commissions be made real process of law and not a process of mere discretionary practical judgment on the part of those who compose them. This is the true meaning for us of the old Jeffersonian principle "as little government as possible." For us that maxim means as little government by executive choice and preference, as little government as possible of the kind that varies the footing upon which interests are dealt with, which chooses its measures differently, instance by instance, leaves some untouched and brings others up with a sharp turn. It means as little government by discretionary authority as possible. It is not hostile to regulated and equalized freedom or to any process of law which is a calculable process of rule and proceeds by definite standards.

Take again the question of the power of the general government as against the power of the governments of the States. We should not waste our time upon any pedantic discussion of what constitutes State rights. We known [know] that we still have a singularly various country, that it would be folly to apply uniform rules of development to all parts of the country, that our strength has been in the elasticity of our institutions, in the almost infinite adaptability of our laws, that our vitality has consisted largely in the dispersion of political authority, in the necessity that communities should take care of themselves and work out their own order and progress, and we know that in stating these things we are dealing with facts, not with abstract principles, and that out of these facts we can draw a very definite rule of action, namely, that in all that we do we should prefer a dispersion of governmental power to a concentration of it, that "home rule" should be the normal rule of life with us and that centralized authority should be the exception. We should not be afraid of it, as of a bugaboo, but we should not be in haste to set it up and should be very sure that we were ready for a general rule before we set up a general authority.

And then, to take a final instance, I think that we can be sure that we are not done with the principle of individual initiative, of individual right. We can still be very sure that any set of measures based upon the purpose of allowing the government to coach or dictate to the individual unnecessarily, where individual action is still possible, will certainly turn out to be measures for the impoverishment of the nation in respect of everything that goes to make for its variety and energy and enrichment. It is hard to find the individual in many cases amidst the present confusion of conditions, but we know that he is the source of energy for the nation nevertheless, and that to smother him is to produce a general mediocrity and inertia. Any form of collectivism which submerges him will certainly be fatal to our progress no less than to our liberty. Whatever laws we may devise, we must make sure not to lose him by any collective process.

Such should be our handling of old principles. In this way should they be made our guides, not to recovering the past, for we are not going in that direction and do not wish to recover it, but to threading the present and making sure of a wholesome and secure development in the future.[1]

Printed in *Year Book of the New York Southern Society for the Year 1909-1910* (New York, 1909), pp. 17-25.

[1] There is a WWhw and WWsh outline of this address, dated Dec. 9, 1908, in WP, DLC.

From Charles Duke Atkins

My dear President Wilson: Philadelphia. Dec. 9, '08.

We are very much pleased to receive your kind letter of Dec. 7th, accepting our invitation to address the Society at its Nineteenth Annual Meeting in March. Of the dates you mention as

convenient, we have selected Friday, Mar. 12th. Will you kindly
reserve this.

As desired, I will send shortly a suggestion as to subject, giving
then also the topics of addresses at our similar meetings in other
years.

Thanking you heartily for the consideration you show us, we
remain,   Respectfully yours,   Charles D. Atkins.

TLS (WP, DLC).

From John Lee Tildsley

My dear President,   [New York]   Dec. 11, 1908

I am delighted that you can speak to the high school teachers
of this city on January 9th. on the lines suggested. We are
desirous of a good attendance not only of high school teachers
but of other teachers and superintendents. To this end I wish
to send out advance notices at once. Will you not therefore send
me the wording of your topic so that I may send out the first
announcements early next week?

I was chosen principal of the De Witt Clinton High School
last Wednesday and begin work there next Monday. Would it not
be possible for you some time this year when you are in New
York to talk to the boys of this school? The school is in session
from 9 to 2.30 and I could call it together at almost any hour to
hear you? This does seem an imposition but I believe that if you
could spare the time you would enjoy the experience.

Again thanking you for accepting our invitation I remain
                         Very truly yours,   John L. Tildsley

(Could you talk as early as 10.30?)

ALS (WP, DLC).

To John Lambert Cadwalader

                                    Princeton, N. J.
My dear Mr. Cadwalader: December 12th, 1908.

I have several times read the Report of the Committee on
Plan and Scope of the Committee of Fifty, presented to the
Trustees on October 15th last,[1] and have given it a good deal
of careful thought. I feel, therefore, that I am ready to comply

1 It is printed at this date.

with your request that I submit to you my opinions concerning its recommendations.

In the first place, I think that it would be very unwise to consent to the name The Graduate Council. You will remember that a graduate council was proposed at the time the very much better arrangement now embodied in our Alumni Representation in the Board was substituted, and I think that you will agree with me that it would be very undesirable to multiply the bodies which are to be concerned either directly or indirectly with the management of the University; and that, whatever might be the first gift of powers to this new body proposed, or rather to this altered Committee of Fifty, the very name "Council" would carry with it many implications and lead to the assumption that its powers were to be considered part of the constituted machinery of the University itself; and this report, you will observe, brings this body into a very formal constitutional relation with the Board of Trustees in respect of the nomination and election of its members and gives it altogether an appearance of permanency which I think highly undesirable.

Of course, the primary purpose of this body, as of the Committee of Fifty, will be the raising of funds, and it will be influential in proportion as the amount it raises is large or small. It seems clear to me, as I know it seems clear to you, that we must not for very many years more depend upon such an instrumentality for defraying the enpenses [expenses] of the University. We must, if we would put the University upon a sound basis, secure within the next few years an endowment sufficient to relieve us from the necessity of employing such an agency as the Committee of Fifty permanently and as an indispensable aid to the maintenance of our work.

I would, therefore, suggest that the name be, not The Graduate Council, but the Alumni Commission, in order to suggest that it is an agency of the Board of Trustees, a commission to which the Board entrusts certain very important interests, but from which the Board may withdraw functions at any time. I think that the name I suggest has both dignity and significance. I would suggest, also, that your committee give very careful consideration to the advisability of connecting the constitution of this body in any formal way with the Board of Trustees.

Passing to the sub-committees proposed, I feel that it would be distinctly inadvisable to commit the matter of publicity, that is to say, the advertising of the University, to any body outside the immediate organization of the University itself. The selection of the things connected with the University to which public attention is to be drawn, and the determination of the way in which public attention is to be drawn to them, should belong to the office of the Secretary of the University, and in my opinion we should, as soon as possible, furnish that office with the funds necessary for maintaining a well managed bureau for this purpose. My judgment upon this matter is very definite. I believe that the University has been greatly harmed in the minds of the most judicious part of the public by the things we have chosen to make most of in calling attention to Princeton. I think that you will agree with me that Princeton has come very much more into notice within the last five or six years than she was before, and this has happened because Princeton has been undertaking and doing serious things of noticeable scope and importance. She is getting the notice she deserves, but no more, and my conviction is that the only effectual means of drawing attention to Princeton is to do things and do them well and soberly, in short that achievement is her only sound advertisement. To whatever she achieves public attention should, of course, be carefully drawn, but the attention drawn to her achievements should be the attention of those who are seriously interested in university advancement as such. I think that I can say that I know that the effect of such publicity as we have sometimes attempted is to bring us no solid credit at all. I could not consent, as the responsible officer of administration, that anyone but the responsible officers of the University should determine the field and method of publicity.

I should think that the committee proposed on Preparatory Schools should also be drawn into very close relations with the officers of the University. I find that some of our school principals smile rather significantly at some of the attempts made to draw the attention of their students to Princeton.

The other suggestions of the Report seem to me most interesting and entirely worth adoption.

You spoke to me the other day about seeing some member of the faculty about this matter. I think you were under a misapprehension. Professor John G. Hibben, who is a member of the faculty, is also a member of the committee which signed this report, but he belongs to the Committee of Fifty and to this sub-committee, not as a member of the faculty but as the President of the Class of 1882. I do not think that you need feel under any more obligation to consult with him than with any other of the gentlemen who have signed this report.

I shall hope to have an opportunity to discuss these matters with you more directly before your committee reports to the Board.[2]

With warmest regard,

Faithfully and sincerely yours,   [Woodrow Wilson]

CCL (WWP, UA, NjP).
    [2] See the report printed at Jan. 13, 1909, and n. 1 to that document.

From Charles Duke Atkins

My dear President Wilson: Philadelphia. Dec. 12, '08.

We venture to suggest the following as topics that would prove very interesting for the subject of your address to the Annual Meeting:

Academic Ideals and Public Service

The Scholar and The People

University Scholarship and Popular Education

Living Problems and Academic Ideals

The Scholar in the World

The following paragraph is from a letter on the subject from one of our former Presidents,—Mr. Charles A. Brinley[1]—

"At the present time I am particularly interested in what the newspapers call "The Awakening of the Public Conscience." I should like to know, if in fact the public conscience has been quickened in respect to morality in politics and business, and what opportunity there is for the educational appliances of the country to encourage the growth of honesty in all relations of life."

Some of the subjects at past meetings include "The Function of the University in the Modern World," by Dean Muir, of Liverpool University;[2] "Literature and National Feeling," by Professor Bliss Perry; "Libraries, Librarians and University Extension," by Mr. Herbert Putnam; "University Extension in England," by Mr. W. Hudson Shaw, of Oxford.

We offer the above merely as suggestions and shall be glad to adopt your preference. If we knew the subject within the next two weeks, we could announce it in the Winter Announcement which reaches all interested in the Society's work and which goes to the printers just before Christmas.[3]

Sincerely yours,   Charles D. Atkins.

TLS (WP, DLC).
    [1] Charles Augustus Brinley, at this time President of the American Pulley Co. of Philadelphia.

[2] Ramsay Muir, formerly Dean of the Faculty of Arts at the University of Liverpool and at this time Professor of Modern History at the same institution.
[3] Wilson spoke on "Academic Ideals and Public Service." A news report of his address is printed at March 13, 1909, Vol. 19.

From Cyrus Hall McCormick

My dear Woodrow: Chicago   12 December 1908.

On February twelfth, next, Chicago is to celebrate in a most dignified and befitting manner the centenary of Lincoln's birthday, and as Lincoln was an Illinois boy it goes without saying that the Lincoln celebration in Illinois will be of quite as much importance to the country at large as any other celebration which may be held in other parts of the country.

A Committee of one hundred representative citizens have been formed to take this matter of celebration in charge and it is their purpose to have a three day's celebration, but the chief address is to be delivered on February twelfth, which is Lincoln's birthday and it is the unanimous wish of the Committee that you should deliver the chief address on this occasion.

Not only because of your admirable personal fitness for this stirring occasion; not only because of the warm appreciation in which you are held here by reason of your former addresses at the Young Men's Christian Association celebration last spring and at the Princeton dinners which have been held here; not only because in your studies of history and government you are already well equipped to deal with a subject of this importance is the invitation so spontaneously and cordially sent to you, but also because you as a southern born man would speak with peculiar delicacy, as well as force, on a theme of such national and even worldwide importance.

I have telegraphed you,[1] asking if February twelfth is free among your engagements because only today has the meeting of this Committee been held and they have asked me to assist them in putting this matter before you in the very best light.

I can assure you that the occasion will be one in which you will be much pleased to take part if you have the time and the strength to make the necessary preparation, and if this invitation comes within the line of those appointments which you would be glad, for your own sake and for that of the University, to accept.[2]

With kind regards to you and Mrs. Wilson, I am

Very cordially your friend,   Cyrus H McCormick.

TLS (WP, DLC).
  [1] His telegram is missing.
  [2] After further correspondence, Wilson agreed to deliver the address which he entitled "Abraham Lincoln: A Man of the People." The text is printed at Feb. 12, 1909, Vol. 19.

From Cleveland Hoadley Dodge

Dear Tommie   Dodge Lodge[1] Sunday Evg [c. Dec. 13, 1908]

I am broken hearted not to have seen you but I caught a bad cold in Washington & my family physician (Mrs CHD) has not allowed me to go out yesterday or today. I had nothing [']tickler to say except to urge you to take care of yourself & to see if we couldn't arrange to have you go away for a long & real rest. Why can't you go off for three or four months. It would come hard but would pay all around. God bless you dear old chap & make you *all* well. Don't fail to let me see you if you come to N. Y. during the Holidays

Ever affly   C. H. Dodge

I met hosts of interesting men in Washington & it would have done your heart good to have heard what they said about Princeton, the Preceptorial System & *you*[.] I lunched at the White House with T. R.[,] Mr Bryce & Mr Root; & Theodore told us how much he admired you, your writings your ability &c *"But I cannot say that I like his political utterances"*

À Dios

I had told him that I had sat next to Coddie Peabody[2] two nights before & he had informed me that he had written Roosevelt urging him to send his son Kermit—6th form at Groton—to Princeton rather than Harvard[3]

ALS (WP, DLC).
  [1] Dodge's house in Princeton at 24 Bayard Lane.
  [2] The Rev. Dr. Endicott Peabody, founder and Headmaster of the Groton School, Groton, Mass., since 1884.
  [3] Actually, Kermit Roosevelt went to Harvard and was graduated with the Class of 1912. He completed his undergraduate course in two and a half years.

To Cyrus Hall McCormick

My dear Cyrus: Princeton, N. J.   December 14th, 1908.

When your telegram arrived, my immediate impulse was to reply that I would make the address which the gentlemen preparing for the celebration of the One Hundredth Anniversary of Lincoln's Birthday in Chicago have so kindly asked me to make, but upon reflection I saw that it was really impossible for me to do so.

The fact is that I have already declined half a dozen invitations for that occasion. I have been asked to speak in Brooklyn, at the official celebration in New York, and at many other celebrations for which programmes are being prepared elsewhere, and I have replied to all of them that I expected to be out of the country at that time. It now looks as if it would after all not be possible for me to take the midwinter vacation, which has been so serviceable to me the last two winters, but you will see that it would be very seriously misunderstood, if I should, after declining these very important invitations, put in an appearance in Chicago as the chief speaker there.

I should consider it a great honor and a real privilege, but I think that you will agree with me that in the circumstances I am estopped. I am still hoping with a vain hope that it may be possible for me to take the vacation I covet, and therefore I can still say that I am reserving February for that purpose. But this hope would not deter me from accepting the Chicago invitation, if it were not for the circumstances I have explained. To accept it would involve a very serious discourtesy to many associations and cities of the first consequence.

I have been a little uneasy at not hearing about Cyrus, Jr. I sincerely hope that he has made satisfactory progress to recovery and that his illness is not going to be a serious embarrassment to him in his studies. My thoughts have turned to him very often.[1]

Please give my warmest regards to Mrs. McCormick, and believe me,

Always faithfully and affectionately yours,
Woodrow Wilson

TLS (WP, DLC).
[1] See C. H. McCormick to WW, Dec. 17, 1908 (second letter of that date), n. 1.

From Wilson Farrand

Newark, N. J.
My dear President Wilson: December 14, 1908.

I write at this time to say that the Executive Committee of our Alumni Association after careful consideration decided to go ahead with the annual dinner at the time arranged, in spite of my father's death.[1] They are, therefore, making all their arrangements for the dinner on Friday, January 15, and are counting a great deal on your presence.[2]

While the dinner cannot be a celebration in honor of my father, it is but natural that it should, to a considerable extent, follow the original plan, and undoubtedly the key note of the evening will be my father's work and the educational principles that he stood for, and that we hope and intend shall be maintained here in the future. I speak of this simply as a hint for you in thinking of what you will say. I had hoped to see you at the Wednesday Club this week,[3] but find that I am not able to be there. Later I will write you in regard to the arrangements here for the dinner, for meeting you, etc.

With best wishes,

Sincerely yours,   Wilson Farrand

TLS (WP, DLC).
  [1] Samuel Ashbel Farrand, for many years Headmaster of the Newark Academy, who died on November 7, 1908.
  [2] A news report of Wilson's address is printed at Jan. 16, 1909.
  [3] A news report of his address to this businessmen's club of Newark is printed at Dec. 17, 1908.

To Oscar Henry Cooper[1]

Princeton, N. J.
December 15th, 1908.

My dear President Cooper:

The theme upon which you ask my opinion is a very broad one, and I am afraid that I can give only a very brief and imperfect expression of my opinion about it in a letter.

If by college ideals you mean ideals of study, I think that college ideals are distinctly on the decline; but if you mean the ideals characteristic of college life, I think that they are not at all on the decline, but are in many ways very wholesome and reassuring.

The trouble, to my mind, is that the extracurriculum activities of college life have so multiplied and have become so interesting and intensive, themselves involving a certain training and preparation for life, that they have dwarfed and subordinated the main purpose of college life, namely, serious study and a thorough orientation in the things of the mind. I believe that it is an imperative necessity now that we should draw the students of our colleges together into a vital academic family which, through the influence of informal as well as formal contact between teacher and student, will restore the consciousness of what a college is and what life in it should mean by way of training and enlightenment.

In brief, I do not think that college ideals are on the decline, but that they are looking in the wrong direction, or, rather, exaggerating things which should be incidental, not the business of the place but its relaxation.

With much regard,

Sincerely yours,   Woodrow Wilson

TLS (deCoppet Coll., NjP).
[1] President of Simmons College, Abilene, Texas.

To Robert Bridges

My dear Bobby: Princeton, N. J.   December 15th, 1908.

I can only guess what would be the feeling of graduates and undergraduates about the substitution of tigers for the lions in front of Old North, but I should guess that it would be favorably, if not enthusiastically, received. The feeling of the class itself in the matter, I think, is a pretty sure guide, and the fact that for a good many years regrets have been expressed not infrequently that lions should have been put there in the first instance rather than tigers, and the constant need to explain that the tiger had in our day not become the emblem of the University in the definite way in which it is now recognized, would seem to indicate that the propriety of the change would be at once acknowledged and that whatever feeling of regret there might be would be more than offset by that feeling of propriety.[1]

I wish very much that I could attend the Burns dinner,[2] but I have declined all invitations for the latter part of January and the early part of February in the hope that I could again take a midwinter vacation. That is the only time of the year when it is possible for me to do so, and I have declined so many invitations for that week and obliged so many persons to change dates for my convenience, that I should feel very much embarrassed by appearing in public at that time, even if it should turn out to be impossible for me to get away.

I have received a very kind letter from Mr. Foord[3] and have explained the matter to him also.

Always affectionately yours,   Woodrow Wilson

TLS (WP, DLC).
[1] For a discussion of the plans of the Class of 1879 to give a pair of bronze tigers for the steps of Nassau Hall, see the news report printed at Feb. 19, 1909, Vol. 19.
[2] The Burns Society of the City of New York was planning a banquet at Delmonico's Restaurant on January 25, 1909, to celebrate the sesquicentennial of the birth of the Scottish poet.
[3] John Foord, Scottish-born journalist of New York, former Editor-in-Chief of the *New York Times* (1876-83); at this time a member of the editorial staff

of the New York *Journal of Commerce* and President of the Burns Society of the City of New York. His letter is missing.

From Rudolph Grossman

My Dear Dr. Wilson: New York, Dec. 16, 1908.

An unusual pressure of work has prevented me from acknowledging sooner the receipt of your very kind letter of the 30th ult. I appreciate most highly your very courteous acceptance of my invitation to deliver an address before my people. The date you suggest, March 18th, is entirely satisfactory to me, & the subject, "Americanism" is exactly what I would want. We look forward with great pleasure to your coming to us, & I shall take the liberty of writing you again a week or so in advance, merely as a reminder.

Again assuring you of my deep appreciation of your kindness, believe me to be,

Very Sincerely Yours,   Rudolph Grossman

ALS (WP, DLC).

From Arthur Ledlie Wheeler[1]

My Dear Dr Wilson: Philada., Pa.   Dec'r 16. 1908

As the chairman of the Committee in charge of the Annual dinner of the Princeton Club of Philadelphia, I am writing to extend to you a cordial and pressing invitation to attend our dinner next March and speak on whatever subject you may select.

We have an option on the "Clover room" at the Bellevue-Stratford for the first three Fridays in March (the fifth, twelfth and nineteenth) and will be glad to have you select the date which will be most convenient to you. On general principles we would prefer not to have the fifth as it is the day following the Inauguration at Washington which might prevent some of our members from attending.

It is now two years since we have had the pleasure of hearing you speak at our dinner[2] and we all sincerely hope that you will be able to accept.[3]

With kind regards, I am,

Yours very truly,   Arthur L. Wheeler

TLS (WP, DLC).

[1] Princeton 1896, of Winthrop, Smith & Co., bankers and brokers of Philadelphia.

2 Two news reports of Wilson's address on this earlier occasion are printed at Feb. 15, 1907, Vol. 17.
3 Wilson chose March 19, 1909. A news report of his address is printed at March 20, 1909, Vol. 19.

A News Report of an Address in Newark

[Dec. 17, 1908]

BUSINESS MAN IS TOO SELFISH
ADDRESSES WEDNESDAY CLUB

That the great trouble with the American business man in relation to his nation is that he is too selfish was the declaration made by President Woodrow Wilson, of Princeton University, at a monthly dinner held by the Wednesday Club at the Continental Hotel last night. The subject under discussion was "The Business Man and the Nation." G. Wisner Thorne[1] acted as toastmaster. . . .

In introducing Dr. Wilson, Mr. Thorne spoke of him as a thorough-going business man, as well as one capable of dealing with the affairs of the nation. That this latter fact was appreciated by the people of this State and the nation, he said, was shown when his name was urged as that of a candidate for the United States Senate and again recently for the Democratic Presidential nomination.

Dr. Wilson said it would be with a degree of temerity that he would attempt to discuss such a large subject as the one selected if it were not for the fact that he could treat it broadly and talk for a long time without saying much of anything. The topic was one, he said, that arises out of the general talk of the time which has stirred the conscience of the people about the civic responsibility of men in business. The reason for the general thought given this subject, he declared, was that there has been a drifting into certain practices of a demoralizing character that appear to threaten the nation itself.

"A great change has come over our country," continued Dr. Wilson, "since its foundation. We would not say that at the time of the Revolution our nation's characteristic was economics. There were not so many merchants at that time as farmers and they did not dream of conquest in the field of arms or commerce. It was a regard for the rights of man that was paramount and it was this feeling that brought about the Revolution in demand for a return to the old stand of English liberty.

"To-day the characteristic American is the American business man. What is he going to do with the country he has made?

The [?] of the land, if it is to be practical, must come out of the consent of the business man. You can secure business on no other terms, and not until such is brought about will our fears pass and our hopes revive. Our wrong practices are not due, I believe, to the prominence of a great number of wicked men, for the proportion of them is not greater now than in any other generation. In fact, these wicked men are needed for the good men to cut their eye teeth on, and they are valuable because of the counter-tendency produced just as any irritant is valuable in our body politic.

"I think that our troubles are due not so much to a disregard of law as to pure selfishness. That abominable phrase, 'Business is business,' is too often made the maxim of the business man in his transactions that are not inspired with a public spirit and are not conducive to the public good. It is because men shut themselves up in their offices, shutting out the world, and concentrate their minds on labor and business, giving no thought to the United States, that conditions undesirable are brought about. I do not mean to say that this act qualifies them for the peniten[ti]ary, but it is productive of failure. By it you multiply your enemies and decrease the number of your friends, narrowing the field of your operation."

The salvation of the corporations, Dr. Wilson said, was universal candor, and if they would endure, he declared, they must lay all their cards above the table. Advice should be given the Legislatures by corporation lawyers, he said, as to the proper laws to be enacted. If they do not someone who does not understand the situation as they do will, and the result will be the ruin of corporations.

"The power of a nation," Dr. Wilson continued, "is in its ability to purify, elevate, and vary itself. It does not lie in [the] things it possesses, but in the things it is. This is being realized in America, and in our awakening we shall come from the seclusion of selfish effort to direct our fellow-men. The whole nation feels the impulse of that day which is dawning, and when it comes we shall know a new age of achievement and triumph."

Printed in the *Newark Evening News*, Dec. 17, 1908; one editorial heading omitted.

[1] Gabriel Wisner Thorne, President and Treasurer of the Newark Call Printing and Publishing Co. and publisher of the *Newark Sunday Call*.

Two Letters from Cyrus Hall McCormick

My dear Woodrow: Chicago   17 December 1908.

I thank you for your very full letter of the 14th, the substance of which I have conveyed to the Committee of One Hundred here. You may perhaps know that Chicago is noted for a moderate amount of persistency and you will, therefore, not be surprised that the Committee and I do not fall in as readily with your reasoning as might be expected. In other words, under the circumstances as stated by you, we do not agree that you are estopped from accepting the Chicago invitation. When you declined the other invitations in the East, it was for a definite reason,—that you expected to be out of the country. The fact that your plans have been necessarily modified since then alters the conditions under which you made your former declinatures, but, in the meantime, the other Committees have undoubtedly completed their arrangements for other speakers, and this invitation comes to you practically at the last moment. This reason seems to me so clear that, if I were a member of a Committee of one of the Associations which had invited you before and if I learned that you had accepted a subsequent invitation under the circumstances under which this comes, I do not see how I could find fault with you or feel that you were in the least inconsistent in having accepted one invitation of this nature after you had declined others.

The explanation which I should think ought to be satisfactory to any one lies in the fact that your own conditions have materially changed in the meantime. So strongly does this appear to me to be the case, that I should not even have any objection to your communicating, by telephone or otherwise, with at least one of the Committees whom you have already declined, to ask them if they think you would be put in an unreasonable position by the acceptance of the Chicago invitation; and I am quite satisfied that they would say that you were free to accept it, much as they might regret that they could not have had you themselves.

The only reason that I can see for your declining this interesting invitation would be the question of your own health or strength. If on this score you feel that you can accept the invitation, would you not review the matter even to the extent of confidentially sounding one of the parties to whom you assume you would be discourteous in accepting the Chicago invitation, to test the ground for your feeling on this subject? If this could be done without much delay, the Chicago Committee would be very glad to wait a little further in the hope that you would send an acceptance. I assume that, under the modified conditions as they now stand, you would probably be able to take your vacation immediately after the twelfth of February, even if not before.

I am   Most cordially yours,   Cyrus H. McCormick.

My dear Woodrow: Chicago   17 December 1908.

Cyrus, I am glad to say, is quite recovered and is at home recuperating under the care of our physician. He is taking lessons daily with a tutor to the end that he may be able to pass the examinations February tenth at Princeton and rejoin his class. By diligent work he hopes to be able to overtake his class by that time. And, in any event, the physician would not permit him to return to college before the middle of January.

I have written the registrar, H[enry]. N[evius]. van Dyke, also Dean Fine, advising them of the status of Cyrus' case and saying that I will inform them just as soon as I can about his return. Our physician thinks that he is making a good recovery and that with time he will feel no ill effects from his hard siege of fever.[1]

With warmest regards from Mrs. McCormick, I am
        Most cordially yours,   Cyrus H. McCormick.

TLS (WP, DLC).
    [1] Cyrus McCormick returned to his classes for the spring term and was graduated with his class in 1912.

From John Lambert Cadwalader

My dear Mr. President: New York, 17 December, 1908.

I duly received your letter concerning the proposed Alumni Council, and I am to have a meeting with Thompson and Garrett, who are coming here for the purpose within a week or ten days, and we are going over the entire subject.

Your letter as to the payment of the Sage money was forwarded at once by me to Henry de Forest, a very sensible business man, who had said to me that he saw no reason why the money should not be paid over, I saying to him that we would receive the amount, or any part of it, keep it separate from other funds, draw upon it solely for this dormitory, and if any further amount was required to complete the building, pay it ourselves.

He now writes me the enclosed note.[1] The whole business with Mrs. Sage has been unfortunate. We have never had anybody *in charge of it* and I fear that our methods will not commend themselves to her. I appreciate, however, at the same time, that she is an old lady, who rather thinks she ought to be consulted and is unable to do her part to meet the consultation. Dodge told me the other day he was going to see her, and I rather suggested to him not to until this thing was closed out.

I should, under this suggestion of Henry de Forest's, meet his views at once, and I think I should send someone to see him, with the plans, who can make the proper explanations, etc., and it ought to be, it seems to me, someone connected with the architects. De Forest himself has had the idea that the building was to be too near the street.

Yours faithfully,   John L. Cadwalader

TLS (WP, DLC).
[1] It is missing.

From Melancthon Williams Jacobus

Hartford [Conn.]

My dear President Wilson: 17th December 1908

I doubt not that you have felt the same regret that I have felt at Mr. Cadwalader's decision not to stand for renomination as an Alumni Trustee. I take for granted that his published letter[1] commits him beyond any reconsideration; in this case the matter of most moment is the choice of the Alumni in his succession. Have you any idea as to the direction in which this choice is likely to lie, and is there anything that can be done to wisely influence it? Alumni Trustees count as all other members of the Board in its counsels and its decisions, and we need constantly and consistently the strongest men we can get.[2]

In view of the new arrangement for Commencement[3] will it not be wise for us to see that a strong list of honorary degrees is prepared for next June? Can you not, out of your wide acquaintance with scholars & leaders in this and other countries provide us with nominations at the January & April meetings? We should make this coming Alumni Banquet, with its "degree" speakers a most notable one. It is a great opportunity and we should not miss it for the University's sake.[4]

Day before yesterday I took my first lecture hour at the Seminary since the middle of last October, and find that I must go very slow for the present. Whether I shall be able to get to Princeton for the January meeting is yet open to question; though I truly hope I shall be able to make the journey. Might I ask, however, as a precautionary arrangement that the meeting of the Curriculum Committee be placed for Wednesday *afternoon* rather than Wednesday evening preceding the session of the Board.

With kindest regards and best wishes for all the happy Christmas time

Yours very cordially   Melancthon W. Jacobus

ALS (WP, DLC).
[1] J. L. Cadwalader to C. W. McAlpin, Nov. 28, 1908, *Princeton Alumni Weekly*, IX (Dec. 9, 1908), 165.
[2] He was succeeded by Wilson Farrand.
[3] The Board of Trustees had voted on October 15, 1908, to shorten commencement week by condensing the activities formerly held on Tuesday and Wednesday into one day, Tuesday. The chief effects of the change were to place the commencement ceremony itself on Tuesday morning, followed by the alumni luncheon and the President's reception. One of the avowed objectives of the new schedule was to enable the distinguished recipients of honorary degrees to be the principal speakers at the alumni luncheon. Previously, the alumni luncheon had been held on the day before commencement, and the speakers had usually been representatives of the various Princeton classes holding reunions, along with the President of the university.
[4] For Wilson's list of nominees for honorary degrees at the commencement of 1909, see WW to the Board of Trustees of Princeton University, Jan. 14, 1909.

From William E. Johnson[1]

My dear Doctor,   New York, Dec 17 1908

I was a guest at the Wednesday Club Banquet in Newark last night & I was so pleased with what you said that I cannot refrain from telling you so.

I am not a college bred man, but if I were to enter on a college course, I would be glad to enter where I could gain ideas from so clear a head as yours.

For many years I have been considered a kind of lost sheep by my family because I forsook the Rep. coral & since my twenty first birthday, I have been unable to tell exactly what fold I did belong to & I am like the man, whom the minister asked if he was sure what place he was going to & he replied, "it made but little difference, he had so many friends in both places"

It did me a world of good to hear a man in your position, where you can do so much good, give vent to ideas that have been mine so long, & I hope you will increase in power, & have the magic to put into the hearts of young men, ideas that will not only make them grow & expand & blossom for the benefit of all, but that you may penetrate into the leather lined think tanks of the hard bald headed variety, for whom, "what was good enough for father is good enough for me"

Yours very truly   Wm. E. Johnson.

ALS (WP, DLC).
  1 A partner in the firm of Watson and Johnson, Real Estate, Mortgage Brokers & Appraisers, 38 Park Row, New York.

From Francis Xavier Dercum[1]

My dear Prof. Wilson,   Philadelphia   Dec. 17 '08

I have learned through Mr. Ax[s]on of your willingness to permit me to show you the buildings, laboratories and hospital of Jefferson College. I write to say that I would be most happy to have you come on such day as is convenient to yourself. I can arrange my time so as to be at liberty on any day from Monday the 21st on. Would a day before Christmas be agreeable to you or would you prefer a day during Christmas week?

I would be delighted if you could arrange your time so as to take lunch with Mrs. Dercum[2] and myself before we go to the College and indeed more than pleased if you could make it convenient to remain to dinner.

I am with kind regards,
                    Very Sincerely Yours   F. X. Dercum

ALS (WP, DLC).
  1 Francis Xavier Dercum, M.D., Ph.D., practicing physician in Philadelphia and Professor of Nervous and Mental Diseases at Jefferson Medical College. As future documents will disclose, some of the Princeton trustees and officers of Jefferson Medical College were considering the possibility of the latter becoming the medical school of Princeton University.
  2 Elizabeth Comly Dercum.

To John Lambert Cadwalader

                              [Princeton, N. J.]
My dear Mr. Cadwalader: December 18th, 1908.

I regret as much as you do that there has been any further mistake in the matter of our dealings with Mrs. Sage. I have all along understood it to be a tacit agreement that you were in charge of our dealings with her, and I am extremely sorry that anything should have occurred to embarrass you in the matter. Except for carrying out the suggestion we all agreed upon, namely that Mrs. Sage was to be invited to Princeton, I have been myself careful to remember that everything should go through you, and I wish everybody else had done the same.

I will immediately write to Messrs. Frank Miles Day and Brother, the architects, and ask that they send a man up, either to your or to Mr. DeForest's office as you prefer, at any time that will suit your convenience. So soon as you can let me know by telephone or by telegraph what time next week the plans should be sent, I will communicate with the architects as to the date. I am writing them today to prepare them for the appointment.

   With warmest regard and appreciation,

                              Sincerely yours,   [Woodrow Wilson]

CCL (WWP, UA, NjP).

To Frank Miles Day and Brother

My dear Sirs: Princeton, N. J.   December 18th, 1908.

   It turns out to be very desirable that Mrs. Russell Sage should see, at as early a date as possible, the plans you have prepared for the dormitory for which she is to pay. I do not know exactly what day will suit Mrs. Sage's convenience, but I am writing to ask if it would be possible for you, should I telephone or telegraph next week, to send the plans up to New York with someone who could fully explain them to Mrs. Sage or to Mr. DeForest, her representative. It is the elevations particularly in which Mrs. Sage is interested.

                              Sincerely yours,   Woodrow Wilson

TLS (WC, NjP).

From John Fairfield Dryden

Dear Sir: Newark, N. J., December 18, 1908.

   As you are doubtless aware, a movement was started in the State some months ago, having for its object the erection of a monument to the late Grover Cleveland at Princeton, New Jersey. A Committee was appointed, of which I was made Chairman, and this Committee has set about raising funds for the proposed monument. It is thought that about $100,000 will be needed and that the same should be obtained by voluntary subscription. Arrangements have already been made for soliciting subscriptions in some of the Counties of the State and we hope to soon cover the whole State.

   We have concluded that to handle the matter properly, it will be necessary to form an incorporation under the Non Pecuniary Profit Act of the State of New Jersey, and we have had a certificate for this purpose prepared, a copy of which I enclose you herewith.[1] It will be necessary for us to name in the certificate of incorporation the Trustees to serve for the first year, and we have consequently selected twenty-four representative citizens, whom we are inviting to become Trustees. I enclose you a list of the same herewith[2] and I greatly hope that the object and scheme will commend themselves to you and that you will consent to serve as one of the Trustees.[3]

We believe that we shall be able, within a short time, to raise the necessary funds and erect a monument that will do credit to the State and Nation and adequately express the regard and veneration of the people for the life and character of Mr. Cleveland.

Kindly let me hear from you at your earliest convenience, and oblige,   Yours very truly,   John F. Dryden

TLS (WP, DLC).
    [1] "Certification of Incorporation," CC MS (WP, DLC).
    [2] "Proposed Trustees of Cleveland Monument Association," CC MS (WP, DLC).
    [3] Wilson's reply is missing; however, J. F. Dryden to WW, Jan. 19, 1909, reveals that Wilson accepted the appointment.

To Melancthon Williams Jacobus

[Princeton, N. J.]

My dear Dr. Jacobus: December 19th, 1908.

I have been deeply distressed by your long illness. It is delightful to hear that you are out again and are attempting some of your professional duties, but I beg that you will be exceedingly prudent and go very slowly indeed in resuming your full activity. I sincerely hope, also, that the doctor who has you in hand is seeing to it that you are thoroughly put in shape again. I have thought of you often and most affectionately and have been very impatient for this news that you were decidedly better.

I feel so much delicacy about making any suggestions, particularly at the present time, with regard to alumni representation in the Board, that I have said and asked very little about Mr. Cadwalader's probable successor. The only name I have heard mentioned at all is that of Mr. John Pitney of Morristown,[1] who, so far as I can see, would make an excellent man for the place and in whose selection the New York as well as the New Jersey men might be willing to join. He is an opponent, I understood, of the quad plan, but I do not think that in the case of honest and open-minded men we should let that count in our judgment.

I think, as you do, that with the new order of things we are setting up next Commencement our list of Honorary Degrees assumes a new importance, and I will certainly try to make suitable suggestions to the committee before the next Board meeting. I will also keep in mind your suggestion that the Curriculum Committee meet in the afternoon instead of in the evening, and I shall hope most warmly that you may be able to be here and that by that time you will be feeling very much stronger again.

Mrs. Wilson joins me in warmest regards, and I am always,

Faithfully and affectionately yours,

[Woodrow Wilson]

CCL (RSB Coll., DLC).
[1] John Oliver Halsted Pitney, Princeton 1881, who lived in Morristown, N. J., and practiced law in Newark.

From William Henry Grant[1]

My dear Doctor Wilson: New York December 19, 1908.

In connection with the Annual Conference of Foreign Missions Boards of the United States and Canada we are preparing for a "China Dinner" at the Hotel Astor, Thursday evening, January 14, 1909. The subject is "Christian Education in China."

It is proposed to have several men who are engaged in the work, and Prof. Harlan P. Beach of Yale,[2] who has recently visited most of the higher educational institutions in China, speak upon "Christian Education in China" as an efficient arm of missionary propaganda, giving us a survey of the work as it exists, and illustrations of its character and effect.

We would ask one of them to speak on "What the college is to the Church," another on "Student Life in our Colleges and Schools," another on "The necessity and value of trained Christian teachers," another on "Union, federation and coordination in educational work," another on "Personal work with students and student Christian Associates and students going abroad."

The Committee are very desirous to secure your attendance at this dinner and to have you speak, as it were, for the nation, as to what should be our induction from the facts and how we should meet this opportunity. The Committee are certain that you are the man to speak for us on this occasion, and that you will say something from your own study and observations which will constitute a message to the whole church.

We are making an effort to secure the attendance of Ambassador Tang Shao Yi to hear and respond to a short memorial address on the late Empress Dowager and Emperor, which will give a little Chinese flavor to the occasion.[3]

If there is any hesitancy in your mind regarding this would you not before you give any decision permit us to come and see you.[4]

Sincerely,   W Henry Grant
Chairman of Dinner Committee
& Secretary of Conference.

TLS (WP, DLC).

[1] Grant was a man of independent means who was deeply involved in foreign missionary work. He had recently been an unpaid secretary and "Honorary Librarian" of the Presbyterian Board of Foreign Missions in New York. In 1908 he still listed his business address as that of the board although he was no longer officially connected with it. His only title at this time seems to have been that of Secretary and Treasurer of the Trustees of the Canton Christian College.

[2] The Rev. Dr. Harlan Page Beach, missionary to China, 1883-90, and at this time Professor of the Theory and Practice of Missions at Yale Divinity School.

[3] The Chinese Ambassador was unable to attend.

[4] Wilson attended and spoke at the China dinner on January 4, 1909. For the gist of his remarks, see the news report printed at Jan. 28, 1911, Vol. 22.

From George Howe III

Chapel Hill, N. C.
December 21, 1908.

Dear Uncle Woodrow:

Our institution[1] has made many attempts to get you to pay us a visit and is now making one more. There is to be a holiday on Lee's birthday, January 19, and a speaker of unusual attractions is desired. It is of the utmost importance to the University to make the day a success, because it will be the only opportunity to bring members of the committees of the Legislature to take a look at what we are doing. It is out of the ordinary to declare a holiday on that day, but there is special reason for it this time. And it must be made a big day. The President[2] instead of writing to you himself has, for various reasons, appointed a committee to attend to it for him, and this letter is the official invitation. You were chosen not simply as a drawing card for the Legislature, but also because every one here has a warm place in his heart for Princeton and sincerely admires her work and her President. We have always failed to get you in June and in October; can we not have you in mid-session?

You would be expected to speak on some subject suitable to the day. The maximum length of time allowed you would be forty-five minutes. There would be but one other speech—the speech of introduction. Of course all your expenses would be paid, but no more.[3]

I have written a very frank invitation, knowing that that sort always makes the strongest appeal to you. Let me also add a personal one. You can hardly estimate how much it would mean to Maisie[4] and me to have you even for a single night. We have hoped more earnestly than you know that you would accept past invitations, and have been deeply disappointed that you did not. Our hopes are soaring once more; do not disappoint us again. Make a special effort this time. I think it would do Princeton good in this part of the country. And I know it would do us personally a world of good. Of course it will mean a great deal for our University to have you.

I freely confess that my main desire in the matter is to see you and to have you in our home. I would not have written thus to any other choice of the committee's. Write as soon as you can that you will come to us for a week's stay, or a couple of days, or even for one night.

We are both well and busy. We are going to Columbia for Xmas but will stay only a few days. My work is running along smoothly. I hope to have a little book out before long, though it will not amount to much.[5]

Maisie joins me in all good wishes of the season and in the warmest love to each and every one of you.

Affectionately,   George Howe

TLS (WP, DLC).
[1] The University of North Carolina.
[2] Francis Preston Venable.
[3] Wilson accepted, as the documents will soon reveal. The text of his address, on Robert E. Lee, is printed at Jan. 19, 1909.
[4] His wife, Margaret Smyth Flinn Howe.
[5] He was referring either to his *Nature Similes in Catullus* (Chapel Hill, N. C., 1911) or to his *Latin Sight Reader* (Raleigh, N. C., 1912).

To Cyrus Hall McCormick

My dear Cyrus: Princeton, N. J.   December 21st, 1908.

I surrender, though with some misgivings as to the consequences. I will explain the matter as well as I can to one or two others, but in the meantime I agree to accept the kind invitation conveyed to me by your letter and Mr. Bancroft's.[1]

I am delighted to hear that Cyrus has made such good progress towards recovery and hope most sincerely that he will not find that he is embarrassed in keeping up with his class. I know how mortifying that is to a boy. Please give my warmest regards to Mrs. McCormick, and believe me, as always,

Affectionately yours,   Woodrow Wilson

TLS (WP, DLC).
¹ This letter from Edgar Addison Bancroft, Chicago lawyer, civic leader, and author, is missing.

From Walter Lee McCorkle

My dear Bro. Wilson: New York   December 21st, 1908.

I have no doubt but that Dr. Wyeth and Mr. Verdery have fully advised you that the Executive Committee of the New York Southern Society have such hearty appreciation of your splendid remarks upon "Conservatism, True and False" that they desire to have a correct copy of your address delivered at the 23rd annual banquet of the Society, on the 9th of December.

I have been waiting to hear from Dr. Wyeth or Mr. Verdery as to whether they had a copy of your address, for every copy that you gave me I gave to the newspapers and the newspapers gave us, this year, more extended notice than we have had in a long, long time.

Your address has been referred to all over the country with most favorable commendation and I am writing you this morning to enclose a copy from one of the newspapers¹ and I would like for you to go over it together with any personal memoranda you have and forward to me at your earliest convenience a complete and correct copy that we might use it for our year book.

I assure you that I did personally enjoy your remarks although they were a year late being delivered and every member of the Society, together with the officers and particularly the Dinner Committee were simply delighted to hear your address and to have you with us.

Trusting you can give me a prompt reply and with the compliments of the season, I am

Very sincerely yours,   Walter L. McCorkle.

TLS (WP, DLC).
¹ This enclosure is missing.

From Franklin Zeiger¹

Dear Sir: Paterson, N. J.   Dec. 21, 1908.

I beg to inform you that the teachers of the Paterson High School are planning a dinner in honor of the twenty-fifth anniversary of the services of the Principal, Dr. J. A[lbert]. Reinhart, and to extend you in their behalf a very cordial invitation to attend as the chief speaker. We are planning to have it next spring on the evening of some date after March fourth, but we desire the further determination of the date to be according to your convenience. . . .

We desire you to choose the subject for your address with entire freedom, if you accept the invitation; and may I add that we are very desirous of having you accept it, not only for the sake of having your address, but also because you are the President of the greatest University in our State, and one of the most distinguished scholars and educators of the time. We presume that in Paterson there are more graduates of your University than of any other, and we are hoping to see the number increase in the immediate future.

Of course we should desire to arrange for your entertainment when in the city, and to meet all expenses of the trip.[2]

Hoping for a favorable reply, I am

Yours respectfully,   Franklin Zeiger.

ALS (WP, DLC).
[1] Teacher of Latin at the Paterson High School.
[2] Wilson accepted; a news item about his address, "The Schoolmaster," on April 23, 1909, is printed at April 24, 1909, Vol. 19.

From Arthur Ledlie Wheeler

My dear Dr Wilson: Philada., Pa.   Dec., 22nd., 1908.

We are all delighted that you are to be with us at our annual dinner and we have definitely engaged the Bellevue-Stratford for the 19th of March. I feel sure we shall have a most successful dinner.   Yours very truly,   Arthur L. Wheeler

TLS (WP, DLC).

From Cyrus Hall McCormick

My dear Woodrow: Chicago   23 December 1908.

I wish you a very happy Christmas, and you have made a large circle of your friends here happy by your letter in answer to our persistent appeal to you.

Of course I take it for granted that you understand that you will stop at our house, as you must always consider that your home when you are in Chicago.

I am   Affectionately yours,   Cyrus H. McCormick.

TLS (WP, DLC).

From John Lambert Cadwalader, with Enclosure

Dear Mr. President,   [New York]   23 Decr [1908]

There! That is settled again. But let somebody take a set to De Forest and have them with him—or do what he wants. He is a very reasonable person and is simply doing something suggested by Mrs. Sage. Pardon this undignified scrawl to a President. All good wishes.   John L. Cadwalader

ALS written on H. W. de Forest to J. L. Cadwalader, Dec. 22, 1908.

E N C L O S U R E

Henry Wheeler de Forest to John Lambert Cadwalader

Dear Sirs: New York   December 22, 1908.

I have yours of the 21st and return President Wilson's letter.

The question of architect, as you know, was settled long ago. You were quite right in supposing that Princeton was "to go on with the matter." Except for Dodge's having spoken to Mrs. Sage about the plans and expressing surprise that they had not been shown her, I don't suppose this question would have been raised, and all I want, as I wrote you, is a set of plans. If President Wilson will send me these there is no possible reason why they should be accompanied by a man from the architect's office unless they want to send him.

Sincerely yours,   H W de Forest

TLS (WP, DLC).

To Andrew Carnegie

My dear Mr. Carnegie,   Princeton, N. J.   26 Dec., 1908.

I know that the Phillips Academy at Andover, Mass., is expecting to appeal to you for assistance in making a very necessary addition to their property, and I take pleasure in saying that in my judgment it is in every way thoroughly worthy of aid by all who are interested in the educational advancement of the country.

It stands quite apart from the ordinary academy in character. It was founded one hundred and thirty years ago, has been built up from generation to generation with unusual intelligence, and has for a long time been, and deserved to be, one of the most famous institutions of the kind in America. Its fame is national because its patronage and its influences have been national. College men everywhere look to it for the kind of work which is the essential foundation for all higher education, and would rejoice, I am sure, in a gift made to it as in a gift made where it would be sure to tell for good. It is a privilege to commend it.[1]

With warmest regard,

Cordially and sincerely Yours,   Woodrow Wilson

ALS (A. Carnegie Papers, DLC).

[1] Carnegie gave $25,000 towards the sum of $250,000 being raised by the Phillips Academy for the purchase and renovation of the buildings and grounds of the Andover Theological Seminary, which had recently moved to Cambridge, Massachusetts. See Claude M. Fuess, *An Old New England School: A History of Phillips Academy, Andover* (Boston and New York, 1917), pp. 508-11.

Notes for an Address of Welcome

MODERN LANGUAGE ASSOCIATION,[1] Princeton, 28 December, 1908.

Welcoming address.

Welcome to Princeton.

We should be glad to see Princeton looked to as the natural foster mother, with her remove, her peace, her sedateness, of conferences of this kind.

Reception. Local invitation.

But qui bono? We are assembled here, I take it, not as teachers, but as those escaped from teaching into the freedom of learning. What is it we seek to learn?

Facts? No fact is in itself final. It might have been otherwise.

Sequences? No sequence is in itself conclusive. It might have been different.

In associations like this we are studying either

Tools,—tools of the human spirit; or

The human spirit itself, as expressed within the terms of life or outside of them.

Much literature is outside actual life: is an expression merely of what we uhould [should] have liked to be or to believe.

Learning is either a diversion or a narcotic or a contribution to life. I am a little interested in it as a diversion; I am profoundly interested in it as a contribution to life, its clarification, its illumination, its consummation.

Led to these reflections because it is my birthday, and one is tempted to ask of everything on one's birthday, What's the use?

WWT and WWsh MS (WP, DLC).

[1] Which met in Princeton, Dec. 28-30, 1908.

From Henry Thompson Kent[1]

My Dear Doctor: St. Louis. December 29, 1908.

Being a member of the Executive Committee of the Civic League, I have learned with much pleasure that you will deliver an address at the annual meeting of the League on March 9th next. As President of the Virginia Society in St. Louis, I am requested to extend you a cordial invitation to be their guest on Wednesday evening, March 10th, and to address the Society on that occasion. It is proper to say that this banquet is entirely confined to men, and in addition to the members of the Society, amongst whom there are many men of high standing and influence in the city, we will have as invited guests, if you will favor us, leading citizens of the city not members, especially, Editors of papers and prominent Educators. We will make the affair in every respect a dignified occasion, and one so recognized in the city.

At the last banquet we had for our guest Dr. Alderman, of the University of Virginia, with whose address we were all much delighted. As to the subject of your address, we leave that to you for you know full well what will be appropriate on such an occasion. Our mutual friend, Mr. McPheeters,[2] a member of our Society, heard you a few years ago deliver an address before the Southern Society of New York with which he was much pleased.[3] In a measure you will address the same type of people here.

Looking at it from the standpoint of Princeton, as I recognize your visits over the country are in their nature representative, I am sure you will address a group of gentlemen that will be strongly appreciative, and that you may sow seed that will bear good fruit. I am confidently relying upon your being with us at the above date. I can assure you that you will receive a hearty Virginia welcome.[4]

I am,   Faithfully yours,   Henry T. Kent

TLS (WP, DLC).

[1] Lawyer of St. Louis. Born in Louisa County, Va., he had been educated in law at the University of Virginia (LL.B., 1872).

[2] Thomas Shanks McPheeters, businessman of St. Louis. See T. S. McPheeters to WW, Sept. 27, 1899, Vol. 11.

[3] Prior to his address to the New York Southern Society on December 9, 1908, Wilson had spoken to that organization on two occasions—on December 9, 1903, and on December 14, 1906. See the news reports printed at Dec. 10, 1903, Vol. 15, and Dec. 15, 1906, Vol. 16.

[4] Wilson accepted the invitation. A brief report of his address is printed at March 11, 1909, Vol. 19.

From John David Davis

My dear Doctor Wilson: St. Louis   Dec. 31, 1908.

Mr. Kent, President of the Virginia Society, showed me a copy of a letter he had just written you, inviting you to deliver the principal address at the banquet of the Society to be held on Wednesday, March 10th. I agree with Mr. Kent that the occasion will be an opportune time for you to meet a large number of our leading citizens; and I think, looking to the interests of the University, that your address on that occasion would be of more value to the University than an address before Princeton men alone. I would therefore be very glad if you could accept their invitation. I think we can arrange an informal meeting of Princeton Alumni immediately following the annual meeting of the Civic League on March 9th, and I think most of our Princeton graduates will be able to attend the dinner of the Civic League, as all will be invited to do so, and thus have an opportunity to hear your address on that occasion.

I am looking forward with great pleasure to having you as my guest during your stay in St. Louis, and if nothing prevents, I will see you at the meeting of the Trustees on January 14th.

Please present my compliments to Mrs. Wilson and wishing you both a very happy New Year, I remain,

                          Very sincerely yours,   Jno D Davis.
TLS (WP, DLC).

From John Lambert Cadwalader

Dear Mr. President: New York, 31 December, 1908.

I have your letter returning to me the pamphlet showing the formation of the Columbia Council.

As I explained, I found the members of the Committee of Fifty who had made the report entirely disposed to meet any criticisms—of which there were several by the Committee of the Board—as to this new organization; and I feel quite satisfied that we are not over-confident in the opinion that we shall be able to meet the wishes of the alumni without sacrificing anything real. In fact, as the Board of Trustees actually require the active services of the alumni, and something quite beyond their sympathy and good-will, it will be wise to give them, as far as we may, *and without sacrificing our position*, proper tools to work with.

I will draw up a report and send you a copy of it for your further criticism.

                    Faithfully yours,   John L. Cadwalader

P.S. I suppose that de Forest was furnished yesterday with the information he desired about the plans for Mrs. Sage's building; and as he is going away for two or three weeks on Monday I am now asking him please to arrange the money matter.

TLS (WP, DLC).

To the Board of Trustees of Princeton University

[Princeton, N. J.] JANUARY 1st, 1909

GENTLEMEN OF THE BOARD OF TRUSTEES:

I have the honour to submit my annual report for the year 1908.

The year which has elapsed since my last report was prepared has been marked by the death of two members of this Board: Dr. Elijah R. Craven died on the fifth of January, and the Hon. Grover Cleveland on the twenty-fourth of June, 1908.

Dr. Craven had been a member of the Board since 1859, a period of nearly half a century, and throughout almost the entire length of his connection with it had acted as its Clerk, an office to the performance of whose duties he gave the painstaking care so characteristic of him. He was guided and stimulated in his service of the University, not only by his always exacting conscience, but also by a very deep and ardent affection for the University under whose influence he had been bred, and by an intelligent comprehension of her needs and obligations. There was a touch of stern precision in him which made him often the mentor of the Board when it showed any inclination to make haste carelessly or with too little regard for the forms of business; but that did not obscure, for those who really knew him, the essential kindness and passion for fair play which were for him the sources alike of judgment and of action. He was just and temperate in counsel, and in whatever he stood firm upon never forgot to be loyal and open.

Mr. Cleveland's death was so great a loss to the country, deprived so many interests and causes of his elevating counsel and example, that it is hard to assess our separate loss and distinguish it from what the whole nation felt. But he did do the University a special service, and it seemed, to us at any rate, when he died, to suffer a special loss. We felt the power of his character in all our deliberations, whether he took a leading part in them or not. We depended upon his suggestions for the wisest settlement of many delicate and perplexing matters. We were conscious of his guidance and his stimulating force in whatever he gave his special attention to. There was an unmistakable tonic in mere association with him; and when, as in matters affecting the Graduate School, he threw his weight into any piece of business, we always profited by the momentum he gave it and were always instructed by the clarification it received at his hands in the phrasing of his reports. He did much more than give the prestige of his great name to the University: he served it with thoughtful intelligence and conscientious devotion. His death has robbed us not only of an honored colleague whom we had learned both to admire and to love, but also of a great force and the influences of a great mind as well; and those of us who received his counsel here will always feel the poorer by reason of his absence.

Professor Charles Augustus Young, Emeritus Professor of Astronomy and for so many years one of the ornaments of the faculty of the University, died at his home in Hanover, New Hampshire, on the third of June, 1908, in the seventy-fourth year of his age. Professor Walter Augustus Wyckoff, Assistant Professor of Political Economy, died in Princeton on the fifteenth of May, 1908, in the forty-fourth year of his age, leaving us to mourn the loss of a man of unusual gifts and character.

I have elsewhere spoken of the work and character of Professor Young. The loss we felt in his death is proportionate to the great honour and love in which we held him while he lived and labored in modest achievement amongst us. Professor Wyckoff's failure in health when apparently at the age of greatest energy and efficiency, just as he was rising to the best work of his life in the classroom and in the community, was a deeply painful shock and surprise to all his friends and colleagues. He had always conceived his duty in a very fine spirit of devotion. He had always performed it with remarkable spirit, independence, and intelligence; he had been a student equally of men and of books, and had made himself an eminently useful citizen as well as a thoughtful scholar; and in all that he did he won the admiration and affection of those with whom he was associated and those whom he served. He seemed to go untimely. It was hard to part with him. It will be stimulating and satisfying to remember him.

Two of the most valued members of the faculty of the University, Professor Garfield and Professor Lovett, left us at the close of the last academic year, Professor Garfield to assume the Presidency of Williams College and Professor Lovett to undertake, as President, at Houston, Texas, the establishment and development of the Rice Institute of Arts and Sciences, recently provided for by the will of the late William M. Rice.[1]

Professor Garfield had been in Princeton only five years, but in that time had so established himself in our confidence, had made himself so essential a part of our counsels and of the daily processes of our university life, that his withdrawal from the faculty seemed to tear away some parts of the indispensable structural fabric of the university administration and instruction; but he returned to his Alma Mater in response to a clear call of duty, at the unanimous desire alike of the alumni and of the Trustees of Williams College, and it was plainly our duty to bid him godspeed with hearty willingness to spare him for his great task there. It is an interesting fact that Professor Finley went from the same chair five years ago to the Presidency of the College of the City of New York.

Professor Lovett came to Princeton in 1897 as Instructor in Mathematics; was elected Assistant Professor of Mathematics the following year; became Professor of Mathematics in 1900, and 1905, upon the retirement of Professor Young, was transferred to the chair of Astronomy. He had grown in reputation and in mastery of his subject with singular rapidity, carried forward by a most engaging eagerness in study and an irresistible impulse to learn and push inquiry to its limits; and yet he had shown himself fit for counsel also and a man whose disposition inclined him to the close companionships of academic life. When the trustees of Mr. Rice's bequest sought a man to take charge of the great institute of technical and liberal learning he had provided for in his will, it was hard to be generous and recommend Professor Lovett to their attention; but he has gone to his new work a thorough Princeton man, and it would indeed be churlish not to be willing to contribute our best men to the great educational work now so hopefully going forward in the South.

At the close of the last academic year, Dr. Cyrus Fogg Brackett resigned the Henry Professorship of Physics which he had filled with such unusual distinction since 1873, a period of thirty-five years. Few college careers have been more notable than his. He worked in the quiet field of mind whose achievements are not talked about outside the circle of those who are intent upon science or letters, and gave his brilliant gifts to the work of teaching and organization rather than to the work of investigation for which he was so admirably fitted; but the application of

[1] About William Marsh Rice and the founding of Rice Institute, see E. Raphael and J. E. McAshan to WW, Jan. 10, 1907, Vol. 16.

his fine force to the work he had to do produced remarkable results in developing the study of physics at Princeton. He may be said to have built the whole fabric of the department of which we are now so proud; and it was a fitting culmination of his career as teacher and leader, alike of those who studied and of those who taught here, that Mr. Palmer's great laboratory should be built in the very year of his retirement, as if in fulfillment of all he had hoped and planned for. It is because of what he did and has inspired us to do also that we are looking forward to the development, in the near future, of the Electrical School which he created at the behest of generous benefactors of the University, and to which he gave such an invaluable reputation for thoroughness and the love of essentials.

PALMER PHYSICAL LABORATORY.

The Palmer Physical Laboratory was opened for class-room and experimental work on the nineteenth of October, 1908, less than one year after ground was broken for the building. Two months' use of it has shown that singularly few mistakes were made in plans or construction, and has served only to heighten the expectations of those using the building as to its great future value to the University.

I am indebted for this account of the Laboratory to my colleague, Professor Howard McClenahan.

In planning the Laboratory, attention was constantly given not only to the present necessity of providing for the needs of the Departments of Physics and Electrical Engineering but also to a possible future development of engineering in the University which would entail a greatly increased amount of work in physics. All of the courses in physics required by an engineering school with 800 or 900 members, in addition to the courses given for general scientific training in modern graduate instruction, could be carried on in the new building with comfort. Over 600 students are now working in the building, one-half of whom are doing experimental work. Ample provision has also been made for growth in the research work of the departments.

The three floors of the building which are already in use constitute an area of approximately 85,000 sq. ft. An additional floor space of about 25,000 sq. ft. is available in the spacious attic. Advantage has been taken of the slope of the land on which the building stands, so that, while on the front the building shows but two stories, on the back it shows three, the full height of the basement being above the ground. For many purposes this story is the most useful in the building.

With the exception of the trim of the doors and windows, the building is thoroughly fireproof. The walls are very massive and of brick; where plastered, they are furnished with terra cotta tiling, upon which the plaster is spread; the floors are constructed throughout of steel girders, vitrified brick arches, and concrete. The steel frame of the roof supports a covering of tiles, upon which the slate is nailed.

About one-half of the building is devoted to the work of under-graduate instruction. This part includes two large and two small lecture rooms, seven recitation rooms, and ten laboratories. The rest of the building is given up to class rooms and laboratories for the School of Electrical Engineering, private laboratories for the teaching staff and for graduate students, machine shops, constant temperature rooms, accommodations for the special departmental libraries, a chemical laboratory, balance and store rooms, photographic, photo-metric, and optical dark rooms, a room for the ventilating machinery, a room for the electrical charging machinery and the liquid air plant, and switchboard and battery rooms.

The distinctive features of the laboratory, due to its construction, are the remarkable absence of vibration from all its parts, the abundance of light and air, the complete system of ventilating ducts which may be utilized for the artificial ventilation of any, or all, parts of the building, and the perfect acoustic properties of the large lecture rooms.

Some of the features of the equipment which call for comment are the following: The unusually large and thoroughly equipped machine shops; the thermostatic control of the heating system, by which the temperature of any room can be kept constant for an indefinite period; the conveniently controlled and intense illumination produced by the electric lighting system; a system of vacuum and pressure pumps and tubing, by which a vacuum pressure of $1/20$ of a pound per sq. in. and a pressure of 15 lbs. per sq. in. can be obtained at any time in any part of the laboratory; an electric elevator running to all floors of the building; a liquid air plant; constant temperature rooms, which can be maintained at any temperature between $0°$ F. and the atmospheric temperature; a Foucault pendulum for showing the rotation of the earth; an inter-communicating telephone system joining the separate sections of the laboratory; a modification of the ventilating system in one wing, by which the humidity of the air in certain rooms can be controlled and kept at some desired value; and, especially, the extraordinarily generous supply of batteries, charging machinery, and electrical circuits.

In addition to the fixed equipment, an abundance of portable apparatus for almost all the measurements of physics or electrical engineering has been supplied by the donor of the building.

The Palmer Laboratory is not notable for the novelty of its construction or equipment, though it is believed that the best features of the existing laboratories have been embodied in our building. It is notable, rather, because of the successful attempt to have only the best of everything used in its construction and equipment, without apparent regard for cost. It is marked by the lavish provision made for convenience of experimental work and of teaching. For example, two gas outlets are usually deemed sufficient for a small research room; here, seven are provided. This is typical of the equipment.

This laboratory is distinguished above all else, by its system of electrical circuits and necessary accessories. Four storage batteries of sixty cells each, with motor-generator and booster sets, required for transforming alternating into direct currents, have been installed. Such is the arrangement of batteries and of circuits that in every room, except those which are used for quizzes, stores, libraries, or the like purpose, direct currents with any voltage between two volts and 480 volts, in steps of two volts, and single phase and two-phase alternating currents with an electro-motive force of 110 volts, or 220 volts, are procurable at any moment.

The Palmer Laboratory is probably superior to any other university or college physical laboratory. Its equal is to be found, if at all, only among the testing laboratories supported by our own, or other, national governments.

STAFFORD LITTLE LECTURESHIP.

By Mr. Cleveland's death the Stafford Little Lectureship on Public Affairs, which Mr. Stafford Little had founded in honour of Mr. Cleveland and which Mr. Cleveland had honoured us by filling since its foundation, fell vacant, and the Board has thought it fitting that Mr. Cleveland's successor upon this interesting foundation should be the Honorable George Brinton McClellan, who in high positions of public trust has exhibited a sturdy courage and regard for principle like Mr. Cleveland's own, and whose gifts as a writer and speaker especially qualify him for the functions of the lectureship. Mr. McClellan will deliver his first lectures on the foundation at some time during the coming spring.

ADDITIONS TO THE TEACHING STAFF.

Since my last report to the Board the following additions have been made to the teaching staff of the University.

Professor Frank Frost Abbott, Professor of Classics, who was graduated Bachelor of Arts from Yale University in 1882; was Clark and Larned Scholar at Yale from 1882 to 1884, and Tutor from 1885 to 1891; who studied at the Universities of Berlin and Bonn from the spring of 1889 to the autumn of 1890; and who became Associate Professor of Latin and Examiner in the University of Chicago in 1891, and Professor of Latin in the same institution in 1893. During the year 1901-1902 he was Professor of Latin in the American School of Classical Studies in Rome. He is the author of the following books: A History and Description of Roman Political Institutions; The Selected Letters of Cicero; The Toledo Manuscript of the Germania of Tacitus; A Short History of Rome; Handbook for the Study of Roman History; and The Use of Repetition in Latin. He is also the author of many technical articles in the *American Journal of Philology*, the *American Historical Review*, the *American Journal of Theology*, the *Archiv für lateinische Lexicographie und Grammatik*, the *Classical Journal, Classical Philology* and the *Classical Review*, and has contributed to the *Sewanee Review*, the *New England Magazine*, the *Arena*, the *Yale Review*, and *The Nation*. He is Associate Editor of *Classical Philology*. Professor Abbott comes to us with the highest and most deserved reputation as a classical scholar. His addition to the faculty of the University completes our faculty of Classics in a way upon which I think we should greatly felicitate ourselves.

Professor Edwin Grant Conklin, Professor of Biology, was graduated Bachelor of Science from Ohio Wesleyan University in 1885, Bachelor of Arts 1886, Master of Arts 1889; was a graduate student at Johns Hopkins University from 1888 to 1891, a Fellow of that University from 1890 to 1891, and received the degree of Doctor of Philosophy from the Johns Hopkins University in 1891; became Professor of Biology in Ohio Wesleyan University in 1891, Professor of Zoölogy at Northwestern University in 1894, and Professor of Zoölogy at the University of Pennsylvania in 1896. He received from the University of Pennsylvania in 1908 the Honorary Degree of Doctor of Science. He was a member of the staff of the Marine Biological Laboratory from 1892 to 1897, and since 1897 has been a Trustee of that Laboratory. He was President of the American Morphological Society in 1899, Vice-President of the American Association for

the Advancement of Science in 1906, Secretary of the American
Philosophical Society from 1901 to 1908, and has been Vice-
President of the Academy of Natural Sciences of Philadelphia
since 1901. Since 1905 he has been a member of the Advisory
Board of the Wistar Institute of Anatomy, and since 1908 has
been a member of the National Academy of Science. He was
editor of the *Contributions from the Zoölogical Laboratory* of the
University of Pennsylvania from 1897 to 1908, and is at present
one of the editors of the *Journal of Morphology*, the *Biological
Bulletin*, and the *Journal of Experimental Zoölogy*. In acquiring
the services of Professor Conklin we have added to our teaching
force one of the most distinguished biologists in America.

Professor Henry Jones Ford, Professor of Politics, was graduated at the Baltimore City College in 1868. After graduation he
took up journalistic work and continued to be connected with the
editing of newspapers until 1905. In 1872 he became a member
of the staff of the *Baltimore American*, of which he eventually became Managing Editor. From 1880 to 1883 he served on the staff
of the *New York Sun*. From New York he went in 1884 to Pittsburgh to join the editorial staff of the *Pittsburgh Gazette*, eventually becoming Editorial Manager of that paper and also of the
Chronicle-Telegraph, both papers belonging to a corporation in
which Mr. Ford had an interest. In 1905 he disposed of his
interest in this corporation and returned to Baltimore, where
he became an editorial writer on the *Baltimore News* and
Lecturer on Political Science at the Johns Hopkins University.
In 1906-07 he delivered a course of lectures at the University
of Pennsylvania on the Theory and Practice of Politics. He has
recently been appointed Blumenthal Lecturer at Columbia University for the year 1909-10. Mr. Ford's principal publications in
political science have been The Rise and Growth of American
Politics, 1898, a book which has attracted the widest attention
and become authoritative in its field, and numerous articles published from time to time in *The Annals of the American Academy
of Political and Social Science, The Political Science Quarterly*,
and the *Proceedings of the American Political Science Association*. He has also contributed articles on political subjects to *The
Independent, The Bankers Magazine*, and *The World's Work*, and
has done a great deal of book reviewing for various periodicals.
He is at present on the staff of reviewers of the New York *Evening Post*. Professor Ford comes to take up the work laid down by
Professor Garfield, and comes equipped with abundant knowledge and commended by a very extensive reputation.

Professor Malcolm MacLaren, Professor of Electrical Engineering, was graduated Bachelor of Arts from Princeton University in 1890, Electrical Engineer in 1892, and Master of Arts in 1893. In 1893 he took up the active pursuit of the profession of electrical engineering. From 1893 to 1897 he was engaged in Pittsburgh designing electrical machinery for the Westinghouse Electric and Manufacturing Company. The years 1897 to 1901 he spent in London as Electrical Engineer for the Westinghouse Company, and from 1901 to 1905 was in Manchester, England, as Chief Electrical Engineer for the British Westinghouse Electric and Manufacturing Company, to which position he had been appointed upon the formation of the company. He organized its engineering department and was responsible for the development of the designs of all classes of electrical machinery manufactured there. From 1905 to 1908 he was in Pittsburgh in charge of the General Engineering Section of the Railway Engineering Department of the Westinghouse Company, having supervision of all engineering recommendations made by that company for railway installations. He is a member of the Institute of Electrical Engineers of Great Britain and an associate member of the American Institute of Electrical Engineers. Professor MacLaren comes to us with the highest reputation as an engineer and has undertaken the work of Professor of Electrical Engineering with an enthusiasm which shows his devotion to the University and School which bred him.

Professor Royal Meeker, who succeeds the late Professor Wyckoff as Assistant Professor of Economics, was graduated Bachelor of Science from Iowa State College in 1898. From 1899 to 1902 he was a graduate student at Columbia University, being Fellow in Finance during the year 1901-1902. From 1903 to 1904 he pursued advanced studies at the University of Leipzig, and in 1904 was appointed to the chair of History and Political Science at Ursinus College, whence he came to Princeton in 1905 as Preceptor in History, Politics, and Economics. He received the degree of Doctor of Philosophy from Columbia University in 1906.

Professor Edwin William Pahlow, who was last year Instructor and who this year has become Preceptor in History, Politics and Economics, was graduated Bachelor of Letters from the University of Wisconsin in 1899 and Master of Letters in 1900, and received the degree of Master of Arts from Harvard University in 1901. From 1903 to 1904 he was Assistant in History at Radcliffe College; from 1904 to 1905 Assistant in History at

Harvard University and Instructor in History at Simmons College, Boston; from 1905 to 1906 Instructor in History at Wisconsin University; and from 1906 to 1907 he pursued graduate studies at the University of Munich, Germany. In 1907 he became Instructor in History, Politics, and Economics at Princeton.

Professor John Gale Hun, Preceptor in Mathematics, was graduated Bachelor of Arts from Williams College in 1899, and received the degree of Doctor of Philosophy from Johns Hopkins University in 1903. During the year 1901-1902 he was Student Assistant in Mathematics in Johns Hopkins University, and Fellow in Mathematics for the year 1902-1903. Since 1903 he has been Instructor in Mathematics at Princeton.

Professor Charles Ranald MacInnes, Preceptor in Mathematics, was graduated Master of Arts from Queens University, Canada, in 1896, and Doctor of Philosophy from Johns Hopkins University in 1900. From 1900 to 1901 he was Tutor in Mathematics and Physics at Queens University; from 1901 to 1903 Instructor in Mathematics at Manitoba College; and from 1903 to 1905 Director of the Gymnasium at Johns Hopkins University. In 1905 he came to Princeton as Instructor in Mathematics.

Professor Carl Eben Stromquist, Preceptor in Mathematics, was graduated Bachelor of Arts from Bethany College in 1899, and Doctor of Philosophy from Yale University in 1903. Since 1903 he has been Instructor in Mathematics at Princeton.

Professor Raymond Smith Dugan, Assistant Professor of Astronomy, was graduated Bachelor of Arts from Amherst College in 1899, Master of Arts in 1902. In 1905 he received the degree of Doctor of Philosophy from the University of Heidelberg. From 1899 to 1902 he was Instructor in Astronomy and Mathematics and Acting Director of the Observatory at the Syrian Protestant College at Beirût, Syria. From 1902 to 1904 he was First Assistant at the Grand Ducal Observatory, Königstuhl-Heidelberg, during his service at which university he discovered sixteen asteroids, of which two received the names "Princetonia" and "Nassovia". In 1905 he was a member of the Lick Observatory Solar Eclipse Expedition to Spain. From 1905 to 1908 he was Instructor in Astronomy at Princeton.

Professor Henry Norris Russell, Assistant Professor of Astronomy, was graduated Bachelor of Arts, *insigni cum laude*, from Princeton University in 1897, Master of Arts in 1898, Doctor of Philosophy, *summa cum laude*, 1900. He was a Fellow in Mathematics in Princeton from 1897 to 1898, Fellow in Astronomy from 1898 to 1900, Research Student at Cambridge

University, England, from 1902 to 1903; Research Assistant of the Carnegie Institution and Honorary Assistant at the Cambridge University Observatory, England, 1903 to 1905. From 1905 to 1908 he was Instructor in Astronomy at Princeton.

Professor Gilbert van Ingen, Assistant Professor of Geology, studied at Cornell University from 1886 to 1888; was Assistant Geologist on the United States Geological Survey, 1889 to 1891; Assistant in Palæontology at Cornell University, 1891-1892; student at Yale University, 1892-1893; Assistant in Palæontology at Columbia University, 1893-1895; Curator of the Geological Collections, Columbia University, 1895 to 1901; Special Assistant to the State Palæontologist of New York, 1901-1903, and since 1903 he has been Assistant in Geology and Curator of Invertebrate Palæontology at Princeton. He was editor of the New York Academy of Sciences from 1897 to 1901, and editor of the Departments of Geology and Palæontology for the New International Encyclopedia from 1901-1903.

During the present academic year Professor Henry van Dyke, Murray Professor of English Literature, and Professor William Kelly Prentice, Professor of Greek, are away on leave of absence.

The following have received appointments as Instructors or Assistants or Teaching Fellows in the University: Charles Delahunt Mahaffie, A.B. King Fisher College, Oklahoma, 1905, B.C.L. Oxford, second class, 1907, *Instructor in Jurisprudence*; George Byron Louis Arner, Litt.B. German Wallace College, 1904, Master of Arts Columbia 1906, Ph.D. Columbia 1908, *Instructor in History, Politics, and Economics*; Ralph Claude Willard, A.B. Hobart College 1904, A.M. Cornell University 1905, A.B. Oxford University (School of Modern History) 1908, *Instructor in History, Politics, and Economics*; Henry Bronson Dewing, A.B. University of California 1903, M.A. 1905, Ph.D. Yale University 1908, *Instructor in Classics*; Charles William Kennedy, A.B. Columbia University 1902, Ph.D. Princeton University 1906, Instructor in English at Princeton 1906-1907, Porter Ogden Jacobus Fellow in English 1907-1908, *Instructor in English*; Raymond Watson Jones, A.B. Cornell University 1905, Fellow in German at Cornell, *Instructor in Modern Languages*; Frank Irwin, A.B. Harvard University 1890, S.B. 1891, A.M. 1894, Ph.D. 1908, Instructor in Mathematics, Harvard University, 1894, *Instructor in Mathematics*; Donald Pritchard Smith, A.B. Williams College 1902, Research Assistant, Massachusetts Institute of Technology 1904, Ph.D. Göttingen 1907, *Instructor in Chemistry*; William Lewis Perdue, B.S. Alabama Polytechnic Institute 1907, *Assistant in Chemistry*; Guy Chester Crampton,

A.B. Princeton University 1904, A.M. Cornell University 1905, Ph.D. University of Berlin 1908, *Assistant in Biology;* John Havron, Jr., C.E. Princeton University 1908, *Instructor in Civil Engineering;* George Gilbert Cornwell, C.E. Princeton University 1908, *Instructor in Civil Engineering;* and Harris Franklin Mac-Neish, B.S. University of Chicago 1902, M.S. 1904, *Teaching Fellow in Mathematics.*

New Dormitories.

The reports of your Committee on Grounds and Buildings have informed you with regard to the rapid progress being made toward the completion of the dormitory which is being erected by the generosity of the Class of 1877, and of the practical completion, by the architects, Messrs. Frank Miles Day and Brother, of the plans for the dormitory to be presented to the University by the thoughtful and generous kindness of Mrs. Russell Sage. There are three hundred and forty-five of our students outside the dormitories taking their chances in the lodging houses of the town, and these two new buildings will greatly contribute to their comfort and morale. The dormitory being provided by the Class of 1877 will accommodate sixty-two students, the dormitory provided for by Mrs. Sage's gift should accommodate one hundred and ten students. The Seventy-Seven Dormitory should be ready for occupation by the opening of the next academic year, the Sage Dormitory by the opening of the academic year 1910-11, and their completion may confidently be expected to lower the rates of rental and increase the range of choice of desirable rooms in the town. It is greatly to be desired that so soon as possible dormitory accommodations should be provided for practically all the students of the University by the University itself.

Mrs. Sage made her generous offer of this gift in the following letter:

New York, April 7, 1908.

To the Trustees of Princeton University:

Dear Sirs—I have felt for some little time past that your University was perhaps lacking in suitable dormitory accommodation on your College campus for members of your Freshman Class, and with the view of supplying such want, if it exists, I have decided to make the following offer, viz.:

I will donate to your University a sum not to exceed $250,000, for the purpose of erecting a dormitory building on the College campus, the primary use of which shall be for members of the

Freshman Class. I can fully understand that, for various reasons, it would not be practicable to have a dormitory used exclusively for Freshmen, and this point could be easily covered by having it understood that to the extent the new dormitory be used for members of other classes like accommodation would be provided for Freshmen in other dormitories.

If you should decide to accept my gift, I should wish to reserve the right to approve of the choice of architect, and I should also wish to have the plans submitted for my approval before final adoption.   Yours very truly,

MARGARET OLIVIA SAGE.

HONORS COURSE IN THE CLASSICAL HUMANITIES.

Some two years ago I reported to you the institution of an Honors Course in Mathematics and Physics, by which we sought, and have sought successfully, to stimulate and concentrate the work of some of our abler and more serious students in the field of the exact sciences. I can now report to you the successful institution of an Honors Course in the Classical Humanities. As the faculty has conceived this course and as you have sanctioned it, it is something more than a special course in Classics for those students who wish to make a specialty of classical training. It is an effort to put interesting and stimulating classical study at the service of all undergraduates who are able to use the classical languages with some ease and pleasure, whatever Department they may have chosen as their main field of work.

It is open, in part at least, both to those who wish chiefly to study in the field of Classics and to those who are in related literary departments. To special students of the Classics who wish to qualify for honors, it extends the privilege of limiting the number of their electives to four instead of five, the number required to pass students. At least two of the four courses thus chosen must be in the field of Classics; one must be outside of that field, upon the principle of broad and varied choice upon which we everywhere insist; the fourth may be in Classics or in any other Department, as the student prefers. All such candidates for honors in Classics are to be enrolled, besides, in the pro-seminary in Classics, in which special themes or readings in classical authors are assigned for individual study and report. This course is open at the beginning of Junior year to all candidates for the degree of Bachelor of Arts or for the degree of Bachelor of Letters who have completed the Sophomore year with an average standing in their classical studies not lower than third group; and the list of classical electives open to such men has been very much enlarged and enriched, while men who have fallen below third group in their Classics in Freshman and Sophomore years are restricted in their choice of classical electives to the present limited number of courses.

Juniors who are qualified by their previous standing in Classics to seek honors in that Department but who prefer to undertake their main work in Philosophy, in History, in Politics, in Art, or in English are offered the opportunity to read classical authors in the field of their choice as a substitute for some one or more of the regular courses of their own Department. Those students who have chosen the Department of Philosophy, for example, but who would be qualified for classical honors had they selected the Department of Classics, may substitute in their Junior year for some one of the courses in Philosophy a course in Plato under Professor Winans and a course in Lucretius under Professor Basore; and in their Senior year a course in Greek Philosophy under Professor Norman Smith, with readings in the original. Students in History and Politics, similarly qualified, may in like manner substitute for some one course in their own Department in Junior year readings in the Latin Historians under Professor Westcott, or in the Greek writers upon Public Life under Professor Capps; and in their Senior year readings in the Greek Historians under Professor Prentice or in the Latin writers upon Roman Public Life under Professor Abbott. Students in English may, when they are Seniors, take a course in the Classical Influences in English Literature under Professor Osgood with copious illustrative readings in the classical authors done under the classical preceptors.

The general purpose of this arrangement may be said to be to unite classical learning, so far as possible, with the studies of all cognate or related Departments. The method of instruction adopted in the new courses offered is, therefore, not philological or scientific, but literary, historical, political, artistic, philosophical. The aim is to make clear, through lectures and preceptorial conferences and the intimate personal work possible in the pro-seminary, the permanently significant lessons of antiquity and the connections of ancient with modern thought and life. The purpose is to guide the student in his classical reading, as nearly as may be, along the line of his special aptitudes and desires. Certain portions of the reading will be done slowly and critically, but it is intended in most cases rather to develop the practice of fluent and copious reading, particularly in the fields of history and literature.

I think that the Classical Department of the University is to be congratulated upon the liberal way in which they have conceived this new development of the studies of their Department and this new relationship of the Department with the other Departments with which it is most naturally allied. The institution of this course seems to me distinctly a movement in the right direction, towards the vital coördination of the studies of the University, rather than an emphasizing of separate departmental interests and an undue specialization upon particular fields

THE LITERARY SOCIETIES.

The Board will remember that some two years ago we began what we then regarded as the experiment of uniting in some degree the work of the Cliosophic and American Whig Societies with the work of the University, so far as the Freshman members of those societies were concerned. Courses in the study of oratory and debate were arranged for, which Freshman members of the societies could substitute for the regular courses provided for them in English. The work in these special courses was to be done in the halls of the societies themselves, and members of the English Department were deputed to take charge of it. I can now report that this arrangement has passed its experimental stage. It has proved a very gratifying success in stimulating the literary work of the Freshman members of the two societies and has had the expected indirect effect upon the whole life and work of the societies themselves as literary and debating bodies. The work has been most intelligently conducted, with excellent judgment and with genuine enthusiasm, by Professor Hardin Craig in the American Whig Society and Professor Harry F. Covington in the Cliosophic Society, though Professor Covington's work has been unhappily interrupted by ill health; and the younger members of the English staff detailed to assist these gentlemen have played a most useful part. I do not think that it would be desirable to go any further in connecting the required work of the University with the voluntary action of the literary societies, whose strength and vitality really consist in their independence, but both inside the societies and outside it is the common opinion of the University that what we have done has been of the greatest value and significance.

The Sophomore Commons.

At the beginning of the present year we were enabled, by the generosity of friends of the University, to make arrangements for supplying meals to all members of the Sophomore Class in University Hall, as we had two years previously done for members of the Freshman Class. All Sophomores are now obliged to take their meals in that place. The Freshman Commons were established under the management of an undergraduate committee, known as The Dining Halls Committee, a committee consisting of members of the Senior Class and presided over by a Chairman whose duties are really the duties of supervising manager. The jurisdiction of this committee has now been extended to the Sophomore Commons also. The actual conduct of the Commons has been in charge of Mr. John F. Deane, who has proved a most efficient steward. Your Committee on Grounds and Buildings have already reported to you the details of the arrangements made for the Sophomore and Freshman Commons. I need not add to the information they have given you. I wish only to report the very satisfactory result of the experiment. This bringing of the class together at meal times, under physical conditions which favour the maintenance of order and make it possible to serve the tables in a way that is dignified and comfortable, promises to produce among the Sophomores a greater feeling of solidarity and more genuine common spirit than has prevailed among them in recent years. They are supplied not only with dining rooms, but with sitting rooms also; the food furnished is excellent and abundant; and we hope that not only their feeling as a class will be greatly changed by the new circumstances of their life, but that their physical health will be very much less endangered than it was under the very unsatisfactory club system which prevailed among them in previous years. The Dining Halls Committee has administered the new arrangement with judgment and excellent spirit, but our chief debt of obligation for what has been done is due to our colleague, Mr. Andrew C. Imbrie, who, with Mr. Henry B. Thompson, has conceived and executed the plan with an intelligent care for details and an assiduity in the proper execution of them which is worthy of the highest appreciation.

Registration.

The total number of graduate students, which was last year one hundred and thirteen, is this year ninety-one. Of this number forty-seven are devoting themselves exclusively to graduate study, as against forty-six last year, and forty-four are combining graduate study in the University with work in Princeton Theological Seminary. It will be observed, therefore, that the falling off of twenty-two in the total number has been from the number of those who give only a portion of their time to work in the University, and that there has been a gain of one in the number of students devoting themselves exclusively to study in the University. Of these latter, regular, graduate students twelve are in residence at Merwick, as against ten last year; and ten are taking their meals there who are not in residence.

The following table shows the number admitted to the University as undergraduates this year as compared with last:

	1907	1908
Freshmen admitted without conditions	128	157
Freshmen admitted with conditions	230	235
New qualifying students not admitted to regular standing	42	40
Totals	400	432

Of the applicants admitted in 1907 thirty, for one reason or another did not come. The number admitted who did not come was this year the same, thirty. The following is a summary of the figures stated in another form:

	1907	1908
Number of students admitted who did not come	30	30
Total number of freshmen admitted	358	392
Total number who actually entered	328	362
Examined but not admitted	80	75
Preliminary or partial examinations	485	468

The total undergraduate enrolment of the University is 1223 and was last year 1188, an increase of thirty-five. The figures of last year showed a decrease of forty-seven, following a decrease of forty-four the preceding year.

I add the following facts for the further information of the Board concerning the entering class, quoting the report of the chairman of the Committee of the Faculty on Examinations and Standing which was submitted to your Committee on the Curriculum at the October meeting of the Board:

"In the Freshman class there has been an increase of seventeen in the number of A.B. candidates and of forty-eight in the number of B.S. and Litt.B. candidates; but, on the other hand, a decrease of twenty-six in the number of C.E. candidates. The rule that a student may not enter the C.E. Department with conditions in Mathematics, which went into effect last year, and the addition of a second language to the C. E. entrance requirement, which went into effect this year, would, therefore, seem to be having the desired result, namely, that of keeping out of the C. E. Department men who have no serious purpose of studying engineering and of diverting them to the B. S. Department, where they more properly belong.

"It is gratifying to note that this year, as last, two-thirds of the Freshmen have entered college either without conditions or with but one condition.

"Of the entering students thirty-seven per cent. are Presbyterians and twenty-seven per cent. are Episcopalians. There are twenty-seven Methodists, twenty-five Catholics, eleven Congregationalists, eleven Hebrews, nine Dutch Reformed, nine Baptists, eight Lutherans, five Unitarians, two Quakers, one Universalist, one Independent, one United Presbyterian, and one Christian Scientist. More than one-half of the entering students are communicants of the churches with which they are connected.

"The average age of the Freshmen at entrance was eighteen years and nine months."

A New Deanship.

I pass from matters suitable to a mere report to a matter of first-rate consequence upon which I wish to make a recommendation.

The new laboratories with which we are being so generously provided undoubtedly mark the beginning of a new era in the development of scientific instruction in the University. I think that we can now look forward with confidence to the large development not only of work in original research and of courses of advanced study for graduate students who are expecting to teach science or seeking to perfect themselves in studies which lead to special fields of investigation or of expert service, but also of technical instruction in mechanical engineering and the expansion of the work we are already doing in civil and electrical engineering,—the whole along lines thoroughly and characteristically Princetonian: to a great development of technical instruction, in short, upon a plan which will make pure science the basis and informing guide of professional scientific study and that study itself a liberal training. Knowing that we wish this and expect it, we ought to supply the process with right guidance.

For that purpose, I have recommended, through your Committee on the Curriculum, the institution of a new deanship, to be called the deanship of the Departments of Science.

By this broad title I would seek to ignore the antithesis which has been too sharply, not to say artificially, set up between pure and applied science. There is a difference, of course; but the two things should never be separated, and the line which divides them is nowhere, should nowhere be, distinctly traceable. It is our purpose to unite them in all that we do at Princeton for the promotion of scientific professional study, embodying from the outset the newer spirit now observable in the scientific professions. I therefore recommend the creation of a new officer of the University, a Dean of the Departments of Science, who shall be charged with the planning and superintending of the development of technical instruction in science, whether in the Schools of Civil and Electrical Engineering which we already have or in the School of Mechanical Engineering which we hope to have; and who, because we recognize no distinct line of demarcation between pure and applied science and intend to unite them so far as possible in our departmental expansion, unite them in administration as well as in spirit, shall also have general administrative oversight of the Departments of Mathematics, Physics, Astronomy, Chemistry, Biology, and Geology.

I further recommend that the superintendence of discipline now vested in the Dean of the Faculty be vested in a dean to be called the Dean of Discipline, and that the duties of the Dean of the Faculty, the ranking Dean of our university organization, be confined to the presidency of the Faculty in the absence of the President of the University, the exercise of the routine administrative duties of the President of the University in the absence of the President from Princeton or his incapacitation from illness, and the administration of the responsible duties of chairman of the Committee of the Faculty on Examinations and Standing.

I trust that these recommendations will commend themselves to the judgment of the Board and that it will feel at liberty to approve of and act upon them at once.

Respectfully submitted,
Woodrow Wilson.

Princeton, 1 January, 1909.[2]

Printed report. (WP, DLC).

2 There is a WWhw outline of this report, dated Jan. 1909; a WWsh draft, dated Jan. 14, 1909; and a typed copy with WWT additions, dated Jan. 1, 1909, all in WP, DLC.

From George Howe III

Dear Uncle Woodrow,   Chapel Hill, N. C.   January 2, 1909.

When your letter came there was great joy in the camp from the President on down. We are all wonderfully happy over it. I am busy now counting the days until your arrival.

Maisie and I are of course hoping that you can take this opportunity for a rest of a few days, and will stay with us for a longer time than just between trains. But if you must hurry away again you must know the schedule of trains here so as to meet your engagement to speak. I have no means at hand of reckoning it from your end. At ours we have two trains a day, one arriving at about twelve noon and usually late, the other at six-thirty in the evening. The exercises take place on the morning of Tuesday the nineteenth and they are planning to run an extra train that day ahead of the regular. It will be practically necessary for you therefore to get in the night before. That will give us at least one evening at home with you, because I have got the President's promise that you can stay in our house. As for your departure the first train goes out at four in the afternoon, but you will try to plan so as to spend another night with us, and as many more as you possibly can. The morning train, leaving at nine, should put you in Princeton at a convenient hour.

We are delighted at the very thought of seeing you so soon again. And we are very grateful to you for accepting the invitation. May the intervening days pass quickly.

With warmest love from us both to all of you, and with all good wishes for a happy New Year,

Affectionately,   George Howe

TLS (WP, DLC).

To Melancthon Williams Jacobus

My dear Dr. Jacobus: Princeton, N. J.   January 4th, 1909.

It was a pleasure to receive your letter of December 31st,[1] but I am sincerely distressed that it does not report a more rapid and complete recovery of your health. I hope that if the doctor advises a vacation, you will be generous enough to the rest of us to take it and not risk your health by a too early return to your work, and I particularly hope that you will not make any imprudent exertion in connection with the work of the Curriculum Committee. I will undertake to keep you fully informed of the committee's work, if you will put the working ore [oar] in my hands.

I think that any hour you might choose for your own convenience on Wednesday afternoon, the thirteenth, could be made suitable for attendance by the other members of the committee. It seems to me an excellent suggestion that the principle pieces of business to be considered should be mentioned in the call, and those that you refer to are, so far as I know, the chief matters to come up for discussion. Dean Fine and I have very easily arrived at a union of opinion about the duties of the new deanship, that is to say, he has convinced me that he was right in his original position.

As for the plans for the dormitories to be connected with the Sage building, Mr. Day was told by some members of the Grounds and Buildings Committee that inasmuch as the projected buildings were to take the place of University Hall, where the Freshman and Sophomore Commons are, it was desirable that the new building should itself contain commons halls. I think that is the genesis of the part of the plan you speak of. At the same time, I find that Mr. Day, like Mr. Cram, is thoroughly in sympathy with the plans which I have most at heart, and that members of the Committee on Grounds and Buildings like Mr. H. B. Thompson readily concede the point that it would be only fair to make the new commons rooms of a size and sort which would render them suitable for the object contemplated in the quad plan, and eminently unfair to make that plan physically impossible or excessively expensive by constructing the building on a plan which would not be suitable. So far, I think there is a slight sign of progress.

Mrs. Wilson joins me in the warmest New Year's greetings to you all and in the sincere hope that the near future may bring you rapid progress to a complete recovery.

Always cordially and faithfully yours,

[Woodrow Wilson]

CCL (RSB Coll., DLC).
¹ M. W. Jacobus to WW, Dec. 31, 1908, ALS (WP, DLC).

From Philander Priestly Claxton[1]

Dear sir,   Knoxville [Tenn.]   4 January 1909.

I take pleasure in informing you that at the meeting of the Southern Educational Association, held at Atlanta, Ga. December 29-31, you were elected a corresponding member of this Association.

Membership of this class carries with it no responsibilities or fees, but entitles you to a copy of the Proceedings of each meeting and to all the privileges of the Association. The number of corresponding members is limited to twenty-five. Other corresponding members are at present: Mr Robert C. Ogden, Mr George Foster Peabody, Dr Walter Page, Dr Albert Shaw, Miss Jane Addams, President G. Stanley Hall, President C. W. Elliott [Eliot], Sir Alfred Mosely, President James Robertson and Dr Henry S. Pritchett.[2]   Yours sincerely,   P. P. Claxton

TLS (WP, DLC).
  [1] Professor of Education at the University of Tennessee, later United States Commissioner of Education.
  [2] Robert Curtis Ogden, retired businessman, philanthropist, and President of the Southern Education Board; George Foster Peabody, retired businessman, philanthropist, Treasurer of the Southern Education Board; Walter Hines Page, editor of The World's Work; Albert Shaw, editor of the New York Review of Reviews; Jane Addams, social worker, head of Hull House in Chicago; Granville Stanley Hall, President of Clark University; Charles William Eliot, about to retire from the presidency of Harvard University; Sir Alfred Mosely, English educational expert, arranger of exchange visits for teachers between Great Britain and the United States and Canada; James Wilson Robertson, Principal of Macdonald College, Ste. Anne de Bellevue, Quebec; and Henry Smith Pritchett, President of the Carnegie Foundation for the Advancement of Teaching.

From Franklin Zeiger

My dear Dr. Wilson: Paterson, N. J.   Jan. 4, 1909.

Our Committee desires me to thank you on behalf of the teachers of the Paterson High School for your very kind reply to our invitation, and to say that we should be very glad to have you choose any date in April after the eighteenth suitable to your convenience, or one in the first week of May. If a Friday would be just as convenient as any other day, it might have a slight advantage for us, but please do not let this consideration interfere in the least with your convenience. Such a date would be at least as good for us as an earlier one and probably better, our plan having been simply not to have the dinner before March fifth.

If you can name the date and accept our invitation, we shall count ourselves extremely happy in having secured you as our chief speaker, and shall be very grateful and under great obligation to you. When the date is selected, we shall invite the other guests. Whenever convenient for you, we should be pleased to hear the subject of your address, but there is not any hurry at all about this.

Kindly pardon my delay in replying to your note. I was away from the city during the holidays and it failed to be forwarded to me as I had requested. Thanking you again in behalf of the Committee for your very kind consideration, I am

Yours respectfully,   Franklin Zeiger.

ALS (WP, DLC).

From Melancthon Williams Jacobus

Hartford, Conn.,
My dear President Wilson: January 5th, 1909

A meeting of the Curriculum Committee of the Board of Trustees of Princeton University is hereby called for the afternoon of Wednesday, January 13th, at 4:00 o'clock, in the President's office, Seventy Nine Hall.

You are specially urged to be present, as there will be considered at that time the following important items of business:

I. The report of the President as to the action of the Faculty upon the resolution of Dr. McPherson regarding C.E. Entrance Studies, referred by the Board to the Committee, and by them referred to the Faculty for consideration.[1]

II. The report of the President as to his Conference with Dean Fine, regarding the latter's official relationship to the Scientific Studies of the University.

III. The following question submitted to the Committee with the approval of the President, by Mr. Pyne:

> Is it fair to the University, in the resulting popular misunderstanding regarding both the Scientific and Academic Departments that candidates for the Litt.B. degree should be assigned to the Scientific Department for the first two years and then transferred to the Academic Department for the remainder of their course?[2]

Yours sincerely,   Melancthon W Jacobus

TLS (WWP, UA, NjP).

[1] As WW to M. W. Jacobus, Jan. 11, 1909, makes clear, there was much confusion in the minds of some persons involved as to just what Dr. McPherson's resolution was about. However, Dean Fine was able to recall the substance of it (WW to M. W. Jacobus, Jan. 15, 1909), and Wilson later revealed that it was concerned with "entrance requirements in languages for the C.E. course" (WW to M. W. Jacobus, Jan. 23, 1909, Vol. 19). Wilson indicated at that time that he would bring it before "an early meeting" of the Faculty Committee on the Course of Study. At the meeting of the trustees' Committee on the Curriculum on April 7, 1909, Wilson and Dean Fine reported that "inasmuch as they expected presently to undertake a systematic reconsideration of the C.E. course of study, they regarded it proper to postpone the examination of the subject [i. e., entrance examinations in languages for the C.E. course] until that time"

(Minutes of the Board of Trustees of Princeton University, April 8, 1909). As it turned out, a revised set of entrance requirements for the C.E. program was not adopted by the faculty until May 16, 1910, and they were to take effect only with the class entering in the autumn of 1912 (Minutes of the Princeton University Faculty, May 16, 1910).

2 See the Committee on the Curriculum to the Board of Trustees of Princeton University, Jan. 13, 1909.

Henry Burling Thompson to Junius Spencer Morgan

Dear Junius: [Wilmington, Del.] January 5th, 1909.

Have you ever received a notice from the President, suggesting the appointment of a Graduate Committee to represent the Clubs? Wilson wrote to me some four or five weeks ago that he would personally notify each of the Clubs of this action of the Board.

I should be glad to have this information at your earliest convenience, as I want to take the matter up next week if the notification has not been sent.

Yours very sincerely, Henry B Thompson

TLS (Thompson Letterpress Books, NjP).

Henry Burling Thompson to Edward Wright Sheldon

My Dear Sheldon: [Wilmington, Del.] January 7th, 1909.

. . . With regard to another matter. You may remember that President Wilson wrote me that he would personally notify the Clubs of the resolution of the Board, advising the appointment of a Graduate Club Committee. He has never carried out his promise, and the Clubs have not been notified. Ought we to take this up in the Board meeting, asking how and when the notice shall be sent, or would you make it a personal matter with Wilson? I am put in an awkward position, for there were several of the Clubs that proposed to act on the question of Sophomore members, also, with regard to new treaties, and I have had all this held up through the Dean for the very good reason that they would be notified of the Graduate Committee, and matters could properly be taken care of through such a Committee. Whether Wilson has forgotten the matter, or whether he wants to re-consider, I do not know.

Yours very sincerely, Henry B Thompson

P.S. Wilson has also messed the Sage Hall affair badly, through neglect to keep promises. I will give you details next week.

TLS (Thompson Letterpress Books, NjP).

From Melancthon Williams Jacobus

Hartford, Conn.,
My dear President Wilson: January 8th, 1909

As an additional item on the Docket of the Curriculum Committee for its meeting Wednesday afternoon, January 13th, Mr. Pyne as Chairman of the Finance Committee desires that there be considered the assignment of Preceptors to the various Departments, whether too many men have been assigned to any one Department, and if so, which men could be spared. Complaints have been made that some Departments are over-manned and some under-manned. In view of the deficit which is increasing each year, it seems to the Finance Committee vital that no waste should be allowed to occur.

Yours very sincerely, Melancthon W. Jacobus

TLS (WWP, UA, NjP).

From Henry Thompson Kent

Dear Doctor: St. Louis. January 8, 1909.

I acknowledge, with much pleasure, your letter accepting the invitation of the Virginia Society to be our guest at a banquet on the evening of March 10th.

The members of the Society are delighted at your coming and we will do everything possible to make the occasion a success.

As the time draws near I may write you again in regard to some of the details, and any information that you may wish from me, please advise.

I am, Very cordially yours, Henry T. Kent

TLS (WP, DLC).

An Address to the New York City High School Teachers Association

[[Jan. 9, 1909]]

THE MEANING OF A LIBERAL EDUCATION.

Mr. President, Ladies and Gentlemen:

I never know whether to describe myself as a liberal or as a conservative. I believe that many of the alumni of Princeton would now describe me as a radical; yet I deem myself a conservative, for I believe that life is the only thing that conserves, and life is the only thing that does not stand still or retrogress.

Progress, therefore, is part of the essential process of conservation. The constant renewal which is life is a part of the constant process of change. At the same time the processes of change, being processes of life, are not susceptible to very specific intellectual analysis.

There is one sentence with which I always open my classes, a sentence quoted from Burke, in my opinion the only entirely wise writer upon public affairs in the English language. Burke says, "Institutions must be adjusted to human nature; of which reason constitutes a part, but by no means the principal part." You cannot develop human nature by devoting yourselves entirely to the intellectual sides of it. Intellectual life is the flower of a thing much wider and richer than itself. The man whom we deem the mere man of books we reject as a counsellor, because he is separated in his thinking from the rich flow of life. It is the rich flow of life, compact of emotion, compact of all those motives which are unsusceptible of analysis, which produces the fine flower of literature and the solid products of thinking. And therefore when I think of the enormous and complex problem of education, it seems to me that it would be mere presumption to say that we can set it forth in complete analysis, to say that we can lay out a program which covers all the necessities of the growing mind, to say that we are certain at the outset of the exact means which we should use to reach the goal of which we can be only measurably certain.

I suppose that what perplexes every man to-day in every walk of life is the extraordinary complexity of modern life as compared with the life in the midst of which our grandfathers found themselves, as compared with the life in the midst of which the generation immediately preceding ours found itself. The life of the present day is incalculably complex, and so many of its complexities are of recent rise and origin that we haven't yet had time to understand just what they are or to assess the values of the new things that have come into our life. Not only is life infinitely complex in our day as compared with the previous age, but learning is correspondingly complex. In the old days of the fixed curriculum of the college and the school one could say with a degree of confidence that the elements of these curricula did contain the main bodies of knowledge, by specimen at least. But who can say that any curriculum that can be packed into the years of school life and the years of college life combined contains all the elements of modern learning? Modern learning has been so drawn into a score of consequences, has been so extended into a system of uses, that it is a sort of mirror held up to life itself, and the man of affairs now seeks in the laboratory, in the quiet places of counsel, from the scholar, those main elements which shall guide him in accomplishing the particular material tasks which lie immediately under his hand. So that life and learning are equally complex, and they are interlaced with each other, they are related as never before. There is not the scholar on the one side with his door closed and his window open, and on the other side the manufacturer and the man of commerce beating the seas with his ships and searching the distant markets of the world for new stuffs. That is not the contrast which exists to-day. The man of learning has on his table a telephone that connects him with all the activities of the world, and his windows look out on smoky chimneys; he feels that he is one of the many servants to carry on the great tasks of to-day, whether they be material or intellectual. So that these complexities interlock and are the same complexities, the complexity of knowledge and the complexity of life.

It goes without saying that there is an equal complexity of economic effort, of employment, and therefore an infinitely greater difficulty than there used to be in calculating the future orbit of any young person. When you say a young person must be prepared for his life-work, are you prepared, is he prepared, are his parents prepared, to say what that life-work is going to be? Do you know a boy is going to be a mechanic by the color of his hair? Do you know that he is going to be a lawyer by the fact that his father was a lawyer? Does any average and representative modern parent dare to say what his children are going to be? My chief quarrel with the modern parent is that he does not know, and that he hands that question over to the youngster whom he is supposed to be advising and training.

I was at a country hotel, and occupied a room in the quietest corner of the house. A balcony ran around the house, and my room opened on this balcony. Because my corner was the quietest corner, a helpless father brought his boy there to reason with him. He was a small boy, only about five years old. The conversation I overheard was about like this—if you can call that a conversation where one person does all the talking. The father said, "Are you going to be good?" No reply. "Are you going to be good?" No reply. "Are you going to be good?" No reply. Finding myself unable to stand this thing, because I am a man of nervous temperament, I said from within the window, "If you will lend me the boy a minute I will find out." Now, that is a picture of modern life. My course of action has never occurred to the parent—that there are means known almost from the beginning of the world for finding out whether a boy will be good or not. There is a predeterminant resident outside the will of the boy himself, and one of the straightest ways to a boy's conscience is through the cuticle of the skin. This is a type of a modern parent, and when he says he wants his son's training suited to his purpose of life he must admit his son has no purpose in life. Then we are asked to suit our processes to this undestined youth.

With this complexity, what has the modern school attempted to do? It has attempted to do everything at once. It has said: Here are a lot of boys and girls whose future occupations we do not know and they do not know. They must be prepared for life. Therefore we must prepare everybody for everything that is in that life. We haven't found it amusing. We havavt [haven't] found it possible. We have attempted it and we know we have failed at it. You cannot train everybody for everything. Moreover you are not competent to teach everything. There is not any body of teachers suited in gifts or training to do this impossible thing. Neither the schools nor those who guide them have attempted to make any discrimination with regard to purpose or to settle upon methods which will promise some degree of substantial success. That is the situation we are in.

I do not wonder at it. I think it is hardly just to blame those who have brought this situation about, because this change in modern life has come upon us suddenly. It has confused us. We are in an age so changeful, so transitional, I do not wonder that this confusion has come into our education, and I do not blame anybody. I do not see how it could have been avoided, how we could have avoided trying our hands at a score of things hitherto unattempted to determine at least if they were possible or not. Therefore this is not a subject for cynical comment, this is not a subject for criticism. It is a subject for self-recognition. The present need is that we should examine ourselves and see whether this be true or not; and, if it is true, ask ourselves whether the air has cleared enough, and whether our experiment has gone far enough, to make a definite program, to make a radical change, in the things we have attempted. This is the moment for counsel. The thing that is imperative upon our conscience is that we should ask ourselves whether it be possible to do it differently and better.

If we are going to do it differently or better it is imperative that we should distinguish between the two things. It is imperative that we distinguish between education and technical or industrial training. And before we distinguish between these two it is necessary that we distinguish between the individuals who are going to take the one and the individuals who are going to take the other. There is no method in American life by which the state or any public authority can pick out the persons to be educated in the one way or the other. The vitality of American life, and the vitality of all democratic life, lies in self-selection; it lies in the challenge put upon all to make up their minds as to what they want and what they intend to do with themselves. It is absolutely essential that we should start with that or we can never have any system of education.

For a system means a definite thing, it means an organic whole; it means the parts of that whole related to each other in rational fashion, some fixed kind and determined sequence of studies. You cannot get system in any other way. Miscellany cannot be jolted down into a system. If we are going to have any selection, we must have a selection of the individual by himself or herself. I think that the most fatal thing that can happen to anybody is to be taken care of by somebody else. To be carried along by somebody's suggestions from the time you begin until the time when you are thrust groping and helpless into the world is the very negation of education. By the nursing process, by the coddling process, you are sapping a race; and only loss can possibly result except upon the part of individuals here and there, individuals who are so intrinsically strong that you cannot spoil them. There are individuals into whose ears your suggestions are received, it may be, with polite attention, but upon whom you make no impression whatever, and those are the persons safe against the demoralizing processes you are attempting.

Let us go back and distinguish between the two things that we want to do; for we want to do two things in modern society. We want one class of persons to have a liberal education, and we want another class of persons, a very much larger class, of necessity, in every society, to forego the privileges of a liberal education and fit themselves to perform specific difficult manual tasks. You cannot train them for both in the time that you have at your disposal. They must make a selection, and you must make a selection. I do not mean to say that in the manual training there must not be an element of liberal training; neither am I hostile to the idea that in the liberal education there should be an element of the manual training. But what I am intent upon is that we should not confuse ourselves with regard to what we are trying to make of the pupils under our instruction. We are either trying to make liberally-educated persons out of them, or we are trying to make skillful servants of society along mechanical lines, or else we do not know what we are trying to do.

Now, what do I mean by education as contrasted with what I shall call training? Of course, the word training should lie on both sides of the distinction. I will use the word training, however, to indicate specific tasks, as contrasted with what is called liberal education. One of the interesting things about liberal education is that it leaves out of the view altogether the question how anyone can directly make money out of it. We boast in our own time that mind is monarch, that we analyze things before we do them; and yet we give ourselves away in every discussion of this particular thing, and show that we have not analyzed it at all. When we discuss what the elements of a practical training are, and what the elements of a liberal training are, the advocates of a practical training all, you will find, include mathematics in their list of studies. And they do not stop at Arithmetic; they include Algebra, Geometry, and Calculus, even; and they confidently maintain that these higher imaginative portions of mathematics are parts of a practical education. Now, leaving out some of the technical professions like engineering, how many professions can you name that use any mathematics above arithmetic? I do not know of any. They may occasionally. A man who is acquainted with the intricate processes of mathematics may take a short cut in some calculation, but it is not an essential part of his equipment for the business he is engaged in. I can show you a place half-way through the arithmetic where it would be perfectly feasible to stop so far as nine-tenths of your pupils are concerned if they are not going to undertake an engineering profession. Yet you tell me that this is a practical training. I take it on faith from the geometrician that there is no such thing in nature as a straight line, that it is a purely imaginary thing, and yet you tell me that this is a very practical study. Of course, I admit that the imagination plays a practical part in life. But you mean that the principles of geometry used literally are a part of the practical facts of the world. I deny it; they are not a part of the practical facts of the world. And so I say that all that you are doing in using higher mathematics (and I approve of your using them) is to train the human mind to such processes of precision as will correct that loose-jointed, wabbly, incorrect, indiscriminate reasoning to which we are naturally inclined; which will make it demand processes clearly connected with premises, and make it impatient of conclusions that do not flow from the premises. We are trying to rid the human mind of its tendency to accept vague propositions.

Take the gymnasium. I think the gymnasium is intensely practical, and that everybody ought to make more or less use of the gymnastic apparatus. But I never heard of anybody doing things in his office that he had done in a gymnasium. If he did, he would be taken for a lunatic. And when I see men doing the double trapeze with grace and precision, and then am told they are doing this in order to fit themselves for life, I take it for granted that you do not mean that they are going to do the double trapeze in the office with their partners. They are doing simply this: they are getting their nerves and muscles in such shape, they are getting the red corpuscles in the blood so encouraged and heartened, that afterwards they can stand the strains of business, can stand the impact of disappointment, can hold steady in the midst of desperate effort, can work in season and out of season and come out of the greatest trials in possession of their full resiliency and return again to health and efficency [efficiency]. That is what makes the gymnasium intensely practical; it is meant that those who use it shall be in fighting trim and conquer the world so far as their bodies are concerned.

Let that serve as a figure for a liberal education. A liberal education consists in putting the mind in such shape that all its powers, like the muscles of the body, will have been called into exercise, will have been given a certain degree of development, a certain uniformity and symmetry of development, so that the mind will not find itself daunted in the midst of the tasks of the world any more than the body itself, and will be able to turn itself in the right direction, even as the athlete, quickly and gracefully, not overwhelmed by the strain, and able to accommodate the several faculties so that they will unite in carrying the strain. The thing is a mere figure of speech, but it is a figure of speech which in some degree illuminates the matter which I want to elucidate for you.

A liberal training is not a complete body of information. I have never met a man who had a complete body of information, though I have met many who thought they had. But I have never met a man who thought he had whom I would employ to do anything of importance, because I do not go into the lumber room to find a workshop. Every workshop has had rigorously shut out from it all the things that do not belong there. A man who resembles a museum or a lumber room does not resemble a workshop; and the perfectly-informed individual, if you can find him, may not be an educated person. Some of the best minds, some of the minds that I have been most afraid of when it came to any kind of intellectual contest, are minds that would have to look up almost every fact they needed to use; but they had so fed upon reason based upon definite facts that the moment you presented the fact to them they would produce something like a finished work of art. The facts are the crude raw material of the mind, and for the process of training one fact will do as well as another of the same kind.

A liberal education should have the elements of modern learning in it. It should have in it the element of language, it should have the element of philosophy (I follow education to the end of the college period), it should have the element of physical science, and it should have a touch of history. Now, you can, in the school curriculum and in the college curriculum, when they are combined, have all those elements in large quantities, provided you will make up your minds to deny yourselves and not have too much of any one of them, provided you will make up your minds what is the best portion of each, and stick to it.

Establish something like a habit of thought and action in the youth under your instruction, so that if the mind thinks of the phenomena of nature it thinks in a precise way by means of the definite observation characteristic, for example, of the chemical laboratory. Do not, if you haven't the time, try to teach him both chemistry and physics. They are quite unlike each other, but the processes of the one laboratory will establish the habit of mind just as well as the processes of the other. What you are after is to establish those methods of thinking and observation which are characteristic of the modern laboratory.

In the field of mathematics, which I have just used for illustration, you have no laboratory. You have nothing that you can see; you have nothing that you have ever seen when you get into the higher regions of mathematics. Therefore, this is one of the best trainings in the world. That mind is best trained which is obliged to move independently of the easy processes of observation. The pupil can separate with a knife what you put on the table before him, and if you give him a magnifying glass he can see what is invisible to the naked eye, and after a short period of training he can pick out all there is there. But when you submit a complicated proposition nowhere to be observed in physical existence, and ask him to analyze it, then comes the tug-of-war, then you learn whether that mind has precision and discrimination.

And this invisibility of subjects lies in many fields: for instance, the field of government. Nobody ever saw a government. You may in certain places see some one who deems himself the whole government; but, quite contrary to his impressions, he does not constitute the government. There was one occasion when a government was visible,—when all the officials of a government were withdrawn from Richmond on one train. It was a government in dissolution; it was a corpse of a government; the lines had closed in upon Richmond, and this was all that was left. You never see politics. Your imagination cannot conceive it unless you have studied widely enough, and read widely enough, to understand your fellow men.

The peculiarity of a politician is that he is a fellow very much like what you would be in the same circumstances. Therefore, the beginning of your understanding of a politician is an understanding of yourself, and of the broader aspects of psychology. I use the word "psychology" with diffidence, because so many queer things are done in the name of psychology nowadays that I have stopped taking off my hat to it; it has turned into a crank, and when I see a crank I walk on the other side of the street. Psychology in its old, respectable, sedate sense I have great regard for.

The bases of our lives and of our understanding of life is the interpretation which our own experiences put upon it, and the interpretation which the experiences of others put upon it, and the experiences of others as contained in literature. The best expounders of politics I have ever read outside the pages of Burke have been some of the English poets, who have understood politics better than any systematic writer on that subject with whom I am acquainted. They have felt those great impulses of life which really constitute the consciousness of the nation. When you get into the consciousness of a nation, and see the favorite pursuits of a nation, you begin to understand its politics; and practically only the seeing poet can interpret these things to you.

You wish physical nature interpreted to you, and history interpreted to you; and the handmaid of history is literature. You wish the philosophy of life explained to you, what men have said life is, what they have surmised of its origin, what they have forecasted its end to be, and what the philosophers from the beginning have said of this complex and interesting game we are playing. That is the field of philosophy. And you cannot go forth into life with any touch of literary education unless you have heard or comprehended something of that. Here are five or six of the elements of a liberal education, and you can wisely select the representative processes which will acquaint the mind with these various pieces of the modern intellectual content. That is a liberal education, and anybody can go out from a liberal education and at once make money by means of it. The most liberally-educated man can go out and at once make money because one of the elements of making money is to have sense, to know what you are, to know where you are, to know what you want, and to be able to understand a thing when it is explained to you.

The superintendent of one of the chief branches of the Pennsylvania R. R. said to me the other day, "We can get any number of men who can do what they are told to do after it is fully explained to them; but the men we will pay anything for are the men to whom a general system of tasks can be explained and who will not afterwards come back for instructions.["] The kind of men American industrial society craves is illustrated by one of the homely stories from the repertoire of stories about Abraham Lincoln. Lincoln was sending a gentleman on a very delicate mission, and this gentleman had sat up until a very late hour with Secretary Seward and the President going over all the possible contingencies of the case. When midnight came and they found themselves jaded and tired, the gentleman, rising to depart, said, "Well, Mr. President, if there is anything that we have overlooked, are there any general instructions you can give me as to what I shall do?" Lincoln answered him in this way: "When I was in Springfield I had a little girl neighbor who was presented with some beautiful alphabet blocks. She was so fascinated with them that she did not want to part with them even at bedtime, so she took them to bed with her. After she had played with them until she was very sleepy, she recollected that she had not said her prayers. So she got on her knees and said, 'O Lord, I am too sleepy to pray, but there are the letters, spell it out for yourself.'" Now, that may serve as an illustration of a liberal education. Here are the general instructions; for the rest, spell it out for yourself. You have spelled it out in the laboratory, in the philosophy exercise, in all of these sample processes; you are a fool if you cannot spell this out, the particular case. I have been told by an eminent railway official that so far as the administrative staff of the railway was concerned he would rather have men with a classical education than men with a scientific education. They want men who can understand from a ledger the whole system of a great railway; and those are the men who have been accustomed to deal with the invisible things of thought, those are the liberally-trained men.

On the other hand, what is technical education? It is one which condemns all but the extraordinary individual to a minor part in life, to a part not of command or direction but of specific performance, to the difficult manual tasks of the world which require skill, a perfect command of the muscles, a trained eye, a definite knowledge of physical relations and of complex machinery; its pupils are men schooled precisely in the particular processes which they are to apply. One of the drawbacks to American industry is that we do not make such men because we overshoot the mark and try to make them something else besides. The consequence is that neither side of the task is completed or perfected, and we make neither liberally-educated men nor serviceable experts. It is not that we should not wish to do it, it is that no matter how hard we wish we cannot do it. It is absolutely an unpatriotic thing to waste the money devoted to education by trying to do a thing which we know is impossible. The majority of men have to be drawers of water and hewers of wood. The mechanical tasks of the world are infinite, and they must be performed; and that nation which does not perform them with skill, which has not a great body of trained mechanics, is going to fall behind in the race of modern civilization. You may build tariff walls as high as you please, and the tide will come over any wall that you build, provided the men inside of the wall cannot work as intelligently as the men outside of the wall. One of the things we ought to be ashamed of is that we have reason to prefer an article labelled "Made in Germany." We prefer it, not because it is made in Germany, but because the Germans train men to know how to make it. America has not been so thoughtful to train men to know how to make things. We have the stuff with which to make them, but we do not give our men the skill to make them. We try to do everything at once, and do nothing well enough.

Of course, there ought to be combined with technical education just as much of the liberal education and of the book explanations of life as it is possible to combine with it without taking the efficiency out of the thing we are trying to do. I have in mind the Hampton Institute in Virginia, where the literary training is not neglected but subordinated. Where you are trying to give sufficient technical training you must subordinate the literary training, just as, when you are trying to give a liberal education, you must subordinate the technical training. Nobody ought to get married, I suppose, who isn't a bit of a carpenter and is likely to mash his thumb when he uses a hammer; because one thing that results from mashing a thumb is a mental state inconsistent with the peace of the household, and certain remarks which are highly unparliamentary result. I suppose nobody is an acceptable husband who cannot at least drive a nail on occasion, provided he drives it into things and not into persons.

There is another matter which is of as much consequence as all this. We must select the way in which we are going to do these things. I have been talking so far only of programs. We have got to communicate education; we must make up our minds as to the best way to give it. The best way to give it is to make the pupil do the work, instead of having the teacher do the work, as is the case nowadays. Our teachers are becoming more and more educated, and by the time they have turned out fifteen or twenty classes they will be extraordinarliy [extraordinarily] well-trained persons. But what about the classes they have turned out? I remember speaking some years ago—doubtless to you on another occasion[1]—and citing with approbation the case of a teacher who made the boys in his mathematics class do all the work themselves. He refused to do any example for a pupil. He was willing to explain the rule and illustrate it; but the specific examples given out he would not assist them in solving. If a boy did not understand he had to go to one of the brighter boys of the class for assistance. This put the boy on his mettle: he did not care to go to one of his chums for assistance. Now, it happened that those boys learned mathematics, and that the boys in neighboring schools did not learn mathematics. After I had cited this case, a man approached me with a sad countenance and said, "Why that is a radical unkindness to the dull boys; it is a mild kind of torture for them; it makes the dull boy do an unreasonable amount of work." I said, "If you want the boy to go to school to excuse him for using his mind, then using his mind should be against the rule; but if he is sent to do things, then I say if he cannot do them he ought to go to some other place and find something more suited to his intelligence. You cannot tell whether he can do it until he has made the effort. I do not know of any other way of bringing out a mind than by obliging the person who is alleged to have one to use it; that is the only way in which you can determine whether he has one." What we are now engaged in doing is coddling undeveloped minds by developed minds; and that is not a process which develops, it is a process which smothers. I know there are some teachers who

---

[1] Actually, in the address to the Schoolmasters' of New York and Vicinity, printed at Dec. 12, 1903, Vol. 15, p. 88.

help and at the same time stimulate, but they are very rare; and most teachers are most of the time very tired, and stimulating draws blood. You cannot stimulate when you are dead tired, and if you help the pupil when you are dead tired he gets nothing out of it except to be excused from exerting his own powers.

I know that teaching would be a more difficult thing than it now is if these suggestions were acted upon. It is a great deal harder to stimulate other minds to do things than it is to do the thing yourself. If a man cannot find the means of making a subordinate do the work he wants him to do, he is not fit for the job. If a subordinate keeps asking for instructions from his superior, and the superior says, "Never mind, I will do it myself," I think that man is unfit for the job. Never carry him beyond a certain point, for the business will break down if you do. And a teacher who cannot find a means of making a pupil do the work is unfit for the job.

I know a good deal of this is futile, that the public schools of this country are not sustained by the school boards in dropping anybody: society won't pay the taxes if you turn their sons out. Very well then, the only thing we can do is to keep the boy in the same grade for his lifetime, refuse absolutely to stultify ourselves by advancing him. We are willing to teach him this thing until he loses his teeth, but we are not going to falsify the returns and say he is ready to advance to the next grade. If the public wishes to maintain schools which will harbor their children for a lifetime, it is no concern of ours except that they will have to enlarge the schoolhouses and the teaching force.

In other words, Ladies and Gentlemen, we are now face to face with a thing just as complex and just as imperative as that which the statesman is face to face with. Here he finds a complex society in which something is the matter, in which a great many things can be done and are done which are against the public welfare, and it is absolutely obligatory upon him to make up his mind what is wrong and, without trying to upset society, prevent the things which are wrong. And his confusion, his unfortunate experimenting in the field of legislation is due to the fact that he has not analysed to the bottom the economic changes that have come upon society. The school teacher is in the same position. He is trying to carry in his hands more than his hands can hold. He is trying to bunch all the elements of education in one process, and they cannot be bunched in one process. He cannot bunch all the elements of one process in a scheme which will readily accomplish the objects of that process. We must make an analysis of this matter, differentiate our schools, our processes;

make it perfectly definite beforehand what it is we are trying to do and how we are going to do it; because education is, as I began by saying, merely a means to life, and the life of the modern world is in danger of nothing so much as the counsels of men with untrained intelligences.

Modern society depends upon the two clarifying processes of reasoning and of counsel which are to make or unmake modern society. I do not mean we are to supply the elements of counsel, but we are to supply the minds capable of discrimination, suitable for the residence of wisdom, able to find the light, responsive to the light; men who know how to think and where to find the substance upon which their thought shall be constructed. If we do not do that society will some day look back upon the history of an age of catastrophe and ask: Where were the wise teachers in those days, where were the men who should have come to the front in the face of no matter what opposition, in the face of no matter how great a body of prejudice, and have said, "We have got to begin at the bottom and analyse it, reorganize it from top to bottom"? We have all the elements, but they are not used with discrimination. We have all the ends in view, but they are not properly related to each other in value and sequence. And unless the spirit of statesmanship enters into our schools and our colleges, we shall not have an age of statesmen but an age of darkness, compared with which the dark ages shall some day seem bright; for there were men then sitting in silent and quiet places who did see the vision of truth; but we of our day, having no quiet places, overwhelmed by the dense smoke, confused by the din of modern industry, will have gone groping about nowhere, not knowing that in the midst of all that turmoil if we had but opened our windows to the right light, there would have come in the full illumination of wisdom.[2]

Printed in *High School Teachers Association of New York Volume 3 1908-1909* (n.p., n.d.), pp. 19-31.
[2] There is a WWhw outline of this address, dated Jan. 8, 1909, in WP, DLC.

From Melancthon Williams Jacobus

PRIVATE.

Hartford, Conn.,
My dear President Wilson: January 9th, 1909

I failed to notice in Mr. Pyne's letter to me, regarding the infelicitous assignment of Litt.B. candidates to the Scientific Department for part of their course and to the Academic Department for the remainder, that at the close he added a paragraph regarding his desire as Chairman of the Finance Committee to have the assignments of the Preceptors to the various Departments investigated, with a view to correcting any possible waste, which seemed to him to be vital in the present financial condition of the University. I therefore have mailed, yesterday afternoon, an extra item for the Docket, embodying his request.

I enclose herewith a page of the "Princetonian" which he sent me in his letter,[1] illustrating what he feels to be the injustice done to Princeton in this meaningless division of the Litt.B. men between two departments.

At various times since our last meeting, I have received from the Secretary copies of remits to our Committee from the Faculty. These I enclose[2] along with the page of the "Princetonian," because my physician has positively refused to allow me to attend the coming meeting of the Committee. I feel that he is justified in his refusal; and, as my recovery has been so slow, I feel I owe it to him as well as to myself to do as he bids me. So that I shall not venture to make the journey to Princeton at this time.

It was very kind of you to offer to keep me informed of the doings of the Committee, and I shall ask you if you will be so kind as to have sent me a copy both of the minutes of the Committee's meeting and also of their report to the Board. The former I wish to incorporate in my book of minutes, and the latter I shall be glad to see for my personal information.

I am exceedingly glad that you and Dean Fine have seen your way clear to report favorably upon the suggestion of his official relation to the scientific studies of the University. I cannot but believe it will be a great relief to you and give you freer hand and more abundant time for the great work you have as representative of Princeton's educational policy before the world of business as well as of letters. The next few years are going to make great changes in University policies, especially with the readjustments which are certain to follow upon the election of a new President at Harvard.[3] Princeton is in the lead now, as far as ideals are concerned. She will find Harvard come to her side, but she must not fail to maintain the pre-eminence which, through you, has now become her possession.

Mrs. Jacobus[4] is improving slowly, a slight operation on New Year's Day having, I think, given certainty of a favorable issue to her case.

I hope before long to be in working condition myself, and trust that neither you nor the Committee on Curriculum will hesitate in any way to call upon me for my services any time they are needed, here or in New York or Princeton.

With kindest regards and best wishes for the coming meeting of the Board, I am

Yours very sincerely,   Melancthon W Jacobus

TLS (WWP, UA, NjP).
    [1] This enclosure is missing.
    [2] These enclosures are also missing.
    [3] Abbott Lawrence Lowell was elected President of Harvard University on January 13, 1909.
    [4] Clara Cooley Jacobus.

From Harvey Edward Fisk

Dear Doctor Wilson,   [New York]   Jan'y 9th 1909

I want to ask you why it is the officers, faculty and trustees countenance the abominable practice of hazing at Princeton, and especially the refined cruelty of the February renewal of of [sic] the "sport." I assume it is endorsed by you and others in authority as there seem to be regular rules governing it and a set of inquisitors appointed to the duty from the upper classes.[1] Why, after Doctor McCosh had succeeded in eradicating this abuse it should have been revived with the consent and approval of the authorities I cannot understand. Perhaps you can explain.

Another matter about which I would like information is why it should be compulsory for the boys to take their food at the Commons. I am given to understand from many sources that the food is not nourishing, is frequently spoiled and that the service is by dirty servants & in a dirty way. How you can expect to have a healthy set of young men under these conditions is beyond my comprehension.

Here are two abuses which ought to be remedied. Cannot you take the matter up & see that appropriate remedies are applied.

Yours sincerely   Harvey E. Fisk

ALS (WP, DLC).
    [1] As Wilson's reply to Fisk of January 12, 1909, explained, the authorities at Princeton chose to permit certain kinds of "horsing" of freshmen by the sophomores in order to prevent much more severe and secret practices of hazing. Horsing in its more harmless forms consisted of such activities as forcing groups of freshmen to march or run across the campus. However, as Wilson also indicated, it could and often did degenerate into much more serious actions such as compelling freshmen to do things potentially dangerous to life and limb. Under a tacit agreement with the faculty, horsing was to occur only during the first two weeks of the autumn term and during the week including Washington's Birthday. However, in early 1909, the Faculty Committee on Discipline voted to abolish the February horsing. Although accompanied by much grumbling by upperclassmen, the abolition seems to have been successfully accomplished.
    Fisk's remark about "regular rules" governing horsing apparently referred

to the elaborate set of customary rules as to what freshmen could and could not do on the campus. For example, they could not wear the college colors or carry canes; they were required to be in their rooms after 9 P.M.; and they had to wear black skull caps. The *Princeton Alumni Weekly,* IX (Feb. 24, 1909), 309-10, has a list of these rules as well as a discussion of the student reaction to the abolition of February horsing.

From Junius Spencer Morgan

Princeton, New Jersey
My dear President Wilson, Jan'y 10, 1909

After considering the matter carefully, I have decided to write and ask you to present my resignation as Associate Librarian to the Trustees at the meeting of the Board to be held this week, & to request their acceptance of the same.

My reasons for resigning this position, which I have held for twelve years, are various—I do not think it necessary to go into them. I can assure you that I shall always be interested in the Library & that in plans for its growth & development I shall always be glad to render what assistance I can.

Yours very truly J. S. Morgan

ALS (Trustees' Papers, UA, NjP).

To Melancthon Williams Jacobus

My dear Dr. Jacobus: Princeton, N. J. January 11th, 1909.

I am sincerely and deeply distressed that you cannot attend this meeting of the committee and of the Board, but of course it is right that you should obey your doctor most implicitly, and I hope with all my heart that your obedience may yield steady improvement and insure your complete recovery.

I will, of course, take charge of the meeting of the committee and will, so far as possible, carry out the full programme you have outlined.

A very odd thing has happened about Dr. McPherson's request for further light on the entrance requirements to the C.E. course. I found when I tried to put the matter in accurate form that the minutes of the Board contained no reference whatever to the request. I therefore sent over to Lawrenceville to ask Dr. McPherson if he would not re-state it in the form in which he made it, only to find that he had no recollection whatever of making any specific request. He remembered only having had a conversation with the Dean of the Faculty about the C.E. Entrance requirements. In the circumstances, therefore, it does not seem to me that we need take the matter up. It would hardly now be possible to have the matter formulated in time for such action as would be necessary by the faculty.

As to the matter to which Mr. Pyne called your attention—the allotment of preceptors to the various Departments—the terms for which our present staff of preceptors were engaged, most of them, run to the Commencement of 1910. The few whose terms would come to an end sooner are in Departments which are clearly not over-manned. Moreover, I think that this is a matter which should be gone into very systematically and that we should reserve our report on it until the Commencement meeting, instituting the proper processes of inquiry in the meantime.

I will, of course, send you full minutes of the proceedings and recommendations of the committee.

Mrs. Wilson joins me in warmest regard and in the warmest expression of our satisfaction in learning that Mrs. Jacobus is so certainly on the way to perfect health after her light operation.

With warm regard,

Affectionately yours,   [Woodrow Wilson]

CCL (RSB Coll., DLC).

To Cleveland Hoadley Dodge

My dear Cleve: Princeton, N. J.   January 12th, 1909.

I heard only yesterday, when I was in New York, the sad news of the death of your mother,[1] and I write to express my very warm and affectionate sympathy.

I know, of course, that it was a blessed relief for her, but nothing of this kind can be anything but a deep shock and sorrow to those who are left, and I know how your heart must ache because of the vacancy in your life made by your dear mother's departure. I hope that you know how our love and sympathy follow you.

Always affectionately yours,   Woodrow Wilson

TLS (WC, NjP).
[1] Sarah Hoadley (Mrs. William Earl) Dodge, who died on January 10, 1909, at her home in New York.

To Harvey Edward Fisk

My dear Mr. Fisk: Princeton, N. J.   January 12th, 1909.

Allow me to acknowledge the receipt of your letter of January 9th and to say that I, of course, appreciate the gravity of the matter to which it calls my attention.

The whole subject of the relation between the sophomores and the freshmen is one of the extremest difficulty. I do not know any subject it is so hard to handle with wisdom and success. As a matter of fact, hazing never was stamped out. It was at one time successfully driven under cover, and it was in order to save the freshmen from the extreme forms of hazing which went on in secret that we some years ago consented to wink at certain forms of "horsing," as the boys call it, in public, which we thought would be restrained from going to great lengths by the opinion of the undergraduates themselves, if we gave the matter over to the government of that opinion.

For several years it was greatly restrained and did not go beyond the point of silliness, but it is undoubtedly true that it has gone from bad to worse and has not been restrained as we expected it would be. We have again and again applied to the Senior Council[1] in the matter, and they have again and again responded to our appeal so that the horsing has been checked and minimized again and again, always, however, to grow once more into something very bad indeed.

We are clearly aware that something must be done, but we are anxious not to do anything which will again drive the thing into secret practices which would be worse even than what we have at present. It is impossible, without an intolerable system of spies, to stop it altogether. We have taken measures to prevent, if possible, the renewal of the horsing on Washington's Birthday, and are debating the wisest course to pursue with regard to the general restraint and ultimate extinction of the whole practice.

Allow me to thank you for your letter and to assure you that we were already fully aware of the gravity of the situation.

Very truly yours,   [Woodrow Wilson]

CCL (WWP, UA, NjP).

[1] About this organization, see H. B. Thompson *et al.* to the Board of Trustees of Princeton University, April 8, 1908, n. 1.

From Edward Graham Elliott

My dear Dr. Wilson: Princeton, N. J., Jan. 12, 1909

I have given your proposal respecting the Deanship of the College[1] my most careful consideration. I have consulted several of my friends and they have been good enough to urge me to accept. My only desire has been to determine in my own mind the question of my fitness for the position. While not wholly convinced of that fact I do not feel that I can disregard the opinion of those who have been associated with me. I will therefore be most happy to have my name presented.

Allow me to thank you most cordially for the honor and for the confidence you have shown in me.

Very sincerely yours,   Edward G. Elliott

ALS (WP, DLC).
[1] A position about to be created, about which see Chapter IX of the proposed by-laws of the Board of Trustees printed in the Committee on the Curriculum to the Board of Trustees of Princeton University, Jan. 13, 1909.

From Cleveland Hoadley Dodge

Dear Woodrow   [New York]   Jan. 13th [1909]

Heartfelt thanks for your very kind letter.

My dear mother used to deprecate her "useless" life but as I figure over all she has done during the last five years for Princeton, Teachers College, the YMCA & other causes it is almost staggering to think of the forces which she let loose

Your sympathetic words are a great comfort & I appreciate them very much   Yrs affly   C H Dodge

ALS (WP, DLC).

From Franklin Zeiger

My dear Dr. Wilson: Paterson, N. J.   Jan. 13, 1909.

On behalf of our Committee and all the teachers of the Paterson High School I desire to thank you most heartily for your kindness in accepting the invitation to attend the dinner to Dr. Reinhart. We surely shall anticipate your visit with a great deal of pleasure. I shall be very glad to let you know a week or so before the date the full particulars of the arrangements for the dinner with the hour and place, as well as the arrangements for your entertainment.

Thanking you again most sincerely for the great favor, I am
Yours respectfully, Franklin Zeiger.

ALS (WP, DLC).

Proposed By-Laws of the Board of Trustees of Princeton University

Proposed By-Laws   [c. Jan. 13, 1909]

Chapter VII.

Of the Dean of the Faculty.

1. The Dean of the Faculty shall be charged with the administrative oversight under the Pres. of the Univ., of the application and enforcement of the rules and standards of scholarship in the University, and to this end shall *ex officio* be a member of the Committee of the Board on the Curriculum and chairman of the standing committee of the University Faculty on Examinations and Standing

2. He shall, whenever the President of the University is absent from Princeton or incapacitated by illness or any other temporary cause, perform the routine duties of the President of the University, including the duty of presiding over the meetings of the University Faculty.

3. He shall report in writing to the Committee on the Curriculum before the April and Commencement meetings of the Board on the state of scholarship in the University and on all matters relating to the application and enforcement of the rules and standards of scholarship, which may call for comment or action.

Chapter IX

Of the Dean of the College

1. The Dean of the College shall be charged with the oversight, under the President of the University, of the discipline of the University, including attendance upon all university exercises and all matters of personal conduct; and to that end shall *ex officio* be a member of the Committee of the Board on Morals and Discipline, and chairman of the Committee of the University Faculty on Discipline

2. The Curator of Grounds and Buildings shall report to him

concerning all matters affecting discipline, so far as they may come under his notice, and upon all cases of illness occurring within the buildings of the University; and the proctors shall be subordinated to him, as well as to the President of the University, and shall report to him on all matters relating to the deportment of the students.

3. He may assign rooms in the dormitories to such members of the teaching staff of the University and to such Fellows as he may see fit, subject to the approval of the Committee on Grounds and Buildings.

4. He shall report in writing to the Committee on Morals and Discipline before the October and April meetings of the Board on the state of discipline in the University and on all matters relating thereto.

Chapter X.
Of the Dean of the Departments of Science

1. The Dean of the Departments of Science shall have administrative oversight, under the President of the University, of the Departments of instruction in the mathematical, physical, and natural sciences, and to that end shall be *ex officio* a member of the Committee on the Curriculum.

2. He shall have administrative oversight, under the President of the University, of the organization, development and conduct of all work leading to degrees in applied science.

3. He shall report in writing to the Committee on the Curriculum at such times as that Committee may direct or the matters in his care require, concerning whatever within the scope of his duties may call for comment or action or upon which information may be desired by the Board or the Committee.

Chapter XIV.
Of the Registrar

Add

5. The administrative organization and methods of the Registrar's office shall be determined by a committee consisting of the Registrar, the Dean of the Faculty, and the Dean of the College.

WWhw MS (WWP, UA, NjP).

The Committee on the Curriculum to the Board of Trustees of Princeton University

Princeton, January 13th, 1909.

A meeting of the Curriculum Committee was held in the President's office in '79 Hall at 4 P.M., January 13, 1909.

Members present were: The President of the University and Messrs. De Witt, Stewart, Thompson, Palmer and Imbrie.

In the absence of Dr. Jacobus, Dr. De Witt acted as Chairman of the meeting.

The Committee considered the following question submitted by Mr. Pyne with the approval of the President:

> Is it fair to the University, in the resulting popular misunderstanding regarding both the Scientific and Academic Departments that candidates for the Litt.B. degree should be assigned to the Scientific Department for the first two years and then transferred to the Academic Department for the remainder of their course?

Upon motion of Mr. Thompson it was:

Resolved: That the matter be referred to the President for examination and to report at a subsequent meeting of the Committee.[1]

The President reported as to his conference with Dean Fine, regarding the latter's official relationship to the Scientific Studies of the University, and submitted for the consideration of the Committee the following amendments to the By-Laws:

Chapter VII.

Of the Dean of the Faculty.

1. The Dean of the Faculty shall be charged with the administrative oversight, under the President of the University, of the application and enforcement of the rules and standards of scholarship in the University, and to this end shall *ex officio* be a member of the Committee of the Board on the Curriculum and Chairman of the Standing Committee of the University Faculty on Examinations and Standing.

2. He shall, whenever the President of the University is absent from Princeton or incapacitated by illness or by any other temporary cause, perform the routine duties of the President of the University, including the duty of presiding over the meetings of the University Faculty.

3. He shall report in writing to the Committee on the Curriculum

at such times as that Committee may direct or the matters in his care require, concerning anything within the scope of his duties that may call for comment or action or upon which information may be desired by the Board or by the Committee.

Chapter IX.

Of the Dean of the College.

1. The Dean of the College shall be charged with the oversight, under the President of the University, of the discipline of the University, including attendance upon all university exercises and all matters of personal conduct; and to that end shall *ex officio* be a member of the Committee of the Board on Morals and Discipline, and Chairman of the Committee of the University Faculty on Discipline.

2. The Curator of Grounds and Buildings shall report to him concerning all matters affecting discipline, so far as they may come under his notice, and upon all cases of illness occurring within the buildings of the University; and the proctors shall be subordinated to him, as well as to the President of the University, and shall report to him on all matters relating to the deportment of the students.

3. He may assign rooms in the Dormitories to such members of the teaching staff of the University and to such Fellows as he may see fit, subject to the approval of the Committee on Grounds and Buildings.

4. He shall report in writing to the Committee on Morals and Discipline before the October and April meetings of the Board on the state of discipline in the University and on all matters relating thereto.

Chapter X.

Of the Dean of the Departments of Science.

1. The Dean of the Departments of Science shall have administrative oversight, under the President of the University, of the Departments of instruction in pure and applied science, and to that end shall be *ex officio* a member of the Committee on the Curriculum.

2. He shall have administrative oversight, under the President of the University, of the organization, development and conduct of all work leading to degrees in applied science.

3. He shall report in writing to the Committee on the Curriculum at such times as that Committee may direct or the matters in his care require, concerning anything within the scope of his duties

that may call for comment or action or upon which information may be desired by the Board or by the Committee.

Chapter XIV.

Of the Registrar.

Add

5. The administrative organization and methods of the Registrar's office shall be determined by a committee consisting of the Registrar, the Dean of the Faculty, and the Dean of the College.

Upon motion of Mr. Palmer it was

Resolved: That the Committee recommend for the approval of the Board the amendments to the By-Laws as proposed by the President.[2]

Upon motion of Mr. Palmer, it was

Resolved: That the President, having reported to the Committee his intention to nominate Professor Henry B. Fine, now Dean of the Faculty, to be also Dean of the Departments of Science, and having asked the concurrence of the Curriculum Committee, the Committee heartily concurs.[3]

Upon motion of Dr. Stewart it was

Resolved: That the President, having reported to the Committee his intention to nominate Professor Edward G. Elliott to be Dean of the College, and having asked the concurrence of the Curriculum Committee, the Committee heartily concurs.[4]

There being no further business, the Committee adjourned.

Andrew C Imbrie   Secretary.

TRS (Trustees' Papers, UA, NjP).

[1] At the meeting of the trustees' Committee on the Curriculum on April 7, 1909, Wilson proposed a new scheme for the arrangement of students' names in the university catalogue. The new arrangement was approved by the trustees on April 8, 1909, and was first used in the catalogue for 1909-10. What it did in effect was to drop the old separate list of all students in the School of Science and arrange all students by class and by degree sought within each class. However, in the freshman and sophomore years, Litt.B. and B.S. students were still listed separately.

[2] The Board of Trustees adopted these by-laws on January 14, 1909.

[3] The Board of Trustees confirmed this appointment at its meeting on January 14.

[4] The board confirmed Elliott's appointment at the same meeting.

From John Lambert Cadwalader

My dear Mr. President: New York, 13 January, 1909.

I enclose a copy of the report[1] which we propose to present to the Trustees tomorrow on the question of the report of the Committee of Fifty.

The more I think of it the more I am satisfied that if the alumni desire to put themselves in some working condition toward the Trustees and the University, it is not simply permissible but quite an advisable thing to do. And if advisable, then unimportant things, such as the name of the organization, do not figure at all; but the whole business will be, how serious is the organization, what kind of work can they accomplish, and by whom is it to be conducted. If all these are on the plane on which they ought to be, then the organization of the alumni will be a very large assistance to the University.

When we consider that it is only of late years that the University has called on the alumni, as a body, for service, and that in the future they must be reckoned with as one of the prime forces of the University, it will be plain, I think, that they will more and more become prominent not simply in carrying out some particular piece of work which is suggested but as having specific duties and perhaps a permanent existence. In other words, we have gradually evolved alumni Trustees not for the purpose of giving the alumni more hold on the work of the University but solely to interest the alumni as a body, and we shall get along some of these days—not quickly, but gradually— to a condition, perhaps, somewhat like Harvard, which has two bodies—one composed of the people who do the things,[2] the other composed absolutely of people elected by the alumni—that is, the overseers[3]—and practically they are almost as important a body as the alumni at large. We are very far from that now; at the same time, the gradual importance of the alumni as a working force must be counted with. I am quite sure that we can work this body into some form which will not be in any way objectionable.

I am exceedingly sorry that I cannot get to Princeton tomorrow. To tell the truth, I have not been out now for a week owing to an attack of the gout. It is an old story, and I am disgusted that it is so. I have been downtown for about two hours today, for the first time in a week, and I am absolutely afraid to try the business of going to Princeton tomorrow morning. If I had an extra day it would be all right, but I am really afraid to do it.

Believe me,   Yours faithfully,   John L. Cadwalader

per R.

TLS (WP, DLC).

[1] The original of this copy is printed as the following document.

[2] That is, the President and Fellows of Harvard College, commonly known as the Corporation.

[3] The Harvard Board of Overseers.

A Report

REPORT
of the
Committee appointed to consider the Report
of The Committee of Fifty.

At a regular meeting of the Trustees of Princeton University, held on the 15th of October, 1908, a report of the Committee on Plan and Scope of the Committee of Fifty of Princeton University was presented to the Trustees. Thereupon the Secretary was directed to forward a copy of such report to each of the Trustees, and it was resolved that the President appoint a committee of three to consider carefully the report for presentation and suggestions at the meeting of the Board to be held in January, in order that definite action upon the report might be taken at that time. The undersigned committee, appointed pursuant to such resolution, have the honor to report as follows:

The committee have considered the report of the Committee on Plan and Scope above referred to with great care, and have taken every means in their power of informing themselves on the subject. They have consulted the officers of the University, and have looked into the entire subject and formally discussed it with the Committee on Plan and Scope at a meeting called for that purpose, and after such investigations the committee submits the following report.

The report of the Committee on Plan and Scope of the Committee of Fifty, in substance, submits to the Board of Trustees that, to render the Committee an effective organization for increasing the endowment of the University, for the raising of funds or for other purposes, it must have a more effective position and standing; that to further the collection of funds for endowment or otherwise the number of appeals made to the alumni by various quasi-official bodies should be lessened, and, save in exceptional cases, the body which the report proposes to establish should be the main medium through which the Trustees might make public the vital needs of Princeton, and that therefore it has been necessary to apply for contributions practically to make up the yearly deficit, which is regarded as unfortunate; and it is suggested that the Trustees should submit to the body to be organized, at the beginning of each fiscal year, a list of the several purposes for which specific funds would be needed, so that individuals or alumni associations might select particular objects for support, and a much larger interest toward the raising of funds would then be created among the alumni.

It is therefore proposed by the report to establish a body, consisting of one representative from each of the last 35 classes and fifteen members at large, to deal with questions with which the Committee of Fifty have dealt with in the past, and to give the new body such dignity and importance as the representatives of the alumni ought to possess.

With the general objects set forth in the report of the Committee your committee entirely sympathizes. The committee is of the opinion that the general objects and ends aimed at are desirable; that the organization of the alumni in some effective form in order to render the body of the alumni more able to perform the duties which belong to it is desirable and probably necessary, and that as the assistance of the alumni as a working force is a necessary adjunct to the advancement of the University the body of the alumni are fairly entitled to organize in such form as to become effective for their regular work. It is quite true that there can be but a single governing body in the University, but your committee believes that no trouble is to be anticipated in that regard. The committee is therefore of opinion that the Trustees should approve the general course recommended—with such modifications as are suggested in this report, as the committee has some comments to suggest as to certain of the details of the proposed organization.

(1) The name suggested is The Graduate Council. Some criticism has been directed against the name on the ground that the word Council would seem to imply larger powers, perhaps, than should be accorded to any similar body. From the point of view of your committee, the name is not important. Similar bodies exist elsewhere—one at Columbia University, precisely under this name—and, the relation of the organization to the University being clearly established, the matter of a name is not deemed by the committee to be of very great importance.

(2) It is proposed by the report that a Nominating Committee shall present each year to the Trustees of the University the names of seven class representatives and three members at large for election as members of the Graduate Council. The committee is of the opinion that the members of the body should be appointed by the alumni. Naming the individuals to be appointed and having the Trustees solely register the appointments would be neither one thing nor the other; they would not be the real representatives of the alumni nor would they be nominated

by the Trustees. On the whole, the committee is of the opinion that the members of whatever body is established should be appointed by the alumni, subject, if it be deemed desirable, to confirmation or approval by the Trustees.

(3) It is recommended that among the appointments to be made by the new body shall be a Committee on Finance, which shall lay before the several class or alumni organizations objects for which funds are needed and shall report to the Graduate body, for transmission to the Board of Trustees, information as to the specific purposes to which the contributions of such organizations are to be devoted. The committee is of the opinion that, while it may be, and is, desirable that contributors should have large choice as to the particular purpose to which funds are to be devoted, it would not be desirable that any class of subscribers or particular body of the alumni should maintain a particular professorship or preceptorship, as tending to make a particular professor or preceptor beholden rather to the body to be established or to a particular group of the alumni than to the Trustees of the University, but that special contributions may better be obtained toward the support of departments or objects, the application of the fund, however, in every case to be made by the Trustees, as is now done.

(4) A Committee on Publicity is provided for, the purpose of which is to cooperate with the Secretary of the body to be appointed in the maintenance of an efficient press bureau. The committee is of the opinion that it is of doubtful advisability to commit the matter of publicity—that is to say, the advertising of the University—to any organization independent of and outside of the immediate organization of the University itself, but that the selection of matters concerning which public attention is to be drawn, and the determination of the way in which such attention is to be drawn, should belong to the office of the Secretary of the University, who should be furnished with sufficient funds for the maintenance of the necessary facilities, and with whom the secretary of the body to be established should communicate.

(5) The committee is of the opinion that any Committee on Preparatory Schools should also be drawn into close relations with the officers of the University.

(6) The committee is of the opinion that, with a body of such size as is proposed, some Executive Committee will probably be required to act when the Committee is not in session.

On the whole, the committee is satisfied that there will be no great difference on these points between the present committee and the Committee on Plan and Scope of the Committee of Fifty.

The committee has discussed the general questions in friendly spirit, and is satisfied that an agreement can be had upon all the questions which have been suggested, and that a body can be established which will be of great benefit to the University at large, afford an easy means of discussion as to the needs of the University, and draw the alumni more closely together.

The committee therefore reports that the general recommendations contained in the report of the Committee on Plan and Scope should be approved, with the modifications above mentioned and in such respects as may hereafter arise, and that it would be wise either that some further committee should be appointed, with power, or that the existing committee should have power, in conference with the President of the University, to carry out the recommendations herein made.

Respectfully submitted:

John L. Cadwalader
Henry B Thompson
Robert Garrett
Committee.[1]

TRS (Trustees' Papers, UA, NjP).

[1] The trustees voted on January 14 to accept this report and to continue the committee "with power, in conference with the President of the University, to carry out the recommendations made in their report." Another report embodying another plan of organization of the Graduate Council of Princeton University was presented by Cadwalader's committee to the trustees on April 8, 1909, and was approved at that time. This report is printed at March 29, 1909, Vol. 19.

To the Board of Trustees of Princeton University

Gentlemen: Princeton, New Jersey, January 14, 1909.

Your Committee on Honorary Degrees recommend

FOR THE HONORARY DEGREE OF LL.D.

Charles Francis Adams, Historical writer.
Earl Grey, Governor-General of Canada.
Dr. Frank Hartley, '77, Surgeon.
Abbott Lawrence Lowell, President-elect of Harvard University.

FOR THE HONORARY DEGREE OF D.D.

William Henry Steele Demarest, President of Rutgers College.

FOR THE HONORARY DEGREE OF L.H.D.

John White Alexander, Artist.
Samuel McChord Crothers, '74, Author.

FOR THE HONORARY DEGREE OF A.M.

Gutzon Borglum, Sculptor.

Respectfully submitted,   Woodrow Wilson
Chairman.

TRS (Trustees' Papers, UA, NjP).

Three Resolutions

[c. Jan. 14, 1909]

RESOLVED that the Board of Trustees extend to Messrs. David B. and Thomas D. Jones their hearty thanks for the very generous gift of $200,000 for the endowment of the Palmer Physical Laboratory fund, and that the conditions of the said gift as expressed in a letter from the said gentlemen to the Board, dated January 4, 1909, be accepted.[1]

RESOLVED that the Secretary of the University be requested to express to Mr. James Speyer their hearty thanks for and appreciation of his generous gift in the foundation of the Gordon McDonald Fellowship.

RESOLVED that the Secretary be directed to extend to Mrs. Henry Norcross Munn and Mr. Charles A. Munn the hearty thanks of the Trustees of Princeton University for their generous gift in the foundation of the Orson Desaix Munn Fellowship.[2]

T MS (Trustees' Papers, UA, NjP).

[1] D. B. Jones and T. D. Jones to the Trustees of Princeton University, Jan. 4, 1909, TCL (Trustees' Papers, UA, NjP). The conditions of the Jones's gift were that the principal was to be kept and invested in perpetuity, with the income to be devoted "solely for the purposes of the Departments of Physics and Electrical Engineering of Princeton University" for maintenance and enlargement of scientific equipment, for salaries of research staff, and for "implements, materials, books, pamphlets and periodicals as may be needed for the scientific work of these departments." The income was not to be used for maintenance of the building, salaries of janitors or caretakers, charges for heat, light, gas, or water, or for salaries of members of the teaching staff.

[2] The trustees adopted these resolutions at their meeting on January 14, 1909.

From the Minutes of the Board of Trustees
of Princeton University

[Jan. 14, 1909]

The Trustees of Princeton University met in stated session in the Trustees' Room in the Chancellor Green Library, Princeton,

New Jersey, at eleven o'clock on Thursday morning, January 14, 1909.

The President of the University in the chair. . . .

The President of the University presented Mr. Junius S. Morgan's resignation as Associate Librarian. On motion of Mr. John A. Stewart, Mr. Morgan's resignation was accepted with great regret. At the suggestion of Mr. Green the President of the University was requested to prepare a minute expressing the regret of the Board at Mr. Morgan's resignation. . . .[1]

Mr. McCormick announced that it was the intention of the Class of 1879 to present to the University two Bronze Tigers to take the place of the Lions at the main entrance to Nassau Hall.

[1] See the Enclosure printed with WW to C. W. McAlpin, Jan. 23, 1909, Vol. 19.

To Melancthon Williams Jacobus

My dear Dr. Jacobus: Princeton, N. J.   January 15th, 1909.

Mr. Imbrie is going to send you the minutes of our committee meeting, but there are one or two matters not in the minutes about which I am sure you would like to be informed.

Fortunately, we were able to recover, by the assistance of your message[1] and Dean Fine's recollection of an interview with Dr. McPherson, the exact point involved in the question which he raised in the Board. I am sorry that there should have been any slip about the matter. It is a matter, however, which will need the very careful consideration of the faculty, and it would not in any case have been possible to prepare it in final form for this meeting of the Board of Trustees. It will not now slip from our recollection and we shall take it up in the proper committee at a very early date. It is a matter which in any case ought to have been attended to.

You will be interested to know that the Board adopted without objection our full programme with regard to the new deanship and the reconstitution of the existing deanships. Nothing occurred at the Board meeting, indeed, which was in the least untoward, and I think a very general spirit of hopefulness and intelligent cooperation manifested itself. There were a great many expressions of regret that you should be absent and of anxiety that you should take proper care of yourself and come back to us perfectly fit again.

The list of names presented by the Committee on Honorary Degrees and accepted by the Board was as follows:

For Doctor of Laws—
  Charles Francis Adams
  Earl Grey, Governor General of Canada
  Frank Hartley, of your own class
  Abbott Lawrence Lowell.
For the degree of L.H.D.
  John W. Alexander, the artist, and
  Samuel M. Crothers, the essayist.
For the degree of Doctor of Divinity, President Demarest of Rutgers, and
For the honorary degree of Master of Arts, Mr. Gutzon Borglum, the sculptor.

No nomination was made for trustee, and Mr. Sheldon's amendment to the By-Laws, forbidding a vote on such a nomination at the same meeting at which it is made, was adopted.

  Mrs. Wilson joins me in warmest regard, and I am always,
  Cordially and affectionately yours,   [Woodrow Wilson]

CCL (RSB Coll., DLC).
1 M. W. Jacobus to WW, Jan. 13 [1910], T telegram (WP, DLC).

To Lucius Hopkins Miller

[Princeton, N. J.]

My dear Professor Miller: January 15th, 1909.

Among the many things which I have allowed to slip from my memory, amidst a rush of engagements, is the matter of the Chinese students who are to be sent to this country.[1] I think that it is clearly Princeton's duty to take part, so far as she can, in educating these men, if we can arrange to have some of them sent to us, and I am writing to ask if you will not be generous enough to set the business going for me. Will you not be kind enough to find out from some influential Princeton man in Washington what the best way would be of getting the ear of the Chinese Legation in Washington, so that we might be instructed from the legation how to go about getting ourselves put upon some preferred list? I know that your interest and enthusiasm will incline you to comply with this request.

Of course, the only thing Princeton will get out of this business is a grip upon the minds of men who may be influential in guiding the future of the Chinese empire. I do not feel that our facilities for giving them what they want are as great as the facilities of some other universities, but I do feel that it is clearly our duty to take advantage of such an opportunity for influence.

With warm regard,

Faithfully yours,   [Woodrow Wilson]

CCL (WWP, UA, NjP).

1 Students whose expenses were to be paid by the Chinese government out of funds returned to China by the United States government from the so-called Boxer Indemnity.

In the aftermath of the Boxer Rebellion of 1900, the United States in 1901 was granted an indemnity from the Chinese government amounting to over $24,000,-000. However, from the outset it was the unstated policy of the American government that, after the reimbursement of expenses incurred during the uprising and the settlement of all claims of American citizens for injury and property loss, the balance of the indemnity would be remitted to China. On January 15, 1907, Secretary of State Elihu Root formally communicated this intention to the Chinese Minister in Washington. On May 25, 1908, Congress authorized the remittance of nearly $11,000,000 of the indemnity to China. On July 14, 1908, the Chinese Foreign Office informed the American Minister in Peking that the returned funds would be used in large part to send Chinese students to American colleges and universities. In pursuance of this policy, a system of competitive scholarships was set up, and a preparatory school staffed by Americans was established to insure the adequacy of preparation of the applicants. The first Chinese students under this program arrived in the United States in 1909, and others continued to follow until the Second World War.

From John Grier Hibben

My dear Woodrow   Princeton   January 15/09

I wish to lay before you my resignation as a member of the Committee on Discipline, and the Committee on Examinations & Standing.[1]   Sincerely yours,   John Grier Hibben

ALS (WP, DLC).

1 Hibben wrote this letter on the day or soon after Dean Fine told Dean West that the Faculty Committee on the Graduate School was to be reorganized by the elimination of all of West's supporters and the appointment of Wilson men in their stead. Andrew F. West, "A Narrative of the Graduate College of Princeton University . . ." (mimeographed MS, UA, NjP), pp. 41-42. West undoubtedly told the news at once to Hibben, his close friend, and Hibben wrote this letter in protest. There are many documents relating to the reorganization of the Faculty Committee on the Graduate School in Volume 19.

To John Grier Hibben

My dear Jack,   Princeton, N. J.   15 January, 1909.

I have just received your note of this morning. I would come to see you were I not leaving town to meet an engagement. I cannot accept your resignation from the Committee on Discipline or from the Committee on Examinations and Standing, without some explanation. Your note has distressed me deeply. I shall be at home by noon to-morrow: will you not come to see me at my office (where there will be less danger of interruption) at 2.30?[1]   Affectionately Yours,   Woodrow Wilson

ALS (photostat in WC, NjP).
[1] Wilson persuaded Hibben to withdraw his resignations at this time.

To Abbott Lawrence Lowell

My dear Mr. Lowell: Princeton, N. J.   January 15th, 1909.

You will presently receive from the Secretary of Princeton University an invitation to be present at our next Commencement and receive the degree of Doctor of Laws from the University. You will think, no doubt, that this action on the part of our Trustees is merely a desire to honor you in view of your recent election to be President of Harvard University, but I beg to assure you that it is much more personal than that. We had it in mind to vote this action before the Harvard Corporation chose you and without regard to any choice that they might make, wishing to honor you on your own achievements, which everybody now recognizes to be unusual and permanent.

I tried to express in a telegram to you yesterday the very great pleasure that your choice as President of Harvard University has given me personally. I think that Harvard is more to be congratulated than you are. My own experience is that the headship of an active and growing university is a post of very anxious responsibility and involves many burdens which it is almost impossible to carry lightly. But I am sure that you will enjoy many parts of it, and that you will be able to render Harvard a service which no one else within my knowledge would be able to render her. It is a great pleasure to me to think that your assumption of the duties of President of Harvard will increase the chances of my seeing you on various occasions and may draw us even closer together than we have been in the past, so that I may often enjoy the benefit of comparing views with you and of drawing thoughtful counsel from you.

With warm regard,
Sincerely yours,   Woodrow Wilson

TLS (A. L. Lowell Papers, MH-Ar).

From Abbott Lawrence Lowell

Dear President Wilson: Boston.   January 15, 1909.

Your words of welcome into the great fraternity of college presidents are most gratifying. You know how much I have admired your progressive grasp of the college situation, and I hope to have many fruitful talks about it.

Yours very truly,   A. Lawrence Lowell.

TLS (WP, DLC).

A News Report of an Address to the Alumni of the Newark Academy

[Jan. 16, 1909]

ACADEMY BOYS HOLD REUNION

President of Princeton on Education

Glories of Newark Academy as an institution, ideal in the production of American manhood, were extolled by speakers at the twenty-third annual dinner of the school's Alumni Association last night. More than eighty members attended the affair, which was held in the gymnasium of the academy in High street. Dr. Woodrow Wilson, president of Princeton University, was one of the speakers. He described the aims and objects of education and the attributes essential for an educator. He said education was a means of life and not of livelihood. . . .

Dr. Wilson received a great ovation when he was introduced, and at the conclusion of his address three hearty cheers were given. The Princeton men among the diners joined with a tiger yell.

In his address Dr. Wilson declared that a man's life consists not in the things he plans to do, but in his purpose. Every day, he said, man must have a conception of what duties he has to perform. He must make an effort to realize that there is something imprisoned within him which he desires to release. He should also consider, the speaker said, whether he is climbing up or going down hill.

"Education is a means of life," Dr. Wilson said, "and it should never be considered as a means of livelihood. Man must train himself in certain things to obtain a livelihood, but only for the sake of life. There is nothing to enjoy in life if you have no vision of what it is. In order to behold this vision you must look beyond the goal of money making.["]

Dr. Wilson then told of what education consists. He said some people may ask what benefit is derived from Latin and Greek for the modern mind. It may be true, he said, that such studies are of no material aid in the making of money, but the one who is not familiar with the classical authors in Greek and Latin, he declared, does not know the origin of modern intellectual life. . . .

Dr. Farrand possessed all the qualities, said Dr. Wilson, which are requisite in the make-up of an educator, and the school he founded is all that such an institution should be for the forming of character in young men.[1]

Printed in the *Newark Evening News*, Jan. 16, 1909; some editorial headings omitted.
[1] There is a WWhw outline, with the composition date of Jan. 14, 1909, of this address in WP, DLC.

From Hollis Burke Frissell[1]

Hampton, Va.,
January 16, 1909.

My dear President Wilson:

I hear with great pleasure from Mrs. William Potter Wilson[2] that you are planning to be with us on the evening of February twenty-sixth.[3] I feel especially glad to have you speak on that occasion for it seems to me that it is of vital importance that we make both the North and South feel the necessity of industrial training for the negro race.

At this time, when the conservation of forces is so much to the front and the value of industrial training is coming to be so well understood, it seems important that Hampton should endeavor to make clear the sort of work that it is trying to do. In talking with southern men of late I have been very much pleased to see that they are coming to understand as never before that the South cannot take its place unless all its people are trained for service. The economic value of the industrial training of the negro is gradually being appreciated.

Hampton, of course, has only made a beginning, but we have made something of a showing of what can be done along this line. Because of your southern connections and your broad outlook upon educational matters you are especially fitted to present this to a Philadelphia audience.

We all rejoice in the important educational moves that you have been able to make; I was glad to tell the members of the General Education Board, when the matter of rendering aid to Princeton came up, how important it seemed to me that you should be supported in your endeavors.[4]

I wish that we might have the pleasure of seeing you here; while we are far from being or doing what we ought, I am sure that our work is in better shape than ever before and that the belief in the dignity of service pervades the school.

I am sending you our last reports and some other documents which will give you an idea of the work. With sincere appreciation of the interest which you have always shown in Hampton, I am   Very truly yours,   H. B. Frissell

TLS (WP, DLC).
¹ Principal of the Hampton Normal and Agricultural Institute.
² Ellen Dickson (Mrs. William Potter) Wilson, a widow of Rosemont, Pennsylvania, and the mother of Wayne MacVeagh Wilson, Princeton 1898, and Hugh Irvine Wilson, Princeton 1902. She was assisting in the organization of a meeting on behalf of the Hampton Institute to be held at the Academy of Music in Philadelphia on February 26, 1909.
³ Wilson's notes for his remarks on this occasion are printed at that date, Vol. 19.
⁴ About the decision of the General Education Board to aid Princeton, see C. H. Dodge to WW, March 28, 1907, Vol. 17.

Junius Spencer Morgan to Henry Burling Thompson

New York N Y   1/18 1909

Ivy Club governors meet tomorrow   can you send me some information as to what, if anything was done in regard Club matter recent board meeting   Junius S. Morgan

Hw telegram (H. B. Thompson Papers, NjP).

Henry Burling Thompson to Junius Spencer Morgan

Dear Junius: [Wilmington, Del.]   January 18th, 1909.

I have your telegram of even date, stating—"Ivy Club Governors meet to-morrow. Can you send me some information as to what, if anything, was done in regard to club matters recent Board meeting?"

At our Board meeting on Thursday, under "Miscellaneous Business," I asked the President how the Clubs were to be notified of the action of the Board at the October meeting; viz, the resolution suggesting the advisability of the Clubs appointing a Graduate Committee,—such Committee to discuss all matters of present and future interest to the Clubs. President Wilson stated that he had proposed personally to notify the Clubs of this resolution, but that he had forgotten it, and he asked the Secretary to make a note, calling his attention, in order that he could take care of this matter.

A communication was received from Cottage and Cap & Gown, in reference to Sophomore elections. My understanding is that such communications would naturally be referred to that Graduate Committee, who could ask for a conference with the Faculty.

I spoke to McAlpin at lunch with regard to the necessity of keeping Wilson posted, because there was a restlessness among the Clubs, on account of our inaction. I imagine neither the faculty or the Board, in view of the resolution in October, would care to take up matters with any individual Club, but would prefer to discuss all questions with the new Graduate Committee.

I spoke to Dean Fine on Thursday afternoon of the importance of getting this Graduate Committee appointed, and I think he is entirely in sympathy with it.

Yours very truly,   Henry B Thompson

P.S. I mail copy to N. Y. office not knowing your address for tomorrow's meeting.

TLS (Thompson Letterbooks, NjP).

An Address on Robert E. Lee at the University of North Carolina

[[Jan. 19, 1909]]

Mr. President, Ladies, and Gentlemen:

I hope before I enter upon the theme upon which you have asked me to speak that you will give me leave to express the very keen personal pleasure I feel in finding myself in this place.

It is all very well to talk of detachment of view, and of the effort to be national in spirit and in purpose, but a boy never gets over his boyhood, and never can change those subtle influences which have become a part of him, that were bred in him when he was a child. So I am obliged to say again and again that the only place in the country, the only place in the world, where nothing has to be explained to me is the South. (Applause).

Sometimes, after long periods of absence, I forget how natural it is to be in the South, and then the moment I come, and see old friends again, and discover a country full of reminiscences which connect me with my parents, and with all the old memories, I know again the region to which I naturally belong.

So it is with peculiar personal pleasure, and with the sense that you have accorded to me a privilege, that I stand here tonight to speak of General Lee.

In one sense, it is a superfluous thing to speak of General Lee, —he does not need the eulogy of any man. His fame is not enhancad [enhanced], his memory is not lifted to any new place of distinction by any man's words of praise, for he is secure of his place. It is not necessary to recount his achievements; they are in the memory not only of every soldier, but of every lover of high and gifted men who likes to see achievements which proceed from character, to see those things done which are not done with the selfish purpose of self-aggrandizement, but in order to serve a country, and prove worthy of a cause. These are the things which make the name of this great man prominent not only, but in some regards unapproachable in the history of our country.

I happened the other day to open a book not printed in this part of the country, the *Century Cyclopaedia of Names*,[1] and to turn to the name of Lee, and I was very much interested, and I must say a little touched, by the simple characterization it gave of the man: "A celebrated American general in the Confederate service." How perfectly that sums the thing up,—a celebrated American general, a national character who won his chief celebrity in the service of a section of the country, but who was not sectionalized by the service, is recognized now as a national hero; who was not rendered the less great because he bent his energies towards a purpose which many men conceived not to be national in its end.

I think this speaks something for the healing process of time. I think it says something for the age, that it should have taken so short a time for the whole nation to see the true measure of this man, and it takes me back to my own feeling about one's necessary connection with the region in which he was born.

There is an interesting and homely story of Daniel Webster, how after one very tedious and laborious session of the Senate he returned to his home in Boston quite worn out and told his servant that he was going up stairs to lie down, and must not be disturbed on any account. He had hardly reached his room when some gentlemen from the little village in New Hampshire which had been his original boyhood home, called at the door and said they must see him,—that a man's life was involved. They had come down as the neighbors of a lad in his old home, charged, as they believed falsely with murder. They believed

---

[1] *The Century Cyclopedia of Names: A Pronouncing and Etymological Dictionary of Names in Geography, Biography, Mythology, History, Ethnology, Art, Archaeology, Fiction, etc.* . . . (New York, 1894). Numerous later printings and "editions," all with additions and corrections. There is a copy of this work in the Wilson Library, DLC.

in the lad but were confounded by circumstantial evidence; and they thought that there was only one man in the United States who could unravel the tangle of misleading indications; and they had come to seek Mr. Webster. The servant was afraid to call him but yielded to their urgency, and he came down in no pleasant humor. To all their appeals he replied, "Gentlemen, it is impossible; I am worn out. I am not fit for the service, and cannot go." Seeing at last that it was probably hopeless, the spokesman of the little company at last rose and said "Well, I don't know what the neighbors will say."—"Oh! well" said Webster, "if it is the neighbors, I will go!" There came to his mind the vision of some little groups of old men in that village where he had lived as a boy whose comments he could surmise, and that was the particular condemnation he could not face. So all great patriots have had a deep local rootage, and have drawn the sap of their patriotism from that rootage. You can love a country if you begin by loving a community, but you cannot love a country if you do not have the true rootages of intimate affection which are the real sources of all that is strongest in human life. So this 'celebrated American general' had his necessary local rootages, and the sap of his manhood united him with the soil on which he was bred. It was there he won his celebrity and made secure his fame. I think one of the most interesting things to remember about Lee is that he was an ideal combination of what a man inherits and what he may make of himself.

General Lee came of a distinguished family. His father, Light Horse Harry Lee, was of the finest breed of those gallant soldiers who made the country free; and the lad in his boyhood must have been bred to many memories of high deeds and to many fine conceptions of patriotic service at the hearth where his father sat.

I like to think, for my part, that Light Horse Harry Lee was bred under the teaching of Doctor John Witherspoon, the great Scotchman who at that day presided over the college at Princeton, and that there is some sort of Princetonian lineage in the man whom we have met to honor tonight.

But these soldierly traditions, this impulse from a great father, were not what made Robert E. Lee. After all, ladies and gentlemen, what makes and distinguishes a man is not that he is derived from any family or from any training, but that he has discovered for himself the true role of manhood in his own day. No man gains distinction who does not make some gift of his own individuality to the thing that he does,—to the generation which he serves.

This man was not great because he was born of a soldier and bred in a school of soldiers, but because, of whomsoever he may have been born, howsoever he was bred, he was a man who saw his duty, who conceived it in high terms, and who spent himself, not upon his own ambitions, but in the duty that lay before him. We like to remember all the splendid family traditions of the Lees, but we like most of all to remember that this man was greater than all the traditions of his family; that there was a culmination here that could not have been reached by the mere drift of what men remember, but must be reached by what men originate and conceive.

I am not going to try to outline the career of Lee, because I feel the compulsion of that last characteristic of General Lee. I do not want to live, and I do not wish to ask you to live on the memory of what General Lee did. I want to remind you of how General Lee,—as the President of the University has told you,— turned immediately from war, when it was past, to the future which was to come, and said, "I will do my part in trying to make the young men of this country ready for the things which are yet to be done."

We are not at liberty to walk with our eyes over our shoulders, recalling the things which were done in the past; we are bound in conscience to march with our eyes forward, with the accents of such men in our ears saying, "We lived not as you must live. We lived for our generation; we tried to do its tasks. Turn your faces and your hands likewise to the tasks that you have to do." We would not be honoring General Lee if we did not think of him only enough to remind ourselves of what we have to do to be like him. The true eulogy of General Lee is a life which is meant to be patterned after his standards of duty and of achievement. And so I am not going to ask you tonight to look back at General Lee, but, rather. to answer the question—"What does General Lee mean to us?"

It is a notable thing that we see when we look back to men of this sort. The civil war is something which we cannot even yet uncover in memory without stirring embers which may spring into a blaze. There was deep color and the ardor of blood in that contest. The field is lurid with the light of passion, and yet in the midst of that crimson field stands this gentle figure,—a man whom you remember, not as a man who loved war, but as a man moved by all the high impulses of gentle kindness, a man whom men did not fear, but loved; a man in whom everybody who approached him marked singular gentleness, singular sweetness, singular modesty,—none of the pomp of the soldier, but all the simplicity of the gentleman. This man is in the center of that crimson field, is the central figure of a great tragedy. A singular tragedy it seems which centres in a gentleman who loved his fellow men and sought to serve them by the power of love, and who yet, in serving them with the power of love, won the imperishable fame of a great soldier! A singular contradiction!

It is true that we do not think entirely correctly of Lee in supposing that he was compact entirely of gentleness. No man whom you deeply care for or look to for leadership is made up altogether of gentle qualities. When you come into the presence of a leader of men you know you have come into the presence of fire,—that it is best not incautiously to touch that man,—that there is something that makes it dangerous to cross him,—that if you grapple [with] his mind you will find that you have grappled with flame and fire. You do not want sweetness merely and light in men who lead you; and there was just as much fire in Lee as there was in Washington. In Washington it was more upon the surface, but it was not more truly present. Every man who approached Washington had the singular impression that he was in the presence of a man of tremendous passions, yet no man ever saw him yield to those passions. He was always well in hand; but you knew that the man himself was aware that he was driving a mettlesome team, which he had to watch at every movement to avoid sudden runaway, when circumstances were exigent or exciting.

You did not get that impression when in the presence of Lee. I have only the delightful memory of standing, when a lad, for a moment by General Lee's side and looking up into his face, so that I have nothing but a child's memory of the man; but those who saw him when they were men and could judge say that you got no impression of constrained and governed passion such as men got from General Washington. But whenever General Lee was in the field no one dared cross him, no one dared neglect his orders, no one dared exercise a dangerous discretion in the carrying out of his commands. There would flare in the man a consuming fire of anger; those who were in his presence felt it was dangerous so much as to breathe naturally until it was past. There was something of the tiger in this man when his purpose was aroused and in action. It would immediately recede; quiet gentleness would come again, that perfect poise, that delightful sense of ease as he moved from one purpose to another; but you would not forget that moment of exposed fire,—you would know that you had been in the presence of consuming force.

But what strikes me as most interesting in the example of General Lee is that this was not in one sense of the word personal force at all. Touch General Lee about himself and you never saw the flash of fire, but touch him about things he regarded as his duty, and you saw it instantly. So the force that presided in him was no other than that moral force which may be said to be a principle in action. There is a sense, I sometimes think, in which every one of us in whose life principle forms a part is merely holding up a light which he himself did not kindle, not his own principle, not something peculiar and individual to himself, but that light which must light all mankind, the love of truth, the love of duty, the love of those things which are not stated in the terms of personal interest. That is the force and that the fire that moulds men or else consumes them.

You need not be afraid of the fire that is in selfish passion, you can crush that; but you cannot crush the fire that is in unselfish passion. You know that there you are in the presence of the greatest force in the world, the only force that lifts men or nations to greatness, or purifies communities; and that is the consuming fire which we dare not touch. I apply this thought sometimes to existing circumstances. I grow tired often, as I tire of any futility, of hearing certain abuses condemned and not having the condemnation followed by a list of the names of the persons who are guilty of them; for there is not a group of men in this country who could stand the heat of the fire that would scorch those names. You cannot scorch the abuse, but you can consume men by merely exposing them to this moral fire, which they know is the fire of their death; and that is the sort of force that burned in General Lee. All his life through you are aware of a conscious self-subordination to principles which lay outside his personal life.

I have sometimes noted with a great deal of interest how careless we are about most words in our language, and yet how careful we are about some others. For example, there is one word which we do not use carelessly and that is the word "noble." We use the word "great" indiscriminately. A man is great because he has had great material success and has piled up a fortune; a man is great because he is a great writer, or a great orator; a man is great because he is a great hero. We notice in him some distinct quality that overtops like qualities in other men. But we reserve the word "noble" carefully for those whose greatness is not spent in their own interest. A man must have a margin of energy which he does not spend upon himself in order to win this title of nobility. He is noble in our popular conception only when he goes outside the narrow circle of self-interest, and begins to spend himself for the interest of mankind. Then, however humble his gifts, however undistinguished his intellectual force, we give him this title of nobility, and admit him into the high peerage of men who will not be forgotten.

Now that was the characteristic of General Lee's life. It was not only moral force, but it was moral force conscientiously guided by interests which were not his own. You do not need to have me illustrate that. It was manifestly not to General Lee's personal interest to take command of the armies of the South. He could have taken command of the armies of the North; and, in spite of the noble quality of the Southern struggle, every man now sees that the forces of the world were sure to crush the self-assertion of the South; and General Lee knew enough of the force of the world, had been schooled enough in national armies to know upon which side the probability of material power lay and therefore the probability of success in arms. He knew that the South would be weak in that it could not count on the support of the world, and the North could. A man seeking his own aggrandizement would not have chosen as General Lee did. But he did not choose with any, even momentary regard for his personal fortune. He sacrificed himself for the things that were nearest, the things I have illustrated in the homely anecdote about Webster. He thought of the neighbors; he knew that a man's nearest attachments are his best attachments, and his nearest duties his imperative duties. He had been born in Virginia, he was Virginia's. Virginia could do with him as she pleased. And wherever that spirit obtains, wherever men can be found in the State of North Carolina, or in any other State, who conscientiously live upon this principle, that they belong to North Carolina, that they belong to their people and to their State and must see to it that they yield themselves to the needs and commands of their people and do the things that are necessary to be done for their welfare, those are the men who, if they do not look merely to their own fame, will sometime be written upon the roll of honor of the local and national history of this country.

So that there is brought to the surface in General Lee, as it were, the consummate fire of a democratic nation, the perfect product of a common conscience and a common consciousness expressing itself in an instrument excellently suitable because of its own fine quality. You may use a clumsy instrument for the right purpose, but it is better to use a perfect instrument, and this man was like the finest steel adapting himself to the nicest strokes of precision and yet incapable of being snapped or broken by any impact. He was a perfect instrument for a thing which we too little think of.

I do not believe in a democratic form of government because I think it the best form of government. It is the clumsiest form of government in the world. If you wanted to make a merely effective government you would make it of fewer persons. If you wanted to invent a government that would act with speed and quick force, you would be doing a clumsy thing to make it democratic in structure. That is not purposed to be the best form, but to have the best sources.

Did you ever think how the world managed politically to get through the middle ages? It got through them without breakdown because it had the Roman Catholic Church to draw upon for native gifts, and by no other means that I can see. If you will look at the politics of the middle ages you will see that States depended for their guidance upon great ecclesiastics, and they depended upon them because the community itself was in strata, was in classes, and the Roman Catholic Church was a great democracy. Any peasant could become a priest, and any priest a chancellor. And this reservoir of democratic power and native ability was what brought the middle ages through their politics. If they had not had a democratic supply of capacity they could not have conducted a sterile aristocratic polity. An aristocratic polity goes to seed. The establishment of a democratic nation means that any man in it may, if he consecrate himself and use himself in the right way, come to be the recognized instrument of a whole nation. It is an incomparably resourceful arrangement, though it is not the best practical organization of government.

In a man like General Lee you see a common conscientiousness made manifest; and this singular thing revealed, that by a root which seems to be a root of failure a man may be lifted to be the model of a whole nation. For it is not an exaggeration to say that in all parts of this country the manhood and the self-forgetfulness and the achievements of General Lee are a conscious model to men who would be morally great. This man who chose the course which eventually led to practical failure is one of the models of the times. "A nation," Browning says, "is but the attempt of many to rise to the completer life of one; and those who live as the models for the mass are singly of more value than they all."

The moral force of a country like America lies in the fact that every man has it within his choice to express the nation in himself. I am interested in historical examples as a mere historian. I was guilty myself of the indescretion [indiscretion] of writing a history, but I will tell you frankly, if you will not let it go any further, that I wrote it, not to instruct anybody else, but to instruct myself. I wrote the history of the United States in order to learn it. That may be an expensive process for other persons who bought the book, but I lived in the United States and my interest in learning their history was, not to remember what happened, but to find which way we were going.

I remember a traveller telling me of being on a road in Scotland and asking a man breaking stone by the roadside if this was the road to so and so, the man said "where did you come from"; he answered "I don't know whether it is any of your business where I came from." "Weel," said the man "its as muckle as whaur ye're ganging tae.["] (Laughter). There is a great deal of philosophy in that question asked by the roadside. If I am near a cross road and ask if this is the road to so and so, it is a pertinent question to ask me where I came from.

We often speak of a man as having 'lost himself,' in a desert for example. Did you never reflect that that is the only thing he has not lost,—himself? He is there. The danger of the situation is that he has lost all the rest of the world. He doesn't know where the North is, or the South, or the East, or the West,—has lost every point of the compass. The only way by which he can start is to get some fixed and known point by which he can determine his direction. A nation that does not know its history and heed its history has lost itself. Unless you know where you came from you do not know where you are going to.

I am told by psychologists that if I did not remember who I was yesterday I would not know who I am to-day. Now the same is true of a nation. A nation which does not remember what it was yesterday does not know what it is to-day, or what it is trying to do. We are trying to do a futile thing if we do not know where we came from or what we have been about.

We have stumbled upon a confusing age; nothing is like it was fifteen years ago,—certainly in the field of economic endeavor, and we are casting about to discover a new world without any standards taken out of an older world by which we can make the comparison.

I was passing through the city of Omaha during the latter stages of the Presedential [Presidential] campaign and I bought the morning paper, the "Omaha Bee" and found in it an interesting article by my friend Mr. Rosewater[2] in which he made capital fun of a quotation about the tariff from Mr. Bryan. I thought there was something odd about the quotation, and it turned out the next morning that Mr. Rosewater, himself a member of the

[2] Victor Rosewater, editor of the *Omaha Bee*.

Republican National Committee, had been making fun, not of a quotation from Bryan, but of a quotation from the Republican platform. Now the point is, that unless you had an experienced nose in that campaign, if you picked up either of the platforms you had to look at the label to see which it was. The reason is that in recent years we have been looking about for expedients and policies and have not been looking about for principles. (Applause).

If you want me to bid against you for a popular policy I will probably resort to the expedient of matching your bid if I think it a good one; but if I happen to be restrained by certain knowledge of what happened once before, I may choose differently and by a longer measurement. I may say there are certain things going to happen in this; they are going to happen upon well known and ancient principles: having read history I would be a fool if I did not know it. I am going to hark back to those fundamental principles which hold good despite changes of policy. I am not going to hark back to old policies, but I shall try to find out whether there is not some new and suitable expression of those old principles in new policies. Although I may not assist my party to win at the next election by such a course, it is sure thereby to win at some election, at which it will give it such distinction that the country will thereafter for a whole generation recognize in it the only safe counsellor it has.

If you want to win an election which occurs to-morrow probably you haven't time to remind your fellow countryman of the abiding principles upon which they should act; but if you form the habit of basing your advice upon definite principles you will presently gain a permanent following such as you could not possibly have gained upon any bidding for popularity by mere expedients.

I want to say that the lesson of General Lee's life to me is that it is not the immediate future that should be the basis of the statesman's calculation. If you had been in Lee's position, what would have been your calculation of expediency? Here was a great national power, material and spiritual, in the North. In the Northwest there had grown up by a slow process, as irresistible as the glacial movement, a great national feeling, a feeling in which was quite obliterated and lost the old idea of the separate sovereignity [sovereignty] of the States. In the South there had been a steadfast maintenance of the older conception of the union. What in such a case would you have said to your countrymen? "It will be most proper, as it will certainly be most expedient, for you to give in to the majority, and vote for the

Northern conception?" Not at all. If you had been of Lee's kind you would have known that men's consciences, men's habits of thought, lie deeper than that, and you would have said: "No; this is not a time to talk about majorities; this is a time to express convictions; and if her conviction is not expressed by the South in terms of blood she will lose her character. These are her convictions, and if she yield them out of expediency she will have proved herself of the soft fibre of those who do not care to suffer for what they profess to love." Even a man who saw the end from the beginning should, in my conception as a Southerner, have voted for spending his people's blood and his own, rather than pursue the weak course of expediency. (Applause). There is here no mere device, no regard to the immediate future. What has been the result?—ask yourself that. It has been that the South has retained her best asset, namely, her self-respect. (Applause).

Let that great case serve as an example. Are you going into political campaigns of a less fundamental character on the ground of expediency, or are you going in on the ground of your real opinions and ultimate self-respect?

For my part, if I did not, after saturating myself in the conceptions upon which this government was formed, express my knowledge of those principles and my belief in them by the way I voted, I would lose my self-respect; and I would not care to have anybody's company in the poor practice. What this country needs now in the field of politics is principle; not measures of expediency, but principle,—principles expressed in terms of the present circumstances, but principles nevertheless. And principles do not spring up in a night; principles are not new, principles are ancient.

There is one lesson that the peoples of the world have learned so often that they ought to esteem themselves contemptible if they have to learn it again, and that is that if you concentrate the management of a people's affairs in a single central government and carry that concentration beyond a certain point of oversight and regulation, you will certainly provoke again those revolutionary processes by which individual liberty was asserted. We have had so little excess of government in this country that we have forgotten that excess of government is the very antithesis of liberty. So it seems to me that the principle by which we should be guided above all others is this, that we do not want to harness men like Lee in the service of a managing government; we want to see to it that, though there is control, it is control of law and not the discretionary control of executive officials. We want to see to it that while there is the restraint of abuses, it is persons who are restrained, and not unnamed bodies of persons. There is only, historically speaking, one possible successful punishment of abuses of law, and that is, that when a wrong thing is done you find the man who did it and punish him. You can fine all the corporations there are, and fine them out of existence, and all you will have done will be to have embarrassed the commerce of the country. You will have left the men who did it free to repeat it in other combinations. (Applause).

I am going to use an illustration which you can easily misunderstand, but I am going to ask you not to misunderstand it.

Suppose I could incorporate an association of burglars with the assurance that you would restrain their actions, not as individuals, but only as a corporation. Whenever a burglary occurred you would fine the corporation. They would be very much pleased with that arrangement, because it would leave them the service of their most accomplished burglars, who could fool you half the time and not be found out. Such a corporation would be willing to pay you a heavy fine for the privilege. Now I do not mean to draw a parallel between our great corporations and burglars,— that is where you are likely to misunderstand me, (Laughter) because I do not hold the general belief that the majority of the business men of this country are burglars; I believe, on the contrary, that the number of malicious men engaged in corporations in this country is very small. But that small number is singularly gifted (Laughter), and until you have picked them out and distinguished them for punishment you have not touched the process by which they succeed in doing what they wish. You may say that this is a very difficult thing, that there is so much covert, so much undergrowth, the nation is so thickset with organizations that you can not see them and run them to cover.

Perhaps you are right; but that does not make any difference to my argument; whether difficult, or not, it has got to be done. If you don't know enough to do it, it is none the less necessary to find the way.

What have we been doing in the last fifteen years? Trying to remedy things which we have not stopped long enough to understand.

I was talking the other day to a body of men which included a good many persons belonging to the profession to which I used to belong. I used to be a lawyer. I said to these men: "I am sure there are a great many corporation lawyers in this audience and I have something to say to them. You know exactly what is being done that ought not to be done. You complain that the legislators of this country are playing havoc with the industry of the country by trying to remedy things in the wrong way. Now, if you really want to save the corporations, you will tell the legislators you complain of what ought to be done and how. If you do not, they will continue their experiments and destroy your corporations, but having said that to you I must add that I don't expect you to have sense enough to do anything of the kind."

There is a hopeless sort of fidelity in men who are employed as advisers that prevents their seeing the coming of the deluge; and yet it is they who are to blame if it comes. If you and I had this difficult task in hand of regulating the corporations, whom would we call into counsel? The men who had handled the business. And yet they are the very men who will not yield us any service in the matter at all. They are the very men who are neglecting this great example we are recalling to-night. They are acting upon lines of self-interest, closing in the lines of self-interest as about themselves, and about those whom they represent, and forgetting those greater interests which, if they forget, they oppose,—the interests of the nation and of our common life. And so hostility has sprung up where there should be co-operation, and blunders are committed because men who know how the thing ought to be done will not give public counsel.

We must stop long enough to know what we are about and then go fearlessly forward and do it against the guilty individuals.

I think if I had an independent fortune, and could give up my present profession I could find a delightful occupation. I would take up my residence in the city of Washington and would industriously find out from the central bureaux of inquiry what was going on in the larger business world of the United States. Then I would prepare one or two addresses upon the knowledge which I had gained and would make a careful list of the names of the gentlemen who had been doing the things that ought not to be done. They could not do me any harm physically, and I would enjoy the opinion they would have of me. If I could once get their names I would not need the assistance of the criminal law; I would only have to publish the names and prove the facts to put them out of business. Because the moral judgments of this country are as sound as they ever were, and if you direct them in the right channels they are irres[is]tibly effective. At present we are directing them into oratorical channels and not into legislative or judicial channels.

The channels of legislation, the humdrum daily administration of courts of justice are the effective channels of government, and I would rather have government carried successfully on by such means than hear all the fine speeches that have been uttered by the most gifted speakers. I am not depreciating speakers, because that is part of my own business, and I would not ask you to look with contempt upon the humble vocation which I attempt. But I would look with contempt upon myself if I supposed speaking to be a kind of action.

Now, gentlemen, what does it mean that General Lee is accepted as a *national* hero? It means simply this delightful thing, that there are no sections in this country any more; that we are a nation and are proud of all the great heroes whom the great processes of our national life have elevated into conspicuous places of fame. I believe that the future lies with all those men who devote themselves to national thinking, who eschew those narrow calculations of self-interest which affect only particular communities and try to conceive of communities as a part of a great national life which must be purified in order that it may be successful. For we may pile up wealth until it exceed all fables of riches in ancient fiction and the nation which possesses it may yet use it to malevolent ends. A poor nation such as the United States was in 1812, for example, if it is in the right, is more formidable to the world than the richest nation in the wrong. For the rich nation in the wrong destroys the fair work that God has permitted and man has wrought; whereas, the poor nation, with purified purpose, is the stronger. It looks into men's hearts and sees the spirit there; finds some expression of that spirit in life; bears the fine aspect of hope and exhibits in all its purposes the irresistible quality of rectitude. These are the things which make a nation formidable. There is nothing so self destructive as selfishness, and there is nothing so permanent as the work of hands that are unselfish. You may pile up fortunes and dissolve them, but pile up ideals and they will never be dissolved. A quiet company of gentlemen sitting through a dull summer in the city of Philadelphia worked out for a poor and rural nation an immortal constitution, which has made statesmen all over the world feel confidence in the political future of the race. They knew that human liberty was a feasible basis of government.

There is always danger that certain men thinking only of the material prospects of their section, wishing to get the benefit of the tariff, it may be, or of this thing, or of that, when it comes to the distribution of favors, will write only the history which has been written again and again, whose reiteration has been repeated since the world began; from which no man will draw fresh inspiration, from which no ideal can spring, from which no strength can be drawn. Whereas the nation which denies itself material advantage and seeks those things which are of the spirit works not only for each generation, but for all generations, and works in the permanent and durable stuffs of humanity.

I spoke just now in disparagement of the vocation of the orator. I wish there were some great orator who could go about and make men drunk with this spirit of self-sacrifice. I wish there were some man whose tongue might every day carry abroad the golden accents of that creative age in which we were born a nation; accents which would ring like tones of reassurance around the whole circle of the globe, so that America might again have the distinction of showing men the way, the certain way, of achievement and of confident hope. (Applause).[3]

Printed in the University of North Carolina, *Record. Alumni Bulletin No. 2. Anniversary of Lee's Birth* (Chapel Hill, N. C., 1909), pp. 6-21.

[3] There is an undated WWsh outline and a WWhw outline of this address, dated Jan. 19, 1909, in WP, DLC; there is also a typed abstract in WC, NjP.

From John Fairfield Dryden

Dear Mr. Wilson: Newark, N. J.   January 19, 1909.

With a view to perfecting the organization of the Association of which you have kindly consented to become a trustee, and of making final arrangements for expeditiously raising a fund for the erection of a suitable monument to the late Grover Cleveland at Princeton, N. J., a meeting has been called of those who have thus become identified with this laudable enterprise for February 2, 1909, at eleven o'clock in my office in the Prudential Building.

I was personally much gratified to have your acceptance of the trusteeship in this connection, and I trust that it will be entirely agreeable and convenient for you to attend the meeting at the time above stated.

Believe me,   Very truly yours,   John F. Dryden

TLS (WP, DLC).

From Alfred Thomas Carton[1]

Dear President Wilson,   Chicago, Ill.   January 19, 1909

At a meeting of the Executive Committee of the Princeton Club of Chicago held today, I was instructed to request you to honor the Club by your presence at an informal dinner to be held at the University Club of Chicago, 116 Dearborn Street, on Saturday evening, February 13, 1909.[2]

We trust that in view of the Lincoln celebration in Chicago on February 12, this date will be convenient. May I hear from you in reply by return mail or by wire.

Very respectfully yours,   Alfred T. Carton

ALS (WP, DLC).

[1] Princeton 1905, lawyer of Chicago, Secretary and Treasurer of the Princeton Club of Chicago.

[2] A news report of Wilson's speech to the Princeton Club of Chicago is printed at Feb. 14, 1909, Vol. 19.

ADDENDA

To George Haven Putnam[1]

Princeton, New Jersey

My dear Mr. Putnam,
17 March, 1897.

I am uttering no merely formal phrase when I say that I appreciate most deeply your desire to have me contribute the volumes on the United States to the "Stories of the Nations" series, and that I wish very much that I could undertake so attractive a job.

But the truth is, that I have taken the bit in my teeth, and am henceforth dedicate[d] to undertakings wholly of my own planning. I allowed myself to interrupt one such undertaking for the sake of the volume on Washington which I have just published; but I hope that in the future I shall be more constant. I must devote myself to some very serious work which I have long known to be ahead of me, if I were really going to have a try at my own ideals.

Let me thank you for your confidence in me, and beg that you will believe me, with cordial regard,

Faithfully Yours, Woodrow Wilson

WWTLS (G. H. Putnam Papers, WyU).
[1] President of G. P. Putnam's Sons.

An Abstract of an Address to the Chamber of Commerce of Toledo, Ohio

[c. Nov. 27, 1908]

The Business Man and The Community.

A very remarkable civic awakening has marked the last ten years in this country. No one who has watched affairs with the least attention can have failed to perceive it, or to feel, in some degree, the air of change or the ardor of reform which has followed it. It has been an awakening full of happy augury if thoughtful citizens everywhere bestir themselves to make use of it for the betterment of their communities; but it may lead only to hasty and ill-considered change if we be not all cried awake at once. We do not yet know exactly what we would be at. We are in the somewhat confused, interrogatory state of mind of those who have just opened their eyes after long slumber. The sooner we come fully to our senses, the better and more sanely will the day's work be done.

One thing, however, is already clear. Some demoralizing old standards are already discredited: For example, the old maxim that "Business is business." It was never a handsome saying. It mean business is *not* morality, is not public spirit, is not a regard for others, but an eye for the main chance, and every man looking out for himself and only for himself. There is still life and validity to the old saying that "Competition is the life of trade." From the consumer's point of view it certainly is. But on the principle that business is business men came to justify themselves in killing competition, killed it by its own processes, by taking unfair advantage of special relationships which they were able to establish with each other, for example, with transportation companies, with mines and factories and with the lenders of money. But our civic awakening means, among other things, that we now know what has been going on, and the whole of the ugly, selfish process is discredited.

The trouble with the processes of business which we are now more or less intelligently engaged in trying to correct was not so much that they were touched with actual and direct corruption as that they were characterized by utter selfishness and absolute disregard for the general interest. The majority of the men who have been benefitting themselves and the corporations with which they were connected in recent years by doing everything that they could do in restraint of trade and of competition were no doubt perfectly honest men according to the standards time out of mind accepted in business circles, when business was done on a smaller scale and whole communities were not affected by individual transactions. They simply did not change their principles or widen their perceptions with the scope of their business. Moreover, they have held in all sincerity a theory of business which was once accepted by everybody without question: the theory that every one who piled up material wealth, added to the output of mines and factories, swelled the currents of commerce or in any way increased the material resources of the country, was a public benefactor as well as a private success, was doing a thing patriotic as well as profitable; wealth was in the aggregate, not private, but national; the country was being nobly enriched by their efforts, and wealth was welfare.

And so they fought for their privileges with a sort of righteous fervor at which we need not wonder, with which indeed we all once sympathized. Many corporations otherwise perfectly honest in their business methods habitually paid money into the treasuries of local political parties to be let alone by city councils, and of state political machines to be let alone by state legislatures.

It was in their eyes the necessary price of their legitimate liberty, and did in fact often protect them from corrupt and dishonest attack. In the same way and equally apart from their ordinary business morality they made large subscriptions, when it seemed to their interest to do so, to the campaign funds of the national party which was most likely to secure them in the many direct and indirect benefits and advantages which they derived from a protective tariff. Direct payments to be let alone, indirect payments to be helped and made secure of certain artificial advantages, came to be with them matters of course, accepted and never seriously criticised.

No doubt there are many valid and conclusive arguments for a protective tariff in a country whose power is new and whose resources are in the early stages of development; but those arguments when valid are always arguments for the general benefit, never arguments for private interest or the benefit of particular undertakings. There can never be any valid justification for using the taxing power of government for the benefit of anything less than the national interest. But the interests which directly and obviously benefitted by the tariff, inevitably came to look upon it as one of their assets to the preservation of which they were entitled in perpetuity, and when their private interest and the welfare and benefit of the community as a whole cease to be identical the tariffs which sustain them become an actual menace to business morality, their maintenance a process of demoralization and corruption. The present well nigh universal demand that our tariff policy be reconsidered arises from a very general consciousness that we have reached that point. That is one of the general perceptions that marks the civic awakening.

And it is not an awakening confined to those who are detached from great economic undertakings, who are merely the lookers-on at enterprise, and who might under any circumstances be expected to be critics. It has extended to the men of business of all ranks, and standards of success have come to be revised. Men who have made self-interest the exclusive law of business enterprise have come at last to see that such self-centered selfishness is not even enlightened selfishness. They have come to see that it may sometimes be carried to such a length as to be incompatible with self-respect, because self-respect is not wholly a matter of private thought. One's respect for himself is regulated in no small degree by the opinion others entertain of him; his estimate of himself is in large part regulated from without.

We have enlarged our view, and have come to see that prosperity is an organic thing, a thing of the whole community, the whole nation. No man can long successfully separate his interest from the interest of his community or his country. He cannot even separate himself in spirit from the great forces which make for the general welfare without presently feeling the isolation to his disadvantage. Prosperity is an organic thing not only, but a spiritual thing as well, a thing of principle as well as of interest, a thing built upon an enlightened conscience as well as upon a shrewd appreciation of selfish interest.

And so the best feature of the new awakening is that the business man has come to realize once more his real place in the community and the responsibilities that rest upon him, and that chambers of commerce, like this, are becoming the centers of the higher sort of civic endeavor. Business men have come to realize that no man can afford to be as small as his business; that the environment he makes for himself will make him big or little; that the community in which he lives is his place of expression, where his action will determine what he is, his place of stimulation, his atmosphere and medium within which and through which he must make himself whatever he is to become. Once let great instrumentalities like this chamber of commerce become the instruments of every large civic effort, and business men will have found themselves and their true interest, both spiritually and materially. They cannot again forget that they are poor business men when they are indifferent citizens.

The elements of force in a community are contained in its power of self-elevation, its power of self-purification, its power of self-variation. Governments can not lift men; they must lift themselves. Law can not purify them; their purification must be of themselves. No stimulation or restraint applied from without by the organized power of the community can give to the business or to the individual effort, either sufficient strength or sufficient variety to enrich and develop the country. That nation is richest and greatest which produces endeavor and capacity in the greatest variety, and only individual initiative can be relied on to do that. No people has got its strength from being taken care of or coached by its government. We must get every advantage we obtain from our own voluntary action. A country is made great by the affection of its people, the voluntary exertions in its behalf. When chambers of commerce show civic pride, and merchants and manufacturers are glad to think and act for the public interest in the midst of their own efforts for success, it is a sure sign that the vitality and the conscience of the community have been renewed, and wholesome progress is certain. Toledo is to be most heartily congratulated upon its instinctive right action in giving such evidence of its own conscious participation in the general civic awakening. In this fashion shall we have both better politics and better morals.[1]

T MS (WP, DLC).
  [1] There are two undated WWhw outlines of this address in WP, DLC.

INDEX

NOTE ON THE INDEX

THE alphabetically arranged analytical table of contents at the front of the volume eliminates duplication, in both contents and index, of references to certain documents, such as letters. Letters are listed in the contents alphabetically by name, and chronologically within each name by page. The subject matter of all letters is, of course, indexed. The Editorial Notes and Wilson's writings are listed in the contents chronologically by page. In addition, the subject matter of both categories is indexed. The index covers all references to books and articles mentioned in text or notes. Footnotes are indexed. Page references to footnotes which place a comma between the page number and "n" cite both text and footnote, thus: "624,n3." On the other hand, absence of the comma indicates reference to the footnote only, thus: "55n2"–the page number denoting where the footnote appears. The letter "n" without a following digit signifies an unnumbered descriptive-location note.

An asterisk before an index reference designates identification or other particular information. Re-identification and repetitive annotation have been minimized to encourage use of these starred references. Where the identification appears in an earlier volume, it is indicated thus: "*1:212,n3." Therefore a page reference standing without a preceding volume number is invariably a reference to the present volume. The index supplies the fullest known forms of names, and, for the Wilson and Axson families, relationships as far down as cousins. Persons referred to in the text by nicknames or shortened forms of names can be identified by reference to entries for these forms of the names.

A sampling of the opinions and comments of Wilson and Ellen Axson Wilson covers their more personal views, while broad, general headings in the main body of the index cover impersonal subjects. Occasionally opinions expressed by a correspondent are indexed where these appear to supplement or to reflect views expressed by Wilson or by Ellen Axson Wilson in documents which are missing.

INDEX

Woodrow Wilson, cont.

Chapel, Sept. 25, 1908; news report, 421-22

Meditation, talk before Philadelphian Society, Nov. 19, 1908; news report, 518-19

City Government, address before the Municipal Club, Dec. 2, 1908; news report, 530-32; mentioned, 493

Address of welcome to the Modern Language Association in Princeton, Dec. 28, 1908; notes, 566-67

Annual Report to the Board of Trustees, Jan. 1, 1909, 569-87

PROFESSIONAL ACTIVITIES

LL.D. degree conferred by Williams College, Oct. 7, 1908, 347-48, 382-83; citation, 439

Trustee of Cleveland Monument Association, 559,n2,3, 645

Corresponding member of the Southern Educational Association, 589-90

PUBLIC ADDRESSES AND LECTURES

The Ideals of Public Life, address to the Cleveland Chamber of Commerce, Nov. 16, 1907; mentioned, 217, 263; text in Vol. 17, 497-506

Address to the Princeton Alumni Association of Maryland, Arundel Club, Baltimore, March 6, 1908; news report, 10-11

Talk on Good Citizenship to students of Chicago Latin School, March 12, 1908; repeated before students of the University School for Boys, same day; news report, 16-17

Address to the Princeton Club of Chicago, University Club, March 12, 1908; text, 17-34; mentioned, 16, 219

The Government and Business, address to the Commercial Club of Chicago, Congress Hotel, March 14, 1908; text, 35-51; mentioned, 17, 59, 60

The Training of Intellect, Phi Beta Kappa address at Yale University, March 18, 1908; text, 53-59; mentioned, 10, 60, 312

The Government and Business, address to the Traffic Club of Pittsburgh, April 3, 1908; abstract, 221-25; mentioned, 262-63

Law or Personal Power, address at the Jefferson Day dinner of the National Democratic Club, Hotel Knickerbocker, New York, April 13, 1908; text, 263-69; news report, 269-71; mentioned, 59-60, 219-20

The Contribution of the [Young Men's Christian] Association to the Life of the Nation; address to the Chicago

Woodrow Wilson, cont.

Y.M.C.A. at Congress Hotel, April 27, 1908; outline, 276; news report, 276-77; mentioned, 60, 272-73,n3, 274, 313, 545

Address to the Western Association of Princeton Clubs, Pittsburgh, May 2, 1908; text, 280-85; mentioned, 51-52, 218

Address to the Princeton Alumni Association of New England, Hotel Vendome, Boston, May 15, 1908; text, 297-300; mentioned, 295,n1, 303

Mere Science, response to toast at retirement dinner of Cyrus Fogg Brackett, Princeton Inn, May 18, 1908; mentioned, 301

College Work and College Administration, commencement address at the Woman's College of Baltimore (now Goucher College), Lyric Theatre, June 3, 1908; outline, 318; news report, 318-20; mentioned, 278

After-dinner speech on S.S. *California*, June 27, 1908; outline, 347

After-dinner speech at entertainment on S.S. *Caledonia*, Sept. 11, 1908; notes, 418

The Banker and the Nation, address to the American Bankers' Association at Denver, Sept. 30, 1908; text, 424-34; mentioned, 435, 436, 441, 469,n1,2, 470

Address to the Wednesday Morning Club of Pittsfield at the Berkshire Athenaeum, Oct. 6, 1908; mentioned, 436

Address at the Inauguration of Harry Augustus Garfield as president of Williams College, Thompson Memorial Chapel, Oct. 7, 1908; text, 437-39; mentioned, 436

Public Affairs and Private Responsibility, address to the Men's League of the First Congregational Church, Pittsfield, Mass., Oct. 8, 1908; news report, 440-44; announcement, 436; mentioned, 424,n2

Address at the seventy-fifth anniversary of Haverford College, Oct. 16, 1908; text, 459-65; invitation, 67; mentioned, 420

What Kind of Citizens Shall We Be? Talk at Lawrenceville School, Nov. 4, 1908; notes, 482-83; mentioned, 275-76, 278

Address to the University Club of Jersey City at Hasbrouck Hall, Nov. 5, 1908; news report, 485-87

Address to the Jersey City High School, Nov. 6, 1908; news report, 487-89; mentioned, 534-35

The Meaning of a College Education, address at the Hotchkiss School, Lakeville, Conn., Nov. 12, 1908; text, 495-507; mentioned, 509

Woodrow Wilson, cont.

Address to the City History Club of New York, Hotel Plaza, Nov. 13, 1908; news report, 509-10; mentioned, 516

Success and How to Attain It, address before the East Liberty Y.M.C.A., Pittsburgh, Nov. 22, 1908; news report, 520-21; mentioned, 507-8,n3,5

The Contribution of the Young Men's Christian Association to the Life of the Nation, address at the thirty-fourth anniversary services of the East Liberty Y.M.C.A., Pittsburgh, Sunday evening, Nov. 22, 1908; news report, 521-22; mentioned, 507,n4

The Business Man and the Community, address to the Toledo Chamber of Commerce, Valentine Theatre, Nov. 27, 1908; news announcement, 524; news report, 526-28; abstract, 647; mentioned, 530

Conservatism: True and False, address to the New York Southern Society, Waldorf-Astoria Hotel, Dec. 9, 1908; text, 535-40; mentioned, 432,n3, 563

The Business Man and the Nation, address to the Wednesday Club of Newark, Continental Hotel, Dec. 16, 1908; news report, 551-52; mentioned, 548, 556

The Meaning of a Liberal Education, address to the High School Teachers Association of New York City, Jan. 9, 1909; text, 593-606; mentioned, 533

Address to the alumni of Newark Academy, January 15, 1909; news report, 628-29; mentioned, 547-48

Robert E. Lee, address at the University of North Carolina, Jan. 19, 1909; text, 631-45; invitation, 561-62

Abraham Lincoln: A Man of the People, centenary address delivered in Chicago, Feb. 12, 1909; text in Vol. 19; mentioned, 545, 546-47, 553-54, 563, 564

Address at a dinner of the Princeton Club of Chicago, Feb. 13, 1909; invitation, 645-46; news report in Vol. 19

Address at a meeting in behalf of the Hampton Normal and Agricultural Institute at the Academy of Music, Philadelphia, Feb. 26, 1909; mentioned, 629-30; notes in Vol. 19

Address to the Civic League of St. Louis, March 9, 1909; text in Vol. 19; mentioned, 516-17, 532-33, 567, 568

Address to the Virginia Society of St. Louis, March 10, 1909; mentioned, 567, 568, 593; report in Vol. 19

Woodrow Wilson, cont.

Academic Ideals and Public Service, address to the American Society for the Extension of University Teaching, Witherspoon Hall, Philadelphia, March 13, 1909; news report in Vol. 19; mentioned, 525, 545

Americanism, address at Temple Rodeph Sholom, New York City, March 18, 1909; mentioned, 523,n2, 550

Address to the Princeton Club of Philadelphia, March 19, 1909; mentioned, 550, 564; news report in Vol. 19

The Schoolmaster, address at Paterson (N.J.) High School, April 23, 1909; mentioned, 563-64, 590-91, 612-13; news item in Vol. 19

READING

Authors and works read, cited, alluded to, etc.

Frank Frost Abbott, *Handbook for the Study of Roman History*, 575; *A History and Description of Roman Political Institutions*, 575; *Short History of Rome*, 575; *The Selected Letters of Cicero* (ed.), 575; *The Toledo Manuscript of the Germania of Tacitus*, 575

Walter Bagehot, 95; *Physics and Politics*, 88

Robert Browning, 638; *Luria, A Tragedy*, 328n1

Thomas Carlyle, *History of the French Revolution*, 83n2; *Love Letters of Thomas Carlyle and Jane Welsh* (ed. A. Carlyle), 362,n1; *New Letters of Thomas Carlyle* (ed. A. Carlyle), 362,n1; *Reminiscences* (ed. Froude), 362,n2

Rheta Childe Dorr, What's the Matter with the Public Schools? 62,n2, 68,-n1

George du Maurier, *Peter Ibbetson*, 413

Henry Jones Ford, *The Rise and Growth of American Politics*, 208n5, 576

John Richard Green, 89

Alexander Hamilton, *Report of the Secretary of the Treasury on the Subject of Manufactures*, 538

Benjamin Kidd, *Social Evolution*, 443,-n1

Edward Verrall Lucas, *The Open Road. A Little Book for Wayfarers*, 411,n3

Sir Henry James Sumner Maine, *Popular Government*, 103n3

Frederick William Maitland, *The Constitutional History of England*, 356-57,n1

Lucius Hopkins Miller, Modern Views of the Bible and of Religion, 273,n2